D1600984

HISTORIANS
OF THE
CHRISTIAN
TRADITION

HISTORIANS OF THE CHRISTIAN TRADITION

THEIR METHODOLOGY AND INFLUENCE ON WESTERN THOUGHT

Michael Bauman

Martin I. Klauber

BROADMAN
& HOLMAN
PUBLISHERS

Nashville, Tennessee

4211–60
0-8054-1160-7

Dewey Decimal Classification: 270
Subject Heading: Church History
Library of Congress Card Catalog Number: 94-42498

Library of Congress Cataloging-in-Publication Data
Historians of the Christian tradition: their methodologies and impact on western thought / edited by Michael Bauman and Martin Klauber.
    p. cm.
Includes bibliographical references.
    ISBN 0-8054-1160-7
    1. Church history—Historiography. 2. Civilization, Christian.
I. Bauman, Michael. II. Klauber, Martin I., 1956–
BR138.H54   1995
270'.072—dc-20   94-42498
                                                  CIP

1 2 3 4 5 6 00 99 98 97 96 95

CONTENTS

Contents

INTRODUCTION:

THE NATURE AND IMPORTANCE OF RELIGIOUS HISTORIOGRAPHY

MICHAEL BAUMAN

We must see through many ages before we see through our own distinctly.

—*Walter Savage Landor*

History is the most comprehensive horizon of Christian theology. All theological questions are meaningful only within the framework of the history which God has with humanity and through humanity with his whole creation—the history moving toward a future still hidden from the world but already revealed in Jesus Christ.

—*Wolfhart Pannenberg*

The historian who is afraid of terms of value presently will find himself in a world where no norms are recognized.

—*Russell Kirk*

1

If at least part of the task of the Church and of its theologians is to identify what was central to the message of the apostles, then we Christians
must do the work of historians: We must look, listen, analyze and report,
for the Christian message is a fact of history. Because it is, we must, as far
as possible, let the ancients speak for themselves. We must let them tell us
what they said and believed, let them tell us what was or was not at the core
or heart of their proclamation. We must not, even if we fancy ourselves
rather capable philosophers and theologians, establish some standpoint of
our own about what they ought to have said, and then to reject as incon-
sequential or marginal in their message whatever does not suit our private
predilections. Our responsibility as modern Christians, as people who live
many centuries after the founding of their religion, is not to create the
gospel, but to discover its actual shape and content, and then to preserve
it, package it, and present it to our own age as compellingly as we can, and
with as little distortion as possible. To help us discover that shape and to
preserve it, the work of our tradition's greatest religious historians[1] is indispensable, because it shows us how the finest historical minds have gone
about that important task.

I am not saying anything so naive as that historians of religion and of
doctrine can be absolutely objective, or that the historian's personal biases
have no effect upon the historian's work. They do. But neither am I making the equally naive opposite assertion that because of the historian's own
inclinations historical accuracy and historical knowledge are not possible.
We can, and do, know many things about the past. Among the things we
can know is the nature of the earliest Christian witness—what was at its
center and what was on its periphery. We know such things first as historians of theology, not as philosophers, and not even as believers. In that
fact lies one of the chief reasons why the study of history and the practice
of historiography are important to Christians, and why this book was written.

As perhaps its most distinctive tenet, Christian theology affirms that, in
the person of Jesus, God Himself became a man. Because He did, because
God entered human history, because the very Deity Himself is a figure in
the human past, we need only turn around to see Him. God actually stands
behind us. Historical study is one of the means by which we come to see
Him. As Karl Barth once wrote, our "faith has to do with the God who is
Himself historical and has fashioned a decree whose goal is history."[2] As
a result, the work of our tradition's finest historians if executed properly
by them and understood properly by us can be a means of enlightenment,
not only concerning the earliest Christians, but also concerning the God
they served and Who walked among them.

2

Theologically speaking, for the sovereign God of Scripture, history is a tool for His own purposes, the stage upon which the play of God's own making is acted out. In that historical play, in the drama of redemption, God shows Himself such an amazing playwright and director that He can permit His actors to ad lib at will and still lead the entire production and all its characters to His own intended conclusion. He even walks across the historical stage Himself, and the lines He utters are so wonderful and His gestures so sublime that, no matter who appears after Him, He is never upstaged; His thunderous curtain call goes on forever.

In that light, because Christianity is a religion both in history and of history, because its central figure is a historical figure, and because its message is and only can be proclaimed in time, the study of history is of fundamental importance for the Church. Few endeavors of the mind, therefore, prove as productive of insight and of solid common sense as does examining with care, and in precise detail, exactly how the finest and most influential religious historians have done their work. By looking over their shoulders and watching them toil at their craft, so to speak, we learn better how to do our own. By seeing how well, and in some cases how poorly, they served their own age, we can improve the work of the Church in ours. Again, that is why this book was written.

At the beginning of his *Institutes*, John Calvin rightly declared that true wisdom consists of two things: our knowledge of God and our knowledge of ourselves. I have already mentioned how history aids us in the former pursuit. Here I simply say that history is also one of the most effective means of pursuing the latter. Human nature remains fundamentally unchanged, and from all we can see of it, unchangeable, which is why history seems to repeat itself, and why it seems to some to be cyclical. That which led to the fall of leaders and of empires in the past will continue to lead to similar falls in the future. The egotism, self-indulgence and uncharitableness that bring about human calamity are with us always and everywhere. This is not fate or misfortune so much as it is sin. Historians ought not to balk at using that word. A large part of efficient and effective historiography, after all, is learning to call things by their real names. Sin is a fact about ourselves, about our history. Historical study reveals that barbarism, ignorance, and apathy are as old as the race, and that their consequences remain now what they always were. Those who think that somehow technology has served to make us more civilized than our forebears need only reflect that in our technological century the modern nation state has been the cause of more deaths than in any other, over 112 million. Sinners do become saints, no doubt, but those who do are the exception, and that fact of history is full of theological significance. We still are fallen creatures;

we still are the sons of Adam and the daughters of Eve, something C. S. Lewis rightly perceived was glory enough to raise the head of the lowest beggar and shame enough to lower the head of the highest king. Or, in the words of historian Roland Bainton, angel and ape make their abode in the same soul. So speaks history and so ought to speak the historian.

The historiographical upshot of unchanging human nature is that one need not be an antique in order to understand the past, one need only be observant and carefully analytical. A man need not be hundreds of years old to understand what it means to bury his wife or his son, or to preserve them for memory in the poignant words carved on a tombstone or uttered in a tearful eulogy, of which the world has seen perhaps millions. Looking into the past in such cases is like looking into a pool and seeing our own reflection. By preserving the records of such people, therefore, the religious historians help us to see not only our ancestors, but ourselves, and thus aid us in the fuller attainment of the second half of Calvin's two-sided pursuit.

History not only helps us understand both God and humanity; it also helps us better to understand the historical institution in which they most closely meet—the Church. The religious historians examined in these pages invested the lion's share of their professional lives tracing the history and development of precisely that institution. What their research revealed is both fascinating and instructive, at times even surprising. When, for example, Adolf Harnack looked back across the Church's checkered past, he noticed that whenever the masses were let into the Church, the spiritual giants, the saints, fled to the desert. As did some of the medieval monks before him, Harnack realized that, despite the advice of the temporizers in every age, it might not be advantageous for the Church to let down its barriers either to membership or to communion. After all, he said, look at what you let in. Or, in Vance Havner's memorable words, it's one thing to have the boat in the water; its quite another to have the water in the boat. People are not rescued by boats that are sinking; people are rescued from them. The relevance of that fact to an institution like the Church, an institution that has seen itself for nearly two thousand years as an ark, is only too obvious, and is one of the observations brought to light by the scholars whose work we examine in these pages.

To put a different point on it, the editors and authors of this volume are concerned to see how well, and in what ways, the most prominent religious historians in our tradition did their work, to discover to what extent those historians were able to incorporate or even to transcend what Ernst Bernheim, in his *Lehrbuch der historischen Methode und der Geschichtsphilosophie*, identified as the four principal elements of good historical writing:

first, the gathering of relevant historical evidence *Heuristik*; second, the fair and honest analysis and evaluation of that relevant historical evidence *Kritik*; third, the accurate and insightful apprehension of the true significance of that relevant historical evidence *Auffassung*; and fourth, the memorable and precise articulation of one's findings *Darstellung*. Additionally, although its main purpose lies elsewhere, this volume also demonstrates that to be a first-rate religious historian is exceedingly difficult because it demands that one combine a number of talents and characteristics not easily acquired—great learning, patient endurance, scientific precision, theological acumen, penetrating analysis, rhetorical virtuosity, and common perhaps even, uncommon sense.

This volume also makes plain that, even though people are always buying it, reading it, and writing it, history is more than entertainment, more than instruction, more than an enjoyable avocation. It is also a compass for voyagers in a storm-tossed sea, which is an apt description of Christians in nearly every age, buffeted as they are by opposition from the world, and badgered as they are not only by every heresy that threatens to distort their faith, but also by their fellow believers, who sometimes oppose them even more vigorously than do their secular counterparts. As Samuel Taylor Coleridge once observed, we often have more to fear from those who agree with us 90 percent than we do from those who do not agree with us at all. For that reason, the history of the Church has been a history of frequent conflict, some of it not confined to words or ideas. In such conditions, we discover, religious history writing has followed much the same path as has secularized political and social history writing, which seems always to have flourished most remarkably in the wake of war.

Scholars write history in such times not only because historical study helps us to get our bearings amidst the daunting tumult raging around us, but also because they know that whoever controls the past has the best chance of controlling the present. Whoever controls the present has the best chance of controlling the future. An entire procession of notable histories, therefore, has been written both during and after great combat, from the classical histories of Thucydides and Herodotus, written in the shadow of ancient conflict, to the works of H. G. Wells and Arnold Toynbee, written after this century's first world war, on the one hand, and to that of Winston Churchill, written after the second, on the other. This same characteristic is true of religious historians: Eusebius wrote in the midst and in the wake of the empire-wide Arian conflict. The Reformation spawned numerous chroniclers of both Roman Catholic and Protestant persuasion, not the least of whom was John Foxe, who wrote in the midst and in the aftermath of Queen Mary's bloody persecution of his

Protestant colleagues, and whose so-called *Book of Martyrs* has been the source of courage and inspiration for countless thousands. As well, the Puritan revolt in England gave rise in time to Bishop Burnet's two great histories, as well as to that by Lord Clarendon. And so the case goes.

We sometimes forget that the future is history too. It is—but only from our particular standpoint in time—simply history turned on its head. In theology we give history-on-its-head another name. We call it eschatology. Eschatology is the extension of our understanding of history in the opposite direction so that it encompasses the entire range of historical events both human and divine, both past and future. As Christian historians and scholars, we can consider the historical significance of the future because we see that in Christ the future has already broken into the past. The resurrection that awaits us all, and the cosmic reconciliation of which it is a part, have already made their appearance in the human past, in the most remarkable event of history—the resurrection of Jesus. What happened to Him in space and time shall happen to us all. Jesus is the end, or goal, of history. In His life we see not only where history has been, but where it is going. In His past, we see the presence of the future. Because of Him, and by means of Him, we can study the future by studying the past. We can look forward by looking behind us. We know what awaits us and we know Who awaits us. We know Who is coming, though we do not know when. We know such things about our future from our study of history, which is simply to say that Christian historiography agrees full well with what the Queen said to Alice in *Through the Looking Glass*: It's a poor sort of memory that only works backwards.

Further, like the history of the past, the history of the future has the power to generate changes in the present. Our notions of both past and future are powerful notions, for they are the controlling images around which we shape our identity, our calling, our life, our work. Because of their generative potency, our visions of the past and the future are the womb or matrix of the Church. History, whether before us or behind us, is a powerful motivator. It inspires us to rise to challenges that otherwise would have been too daunting and to slay dragons that, had we lacked such inspiration, would have slain us. By tying us to the courage of our ancestors, on the one hand, and to the predictable plight of our descendants, on the other, the study of history helps us to dare things we otherwise would not have dared. For such enlightenment and inspiration, we Christians are deeply indebted to the scholars whose work is considered here.

History's power to inspire us is, of course, primarily a literary power. That is, it inspires us because those who write it well are eloquent, widely informed, people of letters. Almost no Christian can fail to be moved by

Bainton's Luther or by Athanasius's Anthony, two people whose spiritual stature and heroism were captured for all time in stirring, memorable, graphic prose. Great historians, in other words, even though they work with a scientist's precision, are verbal artists. They are painters with words.

And they are polemicists. That which can be used for other purposes can also be made to serve factious or sectarian ends, and to those ends some of the scholars studied in this volume have no doubt put it. In most such cases, historians reduce themselves to mere lackeys of whatever might be the current, or local, or preferred, manifestation of "the reign of lies." Historians, religious historians included, sometimes seem unable to rise above the fracas that surrounds them. They permit themselves to be co-opted for purposes other than truth. In so doing, they become willing enlistees in a battle not properly their own. I am not saying that historical study cannot or should not serve a purpose higher or other than itself; I am saying that when religious historians sacrifice truth for partisanship, the study and writing of history is no longer our friend, it is our enemy. The same thing holds true, of course, for historians whose work is made to serve secularized or anti-religious ends. When the writing of religious history becomes merely the toadying handmaid of factionalism, the results are often tragic because religious historians ought to be the keepers of the ecclesiastical memory. When religious historians sell out, when they permit sectarian theology to deform their work, we forget. Ecclesiastical amnesia is a serious and crippling disease. A Church without a memory is doomed to invent the churchly and the theological wheels anew. The writing of religious history, in other words, is the necessary prop our naked memory requires in order to draw upon the accumulated wisdom of the ages, enabling us to withdraw at our need the deposit of insight and truth generously stored up for us by our predecessors in the faith. By studying that deposit, and by preserving great portions of it for us in written form, our tradition's greatest religious historians aid us in our resolve not to be duped, which is the first obligation of those endowed by God with rational minds. To defer once more to C. S. Lewis, it is the forgotten, not the remembered, past that enslaves us.

But to aid us effectively in remembering that past, religious historians, like their secular counterparts, must remain as disciplined and precise as professional integrity and historical data permit. In many ways, religious historians must learn to play the scientist, to whose efforts and methods their own are surprisingly similar: gathering data, creating and testing hypotheses, revising theories where needed, and articulating and documenting conclusions so that their work can be checked and verified, perhaps even discredited, by their peers. In their historiographical laboratories, re-ligious historians, therefore, must deliberately and consistently set aside whatever prejudices, predilections, and wishes that might serve to skew their work and to distort their conclusions. This volume clearly demon-strates that even the best among them do not always do so. Such detached or disinterested mastery of data and of technique is a talent only rarely achieved, whether by the religious or the secular historian. As Gordon Rupp explained: "Let it be admitted that Church historians have too long undervalued the importance of the material environment. They ought not, as believers in a religion of Incarnation, to be afraid of taking the mass of history seriously. Yet, we may admit that bad history, like bad science, is, when perpetrated by Christians, only too inclined to bring in the Holy Spirit to fill the gap. But the doctrinaire sociologist goes to the other ex-treme."[3]

Occasionally the positions proffered on both sides of the fence that now divides secular from religious historiography are so ludicrous that only un-reconstructed intellectual bigotry could find them convincing. All too of-ten, the philosophically naive application of both theistic and non-theistic theories of historical cause and effect have led to tendentious distortions of the human past. That Christianity is a religion of history means, among other things, that Christians cannot artificially insulate either themselves or their beliefs from historical/critical questions. To that assertion virtu-ally all secular historians would assent. But, if A touches B, B must touch A. That being so, secular historians cannot continue to isolate themselves and their work from either its inescapably theological presuppositions or conclusions, the theological nature of which almost no secular historian ever recognizes, much less takes wisely or fully into account. To function according to consciously God-less principles is as theological a decision and procedure as to include them. Both the historiographical atheism and agnosticism of modern historical writing are shot through with theologi-cal presuppositions and conclusions, most of which are theologically na-ive. But that does not seem at all to matter to many modern historians, who actually pride themselves on what they believe is the superior service-ability of their intellectually myopic procedures. "Secular," they must be reminded, is by no means synonymous with either "objective" or "true," though many historians seem credulously to operate as if it were.

Most of the religious historians examined in this text seem to have un-derstood that no academic discipline functions well or properly in an air-tight compartment and that "separate but equal" works no better in the academy than it did in the old South, where "separate but equal" always meant separate but unequal, and served as a mask for bigotry. But Jim

Crow has come back to campus. To some scholars, even today, it is intellectually respectable to push theology to the back of the bus. In fact, if one may be permitted a personal observation, the religious historians studied in this volume seem far more fully aware of the historical/critical implications of their work than the secular historians seem to be concerning the philosophical and theological nature of theirs. The critical competence of the one side far outstrips the theological sophistication of the other. The failure in view is so widespread that many prominent modern historians cannot even imagine what relevance or impact their extra-disciplinary innocence in this case, theological, can possibly have upon their work. Happily, among the scholars examined here, that egregious failure is quite rare, though not entirely absent. To their impressive and instructive body of work we now turn.

BIBLIOGRAPHY

Ausubel, Herman, J. Bartlet Brebner, and Erling M. Hunt, eds. *Some Modern Historians of Britain*. New York: Dryden, 1951.

Bainton, Roland H. *Yesterday, Today, and What Next?* Minneapolis: Augsburg, 1978.

Barnes, Harry Elmer. *A History of Historical Writing*. New York: Dover, 1937/1962.

Barzun, Jacques. *Clio and the Doctors: Psycho-History, Quanto-History, & History*. Chicago: University of Chicago, 1974.

Bebbington, David. *Patterns in History*. Grand Rapids: Baker, 1979/1990.

Benson, Lee. *Turner and Beard: American Historical Writing Reconsidered*. New York: Free Press, 1960.

Bloch, Marc. *The Historian's Craft*. New York: Vintage, 1953/1964.

Brown, Colin. *History & Faith: A Personal Exploration*. Grand Rapids: Zondervan, 1987.

Butterfield, Herbert. *Christianity in European History*. London: Collins, 1952.

———. *The Whig Interpretation of History*. New York: W. W. Norton & Company, 1965.

Cairns, Earle E. *God and Man in Time: A Christian Approach to Historiography*. Grand Rapids: Baker, 1979.

Cantor, Norman F. and Richard I. Schneider. *How to Study History*. New York: Thomas Y. Crowell Company, 1967.

Carr, E. H. *What Is History?* New York: Penguin, 1961/1977.

Clive, John. *Not by Fact Alone: Essays on the Writing and Reading of History*. Boston: Houghton Mifflin, 1989.

Collingwood, R. G. *The Idea of History*. New York: Oxford, 1956.

Elton, G. R. *The Practice of History*. New York: Thomas Y. Crowell Company, 1967.

Fischer, David Hackett. *Historians' Fallacies: Toward a Logic of Historical Thought*. New York: Harper & Row, 1970.

Fussner, F. Smith. *Tudor History and the Historians*. New York: Basic Books, 1970.

Gay, Peter. *Style in History*. New York: McGraw-Hill, 1974.

Gottschalk, Louis, ed. *Generalization in the Writing of History*. Chicago: University of Chicago, 1963.

Gottschalk, Louis. *Understanding History: A Primer of Historical Method*. New York: Knopf, 1950/1969.

Gooch, G. P. *History and Historians in the Nineteenth Century*. Boston: Beacon, 1959.

Grant, Michael. *The Ancient Historians*. New York: Charles Scribner's Sons, 1970.

Gustavson, Carl G. *A Preface to History*. New York: McGraw-Hill, 1955.

Harbison, E. Harris. *Christianity and History*. Princeton: Princeton University, 1964.

Harvey, Van Austin. *The Historian and the Believer: The Morality of Historical Knowledge and Christian Belief*. New York: Macmillan, 1969/1975.

Hegel, G. W. F. *Reason in History: A General Introduction to the Philosophy of History*. Indianapolis: Bobbs-Merrill, 1953.

Kent, Sherman. *Writing History*. New York: ACC, 1967.

Littell, John Stockton. *The Historians and the English Reformation*. Milwaukee: The Young Churchman Company, 1910.

Manuel, Frank E. *Shapes of Philosophical History*. London: George Allen & Unwin Ltd., 1965.

Marsden, George, and Frank Roberts, eds. *A Christian View of History?* Grand Rapids: Eerdmans, 1975.

McIntire, C. T., ed. *Herbert Butterfield: Writings on Christianity and History*. New York: Oxford, 1979.

McIntire, C. T., and Ronald A. Wells, eds. *History and Historical Understanding*. Grand Rapids: Eerdmans, 1984.

Momigliano, Arnaldo. *Studies in Historiography*. New York: Harper & Row, 1966.

Montgomery, John Warwick. *History & Christianity*. Downers Grove: InterVarsity, 1964/1972.

———. *The Shape of the Past: A Christian Response to Secular Philosophies of History*. Minneapolis: Bethany, 1975.

Nevins, Allan. *The Gateway to History*. New York: Anchor, 1938/1962.

Randall, John Herman, Jr. *Nature and Historical Experience: Essays in Naturalism and in the Theory of History*. New York: Columbia University, 1958.

Renier, G. J. *History: Its Purpose and Method*. New York: Harper & Row, 1950.

Skotheim, Robert Allen, ed. *The Historian and the Climate of Opinion*. Reading: Addison-Wesley, 1969.

Stern, Fritz, ed. *The Varieties of History: From Voltaire to the Present*. New York: Vintage, 1956/1972.

Swanstrom, Roy. *History in the Making: An Introduction to the Study of the Past*. Grand Rapids: Baker, 1978.

Taylor, Hugh. *History as a Science*. Port Washington: Kennikat, 1933/1971.

Tillinghast, Pardon E. *The Specious Past: Historians and Others*. Reading: Addison-Wesley, 1972.

Trevelyan, George Macaulay. *Clio, A Muse and Other Essays*. New York: Longmans, Green and Co., 1913/1949.

Wedgwood, C. V. *The Sense of the Past: Thirteen Studies in the Theory and Practice of History*. New York: Collier, 1960.

Wells, Ronald A. *History Through the Eyes of Faith*. San Francisco: Harper & Row, 1989.

Winks, Robin W., ed. *The Historian as Detective*. New York: Harper & Row, 1968.
Woodward, C. Vann. *Thinking Back: The Perils of Writing History*. Baton Rouge: Louisiana State University, 1986.

NOTES

1. By "religious historians" I mean those historians who deal with theological people, ideas and events in a theologically informed fashion.
2. Karl Barth, *Dogmatics in Outline* (New York: Philosophical Library, n.d.), 28.
3. Gordon Rupp, *Protestant Catholicity* (London: Epworth, 1960), 11.

1

OLD TESTAMENT
HISTORIANS

R. PAUL HOUSE

Historians have never had an easy task. Despite what some non-historians might think, it is no simple matter to tell what has happened to a given person, nation, or civilization. On the one hand, it is difficult to assemble even basic accurate data such as names, places, and dates. On the other hand, it is harder still to assess the causes and effects of events, and perhaps hardest of all to choose which events have been the most significant for the person or group being studied. Mixed into all these issues is the historian's struggle to discern how personal, political, sociological, economic, or religious viewpoints have affected his or her historical analysis.[1]

Old Testament historians had similar difficulties and even had some problems peculiar to their own situations. For example, Hebrew historians had few models for their writing because they were among the first creators of narrative history. Therefore, they were forced to develop patterns and styles of their own. They also had distinct ideas about how history and theology are related. Their God-centered approach to national and international history was sometimes difficult for them to reconcile with the apparent victory of evil over good as when Assyria, Babylon, or Persia dominated the ancient world. Further, Old Testament historians often faced the uncertainties caused by Israel's shifting fortunes. Though not primarily a historian, Moses wrote part of Israel's story, always while sharing the nation's nomadic lifestyle. The author of Joshua, Judges, 1–2 Samuel, and 1–2 Kings compiled his annalistic, biographical, and theological data after Jerusalem had been destroyed. First and Second Chronicles were composed by either an exile or a person living in a less-than-ideal social, political, and religious situation in a Jerusalem ruled by a foreign government. Many of the prophets lived in settings equally undesirable. Finally, Old Testament historians held a monotheistic, covenantal worldview in a polytheistic, nationalistic age. Their world was truly multi-cultural, greatly pluralistic, and totally opposed to their convictions about why events occurred and on what grounds a person or event should be considered significant. Again, their task was complex and, most likely, more than a little frustrating.

Given these obstacles, the achievements of the Old Testament historians are impressive. They managed to present an account that, while focusing on certain major events, spans from creation of the human race to the rebuilding of Jerusalem after the Babylonian exile. Their accounts include other nations, such as Egypt, Assyria, Babylon, and Persia. Thus, the scope of their writings includes the international scene. Their histories are more than bare presentations of facts, for they include a purposeful ideology that offers readers a way of understanding all history. They use sources extensively, yet rarely fail to integrate their materials into a readable, even artistic, coherent narrative. No wonder, then, that the Old and New Testament communities of faith preserved these texts as scripture.

This chapter seeks to illustrate the achievements of Old Testament historiography by examining the work of two of the greatest Hebrew historians: the Deuteronomist, (the writer of Joshua, Judges, 1–2 Samuel, and 1–2 Kings), and the Chronicler. Both the Deuteronomist and the Chronicler chose to survey a lengthy period of time, both utilized source material, both held a theocentric view of history, both lived after Israel's national disintegration, and both wrote with a distinct purpose in mind. Still, the two are sufficiently different for a sense of the diversity in Old Testament historiography to emerge. They vary in tone, detail, purpose, guiding principles, and audience, though they accurately recount many of the same events. These similarities and differences will be explored through a study of the historians' identity, historical methodology, historical setting, personal viewpoint, and canonical writings. A survey of these two historians' work should help us better understand biblical history in general.

CANONICAL PLACEMENT OF
1–2 KINGS AND 1–2 CHRONICLES

One of the major differences between the order of the books in English and Hebrew Bibles is found in the historical books. The Hebrew text lists four: Joshua, Judges, Samuel, and Kings. English Bibles add Ruth and divide Samuel and Kings into four books. English Bibles also include 1–2 Chronicles, Ezra, Nehemiah, and Esther in this section, thus presenting Israel's history from the conquest of Canaan (ca. 1400 B.C.) to the Persian period (ca. 465 B.C.). The Hebrew Bible, by contrast, places 1–2 Chronicles, Ezra, Nehemiah, and Esther in the Writings, at the end of the Canon. Job, Psalms, and the other "poetic and wisdom" books follow Esther in the English Bible, while the Prophets come after Kings in the Hebrew texts.

Why mention these varying orders when the contents of the books are the same? Chiefly because the differing lists reveal how the histories have been interpreted. The English Bible presents the books more as straightforward accounts of events than as interpretations of history. Placing the books together demonstrates the English Bible's interest in detailing events of Israel's history. But, the Hebrew Bible pairs Joshua-Kings with the Prophets, which highlights the commonalities between that history and the prophetic tradition. This decision makes Joshua-Kings both proclamation *and* history. It also helps readers understand why Joshua-Kings discusses the downfall of Israel. These books share the prophets' conviction that the nation's covenant breaking led to its eventual destruction.

The Chronicler certainly consulted the Former Prophets as a source of information. Indeed the Chronicler used the books as more than information, for they operate as a brooding dialogue partner to the more upbeat history found in 1–2 Chronicles. The Chronicler included most of the characters and events mentioned in 1–2 Samuel and 1–2 Kings, yet shaped them much differently than did his partner. For example, Saul makes only a cameo appearance in 1–2 Chronicles (cf. 1 Chron. 9:35–10:14). Why? Because David's importance is heightened. He is portrayed as Israel's greatest king and the one who collected material to build the temple (1 Chron. 28:1–29:20). Solomon's idolatry, which the Former Prophets claim led to the nation's division, goes unmentioned, and even wicked Manasseh is portrayed in a partly positive manner (cf. 2 Chron. 33:10–13). Jerusalem's fall receives only brief treatment (2 Chron. 36:15–21), though the Chronicler did blame the people for the disaster (2 Chron. 36:14).

Both histories are necessary for readers to have a balanced picture of Israel's history. Though quite different, both viewpoints are accurate and appropriate for their intended audience. Certainly Israel's negative actions precipitated their downfall, but the nation still had a proud and productive heritage. Placed at the very end of the Hebrew canon, 1–2 Chronicles encouraged post-exilic readers to maintain hope and to trust God to do great things for them again. Written earlier, and from a prophetic theological stance, Joshua-Kings admonished the nation, basing hope more on change than on the removal of doubt and discouragement. Together the histories present the best and worst of Israel's past, and they do so in a way that rebukes the proud, rewards the humble, and encourages the hurting.

THE DEUTERONOMIST'S IDENTITY AND HISTORICAL METHODOLOGY

The question of who wrote Joshua, Judges, Samuel, and Kings in what manner has sparked lively debate during the past half century. This debate has been divided basically between scholars who think the books were written by a single author who carefully crafted a consecutive history using accurate sources, and those who believe the texts were composed by two, three, or more careful editors writing at different stages in Israel's history.

No author is ever identified in the biblical text itself. Major characters in the accounts could have played a role in the books' composition, of course, but none is singled out as an author in any direct way. Given this situation, one must examine other types of information which the accounts offer in order to determine when they were written, and by whom. Though other factors are also important,[2] two basic factors provide insight into these issues.

The first factor is the *scope of events* covered in the books. At least seven hundred years unfold. Joshua's conquest of Canaan, the history's initial event, occurs no later than 1250 B.C.[3] Second Kings ends with a description of how Jehoiachin, a Judahite king exiled in 597 B.C., is given kind treatment in the thirty-seventh year of his imprisonment in Babylon (2 Kings 25:27–30). This notation places the author of that material beyond 560 B.C. Therefore, it is safe to conclude that the books were completed sometime after that date. Because no further events are described, the author of the books could have written the material by 550 B.C.

The second factor is the matter of the *sources*. Several written sources are mentioned in the books themselves. Joshua 10:12–13 and 2 Samuel 1:17–27 are poetic texts that the author says may be found in the Book of Jashar. It is impossible to know the contents of this source because only these references have survived. C. R. Kraft suggests, "It seems to have been an ancient national song book, the antiquity of which is suggested in part by the relatively poor state of preservation of the Hebrew text of each poem."[4] Regardless of its origin, the author of Joshua and 2 Samuel freely admits using the source, an implicit invitation to check the accuracy of the citation.

Three written sources are mentioned in 1–2 Kings. The Book of the Acts of Solomon is listed in 1 Kings 11:41, and seems to be cited as the main source for most if not all of the Solomon material found in 1 Kings 1–11. The Book of the Chronicles of the Kings of Israel is claimed as a source for every northern king's reign except for Jehoram and Hoshea. The Book of the Chronicles of the Kings of Judah is cited as a source of information on all of Judah's rulers except for Ahaziah, Athaliah, Jehoahaz, Jehoiachin, and Zedekiah.[5] In each instance where these three sources appear the author implies that more details on each king's era were available in those works. This impression leaves the true nature of the source material very much in doubt, which has allowed various scholarly opinions to arise.

In the decades after Julius Wellhausen popularized source criticism of the Pentateuch, several scholars, following Wellhausen himself,[6] sought to divide Joshua, Judges, Samuel, and Kings into numerous sources. Some critics argued that the same J and E sources supposedly found in the Pentateuch also run throughout the books that follow.[7] Other commentators basically rejected the J and E hypothesis, and sought to identify the nature of all the stated and unstated sources used to write the books.[8] Based on the variety of the books' material and the difficulty of determining what the stated sources, much less the unstated sources, contained, most experts correctly concluded that the so-called Pentateuchal sources were not present in the Former Prophets.

Did the books' author use other sources? If so, what was the nature of these sources and of the ones the biblical text mentions? Interpreters must exercise caution and humility when answering these questions. Though only three sources are explicitly revealed, other data may have been used. After all, the stated sources all refer to poems or to the activities of kings. Yet the books also include genealogies, divisions of land, and accounts of battles. Several narratives about prophets also appear, which makes it possible that the author gathered written or oral materials from prophetic sources. As for the contents of the sources named, 1 Kings 11:41 indicates that the Book of the Acts of Solomon "comprised contemporary annals, biographical materials, and extracts from records in the Temple archives."[9] The Books of the Chronicles of the Kings of Israel and Judah probably contained similar details, since they are said to chronicle dates, royal achievements, and important events (e.g., 2 Kings 13:8). Whether or not these "events" include the prophets' lives and teachings, though, is impossible to determine.

Do such conclusions not lessen the historical value of the Former Prophets? No, because archaeological evidence indicates that the historical data is accurate and reliable.[10] The author researched Israel's history, chose appropriate material from available sources, and crafted the data into a coherent whole. Readers are even invited to peruse the documents in order to read more about the kings. Certainly the author wrote from a theological viewpoint, but that fact does not mean the history is inaccurate. Indeed, theological scruples may lead to a greater concern for accuracy and truth. There is no compelling reason, then, to doubt that this openly honest author faithfully used accurate sources to write the books, even though the sources' exact contents and age cannot now be recovered.

Scholars have used the literary and theological aspects of the Former Prophets in attempting to learn more about the person or persons responsible for their final form. Several commentators think a single individual who lived about 550 B.C. collected relevant source data, and then created a narrative framework for these books in order to explain how Israel gained, possessed, and lost the promised land. Other experts think the Former Prophets passed through several editors' hands. These editors are thought to have completed separate histories which had distinct theological viewpoints and distinct conclusions. A later editor then added historical details from his era, smoothed over whatever rough transitions existed, and thereby produced Joshua, Judges, Samuel, and Kings as they now stand.

Though earlier scholars had suggested some of the same points, Martin Noth set what remains the agenda for the authorship discussion.[11] Noth claimed that one author wrote all four books. His theory was clear, concise, and in step with then-current critical opinions on the Pentateuch and the Prophets. He argued that the author was heavily influenced by the language and thinking "found in the Deuteronomic Law and the admonitory speeches which precede and follow the Law."[12] Because of the influence of Deuteronomy's standards on the writer's work, Noth called the author "the Deuteronomist." Further, Noth said the Deuteronomist selected source materials that were then carefully crafted into a unified whole.[13] Part of the crafting process included writing Deuteronomy 1–4 to introduce the history, providing narrative links between "books," and composing strategic speeches that summarize and advance the story.[14] Finally, Noth stated that the Deuteronomist had probably witnessed the fall of Jerusalem (and thus must have penned the history by 550 B.C.)[15] and therefore wrote to explain to future generations how Israel lost its land.[16]

The Deuteronomist was, then, a careful, theologically astute individual who chronicled the negative side of Israel's history.

Many commentators accepted Noth's basic thesis, but modified certain theological or compositional details. For example, Gerhard von Rad and H. W. Wolff observed that the history's theology may be more hopeful than Noth thought. Von Rad claimed that the Deuteronomist emphasized how God fulfilled prophetic predictions in history, and that the great historian believed God would continue to work with and through David's descendants because of the promises made to David in 2 Samuel 7:13.[17] According to von Rad, the partially hopeful ending of the history (2 Kings 25:27–30) implies "that the line of David has not yet come to an irrevocable end."[18] Wolff also located positive theology in the many texts that encourage Israel to repent and turn to the Lord.[19] These passages indicate that God still cares for Israel and calls this nation back to its prior relationship with Him. These, and other,[20] studies helped balance Noth's presentation of the books' theology.

R. K. Harrison provided a mediating, evangelical perspective in his comprehensive *Introduction to the Old Testament* (1969). While agreeing that one person heavily influenced by covenant thinking and the book of Deuteronomy wrote Joshua-Kings, Harrison correctly argued that this conclusion need not be based on an acceptance of source critical theories of the Pentateuch.[21] In fact, "The term 'Deuteronomist' can only be applied . . . in the sense that the author recognized with Moses (Deut. 28:1ff), that obedience to God brought blessing, while disobedience resulted in calamity."[22] Despite these reasonable correctives, Harrison and Noth both stress the unity of the Former Prophets, the books' overriding theology, and their probable composition by 550 B.C.

From the time the seminal writings of Abraham Kuenen and Julius Wellhausen appeared,[23] some scholars have concluded that at least two editors were responsible for collecting the history. Alfred Jepsen located two editors, one with a priestly perspective and one with prophetic convictions.[24] Jepsen could not be sure, though, where one editor spoke and the other did not. Rudolf Smend agreed with Jepsen's concept of prophetic and priestly editors, and added a third compiler who displayed keen interest in the law. Thus, Smend claimed that a prophetic editor wrote an initial history after Jerusalem's fall (587 B.C.), a priestly compiler reworked the history about 580–560 B.C., and a law-oriented editor completed the work after 560 B.C.[25] These individuals were all heavily influenced by "deuteronomic" thought, which explains the books' unity. G. H. Jones basically agrees with Smend's conclusions because he thinks this theory explains both the unity Noth emphasizes and the diversity inherent in the text.[26] Jones therefore believes that a "deuteronomic school," or movement, may have produced this history after several decades of theological reflection.[27]

Following F. M. Cross's suggestion that there is no explanatory text for Jerusalem's fall to match the one for Samaria's demise (2 Kings 17), R. D. Nelson said that one pro-David editor wrote during Josiah's time, and was followed by an exilic writer who explained how and why the monarchy ended. Nelson based his argument on detailed structural, theological, and linguistic grounds.[28] This 1981 volume stated the two-author theory more carefully than it had been stated in the past, yet also generally agreed with other commentators who advocated the multiple-authorship position.[29]

Though it is prudent to be cautious about conclusions regarding the author of an anonymous document, the single-author approach is probably the best answer to the problem. At least four reasons point to this conclusion.

1. *The single-author theory best explains the Former Prophets' unity.* As is evident from the texts themselves, each new "book" in the history is linked to its predecessor. Thus, Moses' death links Joshua to Deuteronomy, Joshua's death ties Judges to Joshua, Samuel's career as Israel's last judge unites Judges and 1–2 Samuel, and David's final days helps 2 Samuel flow into 1–2 Kings. Certain themes also hold the books together, such as the conquering of the promised land, God's promises to David, and Israel's loss of land through idol worship.

2. *The single-author theory adequately explains the history's diversity.* Because the author used source material that spans from the conquest to the destruction of Jerusalem, some diversity is to be expected. It is also true that the author had to include various ideological viewpoints to portray Israel's theological heritage accurately.

3. As Burke Long has argued, *the single-author theory fits the nature of ancient historiography.* Indeed, ancient historians, such as Herodotus, often used diverse types of material to present a series of scenes that created the author's main arguments.[30] Seen this way, what some scholars consider evidence for two or more editors can actually be viewed as part of a carefully structured whole.

4. *The single-author theory retains its scholarly attractiveness without encountering the difficulties of the multiple-author position.* Propo-

nents of multiple editions do not agree on the number, date, or criteria of the proposed redactions. They are forced to posit "schools" that last for decades to account for the books' unity; or, they utilize highly selective and sensitive criteria to separate one edition from the other.[31] These tendencies appear to be based too much on a preference for source criticism rather than on the text itself. Without question, the single-author viewpoint has its own problems, such as accounting for the books' various theological emphases, but it does deal resourcefully with theological, historical, and literary issues.

A fairly distinct authorial portrait emerges from these discussions. The author is an anonymous individual who carefully collected relevant source data and shaped this material into a consecutive account that spans Joshua-Kings. This person finished the work by about 550 B.C. The narrative itself is a sweeping account of Israel's tragic loss of the land it was promised in the Pentateuch.[32] This tragedy occurred because the nation failed to live up to covenant standards, particularly those found in Deuteronomy. Despite this correlation with Deuteronomy, it is unnecessary to conclude that the historian wrote any part of that book. Deuteronomy's influence is sufficient to explain the emphases in Joshua-Kings. Though the loss of the promised land was quite a negative event, the Deuteronomist did not view the situation as permanent. Living after the nation's defeat, this great writer looked to God's eternal covenant with David as proof that Israel was not finished.

With this portrait in place, some tentative conclusions about the author's methodology emerge. First, the author decided to compose a history of Israel based on the theological principles found in Deuteronomy. Second, this individual collected and collated the written sources which the books mention; perhaps other materials not specified in the texts; and unique information the author possessed. Third, the author wove an account that stressed a continuity of leadership and mission from Moses to Joshua, the growth of the monarchy, the promises to David, and the prophets' roles in predicting the nation's demise. Throughout the process the Deuteronomist stressed that God was the one who determined history. Thus, theology and detail were combined in a way that created a worthy history.

THE DEUTERONOMIST'S HISTORICAL SETTING AND AUDIENCE

The Deuteronomist wrote in a way calculated to impact individuals who lived under discouraging circumstances. Israel had experienced its glory days during the reigns of David and Solomon (ca. 1010–930 B.C.). When Solomon died, the nation dissolved into Northern (Israel) and Southern (Judah) segments. In 722 B.C. Assyria conquered Samaria, northern Israel's capital, and overran the entire kingdom (2 Kings 17). Judah survived, but only as an Assyrian vassal, and only in a greatly weakened condition.

Babylon proved the greatest threat during the Deuteronomist's lifetime. Like Assyria, Babylon exerted its power and influence over several centuries. It was during 605–539 B.C. (a plausible life span for the Deuteronomist), however, that this nation impacted Judah the most. In 612 B.C., Babylon conquered Ninevah, Assyria's capital, thus becoming the dominant force in the ancient world. It took the Babylonians until 610 B.C. to eliminate Assyrian opposition,[33] and until 605 B.C. to place Judah under servitude, but once in control they did not relinquish power for nearly seven decades.

Nebuchadnezzar subdued Egypt at Carchemish in 605 B.C. (Jer. 46:2), thus establishing Babylon's control of the region (2 Kings 24:7). Jehoiakim, Egypt's hand-picked ruler (2 Kings 23:31–35), was on Judah's throne. At this time Babylon took some exiles, including Daniel and his friends (Dan. 1:1–2). Jehoiakim served Babylon for three years, then rebelled (2 Kings 24:1). Babylon did not move to punish this rebellion until 598 B.C., the year Jehoiachin succeeded his father (2 Kings 24:8).[34] Nebuchadnezzar removed Jehoiachin from power in 597 B.C., deported more Israelites (e.g., Ezekiel), stripped the temple of its wealth, and placed Zedekiah on the throne (2 Kings 24:10–17; Jer. 24–29). Thus, Babylon gave Judah one more chance to be a loyal vassal.

Zedekiah ruled Judah during its last decade of existence. The only notice 2 Kings offers as to why Babylon finally decided to destroy Jerusalem is the brief comment, "Now Zedekiah rebelled against the king of Babylon" (24:20, NIV). Perhaps nationalistic fervor had arisen, but no clear reason for this rebellion can be discerned.[35] Regardless of the reasons for Zedekiah's actions, Nebuchadnezzar decided to eliminate his troublesome vassal. He captured the city, burned its defense walls and important buildings, including the temple, and appointed his own governor (2 Kings 25:1–24). Zedekiah was blinded, but only after witnessing his son's execution (2 Kings 25:6–7). No part of what was Israel remained self-governing. All twelve tribes were either in exile or subjugated in their own land. Hope for the future remained, but that hope was blunted by the present reality that God had "thrust them from his presence" (2 Kings 24:20, NIV). Jeremiah had predicted a seventy-year exile (Jer. 29), so the Deuteronomist wrote to an audience that was serving a divine sentence for their sins.

It was under such trying circumstances that the Deuteronomist wrote one of the world's first significant narrative histories.[36] The history was written to inform the audience that the prophets were right in their warnings that idolatry would bring exile. It was written so that such mistakes would never again happen. Yet the history was also composed to tell a defeated, discouraged people that divine promises of land and kingship still applied. The author's theological convictions thus transformed the books from annals and lists into a distinct work of history.

THE DEUTERONOMIST'S THEOLOGY

As the preceding sections have indicated, the Deuteronomist's theological perspective impacts his historical presentation. It would be strange if this were not the case, since the author wrote to an audience dealing with exile and national disgrace. Their situation cried out for interpretation. Israel's national predicament caused the people to wonder if any hope for national restoration remained. In this setting history could hardly be told in a detached manner. Past events *meant* something, but what? Though space does not allow a full treatment of this issue, the following themes at least introduce the Deuteronomist's underlying interpretative framework.

First, the Deuteronomist stressed God's gift of the promised land and Israel's forfeiture of it. God promised Abraham that his descendants would eventually possess Canaan (Gen. 12:7) after four centuries of sojourn "in a country not their own" (Gen. 15:13). Exodus describes the nation's movement towards this land; Numbers states why Israel did not conquer Canaan immediately; and Deuteronomy prepares the second post-exodus generation for possession of the promised land.[37] In fact, Deuteronomy is shaped as a covenant between God and Israel, the chief goal of which is to help Israel stay in their new home (cf. Deut. 27–28).[38]

Joshua describes the long-awaited conquest of Canaan. As long as Israel obeys the covenant mediated through Moses, they are allowed to defeat every foe (Josh. 1–6). Only disobedience can check their advance (cf. Josh. 7). Eventually a temple is built in Jerusalem, symbolizing the completion of God's gift of land (cf. 1 Kings 8).

Second, the Deuteronomist advocated monotheism *and* opposed idolatry. If Old Testament theology were to be summarized in one sentence it would probably read, "There is no god but the Lord." This theme emerges in the Bible's opening declaration that "in the beginning God created the heavens and the earth" (Gen. 1:1, NIV). It is re-emphasized in the Ten Commandments, where Israel is told to worship only the Lord (Exod. 20:3) and is warned not to bow down to idols (Exod. 20:4–5). The idea appears again in Deuteronomy 6:4, where Israel's worship, home life, and values system are based on God's unity. In Joshua, idolatry is basically absent, and the people prosper; while in Judges, idolatry is blamed for Israel's periodic plunges into defeat and oppression (cf. Judg. 2). First and Second Samuel never imply that what occurs on earth is not caused by the Lord (cf. 1 Sam. 16:13–14).

First and Second Kings repeatedly oppose idolatry and endorse monotheism. Idolatry is blamed for the nation's division after Solomon's death (1 Kings 11:9–13). Without exception, the kings are judged by whether they promoted, curtailed, or eradicated idolatry in the land. Refusal to obey the prophets' call to turn from idolatry ultimately leads to the destruction of both Samaria and Jerusalem (2 Kings 17:7–41). Clearly, theological failure hastens military failure.

Third, the historian highlighted central worship and opposed worship at "high places," which were sanctuaries where local deities could be worshiped.[39] Besides their obvious polytheistic implications, the high places were a direct rebellion against Jerusalem's temple as God's chosen worship center. Deuteronomy had promised God would pick a central worship site (cf. 12:5, 11; 14:23–25; 26:2; 31:11, etc).[40] Solomon built the temple as a dwelling place for God's name (1 Kings 8:16, 44, 48), and God agreed to place His name there "forever" (1 Kings 9:3) if Solomon kept the Lord's commands (1 Kings 9:4). After Solomon committed idolatry, God divided the kingdom as a punishment, yet spared Judah for David's and Jerusalem's sake (1 Kings 11:13). Second Kings 21:7 reaffirms God's selection of Jerusalem, and 2 Kings 23:27 declares that the city's destruction amounts to a temporary rejection of the chosen capital and its temple.

Fourth, underlying the constant complaints about idol worship and high places, is the conviction that Israel and Judah have broken their covenant commitments to God. Joshua warned against disobedience (Josh. 24:1–27), Judges depicted the early results of rebellion, and 1–2 Samuel presented a contrast between the lives of covenant breakers like Saul and penitent covenant keepers like David. In 1–2 Kings, David (1 Kings 2:3), Solomon (1 Kings 8:53, 56), and the narrator (2 Kings 14:6; 18:4, 6, 12; 21:8; 23:25) all stress the importance of Israel's keeping the Mosaic covenant lest God remove the people from the land. The belief that Israel lost Canaan because of covenant breaking coincides with the threat and promises found in Deuteronomy 27–28.

Fifth, the Deuteronomist underscored the importance of God's covenant with David. In 2 Samuel 7:1–17, a grateful David desires to build a temple for the Lord. Yahweh declines the offer, and instead promises David that his son will build the temple (2 Sam. 7:12–13). More importantly, God tells David his kingdom will endure *forever* (2 Sam. 7:13, 16), which obviously extends beyond Solomon's reign.[41] Though Solomon and all his successors except Hezekiah and Josiah displease Yahweh in some way, God spares the nation "for David's sake" (1 Kings 11:12–13; 15:3–5). Ultimately, however, reprehensible kings like Manasseh cause God to give the people and their king over to judgment (2 Kings 21:10–15). Unfortunately as does the nation itself, the monarchy exhausts the Lord's patience through constant rebellion.

Several prophetic books and many psalms interpret this covenant to mean that the Messiah will come through Davidic lineage, thus providing the fulfillment of the eternal aspect of the promise. Isaiah, Jeremiah, Ezekiel, Micah, Zechariah, and Malachi all highlight the concept.[42] Psalms 89 and 110 indicate the long-term implications of God's promise to David. Of course, the New Testament concludes that Jesus, a descendant of David, fulfills the Old Testament predictions about the Messiah.[43] Therefore, the Bible as a whole teaches that David's kingdom will endure forever because one of his descendants is the eternal son of God.[44] Without question, then, the Deuteronomist conveys the most important promise in scripture.

Sixth, God's absolute sovereignty over history undergirds every theological emphasis in Joshua-Kings. Israel received Deuteronomy's covenant standards because God chose to reveal them to this small nation (cf. Deut. 7:7–8). Israel possessed Canaan because God chose Joshua, Samuel, and David to lead the people. Jerusalem was where Israel should worship because God decided to place His name there (1 Kings 9:3). God called the prophets to warn Israel to repent, and placed each king in power.

Further, the Deuteronomist believed God rules all nations, not just Israel, and directs all human affairs. Even great nations such as Egypt, Assyria, and Babylon do not determine their own destinies. God sends them to do His will. They punish Israel because the Lord wants them to do so (cf. 2 Kings 17). Otherwise, God can defend Jerusalem regardless of the circumstances (cf. 2 Kings 19:35–37). The worst mistake Israel's enemies can make is to assume that Yahweh is merely a regional deity (cf. 1 Kings 20:23–30). By contrast, choosing to serve the Lord is the best decision a gentile can make (2 Kings 5:1–15).

THE DEUTERONOMIST'S WRITINGS

The Deuteronomist combined history, theology, and a concern for readers chiefly by wedding his theology to the historical setting in a creative way. From an exilic point the historian could see that Israel had gained, then lost, Canaan. The Deuteronomist saw that Egypt, Philistia, Syria, Assyria, and Babylon had harassed Israel, and that during reigns such as those of David, Solomon, Hezekiah, and Josiah the nation prospered. It was not overly difficult, then, to apply covenantal theology to Israel's major events. Indeed it was the Deuteronomist's theology that helped him decide which occurrences were most significant.

In Joshua, the historian presents the conquest as a natural result of God's covenant with Israel, the work of Moses, and the nation's obedience (cf. Josh. 1:6–9; 8:30–35). Only God could cause Israel to possess the land, for Israel needed miracles to succeed in this venture (cf. Josh. 6:1–27; 10:1–15). Only disobedience against God on Israel's part could stop the march to victory (cf. Josh. 7:1–26). As long as the people serve Yahweh, all shall be well, even if life is not easy (Josh. 24:1–27). The generation of Israelites who march with Joshua are supremely successful. They follow God, take every military objective, and inherit the land their parents were too fearful to invade.[45]

Judges tells a quite different story, yet it too fits history and the Deuteronomist's theology.[46] The historian knew that Israel experienced economic, social, and military difficulties between Joshua's era and the rise of the monarchy. Religious decay fueled national decline, and new enemies like the Philistines made Israel pay for their weakness. Just as national obedience to the Lord had led to victory in every sphere of life, so now sin led to a miserable existence in the land, according to the Deuteronomist. Israel's chief sin was idolatry, which led to defeat (Judg. 2:1–23). Only when the people repented were they given leaders, called "judges," who delivered them.

Twice in Judges the text blames Israel's lawlessness on the fact that there was no king in Israel (17:6; 21:25). Samuel remedies this lack. Saul and David become Israel's first kings. Together they restored Israel's national fortunes. Saul, a tragic figure,[47] helped the people defeat Philistia and Ammon (1 Sam. 7–11). When God rejected him, it was because of religious, not military, blunders (1 Sam. 13,15). David, by contrast, never worships another god, nor does he usurp the priests' authority. His sins are serious, though of a different nature (cf. 2 Sam. 11). Therefore, God allows him to defeat all enemies, and, most importantly, Yahweh promises him an eternal dynasty (2 Sam. 7:1–17). Again, the Deuteronomist knew history, knew history's ebb and flow, and believed Pentateuchal theology best explained why events happened as they did.

Finally, 1–2 Kings provide the concluding chapter of Israel's pre-550 B.C. history. David and Solomon give Israel their finest days. Yet when Solomon dies, the nation divides because Solomon's idolatry helped cause the nation's fragile political unity to unravel (1 Kings 11:1–43). Syria, Edom, Egypt, Assyria, and Babylon serve as God's agents of punishment

(2 Kings 17:1–17). Jerusalem and Samaria fall not inevitably as greater armies march, but voluntarily as they reject God's word through the prophets. Once more the historian combines theology and events. Every event in 1–2 Kings occurred, so the historians' accounts are accurate. They receive their *meaning*, however, not from their accuracy, but from the historian's understanding of God's sovereignty in history.

THE CHRONICLER'S IDENTITY AND HISTORICAL METHODOLOGY

As with the Deuteronomist, scholars disagree over the date, nature, and extent of the Chronicler's writings. Thus, they also debate whether one or more persons actually composed the history found in 1–2 Chronicles. Despite these problems, there is fairly wide agreement on the Chroniclers' theology and purpose for writing. Thus, some common ground does exist and aids Chronicles research.

Like 1–2 Kings, 1–2 Chronicles covers a vast period of time. In fact, 1–2 Chronicles spans even more centuries than 1–2 Kings, since these books address Israel's history from *Adam* until Cyrus's decree that Israel could return home in 538 B.C. Clearly, the final author of 1–2 Chronicles must have lived after the Jews began to go back to Jerusalem, and this individual must have used sources to compile this history.

At least five types of sources are mentioned in 1–2 Chronicles. The author claims to have had access to genealogies from various clans and kings (1 Chron. 4:33; 5:17, etc.), documents such as letters from foreign rulers (2 Chron. 32:17–20), songs of praise and lament (2 Chron. 29:30; 35:25), eleven different prophetic writings (1 Chron. 29:29; 2 Chron. 9:29; 12:15; 13:22; 20:34; 32:32; 26:22; 33:19; 36:22), and other historical works such as "the book of the kings of Israel and Judah" (e.g., 2 Chron. 27:7; 35:27, etc.).[48] All these references to sources indicate the author has researched the topic thoroughly, has tried to present the events accurately, and in general has been as honest as possible in telling Israel's history. Too, the references imply that the author has fit source material into an overall plan. The history is told for a purpose.

Two other factors found in the text itself may help illuminate the author's identity. First, the book has an obvious, specific interest in religious details such as priestly and Levitical duties. The ark, the temple, and the need to rebuild the temple are quite significant in the story.[49] Consequently, the historian may have been a priest or a Levite. Second, Ezra begins almost where 2 Chronicles ends, then takes the history into the mid-fifth century. This fact and other details led several commentators to conclude that Ezra himself wrote 1–2 Chronicles and Ezra, or at least that someone with similar interests did so.[50]

Recent scholarship has generally questioned linking 1–2 Chronicles and Ezra.[51] The possibility cannot be ruled out, nor can it be validated with absolute certainty. Consequently, this chapter will only deal with 1–2 Chronicles, which stands on its own in the Hebrew canon. Still, as has been stated, a person with concerns like Ezra's might well have written the books.

Estimates vary as to when the history was composed. Because the material begins with the dawn of the Persian era, reckons money in Persian coinage (cf. 1 Chron. 29:7), and presents a six-generation genealogy of Zerubbabel's descendants (1 Chron. 3:19–24), the text could hardly have been completed after 300 B.C.[52] Otherwise the absence of Greek influence is remarkable. Conversely, slightly before 515 B.C., or near the time the temple was rebuilt (cf. Haggai and Zechariah), may be the earliest date for the history, since the story ends with a call to rebuild God's fallen house.[53] Scholars who think Ezra and 1–2 Chronicles are one work set a date of about 400 B.C. for the history,[54] while some experts who claim the books were never a unit settle on that era as well.[55] In each case the scholars believe the genealogical and Persian data in 1–2 Chronicles lead to this conclusion.

Though it is always best to fix a biblical book's date if at all possible, sometimes accuracy cannot be obtained; this appears to be the case with 1–2 Chronicles. Only the general time period 515–300 can be stated with certainty, and about 400 B.C. seems to be a good mediating date. Given this situation, it is important to determine Israel's overall situation during the Persian period.

Fortunately, at least for exegetes, Israel's setting does not alter greatly during these years. In 538 B.C. Cyrus decreed that the Jews could return to Jerusalem and rebuild the temple (2 Chron. 36:23). Some Israelites did indeed return under the guidance of Zerubbabel and Joshua, during about 538–535 B.C. (Ezra 2), but the temple was not rebuilt until about 520–516 B.C., when Haggai and Zechariah urged the people to do so. This new temple was smaller and less attractive than Solomon's, yet God promised that its glory would somehow surpass its predecessor's (Hag. 2:1–9). Despite the presence of the new temple, Israel's attitude toward worship was distasteful to Malachi (cf. Mal. 2:1–9), Ezra (Ezra 9–10), and Nehemiah (Neh. 13) a century later. Similarly, Haggai, Zechariah, Malachi, Ezra, and Nehemiah indicate that Israel's financial situation was difficult during this entire period, and that they had serious problems with neighboring groups.[56] In other words, the Chronicler wrote during a difficult, even depressing, era of Israel's history, regardless of the exact decade in which the work was composed.

Because of the uncertainty concerning date and authorship, scholars also discuss whether one person or several actually wrote 1–2 Chronicles. For example, Braun thinks the temple's rebuilding occasioned a first edition in about 515 B.C., this edition was then expanded into its final form in about 350–300 B.C.[57] Myers allows for "a revision but hardly an extended one" after the books were written about 400 B.C.[58] As with 1–2 Kings, it is important to remember that the author has used sources, so some diversity will by necessity appear in 1–2 Chronicles. Further, the history has a definite plan and design, which Myers ably illuminates.[59] Such unity probably points to one author, not several later redactors. Thus, it seems appropriate to speak of "the Chronicler" as a single individual. If indeed scribal updates or revisions were made, they were minor, and it was the Chronicler who set the books' content, theology, and purpose.[60]

With the preceding information in mind, it is possible to draw a reasonably sound authorial portrait of the Chronicler and his methodology. First, the Chronicler lived during the difficult Persian era (ca. 515–400 B.C.) The people struggled to reestablish themselves in the land, rebuild the temple, and survive economically. Second, the author was a person with great interest in worship. Perhaps, then, the Chronicler was a priest or Levite. Third, the Chronicler had access to extensive historical records. The writer collected this material, shaped it into a very upbeat account of Israel's history, and used it to exhort and encourage the people in Jerusalem.[61] Fourth, the Chronicler viewed the historian's task as one of purposeful accuracy. The account must be true, and must refashion minds and attitudes at the same time.

THE CHRONICLER'S HISTORICAL SETTING AND AUDIENCE

Because several aspects of the Chronicler's situation have already been noted, it is sufficient at this point to state how this setting affected the writer's audience. With either no temple or an unattractive temple the people's religious fervor was hardly at fever pitch. Haggai states that the Jews did not want to rebuild the temple (Hag. 1:1–4), Malachi claims that worship at the new site was hardly worship (Mal. 1:6–2:9), and Ezra laments that the people did not live out their supposed religious convictions (Ezra 9–10). The Chronicler tried to change this situation by discussing the greatness of Israel's religious heritage. The ark was a glorious sign of God's covenant with Israel (1 Chron. 15–16:6). The temple's functionaries, construction, and dedication prove the worth of worship (1 Chron. 22–2 Chron. 8). Clearly, the Chronicler hoped that a positive approach would alter Israel's conduct.

With no king and no solid economy, the people felt in danger and devoid of a future. The Chronicler declared that God had directed Israel's fortunes from the dawn of time (1 Chron. 1–9). God had also strategically placed David in power so that Israel could have an eternal kingdom (1 Chron. 17:1–7). Indeed God had now given Israel the chance to rebuild and reclaim their former glory (2 Chron. 36:23).

With God as their King, with David's heritage, with a new Temple, and with a new attitude, all things are possible, according to the Chronicler. Again, the Chronicler wrote to encourage the audience about possibilities grounded in past successes. Israel's history was not over as long as God was with the people and they decided to move forward (2 Chron. 36:23).

THE CHRONICLER'S THEOLOGY

Theology provides the means by which the Chronicler interprets history for the audience just described. Like the Deuteronomist's readers, these people's situation begs for explanation. Why have the Jews suffered so greatly? When and how will God bless their willingness to return to Jerusalem? What sort of worship pleases God? Does Israel have a political future? Such questions can be answered from a historical base only by a historian who understands Who rules history. Though the Chronicler's theological themes can be sub-divided many times, at least four basic ideas undergird his history.

1. *The Chronicler believed in retribution, or payment for sin.* Saul (1 Chron. 10:13), Hezekiah (2 Chron. 32:26), and Manasseh (2 Chron. 33:10–13) all suffered because of disobedience against God. Jerusalem fell because the people rejected the prophets (2 Chron. 36:15–17).[62] Still, not every difficulty that Israel faced arose because of sin (cf. 2 Chron. 32:1). Raymond Dillard correctly observes that "The Chronicler has not reduced the principle of retribution to its logical extreme, such that it is a barren and unalterable law in his writings. Punishment does not always follow hard on the heels of transgression, not until the prophets come with their warnings and offers of mercy from God."[63] Clearly, then, the Chronicler believed sin is serious, yet left a good bit of room for grace. Perhaps the inclusion of wicked Manasseh's repentance best illustrates this point (2 Chron. 33:10–13). Israel suffers for its sin, but such suffering can be stopped by repentance.[64]

2.   *The Chronicler believed proper worship was absolutely essential for Israel's restoration.*[65] Legitimate worship included having the right people in charge, offering the right sacrifices, at the right place, among the right members of the community.[66] Bogus worship, such as idolatry or Jeroboam's practices, was a sure path to destruction. A return to God-directed religious life meant a return to the land, a return to prominence, and a return to glory.

3.   *The Chronicler shared the Deuteronomist's conviction that David was as important to Israel's future as he was to their past.* Second Chronicles 17:1–15 agrees fully with 2 Samuel 7:1–17: David's "throne will be established forever" (2 Sam. 7:17). Therefore, Israel has a future because of their greatest king. Details of what *forever* means are not given, but an individual as committed to prophecy as was the Chronicler surely agrees with the prophetic writings. A king will come who will save Israel, defeat their enemies, guarantee peace, and restore national glory. Regardless of the author's exact position on eschatology,[67] David was the key. Israel's political past was determined largely by David, and Israel's political, social, and religious future depended on him as well. David conquered enemies and established a dynasty. He also brought the ark to Jerusalem and planned the temple. Only a true son of David can lead Israel to regain, then surpass, its former standing.

4.   *The Chronicler held a high view of God's character.* God is worthy of every effort expended to worship Him. God created humans, chose Israel, and established the chosen people in the land (1 Chron. 1–9). God selected David and Solomon to lead His people (1 Chron.). God dwells among the people (1 Chron. 23:25), yet also dwells in heaven (2 Chron. 6). God reveals His will through the prophets (2 Chron. 36:15–17) and loves Israel (2 Chron. 2:11; 9:8).[68] In other words, the Chronicler presents a God who creates, speaks, cares, and acts. This God deserves Israel's trust. Readers must not doubt that God will lead them to full restoration.

THE CHRONICLER'S WRITINGS

The Chronicler encloses his historical and theological data in a fairly simple literary framework. Basically, the history unfolds in four parts. Each part contains material found in other parts of scripture, yet every segment differs sufficiently from similar texts to demonstrate the Chronicler's own original viewpoint.

First Chronicles 1–9 lists the major figures from Israel's past and provides an overview of God's work in history. Starting with Adam (1:1), the list continues through Jacob's sons (2:1) and includes David's family (3:1). Because David comes from the tribe of Judah, and because Levi's descendants help direct Israel's worship, Judah (4:1) and Levi (6:1) receive special attention. The genealogy ends with a notation of the Levites who worked at the tabernacle (9:2–44). Worship is thereby highlighted from the very start of the history. No other Old Testament book uses genealogies to this extent for this purpose.

Next, 1 Chronicles 10–29 magnifies David's importance. Again, the Chronicler presents certain materials differently than the Deuteronomist. Saul's career only occupies a few verses (10:1–14), thus making Israel's first king a mere prelude to David. David's bringing of the ark to Jerusalem receives more space than in 1 Samuel, and the Chronicler includes a psalm recited for the occasion (16:8–36). David is thus presented as a great supporter of the central sanctuary. Skipping the Bathsheba incident altogether and presenting the census disaster as the means whereby the temple site was purchased (1 Chron. 22), the Chronicler concludes the David story by noting how God's special king (cf. 1 Chron. 17:1–17) made elaborate preparations for the temple's construction. According to the Chronicler (1 Chron. 29:10–20), David was great because of his commitment to God and worship.

Solomon's wisdom and temple building dominate 2 Chronicles 1–9. His life is portrayed in a highly positive light. He asks for wisdom so he can govern well, and God grants his request (1:7–13). Because of Solomon's God-given wisdom, Israel enjoys unprecedented prosperity (1:14–17). Most importantly, Solomon continues his father's concern for worship by building the temple (2 Chron. 2–4). God's glory fills the worship place (5:14), and Yahweh responds favorably to Solomon's dedication prayers (2 Chron. 6–7). Solomon's later idolatries go unmentioned. Instead, the Chronicler stresses Solomon's faithful service to Yahweh (8:13–14), and closes with the queen of Sheba episode (9:1–12). Thus, Solomon dies with dignity, honor, and esteem.

Finally, the Chronicler describes how the nation was sent into exile. Judah's kings are highlighted. Samaria's rulers are only mentioned when they impact Judah, such as when Jeroboam opposes Rehoboam and Abijah (2 Chron. 10–13), or when Ahab serves as Jehosaphat's wicked ally (2 Chron. 18). Hezekiah (2 Chron. 29–32) and Josiah (2 Chron. 34–35) are singled out as particularly righteous kings, just as they are in 2 Kings. Less godly rulers are generally treated more kindly here than in 1–2 Kings. Most notably, Manasseh, the Deuteronomist's prototypical bad king (cf. 2 Kings 21:10–15), repents after a stint in Babylon (2 Chron. 33:10–17). Still, the Chronicler does not gloss over all the kings' faults. Retribution remains an important theme. Rehoboam acts unwisely (10:1–19), Ahaz remains rebellious (28:22–25), and Jeroboam (13:1–12) and Ahab (18:1–34) are depicted as wicked men. These negative assessments demonstrate the Chronicler's basic honesty. Where good things can be reported the author does so. When nothing positive occurs, the author does not fabricate a happy story.

The book's conclusion illustrates the Chronicler's overall philosophy of writing history. Jerusalem's destruction is dealt with honestly, yet briefly (36:11–12). Readers are not asked to dwell on a catastrophe that happened long before their time. Instead, the Chronicler focuses on Cyrus's decree that Israel can return home and rebuild the temple (36:22–23). Indeed the decree is issued as a challenge for people of courage to rebuild, trusting that God will be with them. In other words, the author encourages all who will to rebuild the temple and recapture Israel's lost glory. The same God who helped David and Solomon construct the first temple will help them build a new one.

CONCLUSION

Some scholars openly question whether Joshua-Kings and 1–2 Chronicles can be considered historical when the books take clear theological positions.[69] After all, the authors attribute many events to the sovereignty of God, sometimes without stating extensively how secular matters affected what occurred. Kings are judged more by their relationship to God or their opposition to idolatry than by their economic or military capabilities. Events seem to be selected more for how they fit the author's theological perspective on how Israel disintegrated than for their impact on the overall structure of secular history. Is such writing historical? Three details help answer this question.

First, no history is *fully* "objective." Every historian, no matter how careful and conscientious, has a personal belief or background that affects his or her writing of history.[70] Second, a historian's personal perspective must be judged in part by whether its view of cause and effect fits the course of actual events. The Deuteronomist's belief that the threats found in Deuteronomy 27–28 and the prophets' dire predictions come true matches reality. Similarly, the Chronicler's conviction that David prospered because of his commitment to his religious beliefs can be defended. Third, an author's theology may actually reflect how people act. Certainly

Israel suffered for its mistakes. Political corruption and shortsightedness, coupled with moral depravity, are a deadly sociological *or* theological combination. There is no compelling reason, then, to denigrate the books' historical value because of their theological inflections anymore than if those inflections were secular.

Given their accomplishments, the Deuteronomist and the Chronicler deserve high praise. Certainly questions remain about certain elements of their historiography,[71] but these issues in no way diminish their achievement. In two turbulent eras, with few models to follow, these individuals forged reliable, compelling, and distinctive accounts of Israel's past. In so doing they set a high standard for all future historians, biblical or otherwise.

NOTES

1. Modern historians are currently discussing how all these issues impact the writing of history. Few, if any, historians any longer claim to be totally objective or not influenced by their cultural or educational background. For analyses of these topics, see James T. Kloppenberg, "Objectivity and Historicism: A Century of American Historical Writing," *American Historical Review* (October 1989): 1011–30; Frank Stricker, "Why History? Thinking About the Uses of the Past," *The History Teacher*, 25:3 (May 1992): 293–312; and John Higham, "Beyond Consensus: The Historian as Moral Critic," in Higham *Writing American History: Essays on Modern Scholarship* (Bloomington, Ind.: Indiana University Press, 1970).

2. One such factor is the appearance of the phrase "until this day" (1 Kings 8:8; 9:13, 21; 12:19; 2 Kings 2:22; 8:22; 10:27; 14:7; 16:6; 17:23, 34, 41, which taken at face value could mean that the situation described existed when the books were composed. It is likely, though, that the phrase states what was true when the source being used was written. Cf. Brevard Childs, "A Study of the Formula, 'Until This Day,'" *JBL* 82 (1963): 279–92.

3. This conclusion reflects the latest possible date for the conquest. Some scholars place the exodus itself as early as ca. 1440 B.C., while others believe the event occurred ca. 1290 B.C.

4. C. R. Kraft, "Jashar, Book of," *IDB* (Nashville: Abingdon, 1962), 2: 803.

5. Cf. John Skinner, *1-2 Kings*, CB, rev. ed. (London and Edinburgh: T. and T. Clark, 1904), 23.

6. Julius Wellhausen, *Prolegomena to the History of Ancient Israel*, rev. ed., trans. Menzies and Black (1883; reprint, Gloucester, Mass.: Peter Smith, 1973), 228–94. Wellhausen's theories first exploded on the theological scene in 1878 with the first edition of this volume.

7. For example, Otto Eissfeldt concluded that J, E, and an older lay (L) source are evident in Genesis-Kings (*The Old Testament: An Introduction*, 3rd ed., trans. Peter Ackroyd [New York: Harper and Row, 1966], 241–48, 297–99). Cf. I. Benzinger, "Jahwist und Elohist in den Königsbüchern," *BZAW* II, 2 (Berlin-Stuttgart-Leipzig: Töpelmann, 1921); Gustav Hölscher, "Das Buch der Könige, seine Quellen und seine Redaktion," *Eucharisterion Hermann Gunkel zum 60 Geburstag*, FRLANT 36 (Göttingen: Vandenhoeck and Ryprecht, 1927); and Rudolph Smend, "JE in den geschichtlichen

Büchern des Alten Testament, herausgegeben von H. Holzinger," *ZAW* (1921), 39:204–15 for variations of the J and E theory.

8. Proponents of this type of analysis include S. R. Driver, *An Introduction to the Literature of the Old Testament* (1891; reprint, Gloucester, Mass.: Peter Smith, 1972), 188–89, who adds prophetic and temple sources to the three stated sources, and Skinner, *1–2 Kings*, 23–33, who also adds prophetic, priestly, political, and succession sources.

9. R. K. Harrison, *Introduction to the Old Testament* (Grand Rapids: Eerdmans, 1969), 726.

10. Cf. John Bright, *A History of Israel*, 2nd ed. (Philadelphia: Westminster, 1972), 127 ff.

11. Martin Noth, *The Deuteronomistic History*, trans. David Orton, JSOT Sup 15 (Sheffield: Sheffield Academic Press, 1981).

12. Ibid., 4. Indeed, Noth believed the "Deuteronomist" wrote Deut. 1–4 as an introduction to the then-existing book of Deuteronomy, which then served as an introduction to the history as a whole (Noth, *Deuteronomistic*, 14–17).

13. Noth says, "Dtr. was not merely an editor but the author of a history which brought together material from highly varied traditions and arranged it according to a carefully conceived plan. In general Dtr. simply reproduced the literary sources available to him and merely provided a connecting narrative for isolated passages. We can prove, however, that in places he made a deliberate selection from the material at his disposal" (Noth, *Deuteronomistic*, 10).

14. Cf. Noth, *Deuteronomistic*, 9, for a discussion of how the author created transitions between books, and p. 5 for Noth's opinions about the role of the key speeches in the history.

15. Ibid., 99.

16. Ibid., 90–92.

17. Gerhard von Rad, *Studies in Deuteronomy*, SBT 9, trans. David Stalker (1948; reprint, London: SCM Press, 1963), 74–91. Von Rad thinks that 2 Sam. 7:13 is the first and greatest of eleven prophetic promises in the "deuteronomistic" history.

18. Ibid., 90–91.

19. H. W. Wolff, "The Kerygma of the Deuteronomic Historical Work," trans. Frederick C. Prussner, in *The Vitality of Old Testament Traditions*, ed. Walter Brueggemann and H. W. Wolff (Atlanta: John Knox, 1975), 83–100. Note Wolff's summary of the historian's main theological points on p. 98.

20. Cf. Dennis J. McCarthy, "II Samuel 7 and the Structure of the Deuteronomic History," *JBL* 84 (1965): 131–38, for an analysis of both the positive and negative aspects of God's promise to David within 1–2 Samuel and 1–2 Kings. See Helen A. Kenick, *Design for Kingship: The Deuteronomistic Narrative Technique in 1 Kings 3:4–15*, SBLDS (Chico, Calif.: Scholars Press, 1983) for a representative work on how the "Deuteronomist" shaped important speeches.

21. Harrison, *Introduction*, 732.

22. Ibid. For significant arguments in favor of Mosaic authorship of Deuteronomy, see M. G. Kline, *Treaty of the Great King: The Covenant Structure of Deuteronomy* (Grand Rapids: Eerdmans, 1963); P. C. Craigie, *The Book of Deuteronomy*, NICOT (Grand Rapids: Eerdmans, 1976): 24–69; and Harrison, *Introduction*, 495–541, 637–62.

23. Cf. Abraham Kuenen, *Historisch-Kritische Einleitung in die Bücher des Alten Testaments*, trans. T. Weber (Leipzig: Otto Schulze, 1886–1894); Julius Wellhausen, *Die Composition des Hexateuchs und der historischen Bücher des Alten Testaments* (Berlin: Georg Reimer, 1889); and Wellhausen, *Prolegomena*. For an outstanding summary of these and other multi-redactional theories, see Richard D. Nelson, *The Double Redaction of the Deuteronomistic History*, JSOT Sup 18 (Sheffield: Sheffield Academic Press, 1981).

24. Alfred Jepsen, *Die Quellen der Königsbuches* (Halle: Niemeyer, 1953).

25. Cf. Rudolf Smend, "Das Gesetz und die Völker: Ein Beitrag zur deuteronomistischen Redaktionsgeschichte," in *Probleme Biblischer Theologie: Gerhard von Rad zum 70. Geburstag*, ed. H. W. Wolff (Munich: Chr. Kaiser Verlag, 1971), 494–509; and *Die Enstehung des Alten Testaments* (Stuttgart: Kohlhammer, 1978), 110–25. Smend's ideas were adopted and adapted by W. Dietrich, *Prophetie un Geschichte. Eine redaktionsgeschichtliche Untersuchung zum deuteronomistischen Geschichtswerk*, FRLANT 108 (Göttingen: Vandenhoeck and Ruprecht, 1972) and T. Veijola, *Das Königtum in der Beurteilung der deuteronomistischen Historiographie* (Helsinki: Suomalainen Tieddeakatemia, 1977). Helga Weippert suggests another three-editor theory in "Die 'deuteronomistischen' Beurteilungen der Könige von Israel und Juda und das Problem der Redaktion der Königsbücher," *Bib* 53 (1972): 301–39. Weippert thinks that a first edition appeared at the time of Samaria's destruction (722 B.C.), a second near Josiah's era (640–609 B.C.), and a third after Jerusalem's fall.

26. G. H. Jones, *1 and 2 Kings*, NCB (Grand Rapids: Eerdmans, 1984), 1: 43–44.

27. Ibid., 44.

28. Cf. F. M. Cross, "The Themes of the Book of Kings and the Structure of the Deuteronomistic History," in *Canaanite Myth and Hebrew Epic* (Cambridge: Harvard, 1973), 274–89, and Nelson, *Double Redaction*. John Gray also claims there were two redactions, one ca. 597 B.C. and one after 587 B.C., in *I and II Kings*, OTL (Philadelphia: Westminster, 1963), 38. In *1 Kings*, WBC 12 (Waco, Tex.: Word, 1985), Simon DeVries says that a first edition was written by "a contemporary of King Josiah" (xlii) and was "revised by a member of the same school living during the Babylonian exile, *ca*. 550 B.C." (xliii).

29. Though I do not share Nelson's preference for the double redaction theory, his book is careful, balanced, and quick to point out the weaknesses of other multiple-author positions.

30. Burke O. Long, *1 Kings, with an Introduction to Historical Literature*, FOTOTL 9 (Grand Rapids: Eerdmans, 1984), 16–21.

31. Cf. Jones, *1 and 2 Kings*, 44, and Nelson, *Double Redaction*, 43–98.

32. For two thorough analyses of the role of the land motif in the Pentateuch, see David J. A. Clines, *The Theme of the Pentateuch*, JSOT Sup 10 (Sheffield: Sheffield Academic Press, 1978) and, especially, John H. Sailhamer, *The Pentateuch as Narrative: A Biblical-Theological Commentary*, LBI 4 (Grand Rapids: Zondervan, 1992).

33. Cf. Bright, *History of Israel*, 323 for an account of how Assyria kept trying to defeat Babylon and regain its former authority.

34. For possible reasons for Babylon's delay in chastising Israel, see Noth, *The Deuteronomistic History*, 282, and Bright, *History of Israel*, 326.

35. Cf. Bright, *History of Israel*, 328–329.

36. For an examination of the importance of history in Israel compared to other nations consult DeVries, *1 Kings*, xxix–xxxiii.

37. Cf. Clines, *Theme of the Pentateuch*.

38. See the works cited in footnote 22.

39. G. Henton Davies, "High Place, Sanctuary," *IDB* (Nashville: Abingdon, 1962), 2: 602.

40. For an examination of these and other texts that link ideas in Deuteronomy and 1–2 Kings see Moshe Weinfeld, *Deuteronomy and the Deuteronomic School* (Oxford: Clarendon, 1972), 320–63.

41. C. F. Keil comments that "however unmistakable the allusions to Solomon are, the substance of the promise is not fully exhausted in him. The threefold repetition of the expression 'for ever,' the establishment of the kingdom and throne of David *for ever*, points incontrovertibly beyond the time of Solomon, and to the eternal continuance

of the seed of David" (*1–2 Samuel* Commentary on the Old Testament, vol. 2, trans. J. Martin [1875; reprint, Grand Rapids: Zondervan, 1978], 346).

42. Cf. Isa. 7:14; 9:1–7; 11:1–9; Jer. 23:5–7, 33:14–22; Ezra 34:11–31; Mic. 5:2; Zech. 9:9-13; Mal. 4:1–6.

43. Note that both Matthew and Luke trace Jesus' ancestry through David's lineage (Matt. 1:1–17; Luke 3:23–37).

44. Hans W. Hertzberg, *1 and 2 Samuel*, OTL, trans. J. S. Bowden (Philadelphia: Westminster, 1976), 287.

45. Note the analysis of land as gift or inheritance in Elmer A. Martens, *God's Design: A Focus on Old Testament Theology* (Grand Rapids: Baker, 1981), 97–108.

46. Though his historical reconstructions are debatable, von Rad correctly observes that the Deuteronomist carefully links each book to its successor in the history (*Old Testament Theology*, trans. D.M.G. Stalker [New York: Harper and Row, 1965] 1:331).

47. Cf. D. M. Gunn, *The Fate of King Saul: An Interpretation of a Biblical Story*, JSOT 14 (Sheffield: Sheffield Academic Press, 1980).

48. Note the discussions of the Chronicler's sources in J. Barton Payne, "1, 2 Chronicles," *EBC* (Grand Rapids: Zondervan, 1988), 4: 309–11; E. L. Curtis, *A Critical and Exegetical Commentary on the Books of Chronicles*, ICC (New York: Scribner's, 1910), 17–26; and Jacob M. Myers, *1 Chronicles*, AB 12 (Garden City, N.Y.: Doubleday, 1965), xlv–lxiii.

49. On the importance of the temple for the shaping of the Chronicler's history, see Brian Peckham, *History and Prophecy: The Development of Late Judean Literary Traditions*, ABRL (New York: Doubleday, 1993), 788–93.

50. Jewish tradition ascribed the books to Ezra. For some basic arguments for the Ezra position see W. F. Albright, "The Date and Personality of the Chronicler," *JBL* (1921), 4:104–24.

51. Note the arguments for and against linking the books in Roddy Braun, *1 Chronicles*, WBC 14 (Waco, Tex.: Word, 1986), xix–xxi.

52. Cf. Curtis, *Books of Chronicles*, 5–6.

53. For arguments for an early date for 1–2 Chronicles consult James D. Newsome, "Toward a New Understanding of the Chronicler and His Purposes," *JBL* 94, no. 2 (June 1975): 215–16.

54. Cf. Myers, *1 Chronicles*, lxxxviii–lxxxix.

55. Cf. Harrison, *Introduction*, 1157.

56. Bright, *History of Israel*, 364–92.

57. Braun, *1 Chronicles*, xxix.

58. Myers, *1 Chronicles*, lxxxix.

59. Ibid., xxx–xlv.

60. Cf. Brevard S. Childs, *Introduction to the Old Testament as Scripture* (Philadelphia: Fortress, 1980), 643.

61. Cf. R. J. Coggins, *The First and Second Books of the Chronicles*, CBC (London: Cambridge Univ. Press, 1976), 3.

62. Robert North, "Theology of the Chronicler," *JBL* 82, no. 4 (December 1963): 372.

63. Raymond B. Dillard, "Reward and Punishment in Chronicles: The Theology of Immediate Retribution," *WTJ* (1984), 46: 170.

64. Cf. Braun, *1 Chronicles*, xxxix–xl.

65. Cf. Myers, *1 Chronicles*, lxvii–lxxiii.

66. North, "Theology," 369–72.

67. For various ideas about the Chronicler's eschatology, note North, "Theology," 376–81, and W. F. Stinespring, "Eschatology in Chronicles," *JBL* 80, no. 3 (September 1961): 209–19.

68. Cf. Myers, *1 Chronicles,* lxiv–lxvii.
69. E.g., Coggins, *First and Second Books,* 3–4.
70. See Footnote 1.
71. Raymond Dillard, "The Reign of Asa (2 Chronicles 14–16): An Example of the Chronicler's Theological Method," *JETS* 23, no. 3 (September 1980): 214–18.

2

LUKE

SCOT MCKNIGHT AND
MATTHEW C. WILLIAMS

grammar!

One may not naively read Luke-Acts and formulate Luke's view of history due to the fact that many, if not most, scholars do not think that Luke wrote accurate history. Such a survey would be worthless, in their view. Thus, before one may examine Luke's historiography, one must analyze and interact with pertinent Lukan scholarship concerning Luke's accuracy. Only after this examination will we be ready to survey the major contents of Luke-Acts and Luke's view of history.

We will divide this chapter into four sections: the author, the history of Luke-Acts scholarship, the historicity of Luke-Acts, and the theology of Luke-Acts. The second and third sections will deal almost exclusively with Acts for two reasons. First, the majority of scholarship on the relationship between history and theology focuses on the book of Acts. Second, Acts contains much data that can be tested with other historical documents for accuracy.

The justification for our interest in history, especially that of a biblical author, is that the Christian faith is ultimately based upon historical events. Faith and history are intimately connected—they cannot be separated. Biblical faith is faith with regard to historical events. "New Testament scholars were therefore ill-advised when they allowed themselves to be persuaded that history and kerygma were exclusive alternatives."[1]

THE AUTHOR

Though the books of Luke and Acts are anonymous, they are traditionally attributed to Luke the physician. That Lukan authorship was the early church's consensus is seen by the agreement of the anti-Marcionite prologue, the Muratorian Canon, Irenaeus, Tertulian, Clement of Alexandria, Origen, Eusebius, and Jerome.

W. K. Hobart's *The Medical Language of St. Luke* (Dublin, 1882) lists words and phrases which are used in Luke which are also found in Greek medical writers with the view to show that the author of Luke-Acts was "Luke, the physician." It has been shown, however, that most of these words were also found in the Septuagint, Josephus, Lucian, and other works, showing that these words are not exclusively medical terms.[2] Nonetheless, we ought to observe that Luke-Acts contains a large number of medical terms—a fact that at least confirms a physician's perspective.

Evidence from the book of Acts which might serve to bolster the early church tradition is found in the so-called "we" passages, passages in Acts which seem to indicate that the author was a traveling companion of Paul at certain stages of Acts (16:10–17; 20:5–21:18; 27:1–28:16). Such passages would serve to document well 2 Timothy 4:11 and Philemon 24. We shall discuss these "we" passages below.

HISTORY OF LUKE-ACTS SCHOLARSHIP

It is no exaggeration to say that the majority of scholars from the second century until the Reformation understood Luke-Acts in a literalistic, historical manner. What was recorded was accepted as what really happened. The book of Acts was seen as a historical document, which recorded historical events accurately. Luke was trusted as an accurate historian because that was what he claimed to be doing in his prologue (Luke 1:1–4): ἔδοξε κἀμοὶ παρηκολουθηκότι ἄνωθεν πᾶσιν ἀκριβῶ" καθεξῆ" σοι γράψαι. Acts was then understood to continue this task (τὸν μὲν πρῶτον λόγον).

With the rise of the Reformation and the Enlightenment, however, the book of Acts was studied in a new light. Scholars began to argue that Luke was not as accurate as had been thought. In fact, some even argued that Luke fabricated some or all of his recorded history. While a negative view of Luke's historical abilities grew and even continues today, another group of scholars arose in defense of Luke's accuracy as a historian.

W. M. L. de Wette (1780–1849) was the first major scholar to challenge the essential trustworthiness of Acts as a historical document. He was soon after followed by F. C. Baur, who is well known as the founder of the Tübingen school. Baur argued that there were two groups in conflict in early Christianity: a Jewish (Petrine) Christian party and a Gentile (Pauline) Christian party. Each of the New Testament texts was seen as written either from the perspective of one of these two groups (thesis-antithesis) or from a third perspective which attempted to reconcile these two groups together (synthesis, which he called "Early Catholicism"). He regarded Acts as being written by a "Paulinist" to defend Paul's Gentile mission against the Petrine party. Baur was followed by many of his Tübingen disciples who took this thesis even further, especially as seen by Albert Schwegler (1819–57) and Eduard Zeller (1814–1908). Schwegler said that Acts was written in the second or third decade of the second century, when the struggles increased between the Gentile and Jewish-Christian parties for leadership in the church. It was Zeller, however, who studied Acts carefully under the Tübingen hypothesis. He worked under the assumption that miracles are impossible. Thus, one is not surprised by his almost wholly negative conclusions concerning the historicity of Acts, since it contains miracles throughout.

While many in Germany rejected these views to some degree (discussed below), others took them to even more radical heights (or depths, depending upon one's viewpoint). Bruno Bauer (1809–88) published a study in 1850 in which he argued that both Acts and Paul's *Hauptbriefe* (Romans, 1 and 2 Corinthians and Galatians) are unhistorical. In 1870 F. C. Overbeck (1837–1905) revised de Wette's commentary on Acts. Overbeck, however, is even more negative than de Wette concerning the historical value of Acts. In fact, he thought that the unreliability of Acts was an established fact of criticism. He also dated Acts in the second or third decade of the second century, stating that it was written to explain the Gentile-Christianity of his day.

Thus, we can see two conclusions concerning the historicity of Luke: (1) because the book was written in the second or third decade of the second century, it was virtually impossible for the author, no longer an eyewitness, to be an accurate historian; he was removed from the scene by time; and (2) given this late dating, the purpose of Acts cannot be historical justification of the growth of the Christian Church, but must be seen as the attempt of a later generation of Gentile Christianity to explain itself as a primarily Gentile movement even though it had Jewish roots.

A little later, Martin Dibelius (1883–1947) applied the method of *Formgeschichte* to the study of Acts and early Christianity. The ideas found in his first essay in 1923 were the basis of all of his later work. In it he makes the following observations: (1) the speeches in Acts were mostly due to the literary imagination of the author; (2) an itinerary-document provided the basic framework for Paul's missionary travels in Acts (basically chapters 13–21). To this document Luke may have added other minor fragmentary sources, but he also embellished these when he found it necessary. What about the historicity of Acts? This is where Dibelius makes the interesting jump to the conclusion that one is not to judge the historical value of any part of the book before one does one's study. We see here the influence of the critical scholars examined above. The negative historical accuracy of Luke-Acts seems to be assumed as an assured result of criticism for Dibelius. Luke is attempting *"eine literarisch-theologische, keine geschichtliche Aufgabe"* ("a literary and theological, but not a historical task"). Dibelius also wrote two essays on the speeches of Acts. Concerning the Areopagus speech in Acts 17, he understands this speech not as Paul's speech, but as a model for Christian preaching to pagans in the author's own day. Thus, it is a literary creation of Luke, not a historical report.

Ernst Haenchen took the method of Dibelius and applied it to Acts in his lengthy commentary of 1955. He claimed that the "we" passages do not show evidence that the author of Acts was present with Paul, but are used "merely as a stylistic device to bring the reader into closer touch with the events related."[3] Haenchen goes beyond Dibelius by stating that the author was from a later generation and that he read his own theology back into the history of early Christianity. Haenchen also says that "Luke was not a companion of Paul's at all." He argues this on the basis of irreconcilable differences between the descriptions of the "Lukan" Paul and the Paul of the Epistles (112–6).

Hans Conzelmann is even more skeptical than Haenchen in his commentary on Acts and in his Theology of St. Luke (*Die Mitte der Zeit*, 1954), Conzelmann rejects nearly all of Luke as unhistorical and as the author's literary creations. We shall discuss why Conzelmann thinks this in our section on theology.

But these voices did not go unchallenged. A second group of scholars has been working all along with the theories and hypotheses of the above mentioned skeptical scholars, with differing conclusions. This second group agree that Luke has been treated unfairly. They contend for Luke's historical accuracy, though certainly some thought he was more accurate than others. Unfortunately, all too often these scholars were labeled as "traditional" or "conservative" and were thus ignored by many of the skeptical scholars. There is a growing consensus today that this second group of scholars should no longer be ignored.

The first scholar who deserves mention in this group is Matthias Schneckenburger (1804–48). He studied under Baur at Tübingen and under Hegel and Schleiermacher in Berlin before teaching at Bern (1834–48). In his study of the book of Acts, he admitted that Luke wrote Acts as a Gentile-Christianity apologetic; however, he also argued that the portrait of Paul in Acts is essentially accurate (contra Baur), stating that the author of Acts was a Paulinist who was an eyewitness of many of the events of the latter part of the book, which was written before A.D. 70. Another of Baur's students, Albrecht Ritschl (1822–89), originally held Baur's views, but was persuaded otherwise through his own study of the historical data. At point after point he shows that Baur and the Tübingen critics are incorrect.

The majority of the defense for Lukan historiography came from Britain, rather than Germany. While much of German criticism on Acts was based too much on philosophical ideas, the study of Acts in Britain was based much more upon historical study. Many of the major figures were originally classicists or ancient historians. Thus, they were better able to understand the period in which Luke wrote.

While doing geological and geographical research in the region of the Eastern Mediterranean described in Acts 27, James Smith concluded, in his *The Voyage and Shipwreck of St. Paul,* that "the voyage is an account of real events written by an eye-witness."[4] Henry Alford (1810–71), who introduced German critical views to Britain, nevertheless, argued for the traditional view of Lukan authorship in A.D. 63.

Through his commentaries on the Pauline epistles (Galatians, Philippians, Colossians, and Philemon) and his work on the Apostolic Fathers (Clement, Ignatius, Polycarp), Joseph Barber Lightfoot (1818–89) showed the inaccuracies of the Tübingen hypothesis. Through his study of the Apostolic Fathers, he argued that there was no evidence for the division in early Christianity between Pauline and Petrine groups, as the Tübingen school argued. He also showed that Luke was accurate in the difficult task of assigning the correct titles to individuals in the quickly changing political environment of the first century.

Sir William M. Ramsay (1851–1939) was a classical scholar and archaeologist who accepted the Tübingen view when he began his own study of Acts. Through a careful study of the data of Acts, while attempting to find information on the geographical and historical situation of Asia Minor, Ramsay began to doubt the critical consensus. He found Acts accurate in its description of the region. In fact, Ramsay converted to Christianity based upon his conclusion concerning Lukan reliability. After thirty years of studying the milieu of first-century Christianity, Ramsay concluded that Luke could stand up to the highest scrutiny. And, as Ramsay says, "a writer who proves to be exact and correct in one point will show the same qualities in other matters."[5]

Another defender of Luke's essential trustworthiness is none other than Adolf Harnack (1851–1930), who is known as the founder of "liberal Christianity." He staunchly defends the traditional Luke, a companion and fellow-worker of Paul, as the author of Luke-Acts. Although Harnack did not believe Luke to be infallible, he did consider Luke to be highly accurate. While originally dating Acts to A.D. 80, after further study, he favored an A.D. 62 date.

F. F. Bruce is another example of a classicist turned theologian. In his two commentaries on Acts and in numerous other articles, Bruce defends Luke's historical abilities. One finds in Bruce thorough and critical discussions of the relationship of Paul in Acts in comparison to the epistles, the dating of Acts (A.D. 61), the accuracy of Luke's use of titles for the various officials in Acts, and so forth.

While many other recent scholars (such as C. J. Hemer, M. Hengel, A. N. Sherwin-White, and C. K. Barrett) could be added to this survey, we shall proceed to examine briefly various directions in today's scholarship. There are basically three areas in which scholars work today in Luke-Acts: historicity of Luke-Acts (discussed in the next section of the chapter), theology of Luke-Acts (discussed in the final section of the chapter), and literary analysis of Luke-Acts. The latter seems to be the most current concern.

WAS LUKE AN ACCURATE HISTORIAN?

The question remains, is Luke a "historian of the first rank," as Ramsay says, or was he merely a clever inventor? In order to tackle this question, we must first examine the milieu in which Luke wrote. What were the historiographical methods of his day? Much effort has been put forth in this area recently. Many scholars claim that the historical methods in ancient days were not as accurate as today, and therefore Luke should be understood as a creature of his era. The assumption of ancient historiographical inaccuracy is incorrect. While certainly many ancients can be cited who invented material (for example, Josephus often invented or exaggerated material to fit his purpose), there are many others who are more exact in their historiography. Polybius was a harsh critic of historians who were inaccurate in their records. He called for the personal interviewing of witnesses (and *living* witnesses, no less—12.27.3) in order to ensure the accuracy of the reporting of an event (much as Luke claimed to do in his preface in Luke 1:1–4):

But from all this it is evident that the account he [Timaeus] gives of Africa, of Sardinia, and especially of Italy, is inaccurate, and we see that generally the task of investigation has been entirely scamped by him, and this is the most important part of history. For since many events occur at the same time in different places, and one man cannot be in several places at one time, nor is it possible for a single man to have seen with his own eyes every place in the world and all the peculiar features of different places, the only thing left for an historian is to inquire from as many people as possible, to believe those worthy of belief and to be an adequate critic of the reports that reach him.[6]

Thucydides comments on his own method of interviewing eye-witnesses, which is similar to Polybius's conviction:

But as to the facts of the occurrences of the war, I have thought it my duty to give them, not as ascertained from any chance informant nor as seemed to me probable, but only after investigating with the greatest possible accuracy each detail, in the case both of the events in which I myself participated and of those regarding which I got my information from others. And the endeavor to ascertain these facts was a laborious task, because those who were eye-witnesses of the several events did not give the same reports about the same things, but reports varying according to their championship of one side or the other, or according to their recollection.[7]

Thus, from these two examples we can see that there were ancient historians with high standards of accuracy.[8] These two men seem to be able to differentiate between truth and fiction, between a reliable and an unreliable eye-witness. It is possible that these two historians may have been a minority, but to claim that Luke was inaccurate merely because he wrote so long ago is presumptuous. We must examine Luke on his own terms in order to evaluate his accuracy, especially given that he claimed in Luke 1:1–4 to follow a pattern of investigation and reporting similar to that of both Polybius and Thucydides. As J. B. Lightfoot said, "No ancient work affords so many tests of veracity; for no other has such numerous points of contact in all directions with contemporary history, politics, and topography, whether Jewish or Greek or Roman."[9]

One must examine the details of Luke-Acts in order to determine whether or not he is accurate as a historian in any particular instance. Thus, we shall now examine five examples of what have been seen as problem areas in the accuracy of Luke in Acts: the description of Paul in Acts versus that in the epistles, the chronology of Galatians 2 versus Acts 15, the "we" sections, speeches, and miracles.

F. C. Baur thought that the main discrepancy between the two portraits was that the Paul in Acts was inferior to and dependent upon the Jerusalem apostles. Luke does not use the title apostle for Paul (except in Acts 14:4, 14 of Paul and Barnabas). Yet, we find in Galatians 1–2 (and most of the other Pauline epistles) that Paul claims to be an apostle who is equal to and independent of the Jerusalem apostles. One wonders if this supposed difference is real. And the term apostle is used by Luke and Paul in different manners. Luke uses the term mainly to refer to those who had been with Jesus during his earthly ministry and witnessed the resurrection. Paul seems to use the term more generically, as for those who have been personally commissioned by Jesus the Christ. Thus, Paul can also use the term for Epaphroditus (Phil. 2:25), and James, the Lord's brother (Gal. 1:19). Another supposed discrepancy is that the Paul of the epistles is free from the Law while the Paul of Acts seems to follow the Law. Such an understanding, however, fails to see the depth of Paul's thinking on the Law. There is a huge difference between following the Law voluntarily because of cultural observances (1 Cor. 10:31–32: "give no offense to the Jew") and following the Law out of a sense of legal obligation. Thus, Paul can make a vow or have Timothy circumcised without contradicting his own views. These and other supposed differences between Acts and the Pauline epistles must be seen in the light of the occasional nature of the Pauline epistles. We certainly do not have a systematic biography of Paul in either his epistles or in Acts. Obviously, Luke does not record all of his knowledge of Paul; he chooses only those details that fit his theological purpose. Therefore, the description of Paul in Acts and in the epistles may be harmonized.

A similar problem for some scholars is that Paul seems to present a different chronology of events in Galatians 1–2 than we find in Acts. Specifically, it appears that Paul's visits to Jerusalem do not coincide in the two accounts. Nearly all adherents to the Tübingen view suppose that Galatians 2 and Acts 15 record the same visit of Paul to Jerusalem. As a result, one of the accounts must be incorrect (usually assumed to be Luke's). However, there has been much recent study that has shown that it is certainly possible and even probable that Galatians 2 and Acts 15 do not record the same event. Rather, Galatians 2 may coincide with the Jerusalem visit recorded in Acts 11:27–30. Under this view, Acts 15 occurred after Galatians was written (so, for example, Longenecker, Galatians; Hemer, Gasque, Bruce). This thesis would solve much of the chronological problem between Galatians 1–2 and Acts.

Do the "we" sections (16:10–17; 20:5–21:18; 27:1–28:16) suggest that the author of Acts was a companion during some of the travels of Paul?

While this is the traditional view, scholars, as far back as de Wette, have argued otherwise. Some scholars believe that Luke has merely used a diary of another person as a source for these sections of Acts and has retained the use of the "we" found in the diary. We must ask, however, why Luke would have retained the use of "we" when he shows himself everywhere else to be a much better editor than that? It has been shown that these passages contain the same style as the rest of Acts. It is doubtful that he would have "accidentally" left the "we" in the account. Thus, others (e.g., Haenchen) postulate that Luke used the "we" as a rhetorical device to express vividness. However, why did Luke use "we" only in these particular instances, where vividness for the reader would not be more of a factor than in other areas in Acts? Also, there are few ancient parallels to such a literary use of "we." Are these explanations more plausible than saying that the author of Acts was present with Paul at these particular times and retained the "we" to indicate the same? We do not think so.

A more difficult problem is found when we turn to the speeches of Acts. Since, as mentioned above, Luke has a uniform style throughout the book of Acts, how can the speeches in Acts, by various speakers, be actual accounts of what was said? It appears that the theology and vocabulary is Lukan rather than Petrine, Pauline, and so forth. No one argues that what we find in the speeches of Acts are verbatim reports of the actual words spoken. Rather, they are summaries of what was said. This is apparent from the brevity of the speeches and the amount of material that is obviously left out of the speeches. The question that needs to be addressed is this: did Luke summarize the actual speeches accurately, or did Luke invent the speeches according to his own needs? Scholars who claim that Luke invented the speeches point to the fact that the style, vocabulary, and theology of all the speeches are the same. They also point to ancient historical methods to show that inventing speeches was a common practice. That all historians did not invent speeches is shown in Thucydides. Thucydides, in describing his historiography, says,

> As to the speeches that were made by different men, either when they were about to begin the war or when they were already engaged therein, it has been difficult to recall with strict accuracy the words actually spoken, both for me as regards that which I myself heard, and for those who from various other sources have brought me reports. Therefore the speeches are given in the language in which, as it seemed to me, the several speakers would express, on the subjects under consideration, the sentiments most befitting the occasion, though at the same time I have adhered as closely as possible to the general sense of what was actually said.[10]

It is important to understand the precise nuances of his claim. He said that he gives the general sense of what was actually said. He did not say that he invents the speeches. On the contrary, Thucydides does not invent speeches according to his purpose, which is the claim of some scholars regarding Luke. He claimed to give summaries of the speeches due to the fact that it was impossible to quote a speech word for word. Remember, tape recorders and the like were not around in antiquity. How else could one report a speech than to give a summary of what was said, unless one had a photographic mind? Thus, it is not *a priori* to be rejected that Luke could have given accurate reports of speeches which either he or eyewitnesses heard just because he wrote in antiquity.

Consequently, the similarity in style and theology of all of the speeches in Acts becomes less problematic. While skeptics see these similarities as a major difficulty, we must ask what one would expect given that the speeches are summaries written by Luke. In other words, how much distinction could Luke have retained in the speeches given that he was merely recording a summary of what was said? Is it not more probable that we would expect the summaries to be written in Lukan style and vocabulary? Apart from style and vocabulary, some scholars fault Luke for a supposed similarity in theological content in the speeches. As far back as J. B. Lightfoot, scholars have shown that the speeches are not as similar as is often supposed. Modern scholars have advanced this view. C. F. D. Moule shows that the Christology of the speeches changes with the speaker.[11] Besides, Luke fares well in his recording of speeches in his Gospel, where we can check his accuracy by referring to Mark and Matthew.

A fifth and final general objection to the accuracy of Lukan historiography is the use of miracles in Luke-Acts. Unfortunately, it is all too often an axiom of historical criticism to reject the possibility of miracles. Often, the use of miracle reports is seen as a method used by ancient writers to document the truth of a certain claim. The modern scholar then views the miracle not as a true report but as a literary method or an accommodation by the biblical author to the mind-set of the first-century person. Thus, the modern scholar must discount the "miracle" if he is to find the truth of the recorded event. We must, however, voice a philosophical disagreement in the presupposition which rejects the possibility of miracles *a priori*.

A full discussion of miracles would take us far beyond the scope of this chapter; nevertheless, a few comments can be made. First, if one rejects the possibility of all miracles, one ultimately takes away the entire gospel message because Paul preached Jesus as resurrected (Rom. 1:4, etc.) If one denies the resurrection of Jesus, one is denying the Christian message of

Jesus. Thus, there is ultimately no foundation upon which to hold even an "existential" faith. If Jesus is not raised—if miracles are not possible—there is no Christianity (1 Cor. 15). Second, there is a huge difference between the miracles recorded in Acts and those recorded in the apocryphal Gospels and Acts. The former present miracles to bolster the witness to the power of God and the truth of the witness; the latter present miracles for their own sake (and often absurd miracles at that!). Third, if the New Testament miracles did not really happen, it would have been very easy for others to appeal to such a fact. For example, Paul appeals to the miracles done among the Galatians (Gal. 3:4–5). If these miracles did not occur, his entire argument would be worthless. We must conclude that the miracles actually did take place because of his appeal to them as evidence in a weighty argument. We realize that this is an incomplete study of miracles, but it will remind us that the possibility of miracles should not be denied beforehand, at least as a presupposition of doing "good" scholarship.[12]

Our goal in this discussion is not to give simplistic answers to what are difficult problems in biblical criticism of Lukan historiography, but to show that there are always two ways of looking at things. When all is said and done, we must approach the text, letting the data of the text prove itself. And, given that Luke is accurate in so many places where he can be checked, he should get the benefit of the doubt elsewhere. As F. F. Bruce has written, "A man whose accuracy can be demonstrated in matters where we are able to test it is likely to be accurate even where the means for testing him are not available. Accuracy is a habit of mind."[13]

THE THEOLOGY OF LUKE-ACTS

If one does not think that Luke was an accurate historian, can one really formulate a theology of Luke that is of any value? Certainly some scholars who are skeptical of Luke's accuracy have written on the theology of Luke. However, given that the biblical definition of faith is based upon historical facts, we believe that if one argues against Luke's accuracy, one must also logically conclude that it is impossible to formulate a Lukan theology that has any final value. If Luke was inaccurate, what aspects of Luke-Acts would be used to formulate Luke's theology? If one assumes that Luke was inaccurate, one must doubt every description of Luke—it must all be questioned as to having any historical value. While we may be able to say there is such a thing as "Lukan theology," we must also conclude that this "Lukan theology" was invented, and has no relationship to truth and history. For example, in Haenchen's analysis, Lukan theology is not a theology of early Christianity, but of a later church read back onto the time frame of the events recorded in Acts.

How then does Luke view history? The impetus for examining Luke's view of history started with Hans Conzelmann (*Die Mitte der Zeit*, 1954). For Conzelmann, Luke was a member of the third generation of Christians looking back at the beginning of the church from the standpoint of a later Christianity's problem, the delay of the parousia. In other words, Conzelmann thought that the church, which expected the Lord imminently, had become disillusioned by the delay of the parousia. Therefore, Luke invented a three-period *Heilsgeschichte* (the period of Israel, of Jesus, and of the church) in order to show that the delay of the parousia was intended from the start. He thus tries to establish a role for the church while it awaits the much-delayed parousia. It is important to understand that, in Conzelmann's view, Luke invented this idea.

Later scholars (notably, Oscar Cullmann), however, have shown that Luke did not invent this *Heilsgeschichte*. Cullmann has shown that this idea is found throughout the New Testament, even in the earliest traditions. Thus, contrary to Conzelmann's proposal, Luke has given a historical account of the early church in order to inform his readers of the truth of the gospel message. While Luke has certain theological themes, he has grounded these in history in order that Theophilus "may know the truth concerning the things of which [he has] been informed" (Luke 1:4, RSV).

No matter how much we may disagree with Conzelmann's proposal, we are grateful for his emphasis on Lukan theology. It is on this Lukan theology that we will now focus. It is important to understand that within our summary of Luke's theology, we shall also be examining his view of history, as his theology is determined by his view of history. Though he set out to compose a historical work which would serve to strengthen Theophilus's faith in the things he had been taught, Luke also composed the material in his own unique manner with his own theological tendencies due to the fact that he had his own angle for viewing history.

We shall summarize the major themes of Lukan theology under four main headings: (1) the sovereignty of God over history; (2) Jesus Christ as God's agent of salvation; (3) the Holy Spirit as God's instrument of salvation; and (4) the disciples continue the work of God for salvation.

THE SOVEREIGNTY OF GOD OVER HISTORY

Luke grounds the acts of God in history not because he is merely a historian but in order to show that God is sovereign over history.

The Continuity of God's Plan of Salvation. It is important for Luke to show that God's plan had not changed with time. Therefore, Luke shows that the ministry of Jesus and the Church fulfill Old Testament prophecies and also that the movement of salvation to the Gentiles was foreordained.

Luke makes it clear that the ministry of Jesus fulfilled Old Testament prophecies. Zechariah understood the birth of John the Baptist as God fulfilling His plan: "Blessed be the Lord God of Israel, for he has visited and redeemed his people, and has raised up a horn of salvation for us in the house of his servant David, as he spoke by the mouth of his holy prophets from of old" (Luke 1:68–70 RSV). Luke's programmatic summary of Jesus' mission in Luke 4:16–21 makes it clear that Jesus understood that He came to fulfill God's plan in that He concluded the reading of Isaiah 61:1–2 with these words, "Today this scripture has been fulfilled in your hearing" (Luke 1:21 RSV). Even Jesus' death was ordained beforehand. He was "delivered up according to the definite plan and foreknowledge of God" (Acts 2:23 RSV).

The Gentile mission was also God's plan from the beginning. Simeon prophesied that Jesus was "a light for revelation to the Gentiles" (Luke 2:32 RSV). Acts 1:8 makes it clear that the disciples are to be witnesses to the ends of the earth. In the preaching of Peter, Paul, and others in Acts, we see again and again how they ground the Gentile mission in Old Testament prophecies. Acts 13:47 quotes Isaiah 49:6: "I have set you to be a light for the Gentiles, that you may bring salvation to the uttermost parts of the earth" (RSV). In fact, the movement of salvation to the Gentiles was directly initiated by God. The conversions of both the Ethiopian eunuch (Acts 8:26–40) and Cornelius (Acts 10) were initiated through an angel of God. The gift of the Holy Spirit as Peter spoke in Cornelius's house indicated God's acceptance of the Gentiles. Of course, Paul's calling to the Gentiles confirms their acceptance by God.

The Sovereign Movement of God's Plan. A geographical movement can be seen both in Luke and Acts. In Luke, much of the story is centered around Jesus' travel narrative to Jerusalem, the city of destiny (9:51–19:27). Beginning in 9:51, and repeated in 13:22, 17:11, 18:31, and 19:28, Jesus resolutely sets his face toward Jerusalem. Luke uses δεῖ, "it is necessary" (18 times in Luke compared to 8 times in Matt. and 6 times in Mark; 22 times in Acts), to show the divine necessity of the movements of Jesus and others in fulfilling God's plan. "The Son of man must [δεῖ] suffer many things, and be rejected by the elders and chief priests and scribes, and be killed, and on the third day be raised" (Luke 9:22 RSV). Beyond this, Luke makes it clear that the overall movement of the world is in God's sovereign hands (Acts 17:26, 31, etc.).

In Acts, too, we see a geographical movement as the gospel message progresses from Jerusalem to Judea to Samaria and to the end of the earth (Acts 1:8). The final word in Acts is indicative of this move: ἀκωλύτω": "unhindered." Paul spent two years in Rome "preaching the kingdom of

God and teaching about the Lord Jesus Christ quite openly and unhindered" (Acts 28:31 RSV).

Eschatology. Contrary to Conzelmann, there are both present (Luke 10:11; 21:31) and future (12:38, 45; 13:8) elements in Luke's inaugurated eschatology. The emphasis in Luke, however, seems to be on "today," *shvmeron* (Luke 4:21; 5:26; 19:5, 9; 23:43; Acts 4:9; 20:26—twenty times in Luke–Acts). It is certainly possible that Luke was concentrating on the necessity of living the Christian life today, rather than either being disappointed in a delay of the parousia or in hoping for the future. While Jesus will certainly return in the future, Luke shows us that the present also has a place in God's plan.

JESUS CHRIST AS GOD'S AGENT OF SALVATION.

Jesus is portrayed in Luke-Acts as the agent of salvation (Acts 4:12). This is seen in that His ministry fulfilled Old Testament prophecies (above). In addition, the signs and wonders which Jesus performed showed that God had anointed Jesus as His agent of salvation (Luke 4:18–20; Acts 2:2).

Christology. Luke places a special emphasis upon Christology in order to make it clear that Jesus transcends mere humanity. From the beginning of Luke's Gospel, we understand that Jesus is more than a mere man for He is born of the virgin Mary, through the Holy Spirit, and was to be called the Son of the Most High (Luke 1:26–38). John the Baptist "leaped in [Elizabeth's] womb" at the sound of Mary's voice (Luke 1:41 RSV). Could this be an understanding of the importance of Jesus already by the yet-to-be born John? The shepherds and host of angels announce the importance of Jesus at His birth (Luke 2:8–20). Both Simeon and Anna announce God's day of redemption has come in Jesus (Luke 2:22–40). Jesus is shown by Luke to have a special relationship with God the Father (2:49; 3:22; 9:35; 10:21–22; 23:46). The premier example of Jesus' transcendence is seen in His resurrection from the dead (Luke 24:6–7; Acts 2:24, 32; 3:15, etc.) ascension (Luke 24:51; Acts 1:9), and exaltation to the right hand of the Father (Acts 2:33; 5:31).

Luke utilizes various titles for Christ in Luke-Acts to depict his Christological emphasis. Rather than give a lengthy discussion of each title's background and meaning, it will suit our purposes merely to list these titles (see bibliography for further details). Luke describes Jesus as the Messiah or Christ, Lord, Savior, Son of God, Son of Man, Son of David, King, Servant, and Prophet. Lesser-used titles include Holy One, Leader, Teacher, Righteous One, and Judge.

Soteriology. It is because Jesus is all of these things that He is the focus of the Lukan kerygma. "There is salvation in no one else, for there is no other name under heaven given among men by which we must be saved" (Acts 4:12, RSV). Luke uses σῴζω, "to save," in a spiritual sense more often than either Matthew or Mark. In addition, his use of σωτήρ, "saviour," (1:47; 2:11; Acts 5:31; 13:23), σωτηρία, "salvation," (1:69, 71, 77; 19:9; Acts 4:12; 7:25; 13:26, 47; 16:17; 27:34), and σωτήριο", "salvation," (2:30; 3:6; Acts 28:28) show that salvation is a key theological theme for Luke, as none of these terms occur in the other Gospels. As I. Howard Marshall said, "The key concept in the theology of Luke is 'salvation.'"[14] Luke-Acts pictures Jesus as reaching out to the lost in forgiveness and rejoicing over their return: "For the Son of man came to seek and to save the lost" (Luke 19:10, RSV).

Salvation to the Disadvantaged. Universalism, the extension of salvation to individuals outside of God's chosen people of old, is another key theme in Luke. Even the genealogy of Luke (Luke 3:23–38) hints at the universal offer of salvation in that it carries back the genealogy to God, rather than to Abraham, as in Matthew. The cord of universalism is first struck by Simeon in 2:32, then repeated in 3:6 ("all flesh shall see the salvation of God," RSV). We have discussed above how salvation has been extended beyond the cultural boundary of Judaism to the Gentiles. But we also find that salvation has been extended beyond the social and societal boundaries to Samaritans (10:33; 17:16), tax-collectors (Levi—5:27; Zacchaeus—19:2–10), "sinners" (table-fellowship—5:29–32; 7:36–50; the prodigal son—15:11–32; Acts 8:9–13, 18–24), women (Luke 7:36–50; 8:2–3; 10:38–42; Acts 8:12; 9:36–43), children (Luke 18:15) and the poor (Luke 4:18; 6:20; 16:20; Acts 2:44–45; 11:28–30). Jesus' words to the criminal on the cross next to Him have given hope to many: "Today you will be with me in Paradise" (Luke 23:43 RSV).

The Holy Spirit as God's Instrument of Salvation. Luke has more to say about the Holy Spirit than any other New Testament author. Though all of the Gospels refer to the Holy Spirit, it is Luke who is concerned with initiating the various stages of his narrative under the influence of the Spirit. He mentions the Holy Spirit seven times in the infancy narratives, six times in the chapters concerned with the beginning of Jesus' ministry, and four times in the beginning of the travel narrative (chapters 10–12). After these initial bathings, Luke does not use the term *pneu'ma* in his Gospel. It seems that it was very important for Luke to show that the Holy Spirit was active in each stage of the progression of salvation.

In Acts, however, the Spirit is a consistent theme, beginning with the day of Pentecost, when the Spirit descended upon the disciples. In fact, some have renamed the "Acts of the Apostles" the "Acts of the Holy Spirit." This increased role of the Spirit may be due to the progression of salvation history in that after Pentecost the Holy Spirit is given to all believers regardless of race, gender or occupation (Acts 2:17–21, in fulfillment of Joel 3:1–5). After Pentecost, we find individuals being led by the Spirit (Acts 15:28; 19:21; 20:22), being filled with the Spirit (Acts 2:4; 4:8; 9:17; 13:9, etc.), and missionaries being called by the Spirit (Acts 13:3–4), among other things. Luke makes it very clear that it is through the Spirit that the disciples are able to continue the ministry of Jesus, who Himself was filled with and led by the Spirit (Luke 3:22; 4:1).

THE DISCIPLES CONTINUE THE WORK OF GOD FOR SALVATION

Parallels between Jesus and Disciples. Recent literary studies of Luke-Acts have pointed out numerous parallels between the description of Jesus' ministry in Luke and that of the disciples in Acts (esp. O'Toole, Talbert). These parallels serve to show the reader that the disciples are truly carrying on the work of Jesus. Compare, for example, Acts 2:22, "Jesus of Nazareth, a man attested to you by God with mighty works and wonders and signs which God did through him in your midst," with Acts 2:43, "and many wonders and signs were done through the apostles" (RSV). While there are parallels among the descriptions of Jesus, Stephen (Acts 6–7) and Peter, the main parallel is between Jesus and Paul. O'Toole says that the parallels between Jesus and Paul serve to show us that "Christ, in the person of Paul, brings salvation both to the people and to the Gentiles."[15] In this way, Jesus, who concentrated His ministry on Jews during His life, can fulfill the ultimate goal of His coming: to be a light to the Gentiles. The similarity between the hearings of Jesus (Luke 23:1–25) and Paul (Acts 25–26) is one example of this parallelism.

Becoming a Disciple. While it is true that the disciples carry on the work of Jesus, we must pause and ask, "How does one become a disciple?" We may note three descriptions used by Luke to denote one being saved. First, one must respond in faith to the kerygma (Luke 7:50; 8:48; 17:19; Acts 13:38–39; 16:31). Second, one must repent (noun and verb forms used twenty-five times in Luke-Acts). This denotes a turning from one's former way of life and turning to God. "Repent, therefore, and turn again, that your sins may be blotted out, that times of refreshing may come from the presence of the Lord" (Acts 3:19 RSV). Third, those who believe are to be baptized in the name of Jesus. Sometimes Luke speaks of both believing and being baptized (Acts 2:38); at other times he only mentions baptism (Acts 10:48; 22:16). We should not conclude that baptism was some kind of saving activity by itself, without accompanying faith and repentance. Rather, we should conclude that faith, repentance, and baptism were intimately tied together in the early church. Thus, one could simply refer to one of these terms by itself in order to refer to the entire salvific experience.

The Demands of Discipleship. Discipleship is more than an initial turning to Jesus in faith; it involves a lifestyle of following and imitating Jesus (Luke 5:11). Luke contains two passages on the difficulty of discipleship: the narrative on would-be disciples in Luke 9:57–62 and the high cost of discipleship in Luke 14:25–35 (see also Acts 5:1–11 and 8:4–25). Luke includes a number of specific actions which should be in the Christian's life, though we shall only mention a few. The emphasis on witnessing or proclaiming the good news is a main focus of Luke as seen in Acts 1:8, "you shall be my witnesses . . . to the end of the earth" (RSV). Luke also emphasizes prayer, both in Jesus' life and in others. He refers to prayer twenty-one times in his Gospel, twenty-five times in Acts. The last demand that we will mention is the correct use of possessions by disciples. Jesus tells the disciples to "sell your possessions" (Luke 12:33 RSV), to "renounce all that he has" (14:33 RSV), to "sell all that you have and distribute to the poor" (18:22 RSV). In Acts, the generosity of individuals (Barnabas, Tabitha, Cornelius) shows that "it is more blessed to give than to receive" (Acts 20:35 RSV). It is important, however, to understand that Luke is not saying that it is wrong to have possessions, he is merely making it clear that riches very easily turn one's heart away from heavenly pursuits (Luke 12:33–34; 20:25). The disciple may own possessions, but must understand the danger of them.

We have now summarized some of the highlights of Luke's theology. Luke was an accurate historian who recorded history in order to strengthen Theophilus's faith. Yet, due to Luke's particular view of history, Luke-Acts has its own particular nuances and emphases, as we have seen.

SELECT BIBLIOGRAPHY

Aune, David E., ed. *Greco-Roman Literature and the New Testament: Selected Forms and Genres.* Atlanta: Scholars Press, 1988.

Barrett, C. K. *Luke the Historian in Recent Study.* London: The Epworth Press, 1961.

Bovon, François. *Luke the Theologian: Thirty-three Years of Research (1950–1983).* Translated by Ken McKinney. Allison Park, Pa.: Pickwick Publications, 1987.

Brown, Colin. *Miracles and the Critical Mind.* Grand Rapids: Eerdmans, 1984.

Bruce, F. F. *The Acts of the Apostles. The Greek Text with Introduction and Commentary.* 3rd ed. Grand Rapids: Eerdmans, 1983.

————. "The Acts of the Apostles: Historical Record or Theological Reconstruction?" In *Aufstieg und Niedergang der Römischen Welt*. Band II.25.3: 2569–2603. Berlin: Walter de Gruyter & Co., 1984.

————. *The Book of Acts*. Rev. ed. NICNT. Grand Rapids: Eerdmans, 1988.

————. *The New Testament Documents: Are They Reliable?* 5th rev. ed. Grand Rapids: Eerdmans, 1960 (1943).

Conzelmann, Hans. *Acts of the Apostles*. Hermeneia. Philadelphia: Fortress Press, 1987.

————. *The Theology of St. Luke*. Translated by Geoffrey Buswell. New York: Harper & Row, Publishers, 1961.

Fitzmyer, Joseph A. S. J. *The Gospel According to Luke*. 2 vols. The Anchor Bible 28A–B. New York: Doubleday, 1981.

Gasque, W. Ward. *A History of the Interpretation of the Acts of the Apostles*. Grand Rapids: Eerdmans, 1975; reprint, Peabody, Mass.: Hendrickson Publishers, 1989.

Haenchen, Ernst. *The Acts of the Apostles. A Commentary*. Trans. from 14th German ed. (1965) by B. Noble and G. Shinn; rev. by R. McL. Wilson. Oxford: Basil Blackwell, 1971.

Hemer, Colin J. *The Book of Acts in the Setting of Hellenistic History*. Edited by Conrad H. Gempf. Tübingen: J. C. B. Mohr, 1989; reprint, Winona Lake, Ind.: Eisenbrauns, 1990.

Hengel, Martin. *Acts and the History of Earliest Christianity*. Translated by John Bowden. London: SCM Press Ltd., 1979.

————. *Between Jesus and Paul: Studies in the Earliest History of Christianity*. Translated by John Bowden. Philadelphia: Fortress Press, 1983.

Keck, L. E., and J. L. Martyn, eds. *Studies in Luke-Acts*. Nashville: Abingdon Press, 1966; reprint, Philadelphia: Fortress Press, 1980.

Kee, Howard Clark. *Good News to the Ends of the Earth: The Theology of Acts*. London: SCM Press; Philadelphia: TPI, 1990.

Longenecker, Richard N. *The Acts of the Apostles*. EBC 9. Grand Rapids: Zondervan, 1981.

Marshall, I. H. *The Acts of the Apostles*. New Testament Guides. Sheffield: JSOT Press, 1992.

————. *The Gospel of Luke. A Commentary on the Greek Text*. NIGTC. Grand Rapids: Eerdmans, 1978.

————. *Luke: Historian and Theologian*. Enlarged edition. Grand Rapids: Zondervan, 1989.

Morris, Leon. *New Testament Theology*. Grand Rapids: Zondervan, 1986.

Mosely, A. W. "Historical Reporting in the Ancient World." NTS 12 (1965–66): 10–26.

O'Toole, Robert F., S. J. *The Unity of Luke's Theology: An Analysis of Luke-Acts*. Good News Studies 9. Wilmington, Del.: Michael Glazier, Inc., 1984.

Ramsay, William M. *The Bearing of Recent Discovery on the Trustworthiness of the New Testament*. London: Hodder and Stoughton, 1915; reprint, Grand Rapids: Baker Book House, 1979.

————. *Was Christ Born at Bethlehem? A Study on the Credibility of St. Luke*. London: Hodder and Stoughton, 1898; reprint, Grand Rapids: Baker Book House, 1979.

Sherwin-White, A. N. *Roman Society and Roman Law in the New Testament*. Oxford: Oxford University Press, 1963; reprint, Grand Rapids: Baker Book House, 1978.

Smith, James. *The Voyage and Shipwreck of St. Paul with Dissertations on the Life and Writings of St. Luke, and the Ships and Navigation of the Ancients.* 4th rev. ed. London: Longmans, Green, and Co., 1880.

Stein, Robert H. *Luke.* New American Commentary 24. Nashville: Broadman Press, 1992.

Sterling, Gregory E. *Historiography and Self-Definition: Josephus, Luke-Acts and Apologetic Historiography.* Suppl. to N.T. LXIV. Leiden: E. J. Brill, 1992.

Winter, Bruce W., and Andrew D. Clarke. *The Book of Acts in Its Ancient Literary Setting,* vol. 1, *The Book of Acts in Its First Century Setting* . 6 vols. projected. Grand Rapids: Eerdmans; Carlisle: The Paternoster Press, 1993.

NOTES

1. Martin Hengel, *Acts and the History of Earliest Christianity*, trans. James Bowden (London: SCM Press Ltd., 1979), 43.

2. See esp. H. J. Cadbury, *The Style and Literary Method of Luke.*

3. Haenchen Ernst, *The Acts of the Apostles. A Commentary*, trans. from 14th German ed. (1965) by B. Noble and G. Shinn, rev. R. McL. Wilson (Oxford: Basil Blackwell, 1971), 491.

4. James Smith, *The Voyage and Shipwreck of St. Paul with Dissertations on the Life and Writings of St. Luke, and the Ships and Navigation of the Ancients*, 4th rev. ed. (London: Longmans, Green, and Co., 1880), xlvi.

5. William Ramsey, *The Bearing of Recent Discovery on the Trusworthiness of the New Testament* (London: Hodder and Stoughton, 1915; reprint, Grand Rapids: Baker Book House, 1979), 80.

6. Polybius, *The Histories of Polybius*, XII.4c. 2–5, Loeb edition.

7. Thucydides, I. xxii. 2–3, Loeb edition.

8. See also, A. W. Mosely, "Historical Reporting in the Ancient World," NTS 12 (1965–66): 10–26.

9. J. B. Lightfoot, *Essays on the Work Entitled "Supernatural Religion,"* (London: Macmillan and Co., 1893), 291.

10. Thucydides, I. xxii. 1, Loeb edition.

11. C. F. D. Moule, "The Christology of Acts," in *Studies in Luke-Acts*, 159–85.

12. For further study, see Colin Brown, *Miracles and the Critical Mind* (Grand Rapids: Eerdmans, 1984).

13. F. F. Bruce, *The New Testament Documents: Are They Reliable?* 5th rev. ed. (Grand Rapids: Eerdmans, 1960), 90.

14. I. H. Marshall, *Luke: Historian and Theologian*, enl. ed. (Grand Rapids: Zondervan, 1989), 9.

15. Robert F. O'Toole, *The Unity of Luke's Theology: An Analysis of Luke-Acts*, Good News Studies 9 (Wilmington, Del.: Michael Glazier, Inc., 1984), 68.

3

EUSEBIUS OF CAESAREA

JOHN R. FRANKE

In spite of his prominence as a leading figure of his time, the life of Eusebius is not well preserved. It must be pieced together from a number of sources, and tied with inferences and speculations drawn from his own writings. He is mentioned in the writings of his contemporaries such as Athanasius, Arius, and Alexander of Alexandria. Additional information is also available in the works of Socrates, Sozomen, and Theodoret. But these meager resources leave us with a number of gaps, particularly regarding his early life. Unfortunately, the biography which was prepared by his disciple Acacius has been lost.[1]

LIFE OF EUSEBIUS

Eusebius was born around A.D. 260, probably in the region of Palestine, although this is uncertain. He was baptized at Caesarea and was eventually ordained a presbyter.[2] He was commonly referred to by his contemporaries as either Eusebius of Caesarea, because of his service as the bishop of the church in Caesarea, or as Eusebius Pamphili, due to his close friendship with and admiration for Pamphilus, the major influence on his life.

Pamphilus had come to Caesarea by way of Alexandria, where he had become a committed follower of Origen, the controversial leader of the catechetical school at Alexandria. Upon arriving in Caesarea, Pamphilus established a school similar to that of Origen along with a notable library.[3] Eusebius thrived under the tutelage of Pamphilus and became one of his most capable students and devoted disciples.[4] He received a thorough education and adopted the Origenist opinions of Pamphilus to which he remained committed throughout his life.

While in this environment, Eusebius began work on a number of writing projects, including two of his major historical works, the *Chronicle*, which contains a summary of general history with a table of dates, and the important *Ecclesiastical History*. The influence of Pamphilus on the works of Eusebius is impossible to ascertain with precision, although it is certainly significant. Indeed, it has been suggested that without Pamphilus the compilation of the *History* would not have been possible.[5] This activity was made more difficult early in 303 with the outbreak of the "great" persecution, which continued for the next several years on an intermittent basis. In spite of this disruption and the absence of Eusebius from Caesarea during much of this time, the first decade of the fourth century was the most productive period of his literary life.[6]

Sometime during the fifth year of the persecution, around 308, Pamphilus was arrested and imprisoned. For the next two years, Eusebius was able to spend a considerable amount of time with Pamphilus in prison and the two of them collaborated on a *Defense of Origen* and completed five books before Pamphilus was executed.[7] After the martyrdom of Pamphilus and many of his followers, Eusebius fled to escape a similar fate and was able to complete the work on Origen along with a *Life of Pamphilus* in honor of his teacher. Unfortunately, these works are no longer extant. How Eusebius, one of the best known disciples of Pamphilus, was able to avoid arrest is unknown.

In 311 Eusebius was imprisoned. His confinement was brief, however, and with the advent of the rule of Constantine the harassment of Christians drew to a close. By the winter of 312, Constantine was not only calling the persecutions to a halt but was also encouraging and subsidizing the promotion of the Christian faith.[8] In this atmosphere of toleration, Eusebius returned to his labors in Caesarea where his reputation had grown so much that he was elected bishop of that city, probably around 314.[9] He spent the rest of his life overseeing the affairs of the Caesarean church. The literary output of Eusebius decreased as the demands of his office shifted his attention to matters of church politics and governance.

Around 318 Eusebius became involved in the conflict concerning Arius's teaching that the Son of God was a being created by the Father at a moment in time. To Arius, the Son was not eternal, nor was He the equal of the Father. Rather, His divine title was bestowed on Him by the Father because of His merits. Alexander and Athanasius opposed these views, which led to division among the Alexandrian clergy and the excommunication of Arius.[10] Arius, however, would not back down from his position. He responded to the decision against him with defiance and sought support from other eastern bishops, including Eusebius. Because of his Origenist inclinations, Eusebius was less disturbed by the convictions of Arius than were others. Although he had reservations about the Arian position, he did not believe that it warranted the censure of the church. He wrote a letter on behalf of Arius requesting that he be reinstated.[11] Alexander refused, prompting Eusebius to meet with other Palestinian bishops in Caesarea and authorize Arius to resume his teaching with the proviso that he obey his bishop.[12] This caused an uproar in Alexandria and produced rancor and division in the church. Commenting on this situation years later, Eusebius reported that the scandal of these developments became so notorious that the Christian religion became subject to the "most shameful ridicule" among unbelievers.[13]

In the midst of this controversy, Constantine defeated his rival Licinius at Chrysopolis in 324 to become ruler over the entire empire. He was concerned about the strife caused by the Arian conflict and was determined that it should not compromise the unity of the church and the empire. His efforts to mediate and bring about a settlement led to the Council of Nicaea in 325. Scholars sometimes suppose that Eusebius played a major role as a moderate at the Council in helping settle the issue. It is more likely, however, that Eusebius found himself in the position of having to defend his own orthodoxy at Nicaea because he had earlier been provisionally excommunicated by the Council of Antioch for his refusal to subscribe to its anti-Arian doctrinal statement.[14] Thus it appears that Eusebius' submission of the neutrally worded Creed of Caesarea to the Council of Nicaea was not for the purpose of resolving the Arian controversy, but rather served as his defense against charges that he too was a heretic.[15] That Eusebius was quickly exonerated by the Council was perhaps due in no small measure to the support he received from the emperor.[16]

Concerning the main business of the Council, it thoroughly rejected the theology of Arius and put forward a creedal statement that also spurned even the more moderate position preferred by Eusebius found in the Caesarean Creed.[17] Eusebius was uncomfortable with the language adopted by the Council and was reluctant to commit himself to the document it produced. He believed that it could be used to defend the heresy of Sabellianism if it were interpreted in an extremist fashion. However, after careful consideration and with significant reservation he affixed his signature to the document, though it seems clear that he was not altogether willing to do so. In spite of the efforts and intentions of the Council, the conflict was far from resolved and the tensions in the church over the issue continued to be a source of difficulty and concern. For his part, Eusebius remained suspicious of the Creed and its language while staunch anti-Arians such as Athanasius continued to mistrust Eusebius and suspect him of Arian leanings and disloyalty to the Nicene formulations.[18]

In the remaining years of his life, in spite of the continuing controversy over Arius, Eusebius was again able to turn his attention to writing although he was not as productive as he had been before becoming bishop. Of these later works the best known is his unfinished *Life of Constantine*. In 331, Eusebius was elected to the episcopacy of Antioch, one of the two major sees in the East (the other being Alexandria). He declined, however, citing the fifteenth canon of Nicaea which stated that no bishop should leave the episcopacy of one city for another.[19] It is questionable whether or not Eusebius would have taken the post even without the strictures of Nicaea. He might naturally have felt reluctant to leave Caesarea where he was well-established and had more time to pursue his scholarly interests than would have been the case at Antioch. Whatever his motivation, he chose to accept the authority of the church and continued to serve as bishop of Caesarea until his death sometime around 340.[20]

EUSEBIUS AS CHURCH HISTORIAN

Eusebius is the most important historian of the early church and is often referred to as the "Father of Church history" because of the significance of his *Ecclesiastical History*. This work was the first attempt at composing a complete, continuous narrative of the history of the Christian church and its religion. It is also one of the most important sources of information concerning the history of Christianity from the apostolic age until the first quarter of the fourth century. Much of the knowledge we possess about the early church comes to us only from this work, and without it our understanding of this formative period of Christianity would be considerably impoverished. Without it we know next to nothing about the rapid expansion of the early church, its trials and tribulations, the persecutions and martyrdoms of its members, and the divisions that quickly developed within it. In addition to the *History*, Eusebius' extant corpus includes a number of other significant works: the *Chronicle*, which attempts to provide a summary of universal history by setting forth a comparative chronology for all of Ancient Near Eastern, Greek, and Roman history, and biblical history from the time of Abraham; *The Martyrs of Palestine*, an important source for knowledge of the great persecution; and *The Life of Constantine*, a memorial to the emperor containing much useful historical information. In addition to these explicitly historical projects, Eusebius also authored two apologetic works that contain valuable historical material: the *Preparation of the Gospel* and the *Proof of the Gospel*. Due to space constraints, this essay will focus on the *Ecclesiastical History*, the most important and lasting contribution of Eusebius to the Christian tradition and the most accessible means by which to present his work as a historian.

The *Ecclesiastical History* covers the story of the church from its establishment by Jesus Christ, the Son of God, to the time of the Emperor Constantine. It appears that Eusebius wrote the first edition of the *History* sometime before the end of the third century and that it originally consisted of seven books. The first two books chronicle the origins and foundations of the church, its development as an institution before the Jewish War, and the breach with Judaism. Book Three deals with the Jewish War (66–73), the persecution and growth of the church in the following generation, and the conclusion of the age of the apostles. Books Four and Five carry the history to the end of the second century and frequently appear to be discursive and disjointed. Book Six centers around the great Alexandrian theologian Origen and covers the period from the persecution in the reign of Septimus Severus (193–211) to the Decian persecution (about 250). The seventh and last book of the original work brings the history of the church to the time of Eusebius and symbolically describes the Sabbath of the church, a period of relative peace after years of persecution and harassment. T. D. Barnes notes that in "conformity with tradition, Eusebius remained silent about the deeds and achievements of living contemporaries, and he probably brought the *History* to a close with a brief statement of the names of the bishops who occupied the principal sees at the time of writing."[21]

From the beginning of Book Eight, the tone of the work changes, ceasing to be merely a record of the past compiled from various written sources, though these are still consulted. Eusebius now writes about the events of his own lifetime and he begins to draw on his own experiences and observations as well as on conversations with older contemporaries. The final three books, written sometime after 313, deal with the history of the church from the reign of Diocletian (beginning in 284) through the great persecution to the victory of Constantine and the end of the imperial harassment of Christians.

Within this framework the fabric of the *History* is woven together from a number of different themes set forth by Eusebius at the outset of the work:

> The chief matters to be dealt with in this work are the following: The lines of succession from the holy apostles, and the periods that have elapsed from our Saviour's time to our own; the many important events recorded in the story of the Church; the outstanding leaders and heroes of that story in the most famous Christian communities; the men of each generation who by preaching or writing were ambassadors of the divine word. The names and dates of those who through a passion for innovation have wandered as far as possible from the truth, proclaiming themselves the founts of Knowledge falsely so called while mercilessly, like savage wolves, making havoc of Christ's flock. The calamities that immediately after the conspiracy against our Saviour overwhelmed the entire Jewish race. The widespread, bitter, and recurrent campaigns launched by unbelievers against the divine message, and the heroism with which when occasion demanded men faced torture and death to maintain the fight in its defense. The martyrdoms of later days down to my own time, and at the end of it all the kind and gracious deliverance accorded by our Saviour.[22]

In this opening statement Eusebius identifies five broad subjects: the successions of the apostles, the most important events and persons in the history of the church, the development of heresy, the fate of the Jews, and the persecution and martyrdom of Christians.[23] An additional theme not included here, but acknowledged in another passage and recurring throughout the work is the history of the text and canon of Scripture in the early church.[24]

The first book of the *History*, however, does not deal with the topics announced by Eusebius. Instead it consists of a brief exposition of the foundation that undergirds his interpretation of history as well as his understanding of the church and its role in the plan of God and the history of the world. This book functions as an essential prologue for what follows. In it Eusebius offers an account of the earthly life of Jesus, from birth to ascension, as well as a statement concerning his divinity and pre-existence.[25] Eusebius' intention is to demonstrate that Christianity was not a new religion only recently appearing on the stage of human history, but rather the primeval religion from which all other religions of the world derived.[26]

Jesus of Nazareth, crucified by the Romans, was not merely another man who had fallen afoul of the authorities due to his radical teachings. He was the Divine Word of God and the Light of the world from whom all things were brought into being. Since ancient times, the human race has been divided into two classes: the righteous, who have always worshiped the Son of God and received his teaching concerning the knowledge of the Father by means of the theophanies recorded in the Old Testament, and the majority of the ancients, who neither worshiped him nor were able to receive his teachings. Their error resulted from the disobedience of Adam, which condemned his descendants to a forlorn existence bereft of the knowledge of God and subject to his wrath. However, a small number of persons worshiped God. To them the Word appeared at various times. They sowed the seeds of true religion in the world and from them a whole nation devoted to true religion arose. These were the ancient Hebrews, and to this people, through the prophet Moses, God commanded obedience to religious practices and spiritual principles that gave testimony to a spiritual reality not yet clearly revealed. Their Law became widely known and gradually had the effect of promoting more civil and godly behavior throughout the world.[27] By the time that the Roman Empire appeared, all nations, through the mercy of God, were ready to receive the knowledge of the Father. Therefore, at this juncture the Word of God appeared on earth in human form as the Savior of the world. His birth, life, death and resurrection occurred exactly as foretold by Moses and the prophets.[28]

Eusebius explains that Christians are the ones who worship Jesus Christ, the Word of God, who has been known since ancient times through images and symbols but now in clearly revealed truth. Thus, Eusebius contends that the Christian religion is neither novel nor strange, despite the fact that the church and explicitly Christian teachings had existed for only three centuries. In this relatively brief span of time, the Christian faith had spread dramatically, aided and sustained by the power of God through various trials and tribulations. But the religious beliefs and the way of life practiced by Christians were much older, extending back to the patriarchs, who were Christians in all but name. Eusebius argued that, seen from this perspective, Christianity is the most ancient of all religions and the only true way to worship God.

With this prefatory material in place, Books Two through Ten take up the previously announced themes in a chronological narrative. Concerning the succession of the apostles, Eusebius establishes the line of bishops from the apostles and provides lists of those who held the office in Rome, Alexandria, Antioch, and Jerusalem, although he does not have complete information for the bishops of Antioch and Jerusalem.[29] The framework within which the *History* dates ecclesiastical events is therefore based only on the episcopacies of Rome and Alexandria, which Eusebius correlates with the reigns of Roman emperors in order to provide a structure for the placement of material.[30] An important point worthy of mention here is that Eusebius' depiction of the apostolic succession is purely historical. He did not lay emphasis on the transmission of correct doctrine or on the sacramental nature of episcopacy.[31] According to R. M. Grant, "while Eusebius knows quite a bit about the letters of Ignatius, he describes them in such a way as to neglect entirely their picture of the episcopal office. None of his other sources was likely to point toward high episcopal doctrine. What Eusebius means by 'apostolic succession' is essentially 'the historic episcopate.' "[32]

The knowledge of Eusebius concerning key events in the history of the early church, its leaders and teachers was based largely on sermons, letters, and other writings of church leaders, although he also made limited use of oral tradition.[33] Eusebius records various persecutions and martyrdoms, and he notes the contributions of important individuals. Among the more interesting events Eusebius records are the stoning of James, the brother of the Lord, in Jerusalem; the deaths of Peter and Paul in Rome under Nero; and the exile of John on Patmos and his eventual death in Ephesus. Eusebius emphasizes Alexandria and its leading thinkers such as Philo, Clement, and particularly Origen, whose life and work is the subject of a significant section of Book Six.

Eusebius' preoccupation with Alexandria is due, at least in part, to the nature of his sources. To a considerable extent his choice of materials about events and persons depended on what he found in the library at Caesarea, a library that was Alexandrian in origin.[34] In addition to the limitations imposed on him by his sources, it seems likely also that his interest in Alexandria is the result of his Origenist convictions, which would certainly have inclined him to give special attention to things Alexandrian regardless of the nature of his sources. Whatever the reasons, the result is a picture of the church that is unbalanced and skewed in the direction of Alexandria. Eusebius was also hindered in his treatment of the teachers and literature of the church by his failure to comprehend the historical development of Christian theology. He was not able to conceive that there was progress and growth in the doctrinal conceptions of the Christian religion. In his understanding, the faith had been delivered once and for all to the church. Consequently, no improvement or advancement was possible concerning the truths revealed in Scripture. His account, as a result, reads more like a series of disconnected notes and comments than it does a coherent narrative.[35]

The third theme that Eusebius treats, the various heresies that arose and afflicted the church, is handled in a more cohesive manner. Eusebius believed that the doctrine of the church was simply that which had been taught by Christ and preserved in the apostolic succession. Heresy was the work of the Devil, who intended to use it to "darken the radiance of the universal and only true church," which always held the same doctrines in the same way. Therefore, any teachings that were innovative or were expressed in "manifold and polymorphous" ways were clearly false.[36] Eusebius develops the thesis, echoing Irenaeus, that the earliest heretical sects were all secondary additions to authentic Christianity, which had been maintained in its purest form by the succession of bishops. Following Justin and Irenaeus, Eusebius cites Simon, a magician from Samaria, as "the prime author of every heresy."[37] From this identification of Simon as the fountainhead of heresy, Eusebius chronicles the names and doctrines of those who follow Simon's lead, "pretending to accept that sober Christian philosophy which through purity of life has won universal fame" yet who nevertheless remain "as devoted as ever to the idolatrous superstition from which they seemed to have escaped."[38]

As hinted at above, Eusebius' account of early heresy is largely dependent upon the works of Justin and Irenaeus. He tends to quote Justin and to support him with paraphrases from Irenaeus, upon whom he relies heavily when dealing with figures not mentioned by Justin. Eusebius' views concerning ancient heresy are shaped by the limited number of sources available to him and possess little value apart from the works he quoted or paraphrased. He was not a student of heresies and had neither the inclination nor the means to investigate them thoroughly. In dealing with heretics, Eusebius rarely discusses their doctrines, choosing instead to present information concerning the heretics themselves, whom he describes often in abusive language.[39] His understanding of heresy was simplistic, controlled by the assumption that his own theology was orthodox and by the "notion of a fixed deposit, held by himself and reliable colleagues and rejected by heretics early and late."[40]

The consequences that fell upon the Jews as a result of their treatment of Jesus is the fourth theme addressed by Eusebius in the *History*.[41] Their difficulties began immediately after the crucifixion with the ascent of Caligula to emperor, and they culminated with the destruction of Jerusalem in 70 and its subsequent refounding by Hadrian as a Gentile city off limits to the Jews.[42] This prohibition was still in effect in the time of Eusebius, and he refers to it repeatedly as proof of the historical failure of Judaism. Eusebius interprets these events as God's direct judgment on the Jewish people for their conspiracy to have Jesus killed and for their claim before Pilate that they had no king but Caesar.[43] For Eusebius, historical growth and expansion are the marks of success and divine favor. The disasters that had fallen on the Jews and led to their marginalization in the Empire clearly demonstrated to Eusebius the inferior character of the Jewish religion in comparison with Christianity. In contrast to the failure of Judaism, Eusebius depicts the early church as characterized by considerable growth and success. He writes, "Thus with the powerful cooperation of Heaven the whole world was suddenly lit by the sunshine of the saving word. At once, in accordance with the Holy Scriptures, the voice of its inspired evangelists and apostles went forth into all the earth, and their words to the ends of the world. In every town and village, like a well-filled threshing-floor, churches shot up bursting with eager members."[44] Eusebius does not present the standard modern picture of the early church as a hated and persecuted minority that only gradually attained security and respectability. Rather, the church normally enjoyed the respect and toleration of the Empire from its outset in marked contrast with the consistent hatred and persecution of the Jews.

If his picture of the church as a prosperous institution enjoying the toleration of the Empire was accurate, how did Eusebius explain the persecution and martyrdom of Christians? This is the fifth theme which he considers. Barnes makes an important observation regarding Eusebius' understanding of the persecution of Christians: "For him it was persecution, not (as for moderns) the triumph of Christianity, which represented an aberration from the predictable course of history and thus required an explanation. Hence he presented persecution as a rare and unusual phenomenon which reflected not any underlying hostility by an established order toward a potentially subversive religion but the machinations of the devil, the moral depravity of a Roman emperor, or the envy of despicable individuals."[45] Based on this outlook, Eusebius attempts to chronicle the various persecutions and to give an explanation for their occurrence. He notes that the first Roman emperor to persecute Christians was Nero, whom he describes as a "monster of depravity" driven by a "perverse and extraordinary madness" that led him to the "senseless destruction of innumerable lives," including members of his own family.[46] The next organized persecution, that of Domitian, is also cited as the result of the emperor's depravity. He had many prominent citizens executed without a fair trial and then turned his wrath on the Christians, some of whom he executed and others he exiled.[47] At other times, persecution was due not to the evil nature of the emperor but to political pressure, as Eusebius reports was the case under Trajan. From the reign of Trajan, Eusebius attempts to explain the attitude of each of the emperors toward Christianity. The picture that emerges from the *History* is one in which persecution occasionally occurs in the midst of a generally harmonious relationship between Christianity and the Roman Empire. Eusebius details the various persecutions and martyrdoms for the purpose of providing inspiration for the church and as an apologetic for the faith based on the fortitude of the martyrs and the blessings of God that enabled the church to prosper in spite of such trials.

The final theme taken up by Eusebius does not appear at the outset of the *History* but is a recurring topic: the canon of Scripture. He repeatedly makes reference to the views of early Christian writers concerning their opinions about which documents should be considered part of Scripture. His focus is on the books of the New Testament. Concerning the Old Testament, he is clear that the only inspired books were those included in the canon of the Palestinian Jews, which is identical with the modern Old Testament and did not include the Apocrypha, as did the canon of the Diaspora Jews. Eusebius discusses the Old Testament canon three times, citing Josephus, Melito, and Origen in support of the Palestinian canon.[48]

The canon of the New Testament was a more difficult issue and the subject of continuing debate in the church. Eusebius placed the books into four classes: those which were accepted without dispute (the four Gospels, Acts, the epistles of Paul [including the Epistle to the Hebrews], 1 John, and 1 Peter); those which were disputed but widely familiar (James, Jude, 2 Peter, 2 John, and 3 John); those which he calls spurious (the Acts of Paul, the Shepherd of Hermas, the Revelation of Peter, the epistle of Barnabas, the Teachings of the Apostles); and those "published by heretics under the name of the apostles" (the Gospels of Peter, Thomas, Matthias, and others as well as the Acts of Andrew, John and other apostles). Eusebius does not define with precision the differences between disputed and spurious categories. Although he denies that Peter wrote 2 Peter, he classifies it as disputed rather than spurious.[49]

In dealing with the claims of the spurious writings to be accorded the status of Scripture, Eusebius is generally dismissive without providing any rationale other than the opinion of the church. However, he provides considerably more documentation in establishing the apostolic origins of the books accepted without dispute. Among the more interesting details supplied by Eusebius are his claims that Matthew was the earliest of the Gospels and was originally written in Hebrew;[50] that Mark wrote his Gospel to preserve the preaching of Peter;[51] that Luke wrote his Gospel from the preaching of Paul;[52] and that Paul was the author of the Epistle to the

Hebrews.[53] Concerning the Revelation of John, Eusebius indicates that some included it in the list of accepted books while others declared it spurious.[54] Eusebius himself was suspicious of the book and inclined to exclude it from the canon. Barnes comments: "The cause of Eusebius' unease can readily be diagnosed. Revelation breathes an atmosphere of persecution, with an oppressed minority in a hostile world hoping for a glorious vindication in heaven; Eusebius believed that God intended his church to prosper on earth."[55]

Permeating the entire *History* is the idea of divine providence and grace. God guides history and intervenes in it to ensure that the church will prosper. Throughout the history of the church Eusebius finds evidence of the protection and blessing of God for the church. In addition to strengthening the church and confirming its message, God also manifests his care for the church through divine judgment of the opponents of Christianity: Herod the Great and Herod Antipas,[56] the Jews,[57] those who persecuted the church, especially emperors,[58] as well as bad bishops and those who opposed good ones.[59]

In Books Eight and Nine, Eusebius sees the influence of divine providence in the political history of the Empire. By the grace of God, the Great Persecution came to a conclusion with the reversal of policy by the rulers. For Eusebius, this change of course was not the result of anything human but rather of the intervention of God. Galerius was punished for his policy of persecution and he lifted it; Maximin's empire was struck with drought, famine and plague as God showed his "heavenly alliance" with Christians.[60] The ultimate expression of God's providential care for the church is seen in the conversion of Constantine and the downfall of his rivals Maxentius and Maximin, who had shown themselves enemies of the church.[61] In order to demonstrate the tangible benefits to the church of the course of events he describes, Eusebius includes a collection of imperial edicts in Books Eight through Ten. These edicts document the increasing toleration of Christianity in the aftermath of the Great Persecution and its eventual preeminence under Constantine. Eusebius concludes with a tribute to the emperor who, with the help of divine providence, vanquished the enemies of true religion and brought peace to the church in fulfillment of the purposes of God.[62]

The *History* reads as a simple, straightforward narrative account of the events and persons that shaped the development of the church. Underneath this simplicity, however, are "certain dogmatic presuppositions, of which the story itself is the narrative expression."[63] If Eusebius is to be appreciated as a historian, these implicit presuppositions must be grasped. Although it would be easy to view the *History* as the work of an annalist rather than that of a historian, a more comprehensive consideration of the work indicates that such a notion is mistaken. In the thought of Eusebius, the underlying movement of all human history is the progression from Abraham to Christ, the unfolding of the plan of God to bring blessing to all the world. The goal of this movement was rooted in the promise of God to Abraham, which ensured numberless descendants, territorial possessions, and that the seed of Abraham would be a source of blessing for all the world. Eusebius understood that the fulfillment of this promise would be realized in corporate, not merely individual, salvation. He envisaged a theocracy that included all human beings, one in which God ruled his faithful people.

Eusebius believed that the advent of Constantine during the first quarter of the fourth century was the culmination of this progression. In his works on Constantine, the *Oration in Praise of Constantine* and the *Life of Constantine*, Eusebius sets out to demonstrate the divine origin of his reign. He understands the reign of Constantine as the fulfillment of the promise of God to Abraham that the chosen people would exercise territorial rule. Thus, he sees the empire under Constantine as an extension of the Kingdom of God on earth and as the consummation of history. Based on this conception of the denouement of human history, Eusebius naturally rejected the chiliastic views common in the preceding centuries, and he ridiculed those who held them.[64] With this understanding of the historical process in mind, the intention of Eusebius in composing the *Ecclesiastical History* becomes clear. In the words of Wallace-Hadrill: "Eusebius viewed the course of history from the peak towards which all human history had been moving. The end had been reached, and he saw himself to be in a position to do what none could have done before, to view the process as a whole, to see how the divine purpose had been achieved at each point, and to see the wrong turnings and false starts of pagans and heretics lying off at their varying angles of error from the main highway."[65]

In spite of the grand and noble intentions of its author, the work contains several significant defects. As a literary work the *History* leaves much to be desired: its style is poor, it contains numerous digressions, and it appears to be haphazard in its composition and in its inclusion of material. In some respects, the *History* can be viewed as a collection of extracts from earlier writers loosely held together by the comments and observations of the annalist. Against the view that Eusebius was arbitrary and undisciplined in his selection and placement of material, however, H. J. Lawlor has shown that the fragmentary nature of the work may be accounted for by the close adherence of its author to a careful design,[66] to Eusebius' attempt to structure his narrative around the reigns of Roman emperors and the episcopates of the bishops of the main apostolic sees. Wallace-Hadrill confirms this judgment, commenting that "the material of the *History* is fitted into its framework of interlocking regnal years of emperors and episcopates of bishops with a consistency that destroys real continuity."[67]

Another shortcoming of the work is found in Eusebius' handling of his sources. A careful comparison of the *History* with the documents used as sources discloses several problems. When Eusebius paraphrases, he freely rewrites passages so as to alter the emphasis of the original. When he quotes extant writers directly, he often truncates the source and in many cases alters the meaning. Over fifty quotations, other than citations of Scripture, have been mutilated. In at least thirty-five instances the mutilation obscures the sense of the passage cited.[68] One might also assume that citations from lost documents have been similarly mutilated and altered. In addition, Eusebius sometimes unknowingly used forged or altered documents, as when he failed to detect Christian interpolations in Josephus. Hence, although the *History* contains a wide range of important material, it cannot be taken at face value and must be studied critically.

A final criticism concerns the Eusebian picture of the early church. Because of his understanding of history and the plan of God, he assumed that the church had always been as it was in the late third century: prosperous and respectable with numerous followers. As a consequence, he projected the church of his times back into the first two centuries and produced a portrait of the earliest church that is fundamentally anachronistic. Due to this misconception, Eusebius was unable to discern or to document the crucial transitions in early Christianity. In 180, the Christians were an obscure sect whose beliefs were grossly misunderstood. Yet, within a single generation we find Christians or Christian sympathizers at the imperial court and in the Roman Senate.[69] From that point the church grew steadily in the estimation of Roman society. Individuals such as Tertullian, Cyprian, and Origen established the moral, social, and intellectual respectability of the Christian faith. Further, Eusebius' depiction of the church is unbalanced in that he knew virtually nothing of the early Latin writers. Consequently, he sometimes makes general statements about the nature of Christendom as a whole that are contradicted by the Latin evidence.[70]

In spite of these drawbacks, the *History* remains one of the treasures of the church. It is an important work in at least three respects. First, it provides us with a wealth of information concerning the first three centuries of the church, much of which is preserved only in its pages. No summary can do adequate justice to the plethora of detail it contains. Thus, for scholars of early Christianity and of the Roman Empire, it will always remain a crucial and indispensable quarry of information. Second, it represents the first attempt at writing a continuous full-length narrative history from a Christian perspective. As such, it was the major influence in the formation of a distinctly Christian approach to history that continued to evolve in the works of historians such as Socrates, Sozomen, Theodoret, and Evagrius. An understanding of Eusebius is an essential context for a full appreciation of these early Christian historians and the development of the Christian historiographical tradition. Finally, the work of Eusebius is important because it stands as the only serious ancient Christian alternative to the theology of history presented later by Augustine. Augustine's doctrine of the two cities provided a pragmatic, if theologically brilliant, response to the crumbling of the Roman Empire. In it he denies any notion of genuine historical progress and calls into question the possibility of a fundamental Christian transformation of the secular order. Eusebius, who could not imagine the fall of the Empire, was not so pessimistic: he believed not only that the social order could be reformed from a Christian perspective but that this was an essential aspect of the mission of the church and of God's plan for the world. Although the particulars of Eusebius' understanding concerning the role of the Roman Empire in the plan of God had to be abandoned in the aftermath of its collapse a century later, his vision of a universal Christian society continued to have a formative influence in the Christian tradition. The *Ecclesiastical History* endures as the single most important resource for the study of early Christian history and as a monument to the noble vision of its author.

BIBLIOGRAPHY
WORKS IN ENGLISH TRANSLATION

ECCLESIASTICAL HISTORY

Deferrari, R. J. *Fathers of the Church* 19 (1953); 29 (1955).

Lake, K., and J. E. L. Oulton. *Eusebius, Ecclesiastical History.* 2 vols., Loeb Classical Library. London, 1926, 1932.

Lawlor, H. J. and J. E. L. Oulton. *Eusebius' Ecclesiastical History.* London, 1927.

McGiffert, A. C. "The Church History of Eusebius." *The Nicene and Post-Nicene Fathers,* Second Series, vol. 1. New York, 1890.

Williamson, G. A. *Eusebius, The History of the Church from Christ to Constantine.* New York, 1965.

THE MARTYRS OF PALESTINE

Cureton, W. *History of the Martyrs of Palestine by Eusebius, Bishop of Caesarea, discovered in a very ancient Syriac Manuscript.* London, 1861.

Lawlor H. J. and J. E. L. Oulton. *Eusebius' Ecclesiastical History,* 327–400. London, 1927.

PREPARATION FOR THE GOSPEL

Gifford, E. H. *Eusebii Praeparatio Evangelica.* Oxford, 1903.

PROOF OF THE GOSPEL

Ferrar, W. J. *Eusebius, Proof of the Gospel.* 2 vols. London, 1920.

IN PRAISE OF CONSTANTINE

Drake, H. A. *In Praise of Constantine: A Historical Study and New Translation of Eusebius' Tricennial Orations.* Berkeley, 1976.

THE LIFE OF CONSTANTINE

Richardson, E. C. "The Life of Constantine." *The Nicene and Post-Nicene Fathers,* Second Series, vol. 1. New York, 1890.

STUDIES IN ENGLISH

Barnes, T. D. *Constantine and Eusebius.* Cambridge, Mass., 1981.

_____. "Two Speeches by Eusebius." *Greek, Roman and Byzantine Studies* 18 (1977): 341–45.

_____. "The Editions of Eusebius' *Ecclesiastical History.*" *Greek, Roman and Byzantine Studies* 21 (1980): 191–201.

Baynes, N. H. "Eusebius and the Christian Empire." *Melanges Bidez. Annuaire de l'Institut de Philologie et d'Histoire Orientales et Slaves* 2 (Brussels, 1934): 13–18. Reprinted in *Byzantine Studies* (1955): 168–72.

Chesnut, G. F. "Fate, Fortune, Free Will and Nature in Eusebius." *Church History* 42 (1973): 61–90.

_____. *The First Christian Histories: Eusebius, Socrates, Sozomen, Theodoret and Evagrius. Theologie Historique* 46. Paris, 1977.

Connolly, R. H. "Eusebius, H. E. v. 28." *Journal of Theological Studies* 49 (1948): 73–79.

Cranz, F. E. "Kingdom and Polity in Eusebius of Caesarea." *Harvard Theological Review* 45 (1952): 47–66.

Cross, F. L. "The Council of Antioch in 325 A.D." *Church Quarterly Review* 128 (1939): 49–76.

Grant, R. M. "Eusebius and His Church History." *Understanding the Sacred Text: Studies in Honor of Morton S. Enslin,* 235–47. Valley Forge, 1972.

_____. "Eusebius and His Lives of Origen." *Forma Futuri: Studi in honore del Cardinale M. Pellegrino,* 635–49. Turin, 1975.

_____. "The Case Against Eusebius or, Did the Father of Church History Write History?" *Studia Patristica* 12. *Texte und Untersuchungen* 115 (Berlin, 1975): 413–21.

_____. "Eusebius and Gnostic Origins." *Paganisme, Judaisme, Christianisme: Melanges offerts a Marcel Simon.* 195–205. Paris, 1978.

_____. *Eusebius as Church Historian.* Oxford, 1980.

Gustafsson, B. "Eusebius' Principles in Handling His Sources, as Found in His 'Church History,' Books I–VII." *Studia Patristica* 4. *Texte und Untersuchungen* 79 (Berlin, 1961): 429–41.

Lawlor, H. J. *Eusebiana: Essays on the "Ecclesiastical History" of Eusebius, Bishop of Caesarea.* Oxford, 1912.

Lightfoot, J. B. "Eusebius of Caesarea." *Dictionary of Christian Biography.* Smith and Wace, eds. vol. 2. London, 1880.

Luibheid, C. *Eusebius of Caesarea and the Arian Crisis.* Dublin, 1981.

McGiffert, A. C. "The Life and Writings of Eusebius of Caesarea." *The Nicene and Post-Nicene Fathers,* Second series, vol. 1. New York, 1890.

McArthur, H. K. "Eusebian Sections and Canons." *Catholic Biblical Quarterly* 27 (1965): 250–56.

Milburn, R. L. P. *Early Christian Interpretations of History.* London, 1952.

Momigliano, A. "Pagan and Christian Historiography in the Fourth Century A.D." *The Conflict between Paganism and Christianity in the Fourth Century,* 79–99. Oxford, 1963.

Mosshammer, A. *The "Chronicle" of Eusebius and the Greek Chronographic Tradition.* London, 1979.

Richardson, G. W. "The Chronology of Eusebius: Addendum." *Classical Quarterly* 19 (1925): 96–100.

Stevenson, J. *Studies in Eusebius.* Cambridge, 1929.

Storch, R. "The 'Eusebian Constantine.'" *Church History* 40 (1971): 145–55.

Suggs, M. J. "Eusebius and the Gospel Text." *Harvard Theological Review* 50 (1957): 307–10.

Swete, H. B. *Essays on the Early History of the Church and Ministry.* London, 1918.

Wallace-Hadrill, D. S. "The Eusebian *Chronicle*: The Extent and Date of Composition of Its Early Editions." *Journal of Theological Studies* 6 (1955): 248–53.

_____. "Eusebius and the Gospel Text of Caesarea." *Harvard Theological Review* 49 (1956): 105–14.

_____. *Eusebius of Caesarea.* London, 1960.

Zernov, N. "Eusebius and the Paschal Controversy." *Church Quarterly Review* 116 (1933): 24–41.

NOTES

1. Socrates, *H.E.* 2.4. Note: The abbreviation H.E. refers to the works entitled in English *Ecclesiastical History*. When the abbreviation stands alone it refers to the work of Eusebius, in other cases the author is mentioned beforehand.

2. Socrates, *H.E.* 1.8; Theodoret, *H.E.* 1.11.

3. H. J. Lawlor, *Eusebiana: Essays on the "Ecclesiatical History" of Eusebius, Bishop of Caesarea* (Oxford, 1912), 136–66.

4. Eusebius writes of Pamphilus with genuine affection and high praise for his learning. Eusebius, *H.E.* 7.32.25; *M.P.* 11.1.

5. Foakes Jackson, *Eusebius Pamphili,* 40.

6. For a detailed account of the dating of the works of Eusebius, (see D. S. Wallace-Hadrill, *Eusebius of Caesarea,* London, 1960), 39–58.

7. *H.E.* 6.33.4. Some have assumed that Eusebius was also imprisoned during these two years. However, there is no evidence to support this assumption other than that

Eusebius and Pamphilus must have spent a considerable amount of time together to compose the *Defence*. The fact that Eusebius himself is silent on the matter has led historians to conclude that he merely visited Pamphilus in prison.

8. Wallace-Hadrill, *Eusebius*, 19.

9. On Eusebius' ascension to the office of bishop see the article of J. B. Lightfoot, "Eusebius of Caesarea" in the *Dictionary of Christian Biography*, Smith and Wace, eds., vol. 2 (London, 1880), 312; and A. C. McGiffert, "The Life and Writings of Eusebius of Caesarea" in Schaff and Wace, eds., *The Nicene and Post-Nicene Fathers*, second series, vol. 1: 10–11.

10. Socrates, *H.E.* 1.6.

11. Theodoret, *H.E.* 1.5.

12. Sozomen, *H.E.* 1.15.

13. Eusebius, *V.C.* 2.61. Note: The abbreviation V.C. refers to *The Life of Constantine*.

14. The main source of information concerning the Council of Antioch is found in the synodal letter of the Council. For an English translation see Stevenson, *A New Eusebius*, rev. Friend, 334–37.

15. Kelly, *Early Christian Creeds*, 181, 211ff.

16. Wallace-Hadrill, *Eusebius*, 28. He comments: "The impression given is that Eusebius was very lucky to have so easily escaped ratification of the provisional sentence passed in Antioch, for his defense, based on the Caesarean Creed, was largely irrelevant to the doctrinal point upon which he had been excommunicated. It is possible that the council was glad to pass quickly over the embarrassing matter of passing judgment upon its most learned member and that, as Eusebius suggests in his letter, it readily followed the emperor's lead in effecting his rehabilitation."

17. See Kelly, *Early Christian Creeds*, 226; also Wallace-Hadrill, *Eusebius*, 29–30.

18. For a detailed account of the doctrinal views of Eusebius as they relate to the Arian conflict and the doctrinal formulations of the Council of Nicaea, see Wallace-Hadrill, *Eusebius*, 121–38.

19. Stevenson, *A New Eusebius*, 342, 361.

20. It has been suggested that Eusebius died on May 30, 339; however, this is not certain. Although the exact time of Eusebius death is unknown, we do know that he was no longer living in 341 when we find his successor Acacius as bishop of Caesarea at the council of Antioch in that year (Sozomen, *H.E.* 3.5). In addition both Socrates (*H.E.* 2.4) and Sozomen (*H.E.* 3.2) place his death before that of Constantine II in 340.

21. T. D. Barnes, *Constantine and Eusebius*, (Cambridge, Mass.: 1981), 129.

22. *H.E.* 1.1.1–2. This translation is from G. A. Williamson, *Eusebius, The History of the Church from Christ to Constantine* (New York, 1965), 31–32. However, in this instance I have not retained the manner in which he divides and presents the passage.

23. This list follows that of R. M. Grant, *Eusebius as Church Historian* (Oxford, 1980). Barnes identifies six themes in this passage rather than five. The difference between the two is that Grant's second theme, the events and persons in the history of the Church, is split into two by Barnes: the internal history of the Church and Christian writers and teachers (129). Otherwise their lists are in agreement.

24. *H.E.* 3.3.3. Both Grant and Barnes include this theme in their respective lists. Grant identifies a final theme, "the merciful and gracious help of our Saviour." See *Eusebius as Church Historian*: 142–63, for his delineation of this topic.

25. *H.E.* 1.3.

26. *H.E.* 1.4.

27. *H.E.* 1.2. "Their law became famous and like a fragrant breeze penetrated to every corner of the world."

28. *H.E.* 1.2.

29. For more detail concerning the lists used by Eusebius for all of these cities and the problems involved with each, see Grant, *Church Historian*, 51–55. Grant also notes (59) that Eusebius' concern for the successions at Jerusalem, Alexandria, and Antioch as well as Rome is due to his "desire to broaden the base already laid by Irenaeus and Hegesippus with their emphasis on Rome alone."

30. Barnes, *Constantine and Eusebius*, 130. He notes that with each new Bishop of Rome or Alexandria Eusebius "normally states the number of years the previous incumbent had served and the regnal year in which his successor took office."

31. Swete, *Essays on the Early History of the Church and the Ministry* (London, 1918), 132–42.

32. Grant, *Church Historian*, 59.

33. Ibid., 61–63.

34. Ibid., 72–83.

35. Barnes, *Constantine and Eusebius*, 132.

36. *H.E.* 4.7.13.

37. *H.E.* 2.13.

38. *H.E.* 2.13. For a summary of Eusebius, catalog of heretics and heretical movements, see Barnes, *Constantine and Eusebius*, 133–35.

39. Grant, *Church Historian*, 85. He notes that the use of abusive language may have been the major contribution of Eusebius to the study of heresy. He cites Lucien as one who was critical of the use of abusive language in historical works and maintained that it should be reserved for comedies. Eusebius did not agree and made ample and repetitive use of words such as "abominable," "loathsome," and "shameful" or "unspeakable" practices when describing heretics. His intention was to discredit those who sought to undermine the teaching and unity of the Church. He believed that the worse heretics were made to look, the more radiantly the truth of the Church would shine.

40. Ibid., 87.

41. This theme is dealt with in Books 2–4.

42. *H.E.* 4.6.

43. *H.E.* 2.4–6. Other attempts at explaining the fall of the city had been made by writers such as the Jewish historian Josephus, who attributes it to sedition and the rise of tyrants as rulers. The topic had also been frequently discussed by Christian writers, but the connection between the fall of the city and the death of Jesus had not been made until the third century by Tertullian and Origen. Eusebius certainly derived this idea from Origen on whose work he was dependent for his knowledge of early Christian and Jewish history. See Grant, *Church Historian*, 97–105.

44. *H.E.* 2.3.1–2.

45. Barnes, *Constantine and Eusebius*, 136.

46. *H.E.* 2.25.

47. *H.E.* 3.17–20.

48. *H.E.* 3.9 (Josephus); 4.26 (Melito); 6.25 (Origen).

49. *H.E.* 3.3.1, 4.

50. *H.E.* 3.24.6 and 3.39.19 (Papias); 5.8.2 (Irenaeus); 6.25.4 (Origen).

51. *H.E.* 2.15 and 3.39.15 (Papias); 5.8.3 (Irenaeus); 6.25.5 (Origen).

52. *H.E.* 3.4.6.

53. *H.E.* 3.3.5. Eusebius was aware of the arguments against the Pauline authorship of Hebrews (*H.E.* 6.20.3, 6.25.11). These skeptics maintained that the composition and style of the letter was not Pauline. Eusebius found these arguments invalid and claimed that the letter had been written by Paul in Hebrew and later translated by either Luke or Clement into Greek. Eusebius believed it was Clement due to the "similarity of phraseology shown throughout by the Epistle of Clement and the Epistle to the He-

brews, and the absence of any great difference between the two works in the underlying thought." *H.E.* 3.38.

54. *H.E.* 3.25.

55. Barnes, *Constantine and Eusebius*, 140.

56. *H.E.* 1.8.3; 2.10.1.

57. *H.E.* 2.6; 3.5.

58. *H.E.* 7.30; 8.16; 9.7.

59. *H.E.* 8.1; 6.9.7–8.

60. *H.E.* 9.7.

61. *H.E.* 9.8–11.

62. *H.E.* 10.9.

63. Wallace-Hadrill, *Eusebius*, 168.

64. *H.E.* 3.39.12f. Commenting on Papias's chiliastic beliefs, he writes: "I suppose he got these notions by misinterpreting the apostolic accounts and failing to grasp what they had said in mystic and symbolic language. For he seems to have been a man of very small intelligence, to judge from his books. But it is partly due to him that the majority of churchmen after him took the same view, relying on his early date."

65. Wallace-Hadrill, *Eusebius*, 182.

66. H. J. Lawlor and J. E. L. Oulton, *Eusebius' Ecclesiastical History* (London, 1927), 12–14.

67. Wallace-Hadrill, *Eusebius*, 159–60. He cites the example of Justin whose writings appear in three separate groups, in the reigns of Hadrian, Antonius Pius, and Marcus Aurelius according to the dates of their composition.

68. Lawlor and Oulton, *Ecclesiastical*, 23–26. Lawlor maintains that the reason for these errors is not to be attributed to the intent of Eusebius but rather to the incapacity of the Caesarean copyists to whom he delegated the task of transcribing passages.

69. Barnes, *Constantine and Eusebius*, 142. He mentions that "an apologist could soberly inform a proconsul of Africa that if the proconsul wished to rid his province of Christians, he would need to decimate his own staff and social circle, and a governor of Arabia could ask the prefect of Egypt to send him a Christian teacher for an interview."

70. Ibid., 142–43. In light of Eusebius' wholesale ignorance of the Latin Christian writers, Barnes rightly concludes that the tendency to interpret their works in a Eusebian historical framework must be abandoned.

4

AUGUSTINE OF HIPPO

ALISTER E. MCGRATH

Augustine of Hippo is perhaps the most important theological writer to be included in this volume. His contributions to Christian theology—especially in relation to the doctrines of the church, grace, and the Trinity—are immense. Yet he was a theologian, not a historian. As we shall see, his exercise of historical and historiographical skills was slight. Yet his inclusion in this volume is thoroughly justified. For Augustine was concerned with the interpretation of history—with making sense of the broad sweep of human history, and asking how this could be correlated with the will of God. He asked the big questions—questions which all who are concerned with the history of the church must continue to ask. Augustine is a role model, reminding historians of the need for a theological perspective, and theologians of the fact of their existence in history.

CONVERSION AND EARLY CAREER

The early history of Christianity in the Mediterranean world was troubled by a number of factors, of which the hostility of the Roman authorities was one. Yet by the end of the fourth century, Christianity was respectable, even fashionable. The conversion of Flavius Valerius Constantinus in October 312 was unquestionably of vital importance to the new status of the once-despised religion. When Constantine defeated his rival Maxentius and assumed the title and power of Roman emperor, he created a new and favorable climate for the Christian faith throughout his realm. The conversion of Constantine the Great represented a landmark in Christian history, with dramatic and immediate results for the political history of the Roman *imperium*.

That same century, another conversion took place, which marked another landmark in the advance of Christianity. It related primarily to the world of ideas, rather than to the *realpolitik* of Rome. Yet its long-term influence upon Christian thought has been marked and permanent. The conversion in question is that of Aurelius Augustinus, more generally known as Augustine of Hippo or, most economically of all, simply as Augustine.

In the fourth century, the Roman Empire embraced most of the western Mediterranean coastline, including modern-day Algeria. The Christian faith had become strongly established in this area, strengthened by the witness of martyrs such as Cyprian of Carthage. Although generally regarded as something of a backwater by most educated people, Roman North Africa gave the Christian church one of its most important thinkers in the two thousand years of its history. On 13 November 354, a child was born in the town of Thagaste, now known as Souk-Ahras. His parents were probably north Africans who were entitled to Roman citizenship; they were certainly poor. His name was Augustine.[1]

It soon became clear that Augustine was gifted, and that he would benefit from formal education. This meant leaving the family home and going to a center of learning. His father fostered the idea of sending him to Carthage, the great university town of north Africa. Augustine's mother, Monica, was an enthusiastic Christian, who dearly wanted her son to share her faith. Unfortunately, she could not handle the questions Augustine wrestled with in his youth. Gradually, Augustine began to become alienated from Christianity. He felt it lacked intellectual credibility.

Augustine went to Carthage to further his studies. The key to a successful legal career was a firm grasp of rhetoric and the Latin language. Augustine soon discovered he was good at both, and exulted in his success. His pursuits, however, extended beyond the purely academic: like young students today, he wanted to explore, to test his limits, to be free, to be able to fall in love. Augustine later recalled how freely he indulged himself sensually once he was no longer restricted by his parents. He took a mistress within a year of his arrival, and was soon father to a son (born in 372, when Augustine was 18).

North Africa, however, was home to a religious sect known as the Manichees. Shortly after the birth of his son, Augustine became involved with this sect.[2] This religion resembled Christianity at some points; at others, however, it had little to do with the Christian gospel, teaching, for example, that the God of the Old Testament was malicious and evil, having nothing to do with the God of the New Testament. It was the God of the Old Testament who was responsible for all the evil and suffering of the world. The Old Testament, therefore, was irrelevant to Christians, as it concerned a God inferior to that of the New.

Augustine found Manichaeism enormously attractive, remaining a member of the sect for the next nine years. His mother was horrified and told her son never to come home again. She approached a local bishop for advice on how to cope with her son. He suggested that she leave Augustine alone, so that he could come to his senses. Monica found this advice unbearable. It seemed to amount to abandoning her son to an unknown fate.

Meanwhile, Augustine's career was going well. In 377, he won a rhetorical contest presided over by the proconsul of Africa. He converted some of his friends to Manichaeism and accepted a teaching post at Carthage, seeing this as a useful stepping stone to higher things at Rome itself. It was only a matter of time before he could begin to climb the ladder that led to important imperial administrative jobs in Rome. He might even become governor of a Roman province. His mother asked him not to go to Rome, which she regarded as a worse flesh-pot than Carthage. In 383 Augustine told his mother he was going to see a friend off at the port: in fact, he boarded a ship and sailed to Rome, taking his mistress with him.

Underneath the veneer of success, however, Augustine appears to have been having fundamental doubts about the sect he had joined. He overheard some Christians making criticisms of its ideas in Carthage, and found these criticisms convincing. However, he saw no reason to let his Manichaean colleagues know of his doubts. On arriving at Rome, he got in touch with some local sect members. One of them had contacts in the right places, and through his influence Augustine was soon offered the job of Public Orator in the major northern Italian city of Milan.

On his arrival at Milan, Augustine discovered that Ambrose, the local Christian bishop, had a reputation as a splendid orator. He decided to find out whether the reputation was merited. Each Sunday, he slipped into the cathedral and listened to the bishop preach. Initially, Augustine took a purely professional interest in the sermons as pieces of splendid oratory. But gradually, their content began to take hold of him. His doubts concerning

Manichaeism increased and an interest in Christianity began to develop. "I had yet to discover that it taught the truth," he later remarked, "but I did discover that it did not teach the things I had accused it of."

He began to go through a spiritual crisis. He broke off his relationship with his mistress—a relationship which had lasted 15 years and had given every appearance of stability to his colleagues. Manichaeism no longer had any attraction for Augustine: however, something prevented him from committing himself to Christianity. Something was holding him back; there was a block to his spiritual development. Still, the pressure was building up. Augustine had long been attracted to the writings of the author Marius Victorinus; he now discovered that this writer had become a Christian late in life. A visitor to Augustine's residence told him of how Victorinus had been converted by studying the Scriptures and had insisted on going to church and making a public declaration of faith. The visitor relished the story as a superb piece of gossip; for Augustine, however, it seemed to be the voice of God addressing him in secret.

The crisis came soon afterwards. Augustine found himself wanting to break with his past and begin a new relationship with Jesus Christ. He heard reports of others doing this and wished he could do the same himself. But somehow, the stimulus never came. In his autobiography, Augustine recounts how in August 386 he sat under a fig tree in the garden of his house at Milan, and asked God how much longer this could go on. Why couldn't he set aside his baseness here and now? As if by answer, he heard some children playing in a neighboring garden. They were singing as they played, and the words they sang were, "*Tolle lege! Tolle lege!* Take up and read! Take up and read!" Augustine rushed indoors, opened his New Testament at random, and read these words, which stood out from the page: "Clothe yourselves with the Lord Jesus Christ, and do not think about how to gratify the desires of your lower nature" (Rom. 13:14). He closed the book and told his friends he had become a Christian. Within ten years, Augustine was a bishop in north Africa and had become one of the most influential thinkers that Christianity ever produced. His massive talent was now directed towards the work of the gospel, rather than his own career in the Roman administration. And a vital part of that task was reflection on the nature of history, and the relation of the historical process to the Christian gospel.

THE GOSPEL AND WORLD HISTORY

We must recall that Augustine wrote against the backdrop of the fall of Rome. By the late fourth century, it was clear that the power and authority of Rome were becoming weakened. Internal division within imperial circles led to infighting, further weakening Rome in the face of threats from the north. By 407, the natural barrier of the Rhine had been breached by barbarian invaders; in 410, Rome itself was sacked by the Goths. It was clear to Augustine that he was living and writing at a momentous period in the history of the world. But how was he, as a Christian historian, to make sense of what was happening around him?

It is clear that Christian attempts to write history in this period were initially informed by pagan historiographical models.[3] Roman pagan historiographers tended to avoid contentious issues, such as religion, and contented themselves with providing short accounts of the past history of Rome for the benefit of a readership that was possessed both of an ignorance of the past and of a short attention span. Given the religiously neutral style and content of such works, it was a relatively simple matter for early Christian historians to superimpose material of a more specifically Christian nature on the historical grid prepared for them by such writers. There was a real need for this style of writing: both Christians and potential pagan converts needed to know where Abraham, Moses and Jesus Christ fitted into the world of Hercules, Caesar and Pompey.

An apologetic note can be discerned at this early stage in Christian historiography—the need to justify the historical foundations of Christianity to an educated Roman public, skeptical of its historical credentials. (It is clear that Augustine used, at points, the *Antiquities* of Marcus Terentius Varro in *The City of God*). Augustine himself was acutely aware of the need to date the foundational events of the Christian revelation with reference to "Olympiads and the names of the Consuls". (There is an obvious parallel here with the Gospel of Luke, which dates the opening of the ministry of Jesus Christ with reference to both secular and religious figures: Luke 3:1). In doing so, Augustine was able to draw on the earlier pioneering work of Eusebius and Jerome, who had shown how the events of Scripture could be correlated with secular history, so that Christian history could be seen to be firmly anchored in the real world of concrete events, rather than a fictitious or ahistorical mythological world.

In the early phase of his writing, Augustine is content to draw a distinction between secular history and sacred history, between the history of the world as recounted by secular Roman historians, and the history of redemption in Christ. He is clear that these two styles of history are related to each other, but makes no attempt to explore their relation. Indeed, early works (such as *De doctrina Christiana*) indicate that there is nothing to be gained by the Christian studying secular history, unless it is by way of enhancing an understanding of Scripture, or contributing towards the apologetic tasks of the church.

If anything, this perception is strengthened by the passing of time. In his later writings, Augustine reiterates his belief that there is little to be gained by the study of *historia gentium,* the general secular history of the world, or even of the history of ideas. This history serves little purpose, even, he later suggests, as a *praeparatio evangelica.* In his *Confessions,* for example, Augustine makes it clear that he regards pagan philosophy as something of an irrelevance to believers; why study this philosophy, when it contributes little to faith?

Yet a more detailed examination of Augustine's hostility towards the study of pagan philosophy reveals an insight of considerable importance. Augustine's argument is that philosophy concerns abstract, ahistorical ideas, whereas Christianity is concerned with the actuality and interpretation of historical events. Christianity is concerned with "the history and prophecy of the temporal dispensations of the providence of God for the salvation of humanity."[4] It is therefore necessary to deal with "the actual history of places and times" and "the written experiences of others."[5] The historical anchoring of the foundational and substantive events of the Christian religion therefore necessitates and legitimates the study of history itself. There is an unambiguous and studied rejection of any notion of Christian theology as an engagement with ideas, as if ideas could be detached from their historical origins and stimuli; that, for Augustine, is the error of pagan philosophy. It is therefore clear that Augustine provides a fundamental motivation for the study of history, in that the Christian revelation assumed an historical form.

Yet this idea needs further development. In one sense, Augustine insists, *all* of history is God's history. Any distinction between secular and sacred history other than as distinctive sets of events fails to do justice to Augustine's thinking.[6] His distinction is more nuanced than this. History is not to be understood as "that which happened," but as "the narration of that which happened." In other words, the distinction between *historia sacra* and *historia profana* lies in the manner in which history is interpreted. The writer of sacred history, guided by the Holy Spirit, is enabled to interpret material in a Christian manner, selecting and omitting material in such a manner as to bring out the divine aspects and implications of history as a whole. Augustine thus treats Scripture not merely as historical, in that it relates to historical events, but as a record of sacred history, on account of the interpretation which it places upon these historical events. R. A. Markus makes this important point as follows:

[Augustine] was certainly never without a deep sense of God's everpresent activity in each and every moment of time, as in every moment of space. He often thought of the whole vast fabric of human history as a majestically ordered whole, an extended song or symphony, in which each moment has its unique, if impenetrably mysterious significance. In this sense all history displays the working of God's providence. But in another sense, only 'sacred history' tells us what God has *really* done, what meaning events have within the economy of salvation.[7]

The introduction of an explicitly theological approach to history also has implications for an understanding of the nature of the direction of history. Augustine is committed to the notion of a continous history, and has no place for the notion of *circuitus temporum*, "a cycle of times," which is linked with the notion of limitless time and the recurrence of happenings within it. He explicitly rejects the idea of a "cyclical" history, in which events happen over and over again.

"According to this theory, the Plato who taught his disciples in the school called the Academy at Athens in the fourth century would have reappeared in innumerable centuries in the past, separated by immensely wide yet finite intervals. So the same Plato, the same city, the same school and the same disciples have appeared time after time, and will reappear again innumerable times in the future."[8]

Yet, interestingly, the conclusive argument brought against this cyclical theory of history relates to the death of Christ. Augustine argues that the once-for-all character of the death of Christ must mean that this event is without parallel in the past or future. A Christological criterion is developed against a specific theory of history.

THE DIVISIONS OF HISTORY

How, then, is sacred history—recalling that "sacred history" means "a particular way of looking at universal history"—to be understood? In approaching this question, Augustine proposed a schematization which builds upon and extends existing approaches to the periodization of Christian history. He developed a six-fold understanding of sacred history, which has had a major impact upon western Christian thought.

On the basis of his reading of the Old Testament, especially in the light of the opening genealogy of Matthew's Gospel (Matt. 1:1–17), Augustine distinguishes six periods in salvation history, as follows:

1. From Adam to Noah

2. From Noah to Abraham

3. From Abraham to David

4. From David to the Babylonian Exile

5. From the Babylonian Exile to the labor pains of Mary

6. The birth of Jesus Christ.[9]

The sixth period is understood to extend from the birth of Christ until His coming again in glory. In practice, Augustine tends to blur the distinctions between the first five such ages, treating them as "humanity before the incarnation." "The whole duration of history comprises six ages ... in five [Jesus Christ] was announced by the prophets; in the sixth, he was proclaimed by the gospel."[10]

In many ways, this scheme is traditional; it can be discerned in earlier Christian writers. Nevertheless, Augustine develops it in a number of important directions. The most important development is his correlation of this sequence with the Genesis creation account. The six days of creation are to be directly related with the six periods of salvation history. This periodization also points to a seventh day—a day on which God rested from his labors, and which points ahead to the seventh period of salvation history, in which believers will rest in glory. Some earlier writers had suggested that each of these periods corresponded with an interval of one thousand years, basing themselves here on 2 Peter 3:8, "with the Lord a single day is a thousand years." However, Augustine shows no interest in this millenarianism. The chronological gap between incarnation and parousia is, according to Augustine, of unknown and undefinable duration, known only to God.

Augustine's interest focuses on the sixth day, inaugurated by the birth of Christ and to be ended with the return of the Son of Man in glory. This is the period in history in which the church is located, and which therefore demands the closest of attention. It is debatable whether one aspect of the attention Augustine devotes to it was of much help to the church in its missionary tasks. For Augustine is, quite simply, fascinated by the number "six."

"One and two and three make six. And this number is on that account called 'perfect,' because it is completed in its own parts. . . . And Holy Scripture commends to us the perfection of this number, especially in that God finished his works in six days, and on the sixth day humanity was created in the image of God. And the son of God came and was made the son of Man, that he might recreate us after the image of God in this sixth age of the human race."[11]

For Augustine, it was entirely understandable that God should have chosen to create humanity on the sixth day, just as He should have chosen to redeem it during the sixth era of its history.

Augustine, however, also notes a direct parallel between the six eras of human history, according to Scripture, and the six "ages of man," according to the classical model. These six classical categories are: infancy, childhood, adolescence, maturity, old age, and death. It was a relatively simple matter to rework this model in the light of the Christian revelation, and introduce the idea of a "rejuvenation" or even "rebirth" of humanity through the coming of Christ. The world is now in its old age—yet an old age which, through the coming of Christ, offers the hope of renewal and rejuvenation. The themes of *senectus mundi*, "the senescence of the world," and *mundus senescens*, "a world which has grown old," recur in his writings, especially *The City of God*. Old age brings home the need for renewal, and thus points to the gospel promises in Christ.

THE TWO CITIES

Augustine's conception of history comes to be dominated by the theme of "the two cities," which dominates *The City of God*, written over the period 413–426. This work is perhaps the most significant contribution to the genre of "historical apologetics," which Augustine himself did so much to stimulate. The background to the work is the fall of Rome itself and the questions which this raised. Rome fell in 410; Augustine is known to have begun to plan the work the following year. For many pagan Romans, the fall of their city was to be attributed directly to the replacement of the classical religious cult of ancient Rome with the Christian religion. Carthage became the refuge of many Romans who had fled their city and were not slow to make their feelings about its possible causes known to local Christians. Augustine's task was therefore, at least in part, to demonstrate that the fate of Rome had nothing to do with its adoption of Christianity.

The place of both Rome and its empire had been discussed by earlier Christian writers. Many such writers regarded Rome as the enemy of the gospel, and a force of evil in the world. However, this attitude was not universally shared. Many writers noted that Rome had given rise to conditions under which the spread of the gospel was possible. Before the conversion of Constantine, writers such as Origen had pointed out how the *pax Romana* had given a natural unity and stability to the Mediterranean world, which made possible the propagation of the gospel under favorable conditions.

With the conversion of Constantine, a new era dawned. Some Christian writers, most notably Eusebius, portrayed Constantine as an instrument chosen by the Lord for the conversion of the empire. Others were less effusive; nevertheless, there was a general tendency to view the *pax*

Augusta in terms of the outworking of the divine providence. Ambrose of Milan and Prudentius are examples of a group of writers from this period who referred to Rome in much the same way as some Old Testament writers referred to Zion. Eusebius' "Rome-theology" appears to have had a deep impact upon Christian thinking in this crucial period. The fall of Rome therefore raised a series of potentially difficult questions. Why had Rome been sacked? Augustine addresses such questions in *The City of God*, partly to counter criticisms made from pagan quarters, yet also to discredit a "theology of history" which had become influential in Christian circles.

Initially, Augustine appears to have accepted at least a little of the "imperial theology" which saw Rome as occupying a special place in the providence of God. In 416, Augustine suggested to his Spanish colleague Paul Orosius that he should write a work demonstrating that ancient empires had suffered fates even worse than that which had befallen Rome. This suggestion is most easily understood on the basis of acceptance of at least some aspects of the "Rome-theology" just noted. However, as Augustine began to write *The City of God*, it appears to have become clear to him that he was obliged to counter the arguments of both the Christian "imperial theologians" and the pagan anti-Christians. This dual function of the work underlies much of its more rambling and difficult sections, which has caused its readers much difficulty.

In any event, *The City of God* topples Rome from its position in Eusebius' theology of history. No longer is Rome portrayed as God's chosen instrument for the salvation of the world and the preservation of the gospel. Augustine addresses two quite divergent strands of opinion concerning Rome within the Christian tradition. On the one hand, he is quite clear that the Eusebian tendency to treat Rome in quasi-messianic terms is unjustified scripturally. On the other, he eschews the alternative approach, which vilified Rome as the source of all evil and destruction in the world (an attitude especially associated with certain North African writers, such as Tertullian and Cyprian of Carthage, but which reached its zenith in the Donatist movement). By contrast, Augustine portrays Rome in neutral terms, neither messianic nor satanic.

Underlying Augustine's discussion of Rome is the notion of a tension or dialectic between two cities—the *civitas Dei*, "the city of God," and the *civitas terrena*, "the earthly city." He identifies these two cities as follows:

> Accordingly, two cities have been formed of two loves: the earthly by love of self, even to the point of contempt of God; the heavenly by the love of God, even to the point of contempt of oneself . . . . In the one, the rulers and nations it subdues are ruled by the love of ruling; in the other, the rulers and the subjects serve one another in love . . . . And

therefore the wise people of the one city, living according to human ideas, have tried to profit for their own gain . . . . But in the other city there is no human wisdom, but only godliness, which offers due worship toward God and looks for its reward to the society of saints.[12]

Augustine regards these two cities as juxtaposed in this present age. He makes it clear that there is no place in God's purposes for the restoration of an earthly Jerusalem, excluding any theology of history which saw Rome as somehow fulfilling prophecies relating to Jerusalem. Jerusalem served as an image or foreshadowing of the heavenly city before the coming of Christ. Yet its symbolic role was superseded by that coming of Christ, in that there is no longer any need for such an image. The theological foundation that permitted the identification of Rome and Jerusalem is thus radically undermined.

Nevertheless, Augustine does accept at least one aspect of the "imperial theology of history," which saw the conversion of Constantine as evidence of divine providence. Like many writers before him, Augustine believes that it is God rather than pagan deities who controls the destiny of Rome. *The City of God* is a powerful defense of the sovereignty of God in the face of the rival claims of pagans. Augustine argues that the rise of Rome to supremacy cannot be attributed to pagan gods. Indeed, Rome has been betrayed by its worship of pagan gods, in that it has failed to achieve the virtues which so many ancient Romans sought and honored. "If these [pagan] gods were unknown . . . and [the true God] alone were worshipped and known with sincere faith and virtue, [the Romans] would have a better kingdom here . . . and an eternal kingdom hereafter."[13] Rome's desire for virtue can only find its fulfillment through Christ. The blessings conferred upon Christian Rome were real; yet they are to be seen as pointers to blessings of a totally different order. Still, Augustine does not allow that true worship will necessarily lead to an age of peace and prosperity. He declines to follow the "Rome-theology" at this point, and instead affirms merely that Christianity offers the true fulfillment of Roman hopes and aspirations—aspirations which paganism could never fulfill. The vital theological-historical link between providence and prosperity is thus broken.

HISTORY AND ESCHATOLOGY

As we have seen, Augustine rejected the predominant trend within Christian circles of sacralizing the Roman Empire. For Augustine, it was inconceivable that the destiny of Rome could be allowed such momentous import. The church could not allow itself to be shackled to any human institution in such a manner. If Rome had a purpose to serve in the providence of God, that was well and good; yet it did not follow, for Augustine, that this implied that Rome had a permanent position of honor as a result. Might not God use nations, cities and empires as and when he wished? Was the providential endowment of Rome at one moment in history a guarantee that she would be so privileged in the future? The church could and must survive the fall of Rome.

Augustine's theology of history prevents the church from being dependent upon any secular institution. The city of God is ultimately not dependent upon any earthly city, nor can any earthly city or power be termed "sacred." For Augustine, as we have seen, "sacred history" is not about certain moments or entities in human history as *being* sacred; rather, it is about their history being told from a sacred standpoint. From this perspective, the city of Rome cannot be regarded as sacred, although its history can be read in a sacred manner, as indicating the way in which God is able to work in and through historical events, without being restricted to each or any of them. The fact that Rome may have had its purpose to play in the purposes of God does not mean that Rome is sacred as a result, or that her fall has any negative implications for the Christian understanding of the providence or power of God.

The idea of "historical progress" is therefore to be treated with distrust. Augustine's understanding of divine providence and human history is such that there is room for a radical reversal of fortunes, without the need to give up hope. This brings us to consider the eschatological side of his thought. One of the most important aspects of Augustine's theme of the "two cities" is that the Christian's home is not of this world. The church is not distinguished from the world sociologically, as if a sharp dividing line could be drawn between "the church" and "the world." Augustine recognizes elements of the "city of God" and "the earthly city" at work, to varying degrees, within each. The fundamental distinction is that of *eschatological orientation*—that is, a willingness to look beyond history and to realize that events in human history possess less than ultimate significance.

Augustine develops this important theme in a number of ways. At one level, he stresses the importance of the Christian hope of a final victory over sin and death through the resurrection of Christ. There is an element of "not yet" in his writings, corresponding to this notion of postponement of final Christian gratification. At another, there is the ecclesiological insight, that the church cannot hope to be sharply demarcated from society. But, for our purposes, there is the most historically fundamental insight of all—that one cannot read history and directly transpose from history to providence, or from human happenings to the purposes of God. The most important single case is Rome itself: Augustine insists that its rise cannot simply be attributed to its acceptance of Christianity, nor its fall to any failure on the part of God. The issues are much more complex and must be seen against the backdrop of an eschatological perspective which is at best poorly understood this side of the parousia. The important thing for Augustine is to trust God, rather than any human reading of history.

Perhaps one of Augustine's unacknowledged concerns here was to prepare his readers for Christianity without the benevolent guardianship of Rome. By undermining the theology which affirmed that Roman prosperity was an indicator of divine favour, Augustine opened the way towards reclaiming faith in the promises of God, rather than in the permanent well-being of any human institution.

ASSESSMENT AND EVALUATION

Augustine devoted much thought to the issues of history, but he wrote rather little history himself. In part, this may be due simply to lack of time. Augustine's correspondence is littered with complaints of the lack of time he has for writing and study. One of the few known cases of Augustine *doing* history (as opposed to thinking about history in general) relates to the Donatist controversy, where he is known to have supplemented a dossier of material relating to the movement drawn up by Optatus of Milevus. There is no attempt on Augustine's part to write the history of the Christian church; that task he was happy to leave to individuals such as Orosius.[14] It needed to be done; Augustine, however, did not wish to do it. He clearly felt that his contribution lay elsewhere than in producing a Christian version of the classical historiography of Ammianus Marcellinus.

Augustine's contribution did lie elsewhere. He may not have been an ecclesiastical historian in the style or manner of Eusebius, or, indeed, many of the writers to be surveyed in this volume; he was, however, an interpreter of history, who was concerned with countering improper means of reading sacred meanings into secular events. Augustine is a Pannenberg, not an Oberman. By insisting upon a *theological* reading of history, Augustine was able to introduce a powerful corrective to trends which existed in his day, and which continue to exist in ours. We could summarize them like this.

When things go well, God is with us.

When things go badly, God has abandoned us.

Augustine's interpretative framework indicates that this is neither an exhaustive nor an adequate approach; the eschatological dimension must be recognized. Today's spiritual weakness may turn into tomorrow's revival. A proper theological and historical perspective is in order here. "Revival and reformation in America in the late twentieth century have about as much chance as the likelihood of an obscure provincial sect overturning Imperial Rome."[15]

And finally, Augustine stands as a reminder of the dangers of identifying any human institution with the gospel or the purposes of God. Most fourth-century Christian writers assumed that Rome was an instrument of the purposes of God, and found its decline unbearable and unintelligible. Yet Christianity survived, with Augustine's perspectives providing rational foundations for the explication of this phenomenon. Many nineteenth-century Britons assumed that the British Empire was also an instrument of God, and found the collapse of the British *Raj* to be theologically problematical. And many modern Americans are prone to regard the United States as somehow embodying the will of God. What will the future of that nation be? Nobody knows. But Augustine knew of the dangers of confusing any historical person or institution with the embodiment of the will of God. Perhaps we still need to hear him.

NOTES

1. For valuable studies in English, see Gerald Bonner, *Augustine of Hippo: Life and Controversies* (Norwich: Canterbury Press, revised edition, 1986); Peter Brown, *Augustine of Hippo: A Biography* (Stanford, Calif.: Stanford University Press, 1967); Henry Chadwick, *Augustine* (Oxford: Oxford University Press, 1986); R. A. Markus, *Saeculum: History and Society in the Theology of St. Augustine* (Cambridge: Cambridge University Press, 1970); Jaroslav Pelikan, *The Mystery of Continuity: Time and History, Memory and Eternity in the Thought of St. Augustine* (Charlottesville, Va.: University of Virginia Press, 1986).

2. On the spread of this movement, see Peter Brown, "The Diffusion of Manichaeism in the Roman Empire", *Journal of Roman Studies* 59 (1969): 92–103.

3. See Arnaldo Momigliano, "Pagan and Christian Historiography in the Fourth Century A.D." in *The Conflict Between Paganism and Christianity in the Fourth Century*, ed. A. Momigliano (Oxford: Clarendon Press, 1963), 79–99.

4. *de vera religione* vii, 13.

5. *de Trinitate* IV. xvi.21.

6. For useful reflections, see F. M. Schultz, 'Historia sacra et profana' bei Augustin', *Perennitas: Beitrage zur christlichen Archeologie* in H. Rahner and E. von Severus, eds., (Münster: , 1963), 32–45.

7. Markus, *Saeculum*, 16–17.

8. *City of God* XII, 14.

9. See *de Trinitate* IV.iv.7.

10. *contra Faustum* XII, 14.

11. *de Trinitate* IV.iv.7.

12. *City of God* XIV, 28.

13. *City of God* IV, 28.

14. It is an irony that Orosius' resulting work, *Seven Books of Histories against the Pagans*, bears many resemblances to the kind of "theology of history" which Augustine had tried to avoid! See T. E. Mommsen, "Orosius and Augustinei," in *Medieval and Renaissance Studies* (New York: SUNY, 1959), 325–48.

15. Os Guinness, *The American Hour* (New York: Free Press, 1993), 414–15. See further Os Guinness, "Tribespeople, Idiots or Citizens? Evangelicals, Religious Liberty and a Public Philosophy for the Public Square," in K. S. Kantzer and C. F. H. Henry, eds., *Evangelical Affirmations* (Grand Rapids: Zondervan, 1990), 457–97.

5

VENERABLE BEDE

FRANK A. JAMES III

But what if One, through grove or flowery mead,
Indulging thus at will the creeping feet
Of a voluptuous indolence, should meet
Thy hovering shade, O venerable Bede!
The saint, the scholar, from a circle freed
Of toil stupendous, in a hallowed seat,
Of learning, where thou heard'st the billows beat
On a wild coast, rough monitors to feed
Perpetual industry. Sublime Recluse!
The recreant soul, that dares to shun the debt
Imposed on human kind, must first forget
Thy diligence, thy unrelaxing use
Of a long life; and, in the hour of death,
The last dear service of the passing breath!

—William Wordsworth[1]

Bede (673–735), or "Baeda" as his name appears in the earliest manuscripts, has the distinction of being the only Englishman acclaimed a Doctor of the Church.[2] Furthermore, his last major work, the *Ecclesiastical*

History of the English People, provides the richest treasury of important data for the early history of England, and for which he has been designated the "Father of English history."[3] But Bede's significance is greater still, for he established the fundamental periodization which continues to govern our modern conception of history. That is to say, Bede introduced *anno Domini* as the basic dividing point in human history.[4] This of course tells us immediately that, for this Englishman, the history of the world is measured in terms of the incarnation of Christ. For the Venerable Bede, all history is Christian history.

BEDE'S LIFE

The remotely situated monastery at Jarrow, nestled on a spit of land extending into the river Tyne, was only a few years old when the plague suddenly visited the cloisters in A.D. 686. Every monk succumbed to the pestilence except Abbot Ceolfrid and a "little lad" who had been made a ward of the monastery.[5] Most scholars identify the "little lad" as Bede.[6] The young survivor, if not yet "venerable," was resilient.

Relatively little else is known of Bede's life. Most direct information we possess derives from Bede's own abbreviated account of his life at the end of his most famous work, the *Ecclesiastical History*. The first autobiographical fact (and probably the most important in his judgment) offered by Bede is that he was a "priest of the monastery of the blessed apostles Peter and Paul at Wearmouth and Jarrow." Bede's account continues:

> I was born on the lands of this monastery, and on reaching seven years of age, I was entrusted by my family first to the most reverend Abbot Benedict and later to Abbot Ceolfrid for my education. I have spent all the remainder of my life in this monastery and devoted myself entirely to the study of the Scriptures. And while I have observed the regular discipline and sung the choir offices daily in church, my chief delight had always been in study, teaching and writing. I was ordained deacon in my nineteenth year, and priest in my thirtieth, receiving both these orders at the hands of the most reverend Bishop John at the direction of Abbot Ceolfrid. From the time of my receiving the priesthood until my fifty-ninth year, I have worked, for my own benefit and that of my brethren, to compile short extracts from the works of the venerable Fathers on Holy Scripture and to comment on their meaning and interpretation.[7]

Within this brief framework, it is possible to fill in some of the details of Bede's life.[8] Based on the date given for the completion of the *Ecclesiastical History*, he was born in A.D. 673 in the vicinity of the monastery at Wearmouth, which was established the following year. At the age of seven, the young Bede was given to Abbot Biscop as a child-oblate by his family. Scholars speculate that Bede was entrusted to Abbot Biscop because his parents had died an untimely death. Bede's formative years were spent as a child of the cloister. The twin monasteries of Wearmouth and Jarrow were founded by Benedict Biscop (628–689) in 674 and 681, on land donated by King Egfrid of Northumbria. After the success of the first monastery, established at the mouth of the river Wear in 674, Biscop founded another monastery at Jarrow on the river Tyne.[9] He transferred some seventeen monks from Wearmouth to the new monastery at Jarrow and named Ceolfrid the new Abbot. Like some other monasteries of the seventh century, Wearmouth and Jarrow were considered one monastery, sometimes under one abbot and sometimes under two, but governed by the same monastic rule.[10] Bede makes it clear, when he writes in his *Lives of the Abbots of Wearmouth and Jarrow*, that both monasteries were "built on the understanding that these two houses should be bound together by the one spirit of peace and harmony and united by continuous friendship and goodwill."[11] The two monasteries flourished and at their apex housed six hundred monks.[12]

Within a year of being entrusted to Abbot Biscop, the eight-year-old Bede was transferred to the care of Ceolfrid, the Abbot of the new monastery at Jarrow. Abbot Ceolfrid seems to have been a substitute father for whom Bede had deep affection. Something of the depth of their relationship is evident in Bede's "anguish of mind"[13] when the elderly Ceolfrid decided to leave Jarrow (716) and end his days with a pilgrimage to Rome. So great was his grief, Bede was unable to devote himself to his work for a considerable time.[14]

In many respects Bede was a typical medieval monk. Excavations have revealed that he probably lived in a small cell, in which a low wooden screen separated the prayer area from the rest of the cell.[15] Some of his earliest training involved singing chants, which had been introduced at Wearmouth and Jarrow by John, the Arch-cantor from Rome, who had been brought to Britain by Benedict Biscop.[16] Much of his day was governed by the monastic office. Bede met with his fellow monks seven times a day and once a night to sing or read the scriptures, especially the Psalter. Some scholars believe he eventually became the choirmaster at the monastery.[17] The rest of the day was divided between study and work. Early years were devoted to his education—Latin, Greek, Roman law, chant, mathematical calculation and the zodiac.[18] It appears that Bede's first Latin teacher was Ceolfrid. Bede also mentions Trumbert, an Irish monk of Lastingham, who taught him the Scriptures.[19] One of the great legacies of Biscop was the library at Jarrow, with its varieties of texts of the Bible, commentaries by Augustine, Ambrose, Jerome and Gregory the Great, grammatical works and histories to which the young Bede had access.[20] Jarrow also contained a *Scriptorium* where Bede himself must have spent many hours copying manuscripts. Formed as a scholar principally by the Latin Bible, he spent the best part of his life compiling commentaries from the Fathers for the sake of his fellow monks in Northumbria. His interests in chronology, history, and grammar derived from his study of the Bible.

Bede must have been a successful monk. He tells us that he was ordained a deacon at the age of nineteen, six years before the canonical age.[21] It would appear that occasionally exceptions were made for men of outstanding learning and devotion. His early ordination as deacon may also bear witness to the esteem in which he was held by Ceolfrid. At some point in his career, probably before his ordination as priest, he also served as master of education at Jarrow.[22] Bede was then ordained priest in A.D. 703 and spent the rest of his life as a scholar-monk. Interestingly, Bede was never selected as the Abbot, possibly because all the early Abbots of Wearmouth and Jarrow were of noble lineage. Or perhaps he simply declined offers because he preferred to study and teach.[23]

Unlike his predecessors, Bede seems rarely to have travelled. It was not necessary. From their journeys to Rome, Biscop, and later Ceolfrid, made sure that the libraries of Wearmouth and Jarrow were well stocked with a good number of books, which supplied Bede with the important sources for his *Ecclesiastical History*. As far as can be determined, Bede's only known travels were to the island of Lindisfarne to research his book on the life of Cuthbert, to York at the end of his life to discuss church affairs with Egbert and to the monastery of an Abbot named Wihtred, where he discussed computation.[24]

Fortunately we possess an eyewitness account of Bede's final days from Cuthbert, later Abbot of Wearmouth and Jarrow.[25] Cuthbert's own assessment is that he had never known a man "so diligent in giving thanks to the living God."[26] The conscientious Bede labored mightily until the very end, giving lessons to his students, chanting psalms, making corrections in Isidore of Seville's *On the Wonders of Nature* and translating the Gospel of John into English. On the evening of 26 May 735, he gave away the last of his few possessions to his fellow monks and said his farewell: "I have lived a long time and the Holy Judge has provided well for me during my whole life. The time of release is near; indeed my soul longs to see Christ my king in all his beauty." But then the voice of the young scribe, Wilbertht, pierced the sad silence: 'Beloved Master, there is still one sentence left, not yet written down.' He answered: 'Write it then.' After a short time the boy said: 'Now it is written.' And he [Bede] replied: 'Good, it is finished.'

... And thus sitting on the floor of his cell singing: 'Glory be to the Father and to the Son and to the Holy Spirit' ... he breathed his last."[27]

Bede died as he had lived, writing, praying and singing.

BEDE THE CHURCH HISTORIAN

Although Bede's fame rests primarily on his work as a historian, he was renowned throughout the Middle Ages as a biblical exegete, and indeed most of his life was devoted to commentaries on Scripture. In recent years, scholars have begun to recognize that Bede's scriptural orientation profoundly influenced his conception of church history.[28] Much of his historical work was "unoriginal," insofar as it consisted of the views, often the very words, of his predecessors pieced together along with Bede's own interspersed commentary.[29] His earliest historical writings are very brief and include his *Lives of the Abbots of Wearmouth and Jarrow* and two historical chronicles (lists of the principal events in the history of the world) appended to *De Temporibus* (703) and *De temporum ratione* (725).[30] Bede's most famous historical work, however, and the one on which we shall concentrate our attention, is the *Historia Ecclesiastica Gentis Anglorum (Ecclesiastical History of the English People)*, which offers a panoramic view of the history of the church in England and is considered a "masterpiece of Dark Age historiography."[31]

How did Bede come to write the *Ecclesiastical History*? The immediate inspiration for the writing of the *Ecclesiastical History* came from *Albinus*, Abbot of Saints Peter and Paul, Canterbury.[32] It may well be that the great Eusebius' *History of the Church* also served as both an inspiration and a model. As a biblical commentator, Bede compiled and arranged the statements of the church fathers on particular books of the Bible as well as offering his own comments. This method is also evident in his *Ecclesiastical History*. Once the plan was conceived and basic texts had been gathered and arranged, he continued for a period of years to gather additional material which he then seems to have inserted into the text.[33]

What were Bede's sources? His attitude towards most pagan authors was one of cautious reserve. The chief models and foundations for his work were, apart from the Bible, the works of Christian authors from the fourth century on. Bede drew primarily from the Christian histories, the *Histories Against the Pagans* of Orosius and Gregory of Tours's *History of the Franks*.[34] Perhaps the most important such Christian author was Eusebius of Caesaria, whose *History of the Church* set the standard for all historians of the church.[35] Bede's aim seems to have been to do for the history of the church in England what Eusebius had done for the universal church.

SUMMARY AND ANALYSIS
OF BEDE'S ECCLESIASTICAL HISTORY

In five books, Bede recounts the progress of Christianity in England from the arrival of Augustine of Canterbury in 597 until 731. As Bede delineates, the early progress of Christianity in England was feeble and flickering. By 660 it was established in all the major kingdoms and began to flourish.

Behind Bede's *Ecclesiastical History* is a broad redemptive-historical superstructure. Like Augustine and Isidore of Seville, Bede saw world history divided into six ages which correspond to the six days of creation. Each age was marked by a major redemptive-historical event: Creation, the Flood, Abraham, David, the Captivity of Judah and the birth of Christ, which inaugurated the sixth age. In his *De Temporum Ratione*, Bede enlarged upon his historical scheme to include a Seventh and Eighth Age. The Seventh Age, which ran concurrently with all of the previous Six Ages, was a kind of spiritual intermediate state of departed saints and sinners from the death of Abel until the final resurrection. The Eighth Age is the final and eternal destination of all humankind after the last judgment.[36]

Bede concentrates his attention on the sixth age, within which is yet another substructure of biblical history. Because the *Ecclesiastical History* is principally concerned with the sixth age, which was inaugurated by the birth of Christ, Bede therefore employs a distinctively Christian dating system—*anno Domini* (in the year of our Lord).[37] This dynamic inner substructure, which is at the very core of the *Ecclesiastical History*, encompasses the redemptive-historical movement from Old Testament origins to New Testament maturity and fulfillment.[38] At this point, Bede the biblical commentator fuses with Bede the church historian. The first book of the *Ecclesiastical History* corresponds to the biblical book of Genesis in its focus on origins.[39] Beginning with book two, the vision of Christ's promise in Acts (1:8) that the kingdom of God would be extended beyond Jerusalem, Judea and Samaria "to the ends of the earth" dominates the remainder of the work. Bede functions like a medieval Luke, called to chronicle the establishment and expansion of the kingdom of God in the British Isles. Apostolic authority continued unabated through the episcopate and was validated by miraculous signs. Book two closely parallels the New Testament era of the Gospels which record the establishment of Christianity. Bede's third book describes the expansion of the church in England, replicating the expansion of the Christian church in the Acts of the Apostles. In book four Bede, like Paul in his epistles, encourages consolidation of

the church. The final book of Bede's *Ecclesiastical History* reflects the eschatological tone of John's Apocalypse, with its strong sense of imminent
onset of eternity. This biblical orientation informs and shapes Bede's entire work.

BOOK ONE

The first book covers a much broader span of time than the remaining
four books; it recounts about 650 years of the political and religious high
points of early English history. Noteworthy is the fact that Bede does not
begin with human history. Rather, he begins with a geographic description of Britain, formerly known as Albion, before recounting the ethnic
origins of the early inhabitants of the island. He describes the lavish riches
of the island, its plentiful timber, pasture, birds, fish and minerals, which
has the effect of conjuring up an Edenic vision of an island paradise. Bede
then considers the primitive inhabitants of this island paradise before Roman civilization. First to settle were the Britons (Welsh) in the south.
They were followed by the Picts and the Irish, who occupied the northern
part of the island. The Angles and Saxons arrived somewhat later and settled in the south. Like the book of Genesis, Bede's first book of the *Ecclesiastical History* is about beginnings.[40]

According to Bede, the religious history of Britain really begins in A.D.
156 when Lucius, a British King, wrote to Eleutherus, the Bishop of
Rome, expressing his desire to become a Christian.[41] Christianity thus
came to Britain and thrived for over a century until the church came under
severe persecution in the reign of Emperor Diocletian (286 A.D.). The
high point of book one is Bede's vivid account of Alban's martyrdom during the Diocletian persecutions. Although a pagan, Alban had given shelter to a persecuted Christian whose piety deeply impressed him. When
imperial soldiers came to arrest the Christian priest, Alban donned the
priest's cloak and surrendered himself in the place of the Christian priest.
Boldly defying his captors, he refused to offer sacrifices to pagan gods and
was sentenced to death by decapitation. On the way to the place of execution, the soldiers came upon a river, which caused them to delay as they
searched for a safe crossing. Alban prayed for a swift martyrdom, and miraculously the river dried up making a path to cross. At the sight of this
wonder, the executioner was converted and willingly joined his fate to that
of Alban. Later, Alban prayed for water to drink and water miraculously
bubbled up from the ground. And when the new executioner completed
his wicked duty, yet another miracle occurred. "As the martyr's head fell,
the executioner's eye's dropped out on the ground."[42] The account of the
martyrdom of Alban evinces Bede's strong biblical orientation. Two of the

miracles associated with Alban harken back to Mosaic miracles in the Pentateuch—the parting of the Red Sea and the water from the rock at Rephidim.[43] As Bede describes these miracle stories, he does not appear to be fictionalizing, but rather shaping historical episodes (as reported to him by apparently credible witnesses) according to a redemptive-historical construct.

The fall of Rome in the fifth century A.D. also signaled the end of Roman rule in Britain. The removal of Roman legions had dire consequences for the Britons (Welsh) for it resulted in many years of savage tribal war with the Picts, the Irish, and then later, with the Angles and the Saxons. When the Britons appeal to God for rescue, Bede, with a deft hand, bathes the story in Old Testament images. Reminiscent of the Old Testament judges, national deliverers emerge, first Ambrosius Aurelius and then Germanus of Auxerre.[44] Under Germanus especially, Pelagianism is opposed, true Christian faith is restored and the Britons are led to military victory over their oppressors. In an echo of the strategy of Gideon in the Old Testament, Germanus directs his forces to surprise the enemy with a "mighty shout" causing the enemy to be confused and then routed. It was, as Bede says, "a victory by faith not by force."[45] Despite their victories and validation by the miracles of Germanus, the Britons, like the Israelites of old, turned away from true religion. One of the "unspeakable crimes", as far as Bede is concerned, was that the Britons "never preached the Faith to the Saxons or Angles."[46]

Even though the Britons failed to evangelize the Angles and Saxons, "God in His goodness did not utterly abandon the people whom He had chosen."[47] With this statement, Bede shifts his attention to the main focus of the *Ecclesiastical History*, namely the conversion of the English (Anglo-Saxons).

BOOK TWO

Book two marks a major transition from Old Testament to New Testament themes. Book one is filled with prominently displayed Old Testament images which broadly correspond to the first five ages of the world. Book two reflects the New Testament orientation of the sixth age, which begins with an emphasis similar to the Gospels. At the outset Bede pays tribute to Pope Gregory, whom he designates the "apostle" to the English nation. Bede recounts Gregory's life and accomplishments, especially his Pauline desire for the salvation of the English. In the course of his tribute, Bede relates the traditional story of how Gregory's affection for the English was kindled. Before his pontificate, he happened across some fair-skinned boys being sold as slaves in a Roman marketplace. Having noticed their attractive features, he inquired as to their place of origin. When told they were from the island of Britain and their race called "Angles," Gregory declared: "That is appropriate, for they have angelic faces, and it is right that they should become joint-heirs with the angels in heaven."[48] When Gregory became Pope, he sent Augustine to convert the English. Augustine received a warm welcome from the Kentish King Ethelbert (A.D. 597), who permitted him to preach the Christian faith. Soon King Ethelbert himself was converted, and Augustine was consecrated Archbishop, thus establishing the episcopate and a link to the apostolic era.

Augustine's ministry to the English is confirmed through a distinctively New Testament miracle, the healing of a blind man.[49] Bede describes how the church developed in England through two complimentary means, the episcopate and the conversion of Kings. Archbishop Augustine is succeeded by a series of men who alternate between boldness and timidity. The centerpiece of book two is the conversion of King Edwin of Northumbria, whose realm was unmatched by any previous English King. After carefully evaluating the teachings of Christianity, receiving letters from two popes (Boniface and Honorius) and the approval of Coefi (chief priest of the pagan religion), Edwin "renounced idolatry and professed his acceptance of the Faith of Christ."[50] As evidence of his zeal Edwin evangelizes Earpwald, King of the East Angles.

Book two ends on a somber note—the death and defeat of Edwin at the hand of the British King, Cadwella, described by Bede as "more savage than any pagan." By concluding with the death of a Christian king, Bede not only identifies the English church with the martyrs of the New Testament church, but also reminds his readers that the work of the church in England is not completed.

BOOK THREE

Book three begins with what is perhaps the spiritual nadir of the history of the English church (633–634). The two Christian Kings who succeeded Edwin in Northumbria, Orsic and Eanfrid, aposticized from the faith and "reverted to the corruption and damnation of their former idolatry."[51] These two apostate kings soon find themselves under divine wrath. Orsic and Eanfrid were ravaged by the "godless Cadwalla," king of the Britons, who had delivered the death blow to King Edwin at the battle of Hatfield. So vile and repulsive was the character of these kings, reports Bede, that "all those calculating the reigns of kings have agreed to expunge the memory of these apostate kings and to assign this year to the reign of their successor."[52] These Judas-like traitors gave way in Bede's story to zealous Christians and ultimately to spiritual triumph.

The successor to the apostate kings was one of the greatest Christian kings in Bede's *Ecclesiastical History*, King Oswald, brother of Eanfrid. Oswald's deep Christian piety was demonstrated in his battle preparations before meeting the "savage Tyrant" Cadwalla at the battle of Denisesburn. Much like Constantine's vision of the cross before the battle of Milvian Bridge (A.D. 312), Oswald set up a wooden cross, kneeled and prayed that God would grant victory over Cadwalla. Although Oswald was vastly outnumbered, God granted him a miraculous victory. Oswald's triumph continued and his kingdom was greatly enlarged to include "all the peoples and provinces of Britain speaking the four languages, British (Welsh), Pictish, Irish, and English."[53]

Grateful to God for his victory, King Oswald requested of the Irish church to send him a bishop "by whose teaching and ministry the English people . . . might receive the blessings of the Christian Faith."[54] The Irish sent bishop Aidan, whom Bede describes as "a man of outstanding gentleness, holiness and moderation."[55] Typifying the Acts of the Apostles, Bede proceeds to recount the progressive extension of the gospel among the various peoples and regions of Britain: the missionary labors of Columba among the Picts, of Birinus among the West Saxons, Fursey among the East Angles, King Oswy among the Middle Angles, East Saxons and the Mercians.[56]

With Oswald's death, the two provinces of the Northumbrian kingdom were ruled separately, Deira by Oswine and Bernicia by Oswy, until the unthinkable happened: one Christian king killed another. Oswy "the Christian king" "treacherously murdered" Oswine, described by Bede as a "man of great holiness and piety."[57] Yet despite his "crime," Oswy subsequently played a vital role in extending the kingdom of God in book three. King Oswy brought Christianity to the Middle Angles; won over King Sigbert of the East Saxons; and "converted the Mercians and their neighbors to the Christian Faith."[58] Above all, it was Oswy who called the Synod of Whitby (A.D. 664) and finally settled the recurring Easter problem in favor of the Roman reckoning.[59]

For Bede, the Synod of Whitby was a watershed event in the early history of the English church. When the controversy came to the attention of King Oswy, he initially favored Bishop Coleman's Irish dating for Easter. But Oswy's son, Alchfrid, having been instructed by Bishop Wilfrid, favored the Roman tradition. To resolve the differences, it was decided to hold a synod at the monastery of Whitby, ruled by the pious Abbess Hilda. Bishop Coleman defended the Irish view and Wilfrid the Roman view. In the end, the matter hinged on the apostolic authority of the Roman church. King Oswy issued his judgment: "I tell you, Peter is guardian of the gates of heaven, and I shall not contradict him. I shall obey his commands in everything to the best of my knowledge and ability; otherwise, when I come to the gates of heaven, there may be no one to open them, because he who holds the keys has turned away."[60]

Oswy's final decision was binding on all in his kingdom, which extended to virtually all of Britain. The differences on the dating of Easter, which creates dramatic tension throughout, are finally resolved.

BOOK FOUR

Whereas book three looks outward to expand the church, book four looks inward at consolidating the church. One sees here the powerful demonstration of the growing piety of the church in England, through its bishop-saints, monasteries and miracles. Bede opens book four with the story of one of the greatest bishop-saints in the history of the church in England, Theodore of Tarsus. During his pontificate as Archbishop of Canterbury, the church in England comes of age. Theodore is particularly significant to Bede because Theodore was "the first archbishop whom the entire Church of the English obeyed."[61] Under his leadership, the church was united under firm guidance and enjoyed great success. "Never had there been such happy times as these since the English settled in Britain; for the Christian kings were so strong that they daunted the barbarous tribes. The people eagerly sought the new found joys of the kingdom of heaven, and all who wished for instruction in the reading of the Scriptures found teachers ready at hand."[62]

Theodore's activism is seen in his calling and participating in three Synods, which reinforced unity by formally establishing the practical and moral order of the English church, as well as its allegiance to the Roman dating of Easter.[63] At times Theodore went above and beyond the call of his episcopal office, as he did in negotiating peace between warring factions, the Kings of Northumbria and Mercia.

Of the other saintly bishops in the English church who figure prominently during Theodore's tenure as Archbishop, none was greater than Cuthbert. If any person embodied the virtues of a saint for Bede, it was the "venerable Cuthbert," bishop of Lindisfarne. Cuthbert was not only a hermit who "served God in solitude for many years in a hut surrounded by an embankment so high that he could see nothing but the heavens," but also a humble and reluctant bishop. Refusing all entreaties and many appeals from admirable brethren "begging him with tears," Cuthbert finally and reluctantly succumbed to their supplications and assumed the burden of episcopal responsibility. For Bede there was a sense in which the glory of Cuthbert's life does not begin until his death. After his burial magnificent miracles are linked to his tomb, all of which seem to have a New Testament orientation. Like the paralytics of the New Testament, the monk Baduthegn is cured of his paralysis resulting from a miracle at Cuthbert's tomb.[64] Like the blind men in the New Testament, the diseased eye of a young monk from Lindisfarne is miraculously restored after coming into contact with the "hairs of the holy Cuthbert's head."[65] There is also the curious miracle in which the body of Cuthbert is exhumed eleven years later and found to be without decay: "when they opened the grave, they found the body whole and incorrupt as though still living."[66] This miracle has a clear Pauline tone, for the Apostle had spoken of the resurrected body of Christians as being "incorruptible," signifying immortality and the victory over death. Apparently, Bede sees a New Testament parallel between the incorruptible body of Cuthbert and the incorruptible body mentioned by the Apostle Paul.[67]

One of the distinguishing features of book four is the concentration on monasteries and their formative role in the character of the English church. Monasticism was, in the view of Bede, the backbone of true Christianity and, interestingly enough, it is particularly associated with the role of monastic women. One of the most famous monasteries was that of Whitby, founded and ruled by the Abbess Hilda, whom Bede calls a "Christian servant."[68] At Whitby an extraordinary miracle occurred in the herdsman named Caedmon. One night he had a vivid dream in which he sang "verses in praise of God." The next day, Caedmon awoke with the miraculous ability to turn any scripture passage "into delightful and moving poetry in his own English tongue," even though he had no prior knowledge of poetry. He was brought to Abbess Hilda, who tested his new-found gift. She then invited Caedmon to join the monastery at Whitby, where he spent the rest of his life composing "melodious verse."[69]

Bede concludes book four with the short account of Cuthbert's life and legacy. As Cuthbert, the saints and the monasteries demonstrate, the church in England was alive and well. In this period of consolidation, perhaps the most distinctive feature is the dramatic multiplication of miracle stories.[70] A good number of them are bizarre and superstitious, but there are also a number which bear noticeable resemblance to the characteristic miracles of the New Testament. It would seem that Bede's shaping of the material in book four, and especially the miracle-stories, is designed to draw a link with the early New Testament church and to display divine approval of the piety of the church in England. To be sure, it has not reached full maturity or perfection, as Theodore's dismissal of the bishop of Wynfrid shows,[71] but it was nevertheless a vibrant church for which God showed his miraculous good pleasure.

BOOK FIVE

Book five begins dramatically, first identifying Cuthbert's successor, Ethelwald, and then recounting six successive miracles by Thelwald and John of Beverley. The striking feature of all six miracles is that they are direct parallels with New Testament miracles. Ethelwald's prayer calms a storm; John heals a dumb man, restores a diseased arm of a nun, cures the wife of Thegn, heals the servant of Thegn, and resuscitates a monk who is thought to be dead.[72] All of these miracles function as indicators of the progress and vitality of the church in England during the time of Theodore. Bede states: "the churches of the English made greater progress during his [Theodore] pontificate than they had ever before."[73]

Another important sign of ecclesiastical maturity and progress was the abdication of kings who willingly gave up their power in order to pursue heavenly rewards. Both Cadwalla, king of the West Saxons,[74] and his successor, Ine, abdicated their thrones to embark on pilgrimages to Rome "hoping to merit a warmer welcome from the saints in heaven."[75] Again, Bede recounts two more kings who abdicated their royal prerogatives for spiritual service to the church. Both Coenred, King of the Mercians, and Offa, King of the East Saxons, resigned their kingly scepters for the tonsure and a monastic life.[76] Further indication of the spiritual vigor of the church in England is the successful missionary efforts of Willibrord in Frisia. Now those who were formerly the objects of missionary activity are initiating missionary efforts elsewhere.

One of the most striking features of book five is the description of dramatic visions of the afterlife. The first and most detailed is the vision of Drythelm, who is at death's door when a "man in a shining robe" appears and gives him a guided tour of purgatory. Drythelm's guide pulls back the veil of the seventh age (intermediate state) and allows a glimpse of the afterlife. Reminiscent of Dante, Drythelm observes a two-tiered purgatory, a valley of "burning flames and icy cold" and a "pleasant meadow filled with the scent of flowers." The valley is inhabited by those who "have delayed to confess and amend their wicked ways and who at last had recourse to penitence at the hour of death." These, although they confessed and were penitent only at death, will finally be admitted to the kingdom of heaven on the Day of Judgment. The meadow is occupied by souls who have done good deeds, "but are not so perfect as to merit immediate entry into the kingdom of Heaven."[77] Another vision of the afterlife concerns a solider who repeatedly put off repentance until it was too late. Just before his death, he saw two books. One was a "tiny but very beautiful book," which contained all the good deeds the solider had ever done. The other was "a horrible looking book of enormous size and almost unbelievable weight," which listed all his evil deeds, "not only sins of act and word, but even those of the least thought," and they were written in black letters.[78] These dramatic portraits of hell clearly parallel the New Testament Apocalypse of the Apostle John, with its visions of wrath and judgment. The soldier's vision of the two books closely resembles the books of life and death at the judgment of the great white throne at the end of the Apocalypse of John.[79]

The Apocalypse of John not only pictures wrath and judgment, but also envisions a glorious harmony in the new heavens and the new earth. This same general idea is captured by Bede in the final chapters of book five. There one sees a growing unification between the English church and the Roman mother church. Bede relates a series of success stories of how dissident churches came to accept the Roman dating of Easter: how Adamnan persuaded many of the Irish churches to adopt the Roman dating; how Aldhelm wrote a "notable treatise" which "persuaded many of those Britons who were subject to the West Saxons to conform to the Catholic observance of our Lord's Resurrection"; how Egbert persuaded the monks of Iona to "adopt Catholic ways of life"; and how Nechtan, King of the Picts, adopted the Roman dating for Easter "after assiduous study of Church writings." Bede also includes a very long letter from the Abbot Ceolfrid to Nechtan, offering advice on the "Catholic observance of Easter." Bede's inclusion of the life of Wilfrid was also an important part of achieving the ecclesial harmony between Rome and England, especially on the troublesome matter of the dating of Easter.[80]

Bede concludes his history with a brief summary of the whole book, his autobiography and an assessment of the present state of the English church. Although perfect harmony has not been achieved, for the Britons still "uphold their own bad customs against the true Easter of the catholic Church," yet the English church has attained a certain level of maturity and there is cause for hope in the future.

Peace and prosperity prevail in these days. Many of the Northumbrians, both noble and simple, together with their children have laid aside their weapons, preferring to receive the tonsure and take monastic vows rather than study the arts of war. What the result of this will be the future will show.[81]

APPRAISAL OF BEDE'S ECCLESIASTICAL HISTORY

Perhaps the most salient fact about Bede's *Ecclesiastical History* is that historical data is ordered in relation to a redemptive-historical paradigm.[82] Recent developments in Bede research have shown the vital importance of the biblical categories that shaped his historical understanding.[83] One cannot ignore the fact that Bede was first and foremost a biblical exegete and that his biblical orientation profoundly governed his understanding of English church history. Indeed, the fundamental presupposition of Bede the historian is that the English church was an extension and development of the story of the Acts of the Apostles and of the New Testament. Bede is convinced that he has discerned the redemptive pattern of God's workings among the English, and out of this historical record he fashions a redemptive history of England. As He did with the Jews of old and the Gentiles of Apostolic times, God was redeeming the English people for Himself. Like the biblical writers, Bede recounts the history of that redemption in order to remind the English of what God has done. In the final analysis, there is for Bede no distinction between history and redemptive-history.

It is at this point that miracles, verified by eyewitnesses or credible accounts, are taken as a constituent part of the historical record. Benedicta Ward is correct when she writes: "Bede and other writers who record miracles believed they were recording facts about events. People believed that they had witnessed these events, and they told Bede what they believed happened; there is no question of deliberate fraud or falsehood."[84] With Bede's redemptive-historical paradigm, miracles were to be expected with the coming of Christianity to England just as they had been present in the apostolic church.[85] Imbued with a New Testament ethos, many of the miracles selected for inclusion by Bede are virtual replicas of New Testament miracles—a point which Bede himself recognizes.[86] English history belongs to the same redemptive epoch as Christ's Apostles and is, therefore, part of the redemptive era of divine interventions. For Bede, miracles were not *miracula* but *signa*, signs of the continuance of the New Testament age.[87]

Although Bede's redemptive-historical orientation is important, still he is concerned about historical accuracy. He informs the reader that he has written his book according to the *vera lex historiae* (true law of history).[88] The *vera lex historiae* refers to an accurate historical record which can be verified by the general populace. This "true history," as Bede notes in his preface, stresses the importance of reliable sources for his account. Indeed, historical accuracy is a necessary compliment to the redemptive-history of England. However, this is not naively to suggest that Bede was a precursor to modern historical writing. He belongs to another world of historical writing, in which there is an overarching moral purpose to history.

For if history records good things of good men, the thoughtful hearer is encouraged to imitate the good: or if it records evil of wicked men, the devout, religious listener or reader is encouraged to avoid all that is sinful and perverse and to follow what he knows to be good and pleasing to God.[89]

Bede reveals a twofold purpose in writing. On the one hand, he wanted to present an accurate record of past events. On the other hand, he also had a higher purpose, namely, to persuade and to encourage devotion to God. In his conception, history is a servant of the redemptive agenda. Much of the *Ecclesiastical History* is devoted to inculcating the moral and spiritual virtues which Bede had spent most of his life expounding in his commentaries. For example, in book five of the *Ecclesiastical History*, the horrible visions of purgatory are clearly intended to instill a fear of hell and a love of heaven, as well as to drive home such points as the folly of depending on a death-bed repentance and the certainty that even the least thought or action will be taken into account after death.[90]

Within this twofold purpose is a related theme, namely, the struggle for orthodox unity in the English church.[91] Bede alludes to heretical challenges to the fledgling English church, such as Pelagianism, Arianism and Eutychianism. But the error which caused the most disruption centered on the calculation of the date for Easter. This received the longest chapter both in the third book and the fifth. As far as Bede was concerned, the date of Easter was not a minor point of discipline, but a rift in the unity of the church. That was why any deviation caused by rival calculations of Easter was so unacceptable. Bede's concern, almost obsession, with this issue shows itself repeatedly in his judgments on the Britons (Welsh), the Irish Christians and even Aidan. It also explains the great length Bede granted to the Synod of Whitby, "the dramatic centre-piece of the whole work."[92] The battle for Roman uniformity was still not completely won at the time of Bede's writing. As with Pelagianism, so with the Easter controversy, Bede was writing not only an account of the past, but a tract for his own times.

Three theological ideas are particularly associated with Bede's conception of history: divine providence, divine predestination, and medieval ecclesiology. One of the most obvious and influential theological ideas is Bede's highly developed sense of divine providence.[93] The coming of Christianity to England is seen fundamentally as a work of God, especially working through heroic saints and spectacular miracles. The providence of God is also evident in Bede's formulaic view of Christian history. Characteristically, he demonstrates that those kings who obey God receive victory in battle and peace in their realms. Those who disobey are defeated in battle and lose their kingdoms.[94] The God who providentially "rules" the world is no passive deistic god who winds up the world and then watches from a distance. Rather, Bede sees a powerful God who governs all history. One sees a hint of Bede's own overriding sense of divine providence in the declaration of King Oswy to King Sigbert, King of the east

Saxons. In contrast to the Saxon idols made from stone, the true God is "a being of boundless majesty, invisible to the human eye, almighty, everlasting, creator of heaven and earth and of the human race. He . . . rules and will judge the world in justice, abiding in eternity not in base metal."[95] Within the providence of God, there is also a notable subcurrent of predestinarianism. Bede describes the English as God's "chosen people."[96] But his is not merely a corporate predestinarianism, it also involves individuals. For instance, referring to King Edwin's conversion, Bede specifically ascribes it to "predestination."[97] Clearly, Bede's conception of history was informed by an Augustinian theological orientation.

Besides Bede's Augustinian view of providence and predestination, one also finds his archetypical medieval Christianity, with such notions as the intercession of dead Saints, relics, pilgrimages and meritorious works.[98] Bede, like many medieval churchmen, combined a formal Augustinian conviction of the priority of grace in salvation with a firm practical belief in meritorious works.

CONCLUSION

As the first great historian of the church in England, Bede belongs to a world very different from our own. For him, history was never purely secular, but rather a temporal manifestation of the divine plan of redemption, predestined before the foundation of the world. This was obviously God's world and any honest historical research would reflect that fact. To write history without theological convictions was to Bede utterly ridiculous, not to mention blasphemous. Bede's historical writing was never merely academic, but always had a clear redemptive motive.

Some have judged Bede a "second-rate scholar" because his *Ecclesiastical History* is largely derived from the works of previous church historians. However, this material has been carefully reshaped by a redemptive-historical vision and made theologically coherent so that the sum is greater than its previously derived parts. "It takes a kind of genius to do this sort of thing well," judges one modern medievalist; a kind of genius which Bede undeniably possessed.[99]

BIBLIOGRAPHY
PRIMARY SOURCES

COLLECTED WORKS

The Complete Works of the Venerable Bede in the Original Latin . . . Accompanied by a New Translation of the Historical Works. Edited by J. A. Giles. 12 vols. London: Whitaker & Co., 1843–44.

Bedae venerabilis opera. Various editors. Corpus Christianorum Series Latina (CCSL), vols. 118–20, 122–23, 175–76, to date. Turnhout, Belgium: Brepols, 1960–83.

Venerabilis Bedae Opera Omnia. Edited by J. P. Migne, Patrologia Latina (PL), vols. 90–95. Paris: J. P. Migne, 1850–51. Reprint, Turnhout, Belgium: Brepols, 1980.

HISTORIES

Letter to Ecgbert. Translated in *English Historical Documents, ca. 500–1042.* English Historical Documents, vol. 1, edited by D. Whitelock. 2nd ed., no. 170, 799–810.

Life of Cuthbert. Translation in *The Age of Bede,* edited by D. H. Farmer and translated by J. E. Webb, 39–102. London: Penguin Books, 1988.

Lives of the Abbots of Wearmouth and Jarrow. Translation in *The Age of Bede,* edited and translated by D. H. Farmer, 183–208. London: Penguin Books, 1988.

The Ecclesiastical History of the English People. Translated in Bede, *Ecclesiastical History of the English People,* by L. Sherley-Prince and R. E. Latham, 41–331. London: Penguin Books, 1990.

The Life of Ceolfrid. Translated in *English Historical Documents, ca. 500–1042.* English Historical Documents, vol. 1, edited by D. Whitelock. 2nd ed., no. 155, 758–70.

SECONDARY SOURCES

BIBLIOGRAPHIES

Anglo-Saxon England. Cambridge: Cambridge University Press, 1972. Annual bibliography on works concerned with Bede.

Bolton, Whitney F. "A Bede Bibliography: 1935–60." *Traditio* 18 (1962): 437–45.

Eckenrode, Thomas. "The Venerable Bede: A Bibliographical Essay, 1970–81." *American Benedictine Review* 36 (1985): 172–91.

Rosenthal, Joel T. *Anglo-Saxon History: An Annotated Bibliography, 450–1066.* New York: AMS Press, 1985.

BOOKS

Blair, Peter H. *The World of Bede.* London: Secker & Warburg, 1970.

Bonner, Gerald, ed. *Famulus Christi: Essays in Commemoration of the Thirteenth Centenary of the Birth of the Venerable Bede.* London: SPCK, 1976.

Brown, G. H. *Bede the Venerable.* Boston: Twayne Publishers, 1987.

Campbell, J., ed. *The Anglo-Saxons.* Ithaca, N.Y.: Cornell University Press, 1982.

Duckett, Eleanor S. *Anglo-Saxon Saints and Scholars.* New York: Macmillan, 1947.

Jarrow Lectures. Jarrow, England: Rector of Jarrow, 1958—.

Laistner, M. L. W. *Thought and Letters in Western Europe.*, A.D. *500 to 900*. Ithaca, N.Y.: Cornell University Press, 1966.

Mayr-Harting, H. *The Coming of Christianity to England*. New York: Schocken Books, 1972.

Meyvaert, P. *Benedict. Gregory, Bede and Others*. London: Variorum Reprints, 1977.

Stenton, F. M. *Anglo-Saxon England*. 3rd ed. Oxford: Clarendon Press, 1971.

Thompson, A. H., ed. *Bede: His Life, Times, and Writings: Essays in Commemoration of the Twelfth Centenary of His Death*. Oxford: Clarendon Press, 1935.

Whitelock, D. *English Historical Documents, 500–1042*. English Historical Documents, vol. 1. 2nd ed. New York: Oxford University Press, 1979.

Wormald, P., with D. Bullough and R. Collins, eds. *Ideal and Reality in Frankish and Anglo-Saxon Society: Studies Presented to J. M. Wallace-Hadrill*. Oxford: Basil Blackwell, 1983.

ARTICLES

Campbell, J. "Bede." In *Latin Historians*, edited by T. A. Dorey. New York; Basic Books, 1966.

Davidse, J. "The Sense of History in the Works of the Venerable Bede." In *Studi Medievali* 23 (1982): 647–95.

McClure, J. "Bede and the Life of Ceolfrid." *Peritia* 3 (1984): 71–84.

———. "Bede's *Notes on Genesis* and the Training of the Anglo-Saxon Clergy." In *The Bible in the Medieval World: Essays in Memory of Beryl Smalley*, edited by K. Walsh and D. Wood, 17–30. Oxford: Basil Blackwell, 1985.

Martin, L. T. "Bede as a Linguistic Scholar." *American Benedictine Review* 35 (1984): 204–17.

Ray, R. "Augustine's De Consensu Evangelistarum and the Historical Education of the Venerable Bede." In *Studia Patristica* 16, part 2. Texte und Untersuchungen zur Geschichte der altchristlichen Literatur, vol. 129 (1985): 557–63.

———. "Bede's Vera Lex Historiae." *Speculum* 55 (1980): 1–21.

———. "What Do We Know about Bede's Commentaries?" *Recherches de theologie ancienne et medievale* 49 (1982): 5–20.

Rosenthal, J. T. "Bede's Use of Miracles in His *Ecclesiastical History*." *Traditio* 31 (1975): 328–35.

Stephens, J. N. "Bede's Ecclesiastical History." *History* 62 (1977): 1–14.

NOTES

1. A. F. Potts, ed., *The Ecclesiastical Sonnets of William Wordsworth: A Critical Edition* (New Haven, Conn.: Yale University Press, 1922), 117 (I.23).

2. At the Council of Aachen (836).

3. G. H. Brown, *Bede the Venerable* (Boston: Twayne Publishers, 1987), p. 21.

4. A. D. dating seems to have originated with Dionysius Exiguus (died ca. 527), but it was Bede who gave it universal popularity. See C. W. Jones and T. Mommensen, eds., *Bedae venerabilis opera. De temporibus liber includens chronica minora*, Corpus Christianorum Series Latina (CCSL), (Turnhout, Belgium: Brepols, 1980), vol.123 C, 120–22.

5. Anonymous, *Life of Ceolfrith*, trans. D. S. Boutflower (London, 1912), 65.

6. C. E. Whiting, "The Life of the Venerable Bede," in *Bede: His Life, Times, and Writings (BLTW)* ed. A. H. Thompson (Oxford: Clarendon Press, 1935), 7.

7. Bede, *Ecclesiastical History of the English People*, trans. L. Sherley-Price and R. E. Latham, intro. D. H. Farmer (London: Penguin Books, 1990), appendix following v. 24 (p. 329).

8. Besides the autobiographical sketch provided in Bede's *Ecclesiatical History*, there are two other sources for Bede's life: *Cuthbert's Letter on the Death of Bede* found in Bede, *Ecclesiatical History*, 357–60 and Bede's own *Lives of the Abbots of Wearmouth and Jarrow* found in *The Age of Bede*, ed. D. H. Farmer and trans. J. F. Webb (London: Penguin Books, 1988), 185–208.

9. Farmer, *Age of Bede*, chaps. 1–7 (185–92).

10. The monasteries followed a *regula mixta* (a composite rule), which was generally in accord with the Benedictine Rule. P. Wormald, "Bede and Benedict Biscop," in *Famulus Christi: Essays in Commemoration of the Thirteenth Centenary of the Birth of the Venerable Bede*, ed. G. Bonner (London: SPCK, 1976), 144, states: "Little of what we can find at Wearmouth-Jarrow is actually incompatible with the Benedictine Rule." Cf. H. Mayr-Harting, *The Venerable Bede, the Rule of St. Benedict and Social Class* (Jarrow Lecture, 1976).

11. Farmer, *Age of Bede*, chap. 7 (p. 191).

12. Ibid., chap. 17 (p. 203).

13. Bede, *In Primam Partem Samuhelis Libri IIII*, ed. D. Hurst, CCSL vol. 119 (Turnhout, 1962), 212.

14. Ibid., preface to Book IV, vol. 119 (Turnhout, 1962), 12.

15. Rosemary Cramp, "Monkwearmouth and Jarrow: The Archeological Evidence," in Bonner, *Famulus Christi*, 5–18.

16. Bede, *Ecclesiastical History*, iv.18.

17. Cf. C. W. Jones, intro to Bede's *Opera didascalia*, CCSL, vol. 123 A, viii.

18. B. Ward, *The Venerable Bede* (London: Geoffrey Chapman, 1990), 8.

19. Bede, *Ecclesiastical History*, iv.3.

20. M. L. W. Laistner, "The Library of the Venerable Bede," in Thompson, *Bede*, 237–66.

21. Bede, *Ecclesiastical History*, v. 24.

22. Brown, *Bede the Venerable*, 19.

23. Mayr-Harting, *Venerable Bede*, 16–17.

24. *Letter to Wihtred*, ed. C. W. Jones, CCSL, vol.123 C (Turnhout, 1980), 617–26.

25. *Cuthbert's letter*, in Bede, *Ecclesiastical History*, 355–60. This Cuthbert is not to be confused with Cuthbert, bishop of Lindesfarne.

26. Ibid., 358.

27. Ibid., 359–60. Bede's last effort was spent on translating John 6:9.

28. See R. Ray, "Bede, the Exegete, as Historian," in Bonner, *Famulus Christi*, 125–40.

29. P. Meyvaert, "Bede the Scholar," in Binner, *Famulus Christi*, 42–43.

30. The two chronicles are nothing more than historical lists. His *Lives of the Abbots of Wearmouth and Jarrow* contain brief sketches of five abbots: Benedict, Ceolfrid, Eosterwine, Sigfrid, and Hwaethberht. These biographical sketches are straightforward and not a single miracle is ascribed to any of these abbots. The one thing in common is Bede's use of A.D. dating. There is one other brief historical writing, the *Life of Ceolfrid*, which is generally attributed to Bede, although no author is specified and Bede does not include it in his list of writings at the end of the *Ecclesiastical History*.

31. J. Campbell, "Bede," in *Latin Historians*, ed. T. A. Dorey (New York: Basic Books, 1966), 160.

32. Bede, *Ecclesiastical History*, 42.

33. See J. Campbell, "Bede," in *The Anglo-Saxons*, ed. J. Campbell (Ithaca, N. Y.: Cornell University Press, 1987), 167.

34. Bede also knew Gildas's *The Ruin of Britain*, Constantius's *Life of St. German* and the *Liber Pontificalis*. Cf. Brown, *Bede the Venerable*, 88–89 and W. Levison, "Bede As Historian," Bonner, *Famulus Christi*, 132–38.

35. Bede used Rufinus's Latin translation of Eusebius' *The History of the Church*. Cf. Brown, *Bede the Venerable*, 85.

36. P. H. Blair, *The World of Bede* (London: Secker & Warburg, 1970), 265–69.

37. See footnote 4.

38. J. Davidse, "The Sense of History in the Works of the Venerable Bede," *Studi Medievali* 23 (1982): 647–95.

39. Mayr-Harting in his Latin Sermon to the University of Oxford in 1981, argues that book one is shaped in some measure by Pentateuchal categories. Cf. Bede, *Ecclesiastical History*, i.1.

40. Ward, *Venerable Bede*, 116–17.

41. Bede *Ecclesiastical History*, i.4.

42. Ibid., i.8.

43. Exod. 14:21 & 17:6.

44. Bede, *Ecclesiastical History*, i.16–21.

45. Ibid., i.20. Cf. Judges 7:19.

46. Ibid., i.22.

47. Ibid., i.22.

48. Ibid., ii. 1.

49. Ibid., ii.2.

50. Ibid., ii.9–19.

51. Ibid., iii.1.

52. Ibid., iii.1.

53. Ibid., iii.6.

54. Ibid., iii.3.

55. Ibid., iii.3. Cf. iii.17.

56. Ibid., for the Picts, iii.4; West Saxons, iii.7; East Angles, iii. 19; Middle Angles, iii. 19; East Saxons, iii. 22; Mercians, iii. 24.

57. Ibid., iii.14, 22.

58. Ibid., iii. 24.

59. Ibid., iii. 25.

60. Ibid.

61. Ibid., 2.

62. Ibid.

63. At Hertford, Hatfield, and Twyford (Bede, *Ecclesiastical History*, iv.5, 17 and 28.

64. Ibid., iv. 31. Cf. Matt 4:24; 8:6; 9:2–7; Mark 2:3–12; Luke 5:18–26.

65. Ibid., iv. 32. For various miracles concerning eyes, see Matt. 20:28–34; Mark 10:46–52; Luke 7:21; 18:35–43; John 9:1–11.

66. Ibid., iv. 30.

67. In the New Testament an incorruptible body is specifically linked to those who have secured victory over death and have eternal life in Christ (1 Cor. 15:42, 52).

68. Bede, *Ecclesiastical History*, iv.23. Up to the ninth century, it was not unusual for a co-ed monastery to be ruled by an Abbess. Cf. R. Tucker and W. Liefeld, *Daughters of the Church* (Zondervan: Grand Rapids, 1987), 135.

69. Bede, *Ecclesiastical History*, iv.24.

70. Joel T. Rosenthal, "Bede's Use of Miracles in His *Ecclesiastical History*," *Traditio* 31 (1975): 328–35.

71. Bede, *Ecclesiastical History*, iv. 6.

72. Ibid., v.1–6.

73. Ibid., v.8.

74. Not to be confused with Cadwalla, King of the Britons.

75. Bede, *Ecclesiastical History*, v.7.

76. Ibid., v.19.

77. Ibid., v.12.

78. Ibid., v.13.

79. Rev. 20:12; cf. Phil. 4:3; Luke 10:20.

80. Bede, *Ecclesiastical History*, v.15, 18, 19, 21, 22.

81. Ibid., v. 24.

82. J. Davidse, "Sense of History", 647–95.

83. Ray, "Bede, the Exegete," 125–40. Cf. Brown, *Bede the Venerable*, 81–96.

84. B. Ward, "Miracles and History: A Reconsideration of the Miracle Stories Used by Bede," in Bonner, *Famulus Christi*, 71.

85. Paul Meyvaert, "Bede the Scholar," in Bonner, *Famulus Christi*, 53 writes: "It should be clear that if Bede thought God could work miracles in Old Testament and New Testament times, he would not have considered that God's power to work miracles had diminished in eighth-century Anglo-Saxon England."

86. Bede, *Ecclesiastical History*, v.4. When Bishop John of Beverley cured the wife of a thegn, Bede makes a specific link to a New Testament miracle. Referring to the healing of the wife of the thegn, Bede writes: "the woman immediately got up . . . [and] she brought a cup to the bishop and us and . . . continued to serve us with drink until the close of the meal. In this she followed the example of St. Peter's wife's mother." Cf. Mark 1:29–34.

87. Ward, *Venerable Bede*, 89–90.

88. Bede, *Ecclesiastical History*, preface. Cf. R. Ray, "Bede's *vera lex historiae*," *Speculum* LV (1980): 1–21.

89. Bede, *Ecclesiastical History*, preface.

90. Ibid., v.12–14.

91. Campbell, "Bede," 179–82.

92. D. H. Farmer, "Bede," introduction in *Ecclesiastical History*, 27. See iii.25.

93. L. W. Barnard, "Bede and Eusebius as Church Historians," in Bonner, *Famulus Christi*, 110.

94. For example see Bede, *Ecclesiastical History*, iii.1.

95. Ibid., iii.22.

96. Ibid., i.22.

97. Ibid., ii.14. Also in the first chapter of his *Lives of the Abbots of Wearmouth and Jarrow*, Bede describes Abbot Benedict Biscop as "predestined by Christ," in Farmer, *Age of Bede*, 186.

98. Bede, *Ecclesiastical History*, iii. 22; iv. 14, 29, 31, 32; v. 6, 7.

99. Meyvaert, "Bede the Scholar," 62.

6

JOHN FOXE

DONALD T. WILLIAMS

John Foxe made history simply by writing it. The *Book of Martyrs* (as his *Actes and Monuments of these Latter and Perilous Dayes, Touching Matters of the Church* is more popularly known) is perhaps surpassed only by the English Bible and equaled only by Bunyan's *Pilgrim's Progress* as a book that has shaped the ethos and sensibility of English-speaking Protestantism. Yet most modern readers have encountered this book only in a severely truncated form. The eight massive volumes of small print in the latest complete edition[1] are reduced to a smattering of the more sensational anecdotes, leaving the impression that the whole is a mere catalog of cruelties:[2]

> Some slain with sword; some burnt with fire; some with whips scourged; some stabbed with forks of iron; some fastened to the cross or gibbet; some drowned in the sea; some their skins plucked off; some their tongues cut off; some stoned to death; some killed with cold; some starved with hunger; some their hands cut off alive, or otherwise dismembered; . . . imprisonment, stripes and scourgings, drawings, tearings, stonings, plates of iron laid unto them burning hot, deep

dungeons, racks, strangling in prisons, the teeth of wild beasts, grid-irons, gibbets and gallows, tossing upon the horns of bulls.[3]

Such scenes do abound in the *Acts and Monuments*, as they have in the history of the Church; but they are not its essence. Rather, Foxe was attempting to vindicate the cause of truth by giving a universal history of God's work in building the Church from the standpoint of the testimony of its martyrs. He "set these stories of recent and remembered figures in what was for his own age a convincing, momentous, historical-scriptural perspective, made meaningful by the unfolding context of immediate events."[4] In the process, Foxe articulates both a history of theology and a theology of history that are still worth consideration today.

HIS LIFE

Foxe was born in 1516 at Boston, Lincolnshire.[5] In that year Erasmus produced the first published edition of the Greek New Testament, and the following year Martin Luther nailed his Ninety-Five Theses to the Wittenburg church door. So Foxe came into the world with the Reformation his writings would seek to vindicate. He grew up as it was coming to England: he was eighteen in 1534, when the Act of Supremacy made Henry VIII rather than the Pope supreme head of the church in England. Henry only wanted to change his wife, but his political move gave more spiritual-minded reformers like Cranmer, Latimer, and Ridley the opportunity they needed to begin the reform of the church.[6]

Foxe's mind was nurtured on the theology of the Reformation and the learning of Renaissance humanism, a happy combination he used to good effect in his life's work. He took his B.A. at Magdalen College, Oxford, in 1537, was elected a fellow in 1539, and took his M.A. in 1543. His friends and correspondents at Oxford included Alexander Nowell, John Cheke, and the reformers Latimer and Tindal.

Reformation was a slow process, even before the setback that occurred under Mary. In 1545, Foxe felt constrained to resign his fellowship because of his objections to the requirement of celibacy. He was to fight a running battle with poverty the rest of his life. He was not a party man; Olsen notes Fuller's distinction between the "fierce and fiery" and the "mild and moderate" Puritan and places Foxe in the latter category.[7] In other words, his Puritan sympathies (against wearing the surplice, for example) were just strong enough to hinder his advancement in the church, despite the popularity of the *Acts and Monuments*. In spite of frequently difficult circumstances, Foxe had a reputation for generosity to those even poorer than himself.

In the meantime, Foxe was married to Anges Randall on February 3, 1547. In 1548 he was appointed tutor to the orphaned children of Henry Howard, Earl of Surrey. He stayed in that post for five years, publishing Latin theological tracts advocating reform. In 1550 he was ordained deacon by Nicholas Ridley in St. Paul's Cathedral. But this peaceful period of his life was about to end: With the untimely death of the youthful and pious Edward VI, Mary came to the throne in 1553.

What Foxe was to call "these meek and gentle times of King Edward" were over. He would remember with satisfaction that "amongst the whole number of popish sort, some of whom . . . were crafty dissemblers, some were open and manifest adversaries; yet, of all this multitude, there was not one man that lost his life" for his religion.[8] Such was not to be Mary's policy. The reformers hoped that she would listen to reason, but that hope was quickly disappointed. Foxe records that Ridley visited the new queen and offered to preach before her but was sharply rebuffed:

Bishop: Madam, I trust you will not refuse God's word.

Mary: I cannot tell what ye call God's word: that is not God's word now that was God's word in my father's days.

Bishop: God's word is all one in all times; but hath been better understood and practiced in some ages than others.

Mary: Ye durst not, for your ears, have avowched that for God's word in my father's days, that now you do. And as for your new books, I thank God I never read any of them: I never did, nor ever will do.[9]

The import of the queen's refusal was not lost on the bishop. After the interview, Ridley was offered a drink by Sir Thomas Warton: "And after he had drunk, he paused awhile, looking very sadly; and suddenly brake out into these words: 'Surely I have done amiss.' 'Why so?' quoth Sir Thomas Warton. 'For I have drunk,' said he, 'in that place where God's word offered hath been refused: whereas, If I had remembered my duty, I ought to have departed immediately, and to have shaken the dust off my shoes for a testimony against this house.' These words were by the said bishop spoken with such a vehemency, that some of the hearers afterwards confessed their hair to stand upright on their heads."[10]

In 1554, Mary released the old Duke of Norfolk, grandfather of Foxe's pupils, who fired him as their tutor. The direction from which the wind was now blowing became obvious. That same year, Foxe fled to the continent. He met Grindal—later to become Spenser's ideal bishop, the "Algrind" of "The Shepheardes Calendar"—in Strasburg in July. Foxe had brought with him a Latin manuscript on the persecutions of reformers

1554

from Wycliffe to the present. Grindal was enthusiastic. The book was published in Strasburg, a small octavo of 212 leaves called the *Commentarii Rerum in Ecclesia Gestarum*. It was the first draft of what would become the *Acts and Monuments*. Grindal kept encouraging Foxe to expand this account and supplied him with many of the documents he would use.

At the end of 1554, Foxe moved to Frankfurt, where he found the exiles split over the forms of worship. John Knox, the pastor, recommended Calvin as an arbiter. Foxe supported this proposal, and Calvin urged a compromise. But in 1555 the controversy broke out anew, with the result that Knox left. Foxe then became the head of the Genevan party. But in November he too left for Basel. Already the reformers were finding it difficult to agree on the precise extent of reform they wanted.

At Basel, Foxe worked for the printer Oporinus and continued his writing. In 1556 he published *Christus Triumphans*, a five-act apocalyptic drama in Latin verse. In 1557 came a plea for toleration addressed to the English nobility, *Ad Inclytos ac Praepotentes Anglicae Prioceres . . . Supplicatio*. Foxe wanted them to influence the queen against persecution. "If heretics they were," he argued, "what avail these naked arguments of blood but to confirm them in heresy? Where is the gentleness of Christ?"[11] The testimony of martyrs weighed so heavily with Foxe in part because of his abhorrence of persecution. When his side came to power, he consistently pled for mercy for Jean Boucher, Flemish Anabaptists, even papists. Mozley thinks that the anonymous person in the *Acts and Monuments* (5:860) who pleads for mercy for Joan of Kent was Foxe himself; he was an eyewitness, and the arguments are like those he was known to use.[12] Foxe argued thus to Queen Elizabeth on behalf of the Anabaptists:

"I defend them not: these errors should be repressed . . . It is the manner of their punishment which shocks me. To burn up with fiery flame . . . the living bodies of wretched men who err through blindness of judgment rather than deliberate will, is a hard thing and belongs more to the spirit of Rome than to the spirit of the Gospel."[13]

Reports of the Marian persecutions continued to filter back to Foxe from England. On June 10, 1557, Grindal urged him to complete the history of persecutions through Henry VIII. In 1559, the result was the *Rerum in Ecclesia Gestarum*. The *Book of Martyrs* had now grown to 732 pages in six books. Meanwhile, Mary's death and the accession of Elizabeth in 1558 made possible Foxe's return to England. But the need for continuing the history remained. Mozley remarks that "to us the enthronement of Elizabeth is the beginning of a long period of prosperity and of freedom from the persecution of Rome."[14] But the people of that day did not yet know this; they still needed to be fortified in the truth against a return of persecution.

When Foxe landed in England in October of 1559, the full horror of the Marian persecution must have burst upon him. Men's tongues were loosened at last, and on every hand stories of woe were to be heard. The friends and kinsfolk of the sufferers would be ready enough to tell their tale, and there was nothing now to hinder him from completing this story.[15]

Foxe lost no time completing it. Two years after his ordination to the priesthood in 1560, the English version of *Actes and Monuments* appeared. People continued to send him documents and accounts, and he continued to revise, expand, and incorporate. In 1570 a new edition consisting of two volumes of 934 and 1378 pages appeared. On April 3, a convocation at Canterbury resolved to place copies in all cathedral churches. The resolution was never confirmed by parliament, but was widely implemented nevertheless. In 1576 and 1583, further editions were published containing more revisions and additions but no substantial changes. Posthumous editions based on the 1583 text appeared in 1596, 1610, 1631–2, 1641, and 1684. In 1837, S. R. Cattley edited an eight-volume edition of the 1583 text "slightly bowdlerized and at certain points awkwardly conflated with" the 1563 edition.[16] Josiah Pratt revised Cattley with pagination unchanged in 1870 and 1877; this is the only complete edition available to most scholars today, and it is unfortunately not identical with any of the texts overseen by Foxe himself. Foxe studies continue to be hampered by lack of a first-rate critical edition.

Foxe spent his last years working on his martyrology and developing a reputation for frugality, generosity, and piety. His objections to wearing the surplice denied him the ecclesiastical preferment he had otherwise earned,[17] though at Jewell's suggestion he was made prebend in Salisbury Cathedral. He died in April, 1587, and is buried at St. Giles, Cripplegate.

Foxe has been called "not properly a historian at all," but rather merely a "compiler on a gigantic scale;"[18] and the *Acts And Monuments* has been called a "jungle" of documents, "horrendous woodcuts," and grossly prejudiced propaganda.[19] The massive size of the work—about five million words by one estimate[20]—makes it difficult for readers to perceive its architecture. It is built according to a definite plan nonetheless, and embodies a fully worked out conception of what history is and what the historian's task should be. Helen C. White has rightly called it "more than a history. It is, also, an encyclopedia of the Reformation in England" in which "all the main issues of the English Reformation are fought out before one's eyes."[21] It is essentially an historical apologetic work in the tradition of Augustine's *De civitate Dei*, whose purpose is to give common people a framework for understanding their own times. Within that framework, we analyze Foxe's contributions to Protestant historiography under three main headings: the historian's mission, the historian's method, and the historian's message.

THE HISTORIAN'S MISSION

Foxe was aware of the need to justify his labors in imposing such a huge volume upon the world: "Seeing the world is replenished with such an infinite multitude of books of all kinds of matters, I may seem, perhaps, to take a matter in hand superfluous and needless . . . considering now-a-days the world is so greatly pestered, not only with superfluous plenty thereof, but of all other treatises, so that books now seem rather to lack readers, than readers to lack books."[22]

But his first motive for writing history was a story that needed to be told. He did not want so many "memorable acts and famous doings" to "lie buried by my default, under darkness and oblivion" when they were worthy to be recorded.[23] History then helps to preserve cultural memory—and to ensure its accuracy: when Foxe "considered this partial dealing and corrupt handling of histories" on the part of Roman Catholic writers, he thought that nothing was more needed than the "full and complete story."[24]

Foxe's readers needed to have the story told and preserved because it was *their* story. Haller reminds us that "it was no new thing in the history of Christianity for an upsurge of the religious spirit to find expression in a rewriting of history. History was what Christianity was all about." The very essence of Christian faith is the conviction that "at a particular moment in time a particular event had occurred" which focused the whole meaning of life.[25] Thus part of the Christian historian's task is to enable his readers to "perceive the continuity of the present moment . . . with the whole sequence of providentially directed events since the first day of creation."[26]

Foxe clearly operates within this framework. "The knowledge of Ecclesiastical History" in his mind "ought not to be separate from" the knowledge of God's word, "that like as by one, the people may learn the rules and precepts of doctrine, so by the other, they may have examples of God's mighty working in his church."[27] He wants his readers to connect the Old Testament history and the Book of Acts with "the acts of Christ's martyrs now," plus "other manifold examples and experiments of God's great mercies and judgments."[28] Knowing the history of the Church helps the believer maintain a connection to sacred history by showing the continuing unfolding and outworking of the plan and principles revealed in the Scriptures. In other words, Foxe applied in history the standard Puritan homiletic practice of explicating cases in terms of principles and then applying them to the circumstances of the hearers.[29]

The greatest need Foxe saw in the recent circumstances of his readers was the ability to discern the true church, the skill to defend it, and the courage to die for it if necessary. Hence he preserves not only the stories of the martyrs' deaths for which he is famous but also detailed transcripts of their disputations and trials. And he asks his readers to note "the full pith and ground of all their arguments."[30] As Thompson points out, this was not merely an academic exercise; it was designed to give people practical help in understanding the issues and answering attacks if times of persecution should come again.[31] The main Catholic argument was that the Protestants were guilty of innovation: Where was their "church" just fifty years ago? Foxe responded to this challenge by trying to write a new history "so overwhelming in size, scope, and documented sources that it could claim to provide historical legitimacy for a church only fifty years old."[32] He also tried to define the purpose of history in order to help the faithful to "discern the better between antiquity and novelty. For if the things which be first, after the rule of Tertullian, are to be preferred . . . then is the reading of histories much necessary in the church."[33] Knowledge of history—and nothing else—could show that it was Rome, not the Reformation, which was guilty of innovation.

Perhaps the thing that most separates Foxe from modern historians is not his partisanship (we simply disguise ours more cleverly) or his lack of rigor in methodology (he was, as we shall see, ahead of his time on that score) but his refusal to see history as a merely academic pursuit. Olsen rightly remarks that Foxe was most basically a theologian and a preacher—that is, a physician of souls—who saw history as a handmaid of those disciplines and became a historian to serve those ends.[34] Wooden notes the many ways in which Foxe's history reaches out to children and the unlearned: using children and simple folk as exemplars, providing woodcuts, pointing out the moral "as explicitly as any in Aesop."[35] These are certainly emphases which appear on page after page. Foxe apologized to his fellow academics for not writing in Latin, but "the needs of the common people of our land drove me to the vernacular."[36] The ignorant flock has "long been led in ignorance, and wrapped in blindness" for lack not only of God's word but also for "wanting the light of history." Seeing this, he "thought pity but that such should be helped."[37] Christ's simple flock, especially the unlearned, have been "miserably abused, and all for ignorance of history, not knowing the course of times and the true descent of the church."[38]

Foxe constantly pointed out the moral and practical significance of the events he narrated. "Nations and realms" should "take example" from those in the past who rejected God's truth or persecuted His messengers.[39] Any prince who so desires may follow the good example of King Alfred.[40] From the Norman Conquest we may "note and learn" the dangers of princes' leaving no "issue or sure succession" and the dangers of foreign marriage with other princes.[41] (These were of course pressing concerns during the reign of the virgin Queen Elizabeth.) But by far the bulk of Foxe's concern is for the lessons of history for the layperson who, while reading the lives of the martyrs, may "therein, as in a glass" behold his or her own case. Secular history helps fit us for "warlike affairs"; the history of the church prepares us for better living. In sum, it can "declare unto the world what true Christian fortitude is, and what is the right way to conquer."[42]

For Foxe, the ultimate benefit of church history is spiritual health in its broadest sense: the understanding, wisdom, character, and fortitude that enable us to take our place in the continuing line of witnesses, prepared if need be to seal their testimony to the gospel with their blood, which constitutes the history of the church. "Observing and noting" the acts of God in history will "minister to the readers thereof wholesome admonitions of life, with experience and wisdom both to know God in his works, and to work the thing which is godly; especially to seek unto the Son of God for their salvation, and in his faith only to find what they seek."[43]

He prays that all "true disposed minds" which shall read his book may by the example of the martyrs' life, faith, and doctrine, receive "spiritual fruit to their souls."[44] He exhorts his readers to "draw near to the fire" of the martyrs that "our cold hearts may be warmed thereby."[45] And among the very last of his five million words are a prayer that "the grace of the Lord Jesus work [be] with thee, gentle reader, in all thy studious readings . . . that by reading thou mayest learn daily to know that which may profit thy soul, may teach thee experience, may arm thee with patience, and instruct thee in spiritual knowledge more and more to thy perpetual comfort and salvation in Jesus Christ our Lord; to whom be glory *in secual seculorum*. Amen."[46]

In sum, Foxe joins to the Renaissance idea that history teaches virtue by example, a profoundly Christian concept of what that virtue is and of why it is needed in terms of one's place in the ongoing history of redemption. Ironically, by subordinating history to theology, by subordinating it to higher values, Foxe gives it as high a place as one can conceive for any human study.

THE HISTORIAN'S METHOD

All these pious intentions, however, count for nothing unless the history *as history* is sound. It is precisely at this point that Foxe has been sharply attacked, long dismissed—and more recently defended. His whole approach was calculated to produce strong reactions. They began early. In his own life he complained that "certain evil-disposed persons, of intemperate tongues, adversaries to good proceedings, would not suffer me to rest, fuming and fretting, and raising up such miserable exclamations at the first appearing of the book, as was wonderful to hear."[47]

He was not exaggerating. Thomas Harding, in an aside during his attack on Bishop Jewell, called the *Acts and Monuments* "that huge dunghill of your stinking martyrs," full of a thousand lies. Foxe had "into that huge volume infarced lies more in number and notabler for vanity than ever were raked together into one heap or book."[48]

A strong partisan inevitably must face the question whether or not he doctored or even falsified his data to make them fit his vision of the world, even if unintentionally. For years with Foxe studies it was simply partisan versus partisan, until beginning in 1837, S. R. Maitland published the first detailed scholarly analysis of Foxe's use of sources.[49] The seeming thoroughness of Maitland's work created the illusion that Foxe's honesty and accuracy had indeed been overthrown. "No need henceforward for a reader to rebut any story which he found unpalatable; it was quite enough to murmur something about the proven untrustworthiness of Foxe and pass on."[50] These views were reported as simple fact in the 1929 *Encyclopedia Britannica* and in Sidney Lee's piece on Foxe in the *Dictionary of National Biography*, and thus influenced a whole generation of scholars.

Lee, for example, states that Foxe was "too zealous a partisan to write with historical precision," as if the mere equation were self-evident. Foxe's history is valuable only in that it illustrates the "tone of thought" of Elizabethan Protestantism; its "mistakes" are the result of both haste and "willful exaggeration."[51] In the same vein, others have called the *Acts and Monuments* an "imaginative and credulous book" with "all the qualities that will delight the partisan and that must torment the historian."[52] Perhaps. But when we read that "supremely sure of himself, Foxe believed that truth could be conveyed without taking the reader through the sources, although he did occasionally incorporate a document in the text,"[53] we must wonder what is going on. For the last statement could only have been made by a person who has never actually read the *Acts and Monuments*, which is a veritable library of transcriptions of every original source Foxe could procure.

Indeed, the most remarkable feature of Foxe's historiography is the diligence with which he sought to collect and preserve original accounts of significant events. Mozley's description is accurate: "Firsthand documents jostle one another, that never would have been preserved but for his zeal, documents written by simple folk straight from the heart, giving us the most lifelike and vivid pictures of the manners and feelings of the day, full of details that could never have been invented by a forger."[54]

The eye-witness accounts of recent martyrdoms for which Foxe is chiefly known are only the proverbial tip of the iceberg. He "ransacked documents of all kinds, ancient and modern, printed and unprinted."[55] He took pride in these labors: "I have an old worn copy of the said sermon [preached at Paul's Cross in 1388], written in very old English, and almost half consumed with age."[56] Readers must sometimes make up their own minds about the truth reported in these documents; but if they reject it, "yet I have shown [them] my author."[57] Fussner credits Foxe with making "a distinct contribution to historiography" by printing original sources for the benefit of the common reader, thus extending the Renaissance humanist emphasis on evidence to a larger audience.[58]

The question remains: what use did Foxe make of his sources? Did he check them for accuracy? Did he force their interpretation to fit his partisan bias? Probably the most important event in the history of Foxe studies was the publication of J. F. Mozley's *John Foxe and His Book* in 1940.[59] His defense of Foxe's accuracy and integrity rescued us from the caricature of Foxe the Protestant mythmaker created by Maitland and perpetuated by Lee, and made possible a balanced appraisal of Foxe's work once again.

Foxe gives evidence of caring about accuracy, and his handling of his sources is often demonstrably anything but uncritical. His partisanship is unquestionable, but he was not so biased that he could not include facts damaging to his thesis that the sufferings of martyrs give moral testimony to the truth of the Church's message and help to distinguish the true Church from the false. Along with the accounts of the heroes he also records stories of potential martyrs whose courage failed them,[60] and he quotes Cyprian to the effect that some persecutions come upon the Church for its sins rather than as attacks of the Enemy.[61]

Neither did Foxe believe everything he read. He is skeptical of miracle stories, not only when they involve Roman Catholic saints, but also when they enhance the memory of heroes he considers to be in the line of true witnesses. Yet he never rejects such accounts simply because of the supernatural element they contain, but conscientiously subjects them to the canons of historical evidence. Abdias reports that when Paul's head was struck off, white milk came out instead of blood; but, "this being found in no other history," Foxe rejects it as Abdias' own invention.[62] Foxe recounts the martyrdom of Clement of Rome, but notes that there is "no firm relation in the ancient authors, but only in such new writers of later times, which are wont to paint out the lives and histories of good men with feigned additions," and therefore gives it "less credit."[63] He would like to believe the various miracles reported of Alexander, but, "as I deny not but they may be true, so, because I cannot avouch them by any grave testimony of ancient writers, therefore I dare not affirm them."[64] In other words, he asks for corroboration from other sources and weighs testimony in terms of its proximity to the event and the reliability of the reporter to see if it is "able to abide the touch of history."[65]

Foxe is also apt to question the authenticity of a source if its style or matter seem out of keeping with the times it purports to represent.[66] Here he is consciously carrying on the tradition of Renaissance humanist critical scholarship which descends from Lorenzo Valla, More, and Erasmus.[67] His judgment in such cases is not infallible. He speculates that Cranmer's recantation was faked by the bishops to confuse the people, in a passage which contradicts his own later report of Cranmer's dramatic gesture of holding first into the fire the offending hand which had signed the recantation.[68] Nevertheless, most scholars who have checked him find him to be "well up to the average of historical accuracy in his *Knappe* day,"[69] indeed unusually fair, balanced, and sympathetic for his times,[70] more scrupulous in his use of sources and in verifying their authenticity than his contemporaries,[71] and in fact a pioneer of the "incipient scientific methodology" of history who "aspires to the kind of plainness and truthfulness he sees in the Biblical record."[72]

If the old charge of "willful falsification of evidence" will not stick,[73] Foxe's strong loyalty to the Protestant cause is still a stumbling block for many modern historians. Mozley comments perceptively, "At the very word partizan scientific historians begin always to look uncomfortable. The partizan hardly plays the game of history as they understand it. Not that they are hard men or severe in their judgments. . . . They can forgive much: they can bear any amount of dullness, particularly when buttressed by terrific arrays of footnotes. . . . But partizanship—to have strong feelings and opinions and to show them—this comes near to putting a man outside the pale."[74]

Instead Mozley argues that open and honest partizanship is to be preferred to the veiled variety which masquerades as objectivity. And Foxe certainly makes no effort to hide his feelings of having "no use for such 'impartiality.' He has passed through the fire, and learnt to dread it. . . . He writes with a purpose. . . . He must honor the dead and warn and encourage the living. His book is a blow in the battle against cruelty: and Foxe hated cruelty with all his heart."[75]

Foxe, in other words, believed that truth matters and that historical truth ought to make a difference. He strives to give us not simply a collection of documents and facts but also the vision of life emerging from them, a vision that is profoundly and particularly Christian. As Thompson puts it, he "merges his Reformed bias with the facts." There is no necessary tension between the two, and the result is "a harmonious synthesis of supernatural and human causality, of the biblical version of history with actual events."[76]

THE HISTORIAN'S MESSAGE

Foxe's interpretation of history is solidly within the Augustinian tradition as mediated to sixteenth-century Protestants by John Bale.[77] Foxe's contributions to that framework involve the superimposition upon it of a rather idiosyncratic eschatological scheme, an influential perspective on the role of England in salvation history, and an abidingly significant view (conveyed by his incomparable skill for simple, straightforward, and vivid narration) of the role of the testimony of Christ's martyrs in the ongoing struggle between the forces of darkness and light.

In the earlier pages of the *Acts and Monuments*, Foxe labors to establish a correlation between the progress of church history and a preterist interpretation of the Book of Revelation.[78] After an initial period of "tribulation" (Rev. 13), Satan is bound for one thousand years. This millennium corresponds roughly to the time between Constantine and Wycliffe, a time in which there was no major widespread persecution, a time in which the Roman church was becoming corrupt. With the persecution of Wycliffe and the Lollards, the pope was revealed as Antichrist and Satan was unleashed for a season. In other words, the church reenters a period of widespread persecution of true believers by the false church. This conflict came to a head with the Reformation, and especially with the Marian persecutions, which vindicate the true church and will eventually usher in the Second Coming and the Kingdom of God on earth.[79]

The attempt to read prophecy as history is a perilous undertaking, if in a sense a necessary one for people who look to its fulfillment as indeed the climax of history. Only one such attempt (at most) will be correct, and by the time we know which one it is, it will be too late to argue about it. Foxe's laudable desire to integrate his interpretation of history with his faith and his natural desire to buttress his view of the centrality of martyrdom to the unfolding of history with every means at his disposal led him to read the history he knew into John's prophecy. But the Reformation, important to the story of the church as it is, did not bring in the millennium. Foxe did not in fact live in the Last Days, and his eschatology now seems forced and naive.

Fortunately, Foxe himself seems to have realized that the details of his reading of Revelation were not central to his interpretation of history. McNeill reminds us that it is possible to overstress the importance of "all this apocalyptical apparatus for Foxe himself." He "respects" dates, facts, and sequence and refuses to "juggle" them to force them to fit his scheme.[80] And in the last half of the work it recedes almost completely from view. The attempt at prophetic interpretation remains a weakness, but one which can serve as a warning to us without detracting from more important facets of Foxe's viewpoint.

What was supremely important to Foxe was that history—however periodized or related to prophecy—be understood as the record of the ongoing conflict between truth and error, good and evil, Christ and Satan. "Always," says White, "it is the battle between light and darkness that is the main standard of values, the focus of all issues for Foxe."[81] The protagonists in this struggle have founded two communities reminiscent of Augustine's two cities: Foxe calls them "this world" and "the kingdom of Christ," and early warns his readers that the difference between them is what is "most requisite and necessary for every Christian man to observe and note" in his history.[82]

They must note them carefully because the struggle is not a simple matter of the church versus the world. The world now appears wearing the face of the church, which is precisely what makes the study of history crucial: "Now forasmuch as the true church of God goeth not . . . alone, but is accompanied with some other church or chapel of the devil to deface and malign the same, necessary it is therefore the difference between them to be seen, and the descent of the right church to be described from the apostles' time: which hitherto, in most part of histories hath been lacking."[83]

The two cities become increasingly focused as the two churches, and history describes the descent of the right one in two ways. First is by the comparison of doctrine and practice that shows the continuity between the Reformation and the primitive church. If we think of ordinance and doctrine rather than organization, it shows that "our church was, when this [Roman Catholic] church of theirs was not yet hatched out of the shell."[84] This is why so much more space is given to examinations, trials, and disputations than to actual martyrdoms, because it gives Foxe an opportunity to deal with *ideas* which are ultimately important.[85] But the second way is the one for which Foxe is uniquely remembered. The moral force of the testimony of her martyrs creates its own continuity, which helps to identify the true church and bring into focus the power of her message.

If the possession of a central theme be one of the prerequisites for a great view of human history, then it cannot be denied that Foxe has it. He goes through past history, garnering up every rebel against Rome that he can find whose position can be reasonably interpreted as involving a return to the position of the primitive church, and out of these figures and movements of the past he establishes what he regards to be a continuing tradition of striving for the restoration of the church to the purity of its first days.[86]

In a telling summation, Foxe contrasts the "primitive" and the "latter" church of Rome: a "persecuted church" versus a "persecuting church," a church whose bishops "were made martyrs" versus one whose bishops "make martyrs."[87] Thus the Reformers' martyrdoms at Rome's hands identify them effectively with the primitive church, and the church of Rome with the pre-Constantinian persecuting Empire. The graphic stories of suffering are present not for the love of gore but because they reveal the true character of both sides with its powerful moral testimony to the truth of the one and the diabolical falsity of the other. "For Foxe, his martyrs are people whose characters and behavior may be taken as arguments for the truth of the position they have taken up. The character of their adversaries is clearly the opposite."[88] This Foxe labors unceasingly to bring out: again and again, his martyrs "humbly offered themselves to the hands of their tormentors; and so took their death both christianly and constantly, with such patience as might well testify the goodness of their cause. Wherein is to be noted how mightily the Lord worketh with his grace and fortitude in the hearts of his servants."[89]

For Foxe, then, the blood of the martyrs is not only the seed of the church but also its sign. Persecuted or persecuting: between the active and passive participles lies the clearest difference history shows between the spirit of Christ and the spirit of Antichrist. The fires of Smithfield burned this principle into the mind of Foxe, and through his mind, into the minds of succeeding generations of Protestant believers.

An important subplot to this story for Foxe is the role of England in the historic struggle between the two churches. He sees for his own people a pivotal role in God's plan for the history of the Church. It was Constantine, a "Britayne born" through his mother Helena, who brought an end to the first wave of persecution;[90] it was the Englishman Wycliffe and his Lollards who recovered the gospel in its purity and became the firstfruits of the new harvest of martyrs in modern times leading to the

Reformation;[91] it was the English Mary Tudor who brought the fury of persecution by the Antichrist to its fullest expression; and it is the English Elizabeth who, as the new Constantine, has restored peace and the true church once again.[92] In general, the conflict of Christ and Antichrist is represented on the temporal level by the (usually English) king versus the pope.[93] When English monarchs (even Mary) support the pope and persecution, it tends to get blamed on evil counselors such as Gardiner.[94] On the whole, as Haller summarizes it, "Every examination, as Foxe reports it, tended to wind up in a dramatic scene in which an honest believer was shown pitting the plain truth of the Word against the super-subtle sophistries of hypocritical churchmen and a loyal subject of the Crown was shown asserting his rights as an Englishman against a popish prelate."[95]

England is, in Haller's phrase, the "elect nation" intended by God to lead mankind to righteousness and freedom for true worship. But this is not mere chauvinism: rather, the English king and the English people are judged as they fail or succeed in living up to that role. There is, nevertheless, great hope for success under Elizabeth to match the egregious failure under Mary.

We should not dismiss this element of Foxe's vision as mere Eurocentric Anglophilia in a misguided passion for political correctness. The English-speaking peoples have indeed played a major role in the propagation of the gospel across the world and the creation of the Church's literature—and a larger role than even Foxe could have foreseen in bringing religious freedom to the world through the American experiment. Therefore, while few would follow Foxe in the details (seeing the king as the bulwark of the true faith, for example), the major thrust of his vision here seems almost prophetic. It may indeed have helped to sow the seeds of its own fulfillment by creating a sense of destiny in such terms for the nation and its progeny. We should also remember that scholars such as Haller, who see this theme as the central one of the *Acts and Monuments*, are probably guilty of imbalance. Naturalism is certainly there; but, as Olsen recognizes, it is subordinate to the gospel, which is for all nations.[96] *That* is what ultimately receives its credibility from the testimony of the English martyrs throughout history.

In summary, history as Foxe wrote it had the power to bring key events from the past into focus so as to give an individual or a people a sense of identity, purpose, and destiny. "History, as he wrote it," says Haller, "always came back to the story of an individual . . . yet every individual case was charged with the whole meaning of history as he conceived it."[97] Thompson describes that meaning as a "cosmic vision," always looming in the background, "lending a ritual quality to actions and words." Everything is defined by the struggle of Christ versus Antichrist, the Mass versus the Word, the Sacrifice of the Mass versus the Sacrifice of the Martyrs.[98] If subsequent history has rendered obsolete his way of meshing history with eschatology, it has refined while confirming his high view of the role of England in church history and done nothing to alter his sense of the significance of her martyrs in the proclamation of the Church's message, as the Auca martyrs and others have amply demonstrated in our own generation.

CONCLUSION

The taunt, "You're history!" seeks to relegate its verbal victim to the irremedial irrelevance of the irretrievable past. The final thing to be said about John Foxe is that, for all his faults, he does at times succeed in reversing that commonly accepted meaning. In his book the past lives in the present and charges it with meaning. No one who has met them can ever forget Foxe's martyrs: Anne Askew, who had received from Wriothesly letters offering the king's pardon if she would recant, and who, "refusing once to look upon them, made this answer again, that she came not thither to deny her Lord and Master";[99] Cranmer holding his offending right hand into the flame;[100] and Latimer, saying on his way to the stake, "Be of good cheer, master Ridley, and play the man. We shall this day light such a candle, by God's grace, in England, as I trust shall never be put out."[101] They, being dead, yet speak, and so their cause, as Foxe intended, also lives on.

The *Book of Martyrs's* biggest fault is its sheer size, which daunts all but the most obsessive readers and obscures its structure and theses. Most of the abridgments, which are legion, focus on the dramatic anecdotes and slight the historiographical context that reveals their meaning. A good critical edition for scholars is a desperate need—and then a popular abridgment, based on it, which could bring its sprawling bulk into focus, might even rekindle the light of Latimer's candle once again.

BIBLIOGRAPHY

Alexander, Gina. "Bonner and the Marian Persecutions." *History* 60 (1975): 374–91.

Bainton, Roland H. "John Foxe and the Women Martyrs." In *Women of the Reformation in France and England*, 211–30. Minneapolis: Augsburg, 1973. Reprint (with different introductory paragraph) of "John Foxe and the Ladies." In *The Social History of the Reformation*. Lawrence P. Buck and Jonathan W. Zophy, eds., 208–22. Columbus: Ohio State Univ. Press, 1972.

Bauer, W. E. "John Foxe and Martyrs." *Church History* 3 (1934): 249.

_____. "John Foxe as Historian." Diss., Cornell, 1932.

Breitenberg, Mark. "The Flesh Made Word: Foxe's *Acts and Monuments.*" *Renaisance and Reformation* 25 (1989): 381–407.

Butterworth, Charles C. "Erasmus and Bilney and Foxe." *Bulletin of the New York Public Library* 57 (1953): 575–79.

Collinson, Patrick. *The Elizabethan Puritan Movement.* Berkeley: University of California Press, 1967.

Davies, Catharine and Jane Facey. "A Reformation Dilemma: John Foxe and the Problem of Discipline." *Journal of Ecclesiastical History* 39 (1988): 37–65.

Dickens, A. G. *The English Reformation.* N.Y.: Schocken Books, 1964.

Fairfield, Leslie P. "John Bale and the Development of Protestant Hagiography in England." *Journal of Ecclesiastical History* 24 (1973): 145–60.

Ferguson, Wallace K. *The Renaissance in Historical Thought,* 53–56. Cambridge, Mass.: Houghton Mifflin, 1948.

Fines, John. "A Note on the Reliability of Foxe." Appendix II of "Heresy Trials in Coventry and Lichfield." *Journal of Ecclesiastical History* 14 (1963): 160–74.

Fox, Alistair. "John Foxe's *Acts and Monuments* as Polemical History." *Parergon* 14 (1976): 43–51.

Foxe, John. *Actes and Monuments of these Latter and Perilous Dayes, Touching Matters of the Church.* 8 vols. Edited by George Townsend. London: Sedley & Burnside, 1841. Reprint, N.Y.: AMS Press, 1965.

Fussner, F. Smith. *Tudor History and the Historians.* N.Y.: Basic Books, 1970.

Hageman, Elizabeth H. "John Foxe's Henry VIII as Justitia." *The Sixteenth Century Journal* 10 (1979): 35–43.

Haller, William. *Foxe's Book of Martyrs and the Elect Nation.* 1963. Reprint, London: Ebenezer Baylis & Sons, Ltd., 1967.

_____. "John Foxe and the Puritan Revolution." In *The Seventeenth Century: Studies in the History of English Thought and Literature from Bacon to Pope.* Edited by Richard Foster Jones, 209–24. Stanford: Stanford University Press, 1951.

_____. "The Tragedy of God's Englishman." In *Reason and the Imagination: Studies in the History of Ideas, 1600–1800.* Edited by J. A. Mazzeo, 201–11. N.Y.: Columbia University Press, 1962.

Hargrave, O. T. "Bloody Mary's Victims: The Iconography of John Foxe's *Book of Martyrs.*" *Historical Magazine of the Protestant Episcopal Church* 51 (1982): 7–21.

Jones, Ruth Ann. "John Foxe and the Humanist Concept of History." Diss., Missouri, 1989.

Kain, Richard M. "The Book of Martyrs." *Library Review* (May 28, 1979): 31–32.

Knappen, M. M. *Tudor Puritanism: A Chapter in the History of Idealism.* Chicago: University of Chicago Press, 1939.

Knowles, Elizabeth M. "First Uses from Foxe's *Acts and Monuments* in the *Oxford English Dictionary:* An Interim Case Study." *International Journal of Lexicography* 2 (1989): 15–23.

Lee, Sidney. "Foxe, John." *Dictionary of National Biography.* Oxford: Oxford University Press, 1917, 7:581–90.

Levin, Carole. "John Foxe and the Responsibilities of Queenship." In *Women in the Middle Ages and the Renaissance: Literary and Historical Perspectives.* Edited by Mary Beth Rose, 113–31. Syracuse: Syracuse University Press, 1986.

————. "Women in *The Book of Martyrs* as Models of Behavior in Tudor England." *International Journal of Women's Studies* 4:2 (March-April 1981): 224–32.

Levy, F. J. *Tudor Historical Thought.* San Marino, Calif.: Huntington Library, 1967.

Lewis, C. S. *English Literature in the Sixteenth Century, Excluding Drama.* Vol. 3 of the *Oxford History of English Literature.* Oxford: Oxford University Press, 1954.

Loades, D. M. *The Oxford Martyrs.* N.Y.: Stein & Day, 1970.

Macek, Ellen. "The Emergence of a Feminine Spirituality in *The Book of Martyrs.*" *The Sixteenth-Century Journal* 19 (1988): 63–80.

Maitland, S. R. *Notes on the Contributions of G. Townsend to the New Edition of Foxe's Martyrology.* 3 parts. 1841–42.

————. "On the Personal History of Foxe the Martyrologist." *British Magazine* 23 (1843): 493–500; 24 (1843): 477–89.

————. *Remarks on S. R. Cattley's Defence of His Edition.* 1842.

————. "Remarks on the New Edition of Foxe's Work, and on the Work Itself." *British Magazine* 11 (1837): 620–25; 12 (1838): 6–13, 137–44, 253–59, 376–81, 496–502, 620–27; 13 (1838): 12–20, 122–29, 254–63, 385–89, 613–19.

————. *A Review of Foxe the Martyrologist's History of the Waldenses.* 1837.

————. *Six Letters on Foxe's Actes and Monuments.* 1837. Reprint of the first six "Remarks on the New Edition," *British Magazine,* 1837.

Martin, J. W. "A Sidelight on Foxe's Account of the Marian Martyrs." *Bulletin of the Institute for Historical Research* 58 (1985): 248–51.

McNeill, John T. "John Foxe: Historiographer, Disciplinarian, Tolerationist." *Church History* 43 (1974): 216–29.

Mozley, J. F. *John Foxe and His Book.* London: SPCK, 1940.

Nichols, J. G. "The Reformation and John Foxe." *Transcripts of the Royal Historical Society* 77 (1860).

Oliver, Leslie M. "The *Acts and Monuments* of John Foxe: A Study of the Growth and Influence of a Book." Diss., Harvard, 1945.

Olsen, V. Norskov. *John Foxe and the Elizabethan Church.* Berkeley: University of California Press, 1973.

Patrides, C. A. *The Grand Design of God: The Literary Form of the Christian View of History.* London: Routlege & Kegan Paul, 1972.

Preston, Joseph H. "English Ecclesiastical Historians and the Problem of Bias, 1559–1742." *Journal of the History of Ideas* 32 (1971): 203–20.

Rosen, Barbara. "John Foxe's *Book of Martyrs* and Its Value as a Book for Children." In *Triumphs of the Spirit in Children's Literature.* Edited by Francelia Butler and Richard Rotert. Hamden, Conn.: Library Professional Publications, 1986.

Rupp, Gordon. *Six Makers of English Religion.* N.Y.: Harper, 1957.

Smart, Stefan J. "John Foxe and 'The Story of Richard Hun, Martyr.'" *Journal of Ecclesiastical History* 37 (1986): 1–14.

————. "'Favourers of God's Words'? John Foxe's Henrician Martyrs." Diss., Southampton (U.K.), 1988.

Smith, John Hazel. "Notes on Two Renaissance Authors: Two Early Latin Poems by John Foxe the Martyrologist." In *Brandeis Essays in Literature.* Edited by John Hazel Smith, 25–29. Waltham: Brandeis University Press, 1983.

Thompson, Geraldine Vina. "Foxe's *Book of Martyrs*: A Literary Study." Diss., Oregon, 1974.

Thompson, J. A. F. "John Foxe and Some Sources for Lollard History: Notes for a Critical Appraisal." *Studies in Church History* 2 (1965): 251–57.

Walls, Kathryn. "Spenser's Kirkrapine and John Foxe's Attack on Rome." *Notes & Queries* 31 (1986): 173–5.

Weisinger, Herbert. "Ideas of History During the Renaissance." In *Renaissance Essays*. Edited by P. O. Kristeller, 74–94. N.Y.: Harper & Row, 1968.

White, Helen C. *Tudor Books of Saints and Martyrs*. Madison: University of Wisconsin Press, 1963.

Whitehead, Lydia. *"A poena et culpa:* Penitence, Confidence, and the *Miserere* in Foxe's *Actes and Monuments." Renaissance Studies* 4 (1990): 287–99.

Williams, Donald T. "The Depth of Rightful Doom: The English Reformers' Concept of Justice and Book V of Spenser's *Faerie Queene*." Diss., Georgia, 1985.

Williams, Neville. *John Foxe the Martyrologist: His Life and Times*. London: Dr. Williams' Trust, 1975.

———. *John Foxe*. Boston: Twayne, 1983.

———. "Recent Studies in Foxe." *English Literary Renaissance* 11 (1981): 224–32.

Wooden, Warren W. "Foxe, Shakespeare, and Hamlet's 'Country Matters.'" *Hamlet Studies* 4 (1982): 89–91.

———. "John Foxe's *Book of Martyrs* and the Child Reader." In *The Child and the Story: An Exploration of Narrative Forms*. Edited by Priscilla Ord, 147–56. Boston: Children's Literature Association, 1983.

Yates, Frances A. "Foxe as Propagandist." *Encounter* 27 (1966): 78–86.

———. "Queen Elizabeth I as Astraea." In *Astraea: The Imperial Theme in the Sixteenth Century*, 29–87. London: Routledge & Kegan Paul, 1975.

NOTES

1. John Foxe, *Actes and Monuments of These Latter and Perilous Dayes, Touching Matters of the Church*, ed. George Townsend (London: Sedley & Burnside, 1841; reprint, N.Y.: AMS Press, 1965).

2. See William Haller, *Foxe's Book of Martyrs and the Elect Nation* (London: Ebenezer Baylis & Sons, Ltd., 1967), 252–53 for a description of typical abridgments.

3. Foxe, *Actes and Monuments*, 1:99, 1:109–110.

4. Haller, *Elect Nation*, 57.

5. Sidney Lee, "Foxe, John," *Dictionary of National Biography* (Oxford: Oxford University Press, 1917), 7:581–90. Though biased, Lee's biography is still the most useful collection of the basic facts of Foxe's life, and will be the source of those facts not otherwise documented here.

6. See Donald T. Williams, "Dossier: Thomas Cranmer," *Eternity* (Sept., 1986): 17 for a brief review of the English Reformation.

7. V. Norskov Olsen, *John Foxe and the Elizabethan Church* (Berkeley: University of California Press, 1973), 9.

8. Foxe, *Actes and Monuments*, 5:704.

9. Ibid., 6:354.

10. Ibid., 6:355.

11. Quoted in J. F. Mozley, *John Foxe and His Book* (London: SPCK, 1940), 54.

12. Mozley, *John Foxe*, 35; cf. Neville Williams, *John Foxe the Martyrologist: His Life and Times* (London: Dr. Williams' Trust, 1975), 22.

13. Mozley, *John Foxe*, 86–7.

14. Ibid., 126.

15. Ibid., 128.

16. Haller, *Elect Nation,* 9; cf. Leslie M. Oliver, "The *Acts and Monuments* of John Foxe: A Study of the Growth and Influence of a Book," diss., Harvard, 1945, which, according to Haller in his "John Foxe and the Puritan Revolution," in *The Seventeenth Century: Studies in the History of English Thought and Literature from Bacon to Pope,* ed. Richard Foster Jones (Stanford: Stanford University Press, 1951), 209–24, is the fullest account of the bibliographical history of the *Acts and Monuments. Mozley (John Foxe,* 125) says that while most of the valuable material from the Latin work was carried over into the English editions, "The Latin book must not for this reason be neglected: for in translating it Foxe and his assistants would often omit some point of interest, sacrifice some graphic touch, or even drastically curtail a narrative." Hence, it is still "always worthwhile" to consult the Basel edition.

17. On March 26, 1566, Foxe was summoned to Lambeth to answer for his refusal to wear vestments. When Archbishop Parker required him to subscribe, he "produced a New Testament in Greek. 'To this,' saith he, 'will I subscribe'" (Mozley, *John Foxe,* 74).

18. Ibid., 153.

19. Hyder E. Rollins and Herschel Baker, *The Renaissance in England: Non-Dramatic Prose and Verse of the Sixteenth Century* (Lexington, Mass.: D. C. Heath, 1954), 174.

20. John T. McNeill, "John Foxe: Historiographer, Disciplinarian, Tolerationist," *Church History* 43 (1974): 225.

21. Helen C. White, *Tudor Books of Saints and Martyrs* (Madison: University of Wisconsin Press, 1963), 179.

22. Foxe, *Actes and Monuments,* 1:xxv.

23. Ibid. Cf. Spenser, *The Faerie Queene,* Proem to Book I, where he sets out to sing of gentle deeds whose praises, "having slept in silence long" in antique rolls, must now be blazoned abroad.

24. Foxe, *Actes and Monuments,* 1:xviii.

25. Haller, *Elect Nation,* 130.

26. Ibid., 145.

27. Foxe, *Actes and Monuments,* 1:viii.

28. Ibid.

29. Haller, *Elect Nation,* 153.

30. Foxe, *Actes and Monuments,* 6:511.

31. Geraldine Vina Thompson, "Foxe's Book of Martyrs: A Literary Study" (diss. Oregon, 1974), 191.

32. Mark Breitenberg, "The Flesh Made Word: Foxe's *Acts and Monuments,*" *Renaissance and Reformation* 25 (1989): 397.

33. Foxe, *Actes and Monuments,* 1:xix.

34. Olsen, *Elizabethan Church,* 49.

35. Warren W. Wooden, "From Caxton to Comenius: The Origins of Children's Literature," *Fifteenth-Century Studies* 6 (1983): 307f.

36. Quoted in Mozley, *John Foxe,* 136.

37. Foxe, *Actes and Monuments,* 1:viii.

38. Ibid., 1:xviii.

39. Ibid., 1:91.

40. Ibid., 2:26.

41. Ibid., 2:108.

42. Ibid., 1:xxvi.

43. Ibid., 1:viii.

44. Ibid., 1:xvii.

45. Ibid., 1:207.

46. Ibid., 8:754.

47. Ibid., 1:vi.

48. Mozley, *John Foxe*, 138–39; see also Thomas H. Clancy, S.J., *Papist Pamphleteers: The Allen-Persons Party and the Political Thought of the Counter Reformation in England, 1512–1615* (Chicago: Loyola University Press, 1964), which gives a number of contemporary reactions to Foxe.

49. Olsen, *Elizabethan Church*, 91.

50. Mozley, *John Foxe*, 183.

51. Lee, *Foxe, John*, 588.

52. Philip Hughes, *The Reformation in England*, 3 vols. (London: Hollis & Carter, 1951–54), 2:257–58; cf. Thompson, "Foxes Book," 59–61, and Stefan J. Smart, "John Foxe and 'The Story of Richard Hun, Martyr,'" *Journal of Ecclesiastical History* 37 (1986): 14, for similar reactions.

53. Joseph H. Preston, "English Ecclesiastical Historians and the Problem of Bias," *Journal of the History of Ideas* 32 (1971): 203–20.

54. Mozley, *John Foxe*, 168.

55. Ibid., 130.

56. Foxe, *Actes and Monuments*, 3:292.

57. Ibid., 1:217.

58. F. Smith Fussner, *Tudor History and the Historians* (N.Y.: Basic Books, 1970), 27.

59. C. S. Lewis, *English Literature in the Sixteenth Century, Excluding Drama*, vol. 3 of *The Oxford History of English Literature* (Oxford: Oxford University Press, 1954), 299–300 judges Mozley's defense of Foxe's integrity to be a "complete success": "For the Marian persecution his sources are usually the narratives of eyewitnesses. . . . Men who have seen their friends die in torture are not always inspired by that cooly scientific spirit which the academic researcher so properly demands. But there seems no evidence that Foxe ever accepted what he himself did not believe or ever refused to correct what he had written in the light of fresh evidence."

60. Foxe, *Actes and Monuments*, 1:184–85.

61. Ibid., 1:196–97.

62. Ibid., 1:103.

63. Ibid., 1:111.

64. Ibid., 1:113.

65. Ibid., 1:273.

66. Ibid., 1:149; cf. 1:193.

67. Cf. White, *Tudor Books*, 180–81.

68. Foxe, *Actes and Monuments*, 3:340.

69. M. M. Knappen, *Tudor Puritanism: A Chapter in the History of Idealism* (Chicago: University of Chicago Press, 1939), 495.

70. McNeill, "John Foxe," 228.

71. J. W. Martin, "A Sidelight on Foxe's Account of the Marian Martyrs," *Bulletin of the Institute for Historical Research* 58 (1985): 151.

72. Thompson, "Foxe's Book," 14f.

73. Warren W. Wooden, "Recent Studies in Foxe," *English Literary Renaissance* 11 (1981): 228; cf. Neville Williams, *Martyrologist*, 17–18: "Modern research has done much to confirm the details" of Foxe on Lollardy; Mozley, *John Foxe*, 159–73: Foxe's errors are "small blemishes" compared to the "solid merit" of the whole, and that we know "what manner of man Tyndale was" is due more to Foxe than anyone else, while the same could be said of many other figures he portrays; Haller, *Elect Nation*, 124, etc., who adds that Foxe's information on Elizabeth probably came from her old tutor Roger Ascham; and John Fines, "A Note on the Reliability of Foxe," Appendix II of "Her-

esy Trials in Coventry and Lichfield," *Journal of Ecclesiastical History* 14 (1963): 173–74, who reports that considering his difficulties, Foxe's accuracy is "amazing."

74. Mozley, *John Foxe*, 156.

75. Ibid.

76. Thompson, "Foxe's Book," 250–51.

77. Haller, *Elect Nation*, 62–67, pursues this connection profitably; cf. Paul Christianson, *Reformers and Babylon: English Apocalyptic Visions from the Reformation to the Eve of the Civil War* (Toronto: University of Toronto Press, 1978), 39f.

78. Foxe, *Actes and Monuments*, 1:289ff.

79. Ibid., 2:724–26; cf. Olsen, *Elizabethan Church*, 71.

80. McNeill, "John Foxe," 224–25.

81. White, *Tudor Books*, 146; cf. Haller, *Elect Nation*, 187.

82. Foxe, *Actes and Monuments*, 1:88.

83. Ibid., 1:xix.

84. Ibid., 1:9.

85. White, *Tudor Books*, 157–58; for a thorough study of the theology of the English Reformation, see Philip Edgcumbe Hughes, *Theology of the English Reformers* (Grand Rapids: Baker, 1980); for a more concise overview, see the first chapter of Donald T. Williams, "The Depth of Rightful Doom: The English Reformers' Concept of Justice and Book V of Spenser's *Faerie Queene*" (diss., Georgia, 1985).

86. White, *Tudor Books*, 179.

87. Foxe, *Actes and Monuments*, 1:12.

88. White, *Tudor Books*, 152.

89. Foxe, *Actes and Monuments*, 5:438.

90. Thompson, "Foxe's Book," 26f.

91. Foxe, *Actes and Monuments*, 2:791; cf. 3:311.

92. Francis A. Yates, "Queen Elizabeth I as Astraea," in *Astraea: The Imperial Theme in the Sixteenth Century* (London: Routledge and Kegan Paul, 1975), 29–87, sees the Elizabeth/Constantine analogy as the key to Foxe's whole book; cf. Thompson, "Foxe's Book," 54f.

93. Thompson, "Foxe's Book," 22–23.

94. White, *Tudor Books*, 178; cf. Thompson, "Foxe's Book," 46–49.

95. Haller, *Elect Nation*, 183.

96. Olsen, *Elizabethan Church*, 36–37.

97. Haller, "Puritan Revolution," 217.

98. Thompson, "Foxe's Book," 5.

99. Foxe, *Actes and Monuments*, 5:550.

100. Ibid., 8:90.

101. Ibid., 7:550.

7

See Lightfoot on Baur, cited p 343-344.

F. C. BAUR

JOHN S. REIST, JR.

INTRODUCTION

Near the beginning of what most critics call his "Hegelian" period (1833–41), F. C. Baur, responding to the orthodox biblical scholar D. E. W. Hengstenberg of the University of Berlin, wrote concerning faith and science:

> Both . . . nourish and refresh each other, and as science can only gain from faith, so also faith from science. Only from faith does science learn to purify itself of everything foreign and impure, and to surrender itself undividedly and unconditionally *to the holy affair of truth*; and on the other hand faith has science to thank for the fact that it is not delivered over to an indolent rest but is maintained in a fresh, vital movement, in order to become clearly and immediately conscious of its divine content . . . . All the doubts which the newer criticism has awakened are for faith healthy and fruitful in the highest order; they are to be viewed as a powerful means of its education and formation. Faith ought never to be idle and secure but always to grow and become stronger.[1]

Baur spent his entire academic career trying to discover and to retrieve, by what he called "pure" historical method, the truth of the Christian faith. For him this was a vocation of highest calling, a "holy affair of truth," and he conducted this affair with meticulous research and profound insight, combining the methods of the researcher with the thoughtfulness of the theologian, such that the inscription on his gravestone reads simply "Theologe."[2] Whether he conducted this affair focused on the truth or became ardently infatuated with other unbiblical, but attractive, ideas, we will examine in this study.

Reflecting on G. E. Lessing's dictum, "accidental truths of history can never become the proof of necessary truths of reason,"[3] which exploded the comfortable medieval scholasticism that still lingered after the reformation and which precipitated the modern hiatus between "heaven and here" that all modern theologies have tried to bridge, Baur himself has produced a *corpus* which has been variously judged. W. Dilthey pronounced, "He was the greatest theologian of our century. He was a man of great character and a scholar in the grand style, both in *a single* person."[4] C. C. McCown, on the other hand, called Baur's work, "a false start, led by philosophy instead of science."[5] C. H. Spurgeon, the great evangelical preacher, denounced it as "the German poison;"[6] and Joseph Parker of the City Temple sneered, "Have we to await a communication from Tübingen, or a telegram from Oxford, before we can read the Bible?"[7] W. Geiger, whose 1964 study of Baur disagrees with P. Hodgson's 1966 book (see bibliography), damns him with faint praise: "As a New Testament scholar, Baur was not an exegete, but a 'critic';"[8] and E. Barnikol concluded that he was "no independent historian."[9]

Was Baur a historical scholar whose work, untrammeled by Protestant and Catholic supernaturalism and eighteenth-century rationalism, produced the fundamental and enduring truth of the Christian faith as well as the methodology to discover and rediscover and maintain it? Or was his "whole historical framework . . . an ingenious blunder," as Horton Harris has concluded?[10] Has Baur, the biblical, church, and dogmatic historian, helped us to cross Lessing's big ditch? Or, as A. B. Bruce judges, has Baur, the Hegelian, left us with a fantasy imposed on Christian history? Of Baur's work, Bruce declares: "The account given of the origin of Christianity and its canonical literature is not history, but a gross caricature. It is, to say the least, very improbable that the real course of history should follow so closely the requirements of a philosophical system. The attempt to make it appear as if it did, will almost certainly transform the actors in the historical drama into puppets, mouthpieces of tendencies, passive instruments of 'the Idea.'"[11]

The purpose of this essay is to describe Baur's historical method, to analyze it in the process, and to offer some conclusions about his strengths and defects and their effect on our world today. But first, I will provide a short biography to set his work in personal and professional context.[12]

A NEW DAY DAWNS:
BAUR'S LIFE BRIEFLY CONSIDERED

Certain great theologians are remembered by single images: Augustine in anguish hearing a child chant: "Take and read, take and read," opening his Bible to Romans 13:13–14, and being converted; after thoughtful reflection at a banquet while others were talking and eating, Thomas Aquinas striking the table with his fist and speaking out loudly, "Thus I refute the Manicheans!"; Martin Luther, thundering at the Diet of Worms, or in his *Anfechtung* receiving his inspiration in the *cloaca*; John Wesley feeling his heart "strangely warmed" after reading Luther; and Karl Barth preaching faithfully at Safenwil while the guns of Europe were blasting in the distance.

Baur, too, has been vividly and movingly remembered in the picture which E. Zeller, early leader of the Tübingen School and eventually Baur's son-in-law, gave us: "Summer and winter he arose at 4 A.M. and in winter he usually worked for a few hours in the unheated room out of consideration for the servants, even though—as often happened—on especially cold nights the ink froze; and thereafter the regular midday or evening walk was generally the single long interruption in the day's academic work."[13]

And even though Harris deflates and detracts from the image with his note: "One should perhaps mention that Baur suffered from insomnia and preferred rather to work than remain lying in bed,"[14] still iced ink, cold hearth, and regular daily walk punctuated his lifelong enterprise that developed into one of the most influential theological achievements of the modern world. Just as Baur greeted each new dawn at his desk, so also did a new day dawn in biblical and historical studies through his effort. The Hegelian position (which Baur eventually adopted sometime between 1833–35) asserts that the Spirit manifests itself (i.e., comes to consciousness) not only in external historical phenomena and events, but also in and through perceiving individuals who experience this historical flow and seek to understand it. If this is so, then it is important to know Baur's biography, for he was a singular and perceptive interpreter of the divine dynamic in and through history, especially as that process manifested itself in burgeoning Christianity with Jesus Christ as its founder and originator.

What were the events and persons and circumstances that produced Baur's indefatigable effort to interpret historical theology, history of dogma, and church history (including primitive or ancient, or apostolic-biblical Christianity)?

We know little about Baur's childhood, which began June 21, 1792, as the first son of an orthodox evangelical pastor-father, Christian Jacob, whose energy counterbalanced his mother's intermittent melancholy and depression. Pastor Baur thought that Kant and Fichte were atheists. Ferdinand read more than he played as a child, and was taught Greek, Hebrew, and Latin by his father until he entered Blaubeuren seminary in 1805, where he received marks of "very good" but not excellent.

In 1809, Baur entered Tübingen Seminary where he studied Kant, Schelling, Plato, Aristotle, and Fichte. He was taught by the younger Bengel, whose grandfather was J. A. Bengel, the famous biblical expositor. The younger Bengel taught that Jesus was divine in that He revealed God (not that He was God); that He was a high moral teacher; and that His divinity is to be ascribed to Him rather than being inherent. In 1814, Baur graduated; he became professor at Blaubeuren in 1817; he married Emilie Becker in 1821; they had five children, the eldest of which, Emilie, married E. Zeller. Baur also did pastoral work during this time. In 1823, he read Schleiermacher's *The Christian Faith*, the proportionality and unity of which he admired; but he criticized the author for not openly denying miracles and the supernatural, and he worried that Schleiermacher's concept of dependence was too subjective. He published his first formidable work, *Symbolik und Mythologie* (1824), which examined the universal dependence humans call religion which he had learned from Schleiermacher.

Baur was appointed professor at Tübingen in 1826, but there was much controversy over his consideration. Many, both in academe and the church, thought he had become either a pantheist or a mystic at this time. In a six-year controversy, 1832–38, he rebutted J. A. Moehler's book, *Symbolik* (1832) on the differences between the Roman Catholic and the Protestant church. Although scholars disagree about how Hegelian he actually was at this time, Baur espoused Hegel in refuting Moehler's study. The more important issue to note is that Baur's recognition and adoption of Hegel's dialectic and idealism occurs *after* his pivotal article published in 1831 about 1 Corinthians 1:12, in which he first contended for what became the determining principle (many would say the procrustean bed) of his New Testament history: that Petrine and Pauline factions were constantly in conflict until the latter part of the second century, Peter representing a narrow Jewish Christianity, and Paul arguing for a freedom from the Torah and a universalizing of the gospel to all humanity. Was Baur's understanding of the development of primitive Christianity Hegelian? Evidently, not originally; but his initial interpretation was such, that when he read Hegel's dialectic of thesis-antithesis-synthesis, Baur's view that Petrine legalism (thesis) and its opponent, Pauline freedom (antithesis), which eventually synthesized into late-second-century catholicism, was easily fitted into this mold.

During this crucial decade in Baur's life (1831–41), David Strauss, his former pupil, published his famous *The Life of Jesus Critically Examined* (1835); Baur produced his book on "the so-called pastoral epistles" (1835), in which his first use of Hegel's threefold dialectic to understand primitive Christianity and its development into catholic Christianity appeared; he published his book on Christian gnosticism (1835) which also manifested Hegelian thought; and he issued his great doctrinal treatments of Atonement (1838), and the Trinity and the Incarnation of God (1841–43). Baur developed all three doctrines historically and dialectically rather than systematically and therefore broke new ground in the study of dogma. It is clear from Harris's modern biography of Strauss[15] that Baur was jealous of his former student whose name was either lauded or denigrated throughout the continent (as well as in England). In "Compelled Explanations," an essay published in 1836, Baur denied that he was dependent on Strauss for his own position; and he especially criticized Strauss for merely showing all the discrepancies and errors in the New Testament. Baur argued that historical studies of the New Testament must be constructive; they must analyze sources of stories and statements in the gospels; and they must critique and date biblical books—gospel and epistle—according to their "tendency," by which Baur meant their motive, or standpoint, or perspective. Called *Tendenzcritik*, Baur employed this method to such conclusions as "the Acts is not to be regarded as a purely historical work, but only as a presentation of the history following a certain tendency."[16] This tendency was "catholic," by which the author of Acts ironically sought to describe Peter as Pauline (the conversion of the Gentile Cornelius, a universalizing event, in Acts 10) and Paul as Petrine, who according to the second half of Acts, visited the temple and always preached to the Jews first. Such an *apologia* for catholicity allegedly deprives Acts of historical value, for it reveals an apologetic and reconciliatory tendency; and since it does not reflect the radical conflict between the Pauline and Petrine factions, it must be dated late second century.

Baur's beloved wife died in 1839, after a long sickness; and his close friend Ludwig Heyd and intimate colleague Fredrich Kern passed away in 1842. Even though Strauss had for the while upstaged his former teacher and the three personal losses deeply saddened him, Baur did not resign his work; he produced *Critical Studies of the Canonical Gospels* in 1847, in which he almost certainly wrongly contended that Matthew was the first gospel because it was written largely for Jews and represented the initial Jewish Christianity of the Petrine party. Luke's Gospel is written by and for a Gentile or more universalizing sensibility and is therefore Pauline. And John is the concluding synthesis of catholicity in the late second century. Hegel's threefold dynamic has clearly influenced Baur into making wrong judgments.

The last years of his life (1845–60) were active and productive; he presented *Paul, an Apostle of Jesus Christ* (1845) in which he argued that only Galatians, Romans, and 1 and 2 Corinthians were Pauline and that Acts was not apostolic in origin. From this time forward, he turned his attention largely from biblical studies to church history and the history of dogma. He produced two of his greatest works, *The Epochs of Church Historiography* (1852) and *Church History of the First Three Centuries* (1853). A third important work, *Introduction to Lectures on the History of Christian Dogma*, was published posthumously in 1865–67, but the text is based on manuscripts from the 1840s. By 1853 he had turned from the Christ of Hegel Who carries within Him the divine Idea, to the Kantian Jesus, Whose example, commands and moral teaching distinguish Christianity from all other religions; and he developed a historiography based on the assumption that the historical development of Christianity neither is originated by, nor is it caused by, nor does it reveal any supernatural source or miraculous power operating in historical events. By substituting Hegelian metaphysics for supernatural Christianity, Baur sought an answer to his search for the key or fundamental principle which would make history more than unconnected moments of historical events with no meaning or purpose. Near the end of his career, he left the divine Idea for the moral Jesus.

> The historian who approaches his subject imbued with the faith of the church finds himself confronted at the very outset with the most stupendous of miracles, the fact which lies at the root of Christianity being in his eyes that the only-begotten Son of God descended from the eternal throne of the Godhead to the earth, and became man in the womb of the Virgin. He who regards this as simply and absolutely a miracle, steps at once outside of all historical connection. . . . Historical connection having once been severed at the outset, the same interruption of the historical process is equally possible at any further point.[17]

He then substituted a general revelation of God in all the historical process, an example of which or a significant illustration of which, was to be found in Jesus and the church, what Harris calls "a divine process of education for mankind."[18] Whether such a view constitutes a new dawn for humanity is the issue before those of us who wish to do constructive theology responsibly, and faithful to the call that is given to us, a century and a half later, to conduct "the holy affair of truth."

Baur died on December 2, 1860, after suffering two heart attacks, and he is fittingly buried in the Tübingen cemetery; his gravestone is ivy-covered and stands modestly between two trees. In a touching letter to Baur's son-in-law, E. Zeller, Prof. A. Hilgenfeld, a long-time correspondent and debater with Baur of the issues raised by the Tübingen School, wrote: "One can apply to him the Scriptural word in its fullest sense, that he rests from his labors and his works follow him. When his mortal body—which I have never directly seen—is lowered into the grave, there will still remain an immortal part of him active in the world."[19]

Noting that there is no reference to the resurrection in the letter, I will in the next section seek to determine more fully what his labors were and precisely how "his works follow him."

BAUR'S HISTORIOGRAPHY: "THE PURELY HISTORICAL PRINCIPLE"

In the latter part of his life Baur wrote: "My basic principle is, in short, the *purely historical principle*. It is merely a case of interpreting the historical facts—as far as that is at all possible—in a purely objective manner. . . . I can designate my standpoint only as the purely historical standpoint and the task is thus to interpret Christianity, *especially in its origins*, as a historical event and to understand it as such."[20] Now, Baur knew as well as any one that there is no purely objective standpoint from which one could do historiography, religious or otherwise: "There are as many different views of history as there are different theological vantage points; . . . there can be no comprehensive work in church history whose view of history does not wholly manifest the theological vantage point of its author."[21] Earlier (1847) he had said history is "the eternally clear mirror in which history perceives itself, views its own image, in order to be what it is in itself also for itself, for its own consciousness, and to know itself as the moving power of historical becoming."[22] The question of course is whether or not historical process itself is a clear mirror that yields knowledge of God and also whether or not Baur's historical method was a clear mirror rather than a prism through which he questionably refracted all of New Testament history and the ensuing history of the church. As early as 1824 in *Symbolik* he had indicated that, for him, history must not be just an accumulation of events or phenomena, a consecution of moments that had no origin, point or goal: he declared that "without philosophy, history remains eternally dead and dumb."[23] For a long while, this was considered to show his "Hegelianism;" actually, it shows only that Baur longed for and searched for a principle by which history—"Tomorrow, and tomorrow, and tomorrow. . . . And all our yesterdays" (*MacBeth*, 5.5. 19–22)—might be shown to have purpose. He eventually became convinced that history had point and focus; it was not naked empirical fact, but rather was penetrated and animated and sustained by what Hegel called the "Idea" or *Geist*. It is especially significant that Baur turned to Hegel as early as 1833 for an understanding of philosophy; indeed, it is not only significant, but regrettable; for this Hegelian influence in his later mature New Testament studies caused him to ignore the God of Abraham, Isaac, and Jacob, the God of Incarnation and Resurrection, the personal God of special revelation and general providence and promise which is clearly the biblical concept of God.

From Hegel he learned "that the philosophy of history means nothing but the *thoughtful consideration of it*."[24] The only thought which philosophy brings with it to the contemplation of history, is the simple conception of *reason*; . . . the history of the world therefore, presents us with a rational process. . . . On the one hand, reason is the *substance* of the universe; *viz*, that by which and in which all reality has its being and subsistence. On the other hand, it is the infinite *energy* of the universe."[25] Further, "That this 'idea' or 'reason' is the *true, the eternal, the absolutely powerful* essence; that it reveals itself in the world, and that in that world nothing else is revealed but his and its honour and glory—is the thesis which, as we have said, has been proved in philosophy, and is here regarded as demonstrated."[26] This reason is "that spirit whose nature is always one and the same, but which unfolds this its one nature in the phenomena of the world's existence."[27] Indeed, for Hegel (and *a fortiori*, for Baur) the question of history is the question of knowing God: "But in noticing the recognition of the plan of Divine Providence generally, I have implicitly touched upon a prominent question of the day; *viz*., that of the possibility of knowing God."[28]

Hegel further refers to "our belief that reason governs the world, and has consequently governed its history;"[29] while at the same time he agrees that "the history of the world is not the theatre of happiness."[30] Nor is history in Hegel's understanding of it the means by which the living God of Christianity reveals Himself.

Baur accepts this Hegelian understanding of history and thinks that he has found in it an interpretive principle of philosophy of history; otherwise, he says: "Even if we take the best and most accepted works on the history of Christianity, and examine them with a view to seeing how far they succeed in combining the historical materials which are of so heterogeneous a nature, and have to be collected from such different quarters, to the unity of a whole—how vague and dim do they appear in many respects."[31] Now, given all this, it is important to determine *when* Baur subscribed to Hegelianism, and *what* that meant for his historical method, especially if we would understand the motivating principle of his New Testament studies. In other words, what did Baur know of Hegel, and when did he know it?

Karl Barth forthrightly states: "Baur, too, was not of Hegelian derivation, but had his theological concerns, which he attempted to bring to bear, long before he made the acquaintance of Hegel."[32] And yet, Baur goes on to say that Baur "discovered in Hegelian philosophy the instrument that seemed incomparably apt for his purpose."[33] Rudolph Bultmann contends that Baur "regards backward-directed reflection upon history as the way by which the mind of man comes to itself. . . . according to Hegel's scheme of thesis, antithesis, and synthesis: out of the struggle of the torah-free gospel of Paul (thesis) with the torah-bound Jewish Christianity (antithesis) there finally emerged in a series of compromises the ancient Catholic church (synthesis)."[34] And the learned and influential twentieth-century Catholic theological scholar, Hans Küng, asserts that Baur "showed himself to be a direct disciple of Hegel by applying the master's idea of development to the history of dogma in general and to Christology in particular. . . . Baur applied the idea of development to the gospels, adhering to Hegel's scheme to ascertain the existence of three basic historical tendencies: (a) Petrine Jewish Christianity (Matthew); (b) Pauline Gentile Christianity (Luke); and (c) the early Catholic church."[35]

However, Klaus Penzel asserts "Certainly, Baur's theology and historiography do not stand or fall with his Hegelianism, which, anyway, affected only his understanding of the relationship between God and history."[36] Horton Harris emphatically states: "Not the Hegelian philosophy, but the acceptance or rejection of a transcendent personal God determined Baur's dogmatic and historical investigations."[37] O. Pfleiderer, a formidable nineteenth-century theologian, judged that:

> When Baur thought with Hegel that the development of the religious spirit was identical with the dialectical development of logical categories, and that the rise and growth of dogmas in the Christian church can be adequately rendered in the formulae of Hegelian terminology, this was a decided error by which the value of his learned works was sensibly diminished. . . . We may in fact affirm that Baur's slavery to the formulae of the Hegelian philosophy was a weak point in his treatment of the history of dogma, which only served to obscure the truth and profundity of his conception of history as a true development of the

human mind, and to give the opponents of his principles many apparent advantages.[38]

And Johannes Munck has even more extremely concluded:

The view that the author of Acts was a Gentile Christian is one of the many opinions held by the Tübingen School, founded by F. C. Baur in the first half of the nineteenth century, from which scholars have not yet emancipated themselves. This school made a sharp distinction between Jewish and Gentile Christianity in the churches founded by Paul, and was therefore obliged to maintain that a man showing sympathy for the mission among the Gentiles belonged to Gentile Christianity. . . . Such sympathy was common in the primitive church even among the Jewish Christians in Palestine; accordingly this argument must be considered of no value. . . . All these assumptions had been taken over from nineteenth century research without thorough examination, and they are not correct.[39]

It is possible to note three periods in Baur's historical studies: first, that from 1831 to the early 1840s, which is given primarily to the study of primitive or New Testament Christianity; and second, the ensuing study (1846–53) of biblical literature, history of dogma and later developments of the church, in which Hegelian categories and foundations prevail and then recede. There is clear overlapping, for as early as his book on Christian gnosis (1835) Baur uses Hegelian categories:

For faith the appearance of the God-man, the incarnation, God's birth in the flesh may certainly be a historical fact. From the standpoint of speculative thinking, however, the incarnation of God is no unique historical fact which happened once for all time, but an eternal determining of the nature of God by virtue of which God enters time and becomes man (becomes incarnate in each individual person) only in so far as he is man from eternity. The finitude and painful humiliation to which Christ as the God-man subjected himself, is borne at every moment by God as man. The finished act of reconciliation is no event in time, but God reconciles himself with himself eternally, and the resurrection and exaltation of Christ are nothing other than the eternal return of the Spirit to itself and to its truth. Christ as man, as God-man, is man in his universality, not one particular individual, but the universal individual.[40]

Baur's great doctrinal treatments of Atonement (1838) and Incarnation and Trinity (1841) also are motivated by Hegelian dialectic.

Such overt Hegelianism yields finally to a return to enlightenment categories; and Jesus becomes neither the orthodox incarnation of God with two natures, nor the momentary Hegelian embodiment of the eternal Idea that divinity and humanity are intimately related through the entire historical process by which Absolute Spirit comes to consciousness; rather, Jesus is the Kantian moralist whose high ideals and moral example reflect the divine, inspiring commitment and trust from his disciples. In this third period of this development, Bauer develops the idea that the history of dogma is the history of the inner life of the church, expressed in dogma, which are not dead doctrines but lively expressions in each era of the prevailing, believing faith of the Christian church.

In his first period, beginning in 1831, when Baur discovered alleged Petrine and Pauline parties at Corinth, and then in Galatians, and then reconciled in Acts, he formulated his monolithic singular principle of interpreting and dating New Testament Gospels and Epistles, *before* he read Hegel. This rigorous principle, by which he determined that a Petrine party of narrow Jewish legalism and circumcision constantly opposed and worked to destroy Paul's school of freedom from the law and of the universal destiny of the gospel to the Gentiles, became the sieve through which he sifted all New Testament documents. Later, in 1845, he still claimed: "It can not be doubted that the Jewish Christians saw in the Apostle Paul only the opponent and enemy of the law and of Jewish Christianity as it depended on the continuance of the law, and that they sought to oppose him by all the means at their disposal and in all the Gentile-Christian Churches."[41]

Any document that did not mention or deal with this conflict was to be dated late, from the middle of the second century on, as a "catholicizing" work (e.g., the Gospel of John). This Petrine-Pauline-Catholic dialectic was evidently not specifically Hegelian or derived from him, since Baur began developing his principle in 1831 with his long article on 1 Corinthians 1:12, and there is no evidence that he actually read Hegel until 1833 at the earliest. Yet, it is practically impossible to imagine that, since university life at that time was permeated by Hegelianism, Baur was ignorant of Hegel's dialectic of history. Thus, Hegel's dialectical system of thesis, antithesis, and synthesis and his over-arching Idealism were instruments into which Baur's threefold principle easily fit. And thus Baur was naturally able, without pausing or faltering, to move into his great period of church history and history of dogma from 1845–60 without missing a stride methodologically.

Indeed, for Baur, New Testament ideas and primitive doctrines and beliefs are not initial or original truths or convictions on which depends the veracity of further dogmatic developments; rather, primitive Christian teachings themselves are involved in the historical development of church dogma[42] . Therefore, when Baur determines that the Petrine-Pauline-Catholic dynamic is the measure of all dating and tendency and interpretation of all New Testament documents, he is perhaps submitting New Testament authenticity to a prior standard or criterion of truth. No one doubts that there was a conflict between Peter and Paul over apostolic authority and legitimacy; but were they as extreme and persistent as Baur insists; that is, does he read this into the texts as a procrustean principle or out of the texts in faithful exegesis? What was the criterion of truth by which Hegel interpreted primitive Christianity?

Before I turn to a definition and exposition of and answer to that question, permit me to say that the limits of this essay preclude a detailed description and critique of Baur's conclusions about the historical development of Christian life and faith of the apostolic and sub-apostolic period. J. Munck gives a strong and accurate judgment against Baur and the Tübingen school: "The picture of Paul therefore becomes a picture of a lonely apostle, giving all his strength in the unparalleled effort of calling into life church after church of newly converted Gentiles, but losing those churches at once to the Judaizing emissaries from Jerusalem who follow hard on his heels. . . . Instead of a richly-faceted historical reality, there has been found a colourless homogeneity, caused by making inferences everywhere from a one-sided interpretation of early Christianity."[43]

Horton Harris clearly describes how Baur's arbitrary selection of the Petrine-Pauline controversy prevented him from seeing the variety and complexity and richness of New Testament writings and churches.[44] There were certainly other problems and conflicts in the early church: use and abuse of gifts of the Spirit; eschatological interpretation, anticipation and delay; justification by faith or life in the Spirit; but Baur's insistence that law (Peter) and freedom (Paul) in conflict determined the whole movement of the church into the catholicizing and universalizing of John's Gospel became a construction that led him into such fantastical interpretations that Simon Magus in the Clementine *Homilies* (which Baur dated *circa* A.D. 170) is actually Paul in disguise, pursued by Peter who opposes his teachings, and that this indicates that the Petrine-Pauline controversy continued through the second century. However, earlier in A.D. 96 Clement of Rome, in his letter to Corinth, mentions both Peter and Paul in the same paragraph, with no indication at all of any conflict, previous or present: "Let us set before our eyes the illustrious apostles. Peter, through unrighteous envy, endured not one or two, but numerous labors; and when he had at length suffered martyrdom, departed to the place of glory due to him. Owing to envy, Paul also obtained the reward of patient endurance, after being seven times thrown into captivity, compelled to flee, and stoned."[45] And Harris also points out that Baur's insistence that Ignatius's letters were inauthentic was untrue. Baur's view was necessitated by the fact that Ignatius nowhere in his letters mentions the Petrine-Pauline hostility; in fact, he too mentions both apostles together with no debate or antagonism even hinted: "I do not as Peter and Paul issue commandments unto you."[46] "For I pray that, being found worthy of God, I may be found at their feet in the kingdom, as at the feet of Abraham, Isaac, and Jacob; as of Joseph and Isaiah, and the rest of the prophets; as of Peter and Paul, and the rest of the apostles, that were married men."[47]

J. B. Lightfoot and T. Zahn have demonstrated the genuineness of the Ignatian letters, and thus we have no evidence of Petrine-Pauline conflict in letters at the turn of the first century. Therefore, Baur's argument that such a conflict endured until late in the second century is greatly weakened. Suffice it to say, Baur permitted his assumption about Peter and Paul in 1 Corinthians 1:12, which he used throughout his ensuing criticism of the New Testament as the fulcrum on which he turned his biblical research, to determine the tenor of church life and to cause him to date letters later than necessary.

Baur devoted the last part of his life to historical studies of the development of the life and dogma of the Christian church. In these works he pioneered study of dogma as it develops historically. He required systematic theologians to see that a historical sense is necessary to understand Christian belief; no longer may they use books of the Bible as proof texts for doctrine. Fearing that Schleiermacher's concept of religion as *Gefuhl* or inner consciousness of God would subjectivize Christian knowledge of God; unable to confess or believe in the supernatural God of the church; and unimpressed by the rationalist attempt to explain away how miracles "actually" happened or to redefine or reject what John 1 or Philippians 2:5–11 or Nicaea or Chalcedon "really" say about the Trinity or Christology, Baur developed a radically historical approach to Christian dogma, motivated by Hegel's Spirit, or Idea.

As early as 1824, as we have noted above, he had declared that history without philosophy is dumb and dead; and he spent the rest of his life— daily, in the winter, he wrote with frozen ink and without a fire in the hearth—attempting to discover what he in 1833 began to detect in Hegel; the dynamic, or principle, or Idea or ground or Spirit that permeated history, that drove its movement, that caused events, that accounted for history appearing at all. In *Paul*, vol. 1 (1845) he wrote, "The statement that has the greatest claim to historical truth is that which appears most unprejudiced and nowhere betrays a desire to subordinate its historical material to any special subjective aim."[48] Two years later, in his *Introduction to*

Lectures on the History of Christian Dogma (1847; but not edited and published until 1865–67, by his son), he contended, "Since Christianity belongs to the succession of historical phenomena, what it is in its essence can be determined only in a historical fashion."[49] The historian uses the proper method: "A true historical method can only be one that holds to the object itself, pursues the movement of the subject matter itself, and transposes itself into it wholly, excluding everything merely subjective and arbitrary, everything that is not based on the subject matter itself but belongs only to the mode of representation of the knowing subject."[50]

It must be "a method that should disclose events in their continuity, their movement and development. That movement, however, should not be merely fabricated or imagined, but should be immanent in the subject matter itself."[51]

By *church history*, Baur means something distinct from the mere chronicle of papal successors, or the annals of councils, or the lists of martyrs and heretics. To understand church history one must know more than these phenomena which are mere data if one does not penetrate into and discover the dynamic or power which motivated the procession of their occurrence, for "everything external has its basis in the internal life from which it proceeds."[52] And therefore, "The history of dogma is related to church history, accordingly, as a part of the whole, and here the significance of church history in contrast to it can readily be seen."[53] Dogma, then, is not some abstraction or concept to prove which one goes to the Bible or councils or theologians; "The history of dogma, therefore, is that discipline which enables us to see into the inner concept of church life and which acquaints us with the course of the spiritual movement to which the external phenomena are attributable as their ultimate basis."[54] Thus, dogmatics is "the system of dogmas that determine the content of Christian faith, ensuing as the result of the entire preceding historical development of dogma."[55] It follows that "dogmatics has the . . . interest of bringing what is relevant from the constant flux of history to a stable shore, there to anchor it against the constantly changing element."[56] And thus, "The inescapable fate of dogmatics is that it continually reverts to the history of dogma,"[57] which is "properly a part of church history."[58]

Methodology for Baur is metaphysical as well as mundane, for method has the important task "of establishing in the nature of Spirit itself the movement of dogma, the universal moving principle through which dogma becomes a history of dogma."[59] Baur's definition of dogma is: "Since the concept in itself, as a vital and moving thing, is only Spirit engaged in the activity of thinking, then the concept of Christian dogma, considered in regard to its content, can be known only from the nature of Spirit."[60]

And so "the entire history of dogma is a continual procession of Spirit in never-ending conflict with itself, never able to become truly one with itself; it is a constant binding and loosening, a never-resting work in which Spirit, like Penelope, continually unravels its own web, only to begin anew."[61] And since this language about Spirit and history and dogma is implicitly, if not decidedly Hegelian, it is not surprising that Baur notes a threefold movement in the development of dogma: "there are three major blocks into which the whole body of the history of dogma is to be divided, in accord with the character of the object: the dogma of the ancient church, of the Middle Ages, and of the recent era, beginning with the Reformation."[62]

In this historical process and the examination and interpretation thereof, the task of the historian of dogma is "to reach the inner concept of the subject matter itself, the inner moving principle which can only be thinking Spirit as it struggles, in its relation to dogma, toward a consciousness of dogma, as well as toward self-consciousness."[63] And since "history is found only where something happens and changes. . . . Thus the history of dogma is the history of heretics."[64] The history of the church, then, is philosophically the history of dogmatic development, dogma being the expression of the internal life of the church as it moves through history; and as such, it assumes the existence of the Absolute Spirit, which comes to consciousness through history. "That an absolute Spirit exists, however, and therefore also a consciousness of the Absolute, is the fundamental presupposition of speculative thinking. The Absolute itself must also be the knowledge of the Absolute, for it would not be the Absolute were it not the Absolute for subjective self-consciousness as well. . . the subject can be conscious of the Absolute only because it is essential to the Absolute itself to give this consciousness."[65]

How does this Absolute give itself to the subjective consciousness of the historian—directly, or only through the study of history? This is an important question, for Baur saw the historian as the expression of the search for the Absolute: "whereas on the one hand historical research must immerse itself in the mass of details, . . . on the other hand it must also rise again to the universal, to those Ideas that must be the guiding points of view and illuminating stars on the long journey through the centuries."[66]

Therefore, history becomes interpretive historiography, not to diminish or ignore or manipulate fact, but so that knowledge might emerge: "History is both what happened objectively and the subjective knowledge of what has happened. . . . Historical knowledge first emerges when the event becomes important enough not merely to be known for the moment but also to be transmitted to the enduring knowledge of posterity."[67] The important questions are "the means by which the whole series of phenomena that make up the continuity of causes are joined together in unity; or how the particular is subordinated to the universal; or which Idea serves as the dynamic principle of the whole."[68] Baur's answer is: "Just as the universal differs from the particular not merely quantitatively but qualitatively as well, so also church history can arrive at the universal inherent in its concept not by mere abstraction from the particular but only from the Idea of the church itself, in that as an Idea it must contain in itself the principle of a vital development proceeding from the Idea."[69] Given this, "In proportion as the historian must, on the one hand, become absorbed as deeply as possible in the particular, individual and concrete aspects of historical phenomena, in order to attain the complete reality of historical life, so on the other hand he must also raise himself to the heights of the universal Idea, in order to grasp the particular from the universal and to see in it only the particularity of the universal."[70] In this universal, "if the unity and union of God and man, which is the absolute content of Christianity, were to be perceived in the person of Christ, this would occur only under the assumption that his humanity remained in its full integrity and was regarded as the essential, substantial foundation of what he is as a whole."[71]

It is here that we can observe Hegel's influence on Baur Christologically; for, if primitive Christianity is part of dogmatic history and *Geist* comes to consciousness through the historical process, then Jesus Christ, whoever He is—rabbi, zealot, idealist, wonderworker, incarnate Word, adopted Son, Messiah—he cannot be the absolute final revelation of the supernatural transcendent God, for *Geist* must move on to fuller consciousness through further historical development. Absolute Spirit must continue to posit the world over against itself; to encounter that world and speak to it so that it will speak back; and finally to come to consciousness *for that moment*. But Spirit must negate its negation, its positing something alien to it, and come to itself by realizing itself at that time; but it then must continue to move on. Even though, "When we consider the way in which Christianity grew up, it is plain that it could have had no place nor significance in history but for the person of its Founder,"[72] nonetheless, "The question as to the nature and the reality of the resurrection lies outside the sphere of historical inquiry. History must be content with the single fact, that in the faith of the disciples the resurrection of Jesus came to be regarded as a solid and unquestionable fact. . . . What history requires as the necessary antecedent of all that is to follow, is not so much the fact of the resurrection of Jesus, as the belief that it was a fact. The view we take of the resurrection is of minor importance for the history."[73]

how they came to believe in the "resurrection"

Here Baur's historical method founders. He substitutes imagination and psychologism for historical textual research. Concerning the early church of the disciples and the apostles, he declares:

> Once they had convinced themselves from the Old Testament that Christ was foreordained to suffer and die, then in the necessity of his death was also contained the inner necessity of the resurrection. If one can now imagine how this inner necessity in its whole significance must have presented itself to the minds of the disciples, and if one also considers that the religious consciousness of this early period of Christianity was of an extremely ecstatic nature, who then could hold it to be psychologically impossible that the thoughts with which the disciples so busily occupied themselves in their minds were transformed into visions which they believed to be appearances of the Resurrected One? What thrust itself into the consciousness of the disciples in this way and caused them to believe in the Resurrected One was the certainty— which represented itself to them in the form of a given picture of the Person of Jesus—that the cause of truth as God's cause could not be defeated. One can therefore say that if Christ did not rise bodily, then he had to rise mentally in the faith of the disciples.[74]

Baur does not trouble to explain or to account for the astonishing (if not miraculous!) ease by which the disciples, without the historical resurrection, were transformed inwardly from fear and despair into belief—Petrine or Pauline! For all his concern for the "purely historical principle," for objectivity, for "the holy affair of truth," he has dehistoricized the concrete revelation of God in the Incarnation and Resurrection of His Son, Jesus Christ; he has substituted a Hegelian conception of Jesus as the one who was the strongest manifestation and illustration of the Idea that God and humanity are one. He says that for the primitive church, this perception was founded on their view that in Jesus there had come to consciousness a full expression of the Idea of the unity of God and humanity. Baur is not purely historical here at all; his historical research is animated by the view that there is no infinite transcendent God who acts freely and sovereignly in His world, and this is a *parti pris* argument; such a reductionism does not cross Lessing's big ditch; it falls into it, and treads water in the quicksand of a historiography that arbitrarily ignores the revelatory acts of the transcendent God of the Bible.

Wolfhart Pannenberg is far more open and historical, without being psychologistic and reductionistic, about these matters: "If the historian approaches his work with the conviction that 'the dead do not rise,' then it has already been decided that Jesus also has not risen (cf. 1 Cor. 15:16)."[75]

Pannenberg

The possibility of the historicity of Jesus' resurrection has been opposed on the grounds that the resurrection of a dead person even in the sense of the resurrection to imperishable life would be an event that violates the laws of nature. Therefore, resurrection as a historical event is impossible. Yet it appears from the perspective of the presuppositions of modern physics judgments must be made much more carefully. First, only a part of the laws of nature are ever known. Further, in a world that as a whole represents a singular, irreversible process, an individual event is never completely determined by natural laws. Conformity to law embraces only one aspect of what happens. From another perspective, everything that happens is contingent, and the validity of the laws of nature is itself contingent. Therefore, natural science expresses the general validity of the laws of nature but must at the same time declare its own inability to make definitive judgments about the possibility or impossibility of an individual event, regardless of how certainly it is able, at least in principle, to measure the probability of an event's occurrence. The judgment about whether an event, however unfamiliar, has happened or not is in the final analysis a matter for the historian and cannot be prejudged by the knowledge of natural science.[76]

If, as Pannenberg contends, it "is a matter for the historian," one would think that Baur, *qua* historian, would go about his work on the basis of the "purely historical principle." However, Baur will have practically none of this. For him, all of history is revelatory of the Divine. In his lectures on the history of dogma he states: "The historical process, in which Christianity comes to historical manifestation, is simply an element in the general process which is the life-process of God himself, in which the idea of God explicates itself in the distinction of its moments. . . . As triune, God is the Absolute Spirit mediating himself with himself in the process of thought. Historical Christianity is simply an element of the same course in which the process immanent to the nature of God explicates itself historically."[77]

Thus special revelation is demoted, if not totally ignored and destroyed, to being only another example of the divine realization of itself in all of history. Jesus is not the Incarnate Word, or the Resurrected Lord. He is an illustration of the permanent truth that the Absolute Spirit externalizes itself and comes to consciousness in all of history.

BAUR'S ENDURING CONTRIBUTION

Doubtless Baur thought that even with the demise of supernatural Christianity there was a nugget of enduring truth which, once discovered, could sustain the church. Jettisoning traditional belief in the transcendent God of the Hebrews and the Christians and substituting Hegel's Idea as the principle of historical events and phenomena, then accepting the moral idealistic Jesus in the latter part of his life, Baur conducted what he called "the holy affair of truth;" given the acuteness of his mind, the diligence of his research, and—in its own way—his Christian faith, it is remarkable and disappointing that he eviscerated the Christian faith of its fundamental truth claims about special revelation and history. Nonetheless, he made positive contributions to historical and theological studies, even if many of his findings no longer are accepted and his rejection of the transcendent God of historic Christianity will never gain the church's benediction.

As a pioneer in historical studies, Baur showed conclusively that it is necessary to study theology historically (diachronically) as well as systematically (synchronically). He showed us that the New Testament texts themselves—not just the Epistles, but the Gospels and Acts, also—were *Tendenz* works, not purely historical. (Would that he had seen this about his own historical approach!) Each document has a tendency, a point of view, a theology, which determines the author's presentation of the gospel. He required that all Christian theology and dogma—including Scripture—be studied critically and rationally. This led to his view that the Bible is more human than divine and that the views therein were not dogmatically authoritative.

Baur also showed the complexity of the relationship between Jesus and Paul; he raised the question of how Paul's alleged harsh attitude toward the law could follow morally and theologically from Jesus' acknowledgment and "fulfillment" of it, and how the historical itinerant moral teacher and wonderworker could be transformed into the Christ of Paul's faith (and ours); for while it is true that Paul refers to the historical Jesus, he does not do so as much as one might expect.

Baur insightfully saw the difference between John and the synoptics; yet he wrongly dated Matthew as the first gospel; he dates many of Paul's letters too late; he wrongly restricted Paul's genuine epistles to Romans, Galatians, and 1 and 2 Corinthians; and his whole perception of the Petrine-Pauline controversy was too extreme in substance and too extended chronologically.

For Baur, history and dogma were alive; but in his search for the vital principle which moved them, Hegelianism became (until around 1850) a procrustean bed for his theological development and his historical research. Thus, for Baur, as for Hegel, God becomes the Absolute Spirit that is externalized in the historical process as it comes to consciousness in and through that process, which really leads to a-theism (God's aseity and transcendence become immersed pantheistically in the world); or else the

Absolute Spirit swallows the world (its past, present, and future) into its metaphysic maw, such that history or the universe ceases to exist discernibly and meaningfully over against the Absolute, which means a-cosmism. The attempt to interpret Baur and Hegel panentheistically does not solve this problem. That is to say, Baur's Hegelianism led to the view that either there is no God but only the universe with which it (Spirit) is identified, or there is no cosmos or history, but only the Idea. His later return to the Kantian ethical Jesus preserved the historical human Jesus as an impressive figure of moral vision and discernment, but reduced Jesus to something other than what the kerygma proclaims about Him.

In conclusion, Baur's use of Hegelian dialectic, his misunderstanding of the Petrine-Pauline conflict, his later reductionistic acceptance of the ethical Jesus, and his "purely" historical principle (which) meant not objectivity, but antisupernaturalism) that shut him off from the God of Abraham, Isaac, and Jacob, became a "holy affair of truth" in intention, but not in achievement, however capacious, brilliant, serious, provocative, and sincere his work was. We remain grateful to a man who, finally, wished to be known only as "Theologe," however cloudy the new dawn that his work precipitated turned out to be; he showed that theology must be done historically, and that the documents of the New Testament are not only historical, but theological. For this we remain in his debt; and, indeed, we are thankful.

BIBLIOGRAPHY

BIBLIOGRAPHIC SOURCES

There are three main bibliographical sources for Baur's *corpus*. They are:

Harris, Horton. *The Tübingen School: A Historical and Theological Investigation*, 263–84. Grand Rapids: Baker Book House, 1990.

Hodgson, Peter C. *The Formation of Historical Theology: A Study of Ferdinand Christian Baur*, 285–94. New York: Harper & Row, 1966.

Smart, Ninian, *et. al.*, eds. *Nineteenth Century Religious Thought in the West*, 287–89. (Cambridge: Cambridge University Press, 1985).

PRIMARY SOURCES

Following is a selective chronological list of Baur's works for those who read German:

Symbolik und Mythologie, oder die Naturreligion des Alterthums. 2 vols. in 3 parts. Stuttgart, 1824–25.

"Die Christuspartei in der korinthischen Gemeinde, der Gegensatz des petrinischen und paulinischen Christenthums in der ültesten Kirche, der Apostel Petrus in Rom." TZTh, V:4 (1831): 61–206.

"Abgenüthigte Erklarung gegen einen Artikel der *Evangelischen Kirchenzeitung,* herausgegeben von D. E. W. Hengstenberg, Prof. der Theol. an der Universität zu Berlin. Mai 1836." TZT*h,* IX:3 (1836): 179–232.

"Das christliche des Platonismus oder Sokrates und Christus." TZT*h,* X:3 (1837): 1–154.

Die christliche Lehre von der Versohnung in ihrer geschichtlichen Entwicklung von der altesten Zeit bis auf die neueste. Tübingen, 1838.

Die christliche Lehre von der Dreieinigkeit und Menschwerdung Gottes in ihrer geschichtlichen Entwicklung. 3 vols. Tübingen, 1841–43.

Paulus, der Apostel Jesu Christi. Sein Leben und Wirken, seine Briefe und seine Lehre. Ein Beitrag zu einer kritischen Geschichte des Urchristenthums. 1st ed. Stuttgart, 1845. 2nd ed., edited by Eduard Zeller. 2 vols. Leipzig, 1866–67.

Paul the Apostle of Jesus Christ, His Life and Work, His Epistles and His Doctrine. A Contribution to a Critical History of Primitive Christianity. Translated from 2nd German ed. 2 vols. Vol. 1, London and Edinburgh 1873 (1st ed.), 1876 (2nd ed., revised by the Rev. Allan Menzies). Vol. 2, translated by the Rev. Allan Menzies, London and Edinburgh, 1875.

Kritische Untersuchungen über die kanonischen Evangelien, ihr Verhaltniss zu einander, ihren Charakter und Ursprung. Tübingen, 1847.

Lehrbuch der christlichen Dogmengeschichte, 1st ed. Stuttgart, 1847. 2nd ed. Tübingen, 1858. 3rd ed., identical with 2nd. Leipzig, 1867.

Die Epochen der kirchlichen Geschichtschreibung. Tübingen, 1852.

Geschichte der christlichen Kirche.

Vol. 1: *Das Christenthum und die christliche Kirche der drei ersten Jahrhunderte.* Tübingen, 1853 (1st ed.), 1860 (2nd ed.), 1863 (3rd ed., identical with 2nd, published under title *Kirchengeschichte der drei ersten Jahrhunderte*).

The Church History of the First Three Centuries. Translation from 3rd German edition, edited by the Rev. Allan Menzies. 2 vols. London and Edinburgh, 1878–79.

Vol. 2: *Die christliche Kirche vom Anfang des vierten bis zum Ende des sechsten Jahrhunderts in den Hauptmomenten ihrer Entwicklung.* Tübingen, 1859 (1st ed.), 1863 (2nd ed., identical with 1st).

Vol. 3: *Die christliche Kirche des Mittelalters in den Hauptmomenten ihrer Entwicklung,* edited by Ferdinand Friedrich Baur. 1st ed. Tübingen, 1861. 2nd ed. Leipzig, 1869.

Vol. 4: *Kirchengeschichte der neueren Zeit, von der Reformation bis zum Ende des achtzehnten Jahrhunderts,* edited by Ferdinand Friedrich Baur. Tübingen, 1863.

Vol. 5: *Kirchengeschichte des neunzehnten Jahrhunderts*, edited by Eduard Zeller. 1st ed. Tübingen, 1862. 2nd ed. Leipzig, 1877.

Die Tubinger Schule und ihre Stellung zur Gegenwart. 1st ed., Tübingen, 1859. 2nd ed. Tübingen, 1860.

Vorlesungen über neutestamentliche Theologie, edited by Ferdinand Friedrich Baur. Leipzig, 1864.

Vorlesungen über die christliche Dogmengeschichte, edited by Ferdinand Friedrich Baur.

Vol. 1, bk. 1: *Das Dogma der alten Kirche von der apostolischen Zeit bis zur Synode in Nicäa.* Leipzig, 1865.

Vol. 1, bk. 2 *Das Dogma der alten Kirche von der Synode in Nicäa bis zum Ende des sechsten Jahrhunderts.* Leipzig, 1866.

Vol. 2: *Das Dogma des Mittelalters.* Leipzig, 1866.

Vol. 3: *Das Dogma der neueren Zeit.* Leipzig, 1867.

Ausgewählte Werke in Einzelausgaben, edited Klaus Scholder. 5 vols. Stuttgart-Bad Cannstatt, 1963–.

SECONDARY SOURCES

Following is a list of secondary works about Baur and about the hermeneutical issues:

Barth, Karl. *Protestant Theology in the Nineteenth Century*, 499–507. Valley Forge: Judson Press, 1968.

Bruce, A. B. "Ferdinand Christian Baur and His Theory of the Origin of Christianity and of the New Testament Writings." In *Living Papers Concerning Christian Evidences, Doctrine, And Morals.* Vol. 7: 3–58. Cincinnati: Cranston & Stowe, 1886.

Bultmann, Rudolph. "Is Exegesis Without Presuppositions Possible?" In *Existence And Faith*, edited and translated by Schubert Ogden, 289–96. Cleveland: The World Publishing Co., 1960.

———. "The History of New Testament Theology as a Science." In *Theology of the New Testament.* Vol. 2 translated by Kendrick Grobel, 241–55. New York: Charles Scribner's Sons, 1955.

Case, S. J. *The Evolution Of Early Christianity.* Chicago: University of Chicago Press, 1914.

Craig, Clarence T. "Biblical Theology and the Rise of Historicism." *Journal of Biblical Literature* 62 (1943): 281–94.

Dilthey, W. "Ferdinand Christian Baur." *Gesammelte Schriften*, Vol. 4, 2nd ed., 403–32. Leipzig: B. C. Teubner, 1925.

Fitzer, J. *Moehler and Baur in Controversy, 1832–38: Romantic-Idealist Assessment of the Reformation and Counter-Reformation.* Tallahassee: American Academy of Religion, 1974.

Frei, Hans W. *The Eclipse Of Biblical Narrative: A Study in Eighteenth and Nineteenth Century Hermeneutics.* New Haven: Yale University Press, 1974.

Furnish, Victor. "The Jesus-Paul Debate: From Baur to Bultmann." *Bulletin of the John Rylands Library* 47 (1965): 342–81.

Geiger, Wolfgang. *Spekulation und Kritik: Die Geschichtstheologie Ferdinand Christian Baurs.* Munich, 1964.

Gerrish, B. A. *Tradition in the Modern World.* Chicago: University of Chicago Press, 1978.

Harris, Horton. *David Friedrich Strauss and His Theology.* Cambridge: Cambridge University Press, 1974.

———. *The Tübingen School: A Historical and Theological Investigation of the School Of F. C. Baur.* Grand Rapids: Baker Book House, 1990.

Harvey, Van A. *The Historian and the Believer: The Morality of Historical Knowledge and Christian Belief.* New York: Macmillan Co., 1966.

Hefner, Philip. "Baur Versus Ritschl on Early Christianity." *Church History* 31, 1962): 259–78.

Hegel, G. W. F. *The Philosophy of History.* Translated by T. M. Knox. Vol. 46 of Great Books of The Western World. Chicago: Encylopedia Britannica, 1952.

Hodgson, P. C., ed. and trans. *Ferdinand Christian Baur on the Writing of Church History.* New York: Oxford University Press, 1968. This volume contains translations of Baur's *The Epochs of Church Historiography* and *Introduction to Lectures on Christian Dogma.*

———. *The Formation of Historical Theology: A Study of Ferdinand Christian Baur.* New York: Harper & Row, 1966.

———. "The Rediscovery Of Ferdinand Christian Baur: A Review of the First Volumes of His *Ausgewahlte Werke.*" *Church History* 33 (1964): 206–14.

Jodock, D. *F. C. Baur and Albrecht Ritschl on Church History.* Ann Arbor: University of Michigan Microfilms, 1970.

Johnson, Sherman E. "The Emergence of the Christian Church in the Pre-Catholic Period." In *The Study of the Bible Today and Tomorrow,* edited by H. R. Willoughby, 345–65. Chicago: University of Chicago Press, 1947.

Kümmel, Werner G. *The New Testament: The History of the Investigation of Its Problems.* Translated by S. MacLean Gilmour and Howard C. Kee, 120–84. Nashville: Abingdon Press, 1972.

Küng, Hans. *The Incarnation of God: An Introduction to Hegel's Theological Thought as a Prolegomena to a Future Christology.* Translated by J. R. Stephens. New York: Cross-Road, 1987.

Lessing, G. E. *Lessing's Theological Writings.* Edited by Henry Chadwick. Stanford: Stanford University Press, 1957.

161

Liebing, Heinz. "Historical-Critical Theology. In Commemoration of the One Hundreth Anniversary of the Death of Ferdinand Christian Baur, December 2, 1960." In *Distinctive Protestant And Catholic Themes Reconsidered*, edited by Robert Funk, 55–69. New York: Harper & Row, 1967.

Luedemann, G. *Opposition to Paul in Jewish Christianity.* Minneapolis: Fortress Press, 1989.

MacKay, R. W. *The Tubingen School and Its Antecedents: A Review of the History and Present Condition Of Modern Theology.* London: Williams & Norgate, 1863.

Martyn, R. W. "Paul and His Jewish-Christian Interpreters." *Union Seminary Quarterly Review* 42 (1988): 1–15.

Morgan, R. "Ferdinand Christian Baur." In *Nineteenth Century Religious Thought in the West.* Volume 1. Edited by Ninian Smart, et al., 261–89. Cambridge: Cambridge University Press, 1985.

Morgan, R., with J. Buxton. *Biblical Interpretation.* Oxford: Oxford University Press, 1989.

Munck, J. *The Acts Of The Apostles.* Vol. 31 of *The Anchor Bible.* New York: Doubleday, 1967.

Neil, W. "The Criticism and Theological Use of the Bible, 1700–1950." In *The Cambridge History of the Bible.* Vol. 3. Edited by S. L. Greenslade, 238–93. Cambridge: Cambridge University Press, 1963.

Neill, Stephen, and Tom Wright. *The Interpretation of the New Testament 1861–1986,* 1–64. New York: Oxford University Press, 1988.

Pannenberg, Wolfhart. *Jesus—God and Man.* Philadelphia: Westminster Press, 1968.

Pattison, Mark. "Present State of Theology in Germany." In *Essays by the Late Mark Pattison.* Vol. 2. Edited by Henry Nettleship. Oxford: Clarendon Press, 1889.

Penzel, K. "Will the Real Ferdinand Christian Baur Please Stand Up?" *Journal Of Religion* XLVIII (1968): 310–23.

Pfleiderer, O. *The Development of Theology in Germany Since Kant and Its Progress in Great Britain Since 1825.* Translated by J.F. Smith, 224–32, 284–98. London: Swan Sonnen-Schein & Co., 1890.

Richardson, Alan. "The Rise of Modern Biblican Scholarship and Recent Discussion of the Authority of the Bible." In *The Cambridge History of the Bible.* Vol. 3. Edited by S. L. Greenslade, 294–338. Cambridge: Cambridge University Press.

Salvatorelli, Luigi. "From Locke to Reitzenstein: The Historical Investigation of the Origins of Christianity." *Harvard Theological Review* 22 (1929): 263–369.

Schweitzer, Albert. *Paul and His Interpreters.* New York: The Macmillan Co., 1951.

———. *The Quest of the Historical Jesus.* New York: The Macmillan Co., 1961.

Teselle, E. *Christ in Context.* Philadelphia: Fortress Press, 1976.

Troeltsch, Ernst. "Adolph von Harnack and Ferdinand Christian von Baur 1921." In *Harnack and Troeltsch Two Historical Theologians*, edited by Wilhelm Pauckk, 97–115. New York: Oxford University Press, 1968.

Welch, Claude. *Protestant Theology in the Nineteenth Century*. Vol. 1, 1972; vol. 2, 1985. New Haven: Yale University Press.

NOTES

1. Quoted in Peter Hodgson, *The Formation of Historical Theology: A Study of Ferdinand Christian Bauer* (New York: Harper & Row, 1966), 180. Italics mine. Science here, of course, does not mean natural science, but all of modern methods and learning which have produced the "science" of historical-critical theology.

2. Robert Morgan, "Ferdinand Christian Bauer," in *Nineteenth Century Religious Thought in The West*, vol. 1, Ninian Smart, *et al.*, eds. (Cambridge: The University Press, 1985), 261.

3. *Lessing's Theological Writings*, Henry Chadwick, ed. (Stanford: 1957), 53.

4. *Gesammelte Schriften*, 4 (Leipzig: B.G. Teubner, 1925): 431.

5. Quoted in W. Neil, "The Criticism and Theological Use of the Bible, 1700–1950," *The Cambridge History of the Bible*, vol. 3 (Cambridge: The University Press), 277.

6. Ibid., 279.

7. Ibid., 286.

8. Quoted in E. Ellis, foreword to Horton Harris, *The Tübingen School*, (Grand Rapids: Baker Book House, 1990), xv.

9. Ibid.

10. Ibid., xxvi.

11. "Ferdinand Christian Baur and His Theory of the Origin of Christianity and the New Testament Writings," in *Living Papers*, vol. 7, (Cincinnati: Hunt & Eaton), 33.

12. For the biographical sketch which follows, I rely on Hodgson, *Formation*, 8–36; and Harris, *Tübingen School*, 8–54.

13. Quoted in Harris, *Tübingen School*, 51.

14. Ibid., n. 64.

15. Horton Harris, *David Friedrich Strauss and His Theology* (Cambridge: The University Press, 1973).

16. F. C. Baur, *The Church History of the First Three Centuries*, (vol. I; Allan Menzies, transl. London: Williams and Norgate, 1878), 32.

17. Baur, *Church History*, 1:1.

18. Harris, *The Tübingen School*, 20.

19. Ibid., 53.

20. Ibid., 251.

21. F. C. Baur, *The Epochs of Church Historiography*, in *Ferdinand Christian Baur on the Writing of Church History*, Peter Hodgson, ed. and trans. (New York: Oxford University Press, 1968), 49.

22. Quoted in Peter Hodgson, "The Rediscovery of Ferdinand Christian Baur: A Review of the First Two Volumes of His *Ausgewahlte Werke*," *Church History* XXXIII (June 1954): 212.

23. Quoted in Hodgson, *The Reformation of Historical Theology* 15.

24. G. W. F. Hegel, *Philosophy of History*, vol. 46, T. M. Knox, transl.,Great Books of the Western World(Chicago: Encyclopedia Britanica, 1952), 156. Italics his.

25. Ibid., 157. Italics his.

26. Ibid. Italics his.

27. Ibid.

28. Ibid., 159.

29. Ibid., 164.

30. Ibid., 165.

31. Baur, *Church History*, 1:xi

32. Karl Barth, *Protestant Theology in the Nineteenth Century* (Valley Forge: Judson Press, 1973), 499.

33. Ibid.

34. Rudolph Bultmann, *Theology of The New Testament*, vol. 2, trans. Kendrick Grobel, (New York: Charles Scribner's Sons, 1955), 245.

35. Hans Küng, *The Incarnation Of God*, trans. J. R. Stephenson (New York: Crossroad, 1987), 475–76.

36. "Will the Real Ferdinand Christian Baur Please Stand Up?" *The Journal of Religion*, XLVIII (1968): 315.

37. Harris, *Tübingen School*, 252. Harris argues that Baur did *not* believe in a transcendent personal God.

38. O. Pfleiderer, *The Development of Theology in Germany Since Kant and Its Progress in Great Britain Since 1825*, trans. J. Frederick Smith (London: George Allan & Unwin, Ltd., 1909), 286.

39. *The Acts of the Apostles*, vol. 31 of *The Anchor Bible* (Garden City: Doubleday & Company, Inc., 1967), xxx, lxii.

40. F. C. Baur, *Die christliche Gnosis*, quoted in Harris, *Tübingen School*, 170.

41. F. C. Baur, *Paul the Apostle of Jesus Christ*, vol. 1, trans. Eduard Zeller, revised by A. Menzies (London: Williams and Norgate, 1867), 240.

42. Compare Barth, who asserts: "In the Bible history is to be understood as an answer, but in the history of the church, of dogma and of theology it is to be understood as a question . . . . The Bible is the criterion of all learning." *Protestant Theology*, 507.

43. Quoted in Stephen Neill and Tom Wright, *The Interpretation of the New Testament*, 2nd ed. (Oxford: Oxford University Press, 1988), 63.

44. Harris, *Tubingen School*, 181ff.

45. "The First Epistle of Clement," in *The Ante-Nicene Fathers, The Apostolic Fathers with Justin Martyr and Irenaeus*, the Rev. Alexander Roberts and James Donaldson, eds. (Grand Rapids: Wm. B. Eerdmans, n.d.), 6.

46. "Epistle Of Ignatius to the Romans," ibid., 75.

47. "Epistles of Ignatius to the Philadelphians," ibid., 81.

48. Baur, *Paul*, 5.

49. In Hodgson, *Formation*, 261.

50. Ibid., 283.

51. Ibid.

52. Ibid., 262.

53. Ibid., 261.

54. Ibid., 262.

55. Ibid.

56. Ibid., 263

57. Ibid., 265.

58. Ibid., 261.

59. Ibid., 283–84.

60. Ibid., 297.

61. Ibid., 300.

62. Ibid., 309.

63. Ibid., 305.

64. Ibid., 364.
65. Ibid., 364.
66. Baur, *Epochs*, 44.
67. Ibid., 46.
68. Ibid., 47.
69. Ibid., 256–57.
70. Ibid., 257.
71. Ibid., 252.
72. Baur, *Church History*, 1: 38.
73· Ibid., 42.
74. Quoted in Harris, *Tubingen School*, 178.
75. Wolfhart Pannenberg, *Jesus—God and Man* (Philadelphia: The Westminster Press, 1968), 97.
76. Ibid., 98.
77. Quoted in Hodgson, *Formation*, 146.

8

JEAN HENRI
MERLE D'AUBIGNÉ

JOHN RONEY

INTRODUCTION

Jean Henri Merle d'Aubigné[1] (1794–1872) was arguably one of the most popular church historians of the nineteenth century. Philip Schaff claims that Merle's histories "had a wider circulation, at least in the English translations, than any other book on church history."[2] *Histoire de la Réformation du sieziétme siécle* (5 vols., 1835–1853), his first work, became very popular with the English edition, *History of the Reformation of the Sixteenth Century* (5 vols., 1846–1853). These five volumes form the first series of a larger Reformation history. *Histoire de la Réformation en Europe au temps de Calvin* (8 vols., 1863–1878), continues as a second series; and in English, *History of the Reformation in Europe in the Time of Calvin* (8 vols., 1863–1878).[3] With Genevan heritage, he first attempted to write to the French-speaking audiences of Switzerland, France, and Belgium, but he soon found a much larger audience with the English-language versions— some original—as well as translations for the German lands, the Netherlands, and Scandinavia. He became the most important historian of the Reformation for nineteenth-century Evangelical Protestants.

167

Merle also published modern historical works: *The Protector: a vindication* (1847), published later in French (1848); and *Germany, England, and Scotland; or, Recollections of a Swiss Minister* (1848), also published later in French (1850).[4] In addition, he published eighty-five other works, including shorter historical writings, discourses, letters, articles, and sermon collections.

BIOGRAPHY

On 16 August 1794, Jean Henri was born to Susanne Marie Elisabeth (Barbezat) and Aime-Robert Merle d'Aubigné of Eaux Vives, Geneva.[5] At age 19, in 1813, Merle began his theological study in the Academie de Genève. The reading and study of the Holy Scriptures was rare, however, and the Academy practiced an "Enlightened Orthodoxy" with Socinian and Unitarian elements. In his four years of theological study, "not one hour was consecrated to the study of Holy Scriptures."[6] Instead of the Bible, he stated that the sources most quoted were Plato, Cicero, and Seneca. The students commonly called them Saint Plato, or Saint Seneca. Despite some "orthodox" pastors and parishioners, in general, religion in Geneva was no longer a model for Calvinistic orthodoxy. Between 1813 and 1820, an awakening of religion occurred in Geneva.[7] Inspired by a Europe-wide *Réveil* (revival), three alternative churches began.[8] At first Merle remained solidly within the established church.[9] Not until the visit of Robert Haldane, from November 1816 to June 1817, did Merle begin to support the Réveil. On 3 July 1817, at age 23, Merle was ordained in the established Church of Geneva (Reformed).

During autumn 1817, Merle traveled throughout the German lands. He attended the celebration of the tercentenary of Luther in Eisenach, where he was confronted for the first time with a powerful demonstration of the German Reformation of the sixteenth century. He was struck by the apparent joy at the remembrance of this great man, but he became disappointed when Luther was praised only for his rebellion against authority.[10] This experience raised serious questions about how to recover a better sense of the past.

With new resolve to search for a way to understand religion in history, Merle traveled to the University in Berlin to study with August Neander (1789–1850)[11] and Friedrich Schleiermacher (1768–1834).[12] Merle's real mentor was Neander, who founded a new school of "Mediatory Theology" (*Vermittlungstheologie*),[13] seeking a faith influenced by both pietism and orthodoxy on the one hand, with science, on the other.

Between 1818 and 1823, Merle pastored the French Reformed Church in Hamburg, then became court preacher to the Dutch King Willem I in

L'église du Musée in Brussels until 1831. In both churches he grew in theological maturity, as well as in establishing a revival of religion.[14] On 22 October 1829, Merle married Marianne Brélaz, daughter of a Portuguese family who had moved to Geneva. In June 1831, following the revolution begun in 1830, they left Brussels for Geneva to become part of the new *École de théologie* established by an orthodox group, the *Société évangélique*, in the Church of Geneva.[15] The *Société* opened the *École* to train pastors and evangelists within a more orthodox milieu, but these activities were seen by the Venerable Company (leadership) as those of a rival church, and in November 1831 the Company suspended the pastors Louis Gaussen, Antoine Galland, and Merle.

For more than fifty years, Merle worked as a teacher, pastor, statesman, and ecumenical leader. He made what he called "Evangelical catholicity" one of his principal goals. Two organizations demonstrated to him the new work of Evangelical catholicity: the *Société évangélique*, which developed societies in many countries, and the Evangelical Alliance, which from the beginning was a gathering of nationalities.[16]

Merle's family life was at times very happy, though he also knew tragedy. Four of Merle's children died at a very young age, and on 12 June 1855, his wife died after a long illness.[17] This left him alone for a time to raise three children.[18] After three years, he met Frances Charlotte Hardy (1826–1904), from Ireland, whom he married in Dublin on 14 August 1858. They were able to have another family because, although Merle was then 64, Frances was only 32. He and Frances had four children.[19] In November 1872, Merle passed away, apparently without distress.

HISTORY OF CHRISTIANITY: A NEW FIELD

Although Merle wanted to write a history of the Reformation in 1817, he did not really begin the venture until he became a teacher in 1831. Already in 1818 Merle claimed that he would begin collecting materials for his history of the Reformation.[20]

Nineteenth-century historians recognized that, despite the growth of scientific history in the eighteenth century, they wanted to study the past again with a new historical consciousness and reliable sources. History began to be seen as a discipline, and a historian became part of a profession. Leopold von Ranke (1795–1886) was the most well-known historian of this new field, and he believed that "modern history ought to be torn to pieces and entirely re-written from manuscript sources."[21] Ranke perfected the earlier historical work characteristic of Göttingen and Berlin with his new historical method known as Historicism. His goal for a historian combined science with art: this applied the scientific method to history and incorporated a unique "understanding" (*Ahnen*) of human experience with the "connected-ness" of historical events (*Zusammenhang*) and a literary narrative style.[22] Many historians writing between 1830 and 1860 were influenced by Romanticism, and historicism drew heavily on this new way of viewing knowledge.[23] From time to time, Merle commented on the work of Ranke in comparison with his own work; although the number of references to other historians remains thin, Ranke was one of the contemporary historians he most frequently used as a secondary source.[24]

We must bear in mind that Merle was trained as a historical theologian, and not according to the modern twentieth-century model of a historian. His official academic title was *"Docteur en théologie,"* an honorary degree which he received from the College of New Jersey (Princeton) in 1838, and from the University of Berlin in 1846. Unlike Ranke, he was a historian of Christianity with an orientation in theology, not social or political history.[25] Therefore, Merle's history is structured by theological discourse, and it is difficult to recognize change in his historical thinking after the time he began to teach (1832). Merle was specifically interested in the religious nature of history: "Men for whom I feel much esteem appear to attach greater importance to a literary or political history of the Reformation, than to an exposition grounded on its spiritual principles and its interior springs of action. I can well understand this way of viewing my subject, but I cannot participate in it. In my opinion, the very essence of the Reformation is its doctrines and its inward life."[26] Merle's method is not a totally new way of studying history, nor is he a founder of a school of historical study pioneering new methods. In fact, apart from his explicit acknowledgment of the influence of Neander, Merle is strangely silent about whose works he was reading and how he would review their work.[27] Rather, as a teacher and pastor, his histories were not meant to rival other historians' narrative interpretation.[28] His essential task was not to spend his time refuting contradictory opinions, rather it was to teach the "truth"—instruct.[29]

As Merle saw it, history as a discipline had developed with an examination that ignored the study of the supernatural and the role of providence in history. Historians influenced by the eighteenth-century Enlightenment had questioned the entire Christian understanding of history. Jacques Bénignes Bossuet (1627–1704), best known for his *Discours sur l'histoire universelle* (1700) and *L'Histoire des Variations des protestantes* (1688), in Merle's opinion, was "one of the most eminent Christian geniuses"[30] who had taken note of the direct hand of God in history.[31]

The distinction between an external and an internal focus of history was not previously unknown. Johann L. Mosheim (1694–1755) employed the term "external" history, meaning "all changes, vicissitudes, and events, that have diversified the external state and condition of this sacred community,"[32] and placed discipline and doctrine as internal study. Providence was conceived as a very general work of God in the world.[33] Likewise, Gottlieb J. Planck (1751–1833), Neander's mentor at the University of Göttingen, distinguished an internal study as an examination of key individuals, which enabled a more thorough understanding of the irrational forces. While Planck tried to explain the politics of the Reformation, he often avoided a deeper consideration of the inner religious motivations of the reformers.[34]

In contrast, Merle believed that the internal elements of his history contained two aspects which had to be addressed: The first was the "divine" aspect, which was the direct activity of God, and the second was the "soul" of history, which contained a record of how humans felt, thought, and responded to divine activity. Merle believed that he was enabled to probe the internal and sacred aspects because, as a Christian historian, he was able to discern the "spirit" and the work of God in history; his motto was "God in History."[35]

The second aspect of the internal focus he called the "soul" of history, that is to say, the moral and emotional elements in historical figures,[36] or human emotions and affections. In order to understand historical events and human actions, the historian must go beyond the "facts."[37] He clearly stated that "it is the historian's duty to combine these two great elements in the picture he presents to his readers."[38]

On a secondary level, Merle sometimes used the term "new field" to mean simply an interest in highlighting Genevan history. He never lost interest in the religious history of his native city, and he wanted to show its struggle as an independent Protestant city of the Reformation. Geneva was, certainly in Merle's view, one of the greatest Reformation cities. His was the first detailed study of the Reformation written in French that adequately covered the French-speaking world.[39]

Following Neander's method, Merle did not want to "banish science on account of the dangers to which it exposes us."[40] Science was at the very foundation of historical study for Merle, and without it no certainty of the events of the past was possible.[41] Merle condemned the method of Rationalism because criticism can easily turn into "hypercriticism, which not only denies what is false, but even what is true."[42] In order to correct this hypercritical tendency, a combination of faith and science producing a moral element, is necessary. If one or the other is left out, "religion easily produces fanatics, and science unbelievers."[43] The moral element uses science in the historical method, but it must discern "diverse elements" and be humble in its knowledge.[44]

Merle meant several things when he used the term "science." He meant, first of all, the gathering of evidence and careful attention to sources. He used the words *authentic* and *original*, and made reference to the original words and testimonies of historical figures.[45] Merle used other sixteenth-century observers to validate the events and words: John Foxe and Johannes Sleidan appear often, as well as other authors such as François Bonivard, Simon Fontaine, Antoine Froment, and Florimond de Rémond. He also used seventeenth-century authors such as Gilbert Burnet, Thomas Fuller, Johann Hottinger, Louis Maimbourg, Veit Ludwig von Seckendorf, Jacob Spon, and John Strype.

A second meaning of the term *science* is the critical collection of what he called "facts" or "details," because they show evidence that a certain event or action occurred. Merle told of his meeting with François Guizot in Paris, in which Guizot asked him to include as many "details" and descriptions as possible in his history of the Reformation.[46] Merle claimed that it is important to locate the most accurate texts, that is, the actual speeches or words of famous historical individuals. "History is a faithful description of past events . . ." Merle affirmed, and with the exact language, that the historian "is more certain of describing them just as they were."[47] The historian must continue to collect more evidence that could be found in state archives which only in the nineteenth century were becoming open to the public[48] or new published collections of previously unedited documents.[49]

Merle followed Neander's method of historical understanding by mentioning that "it is necessary to try to discover what the writer or orator wanted to say in the given historical circumstances. That alone enables us to understand the true sense of the words."[50] Through a sympathetic understanding of the actor's thoughts and feelings, and a knowledge of the context, Merle believed that he could discern the true sense of the words. Paralleling the rules for biblical interpretation, a truthful narrative, for Merle, must be "true in its facts and in the spirit by which it is animated."[51]

A third meaning of the term *science* is the desire for an impartial or unprejudiced study, one free from polemical interests.[52] His wish, however, was never fully realized because he was part of the anti-papal Evangelical movement of the nineteenth century, and this imbued him with their contemporary party politics.[53]

DIVINE AND HUMAN AGENCY IN HISTORY

One of the most important themes in Merle's writings is the intervention of divine providence in human affairs.[54] In order to grasp divine action, Merle made a fundamental distinction between primary causes and secondary causes. Divine providence, or God's will, is always the primary cause in the world, but no less important, human will and action are always the secondary causes. Merle's reference to secondary causes underlined his recognition of a multitude of factors in the events of history. Although Merle's goal was to show the work of God in the Reformation, the reformers, the people, and the political leaders were the major subjects of his histories.[55] Many factors interacted in history; "the part which Geneva played in the sixteenth century is not explained by the character of one man alone; but by many concurrent circumstances both moral and political."[56] Merle believed that the task of the historian was not to predict divine action, nor was it to attribute all cause to divine will alone. The historian had the duty to discern the primary cause as it was manifested through secondary causes.[57] The very fact that God's hand is invisible necessitates the historian's discernment of divine action through those things that are visible, namely, the multitude of secondary causes. Even though God's hand is invisible, Merle saw that human wisdom still possesses a "presentiment" of God's activity.[58] This presentiment allows the historian to begin to search for divine providence in the multitude of secondary causes.

In addition to the religious and theological issues that he confronted in history, he was interested in the political events that gave direction to the course of the Reformation. Merle's criticism of the students at the tercentenary of Luther in 1817 was not that they highlighted the political aspects of the Lutheran conflict, but that the students had reduced a complex situation to this single factor.[59] Merle did not want to see only theological motives behind the Reformation conflict; certainly political problems had to be resolved which were significant factors in history and provided the context.[60] One way he used to show a political movement was to personify "Liberty" as a causal agent: "Liberty was beginning to raise her head in one of the smallest but most ancient cities of the Empire and the Church."[61] Long before the French Revolution, liberty was a moral force that had been growing for a number of centuries, and it prepared society for a political and religious reform.[62]

Merle's fundamental belief was that a religious reform was tied to, or supported by, a political reform. With his own experience of the recent European revolutions, he went so far as to say that "never perhaps has a reformation been accomplished among men without some mixture of revolution."[63] While political reform often supported religious reform, Merle pointed to a precarious relation existing between the two. Motives for change were not always pure, and any reform has not only many causes but many means to achieve its goal. In order to probe beyond what might appear to be the manifest cause and effect,[64] Merle introduced what may be called "unintended consequences" to his concept of secondary causation. He pointed to certain actions or events that might have had the "opposite consequences to what its authors had hoped."[65]

When Merle explained God's presence, he used the phrase the "real presence of Jesus Christ," which was not limited to a eucharistic understanding, because he believed that Christ is present "in the Church, in history, in human hearts."[66] The plan of God is revealed at all times in the world: There is a natural order of things which God created, and there are times when God works by supernatural means. Many times without knowing it, the rulers of this world carry out the divine plan because God's overall plan will be fulfilled.[67]

Although Merle believed that God is always present in the world, and God's laws are fulfilled in the natural order, his concern was to show how God directly worked in the world. Not only will God's goals for the world be ultimately fulfilled, but He continually watches and regulates the changes and developments of human society. General or natural laws were not sufficient in themselves to bring society to a mature understanding of God.[68] More direct action by God was needed, but one which did not abrogate the natural order.

In common with Romanticism, Merle's conception of direct divine action followed the organic model. He employed the imagery of seeds to symbolize the growth of certain ideas, desires, or tendencies. One of Merle's dominant axioms is that God uses the smallest means to accomplish the greatest ends. God follows this law; this is demonstrated by the incarnation of Jesus Christ to His choice of the reformers in the sixteenth century.[69]

RELIGIOUS CONSCIENCE: THE POINT OF CONTACT

The conscience is the most internal aspect of the human mind where, according to Merle, God communicates His will and initiates His work in the world. Merle continually pointed out that the "conscience, which is the voice of God, is higher than all the voices of men,"[70] and that, as in the example of Calvin, "the thought that it was God's will that he should be there was constantly presenting itself to his conscience."[71] God speaks to the human conscience, and for this reason it can be considered a "religious conscience" because it is the organ which responds to divine initiative.[72] The conscience is that part of an individual's inner spiritual core that possesses the capacity for direct divine communication: "Religion penetrates into man by the depths of his conscience; thence it rises to the height of his knowledge, and finally pervades the activity of his whole life. The conscience of man had been seared not only by the sin which clings to our nature, but also by the indulgences and mortifications imposed by the church. It required to be vivified by faith in the atoning blood of Christ."[73]

Merle quoted Calvin to explain that "We have a consciousness of divinity graven so deeply on our minds, that we cannot erase it."[74] By God's design, conscience can call forth an "instinctive feeling," a receptive state, or a preparedness for divine reform.[75] The conscience has been so corrupted by sin, however, that it needs to be revived continually by divine impulse.[76] In the sixteenth century God used this "Christian conscience" to call for a reform in religion and society.[77] Merle summed up the work of the great reformers as the restoration or awakening of conscience.[78]

Where is this "awakened" human conscience? Merle usually connected the conscience with the human soul, or spirit. He wrote: "If the conscience of man was awakened and sanctified by Christianity, then and then only the world would stand. . . . The human soul discovered that this was what it wanted; and was touched, captivated, and finally renewed."[79] The seed has already been planted in the universal possession of conscience, and the heart and conscience are the instruments God uses to direct human action according to His Will.[80] The human conscience and heart were from the beginning created to work in conjunction with God.[81]

The study of conscience as a fundamentally religious category was a central feature of many early nineteenth-century thinkers who were influenced by Romanticism. Already in the eighteenth century, Jean-Jacques Rousseau had set the stage for a greater appreciation of the interior life of individuals. Rousseau turned to the soul, or that element distinctive from the body in a Platonic understanding,[82] which possessed the capacity for judgment of the good.[83] The conscience is able to recognize the good because it is a divine instinct that all people possess.[84] Merle's education was deeply influenced by Rousseau, and he appears to follow him when he pointed to the conscience as that vehicle of communication between the creator and creature; a knowledge of God is due to an imprint left in the human conscience.[85] Both Rousseau and Merle seem to reflect the legacy of the Genevan intellectual tradition; in the end, however, they responded in very different ways.[86] Rousseau believed that the conscience was located in the sentiment, and allowed human recognition of the presence of God in the world, but did not prove God's existence.[87] Humans perceive God, not because of a mental need, but because at the very foundation of being, the conscience, they are prompted by the inner voice of God.[88] Merle differed with Rousseau over the foundation of metaphysical knowledge: Rousseau added reason to the conscience in a way that Merle would have found excessive.[89] Merle, by contrast, restricted all metaphysical knowledge to revelation through Scripture. Merle's use of the word *conscience* (as with such other contemporary concepts as liberty, progress, and democracy) did not carry the same connotations, but served to bridge the gap between the focus of current thought and the restatement of older doctrines.[90]

Schleiermacher, like Rousseau, supported the idea that conscience was an innate quality of God which is at the foundation of human nature: "The general awareness of God constitutes what Schleiermacher called the 'original revelation;' it is distinct from the special or historical revelation in Christ but in Christian experience cannot be separated from it."[91] Merle disagreed with both Schleiermacher and Neander because he reflected the older orthodoxy, which affirmed the dual nature of Christ and traditional interpretation of Scripture.[92] Schleiermacher and Neander, like Rousseau, elevated the Christian conscience to a supreme role in religious knowledge. Merle disagreed with their conception that, in the final analysis, conscience confirmed Scripture. In Merle's conception, Scripture confirmed conscience. Merle pointed out his difference with Neander about the roles of divine and human agency in a discourse entitled *Quelle est la théologie propre à guérir les maux du temps actuel?* For Merle, God must always initiate and humans must follow;[93] therefore, divine revelation through Scripture must confirm human conscience. Merle's attention to the centrality of Scripture and his use of contemporary categories was similar to other Reformed orthodox thinkers, and we can see parallels with the Princeton School.[94]

Merle viewed the process by which God awakens the conscience as a theological mystery revealed in Scripture.[95] God initiates the process that awakens the conscience or heart and soul but does not transform the body, or human character.[96] It is necessary for the Holy Spirit to provide the first impulse in order for the conscience to be awakened. Merle used various images when speaking of the action of the Spirit "moving human souls," "communicating to human hearts," "infusing the sap of heavenly juices," or "speaking through human organs."[97] When Merle referred to the religious conscience, he stressed that he was rejecting all ideas that viewed human conscience as possessing the potential to lead this religious impulse in any direction whatever.[98] Merle insisted that people should avoid a reliance on sentiment alone to guide conscience; he also warned against reliance on reason alone. When divine light shines in the human spirit, it is not by reason that faith accepts the divine will, but by the conscience, which recognizes the divine origin.[99]

Merle used his theory of divine initiative and human conscience to stress the importance of maintaining a conscience that is responsible to

God alone. In no way should any human power attempt to force a religious decision in the human conscience. Throughout history, however, Merle saw that human powers have tried to dominate conscience and direct its attention away from the light of the gospel.[100] It is a "Christian duty" to resist all such human domination,[101] and nowhere does Merle find this constraint more prevalent than during the beginning of the sixteenth century. Although Merle recognized that the Roman Catholic Church possessed the core of true Christianity, the fundamental problem with the sixteenth-century church was that human conscience was bound by human power instead of divine power. In contrast, Merle proclaimed that "all Christian conscience is independent, in matters of faith, to all human power: it relies only on the Word of God, and does not submit to other control. No power is able to impose on them its yoke, neither tradition, nor pope, nor nobles, nor the state."[102] In the sixteenth century, universal human conscience began to recognize the need for freedom.[103] A "consciousness of justice, truth and liberty was awakening" in Europe that called for a new social order in which conscience could be free.[104] This initial consciousness of the need for freedom was at first indistinct,[105] but as the "divine light shown more and more clearly,"[106] individuals gradually began to understand the divine mysteries.

Merle strongly believed that divine providence was at the foundation of all activity in the world. In affirming the omnipotence of God, however, he did not want to advocate a deterministic structure. Rather, he pointed to the necessary role of human agency in the history of the world.[107] Merle believed that if God has chosen to be known to humans by His revelation, then it was necessary for God to operate in the world through an incarnation, that is, a union of the divine and human. The doctrine of incarnation was the foundation of Merle's understanding of how God works in history. Historians study human behavior and appearance, but upon closer scrutiny, human action is in harmony with invisible divine action in a mysterious relationship.[108] Merle drew an analogy between the divine and human mystery: Jesus Christ is in a mysterious relationship with the divine and likewise all humans who have become Christians affirm that Christ lives in them.[109]

THE SIXTEENTH-CENTURY REFORMATION

Merle's first series of books on the Reformation covers the earliest events leading up to the reform and the early work of Martin Luther. He began to publish these works in 1835, and he finished volume five by 1853. The first series showed how a unified movement of reform had occurred in the German lands, Switzerland, and France. Merle began his discussion of the Reformation by affirming the divine preparation for change.[110] This preparation pertained to a multitude of areas: "religious beliefs, political opinions, civilisation, letters, science, morals, and industry."[111] Due to his many obligations as father, teacher, pastor, and statesman, and with other historical works in progress, Merle did not continue his Reformation series again until 1863. He continued a chronological account of the Reformation in the German lands, Switzerland, and England in a way similar to the first series. By the fifth volume he managed to reach the experiences of Farel and Calvin in Geneva (1535–1536). Although Merle had collected materials and sketched out a thorough manuscript of volumes 6, 7, and 8, he died in 1872, leaving the final editing to his son-in-law Adolophe Duchemin, who published them in 1875, 1876, and 1878.

Merle saw the sixteenth century as a time when divine providence was present in full power. God had always sustained the world, but the sixteenth century was a special time when the intended growth of the seeds that God had planted "accelerated . . . so that no human power is able to resist its progress."[112] Merle chose to use the words "mighty hand" or the "hand of God"[113] or the "finger of God"[114] to show direct divine action. During a slow and steady time of preparation, God collected a body of people—ordinary individuals—whose commitment to His will became directly manifest through their actions. Merle referred to this body of people as a "spiritual church" that proclaimed "truth and life."[115] Because God's hand is invisible, however, many have not recognized it in historical events. Merle saw this as Rome's greatest problem: Roman Catholic leaders were so intent on preserving the visible church that they failed to recognize the invisible church that was being gathered from within the walls of the visible church.[116] Merle also saw that, in order to support religious reform, God enabled certain political leaders to create a proper environment.[117]

Merle cautioned that it is not an easy task to show direct divine action. The invisible God is at work in the world and His timing and purposes are often obscured because His ways are "profound and mysterious."[118] God worked in a direct way in the sixteenth century, and nothing could thwart His goal because "even the passions which God condemns, were directed by his almighty hand to the accomplishments of his designs."[119] Even when it appeared that the way was uncertain, the divine work through secondary means was always accomplished, "having no other power than the Word of God."[120] Because of his training as a theologian, and because of his own experience, which inclined him toward a sympathetic understanding for religious phenomena, Merle was confident that divine providence had been the primary cause of the Reformation. Because of his training as a historian and his study of human action and variation, he recognized that humans are responsible for the unique course of history, and therefore their role in secondary causation accounts for the variations in history.

In its origin, "Christianity" is absolute and perfect; because it is a "heaven-descended movement" of God in the world.[121] "Christianity" is the direct agency of God in the world, "operating its work of regeneration."[122] Merle could say with confidence that Christianity is the perfect and divine form of religion because he denied that any church, as only one manifestation of Christianity, could be a complete representation.[123] He could then suggest that Christianity must become manifest throughout the world, for it allowed all people in all cultures—though used in a nineteenth-century provincial sense—to respond in faith.[124] The influence of Christianity had to be carried "into every sphere of existence—into literature and science, into domestic and public life, into commerce, into the navy and army, and into politics."[125]

The power of Christianity is first manifest in the individual and then in the people. Merle used Augustine's conception of the church to distinguish these "people"—ordinary Christians from all levels of society—as the "invisible church."[126] The invisible church had as its head Jesus Christ, "whose grace operated silently but with the same efficacy on the banks of the Elbe, the Rhone, and the Guadalquivir."[127] Neither the Renaissance nor the Catholic Church had been able, in Merle's opinion, to revive society in the sixteenth century by building a spirit of unity, which must begin with individual commitment. Christianity, by contrast, had the power to transform lives and recreate sixteenth-century society; the power inherent in Christianity reformed morals and doctrine and freed the individual conscience.[128]

Merle distinguished between the papacy and the Roman Catholic Church.[129] This was necessary if he was to claim that Luther possessed the "ancient faith of the Catholic Church, of which he was then the representative."[130] The faith that was the core of Christianity—the invisible church—was manifested in various ways. Some individuals or groups were closer to its original meaning, and others were farther away: "It is an error to believe that Christianity did not exist before the Reformation, save under the roman-catholic form, and that it was not till then that a section of the church assumed the form of Protestantism. Among the doctors who flourished prior to the sixteenth century, a great number no doubt had a leaning towards the system which the Council of Trent put forth in 1562; but many also inclined towards the doctrines professed at Augsburg by the Protestants in 1530; and the majority perhaps oscillated between these two poles."[131] Even Protestantism, from its inception, produced an internal, or direct manifestation of Christianity, and an external, or an institutional reflection of the Protestant religion.[132]

When God acts in the world, He acts by human instruments who are responsible for their actions, for either they help or hinder divine will. Certain people, however, are specially chosen to act in specific ways. God chose certain people in the sixteenth century to influence and lead society in a particular direction.[133] Merle believed that God's presence is best represented by people who possess special and superior abilities: "Heroes who spring from society at appointed epochs . . . and around whom, as around a superior and mysterious power, nations and individuals unhesitatingly gather?"[134]

Merle further explained that the union of divine and human elements in history is such a fundamental principle of how God has chosen to act in the world that humans are not able to experience their own creative potential without divine infusion.[135] God gives humans the freedom to act according to the potential with which they were created,[136] and in this way divine initiative is a necessary part of true human freedom. Merle believed that prior to the Reformation: "Reflection, will, feelings, all the faculties of the human being, which, subjected to the Word and Spirit of God, should work and bear fruit freely, were deprived of their liberty, and constrained to expand in shapes that had been determined upon beforehand."[137] When God interacts with His creation, it is as if "two worlds meet face to face, in one light abounds, in the other darkness."[138] Because these two worlds are initially incompatible, a time of preparation and cleansing must take place before God can properly work through human agency.[139] In Merle's view, the preparation for both individuals and society is often hidden, and during the time of preparation divine will can be accepted or rejected. When God acts in special ways, however, the human mind is ready to receive divine power, to choose the way of divine will.[140]

The sixteenth-century reformers were heroes because they exemplified the Christian spirit which had properly responded to the divine initiative. The work of God, Christianity, became established through their own spiritual renewal and reform. Martin Luther started the renewal, and represented one way that individuals respond, the way of "great struggle." Zwingli, by contrast, did not experience these spiritual-psychological struggles; he glided "softly down the stream."[141] Luther's greatest contribution, Merle understood, was his oath of allegiance to Scripture alone. This had the effect of freeing other individuals to be more attentive to the Word of God.

John Calvin was Merle's greatest hero. He represented the ideal reformer. The image of Calvin (as well as of Luther) generally accepted by the nineteenth century did not appreciate his personal and spiritual struggles. Rather, Calvin was often depicted as a harsh leader of a Genevan theocracy; therefore, in Merle's opinion, "There is no character in history more misunderstood than he [Calvin]."[142] By contrast, Merle's image of Calvin was that of a man who deeply felt the presence of God. Calvin's greatest contribution, in addition to a fully developed Protestant theology, was the establishment of a Christian Commonwealth.[143] If Luther reformed the individual, Calvin reformed the church and society.

Merle's conception of the necessity of both divine and human agency is further defined by his disapproval of other ways of understanding this relationship. Merle criticized those who subsumed all human action under divine action. The "Spirituals" of the Radical Reformation were, in Merle's opinion, pantheistic because they said that "in place of our souls it is God who lives in us, and does in us all the actions pertaining to life."[144]

Merle contrasted these examples of an unbalanced view of the relationship between divine and human elements in history with his own view. He believed that he properly interpreted and understood Calvin, and he underlined the importance that Calvin placed on divine initiative and human responsibility: "But although he [Calvin] attributed the victory to God he himself must fight. This observation applies to his whole life. Of all men in the world Calvin is the one who most worked, wrote, acted, and prayed for the cause which he had embraced. The co-existence of the sovereignty of God and the freedom of man is assuredly a mystery; but Calvin never supposed that because God did all he personally had nothing to do. He points out clearly the two-fold action, that of God and that of man."[145] Although God initiates certain actions in order that His will be done in the world, Merle chose to speak about the entire process as a combination, or union, of divine and human.[146] Human responsibility for action in the process is so important that if humans deny divine initiative, the will of God is temporarily blocked. At stake is the existence and character of the church, so that "God alone gives life. But we must act with him . . . [for if] we abandon with indifference the church, if we do nothing ourselves, it will perish."[147]

Merle did not think that God had stopped His special work in the sixteenth century. A reform was going on in the church of the nineteenth century; he called it a "second reformation."[148] In contrast to Edward Gibbon's well-known thesis that Christianity had so weakened Rome that it fell, Merle underlined the strength that Christianity brought to society. Rather than a "Reformed aristocracy," Merle supported the establishment of a new "Christian democracy," which recognized liberty for the people, and freedom for the gospel.[149] In response to the cataclysmic events of the French Revolution, Merle reiterated that Christianity is necessary to liberty, and liberty is necessary to Christianity. Manifested in a powerful way in the sixteenth century, it continued the work of God in a constantly reforming church.

BIBLIOGRAPHY

PRIMARY SOURCES

History of the Reformation of the Sixteenth Century, 5 vols. in 1. Grand Rapids: Baker Books, 1976. French: *Histoire de la Réformation du sieziéme siécle,* 5 vols. Paris-Genève: Firmin-Didot, M. Ducloux, 1835–1853.

History of the Reformation in Europe in the Time of Calvin, 8 vols. (Posthumous vols. 6–8 were translated by William Cates) London: Longman, Green, Roberts, 1863–1878. French: *Histoire de la Réformation en Europe au temps de Calvin,* 8 vols. Paris: Michel Lévy frères, 1863–1878.

The Protector: A Vindication. Edinburgh: Oliver and Boyd, 1847.

French: *Le Protecteur, ou, La République d'Angeleterre aux jours de Cromwell.* Paris: Firmin Didot frères, 1848.

Germany, England, and Scotland, or, Recollections of a Swiss Minister. London: Simpkin, Marshall, 1848. French: *Trois Siècles de Luttes en écosse, ou Deux Rois et Deux Royaumes.* Genève: Béroud et Guers, 1850.

SECONDARY SOURCES

Biéler, Blanche. *Une famille du refuge; Jean Henri Merle d'Aubigné, ses origines, ses parents, ses frères.* Clamart: 'Je Sers,' 1930; *Un Fils du refuge; Jean Henri Merle d'Aubigné; ses origines, sa vie, son oeuvre.* Pari: 'Je Sers,' 1934.

Reid, W. Stanford. *The Reformation: Revival or Revolution?* New York: Holt, Rinehart and Winston, 1968.

Roney, John B. "Jean Henri Merle d'Aubigné: Historian of Christianity in an Age of Revolution." Ph.D. dissertation, University of Toronto, 1989.

Roney, John B. *The Inside of History: Jean Henri Merle d'Aubigné and French Historical Writing.* Studies in Historiography Series. Westport, Conn.: Greenwood Press, forthcoming.

Winkler, Jochen. *Der Kirchenhistoriker Jean Henri Merle d'Aubigné: Eine studie zum Genfer Réveil.* Zürich: EVZ-Verlag, 1968.

NOTES

1. The name Merle d'Aubigné combined the tradition of two families. In conformity with French usage, I have chosen to use Merle. English-speaking authors often refer to him as Mr. d'Aubigné, but he corrected this in *The Protector: a vindication* (Edinburgh: Oliver and Boyd, 1847), 10. Merle d'Aubigné should be listed under M in an index.

2. Philip Schaff, *History of the Christian Church*, 13 vols. (New York: Charles Scribner's Sons, 1903), 6:333. Cf. Harry Elmer Barnes, *A History of Historical Writing*, 2nd rev. ed. (New York: Dover Publications, 1963), 133; A. G. Dickens and John M. Tonkin, *The Reformation in Historical Thought* (Oxford: Basil Blackwell, 1985), 189;   J. W. Thompson, *History of Historical Writing*, 2 vols. (New York: Macmillan, 1942), 2:569.

3. Merle's histories will follow these codes: *Histoire de la Réformation du sieziéme siècle*, 5 vols. (Paris: Ch. Meyreuis et Compagnie, 1860–1862) as *Hde*; *History of the Reformation of the Sixteenth Century*, 5 vols. in 1, reproduced from a similar "standard" Oliver and Boyd edition of 5 v. in 1, 1853 [by Merle's approval] (Grand Rapids: Baker Books, 1976) as *Hof*; *Histoire de la Réformation en Europe au Temps de Calvin*, 8 vols. (Paris: Michel Lévy Fréres, 1863–1878) as *HdeC*; *History of the Reformation in Europe in the Time of Calvin*, 8 vols. [posthumous vols. 6–8 were translated by William Cates] (London: Longman, Green, Roberts, 1863–1878) as *HofC*. See Blanche Biéler: *Une famille du refuge; Jean Henri Merle d'Aubigné, ses origines, ses parents, ses frères* (Clamart: 'Je Sers', 1930), and *Un Fils du refuge; Jean Henri Merle d'Aubigné; ses origines, sa vie, son oeuvre* (Paris: 'Je Sers', 1934). Jochen Winkler, *Der Kirchenhistoriker Jean Henri Merle d'Aubigné: Eine studie zum Genfer Réveil* (Zürich: EVZ-Verlag, 1968).

4. See Merle, *The Protector: a vindication* (Edinburgh: Oliver and Boyd, 1847), (French) *Le Protecteur, ou, La République d'Angeleterre aux jours de Cromwell* (Paris: Firmin Didot fréres, 1848); and *Germany, England, and Scotland; or, Recollections of a Swiss Minister* (London: Simpkin, Marshall, 1848), (French) *Trois Siècles de Luttes en Écosse, ou Deux Rois et Deux Royaumes* (Genève: Béroud et Guers, 1850).

5. Apparently Merle's uncle Jean-Louis, a businessman in Marseille, first combined his mother's name d'Aubigné with his father's name Merle in order to distinguish himself from the many other Merles. Aime-Robert, who also travelled frequently to that city, also took this double name. See Biéler, *Un Fils*, 19.

6. See Merle, "Souvenir de sa vie," Archives de la Bibliothèque Publique et Universitaire de Genève (BPU), MS 560: 72. Socinianism was a rationalist movement founded by Lelio Sozzini (1525–1562) and Fausto Sozzini (1539–1604), seeing Christ as a revelation of God but only man. See Henri Heyer, *L'église de Genève, 1535–1909* (Genève: Jullien, 1909), 112–113n; Auguste Breyton, *Le Pietisme à Genève* (Genève: Wyss et Duchene, 1896), 44.

7. See Merle, *Les trois écoles du protestantisme actuel* (Genève: Emile Béroud, 1863), 4. See also Henri Dubief, "Reflexions sur quelques aspects du premier Réveil et sur le milieu où il se forma," *Bulletin de la Société de l'Histoire du Protestantisme françis* 114 (1968): 392; Ernest Rochat, *Le mouvement théologique dans l'église de Genève au cours du XIXe siècle* (Genève: Georg, 1933).

8. In 1818, L'Eglise du Bourg-de-Four (300 members), included Henri-Louis Empaytaz, Henry Pyt, Jean Gonthier, Emile Guers, and Felix Neff. Ami Bost started a second group in Carouge. César Malan led a third group of strict Calvinists—the Chapelle du Témoignage. See Ami Bost, *Memoirs pouvent servir l'histoire du réveil religieux*, 2 vols. (Paris: Meyreuis et C., 1854), 2:85–213; Hermann de Goltz, *Genève religieuse au dix-neuvième siècle*, trans. C. Millan-Sillem (Genève: H. Georg, 1862), 182–201; Emile Guers, *Le Premier Réveil et la Première Eglise Independente à Genève* (Genève: Béroud et Kaufmann, 1871), 104–127; Heyer, *L'église de Geneve*, 124–33, 148n; Léon Maury, *Le réveil religieux dans l'église Reformée à Genève et en France (1810–1850): étude historique et dogmatique*, 2 vols. (Paris: Fischbacher, 1892), 1:75–149, 355–367; Alice Weymss, *Histoire du Réveil 1790–1849* (Paris: Les Burges et Les Mages, 1977).

9. See Merle, BPU, MS 560:75,76. See also Merle, *Germany*, 17; *Les Trois Écoles*, 16.

10. Merle, *Germany*, 27 ("What called forth the enthusiasm of these young men was far less the faith of Luther than the reveries of demagogues").

11. See Merle, BPU, MS 562:39. See George Adams, "Life and Character of Dr. Neander," *Bibliotheca Sacra and American Biblical Repository* 8 (April 1851):384–411; John F. Hurst, *History of Rationalism*, 3rd rev. ed. (New York: Carlton and Porter, 1867); Philip Schaff, *St. Augustine, Melanchton, Neander: Three Biographies* (London: James Nisbet and Co., 1886); (Rev.) Sears, "Neander's Church History," *Bibliotheca Sacra and Theological Review* 4 (May 1847):386–402.

12. See *On Religion; Speeches to Its Cultured Despisers*, trans. J. Oman (New York: Harper and Brothers, 1958); Merle, *Sommaire de l'histoire des Dogmes* (Genève: Société évangélique de Genève, 1851), 219–49; Brian Gerrish, *The Old Protestant and the New* (Chicago: University of Chicago, 1982); and Richard Niebuhr, *Schleiermacher on Christ and Religion* (New York: Charles Scribner's Sons, 1964).

13. Representatives of the Mediatory School were Friedrich Tholuck (1799–1877), Issac Dorner (1809–1884), Karl Hagenbach (1801–1874), Richard Rothe (1799–1867), and Christian Bunsen (1791–1860). See Karl Barth, *Protestant Theology in the Nineteenth Century*, trans. B. Cozens and J. Bouden (London: SCM, 1959); Colon Brown, *Jesus in European Protestant Thought, 1778–1860* (Grand Rapids: Baker Books, 1985), 239–76.

14. See H. Elisabeth Kluit, *Het Protestantse Réveil in Nederland en daarbuiten, 1817–1854* (Amsterdam: H. J. Paris, 1970).

15. In January, 1831, a group of prominent Genevans, under the guidance of Louis Gaussen, formed the Société évangélique de Genève in order to give clear expression to the past orthodoxy of the established church. Merle felt strongly about remaining in the Reformed Church. In a discourse, *Du caractére nécessaire au théologien et au chrétien en général, dans l'époque actuelle* (Paris: Delay, 1845), 16. See Gabriel Métzenberg, "Louis Gaussen et les debuts," in *Genève protestante en 1831*, ed. Olivier Fatio (Genève: Labor et Fides, 1983), 68; and Biéler, *Un Fils*, 126–27, 135.

16. Merle, "Latitudinarianisme-Antichristianisme," *Circulaire de la Société évangélique de Genève* 3, no. 22 (10 November 1855): 11, and *Caractére du réformateur et de la réformation de Genève* (Genève: H. Georg, 1862), 5. The Alliance began in London 1846, and held meetings in Paris 1855, Berlin 1857, Geneva 1861, New York 1873, and Montreal 1888. See the published reports of these meetings beginning with *Report of the Proceedings of the Conference, Held at Freemasons' Hall, London, from August 19th to September 2d Inclusive, 1846.* (London: Partridge and Oakey, 1847); and D. Tissot, ed., *Les Conferences de Genève 1861: Rapports et Discours publiés au nom du Comité de l'Alliance Evangélique*, 2 vols. (Genève: Henri Georg, 1861). See also Merle's role in the International Red Cross: Gabriel Métzenberg, *Henry Dunant: le predestiné* (Genève: Robert Estienne, 1984).

17. See Merle, *Souvenir des derniers jours de Marianne Merle d'Aubigné née Brélaz* (Genève: Fick, 1855).

18. Children: Oswald (1836–1875), Anna (1841–1912), and Emile (1846–1884).

19. See Julia Merle d'Aubigné, *Madame J. H. Merle d'Aubigné 1826–1904* (Paris: n.p., 1905) [memory of Merle's second wife Frances Hardy]; and *Emile Merle d'Aubigné-Ingenieur, 1846–1884* (n.p.: n.d.), booklet (11p.), Andre Biéler Papers, Queen's University, Kingston, Ontario. Children: Jean-Henri (1859–1935), Frances Charles (1861–1948), Marie Blanche (1864–1958), and Julia Ehoumasina (1868–1935).

20. See Merle, BPU, MS 561: 53, "Je vais commencer à recueiller des matériaux." No doubt the various countries in which he lived offered primary research. See *Hde*, 1:15.

21. Ranke, summarized by Herbert Butterfield, in *The Origins of History*, ed. and intro. Adam Watson (London: Eyre Methuen, 1981), 197. See Georg Iggers and Konrad von Moltke, eds., *The Theory and Practice of History: Leopold von Ranke* (Indianapolis: Bobbs-Merrill, 1973); Leonard Krieger, *Ranke: The Meaning of History* (Chicago: University of Chicago Press, 1977); Theodore von Laue, *Leopold von Ranke: The Formative Years* (Princeton: Princeton University Press, 1950); and Hayden White, *Metahistory:*

The Historical Imagination in Nineteenth-Century Europe (Baltimore: Johns Hopkins University Press, 1973), 161–91.

22. See Ranke, *History of France*, quoted in *Leopold von Ranke, The Secret of World History: Selected Writings on the Art and Science of History*, ed. with trans. Roger Wines (New York: Fordham University Press, 1981), 258.

23. See Bernard M. G. Reardon, *Religion in the Age of Romanticism* (Cambridge: Cambridge University Press, 1985); H. R. Trevor-Roper, *The Romantic Movement and the Study of History* (London: The Athlone Press, 1969).

24. Merle referred to Ranke approximately 32 times in both *Hde* and *HdeC*.

25. See the title page of Merle, *Discours sur l'étude de l'histoire du christianisme et son utilité pour l'époque actuelle* (Genève: Cherbuliez, 1832).

26. *Hof,* 307/ *Hde.*

27. The difficulty of placing Merle in a school of thought is partly his grounding in the experience of the French-speaking world, which differed from the German-speaking world, and partly his non-confrontational style toward other Protestant theologians within either Mediatory, Erlangen, or Confessional schools. In *Germany,* 31–36, he called these the "Scientific," "Symbolic," and "Ecclesiastical" schools.

28. *Hof,* 6/ *Hde,* 1:15. [I will refer to both versions for comparison].

29. See Annie Marion Osborn, *Rousseau and Burke: A Study of the Idea of Liberty in Eighteenth-Century Political Thought* (London: Oxford University Press, 1940), 7, for a comparison with Edmund Burke, whom Merle followed.

30. *Hde,* 1:414. Cf. Karl Léwith, *Meaning in History* (Chicago: University of Chicago Press, 1949), 138–39, compared with Augustine's *City of God.*

31. See Jean Calvet, *Bossuet,* ed. Jacques Truchet, new ed. (Paris: Hatier, 1968); Thèrese Goyet, *L'Humanisme de Bossuet,* 2 vols. (Paris: C. Gabriel Beauchesne, 1910); Paul Stapfer, *La Grande Prédication chrétienne en France: Bossuet, Adolphe Monod* (Paris: Fischbacher, 1898). Merle also saw some affinity with his spirituality. *HofC,* 5:141.

32. Johann Lorentz Mosheim, *An Ecclesiastical History,* trans. Archibald McLaine, 6 vols. (London: R. Baynes, 1819), 1: 2.

33. Mosheim, *Ecclesiastical History,* 1: 1, 13. In this way, Mosheim adds the notion of relativity into an explanation of the historical events.

34. Cf. Ferdinand Christian Baur, *Ferdinand Christian Baur: On the Writing of Church History,* ed. and trans. Peter C. Hodgson (New York: Oxford University Press, 1968), 193.

35. *HdeC,* 6:413. See also *Hde,* 1:4; *HdeC,* 4:v; *L'étude de l'histoire,* 15. Merle singled out Johannes von Mueller as the "greatest of modern historians, fully to comprehend his subject" because he was able to discover God's work in history. *Hof,* 4/ *Hde,* 1:8. See Johannes von Mueller, *Sammtliche Werke,* 40 v. in 20 (Stuttgart: Cotta, 1831–1835).

36. See *HdeC,* 3:xii–xiii.

37. See *HofC,* 1:1/ *HdeC,* 1:1.

38. *Hof,* 2:1/ *Hde,* 1:4.

39. See *HdeC,* 1:ix–x; 3:ix. See also G. E. Ellis, "D'Aubigné on the Reformation," *The Christian Examiner* 32 (March 1842): 35, "He is the first historian who has distinctly claimed and proved for France the honor of having the priority in point of time over all other nations, in advancing doctrines at war with the Papal system;" and "Recent French Literature," *The London Quarterly Review* 39 (October 1863): 186.

40. *HofC,* 6:38/ *HdeC,* 6:40–41.

41. Merle, *L'autorité des écritures inspirées de Dieu* (Genève: Kaufmann, 1850), 142.

42. *HofC,* 5:viii (Eng. only).

43. *HofC,* 3:73/ *HdeC,* 3:80. See also Merle, *Foi et Science* (Genève: Susanne Guers, 1835), 23–24.

44. See Merle, *Foi et Science*, 12,19,28; "Un mot sur les moyens de faire renaétre une véritable vie théologique et religieuse dans les églises évangeliques de France," *Archives du Christianisme au 19ième Siècle* 2 (1819): 46–47.

45. "Authentique," "originaux." See *HdeC*, 1:x, 2:29–30, 3:204, 5:xi; *Hde*, 2: 248n; *Le christianisme au trois premièrs siècles* (Genève: Emile Béroud, 1857), 210; *Caractère du Réformateur*,9; *Protecteur*, pref. iv, 19.

46. See *HdeC*, 3:xviii.

47. *HofC*, 1:xii–xiii/ *HdeC*, 1:xi–xii.

48. *HofC*, 4:xi/ *HdeC*, 4:ix. See also *HofC*, 8:152/ *HdeC*, 8:159. The following archives have been mentioned in Merle's footnotes: Geneva (Choupard MSS, Gautier MSS, "Mémoires de Du Bellay," "Registres du Conseil," and state papers, and the Mallet-Romilly Collections possessed by Cellérier) and other Swiss archives (Basel, Berne, Lausanne, Neuchàtel, Strasbourg, and Zurich), French archives (Lyon, Meaux, Paris— Bibliothèque Royale and St. Geneviere), and others such as Turin (archives générale du Royaume d'Italie), the Vatican, Danzig, London (British Museum), Cambridge (Corpus Christi College), and Bristol (Museum of the Baptist College).

49. Merle used the new collection of Louis Vulliemin (1797–1879) in his earlier histories. See Louis Vulliemin, ed., *Le Chroniqueur. Recueil Historique et Journal de l'Helvétie Romande* (Lausanne: Marc Ducloux, 1836). He also used other new collections as they appeared after 1850. See Jules Bonnet, ed. *Lettres de Jean Calvin* (Paris: Ch. Meyrueuis, 1854); Karl Gottieb Bretschneider, ed., *Opera [Philipp Melanchthon] quae supersunt omnia* (Halis Saxonum: C. A. Schwetschke); *Bulletin de la Société de l'histoire du Protestantisme Francais: documents historiques inédits et originaux XVIe, XVIIe, XVIIIe siècles*, Première année, 1853; Aime Louis Herminjard, ed., *Correspondance des Réformateurs dans les pays de Langue française, recueillie et publiée avec d'autres lettres relatives à la Réforme et des notes historiques et biographiques* (Genève: H. Georg; Paris: M. Lévy frères, 1866–).

50. Merle, *Le témoignage de la théologie; ou, le biblicisme de Néander* (Genève: Kaufmann, 1850), 27.

51. *HofC*, 5:xv (Eng. only).

52. See *Hof*, 498, (Eng. original). See also Merle, *Protecteur*, 290–91; *HdeC*, 1:470.

53. See C. T. McIntire, *England Against the Papacy 1858–1861* (Cambridge: Cambridge University Press, 1983); E. R. Norman, *Anti-Catholicism in Victorian England* (London: George Allen and Unwin, 1968); Philip Schaff, "The Progress of Church History," *Bibliotheca Sacra and Theological Review* 7 (January 1850): 84–85.

54. Merle used the words "divine intervention in human affairs." See *Hof*, 3/ *Hde*, 1:7.

55. Merle's histories are replete with examples. See *HdeC*, 5:1; 5:516; 6:345–46; 6:284.

56. *HofC*, 6:270/ *HdeC*, 6:284–85.

57. *Hof*, 2/ *Hde*, 1:4.

58. See *Hof*, 49;/ *Hde*,1: 132.

59. See *Hde*, 2:104.

60. See *HdeC*, 6:459.

61. *HofC*, 1:203–04/ *HdeC*, 1:220.

62. See *HdeC*, 3:442. The personification of liberty was most important in nineteenth-century Europe. See Eugène Delacroix's (1798–1863) famous painting of Liberty leading her people.

63. *Hof*, 618 [Vol.4, English original].

64. See for example *Hde*, 5:147.

65. *HofC*, 5:292–93/ *HdeC*, 5:323.

66. Merle, *Le christianisme aux trois premiére siècles* (Genève: Emile Béroud, 1858), 254.

67. See Merle, *Les miracles, ou deux erreurs* (Genève: Kaufmann, 1841), 17.

68. See Merle, *Protecteur*, 242.

69. See Merle, *Les miracles*, 25.

70. *HofC*, 8:190/ *HdeC*, 8:200.

71. *HofC*, 7:12/ *HdeC*, 7:13.

72. See *HdeC*, 2:427; 8:32–33; *Germany*, 81.

73. *HofC*, 1:428/ *HdeC*, 1:464.

74. *HofC*, 3:205/ *HdeC*, 3:225.

75. See *HdeC*, 1:520. Here Merle refers to Guizot, *Histoire de la Civilisation en Europe*, when he said, "La chrétianité ayant un sentiment instinctif."

76. See *HdeC*, 8:157. See also *HdeC*, 3:424.

77. See *HdeC*, 5:377.

78. Luther, *HdeC*, 1:465; Calvin, *HdeC*, 5:596; Tyndale, *HdeC*, 5:288.

79. *HofC*, 2:399/ *HdeC*, 2:429.

80. See *HdeC*, 4:130; *Hde*, 1:128–29.

81. See *Hde*, 3:320.

82. Cf. André Ravier, "L'éducation d'une conscience," in Jean Louis Leuba et al., *Jean-Jacques Rousseau et la crise contemporaine de la conscience* (Paris: Beauchesne, 1980), 388–91.

83. Rousseau, "Profession de foi du vicaire savoyard," Livre Quatrième of *émile, ou de éducation*, in *Rousseau: Oeuvres Complètes*, 3 vols. (Paris: Aux éditions du Seuil, 1971), 3:200.

84. Rousseau, "Profession de foi," 3:201. Cf. Pierre Burgelin, *Jean-Jacques Rousseau et la Religion de Genève* (Genève: Labor et Fides, 1962), 26.

85. See "Profession de foi," 3:198.

86. See Leuba, "Rousseau et le milieu calviniste de sa jeunesse," in Leuba, *Jean-Jacques Rousseau*, 24–25, 34–46; and Burgelin, *Rousseau*, 12.

87. Cf. François Chirpaz, *L'homme dans son histoire: Essai sur Jean-Jacques* (Genève: Labor et Fides, 1984), 36.

88. Cf. Ronald Grimsely, *Jean-Jacques Rousseau* (Sussex: The Harvester Press, 1983), 62; and Jean LaCroix, "La Conscience selon Rousseau," in Leuba, *Jean-Jacques Rousseau*, 94.

89. Cf. LaCroix, "La Conscience selon Rousseau," 95. Through natural reason, humans can know of God's existence. In essence, Rousseau had no need for Christian doctrine or dogmas or even traditional revelation through Scripture. This is the essence of Rousseau's Natural Religion. See Rousseau, "Profession de foi," 3:204; Burgelin, *Rousseau*, 36; and Barth, *Protestant Theology*, 225.

90. Cf. Owen Chadwick, *From Bossuet to Newman*, 2nd ed. (Cambridge: Cambridge University Press, 1987), 98, "To adopt a word is not to adopt a philosophy which that word has often represented." See also Winkler, *Kirchenhistoriker*, 104–105, which claims that Merle: (1) used the very weapons of his enemies against them; and (2) he sent his message to unbelievers, in terms they understood.

91. Brian A. Gerrish, *A Prince of the Church: Schleiermacher and the Beginnings of Modern Theology* (Philadelphia: Fortress Press, 1984), 54. Cf. Josef Altholz, *Protestant Churches in the Nineteenth Century* (Indianapolis: Bobbs-Merrill, 1967), 54, called Schleiermacher the "most complete theologian of Romanticism."

92. Gerrish, *Prince of the Church*, 32. All three scholars were 'evangelical' in the sense that they conceived of a personal experience with God and believed in the centrality of the gospel message. Schleiermacher, however, can be called a "Liberal Evangelical" be-

cause, in addition, he went beyond orthodox theology or "the old expressions" of theology.

93. See Merle, *Quelle est la théologie propre à guérir les maux du temps actuel?* (Genève: Emile Béroud, 1852), 22.

94. Cf. Mark Noll, *The Princeton Theology, 1812–1921: Scripture, Science, and Theological Method from Archibald Alexander to B. B. Warfield* (Grand Rapids: Baker Books, 1983), 25. See also Grant Wacker, *Augustus H. Strong and the Dilemma of Historical Consciousness* (Macon,Ga: Mercer University Press, 1985).

95. See *HdeC*, 1:580.

96. Merle contrasted the Protestant view of the mystery in the sacraments with the Roman Catholic view. *HdeC*, 2:37.

97. See *HdeC*, 4:682; *L'autorité des écriture*, 44; *HdeC*, 6:3; *Biblicisme de Néander*, 29.

98. Merle, *Protecteur*, 103.

99. *HofC*, 4:180/ *HdeC*, 4:196. See also, Merle, *Dépendance et indépendance ou foi et critique* (Genève: Emile Béroud, 1854), 23.

100. See *HdeC*, 4:391; 5:478.

101. See Merle, *Die religiése Freiheit vom christlichen Standpunkte* (Frankfort am Main: K.T. Völker, 1854), 21.

102. Merle, *Trois Siècles de Luttes*, 117.

103. See, Merle, *Protecteur*, 2.

104. *HdeC*, 4:326.

105. See *HdeC*, 1:520.

106. This is a common expression Merle used, for example in *HdeC*, 8:63; and in 4:580–81.

107. Cf. Winkler, *Kirchenhistoriker*, 110–11, points to what Merle saw as two factors responsible for the events of the Reformation: (1) the preparation in history which led to the proper time (Kairos); and (2) a movement among the people.

108. See Merle, *Biblicisme de Néander*, 43–44.

109. See Merle, *Les Trois écoles*, 6–7.

110. See *Hof*, 499; and again in *HdeC*, 2:636; 3:607.

111. *HofC*, 1:36/ *HdeC*, 1:40. See also *Hde*, 1:56, 58, 68.

112. *Hof*, 351/ *Hde*, 3:161–62.

113. "La main de Dieu," see *Hde*, 1:6, 38, 3:10, 42; *HdeC*, 1:455, 5:527, 591, 8:401.

114. "Le doigt de Dieu," see *Hde*, 1:151–52.

115. See *Hde*, 5:267.

116. See *Hde*, 2:10–11.

117. Charles V, *Hde*, 2:75; Frederick of Saxony, *Hde*, 1:61.

118. *HdeC*, 6:655.

119. *Hof*, 25/ *Hde*, 1:67.

120. See *Hof*, 675 [Vol.4, English original, 1846].

121. See Merle, *Le christianisme*, 219. *Hof*, 305/ *Hde*, 3:vi.

122. *Hof*, 5/ *Hde*, 1:13.

123. See *HdeC*, 2:651.

124. See Merle, *L'étude de l'histoire*, 27; *Les miracles*, 11.

125. Merle, *Germany*, 74.

126. See *HdeC*, 4:158.

127. *HofC*, 8:35/ *HdeC*, 8:37.

128. See *HdeC*, 2:429; 4:64, 394, 487.

129. See *HdeC*, 4:106.

130. *Hof*, 160/ *Hde*, 2:14.

131. *Hof*, 30–31/ *Hde*, 1:82.

132. See *HdeC*, 3:122; 468–69.

133. See Merle, *Trois Siècles de Luttes*, 245; *HdeC*, 1:467; 4:279–80.

134. *Hof*, 3/ *Hde*, 1:6.

135. See *HdeC*, 1:86.

136. See Merle, *Protecteur*, 394; *HdeC*, 8:33.

137. *Hof*, 393/ *Hde*, 3:320.

138. *Hof*, 5:ii/ *Hde*, 5:viij.

139. *Hof*, 268/ *Hde*, 2:312.

140. See *Hde*, 1:4; *Trois Siècles de Luttes*, 328; David Dundas Scott, in the introduction to *History of the Reformation of the Sixteenth Century* (Glasgow edition, 1845).

141. *Hof*, 524/ *Hde*, 4:78.

142. *HofC*, 7:102/ *HdeC*, 7:107.

143. *HofC*, 6:328/ *HdeC*, 6:346.

144. *HofC*, 6:358/ *HdeC*, 6:376.

145. *HofC*, 7:70/ *HdeC*, 7:73–74.

146. See *HdeC*, 3:208. See also *Biblicisme de Néander*, 21.

147. Merle, *La Question de l'église à Genève en 1842: Liberté des cultes* (Genève: C. Gruaz, 1841–42), 71.

148. *Hde*, 5:ix; *HdeC*, 4:597.

149. Merle, *Jean Calvin, un des fondateurs des libertés modernes* (Paris: Grassart, 1868), 45; *Protecteur*, vii.

9

JOHN HENRY NEWMAN

DAVID L. RUSSELL

"Let heathens sing thy heathen praise, Fall'n Greece! the thought of holier days in my sad heart abides; For sons of thine in Truth's first hour Were tongues and weapons of His power, Born of the Spirit's fiery shower, Our Fathers and our guides."[1]

John Henry Newman's life spanned most of the nineteenth century. The oldest of six children, he was born February 21, 1801, in London to a well-to-do English family. The Newmans lived on old Broad Street, where John learned the ways of the "Victorian gentleman."[2] His father, a banker, "disliked evangelicalism and religious enthusiasm," but was otherwise open-minded about religion.[3] Newman's mother came from a Huguenot family forced out of France following "the revocation of the edict of Nantes."[4] Reflecting later upon his early life, Newman claimed that he had no formulated religious convictions until he was fifteen years of age. His knowledge of the Bible was attributable to the amount of time that his mother and grandmother spent reading the Scriptures to him.

Newman's parents were devout members of the Church of England, a church to which he would later refer as "the national religion of England." He also identified it as the "Bible religion" since it involved the reading of the Bible "in Church, in the family, and in private."[5] In addition to the strong religious atmosphere of the Newman house, John and his siblings were encouraged to pursue a life of learning through good literature, music, and the arts. These influences instilled in Newman the intellectual focus and passion necessary for his academic success at Oxford and beyond. Like many other boys of elite English culture, John was sent to the boarding school at Ealing on May 1, 1808. Ealing was considered educationally progressive compared to the public schools of this time,[6] yet in Newman's recollection the school did him great damage by failing to give him a deeper background in classical literature.[7] During his time at Ealing, Newman managed to move rapidly through his studies and by age fifteen he claimed that his instructors had nothing more they could teach him. Despite Ealing's failure to challenge Newman, he continued to pursue knowledge on his own. As a fourteen-year-old boy, he had the reading appetite of a learned adult. He enjoyed reading Thomas Paine's criticisms of the Old Testament and finding "pleasure in thinking of the objections which were contained in them."[8] He also read the works of the skeptic David Hume and Voltaire's attack upon the notion of immortality, saying to himself, "How Dreadful, but how plausible!"[9] During this time Newman's theological understanding began to take shape, and before his sixteenth birthday he entertained the idea of the priestly life and celibacy.[10] Newman's experience at Ealing, however, had given him an adequate enough background for a challenging time of study at Oxford. All the qualities of leadership, academic savvy, and spiritual insight were in place for his final stage of professional training.

Newman entered Trinity College, Oxford, in October 1817. His course of study included theology, mathematics, ancient history, and ancient philosophy. At this time there were no courses in modern philosophy, modern history or the natural sciences. Language study at Oxford during Newman's stay included only Greek and Latin. In 1818 he became a scholar of Trinity College and began a regimented program of study, often reading as much as twelve hours a day. This exhausting schedule, however, contributed to his eventual failure in legal studies. Newman returned home to gather his thoughts regarding his career. Reflecting upon his failings at Trinity College, he reset his sights on studying for holy orders. His father had high goals for his eldest son's success in law, but accepted without hesitation his qualifications for the ministry in light of his failings at Trinity and his developing religious passion.[11]

In April 1822, he was given the Oriel Fellowship, an honor Newman considered "to be a turning point of his, and of all days most memorable."[12] Newman's life took on fresh meaning as he began his studies under several tutors who would play a significant role in his intellectual development. When he came to Oxford, his religious affections leaned in the direction of evangelicalism, which often placed him at odds with the faculty.[13] Newman eventually abandoned his evangelical convictions due to the influence of J. B. Summer's *Apostolic Preaching*, loaned to him by his teacher, Edward Hawkins. In Newman's mind, evangelicalism had "been a great blessing for England," and had provided "vital truths of Revelation," not only for himself but for many others. Nevertheless, Newman soon realized that many of his evangelical convictions could not be supported biblically, particularly "the doctrine of imputed righteousness," which he exchanged for "the doctrine of Baptismal regeneration."[14]

The influence of the classics, and especially the church fathers, played a significant role in the development of Newman's theological convictions. During the summer and autumn of 1816, Newman's mentor, Walter Mayers, introduced him to Joseph Milner's five-volume *Church History* (1794–1809). He remarked that he was "nothing short of enamored of the long extracts from St. Augustine and the other Fathers which I found there." [15] Milner's work had a lasting effect on Newman insofar as it rescued him from the snares of theological liberalism. He had a renewed interest in the Fathers and by the summer of 1828, he began a serious study of them chronologically, beginning with Ignatius and Justin. Newman's study of the Fathers resulted in an opportunity for him to provide a history of the principal councils for a Theological Library project at Oxford. He began a study of the Council of Nicaea that later became his first major book, *The Arians of the Fourth Century*.[16]

Newman's study of the Fathers became the basis for his developing criticism of the Church of England and of his eventual involvement in the Oxford Movement (1833–1843). The Oxford Movement (also known as the Tractarian Movement) resulted from the criticisms of a handful of Oxford scholars, led by Newman, against the lifeless state of the Church of England and its absence of a sense of doctrinal history.[17] Newman believed that the Anglican tradition had been negatively influenced by liberalism via rationalism and scientism.[18] In a series of tracts, he and his colleagues attempted to call fellow Anglicans back to a recognition of their Apostolic origins in the writings of the early church fathers. The tract that finally outraged the Anglican hierarchy was Newman's famous "Tract 90," which attempted to reconcile the Anglican Thirty-nine Articles with the Council of Trent. Under great pressure, Newman resigned his post at Oxford in 1843. Following a time of soul searching, he decided to join the Roman Catholic Church on October 9, 1845. After a long and fulfilling life as a servant of Christ's Kingdom, Newman died August 11, 1890, after a battle with pneumonia. He was one of the most significant figures in nineteenth-century Catholicism, leaving behind thirty-six volumes of his collected writings and an enriching spiritual legacy.

A DEVELOPING HISTORICAL CONSCIENCE

In his *Difficulties of Anglicans,* John Henry Newman credits the Fathers with making him a Roman Catholic. Beginning with his reading of Milner's *Church History* (1816) through his involvement in the Tractarian Movement (1833–1843), Newman became increasingly convinced that serious study of the Fathers points to Rome. In addition, Thomas S. Bokenkotter has shown that studying the Fathers also made Newman a historian.[19] Though the teaching of history was all but nonexistent during Newman's student days, he managed to develop his own methodological approach for historical research.

As we have seen, Newman's attraction to the Fathers set him on a life-changing course that led to his eventual reception into the Roman Catholic Church. History, according to Newman, testifies to the blunt reality of apostolic succession from the early Church through the Fathers to the present age. In his *Essay on the Development of Christian Doctrine,* he begins with the following criticism levelled against the appeal to antiquity:

> Some writers have gone on to give reason from history for their refusing to appeal to history. They aver that, when they come to look into the documents and literature of Christianity in times past, they find its doctrines so variously represented, and so inconsistently maintained by its professors, that, however natural it be *a priori,* it is useless. . . hence, they are forced, whether they will or not, to fall back upon the Bible as the sole source of Revelation, and upon their own personal private judgment as the sole expounder of its doctrine.[20]

In Newman's mind, this was a classic example of the Protestant (particularly evangelical) denial of the historical development of doctrine. In response, he set out to prove that despite the discrepancies, inconsistencies, and incompleteness linked to the teachings of the Fathers, that "the Christianity of history is not Protestantism."[21]

Newman, it should be remembered, embraced evangelicalism early in his student days at Oxford, having converted to it in 1816. He acknowledged that evangelicalism had been "a great blessing to England" and had given the English people the "vital truths of Revelation."[22] His adherence to evangelicalism ended in 1826 with the realization of several internal doctrinal inconsistencies. Most dominant, perhaps, was the evangelical notion that one could ascertain the truths of historic Christianity through a private interpretation of Scripture. Newman's understanding of doctrinal development, not to mention his rejection of Protestantism, came directly from his recognition that historic Christianity rests upon an understanding of the Fathers. "To be deep in history," says Newman, "is to cease to be Protestant."[23] Newman's dissatisfaction with evangelicalism and the Church of England resulted in his search for a *via media*, a middle ground between Roman Catholicism and Protestantism. After extensive study of the Fathers and the realization that the Church of England was historically at odds with antiquity, Newman turned to Rome, which was not an admission that Rome was flawless, but rather that it was the most direct link to the "Church of the Fathers."[24]

In 1832, Newman published his first major work, *The Arians of the Fourth Century*. His initial objective was to write a history of the early Church councils from A.D. 325–381, showing the specific importance of the Nicene Creed. In a letter to his publisher, Hugh James Rose, Newman clarified that "to understand it [the Nicene Confession], it must be prefaced by a sketch of the rise of the Arian heresy."[25] In the theological liberalism of his day, Newman recognized the Arian heresy that applied reason inappropriately to the interpretation of revelation.[26] Liberalism had shunned the truths of antiquity in favor of a latitudinarian, individualistic approach to Christianity. The Arians of the fourth century sought to change the established creed in a manner that bypassed recognized church authority. They objected to the use of "words not found in Scripture, in confessions of faith," which, in Newman's mind, was the principal earmark of liberalism.[27] Liberalism, much like evangelical Protestantism, sought to eliminate the tradition of church authority as set forth by the Fathers and the Councils. Newman did not have a detached view of liberalism, but first-hand experience with its insidious method: "The truth is, I was beginning to prefer intellectual excellence to moral; I was drifting in the direction of liberalism. I was rudely awakened from my dream at the end of 1827 by two great blows—illness and bereavement."[28] The following year Newman set out to rediscover the truths of history through an intense study of the Fathers.

At the heart of Newman's developing sense of history was his obsession with the importance of church tradition, a point emphasized by Jaroslav Pelikan, who says that Newman's *Arians of the Fourth Century* is "a case study for the recovery of tradition. . . . For in it Newman sets forth in detailed fashion both the process and implications of that recovery." Newman's reading of early church history convinced him that tradition was the ground "on which the Fathers took their stand." He demonstrated this by quoting Anthanasius, who believed "loyalty to tradition" was the definitive "difference between orthodoxy and heresy."[29] Newman's study of the fourth-century Arians, therefore, was his opening statement in a lifelong pursuit of an historical ecclesiology that included a reacquaintance with tradition.

The recovery of tradition was, for Newman, the essence of the historical position of the church. Unlike his Protestant contemporaries, Newman believed that "the Apostolic tradition" had been handed down from New Testament times and was not a later notion by the Fathers. Protestants had embraced the idea that Scripture alone was the basis for tradition and authority, whereas Newman understood tradition to be "consistent with, but independent of Scripture." This was the consensus of the New Testament church.[30] Newman's historical conscience was the catalyst for his emphasis on tradition, which eventually became the basis for his development of doctrine. Indeed, as Thomas M. Parker points out, "Tradition implies history."[31]

Central to Newman's understanding of doctrinal development was the doctrine of the Trinity. Newman's understanding of the doctrine of the Trinity did not change after he converted to Catholicism. It became more pronounced due to his growing understanding of the teachings of the Fathers. In *The Arians of the Fourth Century*, he tried to show how the doctrine of the Trinity, which was confirmed at the Council of Nicaea (325), was "given to the Church by tradition" as well as the writings of the New Testament. Newman accepted the notion of a precreedal "traditionary system, received from the first age of the Church."[32] This precreedal system made it possible to keep the sacred things of the church intact. Newman kept the doctrine of the Incarnation closely connected to the doctrine of the Trinity. He considered "the incarnation the central truth of the gospel, and the source whence we are to draw out its principles."[33] Nevertheless, the doctrine of the Incarnation only "partly implies and partly recommends the doctrine of the Trinity," because it is a question of only one Person of the Trinity.[34] The importance of the doctrine of the Trinity was based on Newman's study of the doctrinal controversies of the early church. The historical errors of the early church over the issue of the Trinity convinced him that "we must have a whole doctrine stated by a whole Church." The fact that many among the Fathers were professing various doctrines of Christ's divinity in no way added strength to the doctrine of the Trinity, but instead created a number of heresies including Arianism, Sabellianism, Unitarianism, and Tritheism.[35] Tradition, according to Newman, dictated the necessity of a unified consensus on the doctrine of the Trinity. In *An Essay in the Aid of a Grammar of Assent* (1870), Newman sums up "Catholic dogma" by way of the doctrine of the Trinity as taught in the Athanasian Creed: God is simultaneously Father, Son, and Holy Spirit, "each of whom is that One Personal God in the fullness of His Being and Attributes." Father, Son, and Holy Ghost are all that is meant by the word "God," for "such is the prerogative of the Divine Infinitude, that that One and Single Personal Being, the Almighty God, is really Three, while He is absolutely One."[36] Newman insisted that the doctrine of the Trinity must be taught and understood in its purest sense because that doctrine itself is central to understanding the essence of historic Christianity. "Theology has to do with the dogma of the Holy Trinity as a whole made up of many propositions."[37] Christianity at its very beginning condemned the pagan teaching of polytheism. It was imperative, therefore, that the church carefully distinguish itself by making sure that the doctrine of the Trinity defines God as one and not three.[38] The vast writing of Newman regarding the impact of the Fathers on his development of doctrine shows, without question, that he was a historian in the truest sense of the word.

STRUGGLE BETWEEN ROME AND ENGLAND

Newman doubtless had an agenda to justify the theological position of the Roman Catholic Church, stemming from the *Apologia* and more specifically from his *Essay on the Development of Doctrine*. The *Apologia*, which is probably Newman's most personal work, was an attempt to answer his critics regarding his silent movement from the Church of England to the Church of Rome. His most vocal opponent, and ablest foe, was Charles Kingsley of Cambridge University, who, in 1864, accused Newman of teaching that "truth is no virtue."[39] In response, Newman asked Kingsley to justify these accusations, to which a war of words ensued between them in the form of pamphlets. In addition to his theological critique, Kingsley accused Newman of silliness, incredulity, and absurdity. Despite his perceived victory over Kingsley, Newman felt that his reputation needed to be vindicated from the damage done by this war, hence the *Apologia*.[40]

The *Apologia* was not merely Newman's defense of his involvement in the Oxford Movement, nor was it a defense of his move to the Catholic Church. These two things are an important part of the *Apologia*. But more important was Newman's desire to set the historical record straight. It was Newman's intense study of church history, specifically the Fathers, which is at the heart of the *Apologia*. In essence, the *Apologia* is not so much a record of how Newman's mind had changed as it is a record of how his study of antiquity had changed his mind.

Throughout the *Apologia*, Newman confesses that his doctrinal position had changed the more he was exposed to the Fathers. As a young man, he was convinced that the Pope was the Antichrist. His reading of church history, which by 1824 had not been extensive, led him to the following conclusion: "From my boyhood and in 1824 I considered, after protestant authorities, that St. Gregory I about A.D. 600 was the first Pope that was Antichrist, and again that he was also a great and holy man; in 1832–3 I thought the Church of Rome was bound up with the cause of Antichrist by the Council of Trent."[41]

After a time, Newman's position on the Pope changed due to the influence of his friend Hurrell Froude, who encouraged him to reconsider his harsh conclusions. From Froude, Newman "learned to admire the great medieval Pontiffs," and to reconsider "the Council of Trent to be the turning-point of the history of Rome." Soon after, Newman journeyed to Rome and Sicily and found himself deeply touched by seeing many of the historic sites of early Christendom. His imagination was ignited at the sight of "venerable shrines, and marble Churches."[42] These experiences somewhat softened Newman's heart, and even caused him to acknowledge something special about the Church of Rome. As an Anglican, Newman maintained agreement with the Roman Catholic doctrine of celibacy, "which I recognized as Apostolic, and her faithful agreement with antiquity in so many points besides, which were dear to me, was an argument as well as a plea in favour of the great Church of Rome."[43]

Newman's opinion about the Catholic Church as an institution, however, had not changed. Roman Catholicism, though it has roots in antiquity, had failed to fall in line with the tradition and insights of the Fathers. Newman, along with other Anglican leaders in the Oxford Movement, had been accused of "Popery" due to their defense of various Roman Catholic ideals. Newman never denied that the road he had chosen appeared to lead to the doorstep of the Pontiff, yet he made it clear that eventually this road will "come to a deep chasm . . . which makes real approximation impossible."[44] The accusation of Popery was not perceived as a serious criticism by Newman because a number of "Anglican divines had been accused of Popery, yet had died in their Anglicanism." He was not teaching anything that was at odds with them. Newman's theology and criticism of Rome were in agreement with the great Anglican divines who preceded him.

As the Oxford Movement continued to make an impact on the Church of England, Newman's conviction of the importance of historical understanding become more pronounced. The Church of England had been blessed with men of keen intellect who understood the teaching of the Fathers and the development of doctrine. "Primitive doctrine," says Newman, "has been explored for us in every direction, and the original principles of the Gospel and the Church patiently brought to light." Due to outside pressures, however, the judgments and opinions of the divines, to which Newman alludes, have been "obstructed" or incomplete. The Anglican tradition, in Newman's mind, could potentially lay claim to the treasures of antiquity. "All is given us in profusion; it remains for us to catalogue, sort, distribute, select, harmonize, and complete."[45] The truths of antiquity, as set forth by the Fathers, were waiting to be rediscovered and utilized.

Newman's study of history, during the years of the Oxford Movement, led him to conclude that Anglican and Catholic teaching agreed on a number of pertinent points of doctrine. These include the doctrine of the incarnation, atonement, future rewards and punishment, obedience, apostolic succession, original sin, regeneration, the sacraments, and the Trinity. The fact that the church had divided into factions did not convince Newman that the historic faith could not be regained. "The Catholic Church in all lands had been one from the first for many centuries." After a time there developed factions, or "branches," as Newman called them, identified as the "Greek, Latin, and Anglican" traditions. Each tradition has its identity in the early church and unity with each other insofar as they stay linked to the early church. Newman believed that these three traditions were more in agreement than at odds. He criticized the Anglican tradition for its failure to retain "in detail, portions of Apostolical truth and usage."[46] Newman's struggle with the Church of England at this time was in no way indicative of any impending move to Rome. The Tractarians were hopeful that Anglicanism would eventually awake to rediscover its link to the early church, as well as to recognize the dangers of liberalism.

Newman's continuing analysis of early church history led him, in the summer of 1839, to his first major doubt "about the tenableness of Anglicanism." His doubts stemmed from reading "the history of the Monophysites," which he saw as relevant to the Anglican Church of his day.[47] If Newman were going to condemn the heresy of the fifth-century Monophysites, how, then, could he avoid condemning Protestants and Anglicans? The Monphysites believed that Christ's human nature was swallowed up in His divine nature; thus He possessed only one nature. The Council of Chalcedon accepted the orthodox notion of both the divine and human natures of Christ in one person.[48] Protestants and Anglicans had fallen out of step with the orthodox, traditional understanding of the divine and human natures of Christ.

Newman's thinking would never be the same once he began to doubt the validity of the Anglican position. Of the fifth century he painfully writes: "The principles of proceedings of the Church now, were those of the Church then, the principles and proceedings of the heretics then, were those of the Protestants now. I found it so,—almost fearfully." To continue defending Anglicanism after such doubt would be, in Newman's understanding, "forging arguments for Arius and Eutyches, and turning devil's advocate against the much-enduring Athanasius and the Majestic Leo."[49] His thoughts about Roman Catholicism and Anglicanism, as expressed in the *Apologia*, appear to reflect frustration and confusion. He admitted, for example, that he "had seen the shadow of a hand on the wall," and that "the Church of Rome will be found right after all," yet soon returned to his Anglican commitment.[50]

In 1841, Newman decided to set aside the controversy surrounding his struggle with Anglicanism. He began a translation of the works of Athanasius. But controversy returned. While studying Arian history, he noticed that the Arian heresy was as visible in the Anglican tradition as was the Monophysite heresy. He had failed to see this in 1832, when he published his work on the *Arians of the Fourth Century*. "I saw clearly that in the history of Arianism, the pure Arians were the Protestants, the semi-Arians were the Anglicans, and that Rome was now what it was." To add to his painful historical dilemma, Newman was beginning to feel the reproach of the Anglican Bishops against his controversial Tract 90. The reproaches were seen by Newman as outright condemnations.[51] In writing Tract 90, Newman attempted to show, without equivocation, that Anglicanism is directly linked to Roman Catholicism and that the Thirty-nine Articles were compatible with the historic Catholic Church.

The perceived truths of history finally convinced Newman that he could no longer support his Anglicanism. By 1843, he officially resigned his post at Oxford University. Newman remained in seclusion for the next two years and decided that he would begin working on "An Essay on Doctrinal Development." He boldly wagered that "if, at the end of it, my convictions in favour of the Roman Church were not weaker, to make up my mind to seek admission into her fold."[52] Newman was not convinced that he was safe in the Church of England. In a letter to a concerned Anglican, he writes, " The simple question is, can I be saved in the English Church? Am I in safety, were I to die to-night? Is it a mortal sin in me, not joining another communion?"[53] On October 9, 1845, Newman quietly joined the Catholic Church. The years of intense study of antiquity had finally led him home to Rome. Newman's attempt to remain faithful to the Church of England became increasingly difficult in light of what he was deducing from the Fathers. The inevitable conclusion for Newman was that "one Church alone . . . could bear the light of historical fact, the Church of Rome."[54]

HISTORICAL AFTERTHOUGHT: PROGRESS

The criticism that Newman leveled against the liberalism of his day came from his study of antiquity. As we have seen, his liberal contemporaries were guilty of the same intellectual dishonesty as the Arians of the fourth century. They misapplied reason to the study of doctrine. Newman's rejection of the spirit of his day is said to be, perhaps, his most significant criticism of liberalism.[55] In the spirit of Edmund Burke, Newman thought that liberal rationalism would lead society down the primrose path of self-interest rather than virtue.

Newman's view of human history did not include progress, for "our race's progress and perfectibility is a dream." Without a commonly held understanding of morality and virtue, the progress and improvement of society and self is pointless. The liberal progressives, says Newman, "can give no better guarantee for the philosophical truth of their principles than their popularity at the moment, and their happy conformity in ethical character to the age which admires them."[56] His knowledge of early church history gave him the ability to understand the patterns of human behavior. Newman was viewed as a believer amidst the skeptics of his age. Yet, as Aeschliman astutely observes, Newman's doubt regarding overall progress places him in the company of skeptics.[57]

NEWMAN AS HISTORIAN

During Newman's student days, the study of history had not been fully developed as an academic discipline. At Oxford he studied ancient history, but had no background in historical methodology. His sense of the necessity of studying primary sources, however, demonstrated a profound understanding of historical methodology. As we have shown, Newman's study of the Fathers played a significant role in the development of his historical understanding, culminating in his move to Roman Catholicism. Yet the question to be answered is whether or not Newman's understanding of history led him in the right direction.

Newman's move to Roman Catholicism was guided by his conviction that tradition was on the side of Rome more than of Canterbury. He recognized that Roman Catholicism had a number of inconsistencies, but had managed to maintain a more direct line to the early church and the Fathers. Newman's contention that Protestants were off track in their free-wheeling approach to interpreting scripture reveals his misunderstanding of the Protestant reformers' stand on tradition. As we have seen, Newman believed that Protestants, in their rejection of tradition, "fall back upon the Bible as the sole source of Revelation, and upon their own personal private judgment as the sole expounder of its doctrine."[58] Regarding what the reformers actually believed, Newman is far from rendering an acceptable verdict.

In *Reformation Thought: An Introduction*, Alister McGrath discusses three approaches to the question of tradition and scripture: Tradition 0,

Tradition 1, and Tradition 2. Tradition 0 teaches that tradition should be eliminated completely. Scriptural interpretation should be left fully in the hands of the individual. Tradition 1 implies that there is "a traditional way of interpreting scripture within the community of faith." This traditional way must always conform to scripture. Tradition 2 holds to a "dual-source" theory that Christian doctrine is based on both scripture and un-written tradition.[59] Newman inappropriately concluded that all of Protestantism had embraced Tradition 0 and completely rid itself of tradition. The reformers rejected the notion of tradition's equality with scripture, but in no way rejected the idea of tradition altogether. Tradition has its place as long as it does not contradict the teaching of scripture.

The principle of *sola scriptura*, to which the reformers held, has been consistently misunderstood. This principle teaches that "by Scripture alone" we determine what is authoritative. Many have interpreted this to mean that one has the freedom to exercise private judgment regarding scriptural interpretation. Yet, as McGrath has shown, this was not the view of magisterial reformers like Calvin, Luther and Melanchthon. The radical reformers, by contrast, had ultimate contempt for tradition, calling for its complete elimination. Magisterial reformers saw the danger of embracing such an extreme position concerning the authority of scripture. They sought instead to uphold the view that there is a traditional way of inter-preting the scriptures. This was the view held by a number of medieval theologians. Scripture is fully sufficient for the development of all church doctrine. Medieval theologians left room for certain issues only implied by scripture, yet subordinated their final judgment to scripture alone.[60] This view was held by the early Church Fathers to whom the medieval theolo-gians appealed. Irenaeus (A.D. 130–200) was one of the earliest Fathers to observe that scripture needs to be interpreted from a traditional framework stemming from the original Apostles. Scripture could not be interpreted subjectively, but only within the confines of the church's historical posi-tion.[61] Irenaeus was careful to point out that the tradition received by the church comes directly from the testimony of the apostles. Tradition in this sense was not a separate unwritten code equal to Scripture, but an affirma-tion of what already exists in Scripture.[62] The writings of Origen (A.D. 185–255) are especially clear on this point. In his summary of the Christian faith, Origen outlines Christian doctrine beginning with God and His cre-ative attributes to the composition of the Scriptures by the Holy Spirit. He speaks regarding that "which has been handed down from the Apostles through the order of succession."[63] Church tradition, according to Origen, rests completely on what the Scriptures teach.[64]

Despite his acceptance of the equality of unwritten tradition with Scripture, Newman admitted that the church, throughout its history, has been regulated by scripture: "The divines of the Church are in every age engaged in regulating themselves by Scripture, appealing to Scripture in proof of their conclusions, and exhorting and teaching in the thoughts and language of Scripture. Scripture may be said to be the medium in which the mind of the Church has energized and developed."[65]

This conclusion in no way contradicts the position of the magisterial reformers, who said that all authority and truth must be consistent with Scripture. Newman gives examples of how the Fathers appealed to Scripture for support of numerous traditional beliefs: "When St. Methodius would enforce the doctrine of vows of celibacy, he refers to the book of Numbers; and if St. Irenaeus proclaims the dignity of St. Mary, it is from a comparison of St. Luke's gospel with Genesis."[66]

The notion of scriptural authority, according to Newman, is a long-held notion in the church. "All truth, all science, must be derived from the inspired volume."[67] These conclusions, however, fail to square with Newman's contention that "we receive through Tradition both the Bible itself, and the doctrine that it is divinely inspired." In addition Newman says that Christians, "derive their faith" from tradition, not Scripture.[68] If tradition is derived from Scripture, then how do we in turn receive the Bible, its divinity, and Christian faith through tradition? Newman appears to contradict himself on this point by placing the traditional cart before the biblical horse, so-to-speak. If we were to judge Newman by the statements above, we would have to conclude that he stands clearly on the side of Scripture over tradition. Yet his commitment to the equality of unwritten tradition with Scripture is more pronounced.

Doubtless Newman's study of early church history took him to Rome. As a historian, Newman understood the necessity of analyzing the historic documents of the early church and the Fathers for the construction of church doctrine. His struggle with the Church of England and evangelicalism was due to his perception that they had denied the historic faith handed down by the apostles and the Fathers, thereby stepping outside the umbrella of tradition. As Newman studied church history he became more convinced that liberalism had worked its way into the Church of England through rationalism. He attempted to remedy the situation by pointing out the historic position of the church on matters of faith and practice. Whether or not Newman made the right choice in joining the Roman Catholic Church is not the major issue. The question regarding his interpretation of Protestantism, however, is of utmost importance. As we have shown, Newman's understanding of the Protestant position on tradition and scripture was inconsistent. While many Protestants embrace a maverick theology devoid of tradition and historical understanding, most accept authority and tradition within the bounds of Scriptural authority. *Sola Scriptura* is not a recipe for anarchy, but a reference point to keep guard over our frail human interpretations of the faith.

BIBLIOGRAPHY

PRIMARY SOURCES

John Henry Newman: Autobiographical Writings. Edited by Henry Tristram. New York: Sheed and Ward, 1957.

Apologia Pro Vita Sua. New York: Doubleday, 1989.

Conscience, Consensus, and the Development of Doctrine. New York: Doubleday, 1992.

An Essay in Aid of a Grammar of Assent. London: Longmans, Green and Co., 1913.

The Idea of a University. New York: Holt, Rinehart and Winston, 1964.

John Henry Newman: Selected Sermons. Edited by Ian Ker. New York: Paulist Press, 1994.

Letters and Diaries of John Henry Newman. Edited by Charles Stephen Dessain, et al., vols. xi–xxii (London, 1961–72), xxiii–xxxi (Oxford, 1973–7), i–vi (Oxford, 1978–84).

Sermons and Discourses (1825–39). New York: Longmans, Green and Co., 1949.

SECONDARY SOURCES

Bettenson, Henry, editor. *Documents of the Christian Church.* Oxford: Oxford University Press, 1982.

———. *The Early Church Fathers: A Selection from the Writings of the Fathers from Clement of Rome to St. Athanasius.* London: Oxford University Press, 1978.

Bokenkotter, Thomas S. *Cardinal Newman as an Historian.* Louvan: Publications Universitaires, 1959.

———. *A Concise History of the Catholic Church.* New York: Doubleday, 1990.

Chadwick, Owen. *Newman.* Oxford: Oxford University Press, 1983.

———. *The Spirit of the Oxford Movement: Tractarian Essays.* Cambridge: Cambridge University Press, 1990.

Coulson, John, and A. M. Allchin. *The Rediscovery of Newman: An Oxford Symposium.* London: Sheed and Ward, 1967.

Crumb, Lawrence N. *The Oxford Movement and Its Leaders: A Bibliography of Secondary and Lesser Primary Sources Supplement.* Metuchen: Scarecrow, 1993.

Dessain, Charles Stephen. *John Henry Newman.* London: Thomas Nelson, 1966.

Fox, Robin Lane. *Pagans and Christians.* San Francisco: Harper Collins, 1986.

Hall, Stuart G. *Doctrine and Practice in the Early Church.* Grand Rapids: Eerdmans, 1991.

Harrold, Charles Frederick. *John Henry Newman: An Expository and Critical Study of His Mind, Thought and Art.* London: Longmans, Green & Co., 1945.

Ker, Ian. *The Achievement of John Henry Newman.* Notre Dame: University of Notre Dame Press, 1990.

————. *John Henry Newman: A Biography.* Oxford: Oxford University Press, 1988.

————. *Newman and the Fullness of Christianity.* Edinburgh: T. & T. Clark, 1993.

Magill, Gerard, editor. *Discourse and Context: An Interdisciplinary Study of John Henry Newman.* Carbondale and Edwardsville: Southern Illinois Press, 1993.

John Henry Newman: Centenary Essays. London: Burns, Oates and Washbourne, 1945.

McGrath, Alister E. *Reformation Thought: An Introduction.* Oxford: Blackwell, 1994.

Pelikan, Jaroslav. *The Vindication of Tradition.* New Haven: Yale University Press, 1984.

NOTES

1. Quoted in Ian Ker's *Newman and the Fullness of Christianity* (Edinburgh: T. & T. Clark, 1993), 83.

2. Charles Frederick Harrold, *John Henry Newman: An Expository and Critical Study of His Mind, Thought and Art* (London: Longmans, Green & Co., 1945), 2.

3. Charles Stephen Dessain, *John Henry Newman* (London: Thomas Nelson, 1966), 1.

4. Ibid.

5. Ian Ker, *John Henry Newman: A Biography* (Oxford: Oxford University Press, 1988), 3.

6. Dessain, *John Henry Newman,* 2.

7. John Henry Cardinal Newman, *Apologia Pro Vita Sua* (New York: Doubleday, 1989), 10. This information comes from Philip Hughes' introduction.

8. Newman, *Apologia,* 127.

9. Ibid.

10. Harrold, *John Henry Newman,* 6.

11. Ker, *John Henry Newman,* 15.

12. Ibid., 18.

13. Newman mentions in his autobiographical writings a teacher named Charles Lloyd, who occasionally challenged his unpopular evangelical views. See Ker, *John Henry Newman,* 20.

14. Ibid., 23. Another major theological change for Newman was his rejection of the evangelical notion of the distinction between "nominal" and "real" Christians. In other words, he came to reject the distinction between the truly converted and the unconverted. See Ian Ker, *Newman and the Fullness of Christianity* (Edinburgh: T. & T. Clark, 1993), 20.

15. Newman, *Apologia,* 129.

16. Ibid., 145.

17. In the *Apologia,* Newman credits his colleague, John Keble, with initiating the movement. Keble preached the Assize sermon in the University pulpit. It was published under the title of "National Apostasy." "I have ever considered and kept the day, as the start of the religious movement of 1833." See Newman, *Apologia,* 152.

18. Hugh T. Kerr and John M. Mulder, *Conversions: The Christian Experience* (Grand Rapids: Eerdmans, 1983), 121.

19. Thomas S. Bokenkotter, *Cardinal Newman as an Historian* (Louvain: Publications Universitaires De Louvain, 1959), 21.

20. John Henry Cardinal Newman, *Conscience, Consensus, and the Development of Doctrine* (New York: Doubleday, 1992), 49.

21. Ibid., 50.

22. Ker, *Fullness of Christianity,* 19.

23. Newman, *Conscience*, 50.

24. Ker, *Fullness of Christianity*, 7.

25. Gerard Magill, "Moral Imagination in Theological Method and Church Tradition: John Henry Newman," in *Theological Studies* 53 (September 1992): 451–75.

26. Ker, *John Henry Newman*, 48.

27. Ker, *Fullness of Christianity*, 34–35.

28. Newman, *Apologia*, 135.

29. Jaroslav Pelikan, *The Vindication of Tradition* (New Haven: Yale University Press, 1984), 25–26

30. Ibid., 27.

31. Thomas M. Parker, "The Rediscovery of the Fathers in the Anglican Tradition," in *The Rediscovery of Newman: An Oxford Symposium*, edited by John Coulson and A. M. Allchin (London: Sheed and Ward, 1967), 39–40.

32. Pelikan, *Vindication of Tradition*, 27–28.

33. Quoted in the introduction to *John Henry Newman: Selected Sermons*, edited by Ian Ker (New York: Paulist Press, 1994), 28–29.

34. Newman, *Conscience*, 55.

35. Ibid.

36. John Henry Cardinal Newman, *An Essay in Aid of a Grammar of Assent* (London: Longmans, Green and Co., 1913 [1870]), 125.

37. Ibid., 140.

38. Ker, *Fullness of Christianity*, 93.

39. Newman, *Apologia*, 37–93.

40. Owen Chadwick, *The Spirit of the Oxford Movement: Tractarian Essays* (Cambridge: Cambridge University Press, 1990), 105.

41. Newman, *Apologia*, 166.

42. Ibid., 167.

43. Ibid.

44. Ibid., 169. Critics of the Oxford Movement said "that the writing of the tracts and the writings of Fathers" would eventually lead Newman and the others to become Roman Catholics.

45. Ibid., 178.

46. Ibid., 180–81.

47. Ibid., 127.

48. Ker, *Fullness of Christianity*, 107.

49. Newman, *Apologia*, 218.

50. Ibid., 220.

51. Ibid., 239.

52. Ibid., 310.

53. Ibid., 312.

54. Bokenkotter, *Cardinal Newman*, 52.

55. M. D. Aeschliman, "The Prudence of John Henry Newman," in *First Things* 45 (August/September 1994): 36–39.

56. Quoted in Aeschliman, "The Prudence," 37.

57. Ibid., 37.

58. Newman, *Conscience*, 49.

59. Alister E. McGrath, *Reformation Thought: An Introduction* (Oxford: Blackwell, 1994), 134–58.

60. Ibid., 135.

61. Ibid., 135–136.

62. Henry Bettenson, ed., *Documents of the Early Church*, 2nd ed. (New York: Oxford University Press, 1982), 68–69.

63. Henry Bettenson, *The Early Church Fathers: A Selection from the Writings of the Fathers from Clement of Rome to St. Athanasius* (London: Oxford University Press, 1978), 258–59.

64. Ibid. Origen speaks to this directly in his discussion on the relationship of the Holy Spirit to the Father and the Son. "It is not yet clearly decided whether or not the Spirit is to be thought of as begotten or unbegotten, or even as the Son of God; this question needs careful investigation, based on Holy Scripture, and is to be examined with prudent inquiry." See also Stuart G. Hall, *Doctrine and Practice in the Early Church* (Grand Rapids: Eerdmans, 1992), 102.

65. Newman, *Conscience*, 301-302.

66. Ibid., 302.

67. Ibid.

68. Ker, *John Henry Newman*, 142.

10

WILLIAM CUNNINGHAM

JOEL R. BEEKE

Little scholarly research has been undertaken on the mid-nineteenth century theologian William Cunningham (1805–1861), whom Hugh Martin coupled with Thomas Halyburton as the two greatest divines Scotland ever produced. John Macleod called Cunningham "Scotland's theologian *par excellence*."[1] But if modern scholarship has afforded scant recognition to Cunningham as a theologian, even less attention has been accorded his historiographical method and interpretative models. Cunningham's historiography has been brushed aside as restrictive, intolerant, and static due to his insistence on interpreting history through the spectacles of scriptural and Calvinistic thought.[2] A close examination of his major writings (all published posthumously)[3] reveals that though definitive in his historiography and poignant in his argumentation, Cunningham remained scrupulously within the parameters of his Calvinist sympathies. If his Calvinist theology and Presbyterian polity earned him a reputation for being among the ablest defenders of Reformed principles in his day, certainly his Reformation historiography is worthy of detailed study.

Before analyzing Cunningham's historiography, I will briefly sketch the major influences upon his life and theology. After considering his historiography from its objective ground (Scripture) and its interpretative models (corruption, restoration, and explanatory development), I will conclude with an assessment of the influence of Cunningham's historiographical output.

INFLUENCE UPON WILLIAM CUNNINGHAM

William Cunningham's early upbringing and educational background provide no hint of his subsequent Calvinist convictions. Shortly after his birth in 1805 at Hamilton, Scotland, his family moved to Duns, where he received all of his pre-university education. Born and bred a Moderate,[4] he entered the University of Edinburgh at age fifteen. After mastering the usual curriculum, he was licensed for the ministry in 1828.

As a student at Edinburgh, Cunningham became known as a voluminous reader, vigorous thinker, and effective speaker. During these years, he also underwent a thorough change in his religious convictions. This change commenced in his first year at Edinburgh when sin began to trouble his conscience. The question of how a lost sinner might be saved by a holy God pressed in upon him. He heard a variety of ministers, but complained that "not one of them gave me an answer to the questions of my soul." By his last year at Edinburgh, he had fully renounced his Moderate principles in exchange for evangelical ones. That is to say, he now believed in an inerrant Scripture, the centrality of the cross, and the necessity of being converted by the saving work of the Holy Spirit.[5]

The work of three renowned evangelicals played a major role in Cunningham's wholehearted conversion to Calvinism: the preaching of Robert Gordon, the writing of Andrew Thomson, and the teaching of Thomas Chalmers. Furthermore, it appears that Thomas M'Crie and John Brown were also of significant influence upon Cunningham during this formative period.[6]

Cunningham's conversion to the evangelical cause was profound and unequivocal. Shortly after licensure, he was asked to assist Dr. Scott at Middle Church, Greenock, and in 1830 was ordained his colleague and successor. From the outset of his preaching ministry, Cunningham espoused thoroughly evangelical principles. As J. J. Bonar illustrates: "Only a short while before, he had been in converse with no sounder divines than Hoadley, and Balguy, and Bull, and Clarke, and he knew the tenets of the Evangelical School only to repudiate them; yet his *first* sermon is as clear in statement of gospel truth, and as ardent in appeal on gospel principles, as any he preached afterwards."[7] Moreover, in Greenock, Cunningham performed significant service for the evangelical cause at large—particularly in refuting universal redemption and the alleged possession of gifts of tongues and healings.[8]

Cunningham's gifts were publicly recognized when he was called to Trinity College Church, Edinburgh, in 1834, where he ministered for the duration of the Ten Years' Conflict which ultimately led to the 1843 Disruption and the subsequent establishment of the Free Church of Scotland. At Trinity Church, Cunningham became known throughout Scotland for his bold evangelical stand. Taking a leading part in the controversies of the day, his reputation steadily grew for learning, force of mind, and power of speech. Particularly, Cunningham was influential in speaking out against patronage,[9] finally securing a majority of the Assembly to advocate its abolition in 1842.

By 1842, the rift between the evangelicals and Moderates had become irreparable. The evangelicals felt there was only one way to preserve the honor of Christ as sole Head of the church. Hence, on May 18, 1843, they arose in the General Assembly, said farewell to the Moderates, and severed their connection with the Established Church of Scotland. The 451 ministers who seceded immediately formed themselves into the Free Church of Scotland.[10]

Though the newly formed Free Church was instantly placed under the incredible burden of building some eight hundred churches (not to mention parsonages), no delay was allowed in providing a "New College" where men might be soundly trained in preparation for Reformed ministry. The initial professorial foursome of New College, Edinburgh, were Thomas Chalmers, David Welsh, John Duncan, and William Cunningham.[11] Upon the death of Welsh in 1845, Cunningham was made Professor of Church History, and two years later, upon the death of Chalmers, he became Principal of New College, which position he retained until his death in 1861.[12]

Cunningham's professorship and rectorship never caused him to withdraw from the work of the church. His voice continued frequently to be heard in the General Assembly, where he delivered numerous speeches quoted for years to come on subjects of vital interest.[13] His deepest commitment, however, was directed to New College, and the history of this institution must remain intimately associated with Cunningham's life. In particular, his interests both as a theologian and as a man lay in his methods, contents, and principles of teaching. Reformation historiography absorbed his most profound sentiments.

WILLIAM CUNNINGHAM'S HISTORIOGRAPHY

Cunningham's Reformation historiography posits its foundation in the scriptural canon as the *objective* ground for the development of doctrine.

Indeed, it is this objective ground of Scripture—which is guaranteed and controlled by God, and does not extend beyond the apostles with whom the development of doctrine within historical, inspired revelation ceases— that gives meaning and validity to a *subjective* development of Christian doctrine both in individuals and in churches. In his *Discussions of Church Principles*, Cunningham writes:

> There is a subjective development of Christian doctrine both in indi- viduals and in churches, whereby men grow in the knowledge of God's revealed will and whereby theological science is extended and improved. But the result of this development is merely to enable indi- viduals and churches to understand more fully and accurately, and to realize more thoroughly, *what is actually contained in, or deducible from the statements of the written word, and can be shown to be so* [Westminster Confession of Faith, ch. I, art. VI]. This, however, is essentially differ- ent from, nay, it is in a certain sense the reverse of, an objective devel- opment, which changes and enlarges or diminishes the external revelation, the standard or system of faith.[14]

For Cunningham, God's truth is found in its perfection and purity only within the sacred canon. "In theology," he wrote, "there is, of course, no room for originality properly so-called, for its whole materials are con- tained in the actual statement of God's Word."[15] Hence, only when his- torical theology develops along the line of what is already inherent in Scripture does the church make genuine progress. On this ground, Cun- ningham readily accepts an obvious subjective development in such docu- ments as the Nicene Creed and the Westminster Confession, and therefore is such a strong adherent of Reformed theology as a whole:

> We insist that their [i.e., Reformers'] theology, as a whole, and every doctrine which enters into their system, shall be judged of fairly and fully by the standard of Scripture, and of Scripture used and applied according to its real character and design. We embrace the theology of the Reformation just because we think we can prove, that all the partic- ular doctrines which constitute it are taught in Scripture, rightly inter- preted and applied; and while, on the one hand, we undertake the responsibility of asserting and proving this, we must, on the other hand, insist that any one who repudiates the theology of the Reformation, shall distinctly specify what the errors of the system are, and bring for- ward the evidence from Scripture that they are errors.[16]

Moving from the basics of scriptural underpinnings, Cunningham ap- proaches the entire field of historical theology by dealing with its major issues, and to that end conjoins core doctrines with polemical discussions.

This merging of historical and polemic theology was an approach Cunningham settled on for practical reasons.

Robert Rainy identifies three general approaches to the study of historical theology in Cunningham's day: First, it was a reporting form that answers the question, "What was believed and maintained during given periods of the Church's history?" Examples include German compendiums of doctrinal history, such as that by Hagenbach, and Bull's *Defence of the Nicene Faith*. Second, historical theology might focus on the genetic development of individual doctrines, explaining "the nature of each theological tendency, the soil it grew in, and the fruit it bore . . . and to shew how the various influences, inherent in the theology, or working on it from without, explain the course of speculation or of controversy." Examples of this approach include Baur's *History of the Doctrine of the Trinity* and Dorner's *History of the Doctrine of the Person of Christ*. Finally, there is a third method, which "refuses to be content with the bare reporting of the first method; but it also refuses to linger, like the second, over speculations as to causes and consequences. It passes on at once to the practical and ultimate question in which the theologian is interested, viz., What is true?. . . What was truly in debate? . . . and what was it all worth when summed and sifted? . . . This method was the main substance of Dr. Cunningham's course. . . . The charm of historic detail was necessarily sacrificed . . . but the service performed for the student became extremely definite." From this method Rainy goes on to state how Cunningham necessarily subordinated historical theology under scriptural exegesis and systematic theology as third in rank, though taking up "the same body of belief."[17]

By adopting this third approach, Cunningham's most important work, *Historical Theology*, takes giant strides through church history by addressing such major issues as the doctrine of the Trinity, the Person of Christ, Pelagianism, scholastic theology, the Fall, the will of man, justification, the sacramental principle, Socinianism, the Atonement, Arminianism, church government, and Erastianism. In similar fashion, his articles on the Reformation written for the *British and Evangelical Review* and collected in *The Reformers and the Theology of the Reformation* deal with such leading men and issues as Luther, the Reformers and the doctrine of assurance, Melanchthon and the theology of the Church of England, Zwingli and the doctrine of the sacraments, Calvin and Beza, Calvinism and Arminianism, Calvinism and the doctrine of philosophical necessity, and lessons and practical applications from Calvinism and the Reformers. Furthermore, even his *Discussions on Church Principles*, which examines the "Popish,

Erastian, and Presbyterian" systems, reveals his principle of subjecting polemic theology to the revealed will and Word of God.[18]

Thus, the very table of contents in Cunningham's works reveals his general approach of assessing major historical and doctrinal discussions and controversies within the confines of systematics which, in turn, must be fully subject to the Word of God. Historiography must be evaluative; the touchstone of the Word must be applied to the material being tested. Cunningham succinctly states his overarching approach to historical theology as follows:

> The most valuable object which the student of historical and polemic theology can aim at is to endeavour to trace, by a survey of controversial discussions, how far God's completed revelation of His will was rightly used by the church for guiding to a correct knowledge and application of divine truth, and how far it was misapplied and perverted.[19]

All of this is detailed by Cunningham in his address on church history at the inauguration of New College in November 1850. In this address, he reinforces his conviction that the study of historical theology is most profitably pursued by focusing on doctrines that are scriptural (or can be deduced from the Scriptures) and that are of a controversial nature in that they "still continue to divide the opinions of men and churches."[20]

Thus, taking his cue from Calvin, Cunningham set up a hierarchy of Christian truths and heresies. Therefore, his historical texts tend to be expositions of cardinal doctrines rather than non-essential doctrines. He refutes in detail Arminianism, Romanism, and Socinianism, while bypassing smaller theological systems that he would also view as heretical. This hierarchy of truths and errors to be addressed is determined by their prominence in Scripture and according to the need of the hour.[21]

For Cunningham, the confining of historiography within the parameters of Scripture was neither a static nor restrictive principle. Rather, the objective ground of Scripture served as a springboard to give added impetus to the subjective development of doctrine throughout church history. From this springboard, Cunningham developed three interpretative models of the Reformation and post-Reformation era, which lie at the heart of his historiography. These may be designated as the models of corruption, restoration, and explanatory development. The first two of these models will be explained briefly, while the third, which contains Cunningham's most salient contribution, will be examined in some detail.

INTERPRETATIVE MODELS OF
REFORMATION/POST-REFORMATION ERA

First, Cunningham used the model of corruption in his interpretation of the Roman Catholic Church in medieval and subsequent Reformation times. He asserted that the church's early subjective growth in understanding such doctrines as the Trinity and Christology was conjoined with a growth of corruption in doctrine, organization, and worship: "[This is] the great Protestant position, that the Church gradually became corrupted in doctrines, government, and worship by departing from the scriptural and apostolic standard and that this is the true cause and explanation of the palpable contrast between the Church of the first century, and the Church at the beginning of the sixteenth century, or what is the same thing, the modern Church of Rome."[22] Cunningham then explains that the corruption which reached its height in the medieval church had its origin in the agency of Satan and the depravity of man. Orientalism, Platonism, and polytheism were merely influences which at particular periods concurred with the basic abuses, but later modified their operation.

Unfortunately, Cunningham uses a somewhat sectarian approach in placing the bulk of medieval theology and practice under his model of corruption. There are some significant gaps in his scholarship in the pursuit of this model. A comment on Thomas Aquinas, for example, implies that Cunningham had seldom perused his works.[23] Moreover, he freely acknowledges that he was acquainted with the writers of the church between Augustine and the Reformation principally from secondary sources.[24]

By comparison, however, Cunningham's model of corruption is more firmly supported from primary sources with regard to the Romish Church in Reformation times. His *Historical Theology* is of inestimable value for thoroughness of treatment on Rome's theology, particularly on the theological aspects solidified at the Council of Trent.

Second, Cunningham utilizes the model of restoration to characterize the Protestant Reformation. His basic claim is that the Reformation churches contain in restorative form and content the doctrine and life of the primitive church. In *Discussions on Church Principles*, he states:

"We maintain that Protestantism was the Christianity of the apostles . . . and that the Protestantism of the Reformation was, to a large extent at least, a restoration of Christianity to its original, apostolic purity."[25]

According to J. J. Bonar, Cunningham "used to declare that the only credit due to him, either in the pulpit or the chair, was this, and no more: that he had resuscitated Reformation doctrine, like Hodge, and caused the Churches to look at it in its noble features."[26]

This is not to say, however, that Cunningham regarded the Reformers as infallible guides: "We do not set up the Reformers as guides or oracles; we do not invest them with any authority, or believe anything because they believed it." Cunningham believed that the Reformers yielded to various sources of error and were not always purged thoroughly from the corrupting influence of the system in which they had been educated; nevertheless, "with respect to all points in which they were substantially of one mind, [they] may be regarded as being upon the whole entitled to more respect and deference than any other body of men who could be specified or marked out at any one period in the history of the church. . . ."[27]

Finally, and most importantly, Cunningham accented a model of explanatory development when viewing Reformed theology from a perspective of internal growth. In other words, he viewed the internal movement of Reformed theology as primarily positive and constructive until the height of Reformed Orthodoxy was reached, as represented by divines such as Francis Turretin (1623–1687), professor of theology in the Genevan Academy.[28] For Cunningham, this positive, subjective development was a healthy outgrowth of realizing the objective development within the Word of God. Specifically, this explanatory development assumed for Cunningham four steps of advancement: first, the development of Calvin's theology as an outgrowth of the theology of Augustine in general and Luther in particular; second, the development of Bezan theology as an outgrowth of Calvin's exegetical and systematic theology; third, the development of the theology of the Westminster Assembly as an outgrowth of Reformation orthodoxy; and finally, the development of Francis Turretin's theology as an outgrowth of Calvinism in its most soundly developed form.

Cunningham asserted that Calvin's joint utilization of Augustine and Luther enabled him to present a harmonious system beyond the reach of either divine.[29] Consequently, Cunningham unequivocally placed the movement from Luther to Calvin within his model of explanatory development. Of Calvin, he writes: "The systematising of divine truth, and the full organisation of the Christian church according to the word of God, are the great peculiar achievements of Calvin. For this work God eminently qualified him, by bestowing upon him the highest gifts both of nature and of grace; and this work he was enabled to accomplish in such a way as to confer the greatest and most lasting benefits upon the church of Christ, and to entitle him to the commendation and the gratitude of all succeeding ages."[30]

Despite Calvin's personal faults, notes Cunningham, "There is probably not one among the sons of men, beyond the range of those whom God miraculously inspired by His Spirit, who has stronger claims upon our veneration and gratitude."[31] For Cunningham, this high tribute to Calvin is valid along both exegetical and systematical lines of theology, as well as in the specifics of ecclesiology—particularly in worship and proper church organization. In Calvin we first find five principles relative to ecclesiology brought together in one package and ably defended: (1) the forbidding of introducing anything into the government and worship of the church which lacks the positive sanction of Scripture; (2) the organization of the church—its offices, ordinances, worship, and administration—in accord with the prescriptions of the New Testament; (3) the Presbyterian form of church government; (4) the protective and supportive role of the state, while leaving the church "altogether free and independent of civil control;" (5) the freedom of the conscience wherever human laws are not directly "sanctioned by the authority of God."[32]

Cunningham did not believe that Calvin's successor, Theodore Beza (1519–1605), betrayed Calvin's theological perspective. In the salient essay, "Calvin and Beza,"[33] Cunningham unfolds his model of explanatory development by answering proponents of a Calvin-Beza dichotomy on four of their major argumentative doctrines that supposedly posit such a cleavage: the eternal decrees of God, the imputation of Adam's sin to his posterity, the limitation of the atonement to the elect, and justification through grace by faith.

Concerning the first point, Cunningham argues that if the internal Reformed debate over the moral order of the eternal decrees of God (supralapsarianism vs. infralapsarianism)[34] had occurred in his day, Calvin would have leaned toward infralapsarianism. He readily admits that Beza went beyond his mentor on this point, but asserts that it bears no major consequences for theology. Being an avowed infralapsarian, Cunningham adds: "We do not regard this among the services [Beza] rendered to scriptural truth; especially as we are bound in candour to admit that there is some ground to believe that his high views upon this subject exerted a repelling influence upon the mind of Arminius, who studied under him for a time at Geneva."[35]

With regard to the doctrine of the imputation of Adam's sin, Cunningham argues that Beza merely developed what Calvin had asserted in seed form. Calvin by no means denied this doctrine, but focused more on "the transmission and the actual universal prevalence of a depraved moral nature than on the imputation of Adam's sin, which was not then a subject of controversy."[36] Hence, Beza's emphasis was one of explanatory development—not radical departure as frequently alleged. This development Cunningham views positively, based on his exegesis of Romans 5:12–19.

Those who posit discontinuity between Calvin and Beza teach that Calvin advocated unlimited atonement whereas Beza taught that atonement was limited to the elect.[37] Also, they teach that with regard to justification by faith, Calvin limited justification to the remission of sins (i.e., not including acceptance) and never used Beza's twofold distinction in justification (viz., Christ's passive obedience as the ground of pardon, and His active obedience to the law as the ground of acceptance).[38] Cunningham denies the former discrepancy on the basis that Calvin nowhere states unlimited atonement; that as a predestinarian he specifically denies that God in some sense desires, purposes, or intends to save all men; and that several of Calvin's exegetical comments (particularly on 1 Timothy 2:4 and 1 John 2:2) support the position of Beza and later advocates of particular redemption. Moreover, he argues that it is unfair to cite Calvin on a question he never formally addressed.[39]

Concerning justification, Cunningham argues that Calvin's accent on pardon in justification does not exclude his belief in acceptance as part and parcel of it; moreover, though the formal passive-active obedience distinction in Christ's righteousness is not explicitly stated, the material content is present. Thus, in both cases, Beza's positions are explanatory developments of seeds sown earlier by Calvin.[40]

Though Cunningham acknowledges that Calvin's teaching was not precisely identical with that of Beza and later Calvinists on these and other doctrinal points, he denied that Beza altered Calvin's basic direction or emphases. Rather, he argues, a development of doctrine in the Calvinist tradition from Calvin through Beza and on into the Reformed tradition must be viewed from the perspective of clarifying that which Calvin himself taught. That is, had Calvin been alive to read what Beza and later Calvinists wrote, he would have acknowledged that they were merely elucidating to their respective generations what he himself had initially propounded to his own. Cunningham concludes:

> It has been often alleged that Beza, in his very able discussion . . . carried his views upon some points farther than Calvin himself did, so that he has been described as being *Calvino Calvinior* [i.e., more Calvinistic than Calvin]. We are not prepared to deny altogether the truth of this allegation; but we are persuaded that there is less ground for it than is sometimes supposed, and that the points of alleged difference between them in matters of doctrine, respect chiefly topics on which Calvin was not led to give any very formal or explicit deliverance, because they were not at the time subjects of discussion, or indeed ever present to his thoughts.[41]

In defending the continunity between Calvin and Beza, Cunningham's model of explanatory development strikes a contemporary chord, for since 1950 there has been a snowballing of scholarly material advocating a supposed Calvin-Calvinist cleavage dating back to Theodore Beza. From Hans Weber through Ernst Bizer, and from Basil Hall to Walter Kickel and R. T. Kendall, Beza has been condemned as the father of Reformed scholasticism, who spoiled Calvin's theology by reading him through Aristotelian spectacles.[42] Beza has been repeatedly charged with scholastic, non-christological rigidity—not only in general doctrinal *loci* and ecclesiastical discipline, but also particularly in his supposed "innovation" of supralapsarian predestination. In contrast to Calvin's Christocentric, biblical and soteriologically oriented doctrine, Beza is viewed as having developed the theocentric, scholastic, and deterministic doctrines of Reformed Orthodoxy.[43] Cunningham's nineteenth-century answer to this twentieth-century debate has never been directly countered to date, despite the fact that it was his most salient contribution to Reformation historiography.

During the 1970s, a fresh reevaluation of Protestant orthodoxy along the more traditional lines advocated by Cunningham was initiated by Jill Raitt, John Patrick Donnelly, John S. Bray, Olivier Fatio, Marvin W. Anderson, and W. Robert Godfrey.[44] In the 1980s, interest in this fresh reappraisal was sparked especially by Richard A. Muller, who argued that late sixteenth- and seventeenth-century Reformed documents did not support the theory of a "predestinarian metaphysic" that smothered the biblicism of the first-generation Reformers. Rather, Muller asserts that although the theologians of the post-Reformation period used a scholastic methodology to clarify the Reformed theological system, they remained in essential agreement with the first generation of Reformed thought. According to Muller, post-Reformation orthodoxy often disagreed with the content of medieval scholasticism, but advantageously used its organizational structure. Hence, in post-Reformation scholastic orthodoxy, "scholastic" refers to the method of theology utilized, "orthodoxy" to the content and doctrinal intention. Though Reformed scholastic orthodoxy stands in some methodological discontinuity with Calvin, it retains strong affinity with Reformation teaching; indeed, the Reformation is incomplete without its confessional and theological codification.[45]

Predictably, Cunningham also cradled the crystallization of Bezan and Reformed orthodoxy as witnessed in the theology of the Westminster Assembly—the Confession, Shorter and Larger Catechisms inclusive—within the framework of explanatory development. For him, the assembly represented the flowering of Calvin's budding thought a century before, and "contained the very meaning of the Bible."[46] When Calvin and the assembly appeared to disagree, as for example on the subject of assurance, Cunningham leaned on his model of explanatory development. He stated that the early Reformers had not yet seen the necessity of separating the assurance of faith from saving faith itself in the infancy of their movement, partially because of their personal experience as assured believers, and partially because of the ground taken by Roman Catholicism in arguing against them.[47] He summarized as follows: "We believe the whole Calvinism of the Canons of the Synod of Dort, and of the Confession of the Westminster Assembly, and we are willing to attempt to expound and defend, when called upon, the whole doctrine of these symbols, to show that it is all taught or indicated in Scripture. We have been only confirmed in our Calvinism by all the study we have given to this subject."[48]

For Cunningham, full-orbed Calvinism was represented in its purest form in the theology of "the great Protestant divines of the seventeenth century," such as Herman Witsius, Petrus Van Mastricht, and especially Francis Turretin.[49] For Cunningham, these theologians, who base the whole of their theology on the foundations laid by the Reformers, carry Reformation theology "to its completion, and may be said to form the crown and the copestone of theological science, viewed as an accurate, comprehensive, and systematic exposition and defence of the doctrines revealed in the word of God."[50] Cunningham asserts that these divines dealt with each important doctrine of Scripture so accurately and thoroughly that each doctrine "is practically exhausted and conclusively determined."[51]

Here lies perhaps one of the greatest weaknesses of Cunningham's historiography. His viewpoint that Turretin and others offered the final word on all substantial theology compelled him to view the post-Turretin era in Reformed theology very negatively. Consequently, he regarded nearly everything innovative in Reformed systematics subsequent to Francis Turretin as a betrayal of the basic principles of Reformed theology, and therefore not worthy of the name "Reformed."[52]

Cunningham regarded the utilization of scholastic methodology in Reformed Orthodoxy—particularly in Turretin—as essential and profitable. In fact, he incorporated it into his model of explanatory development:

> The Reformers themselves do not make much use of scholastic distinctions and phraseology, as they in general avoided intricate and perplexed discussions; but when, in subsequent times, more subtle disputations upon difficult topics arose among Protestant theologians, it was found necessary, if these topics were to be discussed at all, to have recourse to a considerable extent to scholastic distinctions and phraseology; and it was also found that the use and application of scholastic

distinctions and phraseology were fitted to throw some light upon questions which otherwise would have been still darker and more perplexed than they are. . . . Take, for example, Turretine's system, a book which is of inestimable value. In the perusal of this great work, occasionally some difficulty will be found, especially at first, in fully understanding its statements, for ignorance of, or imperfect acquaintance with, scholastic distinctions and phraseology; but, as the reader becomes familiar with these, he will see more and more clearly how useful they are, in the hands of a man like Turretine, in bringing out the exact truth upon difficult and intricate questions.[53]

In short, Cunningham states his model of explanatory and valid development for Calvinism in terms of personal conviction as follows:

"Calvinism unfolds most fully and explicitly the whole system of doctrine revealed in the sacred Scriptures. It brings out most prominently and explicitly the sovereign agency of God . . . in the salvation of sinners; while it most thoroughly humbles and abases men, as the worthless and helpless recipients of the divine mercy and bounty."[54]

The influence of Cunningham's historiography is difficult to measure. On the one hand, it ought not to be forgotten, as Andrew Drummond and James Bulloch point out, that Cunningham "very largely set the theological tone for the Free Church; . . . he transmitted to many of the younger ministers who trained under him, and even to their spiritual descendants who refused to enter the union of 1900 and constituted the Free Church as it is known in the west Highlands today, his rigidity without his ability."[55] On the other hand, Cunningham's influence was quickly eclipsed as Scottish churchmen opted for the philosophy of the Enlightenment over the theology of the Reformation. Moreover, as Donald Maclean notes, among the professors of New College, Edinburgh, Cunningham "represented the last phase of the Calvinistic tradition in Scotland. . . . Theologies after his day depart from this tradition and show indubitable signs of a great change."[56]

Even Robert Rainy—Cunningham's student, biographer, colleague, and eventual successor as Principal of New College for thirty-two years following Candlish—allows a different ethos to pervade his writings. Unlike Cunningham, whose outlook was little influenced by the winds of change blowing into Scotland from Germany, Rainy read German fluently, having resided in Germany for some time.[57] This German influence became noticeable as early as 1873, the year before Rainy became principal, in his addresses delivered as the fifth series of Cunningham Lectures in Edinburgh, *The Delivery and Development of Christian Doctrine* (1875).[58] In short, Cunningham "was the solid, scholastic High Calvinist of the early Victorian era while Rainy was the cultured, moderate Calvinist of the later Victorian era."[59] Furthermore, beyond Rainy, the tendency of New College professors was to attempt to "hold the premises of German unbelief and draw the conclusions of Scottish evangelical orthodoxy."[60]

The professorial colleague in whom Cunningham would find his happiest friendship and sympathy to the end of his career was Charles Hodge, his transatlantic colleague at Princeton. Each of these theological stalwarts esteemed the other higher than himself. As Macleod wittily notes: "The story is told of one of Cunningham's students who had thoughts of taking a session at Princeton with Hodge. He was a canny Scot and wanted to make sure beforehand that a session taken overseas would count as part of his Divinity course. So he went to see the Principal about it. He stated his case. Cunningham when he heard it, took a pinch of snuff . . . and then gave his answer. . . . His only question about the matter was whether a session taken with Hodge ought not to be counted as equal to two."[61]

As in Hodge, so in Cunningham a scarce brand of scholarship comes to the fore. Hard work was not shirked, and conscience was not left to slumber. The scholar was always the servant of Christ, whose task was not to call into question, not to go in search of some novel idea, not to import the wisdom of the world into the church; but rather to vindicate the claims of the gospel, unearth and explore the profound riches of the Scriptures, and bring every thought captive to Christ.

Cunningham's methodology has sometimes been too easily dismissed as being more that of a dogmatician than a church historian. Seldom has it been realized that for him the church historian *must* be a dogmatician. He accented dogma because he was persuaded that this accent was the best way of doing church history. He believed that church history was essentially the hammering out of dogma in the fires of ecclesiastical controversy. It was this principle—not his alleged ignorance—that freed his lectures from detail in historical theology, for as Rainy has pointed out, his detailed knowledge came out in his Thursday talks with the students, in which he displayed that "no man was fuller than Dr. Cunningham of detail, about churches, men, and books."[62]

In sum, Cunningham's influence has been and continues to be greatest among those who embrace the theology and confessions of the Westminster Assembly and are sympathetic to the old Princeton brand of theology, as can be gathered from the recent reprints of his major works issued by such publishers as The Banner of Truth Trust and Still Waters Revival Books. Though Cunningham's views are too Calvinistic and narrow in scope to gain widespread influence at present, he is still being read and emulated particularly by those who strive in a scriptural and Reformed fashion to wed the claims of faith and the claims of truth.

SELECTED BIBLIOGRAPHY

PRIMARY SOURCES

Animadversions upon Sir William Hamilton's Pamphlet. Edinburgh, 1844.

Defence of the Rights of the Christian People in the Appointment of Ministers. Edinburgh, 1840.

Discussions on Church Principles: Popish, Erastian, and Presbyterian. Edinburgh, 1863; reprinted, Edmonton, 1992.

Historical Theology: A Review of the Principle Doctrinal Discussions in the Christian Church from the Apostolic Age. 2 vols. Edinburgh, 1862; reprinted, London, 1969.

Inauguration of the New College of the Free Church, Edinburgh: November, MDCCCL. London, 1851. (Includes an "Address" by Cunningham as Principal, 39–58, and an introductory lecture on "Church History" as Professor of Theology and Church History, 59–78.)

Lecture on the Nature and Lawfulness of Union Between Church and State. Edinburgh, 1835.

Lectures on the Objects, Nature, and Standard of Ecclesiastical Authority. Edinburgh, 1839.

The Reformers and the Theology of the Reformation. Edinburgh, 1862; reprinted, London, 1967.

Sermons from 1828 to 1860. Ed. by J. J. Bonar. Edinburgh, 1872; reprinted, Edmonton, 1992.

Theological Lectures on Natural Theology, Evidences of Christianity, the Canon and Inspiration of Scripture. New York, 1878.

The Unchangeableness of Christ: A Sermon, After the Funeral of Dr. Robert Gordon. Edinburgh, 1853.

NOTES

1. John Macleod, *Scottish Theology* (Edinburgh: Knox Press, 1943; reprinted, Edinburgh: Banner of Truth Trust, 1974), 118, 269ff.

2. E.g., Peter Toon, *The Development of Doctrine in the Church* (Grand Rapids: Eerdmans, 1979), 25–33.

3. These include his most renowned *Historical Theology*, 2 vols. (Edinburgh, 1862; reprinted, London: Banner of Truth Trust, 1969—hereafter, *HT*), and *The Reformers and the Theology of the Reformation* (Edinburgh, 1862; reprinted, London: Banner of Truth Trust, 1967—hereafter, *RTR*), as well as his *Discussions on Church Principles: Popish, Erastian, and Presbyterian* (Edinburgh, 1863—hereafter, *CP*), and *Theological Lectures on Natural Theology, Evidences of Christianity, the Canon and Inspiration of Scripture* (New York: Robert Carter and Brothers, 1878—hereafter, *TL*). All of the above were gathered and published under the direction of James Buchanan and James Bannerman, in whose hands Cunningham left his manuscripts—the only exception being *TL*, published some fifteen years later than the others under the editorial guidance of Thomas Smith. (See the appended bibliography for several of Cunningham's minor works.).

4. The term "Moderates" has been variously and pejoratively used in Scottish church history, but in this article represents a group of eighteenth-century theologians in Scotland who decried the rigidity of the evangelicals, and sought moderate views on most doctrines. The Moderates were led by William Hamilton, professor of divinity at the University of Edinburgh. They were largely Pelagian in theology, taught salvation by

works, and were very critical of "man-made creeds and confessions." Cf. H. R. Sefton, "Moderates," in *Dictionary of Scottish Church History and Theology*, ed. Nigel Cameron (Edinburgh: T. & T. Clark, 1993), 595–96; Macleod, *Scottish Theology*, 198–205; F. Voges, "Moderate and Evangelical Thinking in the Later Eighteenth Century: Differences and Shared Attitudes," *Records of the Scottish Church History Society* 22 (1986):141–57.

5. "Evangelicalism," in Sefton, *Dictionary*, 306–307. Cf. J. J. Bonar, ed., *Sermons from 1828 to 1860 by the Late William Cunningham* (Edinburgh: T. & T. Clark, 1872), xiii. J. J. Bonar was Cunningham's best friend of student days and his subsequent biographer. Also, cf. J. J. Bonar quoted by Robert Rainy and James MacKenzie, *Life of William Cunningham, D.D.* (London: T. Nelson & Sons, 1871), 25. This is the definitive, though in some respects disappointing, biography of Cunningham.

6. Cf. ibid., 25–31. According to Cunningham's own testimony, it was one of Gordon's sermons on regeneration that "was the means, in the hand of the Holy Ghost, of subduing the enmity of his carnal heart, and making him a new creature by faith in Jesus Christ" (J. J. Bonar, "William Cunningham, D.D.," in *Disruption Worthies* by James Wylie [Edinburgh: Thomas Jack, 1881], 195).

7. Bonar, *Sermons*, xvi; cf. 1–19 for his first sermon on Psalm 23:6.

8. Cf. Rainy and MacKenzie, *Life*, 52ff.

9. Patronage involved the role of landowners in the appointment of ministers. The Moderates tolerated patronage because it was civil law and because they believed this system produced a more educated ministry than could be expected from the laymen being involved with the calling of their ministers. Cf. "Patronage," in Sefton, *Dictionary*, 649–50.

10. Iain Murray, "Two Leaders of 'The Third Reformation,'" *Banner of Truth*, no. 18 (November 1959): 16–17, 20–21.

11. By seceding from the Established Church, Chalmers and Welsh automatically relinquished their professorships in the Edinburgh Divinity Hall, and hence were natural choices for the Free Church College. It appears that Cunningham was also a logical choice on account of his scholarly reputation and firm Calvinistic principles. To these three men, "Rabbi" John Duncan was joined due largely to his gifts in the ancient languages.

12. Murray, "Two Leaders," 21.

13. In 1859 he was appointed moderator of the General Assembly.

14. *CP*, 56.

15. *RTR*, 196.

16. Ibid., 21.

17. Rainy and MacKenzie, *Life*, 226–31.

18. This volume also includes a provocative discussion on the relation between church and state in general, and deals with the historical Free Church context.

19. *HT*, 1:7.

20. *Inauguration of the New College of the Free Church, Edinburgh: November, MDCCCL*. (Edinburgh: Johnstone and Hunter, 1851), 66, 67, 72–73. Cunningham gave two significant addresses on this special occasion: one as principal (39–57), and one as professor of theology and church history (59–78).

21. Cf. D. Macleod, "William Cunningham," in Sefton, *Dictionary*, 229–31.

22. *CP*, 60. Cf. *HT* 1: 34–42, for Romish rejoinder.

23. *HT*, 1: 424.

24. Ibid., 413ff.

25. *CP*, 47.

26. Bonar, *Sermons*, xxi.

27. *RTR*, 6–8. Cf. *HT*, 1: 331, 460–61.

28. See especially his *Institutio Theologiae Elenticae* in *Opera*, 4 vols. (Edinburgh: J. D. Lowe, 1847–48), which is in the process of being published in English as *Institutes of*

Elenctic Theology, trans. by George Musgrave Giger and ed. by James T. Dennison, Jr. (Phillipsburg: P & R Publishing, vols. 1 and 2, 1992; vol. 3 is forthcoming.)

29. Cf. ibid., 296–97.

30. Ibid., 294.

31. Ibid., 299.

32. Cf. ibid., 26–28.

33. First written for the *British and Foreign Evangelical Review* (July 1861), and subsequently collated as essay no. 7 in *RTR*, 345–412.

34. Supralapsarianism, meaning "above the fall," is the belief that God's eternal decree of predestination must morally precede the decrees of creation and the fall. Infralapsarianism, "below the fall," is the belief that God's decrees of creation and the fall must morally precede his decree to predestinate. Both viewpoints maintain the sovereignty of God in decreeing from eternity. Supralapsarianism tends to emphasize the absolute sovereignty of God; infralapsarianism, the responsibility of man. The Arminians attempted to accent the supra-infra differences among the Reformed, but failed to bring a cleavage among them, as the Reformed maintained that both viewpoints fell within the arena of sound biblical theology.

35. *RTR*, 366; cf. 358–71; *HT*, 2: 416ff.

36. *RTR*, 378–79; cf. 371–95.

37. Ibid., 395–402.

38. Ibid., 402ff.

39. Cunningham argues that the only time Calvin appears to make a somewhat formal statement on the question of the extent of the atonement, he clearly sides with Beza: "I should like to know how the wicked can eat the flesh of Christ which was not crucified for them, and how they can drink the blood which was not shed to expiate their sins" ("Concerning the True Partaking of the Flesh and Blood of Christ in the Holy Supper," in *Calvin: Theological Treatises*, ed. J. K. S. Reid [London: SCM Press, 1954], 285).

40. Cf. HT, 2: 14ff., 23, 46ff., 54ff.

41. *RTR*, 349.

42. Hans Emil Weber, *Reformation, Orthodoxie und Rationalismus* (Dormstadt: Wissenschaftliche Buchgesellschaft, 1966), 1: 2; Ernst Bizer, *Frühorthodoxie und Rationalismus* (Zurich: EVZ-Verlag, 1963), 6–15; Basil Hall, "Calvin Against the Calvinists," in *John Calvin*, ed. G. E. Duffield (Grand Rapids: Eerdmans, 1966), 25–28; Walter Kickel, *Vernunft und Offenbarung bei Theodor Beza* (Neukirchen: Neukirchener Verlag, 1967); Brian G. Armstrong, *Calvinism and the Amyraut Heresy* (Madison: University of Wisconsin, 1969), xviii, 38–42, 128–33, 158ff.; R. T. Kendall, *Calvin and English Calvinism to 1649* (Oxford: University Press, 1979), 1–41, 209ff.; and "The Puritan Modification of Calvin's Theology," in *John Calvin: His Influence in the Western World*, ed. W. Stanford Reid (Grand Rapids: Eerdmans, 1982), 199–216.

43. All of this and more has been charged to Beza despite the fact that no serious study was ever undertaken of his theology prior to Kickel's in 1967.

44. Jill Raitt, *The Eucharistic Theology of Theodore Beza: Development of the Reformed Doctrine* (Chambersburg, Pa.: American Academy of Religion, 1972); John Patrick Donnelly, *Calvinism and Scholasticism in Vermigli's Doctrine of Man and Grace* (Leiden: E. J. Brill, 1976); John S. Bray, *Theodore Beza's Doctrine of Predestination* (Nieuwkoop: B. De Graaf, 1975); Olivier Fatio, *Méthode et théologie: Lambert Daneau et les débuts de la scholastique réformée* (Geneve: Droz, 1976); Marvin W. Anderson, *Peter Martyr: A Reformer in Exile (1542–1562)* (Nieuwkoop: B. De Graaf, 1975); W. Robert Godfrey, "Tensions Within International Calvinism: The Debate on the Atonement at the Synod of Dordt, 1618–1619 (Ph.D. dissertation, Stanford University, 1974).

45. Richard A. Muller, *Christ and the Decree: Christology and Predestination in Reformed Theology from Calvin to Perkins* (Grand Rapids: Baker, 1988); *Post-Reformation Dogmat-*

ics, vol. 1 (Grand Rapids: Baker, 1987). Martin Klauber asserts that "this important interpretation recasts the entire period and portrays essential continuity in theological organization in the West from the introduction of Aristotle in the twelfth century to the decline in orthodoxy in the eighteenth century. Muller does for the post-Reformation period what Heiko Oberman has done for the Reformation era in pointing out the aspects of continuity with medieval antecedents" ("Continuity and Discontinuity in Post-Reformation Reformed Theology: An Evaluation of the Muller Thesis," *Journal of the Evangelical Theological Society* 33 [1990]:467).

For the support of Muller's basic reappraisal, but with unique emphases, cf. Donald W. Sinnema, "The Issue of Reprobation at the Synod of Dort (1618–19) in Light of the History of This Doctrine" (Ph.D. dissertation, University of St. Michael's College, 1985); Martin I. Klauber, "The Context and Development of the Views of Jean-Alphonse Turrettini (1671–1737) on Religious Authority" (Ph.D. dissertation, University of Wisconsin-Madison, 1987); Stephen R. Spencer, "Reformed Scholasticism in Medieval Perspective: Thomas Aquinas and Francis Turrettini on the Incarnation" (Ph.D. dissertation, Michigan State University, 1988); Joel R. Beeke, *Assurance of Faith: Calvin, English Puritanism, and the Dutch Second Reformation* (New York: Peter Lang, 1991).

46. Bonar, *Sermons*, xxi.

47. *RTR*, 113–15. Cf. Beeke, *Assurance of Faith*, 19–21, 51–54, 63.

48. *RTR*, 200.

49. *HT*, 1: 7; *RTR*, 411. Turretin has been singled out, as his theology was praised the most frequently by Cunningham (e.g., *HT*, 1: 419, 519, 573, 591, 605, 610; 2: 7, 20, 55, 71, 74, 306, 341, 363, 435, 500, 537).

50. *RTR*, 411–12.

51. Ibid., 412.

52. Ibid., 7.

53. *RTR*, 418–19. This is not to say that Cunningham did not at times find Calvin's views to be wiser and more properly proportioned than Turretin's, et al. (cf. Rainy and MacKenzie, *Life*, 501); nevertheless, he maintained Turretinian Calvinism as the "copestone of theological science."

54. *RTR*, 529. Cf. ibid., 339. Also, J. J. Bonar's comments on xxi of *Sermons*, including that Cunningham holds "Calvinism is solution throughout. . . . He found Calvinism in the Bible, in the Standards, in Philosophy, and in his heart."

55. Andrew Drummond and James Bulloch, *The Church in Victorian Scotland, 1843–1874* (Edinburgh: Saint Andrew Press, 1975), 19.

56. Donald Maclean, *Aspects of Scottish Church History* (Edinburgh: T. & T. Clark, 1927), 145.

57. Even Rainy admits that had Cunningham been able to read German and become more familiar with the whole range of German authorship, "his simple reply would have been . . . that unless the work could be done on more secure principles . . . it was not worth doing at all." Nevertheless, Cunningham did express the conviction that those after him might conduct a "thorough examination of the whole results of German investigation . . . as one of the most important services required at that period" (Rainy and MacKenzie, *Life*, 511).

58. Cf. the summary and analysis by Peter Toon, *Development of Doctrine*, 38–51.

59. Ibid., 38.

60. Cf. the summary and subsequent historical development outlined by G. Collins, *The Heritage of Our Fathers* (Edinburgh: Knox Press, 1974), 74–77.

61. Macleod, *Scottish Theology*, 271.

62. Rainy and MacKenzie, *Life*, 231.

11

I. A. DORNER

TIMOTHY R. PHILLIPS

Germany was facing theological turmoil in the middle of the nine-teenth century. While Friedrich Schleiermacher and G. W. F. Hegel had dominated the scene earlier, Friedrich Strauss's *Life of Jesus* succeeded in wrenching apart their synthesis of Christianity and culture. Historicism's all-encompassing and devastating attack quickly became apparent through F. C. Baur's stream of biblical and historical studies, as he dis-solved the whole of primitive Christianity—the origin of the church, its confession regarding Jesus Christ, and its writings—into immanental historical forces.

The so-called "Mediating Theologians" continued Schleiermacher's quest for an "eternal covenant" in this new historically aware context. Isaak August Dorner (1809–1884) was the most creative and conservative mediating theologian responding to historicism's challenge. His studies at Tübingen (1827–1832) under Baur overlapped with Strauss. Both were tutors at the Protestant *Stift* in Tübingen (1834) as Strauss was writing his *Life of Jesus*. After an appointment to Associate Professor at Tübingen (1838), offers took him to Kiel (1839), Königsberg (1843), Bonn (1847), Göttingen (1853), and finally to Schleiermacher's chair at Berlin (1862), where he remained until retirement just before his death. His academic work ranged from systematics and ethics to historical theology. His most important analyses of Christianity's historical development are two multivolume sets, *History of the Development of the Doctrine of the Person of Christ* and *The History of Protestant Theology*.[1] But the intrinsic connection between historical and theological reflection undergirds all his academic work. Throughout the century after his death these works engaged the greatest theological minds, from Karl Barth to Wolfhart Pannenberg, and continue to draw scholarly interest.

Like Schleiermacher, Dorner was occupied with practical as well as academic concerns throughout his career. A leading churchman in Germany, he also participated in the international Evangelical Alliance. His academic influence was wide. His students came from across the Western world, including such notable American figures as Swiss-born Philip Schaff and Charles Briggs. Dorner's work deeply shaped the theological perspectives of the progressive conservatives in this period, from Augustus Strong and James Orr to P. T. Forsyth.[2]

THE CHALLENGE OF HISTORICISM

The historicism of Baur and Strauss shook the pillars of theology. Nothing, Baur claimed, could count for history unless established through historical-critical means. Historicism's further demand that historical causes account for all events posed a challenge to God's miraculous works including Christology. Furthermore, historicism offered an understanding of reality in which all human situations and ideas are necessarily in flux; nothing is fixed. Developing the implications of this stance, Strauss's *Life of Jesus* interpreted the Scriptures as simply reflecting the myth of that primitive age and undermined their credibility. Revelation was dissolved into the fluidity of history where normative statement are no longer possible.[3]

Conservatives immediately recognized the perils of historicism. If the truth has been given once and for all in Jesus Christ, the conservatives contended, why are subsequent developments even needed? History only betrays a "pathology . . . of the Church," for the true church is unchanging. This ahistorical reaction actually had a long heritage among Protestants. During the Reformation, the Magdeburg Centuriators regarded "the primitive age of the church as that in which its ideal was realized." Subsequent history was viewed as nothing but "increasing declensions, restrained perhaps for a season at the Reformation."[4]

This repudiation of Christianity's historical development was linked to an obscurantist fideism and an epistemological objectivism. Strauss and

Baur had provoked many pietists to regard a theological and historical understanding of Jesus Christ "as an empty and vain undertaking."[5] Others following in Storr's steps claimed that knowledge of the past is available apart from subjective influences and is the foundation for faith. They answered Strauss's destructive biblical criticism on evidentialist grounds.[6]

In the midst of these turbulent times, Dorner sought to bridge and even reconcile the claims of reason, history and revelation. From the beginning of his academic career, Paul's phrase that in Christ "are hidden all the treasures of wisdom and knowledge" (Col. 2:3 NIV) hung in his study. And his life's work was devoted to showing that Jesus is history's destiny and the solution to its problems. Throughout his works, Dorner produced sustained criticisms of ahistorical objectivism and an immanental historicism, and proposed a historiography incorporating the demands of both revelation and history. After outlining the key components in historiography, we shall examine his major historical works.

PRESUPPOSITIONS FOR DORNER'S HISTORIOGRAPHY

HISTORICAL KNOWLEDGE AND REVELATION

Trained by Baur, Dorner knew historical criticism's value in eliminating superstition and delusion. However, he rejected Baur's claim regarding its objectivity. The attempt to attain "an historical objectivity apart from a dogmatical background," Dorner regards as one of the "impossible things with which people deceive themselves and others."[7] Historical inquiry is necessarily "worldviewish." Dorner delights in uncovering these confessional presuppositions in his contemporaries. Strauss's *Life of Jesus*, he notes, used Hegel's idealism and assumed that the entire process of history is the self-mediation of God's consciousness. In this system, Jesus cannot be the unique revelation of God's self-knowledge, for God's consciousness is incomplete as long as history is still progressing. That is why Strauss claims the Idea "is not wont to lavish all its fullness on one exemplar, and be niggardly towards all others," but spreads its riches on the entire race.[8] Consequently, Jesus can have only transitory importance.[9] Such a method is neither objective nor presuppositionless; rather, "here the historic is superfluous and reason has become influential."[10]

Dorner is equally critical of Storr's evidentialism, which attempts to establish *fides divina* on *fides humana*. He regards reason's claim to recognize a historical event as God's act as simply intellectual Pelagianism. Moreover, such proofs focus on revelation's form, not its content, and consequently do not correspond to the life and certainty Christianity offers. For

Christianity does not aim at the "purely historical, past, and dead," but the real in the historic: saving fellowship with Christ.[11]

Because confessionless knowing is an impossibility, the Christian must hold as foundational the reality of saving faith. For the very attempt to establish Christianity's truthfulness by a higher principle reveals that Christianity is not the "absolute religion."[12] And it is solely through the New Testament *kerygma* and the Spirit's work that the believer apprehends reconciliation with God as grounded in Jesus Christ. Unlike Schleiermacher, Dorner does not restrict faith's awareness to the religious self-consciousness. Rather, believers "in Christ" actually have knowledge that they have "obtained access to God; [that] in the Son they had found the Father."[13] While history or reason cannot establish revelation, Dorner's fideistic stance does not discard them. For if historical criticism establishes "the incredibility of the fundamental Christian facts, then faith could no longer stand."[14]

HISTORICAL PROCESSES AND CHRISTIANITY

Dorner accepts a sophisticated analysis of human historicity. Humans are reciprocally related to the world and necessarily participate in their own destiny; consequently, development is inherent to human life. Historical development is even intrinsic to Christianity.[15] While Christ's revelation exists "wholly" in the church, culture has decisively shaped its understanding. For instance, Jesus arrived in the midst of the Jewish and heathen world where His truths were grasped in only "a very incomplete form." But history is the arena where God unfolds and brings conceptual precision to the church's understanding of Christ's revelation. Breakthroughs in the church's consciousness are not merely human discoveries and constructions, but reflect the Spirit's work. Next to revelation, then, history holds the key for progress toward the ideal church.[16]

The model of an organism dominates Dorner's understanding of historical processes. He conceives the histories of creation, humanity and even the church as organisms. As in living creatures, an organism consists of a multiplicity of parts which are reciprocally related, so that changes in one produce an alternation in the whole. Development proceeds internally and is directed toward the organism's *telos*, just as an acorn develops into a tree, not a tire. Consequently Dorner rejects miracles in the supernaturalist sense, where God intrudes in creation to bring about His own extrinsic goal. But he accepts "relative miracles" in which nature is receptive to a higher cause coinciding with the organism's *telos*.[17] With this organic understanding of history, Dorner accepts much of historicism's principle of continuity, namely that change occurs through regular and internal causality.[18] In addition, Dorner learned from Baur and Hegel that change in intelligent organisms occurs by means of dialectical antagonisms, which correct one-sided tendencies through a halting process.[19]

This organic model frames Dorner's understanding of Jesus and His work in terms of the continuity between God and creation. Of course, Dorner rejects the view that Jesus is an immanent historical development, insisting instead that the God-man and His new life of reconciliation is a qualitatively new advent in history. But this is a relative miracle. While the God-man and the new life He establishes cannot be explained by prior historical causes, this is precisely the reality the past sought.[20] In other words, humanity is naturally receptive to and longs for the God-man. In Dorner's theological system, Jesus actually establishes the destiny and *telos* for humankind, which was lacking in the first creation. Then this creative reality advances through normal historical processes. Paralleling Schleiermacher's proposal, this construction subsumes the second creation into the intrinsic receptivity of the first, unifying nature and grace in God's original plan for creation.

Jesus' revelation of reconciliation constitutes the essence of Christianity, containing "Christian truth in its totality, but not in a fully developed form." Through history the church develops this "embryonic knowledge," advancing to a more determinate understanding of revelation. For Christianity was not "planted in the world as a young tree, but as a seed" with its entire future enclosed.[21] It is Christ's revelation that propels the church's advancement in understanding truth and life. Revelation, then, possesses an "inborn conquering might" and a world-shaping force, evidenced by its ability to mediate and resolve the world's challenges.[22]

CHRISTIANITY AND THE HISTORY OF DOCTRINE

This seems a precarious and meager grounding for Christianity. Given the flux of history and faith-stance of knowing, how could the theologian show that Christianity is the truth? Does not history dissolve God's unique work in Jesus Christ into its immanental processes? Dorner's work in the history of doctrine answers these questions.

According to Dorner, faith is inwardly assured that its contents are absolute truth. It does not seek to establish Christianity's truthfulness by a higher principle: "Were it to do so, Christianity could not be the perfect or absolute religion."[23] However, its truthfulness is indirectly reflected through historical processes. In the arena of history, Christian revelation shows that it alone possesses an "inborn conquering might" which fulfills the deepest desires of non-Christian systems while shattering their one-sided errors. In this way faith establishes the universality of its vision, for the first as well as the second creation, and thereby demonstrates that Christ is history's *telos*. However, this argument assumes that Christianity is unique and not derived from other religious systems.[24] Dorner employs two strategies to establish the originality of Christianity, one focusing on Christianity in the context of world history and the second on its internal development.

In contrast to the Hegelian view, Dorner insists that history does not possess its own destiny. History consists of a process in which distortions provoke an equally one-sided error, which calls for a counteraction. But a forward advance is not inherent in this process. Unless a higher power establishes a new reality, history consists only of an eternal rebound and repetition.[25] According to Dorner's analysis, humanity's religious quest for God reflects this circular movement. Once God is so purified from all finitude in deism that He is shut up in Himself, there is an inevitable passing over to the opposite, pantheism. For humanity seeks communion with God and an absolutely hidden God is tantamount to atheism. But the history of humanity's attempts to find union with God through pantheism evidences an equal one-sidedness. There is no inherent progression in religion, only a circular movement. The reconciliation of the divine and the human established by Jesus, however, is an original and creative event in history which breaks through the old impasses of deism and pantheism, establishing Christianity as history's destiny.[26]

Second, Dorner must establish that Christianity's progress derives internally from its central idea, and not from extraneous cultural forces. Dorner readily acknowledges that the church is shaped by non-Christian ideas. Even the canon preserves pre-Christian modes of thought. Such are the processes of history. However, the kerygmatic revelation produces conflicts with these extraneous ideas, initiating an internal purifying process. Through these conflicts, the church recognizes deeper connections, progressively masters faith's content, and haltingly presses toward the whole truth. The *kerygma* contains both the germ "in which the whole lies infolded" and the "inborn conquering might" to achieve this goal.[27]

In sum, for Dorner, Christ as the God-man unites the goal of history and the norm for rationality. As such this One is "bringing about the consummation of the world." Herein lies history's destiny. The task for the historian is to exhibit Christ's world-shaping power and assist the future "unfolding and strengthening of Reason through the power of Christianity."[28]

THE DEVELOPMENT OF CHRISTOLOGY

Dorner's *History of the Development of the Doctrine of the Person of Christ* is his most important work in the history of dogma. Initially published in *Tübinger Zeitschrift für Theologie* in 1835–36 and then ballooning eleven-fold in book form (1845–1856), it suffers the fate of similar compilations: disjunctions and uneven analyses. If abridged, its evaluation would undoubtedly be more compelling; nevertheless it stands as an invaluable work in the history of Christological development.

While still at Tübingen, Dorner began this project to show that the church's traditional confession regarding Christ is secure despite the radical criticism of Baur and Strauss. The strategy outlined above structures Dorner's argument. He must establish historically that Christianity originates solely through the advent of Jesus Christ, and that this idea unfolds through the historical process with an "inborn conquering might," advancing a deeper knowledge of God and humanity. Furthermore, he must conceptualize Jesus so that His advent accords with the first creation or human possibilities. Dorner outlines the genesis of Christology according to four periods: (1) the advent of the God-man in the apostolic church; (2) the post-apostolic period when the affirmation of Jesus' deity and humanity solidified; (3) the post-Nicene period through the eighteenth century, in which the church investigated the unity of the deity and humanity; (4) the nineteenth century, in which the church began to resolve the old difficulties and open new directions for the doctrine.

THE APOSTOLIC CHURCH

Dorner opens this history by showing that Judaism and pantheistic systems point to but do not account for the rise of Christianity. While all religion seeks communion with God, pantheistic systems reduce this to an impersonal union and Judaism so elevates God's holy personality that union with humanity is unthinkable. Jesus offers a qualitatively new reality that fulfills the world's longing. As the apostolic proclamation reflects, in Christianity one apprehends Christ as the Son who mediates absolute reconciliation with the Father, for He is the God-man Who will return as the eschatological judge and establish perfection in a new world.[29]

While this analysis only intends to establish the originality of Christianity and the historical context for the subsequent history of dogma, some commentators fault Dorner for failing to interact with Strauss's criticisms against the authenticity of the Gospels point by point. For instance, Colin Brown concludes that, "Dorner exhibited little awareness of any need to come to terms with Gospel criticism, or indeed to work out a considered view of the relationship between faith and history in the light of historical criticism."[30] This, however, is a rush to judgment. Dorner places weight on the intuited kerygmatic essence of Christianity, not the inspired Scriptures. While admitting the presence of pre-Christian ideas and even myth in the text, he firmly rejects Strauss's skepticism regarding the authenticity of the biblical *kerygma*.[31] Dorner's criticism is devastating: Strauss has simply failed to argue this point historically. Identifying the sufficient cause for every effect is the historian's task. Therefore Strauss must provide an alternative historical explanation for the apostolic church's consciousness of redemption and the origin of these documents.[32] This is a familiar criticism; Baur also noted that Strauss failed to provide "a criticism of the Gospel sources."

POST-APOSTOLIC CHURCH

Once the gospel is implanted in history, error is inevitable. The "masses of heathen and Jewish error" were renounced only in principle wherever Christianity was embraced. Their remaining influence was not eliminated "as by a magic stroke," but only through hard work as the idea of Christianity evolved in interaction with the world.[33] The post-apostolic period solidified the affirmation of Jesus' humanity and deity. In two important arguments, one challenging Baur's reconstruction of the second century and a second focusing on the development of the Trinity, Dorner displays the originality and intrinsic power of Christianity.

While Strauss failed to provide a "criticism of the Gospel sources," Baur proposed a radical reconstruction of the early church's history. The dogmatic deficiencies of the second century permitted Baur to challenge the Apostolic Age's achievement and relocate most of the New Testament writings to the second century. Baur insisted that for Jesus and the disciples Christianity was simply a spiritualized Judaism and essentially Ebionite. The church remained firmly Ebionite until the middle of the second century. The confession of Jesus as the unique God-man originated in the Catholic Church, which developed as the synthesis between the judaizing (Petrine) and hellenizing (Pauline) parties in the church.[34]

Dorner acknowledged the importance and severity of this reconstruction. "Beyond all doubt" the church of the second century is inferior to that of the apostles. But Dorner counters that Baur has not sufficiently examined all the historical evidence, namely the Christological consciousness reflected in the church's practices and beliefs. He carefully demonstrates that the ecclesial practices established by the apostolic fathers in a pagan context evidenced a clear consciousness of Jesus' deity. For instance, the liturgical elements, such as the Lord's Supper, reflect Christ's propitiatory work of reconciliation.

Even the church calendar provides implicit evidence. In contrast to the Jewish memorializing the first creation, Christians worshipped on Sunday to celebrate the second creation which Christ's resurrection had established.[35] Dorner attends particularly to the early church's eschatological expectations, emphasizing that they were not flights from history but ways of envisioning the new future Jesus Christ had established. Eschatology, he argues, is the germ from which the completed idea of Christology unfolds.[36] The apostolic fathers begin with the confession that Jesus is the Judge and King who will return and perfect creation, and soon recognized that this assumes Christ is the Creator and the eternal Wisdom of God. Dorner concludes that there is much "diversity" in the early church, but not one of the apostolic fathers is Ebionite. Rather "myths become history to him (Baur) who treats history as myth!"[37]

Completing his historical argument, Dorner shows how the contemporary heresies disintegrated under the reality of the God-man. Judaistic Ebionism proposed to find the deeper meaning of Christianity in the confession of Jesus' humanity and His new Law. But Jesus' baptism and His purported exaltation as God's Son uncovered an inner contradiction in Ebionism. If Jesus' holiness, which rendered him worthy of this honor, were His own work, then He does not represent a new creative principle in history. Rather Jesus would pose a challenge to humans needing forgiveness, and thus would have no religious significance for sinners. By contrast, if His holiness were due to a higher divine power which united with Jesus, then the humanity had merely symbolic significance. So Ebionism opened the door to its opposite, Docetism, in the form of Gnosticism. But the accidental nature of Jesus' humanity became the crux for Docetism. The more the human nature is trivialized, the less this *gnosis* can be linked with Jesus. Rather it becomes only one divine manifestation among many, undermining Jesus' unique dignity. Dorner concludes that the reality of Jesus as the God-man produced this "decomposing process" of pre-Christian religious ideas, bringing these one-sided ideas "into a right track" and thereby establishing itself as "the truth of all that pre-Christian."[38]

Dorner sees a similar process in the development of the Trinity. While nothing short of confessing Christ's true deity could satisfy those conscious of absolute reconciliation through Him, this seemed opposed to God's oneness, which was equally unassailable. At the end of the second century Christological discussions began impacting the concept of God. The prevailing culture conceived God as abstractly one and unable to enter into true fellowship with humanity. As history demonstrated, its logical end was either a deism that produces an Arian Christology or a pantheism that generates Sabellianism. Dorner astutely shows how the Christian understanding of reconciliation in Jesus Christ, and not philosophical influences, overcame both heresies and arrived at the Christian understanding of God.[39] Such analyses are indispensable to his thesis that Christianity possesses its own originality and is not the synthesis of worldly processes, as Baur claimed.

In Sabellianism, God is self-communicative without being able to distinguish Himself from the world. Consequently Jesus is represented as a mere momentary exhibition of divine power, reducing the incarnation to a theophany and undermining Christ's eternality. This contradicts the Christian consciousness which sees Him as the "eternally constitutive and integrant element" in our reconciliation with God.[40] Arianism, by contrast, sharply distinguished God from the world, because any act of divine self-communication was viewed as imperiling creation's existence. God stands in a holy and alien relation to humanity, but not one of love, again contradicting the Christian consciousness of reconciliation.[41]

Throughout this period, the church rejected these heretical ideas and elevated the Christian understanding of a living personal God. But to eliminate all the heterogenous elements and to arrive at the scientific conception of the Trinity takes time. Nicaea declared that the deity and the hypostatic form of Jesus' higher nature are equally certain to faith. Not until Athanasius were these two theses consistently conceptualized. He and others in the church conceived "the self-consciousness of Deity as consisting in the reciprocal knowledge of the Father and the Son, which is not merely a knowledge which the one has *of*, but which each has *in* the other."[42] The Trinity firmly established the idea of God as a living Person who can lovingly relate to creation without losing His own independent existence.

THE CHURCH FROM THE POST-NICENE TO THE PRESENT

The church's refutation of Docetism and Ebionism and the constructive doctrine of the Trinity provided the foundation for conceptualizing the union of humanity and deity in Jesus Christ. According to Dorner's narrative, initially the deity dominates this union which provokes a corresponding one-sided reaction; finally in the nineteenth century human and divine stand in equilibrium. This is to be expected, Dorner explains. Not only were the original counciliar decisions premature, but the conception of Jesus' personal unity is related to other doctrines including Christ's work and the reality of salvation.[43] Dorner's analysis shows how developments in these other areas reciprocally impacted the church's understanding of Christology.

According to the dyophysites, who succeeded at the Council of Chalcedon, the Ego of the Son unites the two natures as well as subjecting the human nature to its decisions. According to Dorner's analysis of the hypostatic union, if human nature is without its own ego (*anhypostasis*) but finds its personality only in the Son (*enhypostasis*), then the human nature is reduced to an impersonal organ. In the medieval church, this Christology produced an understanding of salvation that joined an overly divine and magical view of God's grace with a piety that focused, not on Jesus, but Mary as the ideal of pure humanity.[44] Unfortunately, these are simply dogmatic pronouncements. Dorner assumes that the modern understanding of personality is equivalent to the ecclesiastical term *hypostasis*, a point that modern interpreters dispute.[45] Similarly, Dorner can portray the medieval period as eradicating the human dimension of Christ's salvific work only by virtually ignoring Anselm's pivotal influence. Dorner's failure to discern the theological insight in the church's insistence on *anhypostasis* is more serious. The point is that Jesus' existence derives wholly from God's action. As John declares, it is the Word that assumed flesh (John 1:14). The Incarnation does not model humanity's cooperation with God, nor human nature's current receptivity for God. Fallen humanity has rebelled against God. Rather, the Incarnation is God's creative action in the land of the dead to reestablish life. But it is precisely those points Dorner cannot accept given his organic model. His framework of continuity and an intrinsic openness to God preclude a supernatural act that recreates a lost receptivity.[46]

The Reformation, Dorner argues, provided new insight into the full reality and necessity of Christ's human nature through the reality of justification by faith alone. In the midst of judgment, God encounters the believer as a true personality instead of as an indifferent object. Even judgment reveals God's love and valuation of humans. Similarly, in saving faith humanity finds its *telos* in union with God in Jesus Christ: human and divine combine just as matter and form are joined.[47] Only Luther developed the Christological implications of this insight. According to Dorner, Luther concludes that the divine and human were so united with each other that Christ was a single person, not that the Son united Himself with two natures. Similarly, God's bestowal of the divine on humanity was not accidental and arbitrary but an act of love, so that humanity might attain its true and perfect form. But these are highly debatable points in view of Luther's acceptance of the traditional Christological doctrine and his distinction between the revealed and secret will.[48] Dorner admits that Luther's insights were not enduring. In his subsequent controversy with

Zwingli, Luther's Christology becomes dominated by the picture of a docetic Christ.[49]

According to Dorner, Luther's early conception of the personal union and the related implications regarding God and humankind represents the principal advance during the Reformation.[50] The Socinians established the emptiness of the Reformed alternative of a hypostatic union. For the Socinian proposal of a human Jesus with divine prerogatives ascribed to Christ as much dignity as the Reformed, where the humanity was the self-less instrument of deity. Once again Dorner's own theological biases are evident, as he rides roughshod over his own evidence and fails to investigate suggestive options. Even he acknowledges that the Reformed scholastics discuss Christ's developing human knowledge and will. But no evidence can contest his caricature of the hypostatic proposal.[51]

The Enlightenment unleashed unaided reason, undermining the dogma of Christology and even orthodoxy. Eventually this subjective impulse shattered reason's own claim to a universally valid groundwork. But these destructive seeds were contained in the history of Christianity. For when the human and divine are severed and placed in antagonism, they perish. Yet the Enlightenment was not entirely destructive. It began to perceive the affinity underlying the human and divine. Kant, for instance, descended to the depths of human obligation, discovering a divine element, and made the appearance of the God-man once again plausible.[52] Dorner is certainly aware that this and similar theories reject the church's understanding of Jesus as the unique God-man. But the development of doctrine is a dialectical process. In contrast to the one-sidedly objective consideration that started from above, it is historically necessary that reflection should also begin from below. Only when one-sidedness is overcome can all the truth be incorporated.[53]

THE NINETEENTH-CENTURY CHURCH

This dialectical process, Dorner claims, was completed in his own century. Three great thinkers of the nineteenth century, Schelling, Hegel and Schleiermacher, built on the assumption that the human and divine are not opposed but possess an underlying union. They established the framework for a great advance. By interacting with their systems, seizing their insights and advances, Dorner outlines a proposal for resolving long standing difficulties in the history of dogma.

The traditional scheme conceived Christology extrinsically, as an accidental and arbitrary supernatural advent into this sinful world, thereby placing the second creation in antagonism to the first. Arguing that this dualism is not credible in a historically aware culture, Dorner uses insights from Hegel and Schleiermacher to reconceive the Incarnation as a necessary expression of God's love and in continuity with history's organic development.[54] God's free act of grace now transposed into a necessary aspect of creation. From all eternity God intended for Jesus as Redeemer to be the head of the second creation, the progenitor of a new humanity who know themselves reconciled to God in Him and humanity's *telos* which was lacking in the first creation. Jesus' uniqueness is not located in His humanity's orientation toward God. For the first creation is inherently receptive to the second. All humanity is created with this quest and openness for God; consequently the law of reason harmonizes inwardly with faith. Rather, Jesus' uniqueness is that in this one God the Logos knows himself as having become man, and has established Jesus as the head of the second creation.[55] Building on Schleiermacher's preliminary sketch, Dorner conceives Jesus as a developing union of the Logos and the humanity who together become one self-knowing and self-willing ego.[56]

SUMMARY

This history of dogma brilliantly demonstrates how revelation—the reality of reconciliation with God through Jesus Christ—shatters heretical options and through the medium of thesis and antithesis unfolds a richer understanding of the truth. Dorner uses the whole range of the Christian life impacted by Jesus Christ, from theory to practice, to sustain the originality and world-destiny force of revelation. His analysis of the genetic development of Christology, especially the early battles with Docetism, Ebionism, Arianism and Sabellianism, always focuses upon the decisive and vital issue at stake. Unfortunately, his view of history's progressive advance dilutes the biblical revelation to an intuited kergymatic essence that attains conceptual precision only later through historical processes.[57] As a result, Dorner's historical framework dominates his understanding of progress in the church. And this scheme forces him to discount the church's traditional confession regarding Christ's *anhypostatos*, ignore its theological rationale and caricature its advocates.

The irony of Dorner's history is the utter failure of his final prophecy and proposal. His Christological proposal was virtually ignored after Albrecht Ritschl burst onto the scene. As the remainder of the nineteenth century reflects, the subjective subsumed and dissolved the objective. Nor can Dorner escape blame for this development. Certainly his own proposal is consistent and creatively supports the uniqueness of God's work in Jesus Christ while acceding to the immanental demands of historicism.[58] But precisely because he accepts the historical paradigm, his Christological framework does not narrate humanity's estrangement, rebellion, and death, but its inherent quest for God and evolving destiny. Furthermore, in this immanental context the advent of Jesus Christ still appears arbitrary. Dorner cannot explain why the Incarnation occurred in this man, at this time. Given the cultural domination of the historical framework and its principle of continuity, isn't the next move predictable, namely, to interpret Christology as simply the church's valuation of Jesus, given their experience of reconciliation?

HISTORY OF PROTESTANTISM

Dorner's *History of Protestant Theology* was commissioned as part of an extensive project to document the history of all the sciences in Germany. Reflecting those demands, this two-volume work concentrates on developments in Germany and concludes with an extensive and still valuable survey of the theological disciplines in the nineteenth century, from biblical studies to practical theology. Dorner's overriding aim, however, is to justify the existence of Protestantism over against Catholic attacks by showing the historical necessity for its appearance as well as its preeminence over other Christian options.

Building on the assumption that the church has developed organically, deepening and advancing its understanding of revelation, Protestantism currently represents the highest stage with its own distinctive principle.[59] This approach dictates the breadth of Dorner's research as well as the structure and focus of his argument. He must show that Protestantism does not consist of "a confused mass of accidental opinions" but a definable essence, the Protestant principle. Because this defining core cannot be explained by national factors, Dorner examines Protestantism throughout Europe, even England and America. This principle identifies purifying as well as distortive developments within the history of Protestantism, providing a ready answer to the more provocative attacks—or smears— which linked the Reformation with Müntzer or Enlightenment rationalism.[60] This approach provides Dorner a rich apologetic resource for answering Catholic challenges. If Protestantism is a higher stage of Christianity, a prior form "cannot turn itself against, nor cut itself off from, the essential element of Protestantism, without doing violence to itself and damaging the germs of its own future."[61]

Again dialectic antagonisms dominate Dorner's narrative. His history includes five important periods: (1) the historical context of Medieval Catholicism; (2) the Reformers' Protestant principle; (3) the distortion of the Protestant principle through one-sidedly objective and then subjective reactions; (4) the Protestant principle's dissolution through the Enlightenment; and finally (5) the reappropriation of the Protestant principle in the nineteenth century.

MEDIEVAL CATHOLICISM

While benefitting the church by establishing the goal of Christ's universal kingdom, Medieval Catholicism promoted a dualistic, even antithetical, conception of the objective and subjective dimensions within religion. Catholicism's hierarchical structures controlled the administration of Jesus' work, supplanting personal fellowship with Christ. Revelation, for instance, was objectified so that faith becomes abject submission, without personal conviction. Because the priest's pronouncement could not bestow the certainty of reconciliation with God, salvation receives a mysterious and impersonal coloring, attached to the altar, not to God himself. Similarly, holiness is defined institutionally, not as ethical and personal reality.

This legalism and objectivism kindled reforming movements within the medieval church. Dorner highlights the mystics' quest for an immediate experience with God, the return to Scripture which challenged the church's authority, and Christian education of the laity, as forerunners of the Reformation. But these protests failed to transcend the old framework: the objective and subjective dimensions still remain opposed. Nevertheless, Dorner established that Medieval Catholicism provoked these reform movements. These movements and their successors, including Protestantism, cannot be blamed on the arbitrary and capricious actions of a few; rather they are organic developments from medieval Catholicism, impelled by the latter's defects.

THE REFORMATION AND
THE PROTESTANT PRINCIPLE

The Reformers' personal experience of salvation by faith transcended the Medieval framework by interconnecting the objective and subjective and thereby opening a new insight into the gospel. Against medieval Catholicism's demand for abject submission, the Reformers realized that every Christian can personally apprehend the normative authority of Scripture. In contrast to an institutional holiness, faith's apprehension of Christ's reconciling and sanctifying grace originates a vital love that sets oneself in service to others. These two—the authority of Scripture and justification by faith—represent the defining core of Protestantism, which Dorner labelled the formal and material principle. Dorner's precise conception of these principles is crucial, for they now become the interpretive framework for understanding the original Reformers, their battles and the Protestant tradition.

Definition of the Protestant Principle. While the church can compel only a legalistic assent, the Reformers emphasized that the saving subject matter of Scripture personally attests its divine reality and power to the believer. The *formal principle* maintains that the Word is apprehended as true only when the historical Jesus is embraced as the present and living Christ. Scripture thus points not to itself, but to its subject, the living Lord.

Faith, the subjective counterpart, is not defined by mysticism or reason but a specific relation to the Word. Faith is a being taken captive by the Word and knowing God's reconciling love in Jesus Christ. The *material principle* insists that the reality of justification begins with God's pardoning love, but does not stay there. This divine love must be reflected throughout the Christian's whole life.

The formal and material principles are inseparably connected. Faith cannot exist by itself apart from the Word's portrait of Jesus. Similarly, Scripture points beyond itself to the living Jesus as apprehended through faith. In addition, these two possess an independent and critical stance toward the other. In salvation the Word creates the believer for mirroring and unfolding the Scriptures. And faith possesses an eye for what is Christian; it can distinguish what is for or against Christ. Nothing that contradicts saving faith can have canonical authority, as Luther's criticism of James reflects.[62]

The Protestant Principle in Action during the Reformation Period. The Reformers' debates with other movements in Christendom featured the Protestant principle. Erasmus and the moderate Catholic reformers, for instance, disputed the material principle. Erasmus' conception of faith was related to his Pelagian understanding of human freedom, where the individual was self-sufficient and independent of God. As a result, Erasmus dismissed the possibility that the Word of God could attest its truth to the believer. This Erasmian idea of freedom reemerged in continental Arminianism, which lapsed quickly into Socinianism.[63]

The sectarians and Anabaptist prophets contested the formal principle. The Anabaptists, Dorner argues, reflect the mysticism originating from Medieval Catholicism, building on its dualistic relation between the objective and subjective. Only now the subjective principle is no longer submissive to the objective, but has broken loose from the church and even Scripture, resulting in enthusiasm. Dorner details the Anabaptists' link with Medieval Catholicism, in terms of faith's relation to works, their concept of the church and a common antagonistic relationship between the first and second creation. As a result, he excludes the later forms of Anabaptism developing from Menno from this history of Protestantism. For he has already established that the movement is not Protestant![64]

The Protestant Principle in the Reformers. While insisting that the Reformers agree on essentials, Dorner admits that differences color their respective apprehensions of this principle. Both Zwingli and Calvin emphasize the formal side of the Protestant principle, and fail to follow Luther's lead in criticizing the canon. Zwingli's opposition to Catholicism's deification of the creature led him to locate salvific causality only in God's act in Jesus Christ. Consequently, in his system the outward Word becomes only a sign of the inner Word. Luther, again demonstrating the deepest insight into the Protestant principle, views the first creation as capable of exhibiting grace: the outward Word is a vehicle of grace for the inner Word. Dorner notes that Melanchthon's educational and scientific pursuits employed this same receptive relation of the first creation from the second.[65] But Dorner criticizes the Reformers for failing to advance the Protestant principle when explicating election.

Two issues confront Dorner's distinctive construal of the Protestant principle. First, he treats the church as only secondary to the Reformers' thought. Dorner tries to meet this criticism by noting that in their view the church is subordinate to the living Word. But so is faith; yet he considers it part of the Protestant principle.[66] Dorner attempts to establish the church's existence in several ways. He stresses that justification impels a love for one's neighbor. That may necessitate a civil community but hardly a church, a community of believers! In other places he explains that the church originates because of the receptivity of the first creation for the second: God deals with us in two ways, by the outward Gospel and the inward Spirit; "the outward order . . . must precede, and the inward come afterwards and *by means of* the outward."[67] But what precludes individualism in this scheme?[68] The church held a far more central location among the Reformers: the church is the means through which Christ accomplishes His salvific work. As Calvin explains, the church is our mother, where we are brought to life and nourished.[69]

Second, in Dorner's understanding of the Protestant principle the receptivity of the first creation for the second is just as central as the personal apprehension of the Word. Admittedly Dorner correctly describes the Reformers as understanding the Word as creative. But like his reconception of miracles, this statement is muted and transformed into a "relative" creative act. Faith is a new experience, yet one grounded in permanent human possibilities. This construal is more indebted to Melanchthon, and Dorner's own theological framework of continuity, than to Calvin and Luther. In Luther, for instance, faith does not absorb God into the believer's possibilities; rather, the believer is taken up into God's possibilities. Indeed, faith is a judgment of death and a resurrection.[70]

Post-Reformation Period. The Reformers' original insights required application throughout all life. But Dorner laments that their theological successors were not equal to the task. The living reality of the gospel was soon lost in the post-Reformation period. While Dorner analyzes Lutheran orthodoxy in detail, he sees the same dynamics operating among the Reformed and English divines. In these theologians the Protestant principle no longer functioned as a living reality—the personal assurance of salvation gained through an encounter with the Word—but as a fixed tradition. An exaggerated formal principle dominates the material, obscuring the reality of justification. Now divine assurance confirms the authority of the inspired canon, not the truth of God's promises to the believer. No longer is the reality of reconciliation through faith in Jesus the Redeemer the central theological truth from which all other doctrines originate. Rather, the inspired Scripture is the external authority containing all these propositions. The justification of the sinner before God through faith becomes just one doctrine among others.[71]

Recent studies have shown that Dorner's censorious portrayal of post-Reformation orthodoxy—one often repeated in history texts—is simply unreliable. Among the leading Lutheran and Reformed scholastics, Scripture's authority is grounded in the realities of God's justifying faith. These salvific realities, which God supernaturally bestows on believers, cannot be equated with a *fides historica.*[72] While inspiration was construed in a variety of ways, the leading scholastics rejected a dictation theory which undermined the human role.[73] Similarly, biblical criticism provoked many reactions, but all, except a few, accepted textual criticism. Some scholastics, including the Reformed Turretin, even admitted the presence of "small errors" in the text.[74] While Dorner's portrayal may fit his "law of history," it is seriously distorted. As recent scholarship has shown, Protestant orthodoxy sought to be faithful to the Reformers.

According to Dorner's narrative, in this objectifying climate, the quest for experiential certainty could not be ignored and unleashed an equally imbalanced subjective reaction. The Methodists rediscovered the Reformation understanding that faith is personal reliance in Jesus which brings assurance of the forgiveness of one's sins. But because the subjective now dominates and obscures the objective, they could not attain the Reformation position of the simultaneous presence of grace and consciousness of sin.[75] Similarly, Dorner hails Spener's recognition that salvation is not simply the forgiveness of sins, but also includes a life of personal holiness. Distortions are inevitable, however, because the material principle now dominates and obscures the formal. As already foreshadowed in his critique of the Anabaptists, Dorner is unable to appreciate the aims of the Pietists. He charges that among the Pietists holiness focuses exclusively on converting and developing piety. Anything that does not directly contribute to this goal is ignored. So the arts and sciences, indeed the first creation, have only an incidental role, if any at all. This antagonism to the first creation, as Dorner argues, indicates that a self-sacrificial love does not motivate Pietism, but a selfish concern for their own salvation. As a result, sectarian tendencies dominate Pietism, even that of Halle.[76]

In the end, both orthodoxy and Pietism coexist in antagonism. Neither could perceive the need for the other. According to Dorner, only the Enlightenment's devastating critique could free the scholastic minds from the "fetters of custom and tradition" and allow the Pietists to recognize the importance of the first creation.

Enlightenment Dissolution of the Protestant Principle. The Enlightenment completed this process of dissolving the formal and material principles, showing itself a perversion of Protestantism. The subjective, now wholly separated from the biblical revelation, pursues unabated its victorious attacks on the objective dimensions of the Protestant principle. The Wolffians attempted to establish the truth of Christianity on rational and historical proofs. But they succumbed to the Enlightenment challenges: the reoccurring challenges with science, Semler's undermining the historical case for the Christian revelation, and finally Lessing and Herder dissolving Christianity into universal religious truths.[77] Kant relocated to the debate from reason to morality, elevating the moral law to the place of God. But again the subjective called into question the objective dimension. Kant denied God's internal gracious work in order to preserve human autonomy, and made revelation superfluous as well as unknowable.[78] Jacobi's aestheticism posed the third antagonism between the human and the divine. Through feeling we directly perceive that God is, but are absolutely incapable of knowing who God is. To speak any more of God is self-contradictory.[79]

Ever the optimist, Dorner argues that even this triumph of subjectivism was not entirely negative. As Fichte demonstrated, this history of an "ever fruitlessly repeated circle" of objectivism and then subjectivism could only be overcome by the union of subject and object. Furthermore, the Enlightenment had overthrown the traditional opposition between the human and the divine, and had begun to point to their underlying unity. Thereafter philosophy pursued the absolute in which both subject and object are intrinsically connected. Now the assumption was that the movement in thought is at the same time movement in reality, and that both

245

exist in a vitally receptive and reproductive relation. In contrast to the immutable God of deism and Spinoza, philosophy recognized that God is animate and that only through God can God be known. These principles of philosophical idealism, Dorner observes, are akin to the Reformation.[80] But as in any intellectual endeavor, the conception of this absolute requires time to mature. In Schelling the absolute is related as the soul of the universe, in Hegel the mind and its dialectical process. Finally, Schleiermacher arises above both with the idea of God as an ethical being governing the world toward a moral end.

Nineteenth-Century Reappropriation of the Protestant Principle. According to Dorner, Schleiermacher establishes the foundation for reappropriating the Protestant principle in modern theology. He recognizes that the formal and material principles cannot stand without each other. Faith is in need of Scripture, for through its historical image of Christ one attains a vital communion with God and Christ's redemption; but faith also possesses its own internal certainty and its own critical independence. Elevating this to methodological importance, Schleiermacher derives every doctrine from this principle. Furthermore, Schleiermacher completes Luther's attempt to integrate the first and second creation. While the advent of Christ is God's creative act, humanity is naturally receptive to this redemptive power and continues through ordinary historical means, transcending rationalism and supernaturalism. Yet Dorner notes that problems remain, especially Schleiermacher's failure to transcend deism and pantheism in his doctrine of God.[81]

In the second half of the nineteenth century, challenges representing both the subjective and objective dimensions continue. But Dorner argues that they are in the process of self-destruction. The historical critics can no longer pretend to evade the reality of Jesus by supposing a post-apostolic origin of the Gospels. Like Renan, sooner or later these critics must confront the issue of Jesus: is He "a fanatic, whose spiritual pride was even blasphemous," or do His eschatological claims reflect "His inmost consciousness" and truth?[82] Dorner confidently concludes that Strauss's mythical view is in its last phase; it has run its course! By contrast, biblical criticism has prompted many supernaturalists to employ the church's authority for propping up the canon. In the process, they have descended to a self-defeating legalistic assent.[83] Only the Protestant principle has answered these challenges of history with a conquering force!

Summary. Dorner's history displays an impressive and wide-ranging knowledge of the Protestant heritage and genuinely wrestles with the question of Protestant identity. But this work illustrates again the situatedness of all historical knowledge, which is accentuated precisely because he reduces revelation to a kergymatic intuition that attains conceptual precision only later through historical processes. Even though Dorner emphatically divides the history of dogma from the history of philosophy, insisting upon the integrity of Christian theology, in this work he finds it difficult to distinguish the Protestant principle from the philosophical idealism pervading the German church: "The *theological problem* as yet left unsolved by the Reformation, viz. *the scientific union of the material and the formal*, of the subjective and objective principles, is only a concrete expression, with reference to the Christian religion of the *philosophical problem* of the union of subject and object, of thought and existence."[84] But is the believer—in this life—ever in the position to treat her own demands as establishing the conditions for the divine object, or of equal importance to this object? Is the reality of Christianity found in the "union of subject and object," or outside us two thousand years ago in God's work in Jesus Christ?

Still, this perspective does help explain why Dorner can virtually ignore the vital role of the Christian community, the church, in the Reformers' thought and mutes the truly creative work of the Word of God. And perhaps this is why Protestant orthodoxy's emphasis upon Scripture's divinely creative authority over against the truth of the sinner's own being—in the seventeenth century context of religious war and political intrigue—appears to Dorner as one-sidedly objective.

Again this work reflects Dorner's supreme confidence regarding history's advance. He never appears to have considered the possibility that historicism might dominate the modern consciousness. Nor is he aware of the social and cultural forces steadily secularizing the German church. Perhaps with hindsight he would have been more sympathetic toward the attempts by the later Anabaptists and Pietists to construct a church that disciples believers to confess Christ as Lord, not culture.

CONCLUSION

As we have repeatedly uncovered, Dorner is not immune from the difficulties afflicting us all: imposing a theological scheme upon the church that suppresses and restricts genuinely biblical alternatives. But Dorner has far greater importance than simply exemplifying this commonplace. His historiography is one of the most thorough explorations by a confessional theologian of the possibilities for theology within the historical paradigm. Contrary to his better known contemporaries, Dorner stoutly defends the Nicene Confession. But in his attempt to retain just as firmly the historical method, Dorner comes perilously close to substituting historical processes in the church for the biblical revelation, creation for grace, humanity's evolving destiny for God's transformation of the believer from death to life.

The historical paradigm, with its search for internal connections and continuities, inevitably seeks to equalize the relationship between the first and second creation, the historian's view with God's salvific work, the subject and the object. More than a century later, historicism's challenge and allure have become even more acute. Evangelicals, however, can learn from Dorner's mistakes by confessing that the Word "became flesh and made His dwelling among us" (John 1:14), and that He alone is the *One who must bring us daily from "death to life"* (John 5:24; Rom. 6:13; 1 John 3:14). Perhaps, then, the difference between God's work in Jesus Christ and His salvific work in sinful believers throughout history will be recognized as a qualitative and irreversible distinction!

BIBLIOGRAPHY

PRIMARY SOURCES

Divine Immutability. Minneapolis: Augsburg Fortress, 1994.

History of Protestant Theology. 2 volumes. Translated by George Robson and Sophia Taylor. Edinburgh: T. & T. Clark, 1871; New York: AMS Press, 1970.

History of the Development of the Doctrine of the Person of Christ. 5 volumes. Translated by William Lindsay Alexander and D. W. Simon. Edinburgh: T. & T. Clark, 1861–63.

A System of Christian Doctrine. 4 volumes. Translated by Alfred Cave and J. S. Banks. Edinburgh: T. & T. Clark, 1880–82.

SECONDARY SOURCES

Barth, Karl. *Protestant Theology in the Nineteenth Century: Its Background & History*. Valley Forge: Judson Press, 1968, 577–87.

Dorner, August J. "Dem Andenken von Dr. I. A. Dorner." *Theologische Studien und Kritiken* 58 (1885):417–52.

Hargis, Charles Lee. "The Conception of the Incarnation of God in the Thought of Isaak August Dorner." Th.D. diss., Union Theological Seminary in Virginia, 1974.

Rothermundt, Jorg. *Personale Synthese: Isaak August Dorners dogmatische Methode*. Gottingen: Vanderboeck & Ruprecht, 1968.

Russell, Stanley H. "I. A. Dorner: A Centenary Appreciation." *Expository Times* 96 (1984): 77–81.

Welch, Claude. *Protestant Theology in the Nineteenth Century, Volume 1, 1799–1870*: 273–82. New Haven: Yale University Press, 1972.

Welch, Claude, ed. *God and Incarnation in Mid-Nineteenth Century German Theology: G. Thomasius, I. A. Dorner, A. E. Biedermann*. New York: Oxford University Press, 1965.

NOTES

1. Isaak August Dorner, *History of the Development of the Doctrine of the Person of Christ*, 5 vol., trans. William Lindsay Alexander and D. W. Simon (Edinburgh: T. &

T. Clark, 1861–63). Isaak August Dorner, *The History of Protestant Theology*, 2 vol., trans. George Robson and Sophia Taylor (Edinburgh: T. & T. Clark, 1871; New York: AMS Press, 1970).

2. Grant Wacker, *Augustus H. Strong and the Dilemma of Historical Consciousness* (Macon, Ga.: Mercer University Press, 1985), 133, 163ff. Charles Lee Hargis, "The Conception of the Incarnation of God in the Thought of Isaak August Dorner" (Th.D. dissertation, Union Theological Seminary in Virginia, 1974), 342ff. Glen G. Scorgie, *A Call for Continuity: The Theological Contribution of James Orr* (Macon, Ga.: Mercer University Press, 1988), 48–51, 155. Mark Stephen Massa, *Charles Augustus Briggs and the Crisis of Historical Criticism* (Minneapolis: Augsburg Fortress, 1990), 37–46. Philip Schaff, *Germany: Its Universities, Theology and Religion* (Philadelphia: Lindsay & Blakiston, 1857), 376–80.

3. Peter C. Hodgson, *The Formation of Historical Theology: A Study of Ferdinand Christian Baur* (New York: Harper & Row, 1966), 12.

4. Dorner, *Protestant Theology*, 2:253, 283, 447.

5. Dorner, *Person of Christ* 1: viii.

6. Isaak August Dorner, *A System of Christian Doctrine*, 4 vol., trans. Alfred Cave and J. S. Banks (Edinburgh: T. & T. Clark, 1880–82), 1:103ff.

7. Dorner, *Person of Christ*, 1:ix.

8. David Friedrich Strauss, *The Life of Jesus Critically Examined*, ed. Peter C. Hodgson (Philadelphia: Fortress, 1972), 779–80.

9. Dorner, *Person of Christ*, 5:143; Dorner, *Christian Doctrine*, 1:115, 252; 4:48–49.

10. Dorner, *Protestant Theology*, 2:447.

11. Dorner, *Christian Doctrine*, 1:104–107, 110, 141.

12. Ibid., 1:162.

13. Dorner, *Person of Christ*, 1:47–48.

14. Dorner, *Christian Doctrine*, 2:233, 283ff.

15. Ibid., 2:80, 125, 142–43, 223.

16. Dorner, *Person of Christ*, 1:46, 49, 76, 82.

17. Dorner, *Christian Doctrine*, 2:163–4.

18. Hodgson, *Formation*, 149.

19. Dorner, *Christian Doctrine*, 1:460; 2:49, 27, 75.

20. Ibid., 1:252, 434; 4:48–49; Dorner, *Person of Christ*, 1:48.

21. Dorner, *Person of Christ*, 1:45–46, 344; Dorner, *Christian Doctrine*, 1:166.

22. Dorner, *Person of Christ*, 1:82.

23. Dorner, *Christian Doctrine*, 1:162.

24. Hargis, "Conception of the Incarnation," 75. Dorner, *Christian Doctrine*, 1:159–68, 171, 434; 2:232. Dorner, *Person of Christ*, 1:viii, 3–4, 82.

25. Dorner, *Christian Doctrine*, 1:124, 128.

26. Dorner, *Person of Christ*, 1:1–45, 78; Dorner, *Christian Doctrine* 2:232–80.

27. Dorner, *Person of Christ*, 1:82, 344–47.

28. Ibid., 1:viii–ix. Dorner, *Christian Doctrine*, 2:205–6, 294.

29. Dorner, *Person of Christ*, 1:50–73, 86.

30. Colin Brown, *Jesus in European Protestant Thought, 1778–1860* (Durham: Labyrinth Press, 1985), 273–74.

31. Dorner, *Person of Christ*, 1:47, 49. Strauss "seeks also for internal contradiction in the Gospel, for the sake of proving thereby their non-historical character. These contradictions being, however, but unimportant, it was obvious that they were not to be regarded as that which, properly speaking, was to determine the point." Dorner, *Protestant Theology*, 2:368.

32. Dorner, *Protestant Theology*, 2:372. Dorner, *Person of Christ*, 1:62.

33. Dorner, *Person of Christ*, 1:82.

34. Ibid., 1:93, 181. See also Horton Harris, *The Tubingen School* (Oxford: Clarendon Press, 1975; Grand Rapids: Baker Book House, 1990), 159–237.

35. Dorner, *Person of Christ*, 1:92, 173.

36. Ibid., 1:145.

37. Ibid., 1:160, 443.

38. Ibid., 1:200–203, 221–24, 230–39, 346, 435.

39. Dorner explicates Christian thinkers from the theological center of their thought, not their philosophical framework. For instance, while acknowledging that Origen found it easy to assert the Son's eternity because of his doctrine of eternal creation, Dorner insists that these doctrines are actually grounded independently. When confessing the eternity of the Son, Origen was articulating the Christian conviction that in Christ believers had attained to unity with God Himself, not a secondary God. Because the Son is God, Origen confesses that there never was a time when the Son was not. See Dorner, *Person of Christ*, 2:111–12.

40. Ibid., 2:169.

41. Ibid., 2:289.

42. Ibid., 2:229, 301.

43. Ibid., 3:86ff, 102.

44. Ibid., 3:269–75.

45. Wolfhart Pannenberg, *Jesus-God and Man*, 2nd ed. (Philadelphia: Westminster Press, 1976), 337ff. Reinhold Seeberg, *The History of Doctrines* (Grand Rapids: Baker, 1977), 1:286ff. Karl Barth, *Church Dogmatics* IV.2.49ff. David F. Wells, *The Person of Christ* (Westchester, Ill.: Crossway Books, 1984), 130–32, 156–57, 177ff. H. Maurice Relton, *A Study in Christology* (New York: Macmillan, 1934).

46. Barth, *Church Dogamatics*, IV.2.49ff., 91. Wells, *Person of Christ*, 130–32, 147, 156–57.

47. Dorner, *Person of Christ*, 4:57–65.

48. Paul Althaus, *The Theology of Martin Luther* (Philadelphia: Fortress Press, 1966), 194. "Luther teaches the impersonality of the human nature of Christ (*an-* or *enhypostasis*)."

49. Dorner, *Person of Christ*, 4:180ff.

50. Ibid., 4:102.

51. Ibid., 4:347ff.

52. Ibid., 5:38, 49–50.

53. Ibid., 5:72, 98.

54. Ibid., 5:166, 237, 297. Hargis, "Conception of the Incarnation," 231–360.

55. Dorner, *Person of Christ*. 5:237–47.

56. Ibid., 5:248.

57. Ibid., 1:76. "Though at first there were wanting exact conceptual expressions, yet the thing itself is from the beginning present in another form, in the form of intuition, which is an element of belief."

58. Hargis, "Conception of the Incarnation," 330–60.

59. Dorner, *Protestant Theology*, 1:1.

60. Johann Adam Moehler, *Symbolism* (New York: Edward Dunigan, 1844), 272ff., 425ff.

61. Dorner, *Protestant Theology*, 1:5.

62. Ibid., 1:220–64

63. Ibid., 1:418ff.

64. Ibid., 1:139ff.

65. Ibid., 1:113–19.

66. Ibid., 2:427.

67. Ibid., 1:142–49.

68. Hirsch hints at this point in his criticism of Dorner's Christology. Emanuel Hirsch, *Geschichte der neuern evangelischen Theologie* (Gutersloh: Gerd Mohn, 1949, 1960). 5.1.386.

69. Calvin, *Institutes*, IV.1.4.

70. Martin Luther, *Luther: Early Theological Works*, Library of Christian Classics, ed. James Atkinson (Philadelphia: Westminster, 1962), 292–93.

71. Dorner, *Protestant Theology*, 2:30, 43, 119ff, 124ff., 128, 211.

72. Robert D. Preus, *The Theology of Post–Reformation Lutheranism: A Study of Theological Prolegomena* (Saint Louis: Concordia Publishing, 1970), 20, 24, 339, 291. Robert D. Preus, *The Inspiration of Scripture* (Edinburg: Oliver and Boyd, 1957). Johannes Wallmann, *Der Theologiebegriff bei Johann Gerhard und Georg Calixt* (Tubingen: J. C. B. Mohr, 1961). Timothy R. Phillips, "Francis Turretin's Idea of Theology and Its Bearing upon His Doctrine of Scripture" (Ph.D. diss., Vanderbilt University, 1986). Richard A. Muller, *Post-Reformation Reformed Dogmatics* (Grand Rapids: Baker, 1987).

73. Preus, *Theology of Post-Reformation Lutheranism*, 281–92. Richard A. Muller, *Post-Reformation Reformed Dogmatics*, 2:256–70.

74. Phillips, "Francis Turretin," 656–726.

75. Dorner, *Protestant Theology*, 2:94.

76. Ibid., 2:215, 218, 220, 227, 248ff.

77. Ibid., 2:269, 287.

78. Ibid., 2:321, 328, 333.

79. Ibid., 2:342ff.

80. Ibid., 2:346–47, 357–62.

81. Ibid., 2:374, 376–77, 385, 390.

82. Ibid., 2:419–21, 423.

83. Ibid., 2:398.

84. Ibid., 2:347.

12

CATHOLIC TÜBINGEN CHURCH HISTORIANS

DOUGLAS MCCREADY

In 1812, the king of Württemberg established a seminary at the University of Ellwangen. He did this to provide a source of priests for the Catholic population added to his domain as a result of the Napoleonic wars. Five years later, this small group of Catholic teachers moved to Tübingen to become part of that famous university. This establishment of the Catholic theological faculty at Tübingen also marked the birth of the Catholic Tübingen School. The school has not been marked by a formal organization, but by a particular theological spirit. Members of the school sought to interact with the philosophy and culture of early nineteenth-century Germany and respond to contemporary concerns without compromising their faith as Catholic Christians. Twentieth century Tübingers have continued this approach. Not every Catholic teacher at Tübingen can be considered a member of the school, however, and some members of the school taught on other faculties (after study at Tübingen).[1] So, as a school, the Tübingers were marked neither by unity of method nor by conclusion, but, as Karl Adam said, by a commonality of spirit.[2]

For the most part, Roman Catholicism had not participated in the Enlightenment or the early responses to it. After trying to ignore the Enlightenment in hope it would go away, the Catholic Church then assumed a reactive and defensive posture. The exceptions to this attitude were overwhelmingly German, and the Tübingers built on earlier Catholics who had sought to make Christianity understandable to philosophers and people of culture. They did not follow Schleiermacher in his concern for the cultured despisers of religion, but neither was their focus on the people in the pews. They wanted to make Christianity intellectually respectable. However, unlike other German Catholic attempts in this direction, the Tübingers were able to retain a legitimate, although not endorsed, view because, as Thomas O'Meara said, they displayed strong attachment to Catholic orthodoxy and loyalty to the church as well as being careful, scientific theologians.

Many members of the Catholic Tübingen School were good systematic and historical theologians, but Johann Adam Möhler and Josef Rupert Geiselmann stand out as church historians. Writing in the early 1800s, Möhler established the reputation of the school and made major contributions to Catholic thought that would not be recognized until the middle of this century. Forced to the periphery of Catholic thought by Neo-Scholasticism in the mid-1800s, Möhler's theology reappeared a hundred years later to have a major influence on the work of Vatican II. Geiselmann, writing between the Second World War and the Second Vatican Council, publicized the school and made the writings of its members accessible to modern readers.

The Catholic Tübingen School drew on Protestants as well as Catholics for its ideas. This willingness to interact with thinkers of various backgrounds without compromising their Catholic faith has been a constant trait of the school. Particularly important for the first generation of Catholic Tübingers were the philosophy of Schelling and the theology of Schleiermacher, both Protestants. They accepted neither uncritically, and rejected many details of Schleiermacher's theology in particular. Later Tübingers responded critically to Hegel's thought, only to return in the middle of this century to a renewed appreciation of Schelling. For two generations, Tübingers tried freely but critically to integrate developments in history, biblical criticism, and philosophy into Catholic tradition. Tübingen's readiness to draw from a range of sources (including non-Catholic) for its theology and its willingness to enter into dialogue and debate with its culture did not endear the school to other Catholics. By the time of the first Vatican council (1869–1870), Tübingen theologians had become outsiders in the face of Roman Neo-Thomism. Between Vatican I and Vatican II (1961–1965),

Tübingen theologians labored under the threat of church censure, and the school went into a period of eclipse. Vatican II, however, restored Tübingen theology to a respected position within Roman Catholicism. In great measure, this was because many of the theologians most influential at the council had read the early Tübingen theologians, especially Möhler.

The primary concern of Tübingen theologians from Drey to the present has been history. This is in no way to minimize their other concerns; it is merely to note their emphasis that Christ lived and died in history, that the church and its members exist in history, and that the Spirit acts in history. Tradition is the church living and developing in history, and revelation has occurred in history. History is the presupposition and medium for the realization of the other concerns expressed by the Tübingen theologians.

Max Seckler notes the Catholic Tübingen School was interested in three dimensions of history. The school had, first, a historical-critical interest in researching the past. When historical reality mediates truth, we need to study the forms and dynamics by which truth is mediated in order to understand better the truth being communicated. The second dimension was the joining of the speculative and the historical. In this, one grasps the logic of history from the inside, inductively studying the parts in order to comprehend the whole. Third, the individual data of faith need to be evaluated and correlated. By themselves, they are "blind and dumb." Bringing many of them together only creates a greater mass of blind and dumb data. The theologian-historian needs to distinguish true from false and important from unimportant. Then he or she must fit the pieces together to create a coherent interpretation. That which does not fit into the interpretation is meaningless to the theologian. This is not, however, a subjective work by the theologian because he or she lives within history and must place him or herself under the history and tradition of the Church. In so doing, the theologian is not merely chronicling names, dates, events, and dogmas, but instead is attempting to integrate, interpret, and apply them to the contemporary church.[3]

The Tübingers expressed their concern for history in terms of living tradition and by drawing from patristic sources. They wanted to resolve the tension between an enduring, meaningful ideal and its multi-faceted, historical presence. They did so primarily through their study of ecclesiology. It is no accident that the two great historians of the school focused their effort on the study of the church because they believed that in this way they could relate God to history and make God meaningful to a society where traditional understandings and expressions had lost their meaning and value. This required a departure from the view of tradition as a once-for-all, unchanging deposit. The Tübingers reconceptualized it as a living whole, and revelation as an organic divine plan unfolding within human history. Both the existence of Protestantism and the challenge of Romanticism and German Idealism called into question the *raison d'ê tre* of the visible, institutional church. In Möhler's day, Schleiermacher and Hegel represented this challenge. In the next century, it was Protestant liberalism and Neo-Romanticism.

When the Catholic Tübingen School appeared, historical criticism of the Bible was still young. The Tübingers recognized that if historical-critical explanations of the Bible and early Christianity could show Christianity to have a historically-conditioned appearance, then the purely historical could be removed, leaving Christianity exclusively a religion of reason. Because they saw this danger in German Idealism, they sought to ground Christianity in a God Who has revealed Himself in a particular person at a specific time and place.[4]

For these Tübingers, historical tradition took on a new significance because history was not merely events that could be analyzed objectively but depended on the living Spirit of God revealed in Jesus Christ. The Spirit bound the church closely to the historical Jesus in understanding history. Reason, feeling, intuition, speculation, and concrete reality took precedence over knowledge, abstraction, rationalism, and the contemplation of delivered truths. Despite their study of romantic and idealist philosophy, the Tübingers grounded their work in church history, notably patristic studies.

Reaching maturity during the Romanticism of nineteenth-century Germany, the Tübingen theologians Johann Sebastian von Drey and Johann Adam Möhler showed concern for a dynamic, organic understanding of reality, an appreciation of human experience and intuition (without denigrating human reason), and an optimistic spirit. They rejected, however, the pantheism, autonomy, and repudiation of tradition characteristic of Romanticism. Thus, the Tübingen use of the romantic spirit was never complete, but was always a critical interaction mediated through Catholic tradition and the Tübingers' interpretation of the Bible. Because some of those with whom the Tübingers entered into debate were less rigorous in their evaluation of contemporary culture, the debate was more often marked by animosity than goodwill. Möhler was caught up in such a confrontation with the Protestant Tübingen historical theologian Ferdinand Christian Baur about the legitimacy of the Reformational churches.

JOHANN ADAM MÖHLER

Möhler was the most prominent figure of the early Catholic Tübingen School. His writings anticipated developments in Catholic theology over the next 130 years, particularly in the areas of doctrinal development, ecclesiology, and liturgy.[5] Recognized a century after his death as a valuable resource for dealing with problems confronting Catholicism, Möhler was a major influence on the decisions of Vatican II.

Johann Adam Möhler was born in 1796, in Ingersheim, Württemburg, the son of an innkeeper. He suffered poor health his entire life and died in Munich in 1838. At age nineteen, he was admitted to the Catholic faculty at Ellwangen to begin theological study to become a priest. When Drey moved the faculty to Tübingen in 1817, Möhler went along. He was ordained in 1819, and spent a year serving two parishes. In 1820, he returned to Tübingen to prepare himself to teach church history on the Catholic faculty. Appointed privatdozent in 1822, he spent half a year visiting the great German universities. He was influenced most by his time in Berlin, where he heard Schleiermacher, Marheineke, and Neander. It was in Berlin that Möhler was introduced to Romantic history and saw how he could use it to study the history of the church. From 1823 through 1835, Möhler taught church history at Tübingen; he continued to teach the subject at Munich until 1837.[6]

Möhler's study with the great Protestant theologians of his day indelibly affected him, but it also made him more self-consciously Catholic. Möhler had been appointed to teach canon law and church history, but he soon began to study and write on the nature of the church. This embroiled him in controversy with Protestant and Catholic alike, and motivated him to further work on ecclesiology. The greatest influence on his developing ecclesiology would be his study of early Christian theologians, particularly Athanasius and Anselm of Canterbury. Geiselmann suggests Möhler's thought went through three stages: a juridical concept of the church as a subcategory of the general category of society; a focus on the interior element of the church over the visible church, where the Spirit is the guiding principle; an understanding of the church as the continuation of the incarnation of the Son of God. In this third phase, the Spirit is the Spirit of Christ, not the vital force of the church.

Möhler's thought can be understood in light of two of his books: *Die Einheit in der Kirche* (1825) and *Symbolik* (first edition, 1832).[7] These books presented sharply different pictures of the church, the first antagonizing the German Catholic hierarchy and the second the Protestant Tübingers. Controversy with Ferdinand Christian Baur over the conclusions of

Symbolik caused Möhler's departure from Tübingen and perhaps hastened his death in 1838.

Only two years after he began to teach at Tübingen, Möhler wrote *Die Einheit in der Kirche*.[8] As the book's subtitle explains, Möhler is approaching the nature of the church in light of the first three centuries of Christian thought. True to Möhler's Romantic views, this volume focused on the Spirit as the originator and sustainer of the church. As a teacher of church history, Möhler could not ignore patristic teachings, but because he played down the centrality of Jesus Christ in patristic thought in favor of a pneumatic interpretation, Möhler distorted this source. Although Möhler would later move away from emphasis on the Spirit, his work in the *Einheit* would help prepare Catholicism for the ecumenical openness of Vatican II.

The understanding of the church in the *Einheit* was formed primarily by romantic idealism. The unifying principle for the church is the Spirit. Tradition, then, is the living process by which the Spirit guides the Church. This Romanticism powerfully influenced the early Möhler and would continue to affect him throughout his life. Romanticism's basic premise was that all human societies (including the church) are living organisms subject to the laws of evolution. It also believed that every area of human society was capable of unlimited progress. That Möhler accepted these premises is evident in the *Einheit*. They would lead Möhler to consider the theme of doctrinal development. Romanticism also led Möhler to study the Fathers; because history is an organic whole, one cannot properly study a later era without going back to its sources. In effect, then, the logic of Möhler's Romanticism would lead to a weakening of that Romanticism in Möhler's theology.

In the *Einheit*, Möhler began his move toward the historical understanding of Christianity that would become more pronounced in his later work. As Rosato says, "In Möhler's eyes, the Church must be seen as the uninterrupted historical community which bears Christ's legacy of grace and salvation to men because of the mystical presence of his Spirit as its continuing life-giving principle."[9] Building on the thought of the early church fathers, Möhler presents the unity of the church as the basic principle of Christianity. As Möhler saw it, Protestantism wanted to restore the primitive church as if sixteen centuries had not passed. He, however, argued that the perfection of the apostolic church did not preclude developments growing out of the original. Möhler's return to the Fathers enabled him to go behind the authoritarian, hierarchical understanding of the Catholic Church that had arisen out of the Counter-Reformation and reaction to the Enlightenment. With this move, Möhler was able to restore the mystical aspect of the church as a valid element of ecclesiology.

An additional response to what Catholicism has always seen as a weakness in Protestantism was Möhler's emphasis on the communal nature of human development. The Christian life does not grow individual by individual, but has a social character in which individual and communal life develop in tandem. The individualistic approach, suggests Möhler, tends to end in heresy because it separates people from the body of the church and, therefore, from the church's living tradition. Although they claim to acknowledge only the Bible, these people cannot understand it properly apart from the tradition through which it has been communicated to them. At its root, says Möhler, this is a misunderstanding of history because it sees history in terms of a succession of externally connected events and not an organic whole.

Reflecting the romantic idealism of the age, Möhler portrayed the church in terms of spirit rather than structure and magisterial authority. A church centered on the Spirit would be open to continuing historical change; this would also mean that its structure was subject to reform. Möhler reversed the Tridentine explanation of the church by picturing it as an organism that grows out of its inner being and out of the inner lives of those who make up the church, not a society defined in terms of its clergy and institutions. This evolutionary emphasis in the *Einheit* meant Möhler focused on the church's constant historical striving for perfection at the cost of minimizing its unchanging aspect.

Möhler's ideas aroused serious opposition within the Catholic Church in Germany. Möhler reflected a contemporary impatience with the condition of a Catholic Church that had frozen in reaction to the attacks coming out of the Enlightenment. As Möhler said in his introduction to the *Symbolik*, his intent in writing the *Einheit* was to defend the divine element in the church that had been denied by the Enlightenment.[10] Möhler was not, however, advocating a charismatic Catholicism where all structure, tradition, and authority were up for grabs. Reaction to the *Einheit*, while it would never cause Möhler to repudiate what he wrote in the book, did lead him to distance himself from these early ideas as he continued to think about ecclesiology.

After the *Einheit*, Möhler turned his efforts toward a more direct study of the church fathers and their ecclesiology. Specifically, he wrote a book on Athanasius (1827)[11] and a long article on Anselm of Canterbury (1827–28).[12] The Athanasius volume was far more substantial than the Anselm article, but together they showed a new direction in Möhler's thought that would result in the first edition of the *Symbolik* in 1832. Between 1827 and 1832, Möhler shifted from a mystical, subjective understanding of

Christian life and doctrine to one grounded in the objectivity of Christian revelation. He accomplished this by stressing the external features and character of the church as displayed in its ecclesiastical authority and magisterium.[13] Although some have suggested this change resulted from Möhler's use of Hegel to balance Schleiermacher's subjectivity, study and appreciation of the church fathers is the more likely cause. However much Möhler may have drawn on these two Protestant thinkers, he never forgot that his perspective was fundamentally opposed to theirs. Whereas they conceived religion in evolutionary terms, Möhler understood Christianity as a project of human restoration.

Because of his changed understanding of anthropology, Möhler made Christology increasingly important in his theology. As the human became more important, so, too, did Christ's humanity. His study of Athanasius caused Möhler to see salvation in terms of deification, with Christ rather than the Spirit being the source of new life. Nonetheless, Christ's deity came first; His humanity was later. Möhler saw this as necessary for protecting the certainty of salvation.

Athanasius der Grosse was a corrective to what Möhler saw as the errors of Hegel and Schleiermacher. It also evidenced Möhler's distancing of himself from them as he reevaluated the *Einheit* in the light of further patristic studies. Viewing Schleiermacher's understanding of the Trinity as Sabellian, Möhler used the patristic rebuttal of the original Sabellianism to challenge Schleiermacher. He concentrated especially on what he saw as a minimizing of divine transcendence, an evolutionary understanding of human salvation, and an implicit agnosticism about God's person. Although he never repudiated the contents of the *Einheit*, Möhler now recognized that his treatment of the Holy Spirit had bordered on pantheism. He moved to refocus his theology on Christ. Rosato says that the critical distance from his contemporaries afforded by the study of Athanasius and Anselm enabled Möhler to reevaluate contemporary religious idealism. As a result, he made the Incarnation, not human subjectivity, the basis for knowledge about God. It was in *Athanasius* that Möhler, recognizing that he might be "seriously misunderstood," described the church as the development of Christ in time. This would become a major theme in modern Roman Catholic ecclesiology.

Anselm was a study of the impact a great person can have on history. The biography aimed to defend Roman Catholicism against both Protestantism and Orthodoxy. In the first part, Möhler discussed church-state relations, not without making application to the contemporary German situation. His special concern was what he saw as unwarranted papal interference in the proper sphere of the local bishop. In the second part, he drew on Anselm to construct a Christian anthropology that would reappear in the *Symbolik* as a criticism of Protestant thought. Anselm would serve Möhler as a source (with Vincent of Lerins) for the understanding of human reason that would underlie his idea of doctrinal development.

In *Anselm*, Möhler was critical of the modern tendency to see earlier ages as inferior to one's own because they lacked the knowledge of modern society. He applied this especially to his contemporaries' view of the Middle Ages: "We view [the medieval theologians], then, in the abstract, and unconnected with circumstances, or perhaps associated with circumstances similar to our own, and conclude that, having departed from the present mode of conduct, their actions must of necessity be erroneous. But every actor in history finds himself placed in certain relations, and surrounded by certain necessities, by which he is held captive; by these and by his own free motives must he be judged."[14]

Möhler intended his *Symbolik*[15] to open a discussion with Tübingen Protestants over the relative faithfulness of Catholics and Protestants to the Christian tradition. Instead, it began a sharp debate with Ferdinand Christian Baur that encompassed three years and several articles and books before Möhler felt compelled to leave Tübingen for Munich. Möhler took the Bible, early creeds, and early conciliar statements as the common property of the two groups. He concentrated, therefore, on the major confessional statements of the Reformation and Counter-Reformation. In the second part of the book, he discussed the statements of what he called the minor Protestant sects. Some of these were no longer minor and others had never been orthodox enough to be considered Protestant.

The increasing clarity of Christian doctrine, suggested Möhler, is a valuable by-product of heresy's challenge to Christianity. Heresy forces the church to clarify the meaning of the gospel. Heresy is unquestionably false, but it performs a valuable function as a catalyst to doctrinal clarity and apologetics. Möhler cites as examples the development of Trinitarian doctrine between Nicaea and Chalcedon, teachings on baptism and confession growing out of the Donatist and Novatian heresies, and understandings of sin and justification resulting from the Reformation. Because he considered that Protestants and Catholics agreed on the doctrinal statements of early Christianity, he concentrated on the major confessional statements of the Protestant churches and of the Catholic Counter-Reformation. Möhler's purpose in the *Symbolik* was to bring back to the Catholic Church those branches of Christianity that had fallen away. He hoped to accomplish this by initiating a discussion of the differences between Protestant and Catholic teachings that would show the fidelity of Catholicism to Christian tradition.

The heart of the debate between Catholics and Protestants since the Reformation had been about justification. How one might be justified before God had been the question that drove Luther out of the Catholic Church, and his doctrine of justification by faith remained a key tenet for the Lutherans on Tübingen's Protestant faculty. Möhler argued that concentration on justification missed the true disagreement between Catholics and Protestants. Therefore, he said that he would focus his study on what the two groups had written about human nature before and after the fall. Möhler focused his concern on Catholic, Lutheran, and Reformed statements, considering the other Protestant groups but minor sects. Among these minor sects were the Anabaptists, Quakers, Methodists, Swedenborgians, Socinians, and Arminians. He discussed them briefly in the short second book of the *Symbolik*. Only after his discussion of anthropology did Möhler consider justification, good works, the sacraments, and the church. Möhler recognized that what one said about these subjects depended on one's understanding of the human condition. This insight was not new with Möhler—both sides understood it quite clearly at the time of the Reformation—but he returned it to the center of religious debate.

The approach Möhler used in the *Symbolik* (and with which F. C. Baur responded) was the idea that the history and doctrine of the church were linked by a single all-encompassing idea. So, instead of attacking Protestantism point-by-point, Möhler sought to contrast the totality he called "Catholicism" with another totality he called "Protestantism." His aim was to show that "Catholicism" was the better interpretive key for the sum of church history and doctrine than was "Protestantism."[16] Concluding that anthropology was the crucial difference between Catholicism and Protestantism, Möhler argued that the Reformers' error at this initial point meant that all the conclusions that followed were similarly flawed.[17]

Möhler began by challenging the Protestant understanding of the human race. It is wrong, he said, to read Genesis 1:26 as equating the image of God and likeness of God in which humans have been created. Following Irenaeus, Möhler defined the image of God as those natural human qualities like reason and personality that made humans resemble God and the likeness of God was the supernatural characteristics that made humans godlike.[18] Luther, said Möhler, failed to distinguish between the natural and supernatural characteristics possessed by humanity as created by God in Genesis 1, but combined them. Thus, for the Reformers, the fall affected the image of God in humans (Möhler says they believed the image was lost), whereas for Möhler the fall's greatest effect was on the likeness because the image was a potentiality instead of a condition.[19] Because Protestants so exalt humans in their original state, they must see the fall as devastating in its effects and the consequent human condition as desperate. The result, as Möhler correctly noted, is that humans can in no way cooperate in their salvation.

Catholicism, by contrast, because it has defined both an image and a likeness of God in humans, does not picture the fall in such stark terms. Humans remain noble creatures and their acts can still become God's acts. They also retain some ability to cooperate in their own salvation because the potential represented by the image of God had not been erased.[20] Because Möhler's patristic studies had led him to accept the historicity of the fall, he now saw the need for a historical redeemer and a historically mediating church.

Probably the most important aspect of the *Symbolik* was Möhler's transfer to Christ of what he had said in the *Einheit* about the Holy Spirit as the inner principle of the church. This Christocentric model led Möhler to conceive of the church as the continuation of the Incarnation. As Geiselmann pointed out, Möhler went on to apply the two-natures teaching of Chalcedon to the church, understanding as the union of the visible (human) and the invisible (divine). This came about because Möhler saw a need to anchor his doctrine of the church in Christology to protect it against the subjective intellectual movements of his day. These movements threatened to make Christianity and the church whatever their author chose to make them. This use of Christology required Möhler to present in some detail his understanding of the person and work of Christ. This was based solidly on Nicaea and Chalcedon because Möhler saw this as the only viable foundation for the theology he had derived from the early church fathers. Patristic study opened his eyes as well to the serious difficulties in the idealism of Schleiermacher and Schelling. Both misunderstood the relationship between Creator and creation.

Just before his death, Möhler attacked D. F. Strauss's categorizing of Jesus in terms of myth as untenable and unacceptable. He said the historical setting of early Christianity did not fit the conditions needed for myths to develop. Further, there was not the time between Jesus' death and the New Testament writings necessary for a Christ-myth to develop. Möhler did misunderstand Strauss's use of myth to mean fantasy, so to this extent his critique was off-base. But Möhler died before he could complete this critique. That task was left for his student J. E. Kuhn.

Möhler is not an easy theologian to characterize. He made significant contributions to Roman Catholicism's understanding of the nature of the church and doctrinal development. Catholic progressives like him for the *Einheit*, but conservatives prefer him for his later writings, which were more deeply grounded in tradition and drew from Christology instead of pneumatology. Although Möhler moved away from the views he had expressed in his *Einheit*, he steadfastly refused to repudiate the book, despite the personal and professional cost of this refusal. Möhler worked his way back to traditional theology because the philosophical and theological speculations that he had entertained in his early career proved insufficient to justify and explain the existence of the church. Further, only a full Chalcedonian Christology could justify an emphasis on the visible church in the face of the Protestant focus on the invisible church. Möhler's theology was traditional, but it was an informed tradition, developed out of the argumentation of the Romantic-Idealist period and the onset of skeptical denials of the tradition. Möhler attempted to be biblical and consistent as well as faithful to Catholic dogma. His great achievement was to affirm convincingly both the essential immutability of the church and its teachings and their historical development. He anticipated many developments associated with Vatican II and inspired many leading European Catholic theologians of this century.

JOSEF RUPERT GEISELMANN

Unlike Möhler, Josef Rupert Geiselmann has not been a major figure in Roman Catholic theology. Geiselmann was primarily a church historian. As such, however, he dedicated himself to making the work and thought of his predecessors in the Catholic Tübingen School available to the scholarly world. Geiselmann wrote a book-length study of the school, prepared critical editions of works of earlier Tübingers, and wrote analyses of their theologies. He also clarified the Roman Catholic understanding of scripture and tradition. Following the example of J. E. Kuhn, who in the nineteenth century attacked D. F. Strauss's hermeneutics, Geiselmann critiqued Bultmann's demythologization project.[21]

Joseph Rupert Geiselmann was born in Neu Ulm in 1890. He studied for the priesthood in Tübingen after the condemnation of Modernism (1907). Geiselmann was a student at Tübingen during a period of eclipse of the Catholic Tübingen School: the glory of the nineteenth century Tübingers was gone and Karl Adam would not arrive until 1919. For four years, Geiselmann served as a parish priest; he then returned to Tübingen as an instructor. In 1930, he was promoted to professor. Four years later, he became professor of scholastic philosophy and dogmatic theology. He succeeded to Karl Adam's chair in dogmatics in 1949 and retired in 1958.

For nearly 40 years, Geiselmann devoted himself to researching and revitalizing the thought of the Catholic Tübingen School. When Geiselmann began his research, no consensus existed regarding the nature of the school. At the beginning of the twentieth century, there was not even agreement that such a school ever existed. Geiselmann showed the Tübingen School existed in a vital relationship with developments from the Enlightenment, Romanticism, and German Idealism. He said the determining characteristic of the school was "the fundamental principle of the historicity of revelation." By this he meant Catholic Tübingen theologians saw historicity as the connection of the whole of that which is mediated to humans through living tradition, a tradition they are responsible for and which they must appropriate according to their particular situation.[22]

The way Geiselmann chose to do this was to refocus Catholic thought on tradition. Drawing on Möhler, he described tradition as something alive and developing over time; this was in stark contrast to the dominant pre-Vatican II view that tradition was a static deposit handed down from generation to generation and jealously guarded by the organizational church. The recovery of this dynamic understanding of tradition was, according to Avery Dulles, a major achievement of Vatican II. Dulles says it enabled the Catholic Church to restructure itself in a way that remained faithful to the past while the church entered into conversation with the present.[23]

When Geiselmann spoke of tradition, he included both scripture and nonscriptural apostolic tradition. This definition of tradition would receive formal expression at Vatican II (*Dei Verbum* 10). According to Geiselmann, the Church did not create a canon as the sole repository of apostolic tradition. Had it been otherwise, the Fathers of the second century would have offered a sharply different teaching; instead, they simply added church tradition as a second, independent form of tradition in the church. Geiselmann did say, however, that tradition's capacity and need for adaptation is not unconditional; where it is a matter of truth, there is no question of adaptation.[24] He said the formation of the canon was an act of the church involving a process of selection. Therefore, the canon makes no claim to include all inspired writings. All it claims is that those inspired writings included have a regulative significance in and for the church.[25]

Through a historical study, Geiselmann clarified the Roman Catholic understanding of the relationship between scripture and unwritten tradition and of the sufficiency of scripture. He showed that for Catholics both scripture and tradition mediate the entire gospel, yet they do so in different ways.[26] He explained that, "it is out of the question that Holy Scripture should give us only fragments of the gospel of Jesus the Christ, the rest being given to us by Tradition."[27] In saying this, Geiselmann challenged the understanding common even among Catholics that divine revelation is found in part in scripture and in part in tradition. Geiselmann showed that the Council of Trent (fourth session, 1546) never declared that revelation occurs "partly in scripture, partly in tradition;" instead, it settled for the noncommittal formula that revelation occurs in "scripture and tradition" without further explanation. Because Catholic doctrine teaches that both scripture and tradition are products of the church, Geiselmann concluded that both constitute the external concrete forms of the mystery of Jesus Christ in the life of the apostolic church.[28]

Geiselmann agreed with modern biblical critics that church tradition does not reproduce Jesus' life or other events it reports with modern historiographical accuracy; instead it recounts them in terms of their significance for the readers and hearers of the gospel. The Spirit acting in the church is the source of this interpretive freedom. This kerygma faithfully passes on the gospel and keeps Jesus alive for us today.[29] But the gospel grounds the kerygma and prevents it from becoming merely an idea or myth. As a result, Geiselmann affirmed the unity of the historical Jesus and the Christ of faith, maintaining this was the "scandal and folly" of Christianity. At this point, Geiselmann criticized Strauss and Bultmann for working from a particular view of history that precluded them from recognizing the divine inbreaking into history in the man Jesus. As he said, they concentrated so completely on the *Historie* that they missed the *Geschichte*.

Geiselmann built his argument on the foundation laid by his predecessor J. E. Kuhn[30] against David Friedrich Strauss a century earlier. Geiselmann said the original apostolic kerygma was based on the historical facts of Jesus' life, even if its primary purpose was not to be an historical report. Although the Gospels were concerned with faith in Jesus, they were grounded in the empirical, historical facts of Jesus' life. In presenting Jesus' life as salvation history, the apostles were creatively reforming history, not denying or misusing it.[31] He went on to deny that because the Gospels are not historically neutral they are unable to serve as reliable sources for Jesus' life. We are required only to take their perspective into account before we use them.

Geiselmann did not limit himself to attacking the demythologization program that saw Jesus Christ as merely human. He criticized equally the opposing opinion that had no difficulty seeing Jesus as God but could not conceive of Him as human. Geiselmann said much of the Catholicism of his day concealed a latent Monophysitism.

Drawing on the Tübingen emphasis on history, Geiselmann noted that history is essential in ensuring that tradition does not become rigid, mindless, and dead. But history acts dialectically with continuity, which keeps it from dissolving into subjectivity. This is because tradition must be something that has an identity subject to change over time and yet remains itself during this process of historical transformation. This transformation was essential if the words of Jesus spoken in a particular time and place were to become meaningful in other settings. The most serious situations facing the church were those heretical teachings that arose within the church and philosophical ideas that invaded the church. These compelled the church to refine and clarify its teachings in a way that took account of the objections raised. This means that doctrine appears in a continually new garb of ideas and terms that represent an advance in the understanding of the gospel.[32]

Geiselmann considered the nineteenth century Catholic Tübingen School as the middle-road of contemporary Catholic theology. Tübingen offered a vital mediating process where recognition of the substantial veracity of the Christian revelation led to its being reformed into new historical shape through accepting and rejecting various historical elements. Geiselmann, while recognizing the inner turbulence and pluriformity of the school, uncovered the unity that encompassed these differences.

Geiselmann was convinced that history and theology are not incompatible. This led him to defend the Christological teachings of Christianity as faithful to the history of Jesus. This work on the historical Jesus created an ambiguity in Geiselmann's attitude toward biblical criticism. He accepted those conclusions he could fit into his credal Christology, but rejected other conclusions less compatible with his theology although the bases for each category were virtually identical.

As the historian of the Catholic Tübingen School, Geiselmann prepared the way for its reentry into Catholic theology by writing a study of the school, editing the major works of two of its most prominent thinkers, and preparing studies of the theological contributions of these theologians. Although Geiselmann retired four years before Vatican II, his work made the writings of the Tübingen School more accessible to the open Catholic Church following Vatican II and he trained some of the young theologians who would rise to prominence in the 1970s. One hundred years after the death of Johann Adam Möhler, Geiselmann both defined the nature of the Catholic Tübingen School and appropriated its lessons for his contemporaries.

CONCLUSION

As church historians and theologians, Möhler and Geiselmann argued for the Catholic Tübingen understanding of living, developing tradition as the basis for Christian belief. For Möhler, the opposition was both Reformation Protestantism and the Lutheranism of his Protestant Tübingen contemporaries; for Geiselmann it was the Catholic Neo-Scholasticism of the age between the Modernism controversy and Vatican II and the Protestant biblical criticism of such figures as Rudolf Bultmann. Church history documented the growth of the Church and its thought from Pentecost to the present through a constant process of development and adaptation to meet changed circumstances and new realities.

As Geiselmann said, the Catholic Tübingen School represents a middle way amid various tendencies in Catholic thought. To those who would dissolve history in favor of some idealist system, Tübingers reiterated the truth and significance of biblical history. To those who would discard the transcendent in favor of some sort of immanentism, they reaffirmed the Christian doctrine of the supernatural. As they began to appropriate some methods and conclusions of modern biblical criticism, the Tübingers said this criticism was intended to understand better the inscripturated form of divine revelation. They have recognized development within history and have sought to present Christian teaching to their generation in ways that have been both meaningful to that audience and faithful to the original proclamation. Interacting with, but never married to any one philosophy, Tübingers have grounded their work in church history, especially patristic studies. As Johann Sebastian von Drey, the founder of the Catholic Tübingen School, said, theological method must have a historical basis, but theology must never be dissolved into history. This statement summarizes well the Tübingen understanding of the interrelationship between church history and theology.

BIBLIOGRAPHY

Both Möhler and Geiselmann were prolific writers and they wrote on a wide range of subjects. Few of their writings have been translated into English; however, for those who can read theological German, Walter Kasper's bibliography of Geiselmann on pages 367–71 of *Kirche und Überlieferung*, edited by Johannes Betz and Heinrich Fries (Freiberg: Herder, 1960) is the best source. Also for readers of German, Paul-Werner Scheele's edited collection of Möhler's writings, *Johannes Adam Möhler*, in the series *Wegbereiter heutiger Theologie* (Graz: Styria, 1969), contains a bibliography of Möhler's writings and of writings about Möhler on pages 367–71. The few English-language volumes include:

PRIMARY SOURCES

Geiselmann, Josef Rupert. *The Meaning of Tradition*. Trans. by W. J. O'Hara. Freiburg: Herder, and London: Burns & Oates, 1966.

——. "Scripture and Tradition in Catholic Theology." *Theology Digest* 6 (1958):73–78.

——. "Scripture, Tradition, and the Church: An Ecumenical Problem," Trans. by John Tashjean. In *Christianity Divided: Protestant and Roman Catholic Theological Issues*, Daniel J. Callahan, Heiko A. Obermann, and Daniel J. O'Hanlon, S.J. ed., 39–72. (New York: Sheed and Ward, 1961).

Möhler, Johann Adam. *The Life of Saint Anselm, Archbishop of Canterbury.* Trans. by H. Rymer. London: T. Jones, 1842.

——. *On the Relation of Islam to the Gospel.* Trans. by J. P. Menge. Calcutta: Ostell and Lepage, British Library, 1847.

——. *Symbolism: Or Exposition of the Doctrinal Differences Between Catholics and Protestants as Evidenced by Their Symbolical Writings* (Fifth Edition). Trans. by James Burton Robertson. London: Gibbings & Company, 1906.

SECONDARY SOURCES

Among the growing number of books and articles about Möhler, Geiselmann, and the Catholic Tübingen School, the following are the most accessible and helpful:

Burtchaell, James Tunstead. "Drey, Möhler and the Catholic School of Tübingen." In *Nineteenth Century Religious Thought in the West*, edited by Ninian Smart, et al, 2:111–39. Cambridge: Cambridge University Press, 1985.

Fitzer, Joseph. *Moehler and Baur in Controversy, 1832–38: Romantic-Idealist Assessment of the Reformation and Counter-Reformation.* Tallahassee: American Academy of Religion, 1974.

Gilmore, George B. "J. A. Möhler on Doctrinal Development." *Heythrop Journal* 19 (1978):383–404.

McCready, Douglas. *Jesus Christ for the Modern World: The Christology of the Catholic Tübingen School.* New York: Peter Lang, 1991.

O'Meara, Thomas F. "Revelation and History: Schelling, Möhler and Congar," *Irish Theological Quarterly* 53 (1987):17–35.

——. *Romantic Idealism and Roman Catholicism: Schelling Among the Theologians.* Notre Dame, Ind.: University of Notre Dame Press, 1982.

Savon, Herve. *Johann Adam Möhler, the Father of Modern Theology.* Trans. by Charles McGrath. Glen Rock, N.J.: Paulist Press, 1966.

NOTES

1. Outside Germany, the Catholic Tübingen School has been relatively unknown in comparison to the influence it has had on Catholic theology. Little has appeared in English on the school. A recent article by James Tunstead Burtchaell, "Drey, Möhler and the Catholic School of Tübingen," in *Nineteenth Century Religious Thought in the West*, ed. Ninian Smart, et al. (Cambridge: Cambridge University Press, 1985), 2:111–139, and the following three books, introduce the history and theology of the school to English-speaking readers: Wayne L. Fehr, *The Birth of the Catholic Tübingen School: The Dogmatics of Johann Sebastian Drey*, AARAS 37 (Chico, Calif.: Scholars Press, 1981); Douglas McCready, *Jesus Christ for the Modern World: The Christology of the Catholic Tübingen School* (New York: Peter Lang, 1991); Thomas F. O'Meara, *Romantic Idealism*

and Roman Catholicism: Schelling and the Theologians (Notre Dame: University of Notre Dame Press, 1982).

2. Robert Krieg says of the Catholic Tübingen School: "The method of the Catholic Tübingen School is one of correlation, directed toward 'the intimate, most intimate synthesis of speculative [theology] with historical theology.' It presupposes that theologians participate in the life of the church and tap three sources: Scripture and tradition, historical inquiry, and contemporary thought. This method produces a theology that is both 'dogmatic and apologetic.'" (From Robert Anthony Krieg, C.S.C., *Karl Adam: Catholicism in German Culture* [Notre Dame, Ind.: University of Notre Dame Press, 1992], 175.)

3. Max Seckler, "Johann Sebastian Drey und die Theologie," *Theologische Quartalschrift* 158 (1978): 103 ff.

4. Klaus Reinhardt, *Der dogmatische Schriftsgebrauch in der katholischen und protestantischen Christologie von der Aufklärung bis zur Gegenwart* (Munich: Ferdinand Schöningh, 1970), 117.

5. Joseph Fitzer, *Möhler and Baur in Controversy, 1832–38: Romantic-Idealist Assessment of the Reformation and Counter-Reformation*, AARSR 7 (Tallahassee: American Academy of Religion, 1974), 1 f.

6. Möhler's lectures on church history were only collected and published in 1992. Earlier editions apparently were taken from student notes rather than Möhler's own lecture notes. See Johann Adam Möhler, *Vorlesungen über die Kirchengeschichte*, ed. Reinhold Rieger, 2 vols. (Munich: Erich Wewel, 1992).

7. As is true for all Catholic Tübingers prior to World War I, few of Möhler's writings are available in English translation, and those that are available are not well translated. The situation is even worse for Geiselmann, for whom only three chapters from one book have been translated.

8. Johann Adam Möhler, *Die Einheit in der Kirche, oder das Prinzip des Katholizimus dargestellt im Geiste der Kirchenväter der ersten drei Jahrhunderte* (Tübingen, 1825). This has not been translated into English. The most accessible edition of *Die Einheit* is Josef Rupert Geiselmann's critical edition of 1957, published by the Wissenschaftliche Buchgesellschaft in Darmstadt.

9. Philip J. Rosato, S.J., "Between Christocentrism and Pneumatocentrism: An Interpretation of Johann Adam Möhler's Ecclesiology," *Heythrop Journal* 19 (1978):58.

10. "More than anyone else J. A. Möhler broke the power of the Enlightenment. A revivification of the study of the Fathers and the church's needs brought the lost deposit of the theology of the early church into a new form." (From Andreas Schmid, ed., *Geheimrat Dr. Alois Ritter v. Schmid: Sein Leben und seine Schriften* [Regensburg, 1911], 296. Alois Schmid was a Catholic theologian at Munich in the late 19th century.)

11. Johann Adam Möhler, *Athanasius der Grosse und die Kirche seiner Zeit, besonders im Kampfe mit dem Arianismus* (Mainz, 1827).

12. Johann Adam Möhler, "Anselm, Erzbischof von Canterbury. Ein Beitrag zur Kenntnis des religiös-sittlichen, offentlich-kirchlichen und wissenschaftlichen lebens im 11. und 12. Jahrhunderts," *Theologische Quartalschrift* 9 (1827):435–97, 585–644; 10 (1828):62–130. This was translated by Henry Rymer as *The Life of Anselm, Archbishop of Canterbury; Contribution to a Knowledge of the Moral, Ecclesiastical, and Literary Life of the Eleventh & Twelfth Centuries* (London: T. Jones, 1842).

13. Henry R. Nienaltowski, *Johann Adam Möhler's Theory of Doctrinal Development* (Washington: Catholic University of America Press, 1959), 32.

14. Möhler, *Anselm*, 50 ff.

15. Johann Adam Möhler, *Symbolik oder Darstellung der dogmatischen Gegensätze der Katholiken und der Protestanten nach ihren offentlichen Bekenntnisschriften*, ed. J. R. Geiselmann (Darmstadt: Wissenschaftliche Buchgesellschaft, 1958). This was translated

by James Burton Robertson as *Symbolism or Exposition of the Doctrinal Differences Between Catholics and Protestants as Evidenced by Their Symbolical Writings*, 5th ed. (London: Gibbings, 1906).

16. Fitzer, *Möhler and Baur*, 2.

17. Möhler was quite right in saying that different anthropologies underlie many of the important differences between Protestants and Roman Catholics. This is often expressed by Catholics as a criticism of Protestants' over-pessimistic view of humanity and its capabilities and the Protestant rejoinder that Catholics fail to take sin seriously enough.

18. As did Irenaeus, Möhler failed to recognize the parallelism of the Hebrew construction of the Genesis passage. Seeing the two terms as different, Möhler then had to provide distinct meanings for them (as had Irenaeus). This led Möhler to misunderstand seriously the views of the Reformers and to attribute some incorrect theological consequences to those views. Möhler charged Luther, Calvin, and Zwingli with both gnostic and pantheistic tendencies. He thus concluded that Schleiermacher was the legitimate heir of the sixteenth century reformers.

Wenham notes that the interpretation of image and likeness chosen by Möhler is the traditional Christian interpretation, but says, "The interchangeability of 'image' and 'likeness' (cf. 5:3) shows that this distinction is foreign to Genesis." See Gordon J. Wenham, *Genesis 1–15*, vol. 1 of Word Bible Commentary (Waco, Tex.: Word Books, 1987), 29 ff.

19. Geiselmann says, "For Möhler the fact that it is necessary to prove God is itself a terrible phenomenon, the most striking proof of the fall of humanity in Adam. But that it is still possible to prove God's existence shows that God's image is not completely abolished in us." (From Josef Rupert Geiselmann, *The Meaning of Tradition*, trans. by W. J. O'Hara [Freiberg: Herder, and London: Burns & Oates, 1966], 71.)

20. Möhler says this ability to cooperate is based on divine grace, but argument reinforces the historic Protestant concern that Catholicism has too weak an appreciation of the effects of the fall and human sin on human spiritual capacity. At several points, Möhler misstates the teachings of the Reformers in a way that a careful reading of their writings would have avoided. Most of his attack, however, was directed at the Protestantism of F. C. Baur, which Möhler described as both badly flawed and untrue to the teachings of the Reformers.

21. Virtually none of Geiselmann's writings has been translated into English. Only *The Meaning of Tradition*, which is the first three chapters of *Die Heilige Schrift und die Tradition; zu den neuern Kontroversen über des Verhaltnis der Heiligen Schriften zu den nichtgeschriebenen Traditionen*, has been translated. Geiselmann's study of the Catholic Tübingen School, his critical editions of Möhler, and his theological studies of Möhler deserve the attention of a good translator.

22. Leo Scheffczyk, "Josef Rupert Geiselmann—Weg und Werk," *Theologische Quartalschrift* 150 (1970): 393, cited in McCready, *Tübingen School*, 187.

23. Avery Dulles, *The Reshaping of Catholicism: Current Challenges in the Theology of Church* (San Francisco: Harper & Row, 1988), 17.

24. In dealing with this matter of truth, Geiselmann wrote, "Without authority there is no tradition concerning what is true. But who are the bearers of this authority and what is it based on? It is founded on the transmitter's standing nearer to the source of what is received. . . . The authority of the ancients is founded on the fact that they have received knowledge from a divine source and handed on what they have received" (Geiselmann, *Meaning of Tradition*, 45).

25. Ibid., 36.

26. Josef Rupert Geiselmann, "Scripture, Tradition, and the Church: An Ecumenical Problem," in *Christianity Divided: Protestant and Roman Catholic Theological Issues*, ed.

Daniel J. Callahan, Heiko A. Obermann, and Daniel J. O'Hanlon (New York: Sheed and Ward, 1961), 49.

27. Ibid., 58.

28. Ibid.

29. Ibid., 57. Geiselmann wrote, "The *paradosis* of the apostolic Church preserves the word of Jesus 'but does not guard it with an archivist's piety, nor is it handed on like the sayings of famous rabbis and provided with interpretations. Indeed one may put it as follows: tradition does not actually repeat and hand on his formally spoken word at all; it *is* His word today'" (italics in the original).

30. Johann Evangelist Kuhn was professor of dogmatics on the Catholic Tübingen faculty from 1839 until 1882. A student of Möhler, Kuhn was a New Testament scholar before he was a dogmatician. It was during his New Testament work that Kuhn wrote a scathing critique of Strauss's Christology. See 83 ff. in my *Jesus Christ for the Modern World* for more about Kuhn.

31. Josef Rupert Geiselmann, "Der Glaube an Jesus Christ—Mythos oder Geschichte? Zur Auseinandersetzung Joh. Ev. Kuhn mit David Friedrich Strauss," *Theologische Quartalschrift* 129 (1949):435.

32. Ibid., 30f. Geiselmann is explicitly rejecting the claim that the so-called Hellenization of the gospel constituted a falsification or perversion of the gospel. He is saying that the use of non-biblical concepts and language is both necessary and legitimate if Christianity is to be understood outside its original Palestinian setting.

13

PHILIP SCHAFF

STEPHEN R. GRAHAM

BIOGRAPHICAL INTRODUCTION

If called upon to name the few most influential shapers of the discipline
of church history in the United States, many would include the name of
Philip Schaff. Well-known for his multi-volume, still-in-print *History of
the Christian Church*, and his contributions to the production of the *Schaff-
Herzog Encyclopedia of Religious Knowledge* and the *Select Library of the Nicene
and Post-Nicene Fathers*, Schaff is appropriately named as the founder of
the discipline of church history in America. Upon his arrival in America as
a young man of twenty-five years old, however, few could have imagined
the impact this immigrant would have on intellectual and church life in his
adopted homeland.

Born in Chur, Switzerland, on January 1, 1819, Schaff's prospects were
not good.[1] An only child, his father died before Philip's first birthday and
left his mother in poverty. When she remarried and moved to Glarus, Philip was placed in a Chur orphanage and seldom saw his mother. He had the
good fortune, however, to find favor with the Reverend Paul Kind, who
took the boy under his wing and nurtured him in the Christian pietism that

was to characterize Schaff's outlook for the rest of his life. He entered the boys' academy in Kornthal, Württemberg at age fifteen and found there the warmth of piety and friendship he needed to grow. He recalled his years at the academy with deep appreciation. "To Württemberg I owe under God my spiritual life and the best part of my education."[2] Years later, on a return visit to Kornthal, Schaff recalled the "unspeakable benefit" he owed to his "spiritual birthplace."[3]

From Kornthal, he went to Stuttgart to continue his studies in the *Gymnasium*. While there he began what would develop into a lifelong friendship with William Julius Mann. Together these two young men attended small gatherings of pietists, where their faith was strengthened and their theological assumptions formed. Schaff looked back on these years as the foundation on which he would build his defense against the attacks of rationalism he would endure during his university years.

In 1837, Schaff entered the University of Tübingen, which was astir with the competing theological currents of the new Lutheranism, rationalism, and the mediating theology. Only two years before, David Friedrich Strauss had published his controversial *Leben Jesu*, which created a storm of protest among the more orthodox. Schaff identified himself with the mediating theologians, a foreshadowing of his ecumenical and irenic interests. He expressed admiration for the intellectual capacities of radical thinkers such as F. C. Baur, and admitted that it was from Baur that he received his first conception of historical development. But Schaff also lamented the "sad havoc" created by Baur's treatment of the apostolic age.[4] His defense against this threat was based on piety. "The best authority against Strauss is an honest soul filled with Christ."[5]

He continued his university studies with six months at Halle and finally moved to Berlin. There he came under the influence of Augustus Neander, whom Schaff called "the most important church historian of our time" and "the father of modern church history."[6] Schaff applauded and adopted Neander's understanding of church history as a discipline involving both the intellect and the heart. He was impressed by Neander's learning and solid research, but also by the spirit of faith and devotion that pervaded his works. From his mentor, Schaff inherited the concepts of "*liberality* and evangelical *catholicity*" that would provide key themes for his own work. Schaff noted that "the most enduring merit of Neander's church history consists in the *vital union of the two elements of science and Christian piety*," along with his view of history as full of "*life and genetic development*."[7]

Yet Schaff went beyond his teacher by insisting that there was an unbreakable connection between knowing the church—which meant familiarity with its history—and knowing Christ. Neander's weakness was that he focused on the inward and ideal and lacked a clear enough conception of the church as an institution; he was "quite too little Catholic, in the real and historical sense of the word." In contrast, Schaff insisted that the inward character of religion can never be separated from its outward manifestations. He pronounced his understanding as a maxim: *"Where Christ is, there also is the church, his body; and where the church is, there also is Christ, her head, and all grace; and what God hath joined together, let not man put asunder."*[8]

Upon completion of his studies at Berlin, Schaff began his work as *privatdocent* in 1842. Despite the struggles of getting started in such a position and the dismayingly long road which might eventually take him to full professorship, Schaff's prospects were good. But a totally unexpected opportunity presented itself. It altered both his career and the shape of theological education in the United States.

In July 1843, two delegates from the German Reformed Church extended to Schaff an intriguing offer. They were searching for a theological professor for their denomination's theological seminary in Pennsylvania, they said, and Schaff had been recommended to them by his professors and friends as a superb candidate. Would he consider the offer? The possibility must have stunned and intrigued Schaff. At Berlin, he was on the bottom rung of a long ladder, but at least his steps were moderately secure. Should he abandon what appeared to be excellent prospects for work in the American wilderness at this tiny unknown seminary? Would immigration to America be the opportunity of a lifetime or a career-threatening disaster? Through much prayer, reflection, and discussion—and not a little youthful chutzpah—Schaff came to see his invitation as similar to that of the apostle Paul's Macedonian call, "Come over and help us!"[9] Providence directed him to the New World.

Schaff arrived in Mercersburg, in the rolling hills of south-central Pennsylvania, in August 1844, and was warmly greeted by students and townspeople. His coming was momentous. With his arrival, the size of the theological faculty had doubled. Schaff was surprised and pleased to find that he and his new colleague, John Williamson Nevin, shared fundamental convictions about the character of the church and its weaknesses in America. Nevin had drunk deeply of contemporary German theology and with Schaff would establish Mercersburg as a center of American theological scholarship. Schaff wrote in his journal. "I think I could not have a better colleague than Dr. Nevin. I feared I might not find any sympathy in him for my views of the church; but I discover that he occupies essentially the same ground that I do and confirms me in my position. He is filled with the ideas of German theology."[10]

Schaff immediately began to share his understandings of the nature of the church with his host denomination, but discovered quickly that some influential leaders did not share either his or Nevin's enthusiasm for their form of German ecclesiology. Schaff had already irritated some with disparaging remarks from his ordination sermon that had preceded him across the Atlantic. His inaugural sermon, preached to the German Reformed Synod at Reading in October, poured fuel on the flames and provoked charges of heresy from ministers who had to be taken seriously. Schaff had to wonder whether his "Macedonian call" might have been a wrong number.

The inaugural sermon focused on "the principle of Protestantism," and while strongly affirming the Protestant character of its author, also revealed strong appreciation of the church in all eras, including the medieval. The Protestant Reformation was a necessary development in Christian history, of course, but it was not the abrupt about-face described by anti-Catholics among the German Reformed—one of whom had insisted precisely that in his sermon a few days before. No, Schaff declared, the Reformation was *the legitimate offspring, the greatest act of the Catholic Church.*[11]

Ultimately, the Synod of York exonerated Schaff after a painful and frustrating series of meetings, but it was obvious that he had his work cut out for him if he intended to share the best of German scholarship within his new homeland.[12]

For the next two decades, Schaff and Nevin labored together to develop a sense of history and a proper ecclesiology among American Christians. Their so-called "Mercersburg Theology" never became widely popular, though it did provide an important alternative both to the strict orthodoxy of "Old" Lutheranism and the Princeton Theology, and to the revivalism that swept through American Christianity like a prairie fire. The Mercersburgers believed that they offered a theology that was orthodox, yet irenic and open to development, and an ecclesiology that was traditional, yet ecumenical. Their goal of "evangelical-catholic" Christianity sought to overcome American individualism and anti-historical bias with a model of the church as an organic whole, solidly rooted in the past and looking forward to development, growth, and unity in the future.

By 1863, Schaff considered his work at Mercersburg completed. He had traveled widely among the German Reformed in America; he had returned to Europe on numerous visits; and he had published voluminously. But the isolation of the Pennsylvania hills had become frustrating and the disturbances of the Civil War clinched his decision. If he were to have the opportunities for study and collegial relationships he desired, a more cosmopolitan location was essential. To that end, he received a two-year leave of absence from Mercersburg Seminary in 1863 and relocated his family in New York City. Schaff ultimately resigned his position at Mercersburg at the end of the leave of absence and lived the rest of his life in New York.

His first position in the city was secretary to the New York Sabbath Committee. He served in that post from 1864 through 1870, and also taught part time at Hartford and Drew seminaries. In addition to his services with the Sabbath Committee, during this period Schaff began to see the fruits of a massive editorial project he had organized with the publication in 1864 of the first volume of the American edition of *Lange's Commentary on the Old and New Testaments*. Another example of Schaff's concern to see a cooperation of the best of German and Anglo-American scholarship: he also moved the project in an irenic and ecumenical direction. To one of the author-editors he wrote, "In all your additions keep in mind the encyclopedic and evangelical catholic features of Lange's *Bibelwerk*. Avoid all that is of a sectarian character." As Schaff resolutely moved the commentary series toward completion in twenty-five volumes, he was heard to remark, "All things come to an end, but Lange."[13]

In 1870, Schaff joined the faculty of Union Theological Seminary as Professor of Theological Encyclopedia and Christian Symbolism. The comprehensiveness of the title led at least one of his colleagues to ponder whether any of the rest of them were truly necessary. While the response to that query is obvious, the breadth of Schaff's teaching remains astounding. In 1873, he transferred to the chair of Hebrew. After 1874 he taught New Testament exegesis as occupant of the chair of biblical literature, and finally in 1887 he became Professor of Church History. He continued in that position until just a few months before his death in 1893.

As part of his ecumenical efforts, Schaff became a member of the Evangelical Alliance in 1866 and supported that organization the rest of his life. The peak of his involvement came in 1873 when New York hosted the General World Conference of the Alliance and Schaff worked countless hours recruiting European and American attenders. On behalf of the Alliance he traveled to Europe no less than four times between 1869 and 1873. His efforts were rewarded with a gathering of international religious leaders exceeding anything previously held in the United States.

In the meantime, Schaff helped organize and lead a project that would have a profound impact on Christianity in the English-speaking world. Largely due to his diligent efforts of mediation and organization, an American committee under his direction cooperated with the British revisers of the Authorized Version of the Bible. Schaff served as president of the American committee and through some tumultuous times he promoted, mustered patrons, soothed, coaxed, and negotiated until finally the revised New Testament appeared in 1881 and the Old Testament in 1885. Schaff called the result "the noblest monument of Christian union and cooperation in the nineteenth century."[14]

As part of his agenda to nurture scholarship and teaching in the area of church history in the United States, Schaff founded the American Society of Church History (ASCH) in 1888. Not only would the discipline of church history be strengthened by the society, but the irenic and ecumenical scholarship promoted by the society would help provide the context for the emergence of evangelical-catholic Christianity in America. One of Schaff's dreams for the Society that became a reality only after his death was the publication of a thirteen-volume set of denominational histories under the sponsorship of the ASCH. The American Church History series and the ASCH stand as legacies of Schaff's historically-informed ecumenism.

During his career at Union, Schaff worked steadily on his *History of the Christian Church* which went through five revisions, the last one completed in 1892. That year marked the fiftieth year of his work as a theological professor, an occasion that was celebrated by tributes from scores of friends and a number of universities and theological seminaries.[15]

The final major event of Schaff's life was his attendance at the World's Parliament of Religions held in Chicago in conjunction with the Columbian Exposition of 1893. Against his doctor's advice and although too weak to read his own paper, Schaff insisted on attending. His theme was the reunion of Christendom and in this, his final appeal, he once again called for Christian denominations to bring to fruition their Lord's prayer for unity. The scope of the union was remarkably wide, embracing Unitarians, the Salvation Army, Greek Orthodox, and Roman Catholics—and every Christian group in between. Schaff even dreamed that perhaps someday the Pope himself, "in the spirit of the first Gregory and under the inspiration of a higher authority, should infallibly declare his own fallibility in all matters lying outside of his own communion, and invite Greeks and Protestants to a fraternal pan-Christian council in Jerusalem."[16]

Having made his final appeal for Christian Union, less than a month later, on October 20, 1893, Schaff died. Schaff's son, David, noted four distinctive interests of his father that summarize well the life and work of this great church historian: "His intermediary mission between the biblical scholarship and church life of Europe and America, his work upon the Revision of the English Scriptures, his advocacy of Christian tolerance and the reunion of Christendom, and his labors as a church historian."[17] Later historians stand on the shoulders of a giant.

HISTORIOGRAPHICAL PRINCIPLES

Throughout his career as a church historian, Philip Schaff employed a set of historiographical principles that were drawn from his German background and modified by his American experiences. His self-understanding as a scholar was consciously shaped by both influences. Less than two years after his arrival in America, he put his ideas into print in a thorough discussion of *What Is Church History?* (1846). Five years later, Schaff published his first major attempt to employ his principles of church historiography with his *Geschichte der christlichen Kirche, von ihrer Gründung bis auf die Gegenwart,* translated two years later into English and published as *History of the Apostolic Church, with a General Introduction to Church History* (1853). In an extensive "General Introduction" to that work, Schaff elaborated and expanded his discussion of historiographical principles.

Schaff decried the appalling ignorance of church history he found among church leaders in America and spent his career arguing for the importance of church history as an academic discipline. A number of causes contributed to the problem, including the American anti-historical bias— which Schaff traced to the Puritans whom he believed had left Americans with a low opinion of history and tradition—and to the "dry, lifeless style" that characterized the study of church history in the few seminaries who ventured to offer courses. What was missing, he insisted, was an understanding of the "main thing in history, the *ideas* which rule it and reveal themselves in the process." Only by understanding the ruling ideas of history can one discover meaning within the seemingly endless series of events.[18]

Neither do American scholars adequately appreciate the principle of "organic development" in history. This failure leads to rampant sectarianism as groups, some of whom have legitimate concerns, push their private interpretations of history and foolishly attempt to cut themselves free from the past. Schaff's job was immense.

How shall we labour with any effect to build up the Church, if we have no thorough knowledge of her history, or fail to apprehend it from the proper point of observation? History is, and must ever continue to be, next to God's word, the richest fountain of wisdom, and the surest guide to all successful practical activity. To reject her voice is to rob ourselves of our own right to exist, or, at least, to condemn our own life; since we owe to her, in fact, whether we choose to do so or not, all that we are and all that we can become.[19]

The main theological issue of the age, according to Schaff and his colleague at Mercersburg, John Williamson Nevin, was the *Church Question*." And the church cannot be known without a thorough knowledge of its history. In fact, Schaff virtually identified the two. "Church and History . . . are so closely united, that respect and love towards the first, may be said to be essentially the same with a proper sense of what is comprised in the other."[20]

Having established the importance of his work, Schaff turned to a survey of developments among church historians in Germany, without question the leaders among theorists of the discipline. At the forefront of German theory was an insistence that ideas "rule in the last instance the History of the World."[21] Schaff advocated a modified Hegelianism, which identified the "primal Truth" with God and added a smaller-scale dialectics to the larger dialectics common to Hegelians. For instance, God shaped the western church through a dialectic relationship between Roman Catholicism and Protestantism and in that way directed the lives of millions of Christians. Yet Providence was also active in more limited spheres such as the dialectical relationships between particular American denominations, directing them toward an ultimate unity, or even in the more narrow arena of the various doctrinal or ecclesiastical discussions within denominations.

God revealed His providential control of the universe primarily through Christianity. "Christianity forms the turning point of the world's history; and Christ, the true pole star of the whole, is the centre also around which all revolves." Christ, said Schaff, is the key "which alone can unlock the sense of all that has taken place before his advent or since."[22] There were realms of secular as well as sacred history, but ultimate meaning was to be found only through an understanding of the sacred.[23] In the "General Introduction," Schaff stresses more forcefully and explicitly the uniqueness of Christianity as "the absolutely true and perfect religion, which is destined to absorb all others."[24] Likewise, the goal of history is a theocracy in which the saints rule all nations. While this principle had been implicit in his earlier work, here it is stated starkly with force acceptable to many of his hearers, but stunning to people with today's pluralistic assumptions about American society.

Schaff also stressed that the church historian must be a believer. While he insisted that the historian of the church must rise above "all prejudice" and "all party interest," he understood those to refer to persons working within the general Christian orbit. For those outside the church in its universal sense, there can be no true understanding of its nature. "He who would know truth, must himself stand in the truth; only the philosopher can understand philosophy; only the poet, poetry; only the pious man, religion. So also the church historian, to do justice to his subject, must live and move in Christianity." His opponents were those, like Strauss, who pretended to serve the church, but actually were unbelievers trying to destroy it. "A church historian without faith and piety can only set before us, at best, instead of the living body of Christ, a cold marble statue, without seeing eye or feeling heart." The rationalist historians suffer from an "*entire want of faith*, without which it is as impossible duly to understand Christianity, its inspired records, and its inward history, as to perceive light and colour without eyes."[25]

Like many of his time, Schaff used periodization and other structures of historical time to help achieve understanding. He also identified three periods in the history of church history: orthodox, rationalistic, and organic development.[26]

The orthodox period, including both Protestant and Roman Catholic forms, assumed that the church in its established doctrine and life—from either a Roman Catholic or Protestant standpoint—was complete and final. Any diverging opinions must be rejected out of hand and proponents of such views must be silenced. Because doctrine and Christian life were immutable, the orthodox position allowed no room for development except geographically as missionary expansion. As Schaff put it in describing this method, "What has once been acknowledged by the Church, is constituted a law obligatory for all time."[27] The great weakness of historians during this period of study, however, was their complete lack of an adequate conception of development in the history of the church.

The next period, the rationalistic, corrected the problem of orthodox rigidity, but moved to the extreme of "*fluctuating heterodoxy* and *unchurchly subjectivity*." The two sides to the rationalist coin were the "pietistic" and the "rationalistic." Though vastly different in their regard for the Christian faith, the pietists over-reacted against orthodoxy by focusing their attention exclusively on subjective, practical Christianity, while the rationalists erred in their rejection of the overweening authority of the institutional church by rejecting the institution itself. While Schaff had sympathy with the goals of the pietists—the nurture of their tradition had been and remained very important in his own life—he denounced the rationalists in no uncertain terms. These scholars "could find no more important work, than to complete the business of destruction upon the Church and her history."[28]

Yet the defects of the previous periods had made possible, through the forces of correction, a new form of historical study, which used the good from the earlier times, eliminated the bad, and opened the possibility of a new history that would relate the story of the church in a fairer and more comprehensive way than was previously possible. "To be complete now, a Church History should unite in proper harmony a thorough use of original sources, clear apprehension, organic development, lively and interesting delineation, strong but liberal and universal church feeling, and fruitfulness in the way of practical edification."[29]

With a glimpse of his own ambition for the work, Schaff described the possibility: "The material is prepared; the plan of the edifice too is ready in its main outline; only the master hand is waited for, that shall put the work together, and cause the parts to appear as a complete, magnificent, and harmonious whole." The key to Schaff's understanding of the modern historiography was organic development. "In this view," he explained, "the word of God also was not at once understood by the church from the beginning, in all its depth and comprehension, but gradually always more and more with the advancing age of the church." History progressively revealed the mind of God as God directed the cosmos through the agency of the church, and the true historian was the one who could interpret this direction. Only that which is dead is done, said Schaff. Life, in contrast, involves "a genesis, movement, process, development."[30]

To illustrate this development, Schaff employed organic metaphors: the plant evolving from seed, to root and branch, to blossom, then fruit; the human person, from embryo, through birth, childhood, youth, adulthood, and old age. He also appealed to the threefold meanings of a German term employed by Hegel, *aufheben*. The term combines an abolition of weaknesses from the initial stage, preservation of the good from that stage, and finally, raising that which is preserved to a higher level. For example, "the child is abolished as a child in the young man, and yet is preserved at the same time, and raised unto a higher stage of life." More importantly, however, "spiritual growth or development is likewise a process of annihilation, preservation, and exaltation."[31] Schaff employed this structure of development to help explain developments as varied as progress in historiography, the relationship between Protestant Christianity and medieval Catholicism, and American denominationalism.

The development of the church is also illustrated by two of Jesus' parables: the mustard seed, which though tiny eventually grows to be a huge plant, and leaven, which works its way through the whole lump of dough. The external spread of the church is described by the parable of the mustard seed. Initially localized in Palestine with a small, unimpressive group of followers, Jesus' teachings eventually reached every part of the globe. Likewise, as yeast permeates dough, the internal influence of the church eventually affects all spheres of life, from politics to intellectual life, from economics to art.[32]

Unlike those who would advocate development beyond traditional Christianity, however, Schaff always insisted that the essence of the church present from the beginning did *not* change. The acorn becomes the oak, he noted, but never an apple tree.

The process of development he understood as following the pattern of Hegelian *"dialectic opposites* and *extremes."* Each movement in the history of the church is attended by overemphasis, which is then challenged by its opposite. The result of this "constant *struggle"* is that the extremes of each are abolished, the good from each is conserved, and their synthesis is a higher, more fully developed form of Christianity than either had been. This explains Schaff's conflicts with his peers in the German Reformed Church, who saw themselves as carriers of the unchanging orthodoxy of their ancestors the Protestant Reformers. What the Reformers accomplished was essential, Schaff agreed, but the development of Christianity continued beyond the sixteenth century. In fact, where the medieval church had overemphasized "objectivity, authority, obedience," the evangelical freedom unleashed by the Reformers had provided a necessary corrective, but itself had "degenerate in fleshly self-will and licentiousness." The answer to contemporary problems, therefore, was neither a return to medieval authoritarianism, nor unbridled reformation liberty, but rejection of the extremes of each, appreciation of their strengths, and development of those strengths into a higher form of Christianity. "The truth," Schaff insisted, "lies not in the extremes, but in the *middle,* or the *deep* rather, in which they may be said to meet!" Neither Protestantism nor Catholicism contain the fullness of Christian truth and Schaff identified the key issue of his time as the development from the two of "evangelical Catholicity or churchly Protestantism."[33]

Not only must the church deal with internal extremes, but it must also respond to external situations. Again using an organic metaphor, Schaff insisted that each stage of development was accompanied by a corresponding disease. "Where God builds a temple, the devil is sure to have a chapel alongside."[34] As the developments attain higher and higher levels, the seriousness of the diseases also increase. Perhaps for once losing his own historical perspective, Schaff identified some forms of German philosophy and anti-theology that elevated humanity to the place of God as the most serious threat in the history of the church. Yet, even here Schaff could say that ultimately even the diseases would be used by God to benefit the church. The cures responding to the diseases would leave the organism even stronger than before. The main stream of development, he insisted, "moves always *forward*." Side currents might regress or dry up, but the main channel, though twisting and turning, always moved toward the goal.

Development also had a geographic aspect. Schaff, like many intellectuals of his day, accepted the dictum that as the sun "moved" from east to west, so civilization and Christian development progressed from east to west. His European mentors were surprised when Schaff had the temerity to identify the United States as the western site for the next great developments in Christianity.

In the final section of *What Is Church History?* Schaff expressed his understanding of the importance of "a right view of church history." Church history, he maintained, is no less than the story of God's unfolding plan of redemption. The historian of the church is charged to discern in history the hand of God directing the cosmos, and must accept with confidence the promise of Jesus to the church, "Lo, I am with you always, even to the end of the world." Schaff speaks a strong word to our culture's individualism and the erosion of community sense, even with the church. "It is a ridiculous, if not wicked, presumption, for any one to exalt his own individuality, as such, over the authority of all history."[35]

Finally, Schaff's overarching concern for church unity was supported by his view of church history. Impartial study of history, he believed, could create greater appreciation for the church in all of its manifestations, as well as humility in personal positions. He concluded,

> Thus we come to the result, that a thorough knowledge of the historical development of the body of Christ, in all its parts, is an indispensable condition to the farther advancement of the church, and to a permanent union of its different branches. The cultivation of Church History, and that of the church itself, go hand in hand together. Here lies the strongest challenge to an unremitting prosecution of the study, for all who are called to take part in the solution of the great church questions of the present time, and who are concerned to build, not upon the sand, but upon an immovable rock.[36]

In his "General Introduction" to the *History of the Apostolic Church*, Schaff outlined the vast scope of the project to write a complete and methodologically modern church history and his intended part in it.

> To present from original sources, in a faithful, clear, and life-like picture, the history of the church of Jesus Christ, the God-man and Saviour of the world; to reproduce, with ardent love of truth and with genuine catholicity, her inward and outward experience, her conflicts

and triumphs, her sufferings and joys, her thoughts, her words, and her deeds; and to hold up to the present age this panorama of eighteen centuries as the most complete apology for Christianity, full of encouragement and warning, of precept and example;—this is a task well worthy the energies of a long life, and offering in itself the amplest reward, but at the same time so vast and comprehensive, that it cannot be accomplished to any satisfaction, except by the cooperation of all varieties of talent. The individual must feel sufficiently fortunate and honoured, if he succeed in furnishing a few blocks for a gigantic edifice, which, in the nature of the case, cannot be finished till the church shall have reached the goal of her militant stage. For science grows with experience, and with it alone becomes complete.[37]

Dedicated to his mentor Augustus Neander, Schaff viewed this volume, covering the years A.D. 30–100, as the first of nine proposed volumes which would take the story to his own time. He divided church history into three ages, each with three periods.

FIRST AGE	
First Period	The Apostolic Church (A.D. 30–100)
Second Period	The Persecuted Church (through A.D. 311)
Third Period	The Established Church (through A.D. 590)
SECOND AGE	
First Period	The Commencement of the Middle Ages (through A.D. 1049)
Second Period	The Flourishing Period of the Middle Ages (through A.D. 1303)
Third Period	The Dissolution of the Middle Ages (through A.D. 1517)

THIRD AGE	
First Period	The Reformation, or Productive Protestantism and Reacting Romanism (16th century)
Second Period	Orthodox-Confessional and Scholastic Protestantism (17th and early-18th centuries)
Third Period	Subjective and Negative Protestantism (mid-18th century to the present)

Significantly, he subtitled the final period "Rationalism and Sectarianism," but in accord with his optimistic view of history, despite the problems within the church, he also called this period a time of *"positive preparation* for a new age in both [Protestant and Roman Catholic] churches."[38]

The arrangement of the book clearly reflects Schaff's debt to Neander and to Schleiermacher with its discussion of "moral and religious life" first, followed by "government," "worship," and finally "doctrine and theology." For this pietist historian, life and worship clearly took precedence over doctrine. Klaus Penzel has also noted Schaff's combination of "empiricism and speculation" in writing history. The historian must be familiar with the sources, but must never be content to leave the "facts" without interpretation, which gives the story its living soul.[39]

Before concluding with a brief survey of church historians in France, England, and the United States, Schaff summed up his historiographical principles drawn primarily from the best German scholars.

Unite now the most extensive and thorough learning with the simple piety and tender conscientiousness of a Neander, the speculative talent and combining ingenuity of a Rothe and a Dorner, the lovely mildness and calm clearness of an Ullmann and a Hagenbach, the sober investigation of a Gieseler, the fine diplomatic wisdom of a Ranke, the vivacity and elegant taste of a Hase;—unite all these, we say, in one person, free from all slavery to philosophy, yet not disdaining to employ it thankfully in the service of Scriptural truth; pervaded and controlled by living faith, and genuine, ardent love; and working, not for himself, nor for a party, but wholly in the spirit and service of the God-man, Jesus Christ, the life-giving sun of history, and for the interests of His bride, the one Holy, Catholic, Apostolic, Church; weaving into a crown of glory for the Saviour all the flowers of sanctified thought, faith, life, and suffering, from every age and clime;—and we have, so to speak, the ideal of a Christian church historian in full form before us.

While all these qualities would probably never be found in one person, all those who pursue the calling of church historian should strive to do their part for the common work of attaining the ideal. In his generation, no person contributed more than Philip Schaff.[40]

HISTORY OF THE CHRISTIAN CHURCH

Throughout the rest of his life, Schaff labored to complete the church history outlined in the "General Introduction" to his *History of the Apostolic Church*. He completed the final revision of his *History of the Christian Church* following a stroke that shattered his robust constitution and within a year led to his death. Of the eight volumes of the most recently reprinted edition which covers the years A.D. 1 through the sixteenth century, Schaff himself wrote six and his son David contributed two volumes on the Middle Ages. While he did not repeat the philosophy of history that was most extensively related in the "General Introduction," the *History of the Christian Church* begins with a restatement of some key points. Sacred history, Schaff insists, stands at the center of secular history, and the development of the Kingdom of God is the controlling force in the universe. The history of the church, then, is "the rise and progress of the kingdom of heaven upon earth, for the glory of God and the salvation of the world."[41]

Schaff enumerated the branches of church history, again placing the history of theology and doctrines at the end of his list. He then discussed the various sources of church history, outlined the periods of church history—which would provide the divisions for the volumes of his work—named the uses of church history, and before ending with a discussion of the literature of church history, sketched the duty of the historian. Again, he emphasized the combination of both factual accuracy and interpretation as essential for the writing of history. "History," he insists, "is not a heap of skeletons, but an organism filled and ruled by a reasonable soul." Throughout the volumes, that interpretive schema is always present. Because of his confidence in the Providential guidance of the church's history, Schaff could interpret controversial, divisive, and destructive events as part of God's overruling purpose in the development of his Kingdom on earth. As Schaff put it concerning the conflicts that led to the development of the Nicene creed, "Upon the bed of lava grows the sweet fruit of the vine."[42]

A clear illustration of Schaff's use of his concept of *aufheben* in the *History of the Christian Church* is his understanding of the relationship between Protestantism and Roman Catholicism in the sixteenth century. The Reformation abolished many of the errors and abuses of medieval Catholicism while the catholic substance remained. Thus the church was raised to a higher level with the addition of a clear concept of evangelical liberty. Schaff distinguished "pre-Reformation Catholicism and post-Reformation Romanism," insisting that the former looked forward to Protestantism and prepared the way for the coming of a higher development of Christianity in the Reformation. On the other hand, the rejection of the Reformation by the Council of Trent and in the nineteenth century by the first Vatican Council, represented a repudiation of legitimate development and caused much of Roman Catholicism to stray from God's intended path of development within the church.[43]

SELECT LIBRARY OF THE NICENE AND POST-NICENE FATHERS OF THE CHRISTIAN CHURCH

An important part of Schaff's work to provide the best sources for study of the history of the church was his work as editor of *A Select Library of the Nicene and Post-Nicene Fathers of the Christian Church*, (1886–1900). The collection includes two series of fourteen volumes each. Schaff served as editor for the first series and co-editor with Henry Wace for the first two volumes of the second series. A prospectus for the first series announces that "the object of the Library is historical, without any sectarian or partisan aim. It will put the English reader in possession of the chief sources and authorities of the faith, practice, worship, and discipline of the Greek and Latin Churches, down to the time of their separation."[44] For many years the volumes set the standard for such collections in the English language. They remain highly useful and in print.

CREEDS OF CHRISTENDOM

Perhaps the most enduring of Schaff's publications is his *Bibliotheca symbolica ecclesia universalis, the Creeds of Christendom* (1877). He wrote the volumes to fill "a vacuum in theological and historical literature," and to combat "sectarian exclusiveness or doctrinal indifferentism."[45] To reject these two problems clearly reveals Schaff's lifelong and deeply-rooted concern for Christian unity, but never at the expense of indifference toward central Christian beliefs. "Nothing Christian is foreign to me" Schaff was fond of saying, and at the same time his affirmations were thoroughly Christian. His purpose was to "combine the ἀληθεύειν ἐν ἀγάπῃ and the ἀγαπα‍ν ἐν ἀλήθεια, and to be mindful of the golden motto, *In necessariis unitas, in dubiis libertas, in omnibus caritas.*" His stated goal reveals many aspects of his philosophy of history: Christian unity in diversity, development in Christian doctrine—including the aspects of *aufheben* discussed above—his optimism and expectation of progress, the primacy of relationship over doctrine, and his central core of Christology.

> May this repository of creeds and confessions promote a better understanding among the Churches of Christ. The divisions of Christendom bring to light the various aspects and phases of revealed truth, and will be overruled at last for a deeper and richer harmony, of which Christ is the key-note. In him and by him all problems of theology and history will be solved. The nearer believers of different creeds approach the Christological centre, the better they will understand and love each other.[46]

The preface to the fourth edition echoes this sentiment from the first. "Creeds will live as long as faith survives, with the duty to confess our faith before men. By and by we shall reach, through the Creeds of Christendom, the one comprehensive, harmonious Creed of Christ."[47]

THEOLOGICAL PROPÆDEUTIC

A final publication that set forth Schaff's historiographical principles virtually unchanged from the 1850s was his *Theological Propædeutic*, which appeared in 1893. This book developed from Schaff's Mercersburg and Union lectures on "Theological Propædeutic," which he defined as combining theological encyclopedia, methodology, and bibliography. "Encyclopædia," he explained, "teaches what to study; methodology, how to study; bibliography, what books to study."[48] Designed as a guide for beginning theological students, the book "gives an outline of the various departments of theology, defines their nature and aim, their boundary lines and organic connection, their respective functions and value; it sketches their history, and indicates the best methods of prosecuting their study."

In his outline, Schaff placed church history within a larger section on "Historical Theology" that was preceded by "Exegetical Theology" and followed by sections on "Systematic Theology" and "Practical Theology." Once again, he identified church history with the Kingdom of God and insisted that the kingdom "is the divine leaven which gradually pervades the whole lump of humanity." There are, in fact, as many departments within church history as there are in human life and society, and they "stand in organic relation to each other and form a living whole."[49]

Theological Mediation
Between Europe and America

From the time that he accepted the call to come to the new world, Schaff identified his role as a theological mediator between the old world and the new, particularly between Germany and America. Indeed, his mentors had sent him forth "as the bearer of a pure German national spirit, to assist in restoring to new life a German population whose national character is already half destroyed by the admixture of foreign elements. . . . You are called to transport German theology in its thoroughness and depth and its strong, free life together with the various branches of learning that stand related to it as a family of full-grown daughters."

He was to fight the "many-headed monster of pantheism and atheism, issuing from the sphere of German speculation . . . in the armor of the shepherd boy of Bethlehem."[50] Most were even less generous than his former professor Isaac August Dorner, who allowed that "In America little has yet been done in the department of theology, but more than is known here. . . . You will tell Germany about them."[51]

The Principle of Protestantism

One of Schaff's earliest efforts to share the latest in German historical thinking was his inaugural address as professor at Mercersburg Seminary which was later expanded and published as *Das Princip des Protestantismus*, then translated into English by Nevin as *The Principle of Protestantism* (1845). It turned out that the German-Americans were not nearly so anxious to hear those ideas as Schaff was to share them, but *The Principle of Protestantism* established a direction in Schaff's theology that would characterize the rest of his career. Guided by his understanding of dialectical development and the process of *aufheben*, Schaff discussed first the Reformation's *"catholic union with the past,"* identified the Catholic Church as *"the legitimate bearer of the Christian faith and life,"* and concluded that *"the Reformation is the legitimate offspring, the greatest act of the Catholic Church."* Having established the catholic substance of the church, Schaff went on to discuss its Protestant principle; historical advance, development, and a growing apprehension of the life and doctrine of Christ and the apostles. The key of the Reformation was freedom. *"It has bound the religious spirit indissolubly to God's grace and God's word, and by so doing set it free from all human ordinances running counter to the same."*[52]

Yet the Reformation was not the final form of Christianity, as some of his colleagues assumed. On the contrary, diseases had appeared within the Protestant churches, which revealed the necessity of further advances—as cures for the diseases emerged, the catholic substance and the Protestant principle would be harmonized and raised to a higher form of Christianity, more like that of Christ and the apostles.[53] The two primary diseases of Protestantism were rationalism and sectarianism. Ironically, the cures to both would come from within the catholic tradition: new appreciation for the orthodox beliefs of the Christian tradition, and a renewed appreciation for the organic unity of the church. "Let us never forget the much that we hold in common with the Roman Church, the bond of union by which she is joined with us in opposition to absolute unbelief, whose wild ravages are displayed also in her own bosom." Likewise with the threat of sectarianism: "What we need to oppose to these, is not our formal principle; for they all appeal themselves to the Bible, though without right; but the power of history, and the idea of the church, as the pillar and ground of the truth, the mother of all believers, with due subordination always to the written word. In this controversy we may be said rather to have the Roman Church, in a certain sense, on our side."[54]

LANGE'S COMMENTARY AND THE SCHAFF-HERZOG ENCYCLOPEDIA

What Schaff hoped for was a "higher order of theology" that would result from the combination of German depth of thought and American practicality and activity. Two major publishing projects of Schaff's career stand out as examples of his work as a theological mediator. Both were international efforts that served to facilitate the exchange of ideas and contacts between scholars from Europe and America. Through both, Schaff hoped to pave the way for the flow of ideas in both directions. From his initial conception that Americans would sit as pupils at the feet of their European—read: German—masters, the "American by adoption" realized that the New World had much to teach the Old. The first project was the massive effort of translation and adaptation of Lange's *Commentary on the Holy Scriptures: Critical, Doctrinal, and Homiletical*. The second effort also involved translation and adaptation, but on a much smaller scale, the *Schaff-Herzog Encyclopedia*. Both of these undertakings involved the transmission of German scholarship to the New World and its adaptation to the American context.

For the *Commentary*, Schaff served as general editor and organized a cadre of translators and commentators to produce a combination of the "scholarship and piety of Europe and America," written in an "evangelical catholic spirit."[55] In the preface to the series, Schaff spoke of both the purpose and spirit of the work. It was to be "a commentary learned, yet popular, orthodox and sound, yet unsectarian, liberal and truly catholic in spirit and aim."[56]

Smaller, yet less dated, is the *Schaff-Herzog Encyclopedia*. Originally published in German and arranged and edited by Johann Jakob Herzog, the American edition was begun by John Henry Augustus Bomberger and taken over by Schaff in 1879. He carried the project to completion and published the "Schaff-Herzog" in three volumes in 1882–84. He was tenaciously devoted to the work as an important cooperative effort to bring together German and American scholarship, despite having to produce it with significant personal financial loss.

MERCERSBURG REVIEW AND DEUTSCH KIRCHENFREUND

Two journals edited by Schaff also promoted his goal to combine the best of German and American scholarship, *The Mercersburg Review* (co-edited by Schaff and E. V. Gerhart, 1857–1861), and *Der Deutsch Kirchenfreund* (founded by Schaff in 1848 and edited by him until 1854). Through both of these, Schaff sought to build bridges between Germany and America in theology and practical church life, and to provide interdenominational forums for theological discussion. Schaff's editorship supported a policy of "true catholicity" for both journals, which provoked harsh criticism from some, and left the journals' identity somewhat unclear. Professor Theodore Appel, of Marshall College, reflecting in 1853 on whether publication of the *Mercersburg Review* should continue, noted the difficulty of maintaining support for a periodical that "rises above denominational limits, and aims at true catholicity."[57] Likewise, according to Schaff's biographer and son, David Schaff, *Der Deutsch Kirchenfreund* successfully promoted cooperation between "prominent adherents of the Lutheran, the Reformed, and the Moravian churches."[58]

GERMANY: ITS UNIVERSITIES, THEOLOGY AND RELIGION

In his book, *Germany: Its Universities, Theology, and Religion* (1857), Schaff provided "a guide to the English and American student through the luxuriant forest of Teutonic systems and opinions." The first section of the book covers German universities and the theological systems of their professors. The second section is a general discussion of the various aspects of "German Theology and Religion" which deals with issues such as church and state, religious freedom, the different theological parties, and church life in Germany. The final section of the book includes biographical and intellectual sketches of leading German theologians and church leaders. It was one of the first books published in America with the goal of "bringing the German and American mind into closer union and friendly cooperation for the advancement of sound Christian literature, theology, and religion."[59]

CHRISTIANITY IN AMERICA

As his career in American developed, Schaff came to believe that rather than a land of undisciplined chaos and confusion in the church and society, the United States would become the location of the most important developments in modern Christian history. In America, the best and worst tendencies from Europe were in conflict, but the result would be something higher and better than Old Europe had to offer. Through the ferment a new person was emerging, the "American," and a new Christianity was also appearing which would utilize the good from the past Christian centuries, cast off the bad, and develop into a higher form of Christianity than the world had seen since the days of the apostles.[60]

AMERICA

In 1854, Schaff was called upon to present the land of his adoption to his mentors and friends in Europe. The lectures were eventually expanded and published as *Amerika: Die politischen, socialen und kirchlich-religiösen Zustände der Vereinigten Staaten von Nord-Amerika.*, later translated as *America: A Sketch of the Political, Social, and Religious Character of the United States of America*, (1854). In what Perry Miller has called, "measured, judicious, intelligent analysis, which by its objectivity and affectionate power is as fine a tribute to America as any immigrant has ever paid," Schaff surveyed both strengths and weaknesses of American Christianity, but concluded that "in America the most interesting experiments in church-history are now made."[61]

America faced serious problems, he admitted, such as "slavery, materialism, and radicalism," and Christians there struggled with rampant "sectarianism." Yet, according to his philosophy of church history, these "diseases" were, in God's Providence, "*negative conditions* precisely of [the church's] *progress*."[62] According to his providential view of history, the "distractions and fermentings of Protestantism" which were most graphically portrayed in America were part of a "necessary transition state to a far higher and better condition, to a free unity in spirit and truth, embracing the greatest variety of Christian life."[63] Christianity in America and the American nation as a whole were in a "state of transition," and observers could expect in the future "something higher and better," since "out of the mutual conflict of all something wholly new will gradually arise."[64]

Schaff's optimism, his understanding of historical development, and a concept of the movement of world and Christian history from East to West allowed him to identify America as the land of the future. America was, he insisted,

> The Phoenix grave not only of all European nationalities . . . but also of all European churches and sects, of Protestantism and Romanism. . . . all the powers of Europe, good and bad, are there fermenting together under new and peculiar conditions. All is yet in a chaotic transition state; but organizing energies are already present, and the spirit of God broods over them, to speak in time the almighty word: "Let there be light!" and to call forth from the chaos a beautiful creation.[65]

DER BÜRGERKRIEG

Schaff's next important statement about Christianity in America is another collection of lectures to European audiences, "Dr. Schaff's Lectures on America Delivered in Europe, 1865," which appeared in *The Christian Intelligencer* during the spring of 1866, and had been translated by C. C. Starbuck from the German *Der Bürgerkrieg und das christliche Leben in Nord America.* (1865). Once the war came, Schaff emerged as a staunch unionist who hoped for victory and an end to the conflict as soon as possible. He urged seminary students to enlist. After all, he sighed, "what are seminaries, colleges, and churches if we have no country and home?"[66] Yet by the end of the war he, like Abraham Lincoln, pondered the ways of Providence who brought a righteous judgment "upon a guilt of South and of North." Through it all, Schaff discerned "the all-directing hand of God."[67]

Even this tragedy could be fit into the plan of the developing Kingdom of God in the world. "Providence . . . gradually unfolded its own programme before the astonished view of the world, and educated the nation, with its worthy President at its head, step by step, to the understanding of its appointed work and to the measures adapted for the discharge of this." Ever the optimist, Schaff put the war into his cosmic scheme of interpretation and was able to see purpose even in the tragedy of war and reconstruction. No purely secular interpretation of these events could grasp their essential meaning. "A country in which so many streams of noble blood have flowed, in which so many sacrifices have been offered by Government and people, and in which the hand of God has so visibly and wonderfully guided events to a happy issue, must, according to all human forecast, have a great future before it. It has endured the fiery trial, and has now first entered upon the age of manly vigor and independence."[68]

CHURCH AND STATE IN THE UNITED STATES

Even in the relationship between civil and religious authorities, Schaff discerned the hand of God directing American Christian history in order to bring about the Kingdom of God. He wrote his *Church and State in the United States, or the American Idea of Religious Liberty and Its Practical Effects, with Official Documents* (1888), as the first attempt to interpret American religious freedom "from the stand-point of a church historian and theologian." Complete religious freedom is America's most distinctive characteristic, Schaff insisted, and its development was no accident of human history. "North America was predestined from the very beginning for the largest religious and civil freedom," he insisted. "Congress was led by Providence to establish a new system," and if this point is missed, one's whole interpretation of the events cannot be but seriously flawed. This situation heralded a "new chapter in the history of Christianity," and the most important contribution of America to the development of Christianity.[69]

With his organic view of history, Schaff had no desire to degrade the European heritage of American religion, and he was quick to identify positive results of the church-state relationship in every epoch of the history of Christianity. The Roman persecution of Christians had led to the conversion of the Empire; the medieval world needed a church which could exercise temporal as well as spiritual power in order to civilize and evangelize the peoples of Europe. Eastern Orthodox caesaropapism also had its time and place, but would be totally out of step with the pluralistic character of modern America. Finally, modern European situations of religious *toleration* were not to be rejected out of hand, even though they were qualitatively different than the situation of religious *liberty* that existed in America. Perhaps, Schaff suggested, Europeans were not ready for religious liberty yet, but neither should they cast aspersions on the American scene. Far from being a regrettable situation because its freedom allowed the profusion of sects—the attitude of most Europeans of Schaff's day— the American concept of freedom of religion was "one of the greatest gifts of God to man."[70]

Schaff viewed the United States as a Christian nation in fact, if not by establishment. Against those who argued for a "Christian amendment" to the United States Constitution, Schaff asserted that there was no need: "A mere verbal recognition of God and Christ might be construed as an empty patronizing formality. Having the substance, we may dispense with the shadow, which might cast suspicion upon the reality."[71]

AMERICAN DENOMINATIONAL SERIES

One of the ways to promote church union, Schaff believed, was to educate Christians about one another. To that end, Schaff organized and promoted a series of American Denominational Histories to be produced under the auspices of the American Society of Church History. The final result of the venture was a thirteen-volume set published 1893–97 which Henry Warner Bowden called "the most valuable literary achievement in an ecumenical vein" produced by the ASCH.[72]

Throughout the planning of the project, Schaff's ideal of denominational cooperation toward church union guided his efforts. The goals of the project, that were set forth in the *Papers* of the ASCH, indicated that the authors of the volumes must be ecumenically minded, first-rate scholars. While they obviously would desire to portray their own denominations as positively as possible, they would also recognize the virtues of other communions. These would be volumes "decidedly irenical in spirit." Cooperation among the authors would set the pattern for the desired effect upon readers. The series would produce "large irenical results" because "a wide reading of histories of all the denominations . . . could not fail to be promotive, in a high degree, of truth and peace."[73]

Characteristically, the series included a history of the Roman Catholic "denomination" and to the author of that volume, Rev. Thomas O'Gorman, Professor of Church History at the Catholic University of America, Schaff wrote, "I sincerely hope that the contemplated series of denominational histories prepared by competent scholars will not only be a valuable authentic contribution to our theological and historical literature, but also tend to remove ignorance and prejudice and to bring Christians nearer together." The same goal held true for the Protestant contributors. For example, Schaff wrote to Williston Walker, who was to write the volume on Congregationalism, "I confess to have a moral interest in the contemplated series as a means of bringing the different churches into closer union and ultimate cooperation."[74]

BIBLICAL EXEGESIS AND REVISION

During the 1870s and 1880s, Schaff turned much of his attention to supervising the production of a revised version of the English Bible. He had come to believe that in America a new era of Christian development was underway and a fundamental part of that development would be an updated version of the Bible. American scholars had important contributions to make in the late nineteenth century and Schaff determined that their voices must be heard along with the British revisers who had initiated the project of Bible revision. Through years of sometimes exasperating and always exhausting work, Schaff labored as mediator, encourager, and scholar. Finally, the Revised New Testament appeared in 1881 and the Old Testament in 1885. During the process Schaff produced *The Revision of the English Version of the Holy Scriptures, by Cooperative Committees of British and American Scholars of Different Denominations* (1875), and he edited a collection of essays called *Anglo-American Bible Revision: By Members of the American Revision Committee* (1879). An additional publication that emerged from his exegetical and translation work was *A Companion to the Greek Testament and the English Version*, first published in 1883, then issued in revised editions in 1885, 1888, and 1892. This volume tells the story of the revision work in detail, and also provides a remarkably thorough discussion of issues related to the Greek language, manuscripts, ancient versions, usages, textual criticism, and translations. It concludes with appendices including a list of printed editions of the Greek New Testament, written by Professor Isaac H. Hall, facsimiles of pages from various Greek editions, a list of British and American revisers, and a book-by-book list of changes suggested by the American committee that were either inserted into the text or placed in marginal notes. Finally, there is a short account of the adoption of the Revised Version by the American Baptists.

Throughout the project, Schaff labored to make the revision committees representative of the breadth of American denominational perspectives, and yet to avoid sectarian animosities and biases. Extremely gratified at the positive reception of the Revised Version, Schaff exulted, "There never was a more faithful and harmonious body of competent scholars engaged in a more important work on the American Continent." Remarkably, he continued, "they never raised a sectarian issue."[75]

CHRISTOLOGY

Basic to Schaff's historiography was his conception of Christ as "the centre around which all [history] revolves." The great error of nineteenth-century rationalists was their effort to go beyond Christ; the genius of Neander's church history was his placing Christ at the center of theology.[76] Schaff carried this legacy forward, particularly in two volumes, dedicated to defending the centrality of Christ in world history against the skeptical arguments of opponents such as David F. Strauss and Joseph E. Renan. In 1861, Schaff published *The Moral Character of Christ, or The Perfection of Christ's Humanity, A Proof of His Divinity*. Four years later he expanded and developed those arguments into what became his most popular book, *The Person of Christ: The Perfection of His Humanity Viewed as a Proof of His Divinity*. [*Die Person Jesu Christi: das Wunder der Geschichte*]. This volume went through twelve editions during Schaff's lifetime and besides the German and English versions, the book was translated into Dutch, French, Italian, Greek, Russian, Bulgarian, Japanese, and other languages. The issue was clear, according to Schaff. "The question of Christ is the question of Christianity . . . it is the question of history, which revolves around him as the sun of the moral universe. . . . The object of this book is to show that the Person of Christ is the great central miracle of history, and the strongest evidence of Christianity."

He was convinced that his intellectual arguments against rationalist programs were compelling, but the surest defense was his experience of the living Christ. "The Person of Christ is to me the surest as well as the most sacred of all facts; as certain as my own personal existence; yea, even more so: for Christ lives in me, and he is the only valuable part of my existence."[77]

Schaff's contributions to the study of church history—indeed, to theological scholarship as a whole—were immense. His work to establish the historical study of Christianity in the United States provided a solid foundation for the strength the discipline has now attained.

Though some of his historiographical principles passed away with his era, his work remains a monument to careful, accurate, comprehensive, and irenic scholarship presented as an offering of gratitude to his church and his God.

SELECTED BIBLIOGRAPHY

PRIMARY SOURCES

America: A Sketch of the Political, Social, and Religious Character of the United States of North America. New York: Scribner's, 1855. Reprint edited by Perry Miller. Cambridge, Mass.: Harvard University Press, 1961.

Anglo-Germanism or the Significance of the German Nationality in the United States. Chambersburg: Publication Office of the German Reformed Church, 1846.

Bibliotheca Symbolico Ecclesiae Universalis, the Creeds of Christendom. 3 vols. 6th ed. Revised. New York: Harper and Brothers, 1931.

Christ and Christianity: Studies on Christology, Creeds, and Confessions, Protestantism and Romanism, Reformation Principles, Sunday Observance, Religious Freedom, and Christian Union. New York: Scribner's, 1885.

Christianity in the United States of America. Document 14 of Evangelical Alliance Documents. New York: Bible House, Astor Place. n.d. (A report prepared for the Seventh General Conference of the Evangelical Alliance held in Basel, Switzerland, September, 1879.).

Church and State in the United States or the American Idea of Religious Liberty and Its Practical Effects with Official Documents. New York: Scribner's, 1888.

History of the Apostolic Church with a General Introduction to Church History. Translated by Edward D. Yeomans. New York: Scribner's, 1854.

The Moral Character of Christ, or the Perfection of Christ's Humanity, a Proof of His Divinity. Chambersburg: M. Kieffer, 1861.

The Person of Christ: The Perfection of His Humanity Viewed as Proof of His Divinity. New York: American Tract Society, 1882.

The Principle of Protestantism as Related to the Present State of the Church. Translated by John W. Nevin. Chambersburg: Publishing Office of the German Reformed Church, 1845. Reprint, Philadelphia: United Church Press, 1964.

The Progress of Religious Freedom as Shown in the History of Toleration Acts. New York: Scribner's, 1889.

The Reunion of Christendom: A Paper Prepared for the Parliament of Religions and the National Conference of the Evangelical Alliance Held in Chicago, September and October, 1893. New York: Evangelical Alliance Office, 1893.

Theological Propaedeutic: A General Introduction to the Study of Theology. New York: Charles Scribner's Sons, 1894.

The Toleration Act of 1689: A Contribution to the History of Religious Liberty. London: James Nisbet and Company, 1878.

The University: Past, Present, and Future. New York: University of New York, 1889.

What Is Church History? A Vindication of the Idea of Historical Development. Philadelphia: J. B. Lippincott and Company, 1846. Reprinted and edited by Charles Yrigoyen, Jr. and George M. Bricker in *Reformed and Catholic: Selected Historical and Theological Writings of Philip Schaff.* Pittsburgh: The Pickwick Press, 1979.

Schaff, Philip, ed. *A Commentary on the Holy Scriptures by John Peter Lange.* 25 vols. New York: Scribner's, 1864–1880.

———, ed. *A Dictionary of the Bible Including Biography, Natural History, Geography, Topography, Archaeology, and Literature.* Philadelphia: American Sunday School Union, 1890.

———, ed. *The International Revision Commentary on the New Testament.* 6 vols. New York: Scribner's, 1881–1884.

———, ed. *The Revision of the English Version of the Holy Scriptures by Cooperative Committees of British and American Scholars of Different Denominations.* New York: Harper and Brothers, 1877.

———, ed. *The Schaff-Herzog Encyclopedia of Religious Knowledge.* 3 vols. New York: Funk and Wagnalls, 1882–1884.

———, ed. *A Select Library of the Nicene and Post-Nicene Fathers of the Christian Church.* First series, 14 vols. New York: 1886–1890. Second series, with Henry Wace, 14 vols. New York and Oxford: 1890–1900.

Schaff, Philip, and S. Irenaeus, Prime, eds. *History, Essays, Orations, and Other Documents of the Sixth General Conference of the Evangelical Alliance, Held in New York, October 2–12, 1873.* New York: Harper and Brothers, 1874.

Schaff, Philip, and David Schaff. *History of the Christian Church.* 8 vols. 5th ed. Revised. Grand Rapids, Mich.: Eerdmans, 1950.

Schaff, Philip, et al., eds. *The American Church History Series. Denominational Histories.* New York: The Christian Literature Company, 1896.

SECONDARY SOURCES

Bowden, Henry Warner, ed. *A Century of Church History: The Legacy of Philip Schaff.* Carbondale, Ill.: Southern Illinois University Press, 1988.

Bricker, G., and C. Yrigoyen. eds. *Reformed and Catholic: Selected Historical and Theological Writings of Philip Schaff.* Pittsburgh: Pickwick Press, 1979.

Fisher, G. P. "Dr. Schaff as an Historian." *Papers of the American Society of Church History.* First Series 7 (1895): 3–11.

Goliber, Thomas J. "Philip Schaff (1819–1893): A Study in Conservative Biblical Criticism." Ph. D. dissertation, Kent State University, 1976.

Graham, Stephen R. "Cosmos in the Chaos: A Study of Philip Schaff's Interpretation of Nineteenth-Century American Religion." Ph. D. dissertation, The University of Chicago, 1989.

———— "Cosmos in the Chaos": Philip Schaff's Vision of America." *American Presbyterians* 67 (winter 1989): 259–72.

————. "Philip Schaff and the Protestant Mind in the Nineteenth Century: A Critique of Religion and Society." *Fides et Historia* 21 (January 1989): 32–49.

Johnson, Kathryn L. "The Mustard Seed and the Leaven: Philip Schaff's Confident View of Christian History." *Historical Magazine of the Protestant Episcopal Church* 50 (June 1981): 117–70.

Nichols, James Hastings, ed. *The Mercersburg Theology.* New York: Oxford University Press, 1966.

————. *Romanticism in American Theology: Nevin and Schaff at Mercersburg.* Chicago: The University of Chicago Press, 1961.

Penzel, Klaus. "Church History and the Ecumenical Quest: A Study of the German Background and Thought of Philip Schaff." Th.D. dissertation, Union Theological Seminary, New York, 1962.

————. "Church History in Context: The Case of Philip Schaff." In *Our Common History as Christians: Essays in Honor of Albert C. Outler,* edited by John Deschner et al., 217–60. New York: Oxford University Press, 1975.

————. "Philip Schaff: A Centennial Reappraisal." *Church History* 59 (June 1990): 207–21.

————. "The Reformation Goes West: The Notion of Historical Development in the Thought of Philip Schaff." *Journal of Religion* 62 (July 1982): 219–41.

Penzel, Klaus, ed. *Philip Schaff: Historian and Ambassador of the Universal Church, Selected Writings.* Macon, Ga.: Mercer University Press, 1991.

Pranger, Gary. "Philip Schaff (1819–1893): Portrait of an Immigrant Theologian." Ph. D. dissertation, The University of Illinois at Chicago, 1987.

Proudfit, J. W. "Dr. Schaff as Church Historian." *The New Brunswick Review* 1 (August 1854): 278–325.

————. "Dr. Schaff's Works on Church History." *The New Brunswick Review* 1 (May 1854): 1–63.

Schaff, David. *The Life of Philip Schaff: In Part Autobiographical.* New York: Scribner's, 1897.

————. "Philip Schaff, the Advocate of the Reunion of Christendom." *Reformed Church Review* 64 (January 1917): 1–13.

Shriver, George H. "Philip Schaff as a Teacher of Church History." *Journal of Presbyterian History* 47 (March 1969): 74–92.

————. *Philip Schaff: Christian Scholar and Ecumenical Prophet.* Macon, Ga.: Mercer University Press, 1987.

————. "Philip Schaff's Concept of Organic Historiography Interpreted in Relation to the Realization of an 'Evangelical Catholicism' Within the Christian Community." Ph. D. dissertation. Duke University, 1960.

Smylie, J. H. "Philip Schaff: Ecumenist; the Reunion of Protestantism and Roman Catholicism." *Encounter* 28 (winter 1967): 3–16.

Trost, Theodore L. "Philip Schaff's Concept of the Church with Special Reference to His Role in the Mercersburg Movement, 1844–1864." Ph. D. dissertation, New College, Edinburgh University, 1958.

NOTES

1. Given the name Philipp Schaaf at birth, he changed the spelling to Philip Schaff sometime around 1847.

2. Quoted in George H. Shriver, *Philip Schaff: Christian Scholar and Ecumenical Prophet* (Macon, Ga.: Mercer University Press), 2.

3. Quoted in David S. Schaff, *The Life of Philip Schaff: In Part Autobiographical* (New York: Scribner's, 1897), 13.

4. See, for example, D. Schaff, *Life*, 19–20, and Philip Schaff, "General Introduction," to *History of the Apostolic Church: With a General Introduction to Church History*, trans. Edward D. Yeomans (Philadelphia: J. B. Lippincott and Co., 1846; reprinted in Charles Yrigoyen, Jr. and George M. Bricker, eds., *Reformed and Catholic: Selected Historical and Theological Writings of Philip Schaff* (Pittsburgh: The Pickwick Press, 1979), 109ff. [285ff.]. The first page number given is from the original edition, that in brackets is from the Yrigoyen and Bricker reprint.

5. Quoted in D. Schaff, *Life*, 24.

6. Philip Schaff, *What Is Church History? A Vindication of the Idea of Historical Development* (Philadelphia: J. B. Lippincott and Co., 1846; reprinted in Yrigoyen, Jr. and Bricker, *Reformed and Catholic*, 78 [94]. The first page number given is from the original edition, that in brackets is from the Yrigoyen and Bricker reprint. See also, Schaff, *History of the Apostolic Church*, 94ff. [267ff.].

7. Schaff, *History of the Apostolic Church*, 97–101 [271–75].

8. Ibid., 101, 104 [276, 279].

9. See his ordination sermon, "Ordination of Professor Schaff," *Weekly Messenger* 9 (September 4, 1844): 1869–1870. The quotation is from Acts 16:9.

10. Quoted in D. Schaff, *Life*, 103.

11. Philip Schaff, *The Principle of Protestantism as Related to the Present State of the Church*, trans. John W. Nevin (Chambersburg, Pa.: Publishing Office of the German Reformed Church, 1845; reprint ed., Philadelphia: United Church Press, 1964), 73.

12. See George H. Shriver, "Philip Schaff: Heresy at Mercersburg," in *American Religious Heretics: Formal and Informal Trials* (Nashville: Abingdon, 1966).

13. Quoted in D. Schaff, *Life*, 233.

14. Philip Schaff, *A Companion to the Greek New Testament and the English Version* (New York: Scribner's, 1883), 494.

15. See *The Semi-Centennial of Philip Schaff* (New York: Privately printed, 1893).

16. Philip Schaff, *The Reunion of Christendom: A Paper Prepared for the Parliament of Religions and the National Conference of the Evangelical Alliance Held in Chicago, September and October, 1893* (New York: Evangelical Alliance Office), 28.

17. D. Schaff, *Life*, 497.

18. Schaff, *What Is Church History?* 5 [21].

19. Ibid., Emphasis mine.

20. Ibid., 9 [25].

21. Ibid., 13 [29].

22. Ibid., 40 [56].

23. See Schaff, *History of the Apostolic Church*, 13–15, and "German Theology and the Church Question," *Mercersburg Review* 5 (January 1853): 124–44, reprinted in Yrigoyen and Bricker, *Reformed and Catholic*, 320–40.

24. Schaff, *History of the Apostolic Church*, 6 [163]; Schaff, *Principle of Protestantism*, 221.

25. Schaff, *History of the Apostolic Church*, 34–35, 101, 113 [197–98, 275, 290].

26. Schaff, *What Is Church History?* 57ff; Schaff, *History of the Apostolic Church*, 36–46 [198–211].

27. Schaff, *What is Church History?*, 46 [62].

28. Ibid., 69 [85].

29. Ibid., 79 [95].

30. Ibid., 79–83 [95–99].

31. Ibid., 85 [101].

32. The mustard seed parable is found in Matthew 13: 31–32. The following verse describes the Kingdom of God as yeast.

33. Schaff, *What Is Church History?* 93–98 [109–114].

34. Ibid., 99 [115].

35. Ibid., 114, 120 [130, 136].

36. Ibid., 128 [144].

37. Schaff, *History of the Apostolic Church*, iii [149].

38. Ibid., 36–37 [199–200].

39. See Klaus Penzel, ed., *Philip Schaff: Historian and Ambassador of the Universal Church, Selected Writings* (Macon, Ga.: Mercer University Press, 1991), 124–25; Klaus Penzel, "Church History in Context," in *Our Common History as Christians*, ed. John Deschner et al. (New York: Oxford, 1975), 217–60, and David W. Lotz, "Philip Schaff and the Idea of Church History," in *A Century of Church History: The Legacy of Philip Schaff* (Carbondale: Southern Illinois University Press, 1988), 1–35.

40. Schaff, *History of the Apostolic Church*, 123–24 [301–2].

41. Philip Schaff and David S. Schaff, *History of the Christian Church*, 8 vols, 5th ed. revised (Grand Rapids, Mich.: Eerdmans, 1950) 1: 3.

42. Ibid., 1: 22; 3: 631.

43. Ibid., 7: 4–5.

44. Philip Schaff, ed., *A Select Library of the Nicene and Post-Nicene Fathers of the Christian Church*, 1st series (New York, 1886–1890) 1: Appendix at the end, 2.

45. Philip Schaff, *Bibliotheca Symbolico Ecclesiae Universalis, The Creeds of Christendom*, 3 vols. 6th ed. revised (New York: Harper and Brothers, 1931) 1:v. (Preface from the first edition).

46. Ibid., 1: v–vi. Combine the "truth in love and the love in truth," and to be mindful of the golden motto, "in necessary things unity, in doubtful things liberty, in all things love."

47. Ibid., 1:viii. (Preface to the fourth edition).

48. Philip Schaff, *Theological Propædeutic: A General Introduction to the Study of Theology* (New York: Charles Scribner's Sons, 1894), 6.

49. Ibid., iii, 244.

50. The statement is from a sermon preached at Schaff's ordination by Dr. Frederick W. Krummacher, quoted in D. Schaff, *Life*, 79.

51. Quoted in D. Schaff, *Life*, 75.

52. Schaff, *Principle of Protestantism*, 59, 71, 73, 123–24. Italics his.

53. David W. Lotz notes that Schaff's conception of history was both linear and circular. It was linear in the sense that history moved forward toward the second advent, but circular because the end of history would also witness the reappearance of the ideal church of the apostolic age. "Philip Schaff and the Idea of Church History," 1–35.

54. Schaff, *Principle of Protestantism*, 137, 154.

55. Quoted in D. Schaff, *Life*, 231–33.

56. John Peter Lange, *A Commentary on the Holy Scriptures: Critical, Doctrinal, and Homiletical, with Special Reference to Ministers and Students*, 25 vols., trans. and ed. Philip Schaff (New York: Charles Scribner, 1864–1880), 1: viii.

57. T. Appel, "The Review and the Quarterly," *Mercersburg Review* 5 (January 1853): 7–8.

58. D. Schaff, *Life*, 163.

59. Philip Schaff, *Germany, Its Universities, Theology, and Religion* (Philadelphia: Lindsay and Blakiston, 1857), 9–10.

60. See Stephen R. Graham, "'Cosmos in the Chaos:' A Study of Philip Schaff's Interpretation of Nineteenth-Century American Religion," Ph. D. dissertation, The University of Chicago, 1989.

61. Philip Schaff, *America: A Sketch of the Political, Social, and Religious Character of the United States of North America* (New York: Scribner's, 1855; reprint, Cambridge, Mass.: Harvard University Press, 1961), xxxv, 213.

62. Schaff, *America*, 5–6; Schaff, *What Is Church History?* 100 [116].

63. Schaff, *America*, 13–14.

64. Ibid., 80–81.

65. Ibid.

66. Philip Schaff, "The Gettysburg Week," *Scribners Magazine* (July 1894): 21–22.

67. Philip Schaff, *Der Bürgerkrieg und das christliche Leben in Nord-Amerika* (Berlin: Berlag von Wiegandt und Griben, 1866), 8–10, 28. An English translation by C. C. Starbuck appeared in the *Christian Intelligencer* 37 (1 March 1866): 2; (22 March 1866): 1.

68. Schaff, *Bürgerkrieg*, 12, 16–17; *Christian Intelligencer* 37 (1 March 1866): 3.

69. Philip Schaff, *Church and State in the United States, or the American Idea of Religious Liberty and Its Practical Effects, with Official Documents* (New York: Scribner's, 1888), 5, 9.

70. Ibid., 15.

71. Ibid., 42.

72. Henry Warner Bowden, *Church History in the Age of Science: Historiographical Patterns in the United States, 1876–1918* (Chapel Hill, N.C.: University of North Carolina Press, 1970), 64.

73. *Papers of the American Society of Church History*, first series 3 (1891): 210. Quoted in Shriver, *Philip Schaff*, 96.

74. Quoted in D. Schaff, *Life*, 465. See also, Shriver, *Philip Schaff*, 95–97.

75. Schaff, *Companion to the Greek Testament*, 395.

76. Schaff, *What Is Church History?* 56, 108, 78–79.

77. Philip Schaff, *The Person of Christ: The Perfection of His Humanity Viewed as Proof of His Divinity* (New York: American Tract Society, 1882), 7–8.

14

GEORGE PARK FISHER

MICHAEL WILLIAMS

George Park Fisher (1827–1909) was a liberal for his time, although I
doubt he would think himself such. He most certainly thought himself a
modernist. He was consciously and conscientiously trying to make sense
of his faith and its history in terms of the new historical science of the late
nineteenth century. While he actively engaged the theological trends
coming out of Germany, often with great appreciation, and while he
sought to bring critical method and evolutionary theory to the study of
church history, Fisher was by no means attempting to reinvent the theological and historical wheel. The New Haven school of thought that Fisher inherited, professed, and sought to expand upon has been labeled
"progressive orthodoxy," and even "liberal orthodoxy,"[1] but today he
would be called an evangelical with a sense of history. Fisher was very
much the product of his New England modernist surroundings, and the
product of his critical engagement with Christian history was altogether
American: optimistic, anti-clerical, moralist, Arminian, and above all individualistic. While none of these are in themselves uniquely American, the
convergence of Whig moralistic parochialism, German criticial methodology, and the Taylorite Arminianism of the New Haven tradition, creates

305

a postmillennialist vision of the future that revolves around the notion of the individual historical agent as the moral and substantive analogue of the divine. The centrality of the individual as historical analogue or reflection of the divine mind is at one and the same time the linchpin of Fisher's thought and that which situates him within the American revivalist tradition.

A Congregationalist minister, Fisher was born in Wrentham, Massachusetts, in 1827. His family traced its ancestry to Samuel Fisher, the noted Quaker apologist, co-worker of George Fox, and—ultimately—martyr. After attending public school, Fisher went to Brown University, where he was converted in an evangelical revival during his senior year. Upon graduation from Brown in 1847, Fisher studied at Yale Divinity School for a year. At Yale he came under the influence of Nathaniel W. Taylor, his teacher of Systematic Theology. He also studied for a time at Auburn Theological Seminary, but he completed his seminary training in 1851 at Andover Theological Seminary, where he studied with Edward Amasa Park. Between his experience at Brown and the influences of Taylor and Park, Fisher was thoroughly indoctrinated into the New School Congregationalist revivalism of late nineteenth-century New England. Quite simply, as Hubert Cunliffe-Jones writes, Fisher "had the best training that the leaders of 'New England Theology' could offer."[2]

Even though Park bitterly resisted the introduction of German critical methods and philosophy at Andover, the young Fisher made the then-unusual decision to seek further graduate education in Germany. From 1852 to 1854 he studied at Halle,[3] a center of the evangelical party in Germany. In order to preserve a remnant of Christian thought in the midst of radical German philosophical trends, the German evangelicals had found allies in Schleiermacher, Hegel, and Moravian Pietism. Studying theology with Friedrich A. G. Tholuck and church history with Johann A. Neander, Fisher would be as influenced by German liberalism and idealism as he was by his native New England New School revivalism.

Upon his return to the U.S., Fisher was ordained a Congregationalist minister and named Livingston Professor of Divinity at Yale College. His duties included pastoring and preaching at the College Church. Fisher resigned this post in 1861 in order to become professor of ecclesiastical history in Yale's Theological Department. From 1878 to 1901 he held the chair of Titus Street Professor of Ecclesiastical History. The first to hold that chair, he would be succeeded by Williston Walker, Roland Bainton, and Jaroslav Pelikan. From 1895 until his retirement in 1901, Fisher served as dean of the Yale Divinity School.

Fisher edited the *New Englander* from 1855 to 1857 and then again from 1866 to 1873. From 1892 until his death he served on the editorial board of the *Yale Review*. In 1888 he and his friend Philip Schaff founded the American Society of Church History. Fisher served as President of that organization in 1898, and was President of the American Historical Society.[4]

One of the most respected American church historians of his day, Fisher was a widely read author, and his work evidences nearly exhaustive familiarity with both the history of the Christian church and its doctrinal formation, and the general political history of Europe and North America. His first published work, however, was not historical but rather apologetic. Fisher wrote *Essays on the Supernatural Origin of Christianity, With Special Reference to the Theories of Renan, Strauss, and the Tubingen School* (1865) to address the challenge of German criticism. While appreciative of much of German historical scholarship, Fisher was concerned about the more radical elements of the movement. He would follow up on his first book in apologetics with *Faith and Rationalism* (1879) and *Manual of Christian Evidences* (1888). In general history Fisher wrote *Outlines of Universal History* (1885) and *The Colonial Era* (1892). His major works in church history and historical theology included *The Reformation* (1873), *The Beginnings of Christianity* (1877), *History of the Christian Church* (1887), and *History of Christian Doctrine* (1896).

Despite his dispassionate and laconic style, fourteen of Fisher's works remained in print twenty years after his death. A contemporary, Frederick Lynch, praised Fisher for the comprehensiveness and accuracy of his work, but also noted that his work was rather unexciting to read. Lynch observed that Fisher's histories "are so packed with fact that the flow of style is impeded and the imagination does not find scope for free play."[5] Fisher was seeking a certain critical distance from his subject. His ideal historian was less an advocate than a critical scholar. Following the late nineteenth-century understanding of "critical" as objectivity, Fisher held that historical work should seek a level of objectivity. At the very least, it should not betray any sectarian sympathies. Rather than function as an advocate for the Christian tradition, Fisher would bring the best critical tools available to the subject, and allow the history to speak for itself. Total impartiality was the critical goal he sought for his discipline. From the introduction to *The Reformation* we read: "There is one explanation further which I am anxious to make respecting the design of this book. It is intended in no sense as a polemical work. It has not entered into my thoughts to inculcate the creed of Protestantism, or to propogate any type of Christian doctrine; much less to kindle animosity against the Church at Rome."[6]

Thus Fisher affirmed the modern historical method. While he confessed the living reality of God revealed in Jesus Christ, he also applied the same canons to church history and the Christian Scriptures that critical studies would apply to any historical materials. The irony here is that Fisher thought that, in order to use criticism in the service of faith, he must first separate critical method from his Christian confession.

In his pursuit of factual and concise history, Fisher followed in the tradition of Leopold von Ranke (1795–1886), the "father of historical science," and the Historical School. Like Ranke, Fisher emphasized the accurate chronicle of historical events—seen as facts.[7] Reacting against Hegel's grandiose vision of the cosmos as history, even divine history, Ranke and the Historical School gave far more weight to individual phenomena and events. Ranke declared that he was not seeking to pass judgment upon the past but simply to report *"wie es eigentlich"* (how it actually was).[8] But while both Ranke and Fisher could on occasion read as if they were devotees of Comte's cult of the fact, it would be a mistake to characterize either as a positivist. The divine, they assumed, stands behind all historical phenomena. Influenced by Kant, Ranke understood history as the actualization of idea, thus positing an organic link between the mundane and the transcendent. Yet fearing the deterministic pantheism implicit within Hegelian thought, Ranke closely guarded the idea of divine providence working through human freedom.[9]

Fisher's approach to history proved remarkably similar to Ranke's. For example, in his introduction to volume one of his *Outlines of Universal History* Fisher wrote: "My idea of such a work was, that it should present the essential facts of history in due order, and in conformity to the best and latest researches; that it should point out clearly the connection of events and of each successive era with one another. . . ."[10]

Following the nineteenth-century urge to see history as scientific, Fisher sought to stand apart from his subject and see it as a series of causes and effects. As such, history was a science, a branch of knowledge having a certain completeness and method.

HISTORICAL REFLECTION

Fisher conceived of reality in terms of a spiritual-material distinction, but a distinction within unity. The spiritual is not opposed to the material, but rather is the principle of the material. Whereas modern evangelicals (like ancient Gnostics) often think in terms of a dualism in which heaven is opposed to the material world and the soul is opposed to the body, Fisher used the same terminology but aligned the elements into a duality in which the material is the necessary complement of the spiritual. Thus behind Fisher's duality of matter and spirit stood a fundamental monism. His organistic understanding of reality and the historical process (and Fisher's liberal theological tendencies) are seen in the fact that the language of historical progress toward unity replaces the classical Christian language of sin and redemption.

Human beings cannot be understood by way of a materialist analysis. As an intelligent being, a soul, the human being transcends the world of material existence. At the core, the human being belongs to the spiritual rather than the material order. The person's religious consciousness of self and God raises the human person above the level of the brute, for in the human soul we find a divine analog within the order of nature: "Our religious beliefs spring out of experiences native to the soul and spontaneous,—out of the natural activity of the moral and spiritual nature which God has given to us, and the likeness of Himself, and the affinity to Him, which are inwrought into our being."[11] The human intellect is a reflection of the divine intellect in the same manner that the phenomenal order is the complement of the moral or spiritual order. Thus Fisher was able to think of history as the material reflection of the spiritual and science as the discovery of the idea in the concrete.

The idea of reflection is crucial to Fisher's ontology. The spiritual and the material are not at odds with one another, nor are they to be seen as categorically disjunctive modes of being. While Fisher does not speak of an *analogia entis*, all the elements of the analogy of being exist in his thought. As history is the extension of the soul into the physical world, so the human soul is a substantive counterpart or analog to the divine mind. This means that the natural order, and man's historical-cultural life in this world, is ultimately a divine order, a divine unity. The visible world reveals God's truth, for the visible world and the totality of reality exist in a microcosmic-macrocosmic relationship. And the macrocosm is fundamentally theistic. In terms of historical method, this means that accumulated historical causes and events can legitimately be used as the basis for deductions concerning the macrocosm. Thus one could move scientifically from induction to deduction, from approximate causes to final causes, from historical narrative to deductions regarding the existence of God, divine moral government, divine providence, and the nature and *telos* of history.[12]

Fisher's organicist-idealist ontology—the phenomenal and historical as the reflection and extension of the spiritual—allows him to infuse the natural world and all historical events with divine meaning. All truth is God's truth, and we live in and live out a divine order, for all events express "a common bond . . . between thoughts and things, mind and world."[13] The modern scientific historian's task is to arrange the thought of the infinite God into a coherent framework. From German idealistic thought, Fisher and his contemporaries at Yale imbibed the conviction that science does not undermine faith. In fact, to be truly scientific is to seek to know God. No tension exists between scholarship and faith because the physical world is replete with divine meaning.

Faith precedes all historical observation of the natural world or even the reading of the Bible, for faith arises in the consciousness of the soul's being the *imago dei*. All scientific induction is possible only by the faith-assumption that the human intellect is a reflex of the divine intellect, that the human soul is an ordered and orderly correlate of the divine mind. These idealist assumptions qualified the older New Haven Common Sense Realism. The inductive method of Scottish Realism now stood upon idealist-analogical assumptions, and in turn led to idealist-deductive conclusions. Scientific induction depended upon the continuity of the human to the divine and the predictability of both. The historian inductively accumulates facts and then uses them as the basis for deductions about the larger metaphysical reality.[14]

Where the older New Haven theology of Nathaniel Taylor was rational-revivalist, the Yale scholars of Fisher's generation merged New Haven's Common Sense Realistic tradition with the idealism gleaned from studies abroad and their readings of Coleridge and Emerson into a new epistemology, something between Romanticism and positivism.[15] Fisher agreed with Schleiermacher that the beginning of religion is the feeling of obligation toward God. Christianity accords with reason, yet its locus is "more practical." First and foremost, it appeals to the conscience and the religious affections: "The citadel of Theism is in the consciousness of our own personality. Within ourselves God reveals himself more directly than through any other channel. He impinges, so to speak, on the soul which finds in its primitive activity an intimation and implication of an unconditioned Cause on whom it is dependent,—a cause self-conscious like itself, and speaking with holy authority in consience, wherein also is presented the end which the soul is to pursue through its own free self-determination,—an end which could only be set by a Being both intelligent and holy."[16] Fisher's revivalist heritage is here tempered with idealism. The beginning of religion is to be sought not in a rational *a priori*, but in the experience of the soul. In order to make full sense of the world below, one must first look to the world above, a world that is found within pre-theoretical religious experience. Without that experience, one will live without any knowledge of God, and no amount of rational argumentation will be sufficient to prove a divine being.[17]

Fisher used such words as *heart, intuition,* and *feeling* somewhat interchangeably. Christianity cannot be reduced to rational or even historical constructions and realities. "Faith in God is primarily a feeling." Fisher was intentionally affirming Schleiermacher here, but even as he agreed with Schleiermacher, Fisher criticized him. Schleiermacher made feeling the whole of religion by "confining piety to the incipient stage of faith." Schleiermacher missed the fact that religious dependence has also "an intellectual element."[18]

Fisher was insistent that Christianity is not a "mystic religion." Rather, it is composed of historical realities and teachings that call for a clear and connected interpretation. Because "we are made to think as well as feel and to act," it is only natural that the gospel stimulates our minds to reflect.[19] Christianity has been deposited "in its objective form" in Scripture. The truths of "natural religion," gleaned from the experiences of the soul, are gathered up and directed by the norm of Scripture. This norm adds "further truths of an abstract nature" and "historical facts" to religious experience.[20] Christianity, then, is the agreement "of spiritual experience and objective authority" between faith and historical knowledge. This means that both feeling and critical reflection have their place within Christianity. While the "most convincing source of faith in the divine origin of Christianity is the impression made on the spirit," it also is true that Christianity is a historical religion. "It includes things done, interpositions of God in history, a signal expression and achievement of love on the plane of human action. In a word, Christianity is historical."[21]

Because the content of faith is historically mediated and is knowable through rational faculties, the critical study of the secondary causes by which God works out His will produce a collaborative witness alongside that of the soul. Fisher believed that the critical study of Scripture and church history could work only to the reinforcement of orthodoxy. Science does not conflict with faith. If our critical studies should demonstrate some error in our doctrinal articulation, "the aid should be to eliminate that error, and do it, if possible, forthwith." Even if science were "carried to the farthest bound, it will never be able to dispense with God. It is plain that the world is a cosmos—a beautiful order."[22]

Like other Americans who studied in Germany, Fisher was seeking an introduction to the the modern critical methods of inquiry that were reshaping the scholarship of the late nineteenth century. While Fisher took advantage of the academic and critical resources of his day, several elements within German critical thought concerned him. The German Historical School taught Fisher how to relate individual historical events to the larger metaphysical whole. The Historical School also provided

Fisher with ways of understanding Christianity as a historical, dynamic process rather than a static deposit of eternal truths. Yet he was aware that there were dangers in the German historical consciousness. Much of Fisher's apologetic work focused on the anti-supernaturalism or positivism of the Tübingen school. Such biblical critics as Renan and Strauss had taken a tact that could only serve to push God out of the universe. Leaving God and the supernatural out of the causal nexus would lead only to "the deeper and more general cause of disbelief, which is none other than the weakening or total destruction of faith in the supernatural."[23] The Humean logic of causality led only to atheism, in Fisher's estimation.

The greatest danger of radical criticism is the loss of the transcendent. Again, although appreciating the way Schleiermacher mined religion as the feeling, even the sentimental feeling of dependence, Fisher was alarmed by the subjectivist and pantheist overtones of German theological trends, trends in which the division between the natural and the supernatural were abandoned. Fisher criticized the pantheistic tendency of speculative German theology on two fronts. First, pantheism is deterministic; history is a necessary, and therefore finally meaningless, unfolding of the divine in time. This is the primary failing of Hegel's dialectical view of history. Second, pantheism collapses the idea into reality in such a way that there is no distinction between the natural and the supernatural, the divine and the human.[24] Of course, this is but the reverse side of Fisher's critique of positivism. Positivism naturalizes the supernatural (humanizes God); pantheism supernaturalizes the natural (deifies humans).

Fisher opens *Essays on the Supernatural Origin of Christianity* with this very concern: the collapse of the distinction between the natural and the supernatural, "the leading form of unbelief in the church." In opposition to the Tübingen school, Fisher begins: "The validity of the distinction between the Natural and the Supernatural is assumed, and the attempt is made, in the Introduction and in various parts of the work, to elucidate this distinction. The fact of the constant presence and agency of God in Nature is held to be perfectly consistent with the proposition that the world is a reality distinct from Him."[25] In a manner very similar to that of positivism, pantheism reduces history to a single dimension. "In the end religion is spun out through a metaphysical process in which the facts of Revelation, if recognized at all, are shorn of historical reality."[26]

Much of Fisher's apologetic writing was devoted to biblical crticism, or more exactly, the defense of Scripture—and particularly the supernatural elements therein—from what he considered destructive and unbelieving criticism. Fisher was not seeking to defend the biblical witness for its own sake. He did not argue that the Bible serves as a formal rule of faith, but rather as a credible witness to Christ, a witness that appeals not to subjective religious feeling or to rational speculation, but to historical events. Christianity, for Fisher, as for the majority of late nineteenth-century modernists, is Christ.[27] But Christ was not some abstract metaphor for mankind, but rather, the objective and supernatural intrusion of God within human history. "The question of the Normative Authority of Scripture is of subordinate interest" to the question of the historicity of the supernatural events in the biblical, Christ-centered record.[28] Fisher argued for the reliability of the biblical witness to miracles as actual historical events. He treated the Bible as the evidentiary base for his claims because he contended that the Bible is a scientific, scholarly authority concerning the events which it reports. "The laws that determine the credibility of history are respected in the composition of the sacred books. Contemporary evidence is furnished; and the departures from this practice are the exceptions that prove the rule."[29] When there is no prejudice against Scripture, it testifies to and vindicates itself: "I have undertaken to show that when we take the Gospels as they stand, prior to researches into the origin of them, the miraculous element in the record is found to carry in it a self-verifying character. On the basis of what must be, and actually is, conceded, the conclusion cannot be avoided that the miracles occurred."[30]

In this way Fisher sought to refute critics such as Renan, Strauss, and Baur who held that the biblical miracles were not actual historical events, and from that contended that Christ was not divine. The defense of biblical miracles established the deity of Christ for Fisher, and further, serves to demonstrate that God stands behind human history, intervening within it when redemptively necessary.

Louise Stevenson points out that Fisher's defense of biblical miracles was not intended as an evangel. Where the older generation of New Haven theologians, influenced by Common Sense Realism, had sought to defend biblical supernaturalism for the sake of their doctrine of biblical inerrancy, Fisher defended the miraculous element of Scripture for the sake of the divine history found within its pages and to demonstrate that criticism need not undermine faith.[31]

AMERICAN HISTORIOGRAPHY

Fisher's approach to history was in many ways representative of the late nineteenth century: evolutionary, progressive, and optimistic. Yet he would reject deterministic and scientific historical theory wherever it violated personal freedom. Although learning much from German critical history, Fisher was first and foremost an American, and a New England

313

Yankee at that. The major input for shaping his understanding of history and agency did not come from German philosophy but from forms of thought that were inherent to the American experience. Whether it came from the New Haven tradition of Nathaniel Taylor and his Arminian reconstruction of New England Congregationalism, Fisher's revivalist experience, or simply his Yankee pedigree, Fisher began with the uniqueness of the individual and the right of private choice. Civilization includes more than organized institutions, nations, and the laws that govern those realities. Civilization consists of all that raises humans above the bestial level, and for Fisher, that which raises humans to uniqueness and civilization is the free, individual moral consciousness.[32] The individual has power to determine events. In his presidential address to the American Historical Association in 1898, Fisher summed up his approach to history. The individual is not the postivistic product of the causal nexus. Moral choice cannot be reduced "to the category of effects." History is a drama in which the individual is a real and meaningful actor. It is not "the growth of that impersonal being called society."[33]

While philosophy works speculatively from "the data of consciousness and builds its structure by a process in which events have no place," history is characterized by the plasticity and contingency of human freedom. And it is history, not philosophy, that gives Christianity its particular character:

> Christianity is an historical religion. At the foundation of Christian theology are facts which occur within the sphere of freedom, and therefore do not admit of being explained upon any theory of necessary evolution. As students of the Gospel we are in a province where the agency of personal beings is the principal matter. It was the love of God to mankind that led to the mission of Christ. It was the free act of love, the bestowal of an 'unspeakable gift.' The method of salvation is a course of self-sacrifice which culminates in the cross. These things cannot be made links in a metaphysical chain. They are not so many steps on a logical treadmill. Their analogue is to be found in the purest deeds of love, patience, and self-devotion which the annals of humanity contain. Nevertheless, the facts of Christianity are not barren occurences. They are capable of an explanation. They are not without significance. They are a fulfillment of a purpose. Their fitness to the end sought, theology with the aid of Scripture seeks to point out."[34]

Although Fisher understood Kantian thought as a useful way of making sense of the organic connection between nature and the divine, he judged Kantianism as being largely reponsible for the speculative and deterministic historical science of the day. Kant understood, but unfortunately limited to the noumenal, the fact that "the seat of moral freedom is deep in the radical self-determinations by which the supreme ends of conduct, the motives of life in the aggregate, are fixed."[35] By removing the contingent and the human from history—or reducing it to a rational order—the radical historicism of the German schools secularizes and de-Christianizes history.

In the opening pages of his *History of Christian Doctrine* Fisher discusses his choice not to write a history of dogma, opting instead for a history of Christian thought. The individual choice gets lost in the former as dogma is the articulation of official or ecclesiastical doctrine. Fisher acknowledges Harnack, his teacher Neander, and his friend Schaff as masters of this genre. Harnack is especially singled out as having produced a work of genius, "whatever opinion may be held as to its theological tendencies." Fisher thought Harnack's approach too speculative and too narrow. The history of dogma approach toward church history (I would use the term historical theology but Fisher considered himself a historian not a theologian) is too specialized, for it attempts to bring history under the *loci* or rubrics of theological system and ecclesiastical judgment. This approach is too concerned for product, official articles of faith, and ecclesiastical traditions, and it too easily misses process, the free historical choice of the moral agent.[36] It is the movement of uncoerced religious thought arising out of historical circumstance and context that Fisher seeks to chronicle and to investigate, for those movements are methodologically and historically prior to dogma.[37]

Fisher's favorite examples of the moral individual influencing events were Luther and Calvin. Real historical power lay not in impersonal laws but in the intellectual and moral person of action. In these two giants of the Protestant Reformation, "the unforced appropriation by the soul, of truth in harmony with its inmost nature and its conscious necessities" came to full historic reality. This is not to say that either Reformer worked without the benefit of divine providence or historical precedents. The Reformation was the product of a long process of both human and divine preparation:

> Events, because they are unexpected and startling, are not to be ascribed merely to some proximate antecedent. The Protestant movement is often looked upon as hardly less preternatural and astonishing than would be the rising of the sun at midnight. But the more it is examined, the less does it wear this marvelous aspect. In truth, never was a historical crisis more elaborately prepared, and this through a train of causes which reach back into the remote past. Nor is it the fact that such events are wholly out of the reach of human foresight; they

cast their shadows before; they are the object of presentiments more or less distinct, sometimes of definite prediction.[38]

But the "general causes" of divine providence and the general flow of history do not obviate the reality and meaningfulness of individual choice and action. If revolutionary change in customary ways of thinking or acting is to take place, "there must be individuals to rally upon; men of power who are able to create and sustain in others a new moral life which they have first realized in themselves."[39]

History flows forward toward a movement of crisis in which the moral decision maker would draw upon tradition and personal moral consciousness, make a choice, and direct the course of history forward. While God's providential direction of history certainly enables and prepares for the human moral choice, it does not determine it. Reformation and revolution result not from impersonal social forces or mysterious metaphysical laws, but from human decisions and actions. "Great men are not puppets moved by the spirit of the time. To be sure, there must be a preparation for them, and a groundwork of sympathy among their contemporaries: otherwise their activity would call forth no response."[40] Thus Fisher sought a middle way between freedom and determinism, and he would find it in the complimentary categories of the divine moral government and the free, moral individual.

From Nathaniel W. Taylor and the New Haven theology Fisher inherited an understanding of divine providence as God's moral government, a reasonable divine command which suited the individualistic and anticlerical ethos of Jacksonian America. The New Haven doctrine of the divine moral government was perfectly suited to Fisher's anthropological notion of reflectivity. Belief in God, self, individuality, the integrity of the soul all go together. Out of one's perception of personal spirituality and personal attributes arises the inner consciousness of an infinite and moral spirit we call God. Our own "inward assurance of freedom" is attended by the complimentary consciousness of the morality of God, and thus God's moral administration of the universe.[41] Fisher preferred the moral argument to all other arguments for the existence of God. The most radical distinction between theism and atheism begins with the question of human morality and the reality of a moral universe. If the human person has no moral history distinct from natural history, any talk about the existence of God is idle. "Ethics must share the fate of religion. How can there be serious belief in reasonable action, when man is not free, and is not even a substantial entity?"[42] While a believer in evolution, Fisher held that any theory of biological emergence is at best one-sided, and thoroughly destructive of theism if not brought under the assumption and direction of the divine moral government. "How can self-seeking breed benevolence, or self-sacrifice and a sense of duty spring out of the 'struggle for existence'?"[43] The evolution and uniformity of the universe is no blind necessity, but rather, the arrangement of moral wisdom: "Nor does the order of nature stand by itself apart from all relations to any thing beyond. It is only one province in the whole divine system. There is a moral administration, as well as an administration of physical laws. Material existences are parts, and subordinate parts, of this broader system."[44]

The assumption of a moral government—especially articulated along lines analogous to biological evolution—made history predictable and progressive for Fisher. History is the product of neither capricious individuals nor impersonal forces, but the moral intiatives of God and the equally moral response of humans: "The history of mankind is not a chaotic jumble of occurrences, but an orderly sequence where one set of events prepares for another, and where rational ends are wrought out by means adapted to them. There is a divine plan stamped upon history."[45] That which makes history a progressive and predictable continuity is the historical application of divine justice in the form of rewards and punishments in accordance with moral conduct: "That moral government which appears in the prosperity accorded to righteousness, and in the penalties that overtake iniquity—that sublime manifestation of justice through all the annals of mankind—declares the presence of a just God. The minds of men, when unperverted by false speculation, instinctively feel that God reigns, whenever they behold these providential allotments."[46]

Taylor's New Haven theology rejected the older federal notions of the imputation of Adam's sin. The classical Calvinistic doctrines of the imputation of original sin to Adam's progeny and the consequent total depravity of all humans were judged as offensive to the individualistic democratic ideal because they rob persons of their status as free moral agents. Sin and depravity are the result of individual choice not federal relationship, and it is only acts—not natures or dispositions—that are sinful. It was simple common sense, for Taylor, that individuals cannot be held responsible for either the acts of others or sinful acts unless they are acts of free choice arising from the moral ability to act to the contrary. God relates to mankind through moral suasion in that he upholds and administers a perfect moral government which urges us toward free moral action and benevolence. God does not relate to man coercively or forensically but by the moral means. The divine law is not a rule of judgment but action.[47]

Taylor's Pelagian construction of God's moral government as the moral complement of free moral agency was reproduced whole in Fisher's thought: "The Christian doctrine of the influence of the spirit of God is in itself not more mysterious or inexplicable than the acknowledged personal influence of one human mind upon another. There is involved in it no more interference with the liberty of the will. The reasonableness of the Christian doctrine as a conception will be questioned only by a frigid, unphilosophical deism, which represents God as standing aloof from the world, and ignores the near affinity of the human to the divine."[48]

God is transcendent, yet active in human moral consciousness and in the events of history. God's influence within human history does not destroy the immanent causal nexus of our experience. The divine works through human agents, and He influences them through moral solicitation, preserving their freedom and respecting all secondary causes. Thus the world about us does not come to us as irrational or unpredictable. "The method of Providence is never magical."[49] In this system, Fisher was able to speak of God as sovereign, but it is a sovereignty that is displayed within the eminently rational system of moral government. By governing free agents through moral influence—the promise of prosperity or the threat of punishments that is known intuitively by moral consciousness—God reveals and promotes the divine law.

While meaning to preserve human moral agency, Fisher's understanding of divine providence via moral means could sometimes appear rather deterministic, even historicist. Political habits, art, and literature are correlates of national character. Here Fisher's idea of the preparation of historical precedents resurfaces. Martin Luther was a free moral agent, but he was also a product of the Germanic spirit. The Germans of the sixteenth century "were not content to approach God by proxy, or put their religion outside of them, in sacraments and ceremonies, in sensuous imposing spectacles."[50] Thus, Luther summed up in himself the Germanic love for personal liberty, inward spirituality, and anticlericalism. In like manner, as the French are logical and systematic, so John Calvin was a logician,[51] and the Swiss Reformation sprang from the Swiss national love of liberty.[52] While at the moment of crisis the free individual makes a personal choice, the individual is nevertheless the representative of tendencies of thought inherent to the nation and race. Thus, in every epoch, the prevailing understanding of the faith corresponds to the particular characterisitics of time and race.[53]

HISTORICISM

Like the New Haven theology before him, Fisher stood within the Whig tradition of historicism.[54] The discipline of history was seen as contributing to the scientific and moral progress of humanity. Calling up the law of human progress, Whiggery saw academia as a moral means to the *eschaton*. As man inevitably increases in knowledge, he will also bring material progress to himself and a civilized millennium to all.[55] Fisher understood Christianity's—and especially Protestantism's—role within society as that of moral leaven. "Religion is not to divorce itself from science, art, industry, recreation, from anything that promotes the well-being of man on earth; but religion is to leaven all with a higher consecration. This is the real creed of Protestantism."[56]

The Christian faith exercises a civilizing power within history. In turn, the civilized society nurtures the seed of the divine in the human moral nature. Fisher shared and supported what Wintrop Hudson called Henry Ward Beecher's "confidence in the power of the culture to nurture and sustain the Christian faith."[57] Like Horace Bushnell, Fisher saw the proper role of society and its institutions as to promote the moral individual as an agent of the millennium. This agency was one of moral example, an example that draws others toward moral improvement. Like Horatio Alger, the Victorian-era writer of morality tales for young people,[58] Fisher believed education produced morality and refinement, which in turn produced personal advancement, which via exemplary power produces moral improvement for all within a society. The greater the moral improvement of the individual, the greater the advance of corporate social life. There is a hint here of the old Puritan congruence of the destiny of the individual and that of the nation. The individual and the community need one another. An individual's success and rewards enhance the moral environment and prosperity of society.

Fisher worked within a tradition at Yale which saw the college as an important religious shaper of its students. The Yale of Timothy Dwight and of Nathaniel Taylor had been deeply affected by the revivalism of the Second Great Awakening. Looking to revival as a primary means of moral development, the faculty of the 1830s often led prayer meetings to encourage spiritual awakening. Stevenson notes that by Fisher's tenure the college replaced the church just as as the intellectual and moral nurture of education replaced the more highly emotional experience of revival.[59]

Fisher plied his trade as a historian in the service of the Yale conception of the college as moral shaper and cultural temple. The study of history gives the students models for personal moral development, and because the individual is a crucial element in the moral growth of society as a whole, the study of historical models aids the development of society. The historian's task is moralistic, to fill the past with proper exemplars for thought and action.[60] Fisher was a typical late nineteenth-century Whig historian. As D. W. Bebbington put it, the aim of Whig history was to "interpret the past in the light of the present and so commend history's winners."[61] Whiggery was typified by a progressivist view of history in which the modernist notion of the emergence of liberty was taken as the unchanging norm of historical development. Under this conception of history, the past tells the story of human improvement via movement toward civil liberty.

Social evolution toward freedom is a divinely ordained process, according to Fisher. The chief engine toward that freedom is Christian faith. In *Discussions in History and Theology*, Fisher claimed that Christianity's aim is the civilization of the human race, and civilization is "all that enters into the improvement of the individual and of society—all elements that unite to constitute an advanced stage of human progress."[62] Fisher's optimistic view of human progress made it incumbent upon him to look for a pattern of human accomplishment within history, a pattern that proved that history is indeed providential and progressive. He was convinced that "progress appeared in history as each successive civilization provided increasingly more opportunity for the self-development of its citizens."[63] The Athens of the fourth century B.C. permitted a greater degree of individual development for its citizens than did ancient Persia. By being victorious over Darius at the battle of Marathon, the Greeks had proven the strength of a free people and vindicated the providential movement toward freedom. The battle "was a conflict between the East and the West, between Asia and Europe—the coarse despotism under which individual energy was stifled, and the dawning of liberty which was to furnish the atmosphere required for the full development and culture of the human mind."[64]

Consistent with his commitment to Christianity as the moral means of progress, Fisher drew the vast majority of his examples from church history, and the history of doctrinal development in particular. While much of Fisher's apologetic energies went into a defense of the truthfulness of Scripture, his concern was not to preserve the Bible as a mature and complete storehouse of doctrinal truth. From John Henry Newman, Fisher picked up the notion of Scripture as a doctrinal seed plot. That which is latent or potential within the original unfolds within history.[65] But whereas Newman saw doctrine as progressing under the guardianship of an infallible church, Fisher took a decidedly different tact.

Newman worked within the high creedal tradition of Catholicism. Within that confessional fence he was able to express his progressivist ideas by stessing the authority of the bishop as source of progressive renewal and continuity with the past. Similarly, Philip Schaff affirmed an organic historical growth of doctrine by allowing the liturgical worship and creedal solidarity of Lutheranism to set the parameters of doctrinal development. But Fisher's Americanist individualism dictated an anticlerical and antisacramental, and indeed an antiecclesiastical, approach to doctrinal development. It is not the church but the suasive power of the gospel to the moral individual and God's providential direction through the Christian nurture provided by academic study that secures the organic and continuous development of doctrine. While no law of cause and effect reigns over the human will, the human soul naturally corresponds to the divine soul of which it is a reflection. Thus even though historical movements and developments are never coercive, we may speak of an orderly succession of ideas and events, even a "plan of history" "by the over-ruling agency of God, which has no need to interfere with human liberty, or to coerce or crush the free and responsible nature of man, but knows how to pilot the race onward, be the rocks and cross-currents where and what they may."[66]

AN AMERICAN MILLENNIUM

The Reformation era served as a vindication in Fisher's opinion of his optimistic view of doctrinal and moral progress, and the emergence of freedom. What could look like, and quite possibly was, a nativist fear of Roman Catholicism,[67] was grounded for Fisher in an Americanist loathing of creedalism and sacramentalism. This was also based on the Historical School and Whig understanding of the evolutionary emergence of liberty. "The spectacle of the physical power, the industry and thrift, the intelligence, good government, and average morality of the Protestant nations" bears witness to the superiority of Protestantism over Roman Catholicism.[68]

The model is to be found in Scripture itself. The system of religion found in the Old Testament, with its cultus and sacrifice, temple and holy days, is an external and coercive concept of religion. This dispensation is declared by the Old Testament prophets to be "rudimental and introductory to a more spiritual system," that of the New Testament. "This character of inwardness belongs to the religion of Christ, which, for this reason, is fitted to be universal. Worship is set free from legal restrictions, and the external and sensuous characteristics of the Jewish ritual."[69] Roman Catholicism represents a return to the externalism and depersonalism of Old Testament priestcraft and rite. Over the centuries Rome gained a vast political power that only served to enslave vast populations to her sacerdotal system and clerical mediation.

The emergence of Christianity attended the individual consciousness of the allegiance of the soul to a higher kingdom.

But the church itself at length erected a supremacy over the individual, inconsistent with the free action of reason and conscience, and even stretched that supremacy so far as to dwarf and overshadow civil society. It reared a theocracy, and subjected everything to its unlimited sway. The Reformation gave back to the individual his proper autonomy. The result is a self-respect, an intellectual activity, a development of inventive capacity, and of energy of character, which gave rise to such achievements in science, in the field of political action, and in every work where self-reliance and personal force are called for, as would be impossible under the opposite system.[70]

The Reformation called people away from the excessive esteem of sacrament and ceremony, and away from a scholastic and dogmatic religion to "something more inward and spiritual." A vast institution had stood between the individual and the objects of religious faith and hope, but the Reformation changed all that. Now by speaking of Protestantism as an inward and spiritual faith, Fisher does not mean to say that it is privatistic (as evangelicals usually use the word "spiritual"), but that it is moral or uncoerced. The Protestant faith is one that calls for moral decision and action rather than cultic and sacramental participation.[71]

History has vindicated the Protestant principle of personal liberty and choice. Protestantism, especially in the American model under its separation of church and state, fosters a religion that is successful by means of example and persuasion rather than coercion. The civil and personal liberty that are implicit in the New Testament, and finally made explicit in the Reformation, come to fulfillment in the United States, the environment that is most conducive to and in fact promotes the Protestant principle of personal freedom.

Mark Trechock has noted that the principle of personal freedom is clearly evidenced in Fisher's anticreedal bias. External controls on orthodoxy were repugnant to Fisher. Making a creed binding only subverts human freedom—what Trechock calls "the right of private judgment"—and sets up a new legalism of dogmatic conformity and punctilious tests of orthodoxy.[72] Creedal statements halt doctrinal discussion and development. As such, history very quickly renders them irrelevant. The Protestant emancipation of mankind from clerical rule also frees us from doctrinaire and enforced rules of belief. Alliance to Christ outweighs and relativizes all denominational ties and doctrinal nit-picking. As Trechock put it: "Jesus Christ remained the universal measure of all things, and because he was, the modern scholar was free from the shackles of confessionalism and the Christian church could be free from the temptation to require belief in what was not essential to Christianity and might be disproved by research."[73] Thus the course that Fisher and the Yale scholars attempted to chart in the late nineteenth century was one that would take them between the rocks of naturalistic humanism on the left and rigid confessional orthodoxy on the right. It is here—on the principles of anticreedal moral consciousness and Newman's organic doctrinal development—that Fisher defended the doctrinal innovations of Nathaniel Taylor and New School Presbyterianism. "In our judgment, it is a grand merit of our New England theologians, that while holding the past in due reverence, they have not bowed down before it, but have expected progress. They have seen that the denial of the hope of progress in theology—that is, in the understanding and expression of the truths of the Bible—would have shut out the Protestant Reformation, as well as every other access of light since theology began to be a science."[74]

The breaking of the chains of creedalism perfectly suited Fisher's American context. He and the other Yale scholars were working from and promoting an antidenominational and even antiecclesiastical movement that would also allow the fundamentalists of the next generation to separate from their parent denominations and find their power bases and confessional centers in Bible institutes and Bible colleges. For Fisher, the confessional center was Yale College. The difference, and that which marked him as a liberal, was that he understood Christian sanctity as the cultural nurture provided by education.

Another area in which Fisher greatly differed from the evangelicalism of the next generation (but not that of his own day) was in his optimistic, even postmillennial, vision of the future. His organicist concept of history implied an understanding of history as the progressive story of mankind's movement toward perfect freedom. All the evidence at our disposal—modern inventions, cultural development, and philanthropic movements—shows that mankind is moving toward its ultimate destiny of unity in diversity. "The path of human progress has led in the direction of *unity* as the ultimate goal. It is, however, a *unity in variety* toward which the course of history has moved. The development and growth of distinct nations, each after its own type, and not less, the freedom of the individual to realize the destiny intended for him by nature, are necessary to the full development of mankind—necessary to the perfection of the race. The final unity that is sought is to be reached not by stifling the capacities of human nature, but by the complete unfolding of them in all their variety."[75] The restraints of Christianity allow for freedom and diversity. And all the evidences of mankind's approaching unity, whether it be industrial development, economic enlightenment, the progress of science and letters, global politics, philanthropy, or the growth of Christian missions, show that it is a unity which is characterized by all the variety of human enterprise and culture. Following the Historical School's penchant for stating the facts of this world and then relating them to the divine whole (working from induction and then leaping to deduction to draw a theistic conclusion), Fisher's *Outlines of Universal History* chronicles the history of mankind in as serial a fashion as he was able and then ends with this glowing prospectus: "The progress made in the past encourages the hope that the unity of mankind, a unity which shall be the crown of individual and national development, will one day be reached. That unity of mankind, in loyal fellowship with Him in whose image man was made, is the community of which the ancient Stoic vaguely dreamed, and which the apostles of Christ proclaimed and predicted— the perfected *kingdom of God*."[76]

While insisting on the supernatural origin of Christianity, Fisher's individualism and organicist and progressivist tendencies led him toward a broad ecumenism that sidestepped the doctrinal debates of his day. He shared the evangelical hope of his more conservative brethren, but he departed from any emphasis on doctrine as the test of religious truth. Lacking any sense of radicalism, Fisher argued for a sane, even reverent, approach to scholarship and criticism: "And how important it is that all progress in knowledge should bring us closer to God! Alas, that the study of the works of God should ever be prosecuted in such a spirit that he is more and more removed out of sight! Alas, that the study of history should ever fail to confirm the scholar's faith in the God, of whose Providence history is the record! Vain, nay, worse than vain, are all our studies, if they fail to deepen our faith in God."[77]

Fisher was a transitional thinker. His synthesis of idealism and Common Sense Realism would not hold. His relative seclusion amidst the parochial spires of Yale College allowed him to hold critical scholarship and German idealism together with a supernatural reality that evidences itself within the historical Christ in a single liberal evangelicalism. In the next generation, the ends pulled apart, and Fisher's organicism expired under the autopsies of a more thoroughgoing liberalism and the belligerent dogmatism of a defensive fundamentalism.

AN INDICATIVE
BIBLIOGRAPHY OF FISHER'S WORKS

Essays on the Supernatural Origin of Christianity, 1865.
Life of Benjamin Silliman, 1866.
The Reformation, 1873.

The Beginning of Christianity, 1877.
Faith and Rationalism, 1879.
Discussions in History and Theology, 1880.
The Christian Religion, 1882.
The Grounds of Theistic and Christian Belief, 1883.
Outlines of Universal History, 3 vols. 1885, 1888.
History of the Christian Church, 1887.
Manual of Christian Evidences, 1888.
The Nature and Method of Revelation, 1890.
The Colonial Era in America, 1892.
Manual of Natural Theology, 1893.
Jefferson and the Social Compact Theory, 1894.
History of Christian Doctrine, 1896.

NOTES

1. Commenting on the "progressive orthodoxy" of late-nineteenth-century evangelical liberalism, Winthrop S. Hudson (in *Religion in America* [New York: Charles Scribner's Sons, 1973], 269) observed that "the striking feature of the liberal movement in Protestantism which began to take shape during the 1870s was its conservative intent. The leaders of the movement were evangelicals, standing firmly within the church, cherishing their Christian experience, and uncompromising in their loyalty to Christ. They had little in common with the earlier rationalistic liberalism which had become dominant in Unitarianism. The central concern of the evangelical liberals was quite explicitly apologetic. They wished to preserve the truth of the gospel as it spoke to the hearts of men. In the face of what many feared might be fatal assaults on the Christian faith, they sought to restate the essential doctrines of evangelical Christianity in terms that would be both intelligible and convincing and thus to establish them on a more secure foundation." Hudson's textbook comment is worth repeating here because it perfectly captures Fisher's career. In both his historical and apologetic writing Fisher defended Yale's evangelical modernism from both positivists and romantic pantheists on the left and sectarian creedalists on the right.

2. Hubert Cunliffe-Jones, ed., *A History of Christian Doctrine: In Succession to the Earlier Work of G. P. Fisher* (Philadelphia: Fortress, 1978), 3.

3. Philip Schaff, Fisher's friend and co-founder of the American Society of Church History (1888), also studied at Halle under Tholuck and Neander from 1839 to 1840.

4. For biographical information, see Louise L. Stevenson, *Scholarly Means to Evangelical Ends: The New Haven Scholars and the Transformation of Higher Learning in America, 1830–1890* (Baltimore: Johns Hopkins, 1986), 150; C. H. Lippy, "George Park Fisher," in *Dictionary of Christianity in America*, Daniel G. Reid, et al. (Downers Grove: IVP, 1990), 441; F. H. Foster, *A Genetic History of the New England Theology* (Chicago: University of Chicago Press, 1907); Roland H. Bainton, *Yale and the Ministry: A History of Education for the Christian Ministry at Yale from the Founding in 1701* (New York: Harper and Bros., 1957).

5. Cited in Cunliffe-Jones, *History of Christian Doctrine*, 3–4. Fisher's dispassionate analysis has not served to recommend his work to later generations. Few references to Fisher and his work are to be found in contemporary American church history and historical theology. And evaluations of his abilities and style have been less than stellar.

Henry Warner Bowden depicted Fisher as a Schaff clone without the latter's vision and energy (*Church History in the Age of Science: Historiographical Patterns in the United States, 1876–1918* [Chapel Hill: University of North Carolina Press, 1971], 66. According to Lewis W. Spitz, "Fisher was gifted with a genial but not a deeply analytical or profound mind." See Lewis W. Spitz, "The Lutheran Reformation in American Historiography," in *The Maturing of American Lutheranism*, ed. Herbert T. Neve and Benjamin A. Johnson, (Minneapolis: Augsburg, 1968), 98. Roland H. Bainton (*Yale and the Ministry*, 189) commented that Fisher's *The Reformation* was impartial, unbiased, and fair—perhaps to a fault, as it communicated a certain sense of detachment and lack of commitment. From examining the correspondence of the New Haven scholars, Louise Stevenson noted Noah Porter ([1811–92] Professor of Moral Philosophy and Metaphysics at Yale, and President of the College from 1871–86) and Fisher were not mutual admirers. Porter had originally opposed Fisher's appointment to Yale on the grounds that the latter was a superficial scholar and "not a first-rate man" (Stevenson, *Scholarly Means*, 24). In his introductory essay, which is dedicated to Fisher, Cunliffe-Jones writes that "Fisher's *History* has held its place, and deservedly held its place, right up to the present, as the best one-volume *History of Christian Doctrine* available for the student" (*History of Christian Doctrine*, 3). Yet after the introduction of the book, Fisher nowhere appears in the essays gathered to be a successor to his *History of Doctrine*.

6. George Park Fisher, *The Reformation* (New York: Scribner, Armstrong, and Co., 1873), vii. See George Park Fisher, *History of Christian Doctrine* (Edinburgh: T & T Clark, 1896), vii, for a similar statement of objectivity and comprehensiveness in good conscience.

7. Before the modern period historians did not consider the accumulation of accurate facts as their primary objective. Paul K. Conkin and Roland N. Stromberg comment that before the modern period, "History was rhetoric plundering the past for instigations to present virtue to action"(*The Heritage and Challenge of History* [New York: Harper & Row, 1971], 65).

8. Cited in Ernst Breisach, *Historiography: Ancient, Medieval, & Modern* (Chicago: University of Chicago Press, 1983), 233.

9. On Ranke's view of history and his response to Hegelianism, see Helen Liebel-Weckowiz, "Ranke's Theory of History and the German Modernist School," *Canadian Journal of History*, 28 (April 1988): 73–93; Herbert Butterfield, *Man on His Past: The Study of the History of Historical Scholarship* (Boston: Beacon Hill, 1955), 86–95, 100–142; Mark T. Gilderhus, *History and Historians: A Historiographical Introduction* (Englewood Cliffs, N. J.: Prentice-Hall, 1987), 44–45.

10. George Park Fisher, *Ancient History*, Part 1 of *Outlines of Universal History* (New York: American Book Co., 1885), v.

11. George Park Fisher, *Faith and Rationalism: Short Supplementary Essays on Related Topics* (New York: Charles Scribner's Sons, 1879), 5; see also 50, 135; *Essays on the Supernatural Origin of Christianity: With Special Reference to the Theories of Renan, Strauss, and the Tubingen School* (New York: Charles Scribner & Co., 1865), xiii; *Discussions in History and Theology* (New York: Charles Scribner's Sons, 1880), 469.

12. See Stevenson, *Scholarly Means*, 68ff. She makes the point that for Fisher, as for New Haven scholarship generally, the historical and scientific methodologies were grounded in German Idealism. Where the New Haven thought of Nathaniel Taylor had been squarely Common Sense Realistic, the later New Haven scholars augmented and directed the inductive tendencies of Common Sense Realism with the Idealism gleaned from studies abroad. The result was that the New Haven scholars "retained the empirical dimension of the Scottish philosophy but assumed that every observable fact of this world had an idealistic correlate" (68). Stevenson makes the point that New Haven historical and scientific methodology was "secular" to the extent that history was

done by investigation of historical causes rather than by recourse to authority, but that investigation invariably led to theistic conclusions.

13. George Park Fisher, *The Grounds of Theistic and Christian Belief* (New York: Charles Scribner's Sons, 1883), 41.

14. Commenting on and quoting Noah Porter, Stevenson captures the perspective and methodology of Fisher as well: "Even though the scientist had never seen God, he could still know him, for he assumed that God had arranged the universe according to certain principles. In contrast to Darwinians, who viewed natural processes as random, wasteful, and savage, Porter's scientist conceived of nature as orderly, uniform, and neat; its means were adapted to ends according to the rules of harmony, beauty, and grace. With these assumptions, induction depended on belief not merely in God but a God who behaved in predetemined ways. 'Induction,' Porter reasoned, 'assumes that the *rational methods of the divine and human intellect* are similar, and that the human intellect is therefore capable of judging of the principles and aims by which the universe was constructed and its laws can be known. More briefly expressed, induction is only possible on the assumption that the intellect of man is a reflex of the Divine Intellect; or that man is made in the image of God" (*Scholarly Means*, 72–73).

15. George M. Marsden, "The New School Heritage and Presbyterian Fundamentalism," *Westminster Theological Journal* 33 (May 1970): 134–35. Marsden suggests that New Haven's movement from Common Sense Realism toward German Idealism and native romanticism was an early manifestation of the modernist movement in the U.S. He notes the irony that the "liberal" theology of Nathaniel Taylor represented staunch opposition to the romantic (transcendentalist) movement during the first third of the nineteenth century. Fisher would, of course, agree with the early New Haven position regarding the pantheistic dangers of transcendentalism.

16. *Grounds*, 71; see also 25–27.

17. *Faith and Rationalism*, 13, 125. See also *Reformation*, 23; *Discussions in History and Theology*, 478.

18. *Grounds*, 33; *Supernatural Origin of Christianity*, 469.

19. Fisher *History, of Christian Doctrine*, 9.

20. In *Faith and Rationalism* Fisher writes: "We give the name of the *Christian Religion* to the sum of beliefs which make up the substance of Christianity in its objective form. They are set forth in brief in the Apostles' Creed. They comprise, as we there see, first, what are termed truths of natural religion; secondly, further truths of an abstract nature, such as the relation of Christ to God, which the Gospel Revelation affirms; and thirdly, the main historical facts of Christianity. We may say in general that the Christian faith, objectively considered, includes doctrines and facts" (1).

21. *Supernatural Origin of Christianity*, 350.

22. *Grounds*, 456–57.

23. *Supernatural Origin of Christianity*, 26f; see also 541–47.

24. Fisher, *History of Christian Doctrine*, 12–14.

25. *Supernatural Origin of Christianity*, iii–iv.

26. Fisher, *History of Christian Doctrine*, 12–13. In *Discussions in History and Theology* Fisher groups pantheism together with atheism and deism under the heading of rationalism (439–67).

27. Ibid., 1–7. See also George M. Marsden, *The Evangelical Mind and New School Presbyterian Experience: A Case Study of Thought and Theology in Nineteenth-Century America* (New Haven: Yale, 1970), 168ff. for a discussion of modernist Christocentrism.

28. *Supernatural Origin of Christianity*, 12. See Mark Trechock, "Orthodoxy for a Critical Period: Five Case Studies in American Theology, Circa 1870," Ph.D. thesis,

Iliff School of Theology, 1987, 105ff. for a discussion of Fisher's response to the German biblical criticism.

29. George Park Fisher, *Beginnings of Christianity* (New York: Scribner, Armstrong & Co., 1877), 405. Compare Fisher's *Manual of Christian Evidences* (New York: Charles Scribner's Sons, 1888), 9–20.

30. *Grounds*, vi.

31. Stevenson, *Scholarly Means*, 98.

32. *Discussions in History and Theology*, 161.

33. Cited in Stevenson, *Scholarly Means*, 90.

34. Fisher, *History of Christian Doctrine*, 7–8.

35. *Grounds*, 15.

36. Fisher, *History of Christian Doctrine*, v–3.

37. As we shall see, Fisher understands ecclesiastical and dogmatic statements of doctrine as authoritarian and therefore ultimately counterproductive to free moral sensibilities.

38. *Reformation*, 2.

39. Ibid.

40. *Universal History*, 1:4.

41. *Grounds*, 1,18.

42. Ibid., v. The moral argument for the existence of God is of course much older than the New Haven theology of the nineteenth century. A version of the argument similar to that of New Haven's can be found in *Analogy of Religion* by Bishop Joseph Butler (1692–1752). Fisher blends the moral argument of New Haven's Common Sense epistemology with the idealist tendencies of Romanticism into a new synthesis. For example, in *Grounds of Theistic and Christian Belief* he wrote: "It is through the feeling of dependence and the feeling of obligation that the existence of a Supreme Being in whom we live, and to whose law we are subject, is revealed in the soul" (26–27). Fisher wrote similarly in *Discussions in History and Theology*: "There is, first, the revelation of God in the soul. There is within us a sense of dependence, and a consciousness of a law imposed upon us by the Power on which we depend—a law moral in its nature, and thus revealing that power as having a preference for right—in other words, as personal and holy. An almost audible voice of God in the soul discloses to us his being, and ultimate relation to ourselves" (478).

43. *Grounds*, v.

44. *Supernatural Origin of Christianity*, xix. See also 495.

45. *Discussions in History and Theology*, 483–84.

46. Ibid., 484.

47. For larger discussions of Taylor's Arminian Congregationalism see Marsden, *The Evangelical Mind*, 46–58; William G. McLoughlin, *The American Evangelicals, 1800–1900* (Gloucester, Mass.: Peter Smith, 1976), 1–5; William G. McLoughlin, *Revivals, Awakenings, and Reform: An Essay in Religion and Social Change in America, 1607–1977* (Chicago: University of Chicago, 1978), 109–18.

48. *Grounds*, 361.

49. *Reformation*, 1.

50. Ibid., 86.

51. Ibid., 199.

52. Ibid., 136. Compare *Discussions in History and Theology*, 45 where Fisher applies the idea of national spirit to Rome during the first century.

53. Fisher, *History of Christian Doctrine*, 13. Stevenson (*Scholarly Means*, 88) suggests that the New Haven scholars of Fisher's generation consciously appealed to historicism in order to free themselves from the mechanistic, static conceptions of the universe and society of the older New Haven theology.

54. Stevenson comments regarding New Haven and Whiggery: "The New Haven scholars spoke for Whiggery—a dominant strain in nineteenth-century social, political, and cultural thought. Whiggery stood for the triumph of the cosmopolitan and national over the provincial and local, of rational order over irrational spontaneity, of school-based learning over traditional folkways and customs, and of self-control over self-expression. Whigs believed that every person had the potential to become moral or good if family, school, and community nurtured the seed of goodness in his moral nature. Richard Jensen identifies Whigs as the party of modernizers who promoted some aspects of the nascent middle-class economy and society while restraining others. The Whig program for desirable social and moral change was three-pronged. Whigs opposed institutions that they perceived as inhibiting or preventing moral development, such as the Catholic Church and southern slavery; they identified and sought to eliminate evils, such as intemperance and overdevotedness to material luxury, that tempted free individuals from the goal of self-development; and they founded and supported institutions, such as Bushnell's and Beecher's ideal family, Horace Mann's common school, and the New Haven scholar's Yale, that promised to encourage the growth of an ideal individual, one who embodied and supported Whig values and beliefs" (*Scholarly Means*, 5–6).

55. *Discussions in History and Theology*, 161.

56. *Reformation*, 552.

57. Winthrop S. Hudson, *The Great Tradition of the American Churches* (New York: Harper & Row, 1953), 108. Hudson notes that it was modernism's very confidence in its own cultural dominance that led to its failure. Unable finally to effect its millennial aspirations, modernism was reduced to little more than a parochial protection of the status quo via its own implicit moralism. See also Martin E. Marty, *Righteous Empire: The Protestant Experience in North America* (New York: Dial Press, 1970), 89–95.

58. See John G. Cawelti, "From Rags to Respectability: Horatio Alger," in *Builders of American Institutions*, ed. Frank Freidel, Norman Pollack, and Robert Crunden (Chicago: Rand McNally, 1971), 2:3–17. Henry Ward Beecher, the most popular preacher of the Victorian era, voiced Alger's "pluck and luck" moral and material optimism: "Even in the most compact and closely-populated portions of the East, he that will be frugal, and save continuously, living every day within the bounds of his means, can scarcely help accumulating." Quoted in George M. Marsden, *Religion and American Culture* (New York: Harcourt Brace Jovanovich, 1990), 109.

59. Stevenson, *Scholarly Means*, 3.

60. *History of Doctrine*, 9.

61. D. W. Bebbington, *Patterns in History: A Christian View* (Downer's Grove: IVP, 1979), 85. For an expanded analysis of Whiggery, see Herbert Butterfield, *The Whig Interpretation of History* (London: G. Bell and Sons, 1931).

62. *Discussions in History and Theology*, 161. Fisher continues: "Whoever believes in the teachings of Christ needs no argument to convince him that Christianity is essential to the enduring life of all that is excellent and noble in the products of human activity. 'Ye are the salt of the earth.' It is clear that Christianity, from the moment it first gained a foothold in the Roman empire down to the present time, has never ceased to exert a profound influence upon Christianity" (162).

63. Stevenson, *Scholarly Means*, 24.

64. *Universal History*, 1:94.

65. *Faith and Rationalism*, 188–89. Stevenson suggests that Fisher may have been influenced in his understanding of the progress of doctrine by his friend Philip Schaff's *What Is Church History?* (1846). It is clear that Fisher owed much to Newman. In the introduction to *History of Christian Doctrine* Fisher discusses Newman's *Essay on Development* (1845).

66. *Grounds*, 16. Cf. 2–6; *Discussions in History and Theology*, 164.

67. Regarding anti-Catholic sentiments during the late nineteenth century, the peak of Roman Catholic immigration, see John Higham, *Strangers in the Land: Patterns of American Nativism* (New York: Atheneum, 1963).

68. *Reformation*, 513.

69. Ibid., 14.

70. *Discussions in History and Theology*, 164–65.

71. Because he believed that Protestantism represented the emancipation of the moral consciousness, Fisher judged Calvin's doctrine of predestination "obnoxious" (*Reformation*, 201). Mark Trechock comments: "Above all, predestination seemed to Fisher, as it has to liberals in general, to subvert the moral agency that belongs to the right of private judgment" ("Orthodoxy," 119).

72. Trechock, "Othodoxy," 99–101, 117.

73. Ibid., 125–26.

74. *Discussions in History and Theology*, 287. See also McLoughlin, *Revivals, Awakenings, and Reform*, 116–17 for other New School examples of the congruence of moral freedom and doctrinal development.

75. George Park Fisher, *Modern History*, part 3 of *Outlines of Universal History* (New York: Ivison, Blakeman, Taylor, & Co., 1888), 647. The notion of eschatological diversity or plastic unity was not unique to Fisher. William R. Hutchison writes: "In the face of repeated admonitions from science and from empirical philosophy that the universe is far more fragmented and changeable than idealists had customarily asserted, the almost standard adjustment of idealism and idealistic theology would be to reinterpret the unitive principle as purpose, as dynamic and in process, not finished or static" (*The Modernist Impulse in American Protestantism* [Cambridge, Mass.: Harvard, 1976], 125).

76. *Universal History*, part 3:651.

77. *Discussions in History and Theology*, 485.

15

J. B. LIGHTFOOT

STEVEN R. POINTER

Standing watch over the entrance to the Divinity School of Cambridge University, the statue of Joseph Barber Lightfoot (1828–1889) is a vigilant symbol of the ideals of Christian integrity and academic excellence which he so marvelously combined in his own person. First as Cambridge scholar and later as Anglican bishop, Lightfoot was a distinguished model for nineteenth-century English Christianity in appropriating historical studies for a better understanding of Christianity's development in its early centuries. Perhaps better than anyone else, before or since, he mastered the entire corpus of early Christian literature, canonical and post-canonical, committed to the historical task of establishing and explicating texts in their proper context.

In spite of his enviable record of meticulous scholarship, twentieth-century biographical attention to Lightfoot has been meager. In part this is because, unlike his friends B. F. Westcott, F. J. A. Hort and Edward White Benson, the bachelor Lightfoot had no sons to produce a "life and letters" biography typical of those times. In part, also, the deficiency is attributable to Lightfoot's own personality. F. W. Farrar knew Lightfoot for over thirty-five years and gave this testimony about his former tutor and long standing friend: "The facts of his inner life were revealed to few, perhaps fully to none. His letters were usually brief and business-like, and touched but rarely on his deepest feelings. . . . His best biography, his truest monument, is the great simple, unselfish life which the world saw, and the thought and toil accumulated in his books."[1]

If it is difficult, then, if not impossible, to recapture the private Lightfoot, it is possible to delineate the more public side of his person.[2] The son of a Liverpool accountant, Lightfoot went up to Trinity College, Cambridge, in October 1847 to begin his university studies. By his second year at Trinity, he had come under the tutelage of B. F. Westcott as were Hort and Benson. At that time, the Cambridge curriculum was still dominated by classics and mathematics, and Lightfoot excelled in both, graduating with honors in both in 1851, especially distinguishing himself in classics, where he was the top student ("senior classic"). Thereupon he was elected fellow of Trinity in 1852, tutor in 1857, Hulsean Professor of Divinity in 1861, and Lady Margaret Professor of Divinity in 1875. In what J. A. T. Robinson has called "a single *annus mirabilis*," 1878–79, the Cambridge trio of Lightfoot, Westcott and Hort simultaneously held the three endowed theological chairs at Cambridge (Lady Margaret, Regius and Hulsean, respectively).[3]

Lightfoot's background in classics served him well, providing him with the highest value for philological exactness, which he transferred to his studies of the Greek New Testament and other early Christian literature as well. Between 1854 and 1859 he was involved in founding, editing and contributing articles and reviews to a new journal, which reflected such interests: the *Journal of Classical and Sacred Philology*. His transition from classics to New Testament lecturer occurred in 1854, when his teaching responsibilities at Trinity College dictated that he focus on the Acts of the Apostles and the Pauline epistles.[4] His determination to wed critical scholarship with Christian orthodoxy—and his obvious success in doing so—soon won him eager audiences of students and appropriate recognition from the university.[5]

Not only was he rewarded with a professorship, but Lightfoot served the university well in other capacities also—for sixteen years he was on the Council of the University Senate. Together with Westcott he helped inaugurate the theological program of studies ("tripos") at Cambridge, and was also one of the government commissioners elected by the university to revise the statutes for Oxford and Cambridge. In 1864 Lightfoot took his Doctor of Divinity degree at Cambridge, and later received honorary doctorates from Durham, Oxford, Glasgow, Edinburgh and Dublin.

More than only an academic, Lightfoot had a tenacious sense of loyalty and duty to the Church of England. As an undergraduate he confessed to being "unsettled" as to which party within Anglicanism would win his commitment, finding fault with the Evangelicals (Low Church) and Tractarians (High Church) alike.[6] Ultimately, Lightfoot's "comprehensive churchmanship"[7] attempted to transcend party labels—low, high or broad—and transform divisive tendencies into affirmations of mutual need. Ordained deacon (1854) and priest (1858), Lightfoot continued to increase his ecclesiastical commitments. In 1862 he was appointed chaplain to Queen Victoria and examining chaplain to the Bishop of London. In 1871 he became canon at St. Paul's Cathedral. From 1870 to 1881 Lightfoot served diligently and effectively with a team of scholars revising the New Testament text and translation of the King James Bible. Finally, in January 1879, Lightfoot, after an anguished decision, accepted a calling to serve church and nation as Bishop of Durham, thereby ending his thirty-two year relationship with Cambridge.

Lightfoot spent the last decade (1879–89) of his life in that post. To the surprise of some, the academic-turned-prelate was an effective bishop. Administrating, reconciling, and instructing fit Lightfoot's personality and gifts for service in the church as well as in the university. His most innovative creation combined aspects of both institutions. Lightfoot made Auckland Castle, his episcopal residence, into a small college of theological study for Oxford or Cambridge graduates preparing for ordination in his diocese. Some eighty students came to constitute this "Auckland Brotherhood," with annual reunions reinforcing their bonds of mutual affection and memory.[8]

Lightfoot's scholarly productivity was slowed but not stopped by his move from Cambridge to Durham. Indeed, if anything, his already strenuous work ethic became even more intense. Holidays were not exempt from academic labors: "There are vivid descriptions of Lightfoot being found in a boat or railway carriage with an Armenian or Coptic grammar in hand or calmly correcting proofs while being driven down precipitous paths in Norway."[9]

Lightfoot's linguistic facility matched his work ethic, as he is reputed to have known English, French, German, Italian, Spanish, Latin and Greek, and had a working knowledge of Hebrew, Syriac, Arabic, Ethiopic, Armenian and Coptic. On one occasion, he is alleged to have remarked to an associate, "Does it not sometimes happen to you that when you have read a book you forget in what language it is written?"[10] No wonder that C. K. Barrett declared that Lightfoot's "equipment as a scholar has seldom been equalled, perhaps never surpassed."[11]

Primarily a historian and not a theologian, part of Lightfoot's genius lay in the breadth of his range of studies. Whereas twentieth-century specialization in scholarship has too often created formidable barriers between New Testament studies and church historians, Lightfoot knew no such boundaries. His immersion in the Christian literature of, especially, the first two centuries resulted in significant publications in both domains—the most notable being his three commentaries on Pauline epistles (*Galatians, Philippians*, and *Colossians and Philemon*) and his multi-volume *magnum opus, The Apostolic Fathers*. These works command the bulk of our attention, though first we must attend to the larger context of Lightfoot's thought and to the particulars of his own background.

The years 1859 and 1860 are regarded as something of a watershed for British Christianity. Charles Darwin published *The Origin of Species* in 1859. The next year, *Essays and Reviews*—a collection of essays by seven authors asserting the necessity of free inquiry in religious matters—aroused its own firestorm of controversy. Together, "they were symptomatic of a social and intellectual shift long since begun."[12] A wave of naturalistic thought, long building, finally crested and crashed onto the British shore with these two publications. They signaled "the triumph of scientific method," not only in the realm of nature, but also "as the sole or chief means of establishing the truth" in any intellectual endeavor.[13] This meant, in particular, that the historical events and documents associated with the foundations of Christianity must be subjected to critical enquiry along the lines dictated by scientific method.

Thus, we can now better understand that problems of history were as acute for Christian theology in late nineteenth-century Britain as any that Darwinism could and did pose. Whereas in earlier epochs the historicity of Christianity had been trumpeted as an advantage by its adherents, "the problems of historicity became more obvious" as history became a more intricate, sophisticated discipline (influenced by the scientific method).[14] Questions of continuity and change over time with the recognition of "development" in doctrine, of the particularity of biblical documents allegedly also having universally revelatory significance, and of supernatural events not conforming to the canons of evidence demanded by modern critical methods—these dilemmas, and a hundred more, challenged British Christianity in vital ways in the Victorian era.

Lightfoot did not shrink from such challenges. On the contrary, he welcomed them by openly embracing the new critical methods. Timidity in subjecting the Bible to modern science or criticism, he told his students at Cambridge, was not commendable piety but unbelief; for if the scriptures are true, they must agree with all truth wherever it is found. "It is not much knowledge, but little knowledge that is the dangerous thing here as elsewhere. From the full light of science or criticism we have nothing to fear."[15]

Of course, such a position made Lightfoot vulnerable because the vanguard of biblical scholarship in his day was emanating from German universities, such as Tübingen, with claims that were clearly inimicable to Anglican orthodoxy. Nonetheless, as early as the mid-1850s, Lightfoot announced his position and threw down the gauntlet: "Though we deprecate their views, we are not at liberty to discard the results of their labours .... A sweeping condemnation of everything that is German is not honest, it is not Christian. . . . If the amount of evil in modern German criticism is to be deplored, the amount of good is at least greater, than anything which we have to show on our parts."[16] In effect, Lightfoot's indictment of British scholarship was as severe as it was of German criticism. The greatest challenge was to himself to rectify the situation. Commentaries on Pauline epistles by British scholars C. J. Ellicott, A. P. Stanley and Benjamin Jowett appeared in 1854–55 and represented, in Lightfoot's judgment, an advance unparalleled "in the annals of theological literature in England."[17] Nonetheless, the deficiencies that Lightfoot also perceived in those works convinced him of the need to elevate English New Testament scholarship to a still higher plane.[18]

The appearance of *Essays and Reviews* in 1860, as previously noted, was a significant challenge to the English Church generally and to Lightfoot personally. The most important point of this liberal manifesto was to urge the acceptance of literary and historical criticism of the Bible, summed up in Benjamin Jowett's simple but provocative hermeneutical slogan to "read the Bible like any other book."[19] For conservatives, the threat that such a hermeneutic posed for the traditional understanding of the plenary inspiration of the Bible automatically discredited its use. For theological moderates, such as Lightfoot and his cohorts Westcott and Hort, the greater danger was that the ill-advised radicalism of *Essays and Reviews* would impugn their contemplated plan of a historical-critical approach to the entire New Testament. Consequently, by early 1861, the trio had agreed to author a work that would constitute a mediating position. After several months, however, Lightfoot "found the task burdensome" and so the project was abandoned. Instead, in keeping with his personality, Lightfoot chose the more constructive and less polemical path of completing work on his first commentary, *The Epistle of St. Paul to the Galatians*, as his reply to *Essays and Reviews*.[20]

If Lightfoot's scholarship was shaped by keeping one eye on the contemporary English scene, it is clear that his other eye was trained on

German scholarship. Probably the earliest extant writing of Lightfoot's (dated 1853 by Geoffrey Treloar and Bruce Kaye) is an essay devoted to refuting David Friedrich Strauss's historicist interpretation of Christian origins.[21] That essay, apologetic in purpose, declared that the careful study of history, in conjunction with an enlivened spiritual discernment ("the testimony of the heart"), was the appropriate antidote to German Rationalism. Convinced that the New Testament Gospels furnished reliable testimony about the life and significance of Jesus, Lightfoot was freed to focus his academic labors on Paul.[22] Thus, his attention thereafter shifted from Strauss to Ferdinand Christian Baur and his Tübingen protégés.

Baur (1782–1860), a German Protestant, was, from 1826 until his death, professor of theology at Tübingen. He is widely regarded as the founder of the Tübingen school, famous for its application of Hegelian principles to the development of primitive Christianity. In particular, Baur denied the authenticity of all Pauline epistles except for four and construed the history of the early church as one of struggle and controversy between divergent views, resolved only by the emerging synthesis of second-century Catholicism.[23]

Because Paul's epistle to the Galatians was one of the four documents acknowledged by Baur as authentic, it made a fitting choice for Lightfoot to challenge the Tübingen position on common ground. Thus, it seems that Lightfoot's choice for his first major academic production was influenced *both* by developments at home in the English Church and by his attentive concern to the mostly unfavorable winds emanating from Continental criticism.

When Lightfoot finished penning his acknowledgements to the first edition of *Galatians* in February 1865 at Trinity College, Cambridge, a decisively new model for New Testament commentaries was inaugurated. Conversant with the entire company of commentators who had preceded him, Lightfoot's dialogue with church history about Galatians was impressive in itself.[24] Nonetheless, the highest priority on Lightfoot's agenda was to establish, as far as possible, the original text of the document. No longer bound by the limitations of the sixteenth-century *Textus Receptus*, Lightfoot enjoyed the able assistance of Westcott and Hort in constructing a new critical edition of the text, that strove to be a closer approximation of the Pauline autograph.[25]

Text preceded meaning for Lightfoot. Only after the meticulous labor of reconstructing the text was accomplished could the commentator move on to explication. That latter assignment was not necessarily the same as explaining what a passage had come to mean; the goal was to recover the original meaning of the text, understood in its own linguistic and historical context. Philology and history, then, were the twin keys in unlocking that meaning. In contrast to Benjamin Jowett, Lightfoot's faith in the exactitude of Paul's language was the starting point for his minute analysis of grammar and vocabulary. Similarly, his recognition of the occasional nature of the Pauline epistles exemplified their historical particularity and therefore demanded an equally detailed investigation of their context. Taken together, the effect was novel. As Geoffrey Treloar put it: "Lightfoot's commentary was quite new in the way history and philology functioned reciprocally. Considerations of language controlled inference as to fact, while circumstantial detail behind the text could be the clue to the language."[26]

Thus, the internal evidence of language precisely dissected and the external evidence of historical context faithfully represented were the two keys needed to decipher, not only the epistles of Paul, but all ancient Christian writings. If this method appears painfully commonplace in the late twentieth century, C. K. Barrett reminds us that it is so, in large measure, because much of Lightfoot's work is so convincing that it is taken for granted as common knowledge today.[27]

The other noteworthy feature of the *Galatians* commentary was Lightfoot's use of "dissertations," or extended essays on issues arising from the text. In the case of *Galatians*, he appended three such dissertations to the commentary: "Were the Galatians Celts or Teutons?" "The Brethren of the Lord," and, most importantly, "St. Paul and the Three." In the preface to the commentary as a whole, Lightfoot made it explicit that "the historical views of the Tübingen school" were within his purview and that he was confident that such views were "too extravagant" to be long-lasting in their persuasiveness.[28] In that third dissertation, detailing the apostle Paul's relationship with James, Peter and John, Lightfoot returned again to do battle with Tübingen. Examining the early history of Jewish and Gentile Christianity, he was convinced that an alternative account, more in keeping with the traditional view affirming a general unity of belief and harmony in the first century church—acknowledged conflicts notwithstanding—would discredit the skeptical and radical conclusions of Tübingen. Moreover, Lightfoot asserted that the Tübingen deficiencies were the result of a faulty relationship between a scholar's presuppositions and his methods. A "habit of suspicious interpretation, which neglects plain facts and dwells on doubtful allusions," was likely to blame for the tendency, alleged by Lightfoot, that the Tübingen school began with its theory and not with the evidence.[29]

The overwhelmingly non-polemical character of Lightfoot's *Galatians* commentary is remarkable. The combination of British reticence, the decorum expected of a Victorian gentleman, and Lightfoot's own gracious personality explain, in part, the tenor and tone. However, we must also remember the larger audience and agenda. Lightfoot fervently believed that the university had a spiritual power and responsibility to serve the church and the nation. One significant way of discharging that duty was to demonstrate the necessity of appropriating the historical-critical study of Christianity in a constructive manner. If Lightfoot's eyes were on the failings of contemporary British and German biblical scholarship, his other senses were attuned to the apologetic need for convincing a larger and more traditionally conservative audience (of clerics and other social elites) as to why such scholarship was necessary at all. Thus, even on those relatively rare occasions when his opposition is explicit, it is couched in the language of rectifying "exaggerations" rather than countering heresy or disbelief. Instead, Lightfoot went to great lengths to argue that "mere denunciation" of threatening views is unwise because "the abnegation of reason is not the evidence of faith but the confession of despair."[30] Perhaps Lightfoot's *Galatians*, then, is best seen as his attempt to model the Christian scholar's responsible use of historical-critical methods and thereby steer a course between the Scylla of flawed contemporary scholarship and the Charybdis of native conservative resistance and wariness.

Over the next decade, Lightfoot produced two more commentaries on Pauline epistles: *Philippians*[31] in 1868 and *Colossians and Philemon*[32] in 1875. Both followed the model of *Galatians*: a newly revised Greek text; introductions that dealt with the history of interpretation, questions of authenticity (which for Lightfoot were always bound up with authorship), and issues of historical context (especially about the recipient congregation and city); extensive exegetical notes on the grammatical constructions and vocabulary of the text; and two or three lengthy dissertations per volume on issues of special concern. Once again, polemical statements or criticism of other scholars were kept to a minimum. Because many Tübingen scholars, following Baur's lead, denied that these epistles were Pauline, Lightfoot felt constrained to voice his decorous disagreement: "I cannot think that the mere fact of their having been brought forward by men of ability and learning is sufficient to entitle objections of this stamp to a serious refutation. They have not the suggestive character which sometimes marks even the more extravagant theories of this school, and serve only as a warning of the condemnation which unrestrained negative criticism pronounces upon itself."[33]

In addition, Lightfoot was satisfied that Baur's criticisms had already been refuted successfully several times by others.[34]

Similarly, Lightfoot's commentaries also eschewed doctrinal or theological discussions; indeed, he valued Paul's epistle to the Philippians precisely because its contents call us away from the distractions of "theological definitions or ecclesiastical rules" and back "to the very heart and centre of the Gospel—the life of Christ and the life in Christ."[35] A private, reticent man, Lightfoot, nonetheless, was more likely to open the window of his soul than he was to engage in theological wrangling.

Lightfoot's preference for historical investigation is apparent on every page of his works. At times his empiricism led him in a positivistic direction. He boasted of history's being "obviously the sole upright, impartial referee" able to adjudicate among the "clamour of antagonistic opinions" on the theological playing field.[36] At other times, his claims for historical epistemology were far more modest: "Every historical question must be decided by striking a balance between conflicting probabilities."[37] In fact, try as he did to avoid systematic theology, he found historical theology unavoidable.

One of the best examples of Lightfoot's excursions into historical theology was his lengthy dissertation on "The Christian Ministry."[38] History seemed to prove conclusively that before the middle of the second century the Christian church had developed a threefold order of ministry (bishops, presbyters and deacons), but when, why and with what authority? And, in particular, how do we account for the rise of episcopacy? Lightfoot concluded that the office of bishop developed gradually and evenly, emerging not from the position of apostle but out of the ranks of presbyters, where the office had, in turn, been adopted by the early church from the Jewish synagogue. Only in the third century, with Tertullian and especially Cyprian, did the sacerdotal view of the clergy develop. Lightfoot's candor was misconstrued by some as an attack on the episcopacy. Consequently, in subsequent editions of *Philippians*, Lightfoot reprinted a collection of passages from other writings in the preface to solidify his Anglican standing.[39]

Regrettably, Lightfoot never published any more commentaries, either on the Pauline epistles or any other part of the New Testament. After his death a volume of his lecture notes on 1–2 Thessalonians, 1 Corinthians (through chapter seven), Romans (also through chapter seven) and Ephesians (through 1:14) was published.[40] Additional lecture notes which focused on the internal and external evidence for the authenticity of the Gospel of John were also posthumously published.[41] Finally, though Lightfoot never realized his hopes to produce a commentary on the Acts of the Apostles, we do have access to his thoughts on that significant New Testament document via published articles and manuscript lecture notes.[42]

In all his studies of the New Testament, Lightfoot combined the scrupulous application of his historical-exegetical methods with a quietly reverential respect for the traditional canonical status of scripture. As a result, some scholars find the latter (his theological presuppositions) to have inhibited the former (his judgment as a critical historian), thereby rendering his biblical scholarship less successful than his work as a church historian among the post-apostolic fathers.[43] To be sure, Lightfoot had theological presuppositions and was influenced by them. In particular, as I have argued elsewhere,[44] the "canonical difference"—the acceptance of the New Testament as inspired scripture—loomed large in Lightfoot's differentiated treatment of early Christian literature (at least, larger than his own self-awareness of such an influence). It did so, not simply because of Lightfoot's traditionalist sympathies with Christian orthodoxy, but even more, I believe, because of his hermeneutical sensitivity to read and hear an ancient document on the basis of what it purported to be. His keen mind and ear could not miss or dismiss the symbiotic character of divine and human elements he found in the New Testament documents. Thus, Lightfoot's scholarship seems to demonstrate his own hermeneutical maxim: "Interpret the documents of early Christianity on the basis of what they purport to be," rather than Benjamin Jowett's provocative call to "read the Bible like any other book."

Lightfoot's recognition of the dual character of Scripture demanded that he come to an understanding of the mutual relationship of its divine and human components. He affirmed the idea of the Bible's "inspiration," but was quick to explain that he understood inspiration to be "a moral and spiritual power," "not a mechanical power or a magical agency." He saw readily enough that different views of inspiration were determined by favoring one element over the other, and was convinced that "the true view is a mean between these extremes, or rather it is a combination of the two." This "both/and" approach to the Bible's inspiration allowed Lightfoot to affirm the progressive character of redemptive history and the complementary, but not contradictory, character of the diversity of New Testament writings.[45]

Beyond this, however, Lightfoot was reluctant to go in specifying the results of inspiration. Early in his career he had been chided by Hort for even hinting that scholarship not disturb any preconceived assumptions of orthodoxy. However much Westcott and Hort might desire and even presume the absolute truth of Scripture, the attribution of "infallibility" could only be done "by unbiased *a posteriori* criticism."[46]Obviously, Lightfoot adopted their position and thereafter disdained any precise position on the implications of biblical inspiration. In fact, his very last letter—written only days before his death in December, 1889—explains to his life-long friend, Edward White Benson, why he had declined the request of his fellow bishops to write a paper on the Church of England's teaching in relation to recent views of biblical inspiration, regarding it as "dangerous on such a topic . . . to make everything right and tight." His faith was still serene even with "a thousand questions [left] open, so long as I am convinced on two or three main lines."[47]

Lightfoot's conviction of the New Testament's inspiration was secure but open-ended. It meant that the origins of such documents could never be reduced *exclusively* to those of a natural, historical setting. Yet, the fact that those writings did have such an origin as well—an origin that gave them an authentically historical character still not sufficiently recognized by traditional orthodoxy, Lightfoot believed—linked the New Testament documents with the world of other early Christian literature. And that linkage meant that both sets of writings lent themselves to a common historical-exegetical method of understanding.

Thus, a common method of inquiry allowed Lightfoot to range freely across the corpus of early Christian literature, with his patristics and New Testament scholarship cross-fertilizing each other. One indication of that mutual pollination comes via the frequency of his citations. The indexes to his five major published volumes in biblical studies (three commentaries on Pauline epistles, *Biblical Essays*, and *Notes from Unpublished Commentaries*) disclose that the top eight authors Lightfoot cited were all from the patristic era. The first modern writer on the list was F. C. Baur from Tübingen at number thirteen.[48]

However congenial Lightfoot found his work of producing commentaries on the Pauline epistles, he, nonetheless, found himself gradually called to a new focus: the extra-canonical Christian literature of the first two centuries. Over the last three decades of his life, that shift in priorities meant that his patristics' studies were not only informing his New Testament scholarship, they had become the centerpiece of his life's work. As a result, the five-volume edition of *The Apostolic Fathers* is, without a doubt, Lightfoot's crowning work. Martin Hengel has pronounced that work "a treasure chamber the riches of which are inexhaustible even for today's reader."[49] Stephen Neill's glowing praise included the recommendation that every first-year theological student read at least five hundred pages of Lightfoot's tome.[50] Indeed, in that exhortation Neill simply echoes Lightfoot's own sentiments: "The Ignatian Epistles are an exceptionally good training ground for the student of early Christian literature and history. They present in typical and instructive forms the most varied problems, textual, exegetical, doctrinal, and historical. One who has thoroughly grasped these problems will be placed in possession of a master key which will open to him vast storehouses of knowledge."[51]

Part 1 of *The Apostolic Fathers*, dealing with Clement of Rome, was published in two volumes in 1869. Part 2, focusing on Ignatius and Polycarp, was issued in three volumes in 1885. A revised and somewhat enlarged second edition of Part 2 was published in 1889, whereupon Lightfoot resumed his revision of Clement, which continued until his death (the second edition of Part 1 was published posthumously in 1890). Two years after Lightfoot's death, J. R. Harmer, his younger colleague and domestic chaplain, collected and edited a larger sampling of texts (together with English translations) in a one-volume work.[52]

How do we explain Lightfoot's shift from the Pauline epistles to the likes of Clement, Ignatius and Polycarp? Prolonged intimacy with the writings of these early Christians had an intrinsic worth that he believed was neglected. Thus, Lightfoot could speak affectionately of "the gentleness and serenity of Clement . . . the fiery zeal of Ignatius . . . the unbroken constancy of Polycarp."[53] Yet, he also understood that the fragmentary remains of early Christian literature outside the canon had a strategic value "wholly disproportionate to their literary merits."[54] Hence, Lightfoot acknowledged that the reason for his long labors in this field was not merely for the "educational value" but to answer radical critics. German criticism, especially from Tübingen, in the previous half-century, was overzealous. It required scholars to rebuild what it had injudiciously tried to destroy. Even though construction would be on "the immediately outlying buildings" of Christendom and not "'the House of the Lord' itself" (i.e. the New Testament), Lightfoot saw sufficient value and linkage to sign on.[55]

The task of re-building involved the same meticulous concern for detail that characterized Lightfoot's biblical scholarship. Establishing the best reading of a text and then employing the same historical and exegetical methods to elucidate the meaning and significance of the text were his preferred way of proceeding. Authentic criticism for Lightfoot was neither reckless speculation nor ingenious theorizing; rather, it was "wholesome self-restraint . . . the sober weighing of probabilities . . . the careful consideration of evidence."[56]

In particular, then, the task of re-building for Lightfoot meant reassessing the authenticity of these documents. Baur's theories about the dating and development of the New Testament canon as largely a late second-century phenomenon required him to deny the authenticity, for example, of all the letters attributed to Ignatius. But Lightfoot recognized that establishing the authenticity of *any* of his letters would have devastating repercussions for such a position.[57] Consequently, in a section exceeding one hundred pages in length, Lightfoot painstakingly reviewed the arguments for and against the genuineness of the Ignatian epistles, as usual, under the twin headings of external and internal evidence. His conclusion, affirming the authenticity of the so-called middle recension of the seven epistles of Ignatius, has remained firm to the present.[58]

Because the historical worth of a document was intrinsically connected to its authenticity (or so Lightfoot believed), he placed great value on ascertaining its genuineness. Again, the primary means to that end was a careful evaluation of the available external and internal evidence. Lightfoot thought that the proper starting point was with all the relevant evidence external to the document itself. That done, a presumption for or against the traditionally attributed authorship could then be tested by the internal evidence of the document. Within the text itself, Lightfoot looked for indications of what the document professed to be, by whom and when it was written, and then he asked: "Is its internal character consonant with this profession? If it is not, then we can no longer trust it as a historical narrative."[59] One such case was the document "A Life of Polycarp," which Lightfoot found full of legends and demonstrably false, for "wherever it crosses the path of authentic history, its falsity is betrayed."[60] On the other hand, explicit and convincing external testimony about authorship offered a strong enough presumption for its authenticity that could only be negated by "clear and indisputable tokens of a later date in the document itself, such as proved anachronisms." Unless, of course, early Christian writings were to be tried by different critical standards than other ancient literature![61]

There can be no doubt that the careful, judicious, even cautious judgments that characterized Lightfoot's historical scholarship also resonated well with, and helped reinforce, his Anglican sentiments. However dispassionate his academic persona might appear, the totality of his personhood (philosophical presuppositions, faith profession, ecclesiastical commitment, personality, temperament, and so forth) clearly shaped his perspective in assessing the evidence of history. As a result, Lightfoot was well disposed to see the essential continuity in the historical development of Christianity, and assertions to the contrary were anathema to him. Thus, for example, the figure of Polycarp was important because "in him one single link connected the earthly life of Christ with the close of the second century. . . . S. John, Polycarp, Irenaeus—this was the succession which guaranteed the continuity of the evangelical record and of the apostolic teaching."[62] Modern radical criticism, by contrast, seemed to view early Christian history through the jaundiced perspective of essential *discontinuity*. "Growth, progress, development"—these Lightfoot could see and affirm, but if he was at all successful in rehabilitating the credibility of the witness of Clement, Ignatius, Polycarp and others, then "all such theories of discontinuity must fall to the ground."[63]

Lightfoot's agenda, in his historical scholarship as well as in his biblical scholarship, was the positive task of modelling the assets of constructive criticism. Some might regret that Lightfoot never engaged his Tübingen adversaries head-on in a point-by-point fashion. That, however, would have given his work a decidedly polemical slant and detracted from his own purposes of demonstrating the virtues of critical scholarship. In fact, on only one occasion—a perceived slander of his friend, B. F. Westcott—did Lightfoot ever condescend to join the fracas of polemics.[64] Nevertheless, the views of Baur and other Tübingen scholars were never far removed from Lightfoot's purview. Strident language was sprinkled throughout his writings, variously referring to the need to resist "academic terrorism," to beware of "the feverish and restless criticism of our day," and to await the restoration of a "healthier tone . . . when criticism has recovered its balance."[65] Nor was his criticism always oblique: "No man has shown himself more ready to adopt the wildest speculations, if they fell in with his own preconceived theories, than Baur. . . . Nothing has exercised a more baneful influence on criticism in the country of critics than the fascination of his name. While he has struck out some lines which have stimulated thought, and thus have not been unfruitful in valuable results, the glamour of his genius has on the whole exercised a fatal effect on the progress of a sober and discriminating study of the early records of Christianity."[66]

Contemporary scholarship on Lightfoot has helpfully connected his ideas and concerns to his own English ecclesiastical context as well as to German criticism.[67] Less persuasive, however, has been the attempt to minimize the differences between Lightfoot and Baur, suggesting that their differences reduced to the latter's philosophical mind-set asking the right questions and the former's philological superiority excelling in answering them.[68] Instead, Martin Hengel's comparison of the two is more on target in arguing that their differences were more striking than their similarities.[69]

Even more contested has been the claim that Lightfoot successfully refuted Baur. The laudatory contributors, especially J. Armitage Robinson and A. C. Headlam, to *Lightfoot of Durham* (1933) first championed Lightfoot's triumph over Tübingen, with Robinson asserting that Lightfoot had "knocked the last 'nail in the coffin of the Tübingen theory.'"[70] Stephen Neill promulgated such a view to much wider circles in the publication of his 1962 Firth Lectures, where he gave Lightfoot prominent attention and, said that Lightfoot had slain Tübingen "stone dead."[71] In response, more recent critics have sounded a revisionist note: far from demolishing the *substance* of the Tübingen hypothesis about early Christianity, all that Lightfoot destroyed was the Tübingen *chronology* (instead of stretching into the second century, the dialectical process that yielded Catholic Christianity was pushed back into the first).[72]

What can be said in response to those conflicting claims? The "triumphalist" side probably "pulled a Mark Twain" in greatly exaggerating the demise of Tübingen. Stephen Neill himself noted, "One of the curious features in German theology is that no ghost is ever laid. A century after his death Baur still walks abroad, and echoes of his ideas are found in all kinds of places."[73] In short, the spirit of Baur is alive and well, present wherever modern critics of early Christianity demand that historical methods be thoroughly rationalistic and divested of theological presuppositions. Nevertheless, the "revisionist" side has its perspective automatically skewed by the philosophical constraints that the above atheological methodology dictates. If, then, Lightfoot's work severely damaged the credibility of the particulars of the Tübingen hypothesis, it can hardly be faulted for not producing a philosophical and methodological consensus for modern criticism as well. Twentieth-century scholarship has continued to produce a plethora of conflicting views about the development of early Christianity, its unity and diversity, the historicity of its records, and so forth. The relationship of the historian and the believer (of whatever sort) in the critical scholar still awaits a definitive resolution.

Lightfoot's accomplishment, however, is best seen in the longevity of his substantive scholarship. In an era where scholarship from the previous decade is often passé and probably out of print, one must note the staying power of Lightfoot's work, both on the Pauline epistles and the early church writers, now well into its second century of influence. That achievement certainly justifies Lightfoot's stature as a consummate craftsman and that stature, not the statue in the Cambridge Divinity School, is undoubtedly his "truest monument." F. W. Farrar was right.

Bibliography

Major Primary Sources

Unpublished:

J.B. Lightfoot Papers, Dean and Chapter Library, Durham Cathedral, Durham, England.

Published:

Acts of the Apostles." In *A Dictionary of the Bible*, edited by William Smith and J. M. Fuller, 1: 25–43. 2nd ed. London: John Murray, 1893.

The Apostolic Fathers. Part 1. S. Clement of Rome. 2 vols. 2nd ed. London and New York: Macmillan, 1890.

The Apostolic Fathers. Part 2. S. Ignatius. S. Polycarp. 3 vols. 2nd ed. London and New York: Macmillan, 1889.

Biblical Essays. London and New York: Macmillan, 1893.

Essays on the Work Entitled Supernatural Religion. 2nd ed. London: Macmillan, 1893.

"Eusebius of Caesarea." In *A Dictionary of Christian Biography*, edited by William Smith and Henry Ware, 2: 308–48. London: John Murray, 1880.

Historical Essays. London and New York: Macmillan, 1895.

Notes on Epistles of St. Paul from Unpublished Commentaries. 2nd ed. London and New York: Macmillan, 1904.

Saint Paul's Epistles to the Colossians and to Philemon. London: Macmillan, 1897.

Saint Paul's Epistle to the Galatians. 10th ed. London and New York: Macmillan, 1896.

Saint Paul's Epistle to the Philippians. 12th ed. London: Macmillan, 1898.

Major Secondary Sources

Barrett, C. K. "Joseph Barber Lightfoot." *The Durham University Journal* 64, no. 3 (June 1972): 193–204.

———. "Quomodo Historia Conscribenda Sit." *New Testament Studies* 28 (July 1982): 303–20.

Dunn, James D. G., ed. *The Lightfoot Centenary Lectures. Durham University Journal* Special supplement (January 1992).

Eden, George R., and F. C. MacDonald, eds. *Lightfoot of Durham*. Cambridge: University Press, 1933.

Hort, F. J. A. "Joseph Barber Lightfoot." *Dictionary of National Biography*, 11: 1111–19.

Kaye, Bruce N. "Lightfoot and Baur on Early Christianity." *Novum Testamentum* 26, no. 3 (1984): 193–224.

Kaye, B. N., and G. R. Treloar. "J. B. Lightfoot and New Testament Interpretation: An Unpublished Manuscript of 1855." *The Durham University Journal* 82, no. 2 (July 1990): 161–75.

Loane, Marcus L. *Three Faithful Servants*. Blackwood, Australia: New Creation Publications, 1991.

Morgan, Robert C. "Non Angli sed Angeli: Some Anglican Reactions to German Gospel Criticism." In *New Studies in Theology*, edited by Stephen Sykes and Derek Holmes, 1–30. London: Duckworth, 1980.

Neill, Stephen. *The Interpretation of the New Testament 1861–1961.* London: Oxford University Press, 1964.

Robinson, John A. T. *Joseph Barber Lightfoot.* Durham Cathedral Lecture 1981. Durham: Dean and Chapter of Durham, 1981.

Savage, H. E. "Bishop Lightfoot's Influence: His Trust in Young Men." Edited with an introductory note by B.S. Benedikz. *The Durham University Journal* 77, no. 1 (December 1984): 1–6.

Treloar, Geoffrey R. "J.B. Lightfoot and St. Paul, 1854–65: A Study of Intentions and Method" *Lucas.* Review of the Evangelical History Association (Australia), 7 (December 1989): 5–34.

Treloar, G. R., and B. N. Kaye. "J.B. Lightfoot on Strauss and Christian Origins: An Unpublished Manuscript." *The Durham University Journal* 79, no. 2 (June 1987): 165–200.

NOTES

1. F. W. Farrar, "Bishop Lightfoot," *The Contemporary Review* (February 1890): 170-71.

2. See Marcus L. Loane, *Three Faithful Servants* (Blackwood, South Australia: New Creation Publications, 1991), 91-92 for a discussion of the available sources.

3. J. A. T. Robinson, "J.B. Lightfoot: The Champion of Critical Scholarship," (typescript of sermon, 7 November 1976, Trinity College Library, Cambridge).

4. G. R. Treloar, "J.B. Lightfoot and St. Paul, 1854-65: A Study of Intentions and Methods," *Lucas Review of the Evangelical History Association* (Australia) 7 (December 1989):6.

5. Hort recalls that "no lecture room then available sufficed to contain the hearers [of Lightfoot's lectures] . . . so that leave had to be obtained for the use of the [Great] hall of Trinity." F. J. A. Hort, "Joseph Barber Lightfoot," *Dictionary of National Biography*, 11:1112.

6. A. C. Benson, *The Life of Edward White Benson* (London: Macmillan, 1899), 1:55–56,59–60,64–66.

7. David M. Thompson, "Lightfoot as Victorian Churchman" in *The Lightfoot Centenary Lectures*, ed. James D. G. Dunn, *Durham University Journal* (special supplement, January 1992):17.

8. See, e.g., H. E. Savage, "Bishop Lightfoot's Influence: His Trust in Young Men," ed. B. S. Benedikz, *Durham University Journal* (December 1984):1-6.

9. J. A. T. Robinson, "Joseph Barber Lightfoot," *Durham Cathedral Lecture 1981* (Durham: Dean and Chapter, 1981), 14-15.

10. George R. Eden and F. C. MacDonald, eds., *Lightfoot of Durham* (Cambridge: University Press, 1933), 118–19.

11. C. K. Barrett, "Joseph Barber Lightfoot," *Durham University Journal* (June 1972):194.

12. Peter Addinall, *Philosophy and Biblical Interpretation* (Cambridge: University Press, 1991), 172.

13. Ibid., 172, 174.

14. Peter Hinchliff, *God and History* (Oxford: Clarendon Press, 1992), 8.

15. B. N. Kaye and G. R. Treloar, "J. B. Lightfoot and New Testament Interpretation: An Unpublished Manuscript of 1855," *Durham University Journal* (July 1990):174.

16. Ibid.

17. J. B. Lightfoot, "Recent Editions of St. Paul's Epistles," *Journal of Classical and Sacred Philology 3* (March 1856):83.

18. For a fuller discussion, see Treloar, "Lightfoot and St. Paul," 7–12.

19. Ibid., 13. See also Ieuan Ellis, *Seven Against Christ: A Study of "Essays and Reviews"* (Leiden: 1980).

20. Treloar, "Lightfoot and St. Paul," 14.

21. G. R. Treloar and B. N. Kaye, "J.B. Lightfoot on Strauss and Christian Origins: An Unpublished Manuscript," *The Durham University Journal* 79, no. 2 (June 1987):165–200.

22. Though Lightfoot did lecture on the Fourth Gospel—posthumously included in *Biblical Essays* (London and New York: Macmillan, 1893)—his attention to the synoptic Gospels was minimal.

23. Scholarship on Baur has been very polarized. For favorable assessments see Peter C. Hodgson, *The Formation of Historical Theology; A Study of Ferdinand Christian Baur* (New York: Harper and Row, 1966), and Robert Morgan, "Ferdinand Christian Baur" in *Nineteenth Century Religious Thought in the West*, ed. Ninian Smart et al. (Cambridge: University Press, 1985), 1:261–89. For a devastating critique of Baur, see especially Horton Harris, *The Tubingen School: A Historical and Theological Investigation of the School of F. C. Baur*, second edition (Grand Rapids, Mich.: Baker Book House, 1990).

24. I consulted the fourth edition of Lightfoot, *Saint Paul's Epistle to the Galatians; A Revised Text with Introduction, Notes, and Dissertations* (London and New York: Macmillan, 1896); see, for example, his assessment of patristic accounts of the collision between Peter and Paul at Antioch (128–132) and his appendix on "The Patristic Commentaries on This Epistle" (227–236).

25. On the textual critical work of Westcott and Hort, see Graham Patrick, *F. J. A. Hort, Eminent Victorian* (Sheffield: Almond Press, 1988).

26. Treloar, "Lightfoot and St. Paul," 17.

27. Barrett, "Lightfoot," 201.

28. Lightfoot, *Galatians*, xi.

29. Ibid., 373, 294.

30. Ibid., xi–xii.

31. J. B. Lightfoot, *Saint Paul's Epistle to the Philippians; A Revised Text with Introduction, Notes, and Dissertations*, 12th ed. (London: Macmillan, 1898), [1st ed., 1868].

32. J. B. Lightfoot, *Saint Paul's Epistle to the Colossians and to Philemon; A Revised Text with Introductions, Notes, and Dissertations* (London: Macmillan, 1897), [1st ed., 1875].

33. Lightfoot, *Philippians*, 74.

34. Ibid., 74–75.

35. Ibid., 73.

36. Ibid., 187.

37. Lightfoot, *Galatians*, 55.

38. Lightfoot, *Philippians*, 181–269.

39. Ibid., xi–xiv.

40. J. B. Lightfoot, *Notes on Epistles of St. Paul from Unpublished Commentaries*, 2nd ed. (London and New York: Macmillan, 1904) [1st ed., 1895].

41. J. B. Lightfoot, *Biblical Essays* (London and New York: Macmillan, 1893). J. A. T. Robinson said in his 1981 Durham Cathedral Lecture on Lightfoot that, in his judgment, Lightfoot's contribution to Johannine studies is still underrated and surmises an eventual return by the consensus of New Testament scholarship to accept Lightfoot's position on the apostolic authorship and essential historicity of the Fourth Gospel. (Lightfoot, 16–19).

42. For Lightfoot's published articles on Acts, see especially "Acts of the Apostles" in *A Dictionary of the Bible*, 2nd ed. ed. William Smith and J. M. Fuller (London: John Murray, 1893), 25–43, and "Discoveries Illustrating the Acts of the Apostles," appendix to *Essays on the Work Entitled Supernatural Religion*, 2nd ed. (London: Macmillan, 1893) [1st ed. 1889; reprinted from *The Contemporary Review*, December 1874–May 1878], 291–302. Lightfoot's lectures on Acts, along with other surviving papers, are housed at the Dean and Chapter Library of the Cathedral in Durham, England. For a laudatory assessment of Lightfoot's work on Acts, see W. Ward Gasque, *A History of the Interpretation of the Acts of the Apostles* (Peabody, Mass.: Hendrickson, 1989) [1st ed., 1975]; for more critical assessments see C.K. Barrett, "Quomodo Historia Conscribenda Sit," *New Testament Studies* 28 (July 1982): 303–20, and Bruce Kaye, "Lightfoot and Baur on Early Christianity," *Novum Testamentum* 26, no. 3 (1984): 193–224.

43. E.g., see Barrett, "Quomodo Historia," 316–19.

44. Steven R. Pointer, "J.B. Lightfoot as a Christian Historian of Early Christian Literature," *Christian Scholar's Review*, forthcoming.

45. Lightfoot, *Biblical Essays*, 224–27.

46. Arthur Fenton Hort, *Life and Letters of Fenton John Anthony Hort* (London: Macmillan, 1896) 1:420; Arthur Westcott, *Life and Letters of Brooke Foss Westcott* (London: Macmillan, 1903), 1:207.

47. Arthur Christopher Benson, *The Life of Edward White Benson* (London: Macmillan, 1899), 2:289. Treloar has succinctly summarized Lightfoot's position as regarding inspiration not "as a dogma to be defined and accepted, but a phenomenon to be studied and measured. Part of the task of interpretations was to fix its means and limits" (Kaye and Treloar, "Lightfoot and New Testament Interpretation," 166).

48. The cumulative number of citations compiled from the indexes of those five volumes results in the following list:

1. Clement of Rome - 56
2. Ignatius - 49
3. Jerome - 47
4. Origen - 45
5. Tertullian - 45
6. John Chrysostom - 42
7. Irenaeus - 39
8. Clement of Alexandria - 36
9. Josephus - 33
10. Philo - 32
11. Polycarp - 30
12. Eusebius - 27
13. F.C. Baur - 23

49. Martin Hengel, "Bishop Lightfoot and the Tubingen School on the Gospel of John and the Second Century" in *The Lightfoot Centenary Lectures*, ed. James D. G. Dunn, *Durham University Journal* (special supplement, January 1992):38.

50. Stephen Neill, *The Interpretation of the New Testament 1861-1961* (New York: Oxford University Press, 1964), 57.

51. J. B. Lightfoot, *The Apostolic Fathers. Part 2. S. Ignatius, S. Polycarp. Revised Texts with Introductions, Notes, Dissertations, and Translations*, 2nd. ed. (London and New York: Macmillan 1889), 1:xv.

52. That work has recently been updated and reissued: *The Apostolic Fathers*, trans. J. B. Lightfoot and J. R. Hurmer, ed. and revised by Michael W. Holmes, 2nd ed. (Grand Rapids, Mich.: Baker Book House, 1989).

53. J. B. Lightfoot, *The Apostolic Fathers. Part 1. S. Clement of Rome. A Revised Text with Introductions, Notes, Dissertations, and Translations,* 2nd ed. (London and New York: Macmillan, 1890), 1:7.

54. Ibid.

55. Lightfoot, *Apostolic Fathers, Part 2,* 1:xv.

56. Lightfoot, *Apostolic Fathers, Part 1,* 1:357.

57. Lightfoot, *Apostolic Fathers, Part 2,* 1:283.

58. Ibid., 328-430. Lightfoot's conclusions, fourteen in all, are found on pages 422–23. For the current state of scholarship on the question, see W.R. Schoedel, "Are the Letters of Ignatius of Antioch Authentic?" *Religious Studies Review* 6 (1980): 196–201, and W. R. Schoedel, *Ignatius of Antioch; A Commentary on the Letters of Ignatius of Antioch* (Philadelphia: Fortress Press, 1985).

59. Lightfoot, *Apostolic Fathers, Part 2,* 1:609.

60. Ibid., 1:643.

61. Ibid., 1:581.

62. Ibid., 1:474.

63. Ibid., 1:475.

64. See Lightfoot, *Essays on the Work Entitled Supernatural Religion.* Stephen Neill has declared Lightfoot's essays to be "the best controversial writing in English" since the 1600s. (*Interpretation of the New Testament,* 37.)

65. Lightfoot, *Apostolic Fathers, Part 2,* xi, 604–5.

66. Lightfoot, *Apostolic Fathers, Part 1,* 1:357–58.

67. See especially Treloar, "Lightfoot and St Paul."

68. Barrett, "Quomodo Historia," 318. More moderately, Kaye, "Lightfoot and Baur" takes this tack as well.

69. Hengel, "Bishop Lightfoot and the Tubingen School," 33–36.

70. Eden and MacDonald, *Lightfoot of Durham,* 133.

71. Neill, *The Interpretation of the New Testament,* 55.

72. Barrett quotes R. H. Fuller, *The New Testament in Current Study* on this point in "Quomodo Historia," 310. For even more forceful revisionism, see Robert C. Morgan, "Non Angli sed Angeli: Some Anglican Reactions to German Gospel Criticism" in *New Studies in Theology,* ed. Stephen Sykes and Derek Holmes (London: Duckworth, 1980), 1–30, and R. Morgan, "Historical Criticism and Christology: England and Germany" in *England and Germany: Studies in Theological Diplomacy,* ed. S.W. Sykes (Frankfurt Am Main: Verlag Peter D. Lang, 1982), 80–112.

73. Neill, *The Interpretation of the New Testament,* 58.

16

THOMAS MARTIN LINDSAY

DONALD K. MCKIM

Thomas Martin Lindsay (1843–1914) was born in Lesmahagrow, Lanarkshire, Scotland in 1843. His parents belonged to the Relief Church, a body deposed by the Church of Scotland's General Assembly in 1752 for defending the right of a congregation to choose its minister.[1] Lindsay studied at the Universities of Glasgow and Edinburgh where he was an outstanding student. In Edinburgh, he became an assistant to Professor A. C. Fraser before beginning his training for ministry in the Free Church of Scotland. After graduation, Lindsay became an assistant with R. S. Candlish at Free St. George's Church, Edinburgh. In 1872 he was elected to the Chair of Church History at the Glasgow Free Church College where he served until his death. From 1902 he was also Principal of the (then) United Free College.

Lindsay was a prolific writer of books and articles. He was a contributor to the ninth edition of *The Encyclopedia Britannica* (1875–88) and also wrote chapters in the Cambridge Modern and Medieval History series. In 1902, Lindsay delivered the eighteenth series of the Cunningham Lectures in Edinburgh, published as *The Church and the Ministry in the Early Centuries*.[2] In these he sought to "pourtray the organized life of the

Christian Society as that was lived in the thousands of little communities formed by the proclamation of the Gospel of our Lord during the first three centuries."[3] He is best known for his two volume history of the Reformation in the International Theological Library series published as *A History of the Reformation: The Reformation in Germany from its Beginning to the Religious Peace of Augsburg* (1906) and *A History of the Reformation: The Reformation in Switzerland, France, the Netherlands, Scotland and England, The Anabaptist and Socinian Movements, The Counter Reformation* (1907).[4] This work has had a continuous printing history and establishes Lindsay as one of the foremost Scottish Reformation historians. His intention was to write an account of the Reformation as "a great religious movement amid its social environment."[5] Among his other works were *Luther and the German Reformation* in the World's Epoch-Makers series, *Revivals* and biblical commentaries on Mark, Luke, and Acts in the Handbooks for Bible Classes series.[6] His son, Alexander Dunlop Lindsay, published a collection of his father's addresses and sermons in 1915.[7]

Lindsay was a friend and supporter of W. Robertson Smith (1846–94), a brilliant Scottish Semitic scholar who was tried for heresy by the General Assembly of the Free Church of Scotland in 1881. It was alleged that his critical views of the Bible undermined the church's doctrine of the inspiration of Scripture. The Assembly removed him from his Chair at the University of Aberdeen. Lindsay was a defender and close advisor to Smith.[8]

Lindsay's social concerns were seen through his involvement in crafting agitation and with labor leaders. In addition, he convened the Free Church/United Free Foreign Missions for fifteen years. He received the D.D. from Glasgow and the L.L.D. from St. Andrews (1906).[9]

THE CHURCH AND ITS MINISTRY IN THE EARLY CENTURIES

HISTORIOGRAPHICAL PRESUPPOSITIONS

Lindsay's 1902 Cunningham lectures at Edinburgh were collected and published in eight chapters plus an Appendix sketching the history of the controversy about office-bearers in the primitive Christian churches.[10] The main features of this work were incorporated in his article on "Ministry" published posthumously in the first (1915) edition of *The International Standard Bible Encyclopedia*.[11] In seeking to portray the organized life of the church during the first three centuries, Lindsay indicated his historical method. He selected writings "which seemed to reveal that life most clearly, and to group round the central sources of information illustrative evidence, contemporary or other." His central authorities were writings providing the most detail. These included Paul's letters, especially First Corinthians; Acts, the book of Revelation and the Pastoral Epistles from the New Testament; the *Didache*, the *Sources of the Apostolic Canons* and the *Epistles of Ignatius* from the second century; and *The Canons of Hippolytus* and the *Epistles of Cyprian* for the third century.[12] While this leads to some repetitiveness, Lindsay believed it also gave readers "the contemporary evidence in the simplest ways."[13]

Lindsay indicated three assumptions or postulates which underlay his lectures, leaving it to his readers to determine if these were right or wrong. The first was that he devoutly believed "that there is a Visible Catholic Church of Christ consisting of all those throughout the world who visible worship the same God and Father, profess their faith in the same Saviour, and are taught by the same Holy Spirit; but I do not see any Scriptural or even primitive warrant for insisting that catholicity *must* find visible expression in a uniformity of organization, of ritual of worship, or even of formulated creed."[14]

While Lindsay recognized the historical continuity of the "Visible Catholic Church of Christ," he maintained that the ground of this historical continuity "does not necessarily exist in any one method of selecting and setting apart office-bearers who rule in the Church; its basis is the real succession of the generations of faithful followers of their Lord and Master, Jesus Christ."[15] This meant, said Lindsay, that he could be devoutly thankful to be able to make this assumption "with perfect honesty of heart and of head," since "it relieves me from the necessity—sad, stern and even hateful it must seem to many pious souls who feel themselves under its power—of unchurching and of excluding from the 'covenanted' mercies of God, all who do not accept that form of Church government, which, to my mind, is truest to scriptural principles and most akin to the ecclesiastical organization of the early centuries."[16] Here, Lindsay does not concede any ground to arguments that base the unity and catholicity of the church on an unbroken, historical "apostolic succession"—an idea Lindsay later called a "legal fiction" which "had its origin in the brains of leaders of the Roman Church." But he does indicate a breadth in his view of the church as not being limited *only* to those who have received the covenant mercies of God and believe in his (Presbyterial) view of the proper form of church organization. In the context of his audience and the history of Scottish Presbyterianism, to make this concession would be a "broader" view.

The second postulate concerns the ministry, that "there is and must be a valid ministry of some sort in the churches which are branches of this one Visible Catholic Church of Christ." But Lindsay went on to say that he did not think "that the fact that the Church possesses an authority which is a direct gift from God necessarily means that the authority must exist in a class or caste of superior office-bearers endowed with a grace and therefore with a power of 'specific, exclusive and efficient,'" and that it *cannot* be delegated to the ministry by the Christian people. Lindsay rejected as false an antithetical way of stating the issue: "Must ministerial character be in all cases conferred from above, or may it sometimes, and with equal validity, be evolved from below?" The false antithesis is to assume that what comes "from below," that is from the membership of the church, cannot come "from above," that is, cannot be of "divine origin, warrant and authority." Lindsay asked rhetorically if the Holy Spirit may "not use the membership of the Church as His instrument? Is there no real abiding presence of Christ among His people? Is not this promised Presence something which belongs to the sphere of God and may it not be the source of an authority which is 'from above'?" The theory of "apostolic succession" holds that "no valid ministry can be evolved from the membership of the Christian congregation." This, Lindsay rejects and postulates that valid ministry may indeed arise from the membership of the church.[17]

Third, Lindsay postulated that "analogies in organization illustrative of the life of the primitive Christian communities can be more easily and more safely found on the mission fields of our common Christianity than among the details of the organized life of the long established Churches of Christian Europe."[18] In support of this, Lindsay recounted his twelve months in India where he saw mission work in that culture, first hand. He felt as though he was transported back (as by the "magic carpet" in the *Arabian Nights*, he said) to the early centuries to "hear and to see what the earliest writers had recounted and described." A visit to the mission fields of an ancient civilization is "the magic carpet which transports one back to the times of primitive Christianity" so one can see the simple meaning of statements which are hard to understand by just reading texts. Similarly, Lindsay saw the experience as teaching one to "distrust some of the hard and fast canons of modern historical criticism, and to grow somewhat sceptical about the worth of many of those 'subjective pictures' which some modern critics first construct and then use to estimate the date, authorship and intention of ancient documents." In a statement mirroring Lindsay's openness to the emerging biblical criticism, he went on to say that one "learns that the modern western mind cannot so easily gauge the oriental ways of thought as it persistently imagines." Thus, Lindsay viewed modern missionary work as "full of helpful illustrations of the life and organization of the early centuries."[19]

Historical Assessments

Lindsay saw the New Testament conception of the church to embrace five great thoughts. These were: 1) the church as a *fellowship*—a fellowship with Jesus Christ, which is the divine element in it; 2) the *unity* of the church which is "something essentially spiritual" and a reality which is "more ideal than material"; 3) the church as a *visible community*, displaying the unity of the church, "not by uniformity of organization, but by the manifestation of the fruits of the Spirit"; 4) the *authority* of the visible community, emerging from Christ himself and given to the "community which formed the local church"; and 5) the church as a *sacerdotal society* in which every member has direct access to the throne of God.[20]

These dimensions helped shape the rest of Lindsay's treatment of the emerging church and its ministry through the early centuries. He went on to describe the three kinds of meetings in which local churches participated. These were the meeting for Edification by prayer and edification; the meeting for Thanksgiving which began with a common meal and ended with the Lord's Supper; and a meeting for conducting the business of the community.[21] Lindsay saw in these the several facets of the early church's life: "The meeting for thanksgiving represents the centre of spiritual repose, the quiet source of active life and service; the meeting for edification, the enthusiastic, eager, aggressive side of the life and work; and the business meeting, the deliberative and practical action of men who recognize that they are in the world though not of it."[22]

As for the government or polity of the churches, Lindsay maintained they were independent and self-governing with never an apostolic allusion to "the need of organization under hierarchical authority" and still less any apostolic prescription of "a form of organization which was to be uniform throughout the whole Church of Christ."[23] The traces of organization found in these early churches pertained to the rudiments of discipline and to forms of ministry. These were two different kinds of ministry, a "prophetic" and a "local" ministry. Those "speaking the Word of God" constitute the first form; the second refers to ministries of local churches through those who came to be called pastors, elders, bishops, and deacons. The practical distinction Lindsay makes between these is that "the prophetic ministry did not mean office-bearers in a local church; while the local ministry consisted of these office-bearers. The one was a ministry to the whole Church of God, and by its activity bound all the scattered parts of the Church visible together; the other was a ministry within a local church, and, with the assembly of the congregation, manifested and preserved the unity and the independence of the local community."[24]

In his third lecture, Lindsay discussed the prophetic ministry of the primitive church wherein the "gift" to "speak the Word of God" took a "foremost place" and was specially honored. This may be termed a "charismatic ministry" (Gk. *charisma*; "gift"), yet not "*the* Charismatic Ministry, as if it alone depended on and came from the 'gifts' of the Spirit; for every kind of service comes (Romans 12:7) from a 'gift,' and the ministry of attending to the poor and the sick, or advising and leading the community with wise counsels, are equally charismatic."[25]

The threefold division in the early church's prophetic ministry was apostles, prophets, and teachers with whom Lindsay dealt in turn. Those who "spoke the Word of God" (*lalountes tou logou tou Theou*) and gave the church its preaching ministry, Lindsay maintained, "were in no sense office-bearers in any one Christian community; they were not elected to an office; they were not set apart by any ecclesiastical ceremony." Rather, "the Word of God came to them, and they spoke the message that had been sent them. They all had the divine call manifested in the 'gift' they possessed and could use."[26] While no strict and fixed divisions should be made among these three kinds of ministries of the Word, Lindsay developed each according to its function and how it fulfilled the early church's needs: "What was needed for zealous missionary endeavour was the distinguishing characteristic of the first class, exhortation and admonition of the second, and instruction of the third."[27]

Biblical accounts of organized local ministries during the first century begin with the appointment of seven men to "the service of tables" and thus to "take care of the poor and to administer the charity of the congregation."[28] Lindsay suggested that "the Seven" here were also the ones appointed by the church as "elders" or "presbyters" in Acts 11 who were charged with the duty of distributing money collected outside Palestine for relief of the poor in Jerusalem.[29] Paul and Barnabas appointed "elders" (*presbuteroi*) were in "every church" according to Acts 14:23, the term "appointed" (*cheirotonesantes*) strictly meaning "to elect by popular vote."[30] In addition, Lindsay saw those who were "natural leaders" in the churches, who "work for their brethren and put some heart into their labour" and were "esteemed highly for their works' sake" (1 Thess. 5:13), as the ones called "those who are over you in the Lord" (*proistamenoi*). Here there were those who exercised ministries of oversight and those who rendered "subordinate service" by obeying. Thus, Paul's letters speak of pastors, overseers, elders and deacons (*poimenes, episkopoi, presbuteroi, diakonoi*) with references to office-bearers of local churches "always in the plural." "The government," reasons Lindsay, "must have been collegiate."[31] After examining evidence about "bishops" and "presbyters," Lindsay concludes (in agreement with J. B. Lightfoot and in opposition to Adolf von Harnack) that by the end of the first century, "bodies of presbyters existed as ruling colleges in Christian congregations over a great part of the Roman Empire" and that "the elder is the name for the office, while bishop is the title describing what the elder has to do"—namely, the task of *episcopos*, which means superintendent or overseer of service.[32]

In the second and third centuries, patterns of ministry changed. Lindsay describes these in his fifth lecture, beginning with the appointment of a "pastor" (*poimen*) or "bishop" (*episcopus*) for a local congregation, at least two elders or presbyters, and deacons. This threefold congregational ministry, seen most clearly in the *Letters of Ignatius of Antioch*, became the norm for churches throughout Asia Minor.[33] Lindsay summarized the changes for ministry as the evolution of:

> The ruling body in every congregation changed from being a session of elders without a president and became a session with a president. The president, sometimes called the pastor, but usually the bishop, became gradually the center of all the ecclesiastical life of the local Christian church and the one potent office-bearer.[34]

> With the rise of heresies and the threats of Marcionites, Montanists and others, the "prophetic ministry" gradually fell silent and congregational life increasingly centered on the bishop who was selected by the local congregation and ordained by it.[35] Elders were ordained by the bishop and assisted the bishop in varying ways. The deacon, however, was the official "who does subordinate services."[36]

Lindsay concluded his sixth lecture by comparing the organization of the third-century church with modern church organizational models: congregational, presbyterian, and episcopal. Presbyterian Lindsay concluded that the early church much more clearly resembled the presbyterian form than the other two.[37]

"Ministry Changing to Priesthood" is the topic of Lindsay's seventh lecture in which he detailed significant changes in the concept of the church and its ministry which emerged during the third century. Lindsay saw conceptions of the local and universal church beginning to change in this period and a new relationship between office-bearers and the Christian community. Now, the church was "defined by the ministry in a way that had not been in earlier times." Similarly, the church "which was in earlier days a 'brotherhood of saints,' became a community over whom a bishop presided. It was defined, not so much by the manner of life led by its members, as by the government which ruled over them." The flow was reversed from people worshiping and living the Christian life together to "teachers who imparted and pupils who received, priests who interceded and sinners who were pardoned through the intercession, rulers who commanded and subjects who were bound to obey."[38]

Analogously, said Lindsay, the concept of the universal visible church also underwent a transformation at this time. Instead of it being a wide unity of "all those who professed the name of Jesus" and lived the life of obedience, it became "a federation of local churches, who believed in the same verities, the truth of which was guaranteed by legitimate rulers, and whose members yielded an implicit obedience to the bishop at the head of every local 'church.' It was the federation of churches which excluded heretics and rebels."[39] Lindsay went on to detail the phases in these changes from the quarrels between Hippolytus and Calixtus, to the work and influence of Cyprian who made visible the principles of the unity of the Catholic Church.[40] Lindsay saw Cyprian's views of a united episcopate as inevitably leading to "a one-man theory of the Church universal" and a "transmission of unique prerogatives to the bishop who was supposed to occupy the chair of St. Peter." While some "may protest against the thought that their theories lead to the conception of a 'bishop of bishops,'" Lindsay claimed that "the unsparing logic of history sweeps their protests aside."[41]

The final lecture dealt with the Roman State Religion and its effects on the organization of the church. Here Lindsay detailed the ways in which synods originated to select and ordain chief pastors and to deal with pressing issues such as, in Cyprian's time, the issue of what to do with the "lapsed"—those who had capitulated in the face of Roman persecution. Synods were the application of the congregational meeting to a wider ecclesiastical context.

"Two ideas of organization co-existed," said Lindsay. Cyprian's "conception of the autocracy of the bishop of the local church" and its ascending scale up to the Bishop of Rome (Pope); and the congregational ideal, beginning with the local church body and ascending through provincial councils to an ecumenical council of the whole church.[42]

Lindsay concluded by examining the question of whether the organization of the Christian church began to model itself and adapt itself to the form and organization of the imperial religious system of the Roman Empire. While "Christianity could not become the religion of the empire until this great state religion had been overthrown and its priests abolished or their offices secularized," the question was whether the churches were so organized that when this time came, "the Christian leaders could at once step into the position of those who held the leading places in it and who formed that great pagan hierarchy?"[43]

Lindsay's answer was that in two ways the Christian church did copy the pagan hierarchy. The first was in the distinction within the ranks of bishops by the introduction of metropolitans and grades of bishops; the second in multiplying lower orders of clergy on the model of the state temple service's organization. Lindsay argued that when Christianity became thoroughly established as the official religion of the Roman Empire, Christian bishops secured for themselves the civil powers and privileges formerly belonging to higher priests of the Imperial Cult.[44] This meant that "when the time of the Church's triumph came, which it did early in the [fourth] century, very little change of previous state arrangements was needed to install the new religion in the place of the old."[45]

Lindsay did not see this as a matter of reproach since "the Church and its leaders had a lofty aim before them in all these changes; and the evangelical life could be and was sustained under this complicated ministry."[46] While later the church's centralized government helped sustain it in the midst of the dissolution of the Empire, Lindsay also saw "evils" as arising too. For "the spirit of compromise with paganism, which this imitation even of the externals of a pagan religious administration could scarcely fail to produce, did lead to much corruption both in the beliefs and in the life of the Christian Church." The chief seeds of evil Lindsay saw as imported from "two pagan ideas introduced mainly by Cyprian of Carthage": the special priesthood whereby a bishop, because of the powers ascribed to him of forgiving sin also claimed the right of implicit obedience from followers; and the notion of a propitiatory sacrament in the Eucharist, being efficaciously independent of faith and the piety of the worshippers. "It was these thoughts," said Lindsay, "not the organization which enclosed them, which were to breed evil more abundantly as the centuries passed."[47]

Lindsay's view of the church at the end of the third century, before it became absorbed within the administration of the Roman Empire, was that it consisted of thousands of "more or less independent" churches "associated in groups according to the divisions of the empire." The state "first gave a thoroughly visible unity to the associated churches" and this "imperial unity was the forerunner of the Papal."[48] As the Empire persecuted those who did not conform to the church, the church itself spoke of itself as "the one Catholic Church of Christ outside of which there was no salvation." Such "strange methods," said Lindsay, "do men think it right to use when they try in their haste to make clear to the coarser human vision the wondrous divine thought of the visible unity of the Church of Christ!"[49]

HISTORY OF THE REFORMATION

Lindsay's writings on the Reformation attempted to set the Protestant movement within its social environment. He viewed the Reformation first and foremost as a "religious revival" set in "a framework of political, intellectual, and economic changes" which cannot be "disentangled from its surroundings without danger of mutilation."[50] The sixteenth century saw "the beginnings of our present social life," said Lindsay, "in almost everything, from our way of looking at politics and our modes of trade to our underclothing."[51] Lindsay's goal with Luther, as with the whole Reformation itself, was "to bring him nearer us than has yet been done."[52]

HISTORIOGRAPHICAL PRESUPPOSITIONS

Lindsay approached his Reformation studies as a historian concerned about five distinct but related things: The social and religious conditions of the age out of which the great movement came; the Lutheran Reformation down to 1555, when it received legal recognition; the Reformation in countries beyond Germany which did not submit to the guidance of Luther; the issue of certain portions of the religious life of the Middle Ages in Anabaptism, Socinianism, and Anti-Trinitarianism; and, finally, the Counter-Reformation.[53] While Lindsay did not find it possible to describe all five of these elements in chronological order, he divided his two volumes into six "books." Volume 1 included materials on the "Eve of the Reformation" and "The Reformation" while volume 2 took up "The Reformed Churches," "The Reformation in England," "Anabaptism and Socinianism," and "The Counter Reformation."

Lindsay attempted to give attention to the fullness of the Reformation movement by describing not only the intellectual life of the times in which it was set, and some of the economic conditions (which in his day were only "beginning to attract attention"), but also "the popular and family religious life in the decades before the great revival." "Few," he said, "have cared to investigate" these dimensions. Yet Lindsay argued, "for the history of the Reformation movement nothing can be more important." When these are accounted for, he believed, "it can be seen that the evangelical revival was not a unique phenomenon, entirely unconnected with the immediate past." For "there was a continuity in the religious life of the period." The "same hymns were sung in public and in private after the Reformation which had been in use before Luther raised the standard of revolt," prayers from Reformation liturgies "came from the service-books of the mediaeval Church," and much of the family instruction received by the Reformers as children were passed on to the next generation. When this is realized, said Lindsay, it will be recognized that "the great Reformation had its roots in the simple evangelical piety which had never entirely disappeared in the mediaeval Church." Moreover, "Luther's teaching was recognized by thousands to be no startling novelty, but something which they had always at heart believed, though they might not have been able to formulate it."[54]

Lindsay did not downplay Luther's theological contributions, set, as they were in an ecclesiastical and cultural context he referred to as "a framework of superstition" where "the Church had been generally looked upon as an institution within which priests exercised a secret science of redemption through their power over the sacraments." Yet, Lindsay maintained, "the old evangelical piety existed, and its traces can be found when sought for."[55] Thus Lindsay's chapters in his study of the context of the Reformation considered the Papacy, the political situation, the Renaissance, social conditions, family and popular religious life prior to the Reformation, and the influence of humanism. All these continue to be significant topics for contemporary historians of the Reformation.

HISTORICAL ASSESSMENTS

Lindsay's view of the Reformation as a "religious revival" meant that he was concerned not only with the historical factors which "triggered" the Reformation, but also with the theological forces which were at work within that history. This intertwining of history and theology can be illustrated in several areas of his Reformation understanding.[56]

For example, Lindsay viewed the Reformation as continuous with the medieval past through what he called "the old evangelical piety." His theological perception of this is summed up in his description of it. He wrote:

> The central thought in all evangelical religion is that the believer does not owe his position before God, and his assurance of salvation, to the good deeds which he really can do, but to the grace of God manifested in the mission and work of Christ; and the more we turn from the thought of what we can do to the thought of what God has done for us, the stronger will be the conviction that simple trust in God is that by which the pardoning grace of God is appropriated. This double conception—God's grace coming down upon us from above, and the believer's trust rising from beneath to meet and appropriate it—was never absent from the simplest religion of the Middle Ages.[57]

Lindsay saw medieval theology as obscuring it "owing to its enforced connection with Aristotelian philosophy, that theology was largely artificial." Yet, "the thought itself had a continuous and constant existence in the public consciousness of Christian men and women, and appeared in sermons, prayers, and hymns, and in the other ways in which the devotional life manifested itself." Rather than writing off the whole medieval period, Lindsay saw this evangelical impulse as found in the sermons of Bernard of Clairvaux, the teachings of Francis of Assisi, and in the simpler Latin and German medieval hymns. He also saw "the utter need for sin-pardoning grace" as "expressed and taught in the prayer of the *Canon of the Mass*." It "found its way, in spite of the theology, even into the official agenda of the Church, where the dying are told that they must repose their confidence upon Christ and His Passion as the sole ground of confidence in their salvation."[58]

The importance of this theologically in Lindsay's historical view of the Reformation is found in this summary paragraph:

> All these things combine to show us how there was a simple evangelical faith among pious mediaeval Christians, and that their lives were fed upon the same divine truths which lie at the basis of Reformation theology. The truths were all there, as poetic thoughts, as earnest supplication and confession, in fervent preaching or in fireside teaching. When mediaeval Christians knelt in prayer, stood to sing their Redeemer's praises, spoke as a dying man to dying men, or as a mother to the children about her knees, the words and thoughts that came were what Luther and Zwingli and Calvin wove into Reformation creeds, and expanded into that experimental theology which was characteristic of the Reformation.[59]

Theologically, Lindsay saw the Protestant Reformation as a revival of this essential, evangelical piety which was smothered in medieval Catholicism by an ecclesiastical theology and bureaucracy—epitomized in the Papacy. While recognizing the contributions of Christian humanists toward the "moral renovation" of humankind, Lindsay argued that "history knows nothing of revivals of moral living apart from some new religious impulse." For "the motive power needed has always come through leaders who have had communion with the unseen."[60] The necessary leader for this time was Martin Luther. In contrast to Humanism, wrote Lindsay, which:

> Had supplied a superfluity of teachers; the times needed a prophet. They received one; a man of the people; bone of their bone, and flesh of their flesh; one who had himself lived that popular religious life with all the thoroughness of a strong, earnest nature, who had sounded all its depths and tested its capacities, and gained in the end no relief for his burdened conscience; who had at last found his way into the presence of God, and who knew, by his own personal experience, that the living God was accessible to every Christian. He had won the freedom of a

Christian man, and had reached through faith a joy in living far deeper than that which Humanism boasted. He became a leader of men, because his joyous faith made him a hero by delivering him from all fear of Church or of clergy—the fear which had weighed down the consciences of men for generations. Men could *see* what faith was when they looked at Luther.[61]

After detailing Luther's life and career through a number of chapters, Lindsay completed his first volume with a study of "The Religious Principles Inspiring the Reformation." Chief among these was Luther's discovery of the nature of true faith. Luther was in anguish, trying to please God and find forgiveness of sins. Despite following the prescriptions of the Church in becoming a monk and celebrating the sacraments, Luther felt that he was, as he said, "the most miserable man of earth; day and night there was only wailing and despair, and no one could restrain me."[62] His breakthrough came with his discovery of faith, not primarily as what to believe *about* God (as the church taught), but faith as "that religious faculty which 'throws itself upon God;' and from the first Luther recognised that faith of this kind was a direct gift from God."[63] In contrast to Roman Catholic Church teaching which conceived faith as primarily intellectual assent to church doctrine, Luther discovered faith as lively personal trust. Lindsay put it this way: "Here we find something entirely new, or at least hitherto unexpressed, so far as mediaeval theology was concerned. Mediaeval theologians had recognised faith in the sense of what Luther called *frigida opinio*, and it is difficult to conceive that they did not also indirectly acknowledge that there must be something like trust or *fiducia*; but faith with them was simply one among many human efforts all equally necessary in order to see and know God."[64]

Yet for Luther, "the real faith, the faith which is trust, the divine gift which impels us to throw ourselves upon God, gives us the living assurance of a living God, who has revealed Himself, made us see His loving Fatherly heart in Christ Jesus; and that is the Christian religion in its very core and center."[65] This led Lindsay to describe "the sum of Christianity" to be: "(1) God manifest in Christ, the God of grace, accessible by every Christian man and woman; and (2) unwavering trust in Him who has given Himself to us in Christ Jesus,—unwavering, because Christ with His work has undertaken our cause and made it His."[66]

Lindsay saw "this conception of what is meant by Christianity" to be "the religious soul of the Reformation." For "it contains within it all the distinctively religious principles which inspired it." Lindsay went on to expound his view of how these theological principles were enacted in the historical experience of the Protestant Reformation itself:

363

It can scarcely be called a dogma. It is an experience, and the phrases which set it forth are the descriptions of an experience which a human soul has gone through. The thing itself is beyond exact definition—as all deep experiences are. It must be felt and gone through to be known. The Reformation started from this personal experience of the believing Christian, which it declared to be the one elemental fact in Christianity which could never be proved by argument and could never be dissolved away by speculation. It proclaimed the great truth, which had been universally neglected throughout the whole period of mediaeval theology by everyone except the Mystics, that in order to know God man must be in living touch with God Himself. Therein lay its originality and its power. Luther rediscovered religion when he declared that the truly Christian man must cling directly and with a living faith to the God Who speaks to him in Christ saying, "I am thy salvation." The earlier Reformers never forgot this. Luther proclaimed his discovery, he never attempted to prove it by argument; it was something self-evident—seen and known when experienced.[67]

For Lindsay, Luther's concept of faith led to what amounted to a virtual rediscovery of the Holy Scriptures. Lindsay argued that the differing conceptions of saving faith between Protestantism and Roman Catholicism enabled the Reformers to find a natural unity in the Bible while the Romanists could construct only an "artificial one" by "placing the dogmatic tradition of the Church alongside Scripture as an equal source of authority."[68] The contrast was that "mediaeval theologians looked at the Bible as a sort of spiritual law-book, a storehouse of divinely communicated knowledge of doctrinal truths and rules for moral conduct—and nothing more. The Reformers saw in it a new home for a new life within which they could have intimate fellowship with God Himself—not merely knowledge about God, but actual communion with Him."[69] The Reformers experienced Scripture as the place where they "could hear their Father's voice, learn their Redeemer's purpose, and have faith in their Lord's promises." This meant "saving faith was not intellectual assent at all. It was simple trust—the trust of a child—in their Father's promises, which were Yea and Amen in Christ Jesus. The one essential thing was to hear and obey the personal God speaking to them as He had spoken all down through the ages to His people, promising His salvation, now in direct words, now in pictures of His dealings with a favoured man or a chosen people."[70] Thus, wrote Lindsay:

> The change of view which separated the Reformers from mediaeval theologians almost amounted to a rediscovery of Scripture; and it was effected by their conception of faith. Saving faith was for them *personal*

trust in a *personal Saviour* Who had manifested in His life and work the Fatherly mercy of God. This was not a mere theological definition; it was a description of an experience which they knew that they had lived. It made them see that the word of God was a personal and not a dogmatic revelation; that the real meaning in it was that God Himself was there behind every word of it,—not an abstract truth, but a personal Father.[71]

Faith was also the crucial dimension for Lindsay in claiming that for the Reformers, a true distinction can be made "between the word of God and the Scripture which contains or presents that word." This distinction was "real and not merely formal; it was more than the difference between the word of God and the word of God written; and important consequences were founded upon it." To use a metaphor, Lindsay said, "the word of God is to Scripture as the soul is to the body." For "Luther believed that while the word of God was presented in every part of Scripture, some portions make it much more evident."[72]

Lindsay was careful to make clear this distinction should not be perverted into "the common mystical illustration of kernel and husk, which husk (the record) may be thrown away when the kernel (the word) has been once reached and laid hold of." Nor does this mean that "one part of the Bible is the word of God and that another is not." For "the Reformers uniformly teach that the substance of *all* Scripture is the word of God, and that what is no part of the record of the word of God is not Scripture." Also, one may not use this distinction to "prevent us saying that the Scripture *is* the word of God." For Lindsay, following Luther, "the copula *is* does not express logical identity, but some such relation as can be more exactly rendered by *contains, presents, conveys, records,*—all of which phrases are used in the writings of the Reformers or in the creeds of the Reformation Churches." The "main thing to remember," said Lindsay, "is that the distinction is not to be made use of to deny to the substance of Scripture those attributes of authority and infallibility which belong to the word of God."[73]

For Lindsay, "the authoritative character and infallibility belong really and primarily to the word of God, and only secondarily to the Scriptures,—to Scripture only because it is the record which contains, presents, or conveys the word of God. It is this word of God, this personal manifestation to us for our salvation of God in His promises, which is authoritative and infallible; and Scripture shares these attributes only in so far as it is a vehicle of spiritual truth." According to Lindsay:

> It is the unanimous declaration of the Reformers that Scripture is Scripture because it gives us that knowledge of God and of His will

which is necessary for salvation; because it presents to the eye of faith God Himself personally manifesting Himself in Christ. It is this presentation of God Himself and of His will for our salvation which is infallible and authoritative. But this manifestation of God Himself is something spiritual, and is to be apprehended by a spiritual faculty which is faith, and the Reformers and the Confessions of the Reformation do not recognise any infallibility or divine authority which is otherwise apprehended than by faith.[74]

The importance of faith for recognizing the infallibility of Scripture was significant for Lindsay since he contrasted this view both to medieval theologians and to "many modern Protestants." For the medievals, "infallibility was something which guaranteed the perfect correctness of abstract propositions; with some modern Protestants it consists in the conception that the record contains not even the smallest error in word or description of fact—in its inerrancy."[75] Yet, affirmed Lindsay;

Neither inerrancy nor the correctness of abstract propositions is apprehended by faith in the Reformers' sense of that word; they are matters of fact, to be accepted or rejected by the ordinary faculties of man. The infallibility and authority which need faith to perceive them are, and must be, something very different; they produce the conviction that in the manifestation of God in His word there lies infallible power to save. This is given, all the Reformers say, by the Witness of the Spirit; 'the true kirk alwaies heares and obeyis the voice of her awin spouse and pastor.'[76]

This view, contended Lindsay, "is a religious conception of infallibility very different from the mediaeval or modern Romanist."[77]

In addition, the distinction between the word of God and Scripture "also serves to distinguish between the divine and the human elements in Scripture, and to give each its proper place."[78] By this Lindsay meant that "infallibility and divine authority belong to the sphere of faith and of the witness of the Spirit, and therefore, to that personal manifestation of God and of His will toward us which is conveyed or presented to us in every part of Scripture." Yet, this revelation is given in the course of human history, in human life and in "a record which in outward form is like other human writings." If, said Lindsay, "every part of Scripture is divine, every part of it is also human. The supernatural reality is incased in human realities. To apprehend the former, faith illumined by the Holy Spirit is necessary; but it is sufficient to use the ordinary methods of research to learn the credibility of the history in Scripture."[79] The Reformers declared that the authority and infallibility of the word belongs to the region of faith and by so doing "made that authority and infallibility altogether independent of questions that might be raised about the human agencies through which the book came into its present shape." This meant, Lindsay contended, that it is not a matter of faith "when the books which record the word of God were written, or by whom, or in what style, or how often they were edited or re-edited." It is not a matter of faith whether the account of Job is literal history, or a poem based on old traditions to illustrate "the problems of God's providence and man's probation." These questions belong to the "human side of the record" and "no special illumination of faith is needed to apprehend and understand them."[80]

Yet, at the same time, Scripture is also "the record of the revelation of God" which God has preserved and guarded. The Reformers always spoke of God's providence in making the Scriptures available to the people so that God's mind and will for their salvation is always present. This recognition, said Lindsay, "for ever forbids a careless or irreverent biblical criticism, sheltering itself under the liberty of dealing with the records of revelation." For "no one can say beforehand how much or how little of the historic record is essential to preserve the faith of the Church; but every devout Christian desires to have it in large abundance." Practically speaking, Lindsay contended, "no one can plead the liberty which the principles of the Reformers secure for dealing with the record of Scripture as a justification in taking a delight in reducing to a minimum the historical basis of the Christian faith. Careless or irreverent handling of the text of Holy Scripture is what all the Reformers abhorred."[81]

T. M. LINDSAY: HISTORIAN OF THE CHURCH

The preceding survey has made it clear that Thomas Martin Lindsay was an important Scottish church historian. His major works in early church and Reformation studies provided a wealth of historical information as well as theological analyses of these important periods. He always saw his historical studies as serving the church by helping it come to a clearer self-understanding.

Lindsay made this point in several ways in a valedictory address delivered at the close of the 1874–75 session of his College. His title was "The Study of Church History" and he began with two presuppositions which he considered crucial: Cultivate personal religion; and live a life with a real and living connection with the Church of God as represented by the parish or congregation.[82] These two presuppositions are explicit expressions of the attitudes that underlie Lindsay's own historical work. He saw the motive of Luther and the driving force of the Reformation to be the personal religious faith and "evangelical piety" of those who responded to God's message of salvation; he explicated the development of the church and its ministry in the early centuries, beginning with the initial postulate that there *is* a "Visible Catholic Church of Christ who visibly worship the same God and Father, profess their faith in the same Saviour, and are taught by the same Holy Spirit."[83] Lindsay told his audience that Germany was an example of "the absence of the connection between the professor's chair and the active work of the ministry, and consequently the absence of connection, save of a very outside kind, between the professional theologian and the Christian congregation." This means, Lindsay said, that while Germany had done much from the standpoint of dogmatic, exegetical, and purely historical criticism (the results of which must be assimilated), Germany still had "failed in a sympathetic construction or development of dogma, just because dogma stands in the closest relation to the common life of the Christian Church or the Christian people, and so cannot be sympathetically apprehended or cultivated apart from that life. It is the life within the Church which makes dogma grow, not external pressure applied ever so skillfully."[84]

Lindsay then went on to urge the church's future clergy to pursue the study of history because, he believed, "history affords a common ground on which naturalism and supernaturalism can meet and wage a not unequal war; and if this be the case, if history be the future battlefield between Christianity and unchristianity, the whole mode of contest must be more or less altered. The old vagueness must in measure depart, and instead of wide, indefinite statements and comprehensive problems we shall have sharp, clear question and answer—we shall have something of scientific precision of statement and argument."[85]

His call here was for those mutually engaged in these scientific, historical studies to work together—each taking parts of historical questions and to use their parish situations to do research on historical problems. Old church records, for example, can provide important historical information about how churches have developed. Lindsay's hope was that "many now before me, in the learned seclusion of highland or lowland manse, will fairly grapple with these problems in a much more thorough-going way than any have hitherto done."[86] More broadly, Lindsay urged the study of medieval history as holding keys to understanding the ways in which Christian doctrine was shaped and formed.

The practical reasons for this study of the church of Christ, Lindsay indicated, were two:

(1) Nothing will enable us to cultivate the feelings of common life which, in spite of innumerable differences, must unite all who believe in

one Lord Jesus Christ as a knowledge that the whole of the present manifold divisions of Western Christendom can be traced back to a common origin and to a common stock. This itself is warrant for the fact that there is more unity than there are differences in the many and separated branches of the Christian church. (2) Nothing more brings home to one's mind the nobility of Christianity than to trace the whole progress of the world's history since Christianity came to play a decisive part in all great historical movements.[87]

The true reunion of the Christian church, Thomas Lindsay believed, did not lie in phrases or in attempts at external union—as if the fifteen centuries of church history prior to the Reformation never occurred. Instead, according to Lindsay, "the true reunion of Christendom must be a union of sympathy . . . and such sympathy can be best arrived at by a dispassionate study of times in which the beginnings of divergence are seen slowly shaping themselves."[88] Lindsay's own labors as a church historian, especially of the early church and Reformation periods, were their own testimonies to this conviction.

SELECTED BIBLIOGRAPHY

PRIMARY SOURCES

"Baptism." In *The International Standard Bible Encyclopedia*, ed. James Orr *et. al.* 4 vols. Chicago: Howard-Severance Co., 1915. Reprinted in *The International Standard Bible Encyclopedia*, ed. Geoffrey W. Bromley et al. 4 vols. Grand Rapids: William B. Eerdmans Publishing Co., 1979–1988.

College Addresses: And Sermons Preached on Various Occasions. Glasgow: James Maclehose and Sons, 1915.

A History of the Reformation. 2 vols. New York: Charles Scribner's Son's, 1906, 1907.

Luther and the German Reformation. Edinburgh: T & T Clark, 1900.

"Ministry." In *The International Standard Bible Encyclopedia*, ed. James Orr et al. 4 vols. Chicago: The Howard-Severance Co., 1915.

"Pioneer and Martyr of the Higher Criticism, Professor William Robertson Smith." *The Review of the Churches* 6, no. 31 (April 14, 1894): 37–42.

"Professor W. Robertson Smith's Doctrine of Scripture." *The Expositor,* ed. W. Robertson Nicoll, 4th series, 10 (1894): 241–64.

Lindsay, Thomas M. *The Church and the Ministry in the Early Centuries.* New York: A. C. Armstrong and Son, 1902.

"The Critical Movement in the Free Church of Scotland." *The Contemporary Review,* 33 (August–November 1878): 22–34.

"The Doctrine of Scripture: The Reformers and the Princeton School." *The Expositor,* ed. W. Robertson Nicoll, 5th Series 1 (1895): 278–93.

SECONDARY SOURCES

Reisen, Richard Allan. *Criticism and Faith in Late Victorian Scotland: A. B. Davidson, William Robertson Smith and George Adam Smith.* Lanham, Maryland: University Press of America, 1895.

Rogers, Jack B., and Donald K. McKim. *The Authority and Interpretation of the Bible: An Historical Approach.* San Francisco: Harper & Row, 1979.

NOTES

1. See *Encyclopedia of the Reformed Faith*, ed. Donald K. McKim (Louisville: Westminster/John Knox Press, 1992), s.v. "Relief Church."

2. Thomas M. Lindsay, *The Church and the Ministry in the Early Centuries* (New York: A. C. Armstrong and Son, 1902). The lectures honored Rev. William Cunningham, D. D., Principal of the Free Church College, Edinburgh, and Professor of Divinity and Church History there. See Lindsay, *Church*, "Extract Declaration of Trust," xiii.

3. Lindsay, *Church*, vi.

4. These works were published in New York by Charles Scribner's Sons.

5. Thomas M. Lindsay, *A History of the Reformation* (New York: Charles Scribner's Sons, 1906), 1:7.

6. See Thomas M. Lindsay, *Luther and the German Reformation* (Edinburgh: T.& T. Clark, 1900) and *Revivals* (London, 1909).

7. Thomas Martin Lindsay, *College Addresses: And Sermons Preached on Various Occasions* (Glasgow: James Maclehose and Sons, 1915).

8. See T. M. Lindsay, "The Critical Movement in the Free Church of Scotland," *The Contemporary Review* 33 (August-November 1878): 22–34; "Pioneer and Martyr of the Higher Criticism, Professor William Robertson Smith," *The Review of the Churches* 6, no. 31 (April 14, 1894): 37–42; "Professor W. Robertson Smith's Doctrine of Scripture," *The Expositor*, ed. W. Robertson Nicoll, 4th series, 10 (1894): 241–64. On Smith's trial, see Richard Allan Riesen, *Criticism and Faith in Late Victorian Scotland: A.B. Davidson, William Robertson Smith and George Adam Smith* (Lanham, Md.: University Press of America, 1985). On Lindsay's relationship with Smith, see John Sutherland Black and George W. Chrystal, *The Life of William Robertson Smith* (London: Adam and Charles Black, 1912), *passim* and Riesen, *Criticism and Faith*, 225 n. 38.

9. On Lindsay, see *Oxford Dictionary of the Christian Church*, ed. F. L. Cross and E. A. Livingstone, 2nd ed. (London: Oxford University Press, 1974), s.v. "Lindsay, Thomas Martin;" *Scottish Dictionary of Church History*, ed. D. F. Wright (Edinburgh: T.&T. Clark, 1994); *Dictionary of National Biography, 1912–1921*, 338–39; *The Fourth Generation: Reminiscences* (London, 1912); and *Letters of Principal T.M. Lindsay to Janet Ross* (London, 1923).

10. The total volume is 398 pages with extensive footnote references.

11. See *The International Standard Bible Encyclopedia*, ed. James Orr *et al.*, 4 vols. (Chicago: The Howard-Severance Co., 1915), 3:2057–62; hereafter cited as *ISBE*. Lindsay also contributed an article on Baptism (Non-Immersionist View) to this important work (1:388–94). *The International Standard Bible Encyclopedia*, rev. ed., ed. Geoffrey W. Bromiley, et al., 4 vols. (Grand Rapids: William B. Eerdmans Publishing Co., 1979–1988) maintained Lindsay's article on Baptism in the revised edition as the "Reformed View," 1:418–23.

12. Lindsay, *Church*, vii.

13. Ibid., viii. Quotations are given in English, using the standard sources of his time. Lindsay writes that this had been done "after consultation with friends whose advice seemed to be too valuable to be neglected"—seeming to indicate he might have preferred to leave the quotes in their original language or, perhaps, to have made his own translations.

14. Lindsay, *Church*, viii.

15. Ibid.

16. Ibid., ix.

17. See Lindsay, *Church*, ix–x.

18. Lindsay, *Church*, xi.

19. See Lindsay, *Church*, xi–xii.

20. See Lindsay, *Church*, ch. 1 for these themes. On church as a sacerdotal society, Lindsay is clear that every Christian offers sacrifices of praise and confession to God and that "there is no trace in the New Testament Church of any specially holy places or times or persons." Believers may "select one from among themselves to be their minister." But while there may be a "*ministering priesthood*," there "cannot be a *mediating priesthood* within the Christian society" for "there is one Mediator only, and all, men, women and children, have the promise of immediate entrance into the presence of God, and are priests" (35).

21. See Lindsay, *Church*, 44ff. Lindsay's evidences for these distinct gatherings rises mainly from 1 Corinthians as supplemented by passages from the *Didache*.

22. Ibid., 58.

23. Ibid., 59–60.

24. Ibid., 65–66. He notes that "in the apostolic and early sub-apostolic church the prophetic ministry was manifestly the higher and the local ministry the lower." In his *ISBE* article on ministry, Lindsay distinguished the two different kinds of ministry as the ministry of "those speaking the Word of God" (*diakonia tou logou*) as "prophets" and the "ministry of tables" (*diakonein trapezais*)—the ministry of "deacons" who carried out various tasks. He then goes on with the prophetic/local division. See *ISBE* 3:2057–60.

25. Lindsay, *Church*, 70. Lindsay notes that "the ministry of the local church, which is the foundation whence has come the present ministry in the Church in all its branches, was as much founded on the 'gifts' of the Spirit as was the ministry of the Word" (n. 3).

26. Ibid., 72–73.

27. Ibid., 73. The apostle Paul was "the highest type of the first order of the prophetic" whose "duties and the authority which lay behind them were what belonged to the *planting* of Christianity." "Prophets" were those "specially filled" with a "wealth of insight, and inspired or 'gifted' to disclose to their fellows the divine counsels and the hidden mysteries of the faith." "Teachers" (*didaskaloi*) were those who had personally received the gift of knowledge which "fitted them to instruct their fellow believers" for the edification of the community. See chapter 3, *passim*.

28. Ibid., 115. The title of Lecture IV is "The Church of the First Century—Creating Its Ministry."

29. Lindsay holds this view against Bishop J. B. Lightfoot with whom he often agreed in other matters, citing other authorities (such as Boehmer, Ritschl, and Lange) in support. He notes also that "the Hebrew village community was ruled by a small corporation of *seven men* (Josephus, *Antiquities* 4.8.14,38), as the Hindu village is managed by the council of the *Five* or the Punchayat" (*Church*, 117). He also cited other missionary examples of native, representational organizations from China and the South Seas.

30. Lindsay, *Church*, 118.

31. Ibid., 152.

32. Ibid., 163–65.

33. See Lindsay, *Church*, 183ff.

34. Ibid., 205.

35. See Lindsay's Lecture VI in *Church* and 246ff.

36. See Lindsay, *Church*, 249. Elders assisted the bishop in conducting public worship, placed their hands on the offering while the bishop prayed the prayer of thanksgiving, stood with catechumens who were being baptized, and introduced them to the congregation. They also were to visit the sick and pray for them, care for the young and exercise discipline. Deacons were to visit the congregation, report cases of sickness to the bishop and to the elders, have special charge over the poor, "especially of the 'secret poor,' widows, orphans and strangers." "Widows" in the church had duties of being sick-nurses of the community and were honored for "these loving services and for their prayers for the whole congregation." Lindsay draws this material from the *Canons of Hippolytus*.

37. See Lindsay, *Church*, 259–61.

38. Ibid., 266.

39. Ibid.

40. See Lindsay, *Church*, 280ff. Lindsay said Cyprian believed that "as each bishop sums up in himself the church over which he presides, the whole Church of Christ practically exists in the whole of the bishops, and the harmonious action of the whole Church can be expressed through the common action and agreement of all the bishops" (314). This agreement was obtained through Church Councils.

41. See Lindsay, *Church*, 318–19.

42. See Lindsay, *Church*, 335–36. He notes that Councils had become a regular part of the organization of the churches before the end of the third century.

43. See Lindsay, *Church*, 350.

44. Lindsay, *Church*, 352–53. Lindsay quotes Theodore Mommsen as saying that "the conquering Christian Church took its hierarchic weapons from the arsenal of the enemy," (353) citing *The Provinces of the Roman Empire* (1886), 1:349.

45. Lindsay, *Church*, 356.

46. Ibid., 356–57.

47. See Lindsay, *Church*, 357–58.

48. See Lindsay, *Church*, 360. He notes that the Roman state did all it could to persecute nonconformist Christians, a "glaringly un-Christian mode of creating and vindicating the visible unity of the Catholic Church."

49. Lindsay, *Church*, 361. These are the concluding words of his lectures.

50. Lindsay, *Reformation*, 1:vii.

51. Lindsay, *Luther*, vii.

52. Ibid.

53. Lindsay, *Reformation*, 1:vii–viii.

54. See Lindsay, *Reformation*, 1:viii–ix.

55. Lindsay, *Reformation*, 1:ix.

56. It is not possible here to summarize completely Lindsay's two volume *History of the Reformation*. The following analysis indicates some important theological elements which inform his historiography and which, at the same time, emerge from Lindsay's studies of the historical sources.

57. Lindsay, *Reformation*, 1:124–25.

58. Ibid., 1:125. Lindsay finds this also in the fourth book of Thomas à Kempis' *Imitatio Christi* where, despite wrong notions of the sacrament, it is clear that "he had a clear conception that God's grace was freely given, and not merited by what man can do" (1:126).

59. Ibid., 1:126.

60. Ibid., 1:190. Lindsay believed the Christian Humanists did not really perceive they were living in a time of revolution where more than moral renovation was needed. Abuses in the church were severe. Yet the Humanists believed that "the path of reformation lay through a great readjustment of the existing conditions of the religious life, rather than through ecclesiastical revolution to a thorough-going reconstruction." This was the Humanist failure. Lindsay also saw the Christian Humanists as naive in seeming to believe "with a childlike innocence that the constituted authorities, secular and ecclesiastical, would lead the way in this peaceful reform, mainly because they were tinged with Humanist culture, and were the patrons of artists and men of learning" (1:187).

61. Ibid., 1:190–91. Lindsay saw Humanist reforms as failing to meet the needs of sixteenth-century people who were constantly visited by the plague and lived in fear of a Turkish invasion, of death and judgment hereafter. "What they wanted," said Lindsay, "was a sense of God's forgiveness for their sins, and they greedily seized on Indulgences, pilgrimages to holy places, and relic-worship to secure the pardon they longed for. The aristocratic and intellectual reform, contemplated by the Christian Humanists, scarcely appealed to them. Their longing for a certainty of salvation could not be satisfied with recommendations to virtuous living according to the rules of Neo-Platonic ethics." Thus "the Reformation needed a man who had himself felt that commanding need of pardon which was sending his fellows travelling from shrine to shrine, who could tell them in plain homely words, which the common man could understand, how each one of them could win that pardon for himself, who could deliver them from the fear of the priest, and show them the way to the peace of God. The Reformation needed Luther" (1:188).

62. *Luther's Works* (Erlangen edition), 31:279 in Lindsay, *Reformation*, 1:428.

63. Lindsay, *Reformation*, 1:429, citing Luther's contrast of the two kinds of faith where faith as "a form of knowledge" is contrasted with faith *"which throws itself upon God,* whether in life or in death," and which "alone makes a Christian man" (*Luther's Works* [Erlangen edition], 22:15).

64. Lindsay, *Reformation*, 1:430. Lindsay wrote that "saving faith in the Reformation sense is not belief in a proposition, but trust in a person—living trust on a living Saviour—a turning of the heart to Christ." See "He Shall Turn the Heart of the Fathers," in *College Addresses: And Sermons*, 117.

65. Lindsay, *Reformation*, 1:430.

66. Ibid.

67. Ibid., 1:432. For Lindsay, this experiential dimension was at the heart of the Protestant doctrine of justification by faith. For the Protestant, he wrote, "justification is a personal experience which is complete in itself, and does not depend on any external machinery; in the other, the Mediaeval, it is a prolonged action of usages, sacraments, external machinery of all kinds, which by their combined effect are supposed to change a sinner gradually into a saint, righteous in the eyes of God. With the former, it is a continuous experience; with the latter, it cannot fail to be intermittent as the external means are actually employed or for a time laid aside" (1:448–49).

68. Ibid., 1:455.

69. Ibid.

70. Ibid., 1:458–59.

71. Ibid., 1:459.

72. Ibid., 1:461–62. He cites Luther's instancing the Gospel of John and First John, the Letters of Paul, especially Romans, Galatians, and Ephesians, as well as First Peter, as being portions of the Bible where the word of God is clearly seen. Luther declared that if Christians possessed no other books than these, the way of salvation would be

perfectly clear. In other portions of Scripture, the word of God shines forth with special clearness, as in the Psalms which Luther called the Bible within the Bible (1:462).

73. Ibid., 1:463–64. This same type of distinction was made by Robertson Smith, who used the careful distinction: "Scripture records or conveys to us the Word of God." See Riesen, *Criticism and Faith*, 140ff. According to Lindsay, Smith's view was to be distinguished from the "Broad Church" view in that "while they regarded some parts of the Bible as God's Word and some parts not, Smith regarded the whole of it, 'even geographical and architectural descriptions,' as necessary to complete the manifestation of God to His people." Smith's views were also distinct from the Princeton School in that "whereas they completely identified the Word of God with Scripture, "Smith distinguished between them. Whereas they by their identification could allow no errors whatever in the Bible, or for that matter any approach to it which recognized errors, Smith allowed himself the freedom to treat some things in the Bible as matters for ordinary human investigation, leaving untouched that which could be apprehended only by faith and the illumination of the Holy Spirit" (Riesen, *Criticism and Faith*, 139).

74. Lindsay, *Reformation*, 1:464.

75. Ibid., 1:464–65. In 1895, Lindsay published a very important article distinguishing the Reformers' views of Scripture with the Princeton School of Charles and A. A. Hodge and B. B. Warfield. This was a sequel to his piece on W. Robertson Smith's *Doctrine of Scripture*. Lindsay believed the Princeton view which emphasized the inspiration and inerrancy of Scripture was a "real departure" from "the theology of the Reformation." Lindsay's main critique included these points: "1) Their purely intellectual apprehension of Scripture; 2) Their reduction of the real distinction between the Word of God and Scripture to a really formal difference; 3) Their formal as opposed to a religious idea of the infallibility and authority of Scripture; and 4) Their still more formal relegation of the strict infallibility of Scripture to unknown and unknowable original autographs of Scripture." See "The Doctrine of Scripture," *The Expositor*, ed. W. Robertson Nicoll, 5th series, vol. 1 (1895): 278–93. For a discussion of this article, see Jack B. Rogers and Donald K. McKim, *The Authority and Interpretation of the Bible: An Historical Approach* (San Francisco: Harper & Row, 1979), 380–85.

76. Lindsay, *Reformation*, 1:465, citing the Scots Confession Article 19. He next mentions Calvin's *Institutes* 1.7.5. Lindsay said he did not care "to use 'error' as applied to the Bible" for "this whole question of the formal inerrancy of Scripture seems to me to be trivial in the extreme. My sense of the infallibility of the Bible is in no way affected by the knowledge that while the author of the Second Book of Samuel says that David bought the threshing floor and oxen of Ornan for fifty shekels of silver, the author of the First Book of Chronicles says that the price was 600 shekels of gold [2 Sam. 34:24; 1 Chronicles 21:35]. I say simply that there is some discrepancy here: how the mistake arose I do not know and I do not much care (*nec anxie laboro*; [Calvin, *Comm. on Matthew 27:9*]). I do not go to Scripture to learn the price of threshing floors and oxen. I go to learn God's wonderful dealings with David, to see the sins, and repentance, and faith, of the man after God's own heart" ("Doctrine of Scripture," 287).

77. Lindsay, *Reformation*, 1:465. He earlier wrote: "Faith is not required to recognise inerrancy. Inerrancy, if it exists, is merely a matter of fact to be recognised by the ordinary reason. But the infallibility which compels the conviction that God is speaking to us infallibly, telling us that if we hear and accept this Saviour we shall infallibly be saved, requires faith. And that is the infallibility which the Bible possesses and which man needs" ("Doctrine of Scripture," 290).

78. Lindsay, *Reformation*, 1:465.

79. Ibid., 1:465–66.

80. Ibid., 1:466.

81. Lindsay, *Reformation*, 1:467. This position enabled Lindsay to support the biblical criticism of someone such as Robertson Smith, who treated the text reverently and whose basic Christian faith was not disturbed by his findings on scientific or historical questions relating to Scripture.

82. In Lindsay, *College Addresses: And Sermons*, 79ff.

83. Lindsay, *Church*, viii.

84. Lindsay, *College Addresses: And Sermons*, 85–86.

85. Ibid., 91.

86. Ibid., 96.

87. Ibid., 98–99.

88. Ibid., 99–100.

17

HENRY C. SHELDON

STEVEN E. WOODWORTH

Henry Clay Sheldon was born March 12, 1845, in Martinsburg, New York, the son of Ira and Fanny Maria (Bingham) Sheldon. Henry grew up on his parents' farm before entering Yale University, where he received a bachelor's degree in 1867 and a master's degree three years later. Continuing his education at Boston University, he became, in 1871, a member of the first graduating class of that institution's Theological School. Subsequently, he was ordained a minister in the Methodist Episcopal Church and pastored one year in St. Johnsburg, Vermont, and two years in Brunswick, Maine, before being invited to fill the Chair of Historical Theology at Boston University's School of Theology. Desiring to prepare himself for this responsibility, he traveled to Europe and studied for a year at the University of Leipzig. Returning to the United States in 1875, he took up the offered position at Boston University and, in the same year, married Louise McLellan of Brunswick, Maine. They eventually had two sons.

Sheldon was a fixture at Boston University's School of Theology for some forty-six years, earning an impressive reputation as a teacher, mentor, and scholar. He was remembered as a quiet and scholarly professor who combined a rigorous demand for accurate work and diligent preparation with a warmhearted sympathy for young theologians in their search for truth. Over the years he was awarded doctorates of divinity by both Wesleyan University and Lawrence University. In 1895 he was given the title of Professor of Systematic Theology within Boston University's School of Theology. In 1921 he retired to West Newton, Massachusetts, where he continued his study and writing until his death in August, 1928. His life had been that of a quiet and retiring scholar, in many ways uneventful, but enormously productive in thought and literature, as his lengthy list of publications demonstrates.

HISTORY OF CHRISTIAN DOCTRINE

In 1886 Sheldon published his first major work on church history, *History of Christian Doctrine*. Shorter than his subsequent *History of the Christian Church*, the history of doctrine runs to some 290,000 words in two volumes.

For the study of doctrine, Sheldon delineates five distinct periods: the "Age of Apology," from the close of the apostolic era to 320; the "Age of Polemics," from 320 to 726, the "Age of Scholasticism," from 726 to 1517; the "Age of Confessions," from 1517 to 1720; and the "Age of Strife and of Attempted Reconciliation," from 1720 to the time at which Sheldon wrote. The first three of these periods are dealt with in the first volume. Beginning in his coverage of the first period a pattern that he follows without exception through the remainder of the work, Sheldon devotes to each period six chapters: "Factors in the Doctrinal Development of the Period," "The Godhead," "Creation and Creatures," "Redeemer and Redemption," "The Church and the Sacraments," and "Eschatology." This repetitive, almost mechanical, progression through a set series of topics lends the work an orderly, methodical element, but, combined with a highly intellectual subject matter and a fairly heavy style, makes the work laborious reading when compared with his later *History of the Christian Church*.

In looking at factors in the doctrinal development of the first period, Sheldon examines the influence of pagan philosophy, particularly stressing the congeniality of Platonism to Christianity and the degree to which the early church fathers admired Plato. Moving to a discussion of heresies of the time, he divides such movements in thought into three groups: (1) Jewish, (2) Gnostic and Manichaean, and (3) Monarchian. Montanism he classes separately and is less inclined to condemn categorically. Finally, dealing with Scripture and tradition, he emphasizes the strong view of biblical inspiration held by the Fathers, and the importance of tradition as well as its clear subordination to Scripture.

With regard to the first period's doctrine of the Godhead, Sheldon points out that the existence of God was, during this period, generally treated as something intuitively obvious. He criticizes such ancient authors as Origen and Tertullian for holding weak views of the transcendence of God, pointing out the nature and reasons of their errors. After a lengthy discussion of the concept of the Logos in pre-Christian thought and of differing ideas of the early church regarding the nature and origins of the second Person of the Trinity, he concludes the chapter with a discussion of the Holy Spirit, stressing the prevailing belief of the early church—isolated and ambiguous pronouncements to the contrary notwithstanding—in His personality and divinity.

Turning to the subject of creation and creatures, Sheldon deals with the nature and origins of angels and demons, the nature of man, and of the Fall. Here it is interesting to note his statement that "the Church of the first three centuries maintained, quite as strongly as does Arminian Methodism, the actual possession of free will by the descendants of the fallen Adam, but on the whole fell somewhat below the latter in stress upon inherited corruption and dependence upon divine grace" (1:108). In like manner, in the following chapter, that dealing with the Redeemer and redemption, the Methodist church historian does not miss the opportunity of pointing out that the Fathers before Augustine had no concept of a predestination to salvation not conditioned upon divine foreknowledge of human choices. Yet Sheldon is far from making early church history a mere justification of his own theological beliefs, as is evidenced by his concession that the early church seemed to view sanctification as a gradual process, quoting Clement of Alexandria in such an un-Wesleyan statement as, "It is probably impossible all at once to eradicate inbred passions" (1:127). Sheldon also points out the first stirrings, during this period, of what would in later centuries become serious distortions in belief regarding salvation, such as excessive reverence for confessors and martyrs and extreme veneration of Mary. He maintains, however, that such elements had not yet become serious distortions during the period under consideration.

Respecting the teaching of the church about itself during this first period, Sheldon carefully notes the as yet latent tendency toward a belief that there could be no salvation outside the institutional church, just as he recognizes other incipient ideas such as baptismal regeneration and infant baptism. On the other hand, he argues at some length that no basis can be found in this era for certain later views of the eucharist: "To discover here the doctrine of transubstantiation (or consubstantiation) require imagination aided by a peculiar dogmatic impulse" (1:141).

A chapter on eschatology concludes the discussion of the first period. Sheldon describes, with a faint note of condescension, the rise and decline, during this era, of the doctrine of chiliasm—that is, "that the end of the present dispensation is to be preceded by the personal reign of Christ upon earth" (1:145). Also discussed are death, resurrection and final rewards.

"The reign of Constantine naturally ushered in the Age of Polemics" (1:159), a period of activity that Sheldon sees as necessary and useful. The church's predilection for the philosophy of Plato continued, and even the less appealing Neo-Platonism was not without its subtle impact. Monasticism, too, helped shaped doctrine by placing a high value on external works, as well as "the marvelous and the magical" (1:173). Finally, the entanglement of church and state tended to impose an "inert orthodoxy" (1:174).

The church in this period retained a strong view of biblical inspiration with the Scriptures seen as the complete and authoritative substance of Christian doctrine, though—especially for the purpose of refuting misuse of the Bible by Arians—the orthodox made increasing claims for the authority of tradition in its interpretation. Doctrine of the era held that God was impassable, immutable, and transcendent, sometimes almost to the extreme of being unknowable.

In contrast to the orthodox preference for the philosophy of Plato was the tendency of Arianism—if not of Arius himself—toward that of Aristotle. Sheldon deals with several other origins of Arianism before describing the heresy's teachings and its sixty-year struggle with orthodoxy.

Of creation and creatures, this era continued to stress creation out of nothing in six literal days, though Sheldon notes Augustine's unusual views on the subject. Angels began to be ranked in hierarchies and, in a faint prefiguring of what was to come, venerated. Man was generally held to be a creature of two, rather than three, parts. As to the Fall, Sheldon differentiates between the views of the Greek church, the Latin church before Pelagius, Pelagius, and Augustine. Sheldon notes that Augustine's doctrine was both an innovation and a reaction against Pelagianism. Sheldon then distinguishes such shades of belief as semi-Pelagianism and moderate Augustinianism, which latter he credits with "the favor of a very large proportion of the best minds in the Latin Church in the centuries succeeding its rise" (1:241).

The chapter on "Redeemer and Redemption" for this period deals with Arianism, Nestorianism, and the creed of Chalcedon. Further attention is given to the predestinarian views of Augustine with—surprisingly—no negative commentary from Sheldon, who continues to note with disapproval a growing tendency toward a doctrine of salvation by works within the church of this period. In his discussion of the church and the sacraments during this "age of polemics," he is careful to stress the absence of a belief in papal infallibility or in transubstantiation, though he does admit that in view of certain high-flown figurative language used by some theologians during this era "the church in this period was evidently drifting through a mystical maze in the direction of the amazing dogma of transubstantiation" (1:280). Turning to eschatology in this era, Sheldon notes the demise of chiliasm, the beginnings of the doctrine of purgatory, and continued consensus of belief in an eternal hell of literal fire.

Sheldon begins his discussion of what he calls "the age of scholasticism," appropriately, with a discussion of that phenomenon, and of the rise and decline of Aristotelian thought that paralleled its career during the Middle Ages. He gives an evenhanded evaluation of scholasticism, praising it as the product of industrious, systematic thought, but finding fault with it for a number of reasons, chiefly its deference to the medieval Roman Catholic system over the Bible. Most striking in Sheldon's treatment of medieval theology, however, is his discussion of the church and the sacraments, for here, he believes, are found "some of the most objectionable features of the scholastic theology" (1:404). The ideas of Thomas Aquinas and his contemporaries regarding the papacy were "admirably suited to serve as a basis of spiritual despotism." While Sheldon concedes that such may not have been what Aquinas and the others intended, he goes on to state that "there is evidence that despotic notions were not altogether foreign to their minds" (1:387). As proof of this Sheldon cites Thomas's teaching on how to deal with heretics. Even stronger criticism, however, is reserved for the doctrine of transubstantiation: "So the *real* body of Christ in the eucharist turns out to be the most unreal and ghostly thing of which human ingenuity ever attempted to draw the outlines. What is meant by eating this body, which so marvelously contradicts the characteristics of body, no ordinary mind can understand, any more than it can understand what is meant by combining circularity and rectangularity into a single notion, and getting the same between the teeth" (1:397).

Of the doctrine of the eucharist as sacrifice he observes that "the beautiful Christian idea, designed to be embodied in the rite, was made to recede behind an inferior Jewish conception" (1:398). And the custom, just introduced at this time, of denying the cup to the laity, he labels a "robbery" (1:399).

The second volume of Sheldon's *History of Christian Doctrine* opens with the fourth period of church history, that stretching from 1517 to 1720 and having as its central feature the Protestant Reformation.

Sheldon's approach to the Reformation is little short of exultant. He calls it "an era in the history of Christian doctrine inferior in importance to none since the age of the apostles,—an era from which one might date, without presumption, the second birth of Christianity" (2:3). Having thus introduced the Reformation, Sheldon turns to his usual progression of topics for each period, beginning, as always, with philosophy. After a lengthy discussion of various philosophers from Hobbes to Locke to Descartes and a number of others, he concludes that their thought had but little impact on the Reformation—so much for philosophy. As for the Reformation movement itself, Sheldon depicts the Lutheran wing as reacting against the Jewish elements in Roman Catholicism and the Reformed wing as reacting against the pagan. He discusses various fringe movements of the Reformation era, such as the Socinians, before moving to a very lengthy treatment of differences in the ways Protestants and Roman Catholics viewed Scripture, tradition, authority, and knowledge. Of even more interest, in view of Sheldon's own theological position, is his discussion of different ways of looking at Scripture within the Protestant movement itself, among Calvinists, Arminians, and Anabaptists. Much the same approach is taken to the doctrine of the Godhead, with Sheldon pointing out the continuing prevalence of the orthodox position but with a number of exceptions who took other views of the Trinity. Among these was, for example, John Milton, whose views Sheldon characterizes as "Arian or Semi-Arian."

As he continues through his regular litany of topics, Sheldon generally gives the views on each subject of Catholics, Lutherans, Calvinists, Arminians, and such fringe groups as the Quakers and Socinians. The Methodist historian is scrupulously just to Calvin and his followers, and though he may quote the statement of one of Calvin's contemporaries denouncing, say, unconditional election, he is quick to point out the ways in which such a statement may not be entirely fair. Sheldon saves his own denunciations for Roman Catholicism and can hardly pass up an opportunity to disparage such doctrines as transbustantiation.

The fifth period in Sheldon's scheme of the history of doctrine he calls the period of strife and attempted reconciliation, a necessary process, he believes, in order that "Christian doctrine be tested at every point" (2:221). He proceeds to the discussion of the era through the use of his by now thoroughly familiar succession of thematic chapters. The first, on "Factors in the Doctrinal Development of the Era," contains an even larger than usual discussion of philosophy. In all, this treatment of the thought of such men as Leibnitz, Hume, Kant, Hegel, and others, takes up well over a fifth of the entire space devoted to the era—all six chapters. Hence

Sheldon proceeds through this era much as through the one before, though in his discussions of particular doctrines a tendency appears for denominations to replace the large theological schools of thought of the Reformation period. The Methodists appear, but receive no inordinate amount of attention. Sheldon describes Methodism's version of Arminianism as that of Arminius himself, less removed from Calvinism, more conscious of divine grace, than some of the later developments upon the thought of the Dutch theologian. Catholicism, by contrast, virtually disappears from discussion in the treatment of this period of the history of doctrine, as Sheldon observes that it underwent little development and remained set in the pattern of the previous era. Turning to the discussion of eschatology, chiliasm becomes, for the first time in Sheldon's parlance for the heading of a topic, millenarianism, and he concedes that a number of scholars have embraced such a view. He maintains, however, that "the weight of theological opinion is against it" (2:389). The work ends in a spirit that is, despite Sheldon's occasional forays against Catholicism and other ideas he believes to be mistaken, characteristic of its overall tone, as Sheldon observes that the wisest statement of man's future state is to be found in the words of the apostle: "Beloved, now are we the sons of God, and it doth not yet appear what we shall be; but we know that, when He shall appear, we shall be like Him; for we shall see Him as He is."

History of the Christian Church

Sheldon's other major work on church history is his *History of the Christian Church*, which appeared in 1895, nine years after the *History of Christian Doctrine*. Sheldon's intention here was to produce a church history that would be useful to scholars without being daunting to laymen. For this reason he resisted the temptation to expand the work endlessly in order to make it more "comprehensive." At roughly 680,000 words (five volumes totaling more than twenty-five hundred pages), it is long enough, though still considerably shorter than the works of some of Sheldon's contemporaries. Keeping the narrative concise was made easier for Sheldon by the fact that he had already completed a history of doctrine and thus he could and did pass lightly over that topic, insisting that it belonged in a separated study. He consciously kept his discussions of the various heresies and doctrinal innovations to the minimum necessary for a sound understanding of the general flow of church history.

The work's usefulness to the modern student is, of course, to some extent limited by its nineteenth-century origins. Sheldon's style, while less pedantic than that of most scholarly writers of his era—or of his previous work—will still impress most modern students as heavy, and his habit of assuming in his readers a knowledge of Greek, Latin, German, and French—and thus leaving most quotations from those languages untranslated, particularly in footnotes—may be irritating to some. Nevertheless, Sheldon is far from dull, spicing his narrative with occasional hints of dry humor, often at the expense of the inflated pretensions of the papacy. His overall scheme of organization is also less stilted than the one he used in *History of Christian Doctrine*, being more flowing and less artificially mechanical.

The first volume covers Christianity until 590, which Sheldon divides into two periods, separated by Constantine's edict of toleration in 313. Striking is Sheldon's tendency to confront head-on the ideas or arguments he deems false. The challenge of those who deny the historicity of the supernatural within the Bible he meets and dismisses with wit and cogency, setting the tone for his treatment of papists, sacerdotalists, those who insist on a certain mode of baptism, and others.

As he progresses from the apostolic to the post-apostolic era within his first general time period, Sheldon discusses at length the struggle, both in ideas and in flesh and blood, between Christianity and paganism. He then passes on to brief discussions of some of the notable heresies of the second and third centuries, including Gnosticism and Manichaeism. Separate chapters on church government and discipline, on the one hand, and Christian worship and life on the other, close out his coverage of the pre-Constantinian period.

Sheldon's second period of church history, also covered in the first volume of his *History of the Christian Church*, extends from Constantine's edict of toleration in 313 to Pope Gregory the Great, 590. In discussing church and state through the century and a half of the "Christian Empire," he reflects insightfully upon the significance and results of such entanglements of the kingdoms of Christ and the caesars. Passing on through various doctrinal controversies, including Arianism, Sheldon turns, in his chapter on the church government of the period, to the first stirrings of hierarchicalism, asserting that the practice was contrary to the scriptural pattern but that this pattern was not intended to be prescriptive. A discussion of the beginnings of monasticism and saint- and relic-worship, as well as a brief chapter on early Christian art, architecture, and music, conclude the first volume.

The second volume is devoted to the "Medieval Church," the history of which he divides into three periods. The first of these extends from the time of Gregory the Great to that of Gregory VII (1073). This segment of the book is primarily devoted to the barbarian tribes and the slow and imperfect spread of Christianity among them. Here Sheldon's more-or-less obligatory chapters on church government, mode of life, and worship are considerably briefer than other chapters in the work.

What Sheldon denotes as the second period of the history of the medieval church—that from Gregory VII to Boniface VIII (1294)—affords him opportunity for fuller discussion. The narrative here centers on the growth of papal theocracy through the careers of such ambitious popes as Gregory VII and Innocent III, as well as such dynamic bishops as Thomas Becket. Throughout this discussion, while frequently manifesting his disapproval of "sacerdotalism," Sheldon is remarkable fair with the powerful men who built and attempted to maintain papal theocracy, admiring their personal qualities. Still, Sheldon is far from even such limited acceptance of papal claims as would allow that the papacy might have been a needed institution for that immature phase of church history. He rarely spares criticism where it is due, and takes particular pleasure in pointing out actions or statements of popes that lend peculiar absurdity to the infallibility subsequently claimed for them.

Sheldon then deals with monasticism, particularly the Cistercians and the mendicants, before turning his attention to the Crusades. Surprisingly little attention is given to scholasticism, which shares a much briefer chapter with mysticism. Thomas Aquinas rates little more than a passing notice, far less than is given to figures of his stature in other eras.

In Sheldon's third period of the medieval church, running from 1294 to the posting of Luther's Ninety-five Theses in 1517, considerable attention is given to dissent within Roman Catholicism. He begins the discussion of the period with what is to be his new obligatory chapter in each large division of the work—replacing his previous standbys on church government and mode of worship and life—the political background of the era. Thence he proceeds to a lengthy discussion of the conciliar movement, before devoting short chapters to the Waldenses, John Wycliffe, John Huss, the mystics, and Savonarola. As almost an afterthought at the end of the period, he adds a brief discussion of the medieval Greek church and a chapter on medieval Christian art, architecture, and music.

The last three volumes of the *History of the Christian Church* are devoted to what Sheldon calls "The Modern Church." Volume three deals with church history from 1517 to 1720, a period that Sheldon divides at the Peace of Westphalia in 1648. The first of these periods naturally focuses on the Reformation, which Sheldon obviously celebrates as a "vindication . . . of justification by faith, and the sole authority of the Scriptures" and "a revolt of the human mind against the despotism of a corrupted hierarchy" and "an untold benefaction" (3:3–5). He concedes that in the turmoil of the Reformation era some excesses may have been committed, but these "by no means nullify its historical worth and grandeur" (3:5). He sees the Reformation as benefiting even Roman Catholicism "by re-acting upon it through its higher moral and religious life," and goes on to state that "Romanism owes no small part of such moral respectability as it has maintained during the last three centuries, to the quickening currents which the Reformation brought into Europe" (3:3). One would look in vain here for any simpering "repentance" for supposed divisions brought about in the church by the great movement of the sixteenth century.

Sheldon sets the stage for the Reformation with a brief sketch of the political situation on its eve, particularly in the Holy Roman Empire, and a much fuller discussion of Renaissance humanism in its relation to the coming of the Reformation. While finding much to commend in Erasmus, Sheldon subjects him to mild criticism for stopping short of full approval of the Reformation, indeed, asserting that the noted humanist was unheroic if not downright cowardly in doing so. Still, allowance is made for Erasmus's advanced age and temperamental unsuitability for the rough work that lay ahead.

Moving to the Reformation itself, Sheldon devotes the greater part of a very lengthy chapter to the life and spiritual pilgrimage of Martin Luther as the centerpiece of a discussion of the outbreak of the Reformation in Germany. Luther is presented in an understanding and favorable light. Attention is also given to Melanchthon, particularly as regards the development of Lutheran doctrine.

Subsequent chapters deal with the Reformation in various other countries: Switzerland, where the development of the reform movement under Zwingli and others concurrent with and independent of Luther is noted; France, where violent conflict brought apparent success but ultimate downfall to Protestantism; Italy, Spain, and the Netherlands, where brutal persecution achieved success or near-success in stamping out Protestantism in some areas; and the British Isles, with their own turbulent history. Chapters on the Counter Reformation and the Thirty Years' War conclude Sheldon's treatment of the Reformation era. In dealing with the former, Sheldon gives a scathing account of the Inquisition and an even more negative depiction of the Jesuits, whose casuistry he abhors.

In the second period covered in volume three, that from 1648 to 1720, one reads of religious developments in the France of Louis XIV, and in the Britain of Commonwealth, Restoration, William III and Anne. Of more interest is his account of the church in Germany and other countries, including as it does a discussion of pietism, and, though strictly speaking his ministry fell outside the years set for the period, its foremost spokesman, Nicholas von Zinzendorf. Though generally sympathetic, Sheldon's account is far from uncritical, faulting Zinzendorf with "one-sidedness in certain particulars" of his doctrine as well as downright bad taste in certain overly sentimental statements about Christ, His passion, and the Holy Spirit. Of some of Zinzendorf's many hymns Sheldon writes that they "deserve only to be forgotten" (3:597), while reserving high praise for others.

As in the case of several of the volumes of this work, Sheldon concludes this one with a brief, almost perfunctory, chapter on the eastern church.

Volume four covers the first part of Sheldon's final period of church history. That period begins in 1720 and continues down to the time of Sheldon's writing. Volume four covers the church history of most countries to about 1820. The volume begins with a chapter on the British Isles, the centerpiece of which is, naturally, the Wesleyan revival (Sheldon refers to it as "The Great Revival"). After a discussion of the growth of deism and of the dismal state of morals in Britain in the early eighteenth century, the author turns to the story of John Wesley and the beginnings of Methodism. The account is, of course, sympathetic, but not to the point of blindness. Sheldon is prepared to admit mistakes on the part of Methodism's founder. Proceeding with his account of the revival, Sheldon devotes sections of the chapter to Whitefield and the Calvinist Methodists, to Charles Wesley and the hymnody of Methodism, and to John Wesley's organization of the movement that was to become, not entirely by his will, a denomination. Attention is given to such critics of Wesley as Augustus Toplady and to such of his defenders as John William Fletcher. The chapter ends, somewhat anticlimatically, with discussions of developments among the dissenters and in Scotland and Ireland.

Sheldon then turns his attention to the history of the church in the United States, noting with approval the distinction observed there between civil government and the ecclesiastical establishments of the various denominations. He observes the influences of the "French Deism" and the countering action of the wave of revivals during the early 1800s. Of the latter movement he is approving though not entirely uncritical "as respects some of their methods and incidents" (5:227). Christianity, he believed, had a greater influence over all classes of American society than over those of any other in the world. While he is inclined to defend the American church against charges of excessive denominational fragmentation—noting that many of the denominations had their origins elsewhere and were imported by immigrants—he is equally quick to condemn the church's partial tolerance of slavery in the United States. A lengthy discussion of that issue, in its relation to American church history, follows.

Most of the remainder of this lengthy chapter, well over one hundred pages, is devoted to "Denominational Movements and Crises in the

United States." Essentially this is a series of individual denominational histories for the nineteenth century. The chapter concludes with brief discussions of church history in Canada and Latin America.

Finally, Sheldon inserts his obligatory short—one might almost say perfunctory—chapter on the eastern church, and then another short chapter giving "a glance" at Protestant missions. In his conclusion to the entire five-volumes, Sheldon admits that much of the history of the Christian church has been acted out at a level considerably below that prescribed in the Gospels, but he maintains that these sordid chapters are far from being the whole story. "As secular history makes but moderate account of intervals of peace, and fills a large share of its pages with stories of armed conflicts, because of the prominence with which these stand out in the memorials of the past, so church history takes comparatively little note of the treasure which Christianity, even in the least favored ages, has brought to multitudes of humble believers" (412–13).

BIBLIOGRAPHY

Sheldon, Henry C. *History of Christian Doctrine*. 2 vols. New York: Harper & Brothers, 1886.
History of the Christian Church. 5 vols.. New York: Thomas Y. Crowell, 1895; reprinted, Peabody, Mass.: Hendrickson, 1988.
System of Christian Doctrine. Cincinnati: Jennings & Pye, 1903.
History of Unbelief in the Nineteenth Century. Cincinnati: Eaton & Mains, 1907.
Sacerdotalism in the Nineteenth Century. Cincinnati: Eaton & Mains, 1909.
Studies in Recent Adventism. New York: Abingdon, 1915.

SECONDARY SOURCES

Rosser, George E. *A New Era in Philosophic Theology*. Macon, Ga.: J. W. Burke, 1934.

18

ADOLF VON HARNACK

LARRY DIXON

All attempts to determine the essence of Christianity, argued church historian Ernst Troelsch, should be avoided by bunglers, the doctrinaire, the fanatics, the narrow-minded, the underlings, and the specialists![1] Adolf Harnack, sometimes referred to as modern Protestantism's most influential church historian, fits into none of Troelsch's categories. He vigorously invested his long and full life precisely in an endeavour to define the essence of Christianity.

Not confining his pursuit to the sterile atmosphere of academia, Harnack grappled with questions of theology and history in the church and in his world of emerging liberal theology. His public pronouncements and his ecclesiastical controversies prompted each criticisms as Tyrrell's oft-quoted judgment that "the Christ that Harnack sees, looking back through nineteen centuries of Catholic darkness, is only the reflection of a Liberal Protestant face, seen at the bottom of a dark well."[2]

LIFE

Born May 7, 1851, in Dorpat, Estonia, Adolf was the older of the twins Adolf and Axel, the second and third of the five children of the distinguished Lutheran scholar Theodosius Harnack and his wife, Anna Carolina Maria Ewers. Theodosius taught church history and homiletics at the Lutheran university, serving also as its rector.

Harnack's mother died in childbirth when Adolf was only six. His early childhood was spent in the towns of Dorpat and Erlangen, the latter a stronghold of Lutheran orthodoxy in Bavaria. His father saw to it that all his sons obtained a solid grounding in history, theology, and philosophy. Perhaps more influential upon Harnack was his mentor and confidant at Dorpat, Moritz von Engelhardt, who taught him Church history, but, more importantly, impressed upon Harnack the value of meticulous textual criticism and source study in church historical problems. Upon completing his secondary education, Harnack wrote of his interest in theology to a close friend:

> You will have heard that I am going to study theology. I do not know whether you are one of those who look down on everything called religion and theology with disdain or indifference. And yet, no matter how one looks at Christianity and possibly regards it as a mistake, is it not of real value to pursue the history of this mistake and to discover which world-shaking events and transformations this mistake has caused? . . . The longer I live . . . the more I discover daily that all problems and conflicts finally go back to the religious dimension . . . and why the Christian point of view can never be quite discarded. That is why I am enthusiastic theologian; I hope to find in this scholarly discipline (*Wissenschaft*) the *way* towards solving the major problems of our life. . . . I do not desire to be given the fulness of ready-made statements of faith, rather, I want to produce every statement in that web by myself and then make it my own.[3]

Harnack pursued the history of this "mistake" all his days. Not only did he personally shun ready-made statements of faith, he also thought it inappropriate that such statements be offered to others. Seeking to liberate Christianity from its theological accretions, Harnack sought to discern "the Gospel in the Gospel," the kernel from the husk.[4] Leaving Dorpat in 1872 to study at the University of Leipzig, he wrote his doctoral dissertation a year later. The following year he completed his habilitation-dissertation on Gnosticism. In 1877 Harnack met Albrecht Ritschl, the theologian to whom Harnack pointed as the one who would rescue theology both from romanticism and irrationalism.

Harnack began his teaching career at the University of Leipzig, at twenty-three. He taught at Giessen (1879-1886) and Marburg (1886-1889) before going to Berlin in 1889, where for forty-two years (until his death on June 10, 1930) he continued his many-faceted work. He twice declined an invitation to assume a full professorship at Harvard University, also turning down an offer in 1921 to become German ambassador to the United States.

His Berlin appointment was challenged by the church for a variety of reasons. His doubts about the authorship of the fourth Gospel and other New Testament books, his unorthodox interpretations of biblical miracles including the resurrection, and his denial of Christ's institution of baptism brought opposition from the orthodox. Although his appointment was upheld by the Prussian cabinet and the emperor, the dispute cast a shadow over the rest of his career. Harnack was denied all official recognition by the church, including the right to scrutinize his own pupils in church examinations. Nevertheless, in light of the breadth and depth of his scholarly activity, Harnack deserves the description as "perhaps the most influential church historian and theologian until World War I."[5]

Through a series of lectures he delivered during the winter semester of 1899-1900 at the University of Berlin, Harnack assessed Christianity in the light of modern scholarship. His audience numbered over six hundred and his lectures were taken down in shorthand. Published in 1900 as *Das Wesen des Christentums*, Harnack's lectures were translated the next year into English under the title *What Is Christianity?* The German original went through eleven editions and was translated into fifteen languages during his lifetime, having sold more than 70,000 copies before Harnack's death. Described as "the book of liberal Protestantism,"[6] the demand for the German edition of 1900 was such that the Leipzig freight yards were jammed for days by boxes of Harnack's book.

Harnack's writings were, as one scholar describes them, "unbelievably numerous." Five years before his death, the titles of his published works, including his books, pamphlets, and articles, totalled 1,658. Many of his writings were large volumes, the overwhelming majority dealing with serious scholarly research.[7] His editorial activity was also impressive. Working constantly with original sources, Harnack became one of the most able editors of ancient writings the church ever had. Gaining early recognition though his edition of the apostolic fathers, Harnack also edited the *Didache*, or *Teaching of the Twelve Apostles*, including with it a notable discussion of the problems of early church organization.[8]

His concern to foster scholarship led to his prompting the Royal Prussian Academy of Sciences to found a commission on the study of the church fathers. Harnack became the leader in publishing a series of well-edited texts of the Greek-speaking Christian authors of the first three centuries, a series that by the time of his death totalled thirty-five volumes.

With Otto von Gebhardt, Harnack also edited texts and studies on early church history (Texte und Untersuchungen zur Geschichte der alt christlichen Literatur). Harnack and Emil Schurer founded and edited the Theologische Literaturzeitung, an outstanding survey and review of publications in all areas of theological study. Harnack's literary production continued without intermission from his collaboration with von Gebhardt and Theodor von Zahn in an edition of the apostolic fathers (1876-1878) to his final study of First Clement (1929).[9]

From 1903 to 1912, Harnack served as president of Evangelical-Social Congress, an organization that worked to interpret Christianity to the ranks of labor. He became the general director of the Royal Library in 1905 (until 1921), carrying out a rebuilding program and a combining of the Prussian university libraries. Convinced that some men who were not effective teachers were nevertheless able researchers, Harnack persuaded the Kaiser and others to establish the Kaiser Wilhelm Institute, a facility for technical research in all lines of study. Harnack, to no one's surprise, was its first president. He received his title "von Harnack" in 1914.

Harnack's full and productive life was not only marked by a literary production of over sixteen hundred titles; he also occupied the position of full professor in some of the most prestigious universities, simultaneously serving as the president of several international congresses, and as the general director of the Prussian Royal Library. By imperial decree he became the first president of the Royal Society. Many of these duties overlapped each other.[10]

Adolf Harnack was driven by his inquiry into the essence of Christianity. Our concern in this chapter is to examine his understanding of history, his desire for a scientific theology, and his relation to orthodox Christianity. We then will briefly survey several of his major publications.

THEOLOGY AND HISTORY

Harnack devoted his life to the pursuit of the relationship between the two disciplines of theology and history. As both theologian and historian, Harnack emphasized that a sound knowledge of the past is the business not only of the historian, but of everyone who wishes to benefit from its wealth and strength.[11] History is an opportunity to free "ourselves from the past wherever it has become a burden, to be enabled to do what is right in the present and to prepare the future suitably and with prudence."[12]

Distinguishing between history and biography (historical research excludes the subjective; biography engages in re-experiencing for the purpose of re-creation), Harnack argues that history offers us something firm and secure. That something is the abundance of significant data the truth of which cannot be questioned (e.g., the occurrence of major events and their succession, monuments and developed institutions, etc.). History, although it moves back into "shrouded antiquity," offers each succeeding age an abundance of certain and significant facts from all dimensions of life. The study of history assuredly does not guarantee anyone accuracy in predictions about what might lie ahead, but its diligent pursuit allows historians to become most certain in their future calculations as they grow in their experience of life and history.

Harnack sees three basic steps in the search for meaning in history. Speaking of both the longitudinal (the direction, strengths, and weaknesses of a movement) and the cross sections (the character and style of any given moment) of history, he argues that these two form the first step in historical research. One ought to inquire about direction in history, not primarily about "right or wrong" or "true or false." Rather than a dull recitation of dictators and dates, a proper approach to history promises life and illumination, particularly in terms of direction: "If the gaze is fixed firmly on historical development, no matter whether it is political, scholarly, artistic, religious, or the like, then the dead succession of events comes not only alive but also open to interpretation and understanding, especially if one takes into account at the same time with what force a phenomenon resisted and overcame its opposition and where and why direction was changed."[13]

We study history ultimately in order to know institutions: "Nothing at all, not even great men and the genius makes a lasting impression on the human community that has not taken form in institutions."[14] Therefore, the second step in the study of history is to recognize that all institutions originate in ideas. Harnack emphasizes that "just as surely as everything which is only ideology and not yet institution is not yet history, so also all of the history of institutions is unprobed as long as the motivating ideas are unknown. The ideas are, however, the spirit."[15] If all history is a history of the spirit, Harnack reasons, "we shall remain wretched and in bondage if we limit ourselves to ourselves; we shall become rich and free if we enter every door of history and make ourselves at home in its spacious rooms."[16]

The third step in the interpretation of history concerns value. Some argue that one can infer from history itself a measure of value for what it produces. Others suggests that the historian avoid all valuation, determining simply what *is* in relation to history but not what *ought to be*. If the premise be granted that life is something of absolute value, then the historian should measure and evaluate the processes of history by a standard of how life is preserved and advanced.

Seeing a form of progressivism operative in history, Harnack rejects the cynical view that history is the meaningless repetition of occurrences. He also rejects "the wretched notion" that in "history one worthless cycle of thinking and striving replaces another and all hope is reduced to the comfortless outlook that the bursting bubble of today will not be the last one."[17] For those who might think that a preoccupation with history leads to personal paralysis in life and work, Harnack argues cogently that "[W]hoever does not want to hear the majestic organ music of world events, as it has sounded through three millennia, must remain satisfied with the bell-stroke of the moment, but that is a bad exchange. History paralyses only when one does not allow its deepest content to touch one's being. As we have seen, that content is to be found in the upward-striving direction, in the development of force, in the striving towards unity and in the great and good personalities. All of these, however, have the inner strength to draw us into themselves and to fill us with life."[18]

Great and good personalities have acted with force in history to teach us that we do not stand helplessly before an immovable fate. On the contrary, history shows us that we can control the most important part of our destiny. Therefore, challenges Harnack, we must "lay hold of destiny with a high spirit and shape it accordingly."[19]

The eighteenth century's great assault on the connection between religion and history has been repelled, according to Harnack, especially by Lessing's principle that historical truth, which is accidental in character, can never become the proof of the truths of Reason. Religion was restored to its proper place when the meaning of history came to be accurately understood. Religion is no ready-made structure, but a growth—a growth that falls within the history of humanity. Its developments are a reality, as are its prophets and founders. Therefore, history ought to be approached with an appreciation bordering on awe. "Reverence for the spirit that prevails in history, and gratitude to all those from whom we have received any benefit—and without it we should have been the poorer in our inner and outer life—must, therefore, govern our views of that science."[20]

Not only has the eighteenth century's assault against the connection between history and religion proved a failure, but the objectives raised to the legitimacy of Christian history are answerable. Harnack lists three prevaling objections to Christian history: (1) because Christianity is only a link in the development of history, its founder cannot have any peculiar or unique position; (2) even though Christianity's founder may have been an incomparable man, He lived many centuries ago (therefore, it is impossible to go to Him with our troubles); and, (3) our idea of Christ, if not destroyed by historical criticism, has been rendered doubtful (i.e., facts of history can never be known with a certainty that would entitle us to make them the foundation of our religious belief).

To the first objection, Harnack replies that only by the tracing of the development of events can we attain a true understanding of history. Even those who condemn the modern science of history cannot escape the influence of its method. But, Harnack insists, Jesus is unique as Son of God and Prince of Life.

To the second objection, Harnack responds that even though Christianity's founder lived many centuries ago, we bring our problems not to a principle, but to a Person. Because religion is a relation of the soul to God, and nothing more, one should find God and possess Him as one's *own* God, should live in the awe of Him, trust Him, and lead a holy and blessed life in the strength of this feeling. That, declares Harnack, is the substance and aim of religion. Doubts and questions have existed as long as the Christian faith has been on the scene, but such questions are resolved by looking with a confident trust to the image of Christ's life.

Harnack acknowledges the force of the third objection: our idea of Christ, if not destroyed by historical criticism, has been rendered doubtful. When we consider the "external historical facts," "we find that the tradition as to the incidents attending the birth and the early life of Jesus Christ has been shattered; and so too has been the credibility of many of the stories which were told of him. We find, too, that criticism cannot allay the ancient doubts raised by the reports of what took place on the first Easter morning. As regards the picture of his life, as regards his discourses and the doctrine he taught, the historical way of looking at them seems to transform them altogether. The man who reads his Bible in a homely way is wont to treat all the characteristic features which he encounters in that book as above and beyond time."[21] But the sense and true point of the sayings of Jesus have lost no particle of their power and validity; they have not been altered by historical criticism. The united testimony of the first Christian community comprises a fifth (unwritten) Gospel, whose "voice is clearer and more effective than those of the other four."[22] The great and simple truths which Jesus preached, the personal sacrifices which He made, and His victory in death, formed the new community, and no historical criticism can alter this simple matter of fact. When one considers evidence for faith, Harnack makes his own position clear: "Woe to us if . . . our faith rested on a number of details, to be demonstrated and established by the historian. . . . it is assuredly true that no detail of the past can attain such a degree of evidential certainty that it could form the foundation for bricks and mortar, let alone a whole eternity. Testimonies, documents, assertions—when all is said, to what do they amount?"[23]

Harnack distinguishes between external, historical details and spiritual value. Agreeing with Lessing that we must beware of coupling matters of the highest moment with the "accidental truths of history," Harnack argues that the whole weight of eternity should not be hung on a spider's thread. But Harnack argues that the spiritual purpose of the life of Jesus Christ brings deliverance. Harnack agrees with Lessing's statement, "Even though we may be unable to remove all the objections that may be made against the Bible, nevertheless, in the heart of all Christians who have attained to an inner sense of its essential truths, Religion remains steadfast and intact."[24]

Under his category of external, historical details, Harnack includes the doctrines of Christ's Virgin Birth, divine sonship, and ascension: "They have been to faith what the prop is to the vine, or a sheltering screen to the tender plant. They have given it support and guidance, or they have protected its growth from the influence of wind and weather; and the service which they have rendered in the past, they still render today to many. The difficulty is that one man's faith requires a strong stake to prop it, or some kind of protective shelter; whilst another finds the prop break in his hands, and his faith bloom only in the free light of the sun."[25] We should consider the history of Christianity with an open mind and a humble heart so that we avoid the dangers of an interpretation that "may readily lead a man to foist his own mind upon history, to confuse the plant with the prop, and so to conjure up grave difficulties; [or] it may deaden the force of historical facts as facts, and the personality of Christ as a real personality." Much of the New Testament, Harnack argues, possesses a deep symbolical significance. The same spirit that reveals to one's eyes the power and the glory of a divine life "has also veiled the truth for us with a delicate web of significant legend, a poetry that moves the heart, and has thus brought it home in picture and parable."[26]

Seeing four stages of scientific knowledge, Harnack pursued a life-long quest for a rigorously "scientific" theology, one which could rightly claim its place in the academy. Science's first and lowest stage is that of determining, analyzing and ordering its data. Its second stage is determined by the knowledge of the original interrelationship among things, for what surrounds us are not forces operating mechanistically; we are surrounded by "life." An understanding of this second stage leads one to what Harnack terms "a sublime metaphysics." The third stage of knowledge is that of investigating life. We must reject the illusion that science encompasses everything worth knowing and offers a complete picture of the world. Science should not only render the totality of phenomena into the well-analyzed environment of humankind but should also grasp that environment's course, ideas and purposes (what Harnack calls its "architectonics"). The fourth stage is directed toward the knowledge of humankind, for history begins only where norms and values come to light. This last and highest stage of scientific knowledge flows into philosophy, which is itself, however, no "science." Harnack argues that "philosophy is an aristocratic activity and cultivates a synthesis which is not everyone's concern. One must not forget that humanity has not found its upward way by the light of the torches of individual insights gained through quantitative examination but under the guidance of men who had a vision of a central sun and had the courage to advance from physics to metaphysics, from history to metahistory, from ethics to metaethics."[27]

Harnack's value as a pivotal historian and theologian cannot be overestimated. Perhaps more than any other theologian of his day, he established *Kulturprotestantismus* as a substitute for the evangelical theology of the churches of the people. He gave his energy to address the cultured despisers of the Christian faith, at the same time joining fully with the liberal assertion that the primary goal of man must be freedom from both intellectual and confessional constraints. That freedom for Harnack included a freedom from the Scriptures, which many theologians considered impediments to their visions of scientific progress.[28]

Harnack labored in a country where one became a church member simply by being born. He contrasted the gospel with contemporary nominal Christianity, insisting that Christianity is a matter neither of inheritance nor culture, but rather of a vital personal religious experience and life. He taught that religion is not first and foremost a doctrine; it is faith, a relation to God, a loyalty to Him.

Harnack's concern with both history and theology is evidenced by his enthroning historical scholarship as a theological discipline. One scholar argues that Harnack's work was done "with an erudition that would probably have been attributed to witchcraft in a more supernaturalistic age."[29]

HARNACK AND BARTH

Harnack's public debate with one of his disillusioned pupils, Karl Barth, led to a significant correspondence in 1923, an interchange one researcher describes as "an encounter of different worlds."[30] Both men delivered lectures at Aarau, Switzerland, on April 17, 1920. Harnack provided a post-World War I audience firm answers along lines of renewed certainty; Barth radically questioned the whole enterprise of building on the kind of foundation his teacher embraced. The experience was a turning point for Harnack; he sought for the remaining years of his life to formulate his "science of understanding."

The issues they debated included Harnackian liberalism versus Barthian dialectical theology, the relation of theology and science, the historical-critical approach to the study of the Bible, and human achievement in the realm of culture and ethics among others. Various charges were exchanged between the two in the publication *Christliche Welt*. Harnack accused Barth of giving "half-baked" answers with neither understanding nor "the courage to witness." He insisted that Barth was "wholly submerged in highly sublime psychology and metaphysics."[31] Harnack acknowledged that an enormous gap separated their understandings. "But then," writes Harnack, "neither my nor your theology matters. What does matter is that the gospel is correctly taught. Should however your way of doing this come to prevail it will not be taught any more; it will rather be given over into the hands of devotional preachers who freely create their own understanding of the Bible and who set up their own dominion."[32] In his postscript to their dialogue, Harnack describes Barth's dialectic as leading to an invisible ridge between absolute religious scepticism naive biblicism. Barth's view presents "the most tormenting interpretation of Christian experience and Christian faith."[33]

Barth's replies to Harnack's challenges reflect his dialectic, which seems to separate the Jesus of history from the Christ of faith. For example, Barth writes that the theology of the Reformers "never raised the question of a historically discernible core of the gospel. We need it, however, because we have fallen into this impossible question through flight from the scandal [of revelation]. I see the theological function of historical criticism especially in the task of making clear to us a posteriori that there is no road this way, and that in the Bible we have to do with testimonies and only with testimonies."[34]

Barth charges Harnack with emptying faith, just as he emptied revelation, "by saying that there is a continuity between history and revelation."[35]

The old discussion of Orthodoxy versus Liberalism appears to have been left behind. This dialogue marked the beginning of a "New Reformation" in terms of questions such as "What is revelation?" and "How do we speak of God?" Seen as an attack on cultural Protestantism and its theological positivism,[36] the Harnack-Barth correspondence of 1923 raised questions of ontology and hermeneutics that continue to engage theologians.

Such an exchange between two of the church's most powerful figures reflects the changing world of late-nineteenth- and early-twentieth-century theology. Although Harnack did not convince Barth of his position, this failure did not lessen his influence on future theologians and historians. As Glick states, "To list the students of Harnack who later became renowned would be, practically, to compile a 'Who's Who' of late-nineteenth- and twentieth-century theologians."[37] Some of those include men like O. Dibelius, E. Goodspeed, O. Ritschl, and D. Bonhoeffer.

HARNACK AND RITSCHL

The "key" to understanding Harnack's approach to theology and history lies in his axiology (the study of value), which he gleaned primarily from Albrecht Ritschl. In fact, Harnack sent the first copy of the first volume of his *History of Dogma* to Ritschl in 1885, writing to him that "without the foundation which you laid, the *Dogmengeschichte* probably would never have been written."[38] Harnack clung to the hope during his Leipzig years of a rapprochement between the Tübingen "History of Religions" school and Ritschlian interpretation. Ritschl scorned the idea, advising his disciples to "trust in God, keep your powder dry, and write textbooks!"[39] Harnack gave up on the idea himself after his strife with the University of Berlin appointment and the debate over the Apostles' Creed.

HARNACK'S DIFFICULTIES WITH ORTHODOXY

In his understanding of the nature of history and its relation to theology, Harnack freed himself from the strict Lutheran orthodoxy so fervently embraced by his father. His father believed that theology ought to hold one to the unity and the purity of the Christian confessions; the younger Harnack, however, viewed theology as a release from such a commitment: "I cannot convince myself that God has guaranteed to his Church a special and differently constituted tradition, authenticated as pure. . . . I can bind myself unreservedly to the creeds. . . . I am no longer able to ignore the fact that even the writings of the New Testament contain a variety of very different forms of teaching, which simply cannot all be harmonized."[40]

Harnack's rejection of orthodoxy appears at three points: (1) his view of miracles, (2) his doctrine of Christ, and (3) his view of the Scriptures. His position on the possibility of miracles is straightforward: "as an interruption of the order of nature, there can be no such things as 'miracles.'"[41] Our incomplete knowledge of forces inherent in matter may also explain miracles, he writes, for the notion of miracles belongs only to the realm of fantasy and metaphor. Such a notion, he laments, will "last as long as religion itself." "Miracles, it is true," Harnack states, "do not happen; but of the marvellous and the inexplicable there is plenty. In our present state of knowledge we have become more careful, more hesitating in our judgment, in regard to the stories of the miraculous which we have received from antiquity. That the earth in its course stood still; that a she-ass spoke; that a storm was quieted by a word, we do not believe, and we shall never again believe; but that the lame walked, the blind saw, and the deaf heard, will not be so summarily dismissed as an illusion."[42]

He gives the following advice to anyone who struggles with the concept of biblical miracles: "If there is anything here that you find unintelligible, put it quietly aside. Perhaps you will have to leave it there for ever; perhaps the meaning will dawn upon you later and the story assume a significance of which you never dreamt. Once more, let me say: do not be deterred. The question of miracles is of relative indifference in comparison with everything else which is to be found in the gospels. It is not miracles that matter; the question on which everything turns is whether we are helplessly yoked to an inexorable necessity, or whether a God exists who rules and governs, and whose power to compel nature we can move by prayer and make a part of our experience."[43] Because true religion is an individualistic, not a miraculous, matter, Harnack concluded that "everything that is dramatic in the external and historical sense has vanished . . . It is not a question of angels and devils, thrones and principalities, but of God and the soul, the soul and its God."[44]

The charge that Harnack has substituted "Jesusology" in place of Christology,[45] seems valid, for he has room only for a human Jesus, not an incarnate Son of God. At age twenty-three, Harnack wrote, "The first question to be asked therefore is certainly not this, what was this Christ in and for himself, but the first and most important question is, 'How can I become his disciple?' "[46] Harnack, disdained a developed Christology: "On the question of 'Christology' men beat their religious doctrines into terrible weapons, and spread fear and intimidation everywhere. This attitude still continues; Christology is treated as though the Gospel had no other problem to offer, and the accompanying fanaticism is still rampant in our own day."[47]

Arguing that the proclaimer has become the proclaimed, Harnack says that Jesus "desired no other belief in his person and no other attachment to it than is contained in the keeping of his commandments."[48] The church has been wrong to put a "'Christology' creed in the forefront of the gospel, and in teaching that before a man can approach it he must learn to think rightly about Christ. That is putting the cart before the horse. A man can think and teach rightly about Christ only if, and in so far as, he has already begun to live according to Christ's Gospel."[49]

Calling it a "perverse proceeding to make Christology the fundamental substance of the Gospel,"[50] Harnack emphasizes that "the Gospel, as Jesus proclaimed it, has to do with the Father only and not with the Son."[51] The title "Son of God" does not demonstrate his divine nature, but only reflects Jesus' consciousness that he as a man knew God as his Father. "Rightly understood, the name of Son means nothing but the knowledge of God."[52] Harnack views the apostle Paul as the second founder of Christianity,[53] for Paul "became the author of the speculative idea that not only was God in Christ, but that Christ himself was possessed of a peculiar nature of a heavenly kind."[54]

Concerning Christ's resurrection, Harnack argues that we are to hold to the Easter "faith" even if the Easter "message" (the empty grave) proves false.[55] The resurrection narratives really mean that "God is just and powerful" and that "the first born among many brethren still lives."[56] One is reminded of his father's warning not to stray from an orthodox position on Christ's resurrection: "Whoever takes the position which you take on the Resurrection is in my eyes no longer a Christian theologian. I simply do not understand how anyone can appeal to history when he indulges in such historical machination, or I understand it only if one thereby degrades Christianity. For me Christianity stands or falls with the Resurrection."[57]

Concerning his view of Scripture, Harnack had also been warned by his father not to allow himself "to be imposed upon, nor to suffer your vanity to be charmed by the negative criticism of the modern theology, in which a leaf can be torn from the Bible, or the whole Bible can be thrown away. Do not follow the consciousness of the time, but rather that of the church, for our only choice is between these two."[58]

The younger Harnack, it is safe to say, tore not simply a leaf, but the whole of the Old Testament, from the sacred canon, suggesting that the most fitting place for the Old Testament would be in the Apocrypha, where it would be functionally more effective. He writes: "To reject the Old Testament in the second century was a mistake which the church rightly repudiated; to retain it in the sixteenth century was a fate which the Reformation could not yet avoid; but to continue to keep it in Protestantism as a canonical document after the nineteenth century is the consequence of religious and ecclesiastical paralysis. . . . [T]o sweep the table clean and honor the truth in confession and teaching is the action required to Protestantism today. And it is almost too late."[59]

Filson argues that Harnack can make little of the Old Testament because he "does not take seriously the biblical conception of redemptive history and of the people of God with which Jesus is organically related." Therefore, Harnack "sees no real unity in the canon. His real canon consists of the selected portions of the Synoptic Gospels, especially the teaching passages, that he uses to define Christianity." Filson continues: "To sustain his position, he has to discount even in these Gospels the features that refer to the Incarnation, the personal claim of Jesus, the redemptive significance of his death, and the climatic importance of the Resurrection."[60]

On the issue of the New Testament, for Harnack the synoptic Gospels have been contaminated by the intrusion of Christology into the early gospel tradition. This intrusion has obscured and distorted the gospel as Harnack understands it. According to Filson, "It is indeed an heroic but futile effort that Harnack makes to extricate from the Synoptic Gospels a non-Christological Jesus and a non-Christological, non-doctrinal gospel. But not a single writing in the New Testament clearly and fully supports him."[61]

Harnack may not have been aware of the impact of his views. As Gossai points out, Harnack was espousing these views at a time that would generate bitter and deep anti-Semitic feelings among the inciters during the time of the Third Reich.[62]

In his rejection of orthodoxy's Christology, Harnack makes little use of the Gospel of John. Believing the fourth Gospel cannot be taken as a historical authority (and for other reasons), Harnack will not allow Christ to be an essential part of the basic gospel. The difficulty of maintaining a Christianity without a high Christology, evidenced by Harnack's rejection of the fourth Gospel as a true representation of New Testament Christianity, seems insurmountable.[63] Harnack acknowledges that the faith and life of the church was Christocentric from the outset. By this Harnack implies that the first Christians did not understand Jesus, thereby making the apostolic church an incompetent witness to its Lord. Again Filson makes a telling point when he argues, "It hardly honors Christ to say that he completely failed to make his message understood and that it was radically distorted from the very first days of the church."[64]

Although Harnack acknowledges that Jesus' death has the value of an expiatory sacrifice[65] and that He leads men to God not only by what He says, but still more by what He is and does, and ultimately by what He suffers, Harnack has an inadequate doctrine of the Cross. He cannot affirm that God acted in Christ to redeem men to Himself, that Jesus was thus the indispensable mediator and redeemer, and is therefore an essential part of the gospel. But the New Testament sees Christ's resurrection as God's defeat of evil and death, its inseparable sequel being Christ's taking His place at the right hand of God as the active Lord of His people. Of course, as Filson states, "This Christocentric picture of Christian life and history does not fit Harnack's non-Christological view of the essence of Christianity."[66]

THE APOSTLES' CREED DISPUTE

One of the most bitter of all the controversies surrounding Harnack was the *Apostolikumsstreit*, a dispute on the Apostles' Creed that broke out in 1892. Harnack was asked his judgment on the "Schrempf case." Schrempf was a young minister who had performed a baptism without using the Apostles' Creed. Harnack suggested that the church prepare a shorter confession, which would be more in line with the Reformation in character and would take into account later understandings of the gospel. Harnack felt that certain elements of the creed cannot be interpreted in their original sense. For example, the phrase "conceived by the Holy Ghost, born of the Virgin Mary" cannot be received by many believing Christians as fact. Harnack said that because this controversy affects future ministers, there should be required in the universities the study of the history of dogma and of symbolics.

During that controversy, Stocker accused Harnack and his supporters of having "no respect for history, no honor for the confessions, no regard for the Church and community. Hypotheses, quite often giddy hypotheses . . . are given greater reality than the foundation beliefs of the Church . . . the confession, biblical authority, and finally the historicity and the personality of Christ himself are thrown into the witches' kettle of frothy criticism."[67]

A BRIEF SURVEY OF THE HARNACK CORPUS

Harnack's literary production continues to impress scholars today. Although his main field was patristics, he wrote on many other areas of church history and theology. His monographs on New Testament criticism set forth several conservative conclusions—his viewpoint that a single author wrote Luke/Acts and his defense of the antiquity of Q, (the presumed source behind non-Markan material common to Matthew and Luke). His three most influential works are probably his *History of Dogma* (seven volumes in English), his study of *Marcion*, and his highly successful *What Is Christianity?*

A major thesis in Harnack's writings is that dogma was a product of the Greek spirit (Hellenization) on the soil of the gospel. He writes in *What Is Christianity?* That "The influx of Hellenism, of the Greek spirit, and the union of the Gospel with it, form the greatest fact in the history of the Church in the second century, and when the fact was once established as a foundation it continued through the following centuries."[68] He traces out that influx in his *History of Dogma*, setting forth the idea that dogma in the early church was the natural outgrowth of the search for standards for membership, a development that obscured the essential nature and practical thrust of the teachings of Jesus. Therefore, we must separate the "kernel" of the gospel, that which is permanently valid, from the "husk" of the changing forms of the church's life and thought in which it was given. One side effect of such a position, reasons Pierard, is that "such a theology left Christians at the mercy of the establishment and enabled Harnack to join with other intellectuals in giving unqualified support to the German war effort in 1914."[69]

After discussing in the *History of Dogma* the prolegomena and the presuppositions of the history of dogma, the relationship of Judaism to the gospel of Jesus Christ, the influence of Gnosticism, and figures such as Marcion, Harnack evaluates the rise of Catholic Christianity and the doctrine of the Logos. He surveys the ecumenical councils in their battles for proper doctrine and focuses particular attention upon Augustine, one of his favorite theologians. Scholasticism, including the dogmatic formulations of Roman Catholicism and Protestantism, precede his positive discussion of the Reformation and Luther.

In the last volume of the *History of Dogma*, Harnack describes the theological work of Luther (in his return to the Scriptures) as the completion of the church's dogmatic development. Luther took up again the inwardness and higher dimensions of Jesus' gospel while, at the same time, he tried to reduce the significance of "tradition": councils, creeds, and canon law. Harnack then states that "the whole development of Protestantism from the end of the seventeenth century till the present day must necessarily appear a mistaken development, nay, an apostasy. It is a pity, only, that almost all thinking Protestants have apostatized, and, for the most part, differ from each other only according to the clearness and honesty with which they admit their apostasy."[70] Harnack wrote his *Outlines of the History of Dogma* in 1889, providing an overview of his multi-volumed study of dogma. That synopsis was quickly translated into English, French, and Russian.

Concerning his work *Marcion*, Harnack's interest in one of the ancient Christian heretics first bore fruit in 1870, when he won first place in an essay contest at the University of Dorpat for an essay contrasting Marcion and Tertullian. Harnack expanded this piece into his monumental study of Marcion, published fifty years later. His work is divided into two sections: the first part consists of a historical and doctrinal study of Marcion and Marcionsim; the second consists of twelve appendices which appear to preserve every quotation and allusion of Marcion in early Christian literature. Harnack responded to reactions to his work in 1923 in *Neue Studien zu Marcion* and issued a revised edition in 1924.

The considerable increase of knowledge about the milieu pertinent to the study of Marcion (such as the Nag Hammadi sources) has challenged Harnack's study. Harnack's work appears to be strongly influenced by his own theological agenda, rather than the evidence available. One example sometimes cited in support of this criticism is his presentation of Marcion as a Luther figure. Harnack appears to read into the past, a practice that affected both his interpretation of Marcion's teaching and the way Harnack reconstructed the evidence. Rather than being the theological hero Harnack thought Marcion to be, the evidence indicates that Marcion was a typical heretic.[71]

Harnack's *What Is Christianity?* was for decades regarded as the classic statement of liberal Protestantism. In this text, Jesus is depicted as a man who had rest and peace for his soul and was able to give life and strength to others. The gospel He preached was not about Himself, but the Father; His gospel concerned the Kingdom, the fatherhood of God, the infinite value of the human soul, the higher righteousness and the command to love. The work was a best-seller and the center of much controversy. In this book, Harnack appears guilty of the charge that he depreciates the ontological elements in Christian teaching along the lines of Albrecht Ritschl.[72]

As an example of Harnack's ability to challenge the orthodox status quo, *What Is Christianity?* brought about, and continues to provoke, strong reaction. This work should be studied by the young orthodox theologian, but not uncritically. As a man of great intellectual ability, Harnack nevertheless perverts the gospel of Jesus Christ, providing a less-than-biblical answer to the question "What is Christianity?"[73]

BIBLIOGRAPHY

PRIMARY SOURCES IN ENGLISH

The Acts of the Apostles. Translated by J. R. Wilkinson. New York: G. P. Putnam's Sons, 1909.

The Apostles' Creed. Edited and translated by Thomas Bailey Saunders. London: A. & C. Black, 1901.

Bible Reading in the Early Church. Translated by J. R. Wilkinson. New York: G. P. Putnam's Sons, 1912.

Christianity and History. Translated by Thomas Bailey Saunders. London: A. & C. Black, 1896.

The Constitution and Law of the Church in the First Two Centuries. Edited by H. D. A. Major and translated by F. L. Pogson. New York: G. P. Putnam's Sons, 1910.

The Date of the Acts and of the Synoptic Gospels. Translated by J. R. Wilkinson. New York: G. P. Putnam's Sons, 1911.

History of Dogma. 7 vols. Translated by Neil Buchanan. London: Williams and Norgate, 1896–9.

Luke the Physician. Translated by J. R. Wilkinson. New York: G. P. Putnam's Sons, 1923.

Militia Christi: The Christian Religion and the Military in the First Three Centuries. Translated by David McInnes Gracie. Philadelphia: Fortress Press, 1981.

The Mission and Expansion of Christianity in the First Three Centuries. Edited and translated by J. Moffatt. New York: Harper and Row Publishers. 1962.

Monasticism: Its Ideals and History and The Confessions of St. Augustine. Translated by E. E. Kellett and F. H. Marseille. London: William and Norgate, 1901.

New Testament Studies. 6 vols. Edited by W. D. Morrison and translated by J. R. Wilkinson. New York: G. P. Putnam's Sons, 1908–25.

Outlines of the History of Dogma. Translated by Edwin Knox Mitchell. Boston: Beacon Press, 1957.

The Sayings of Jesus. Translated by J. R. Wilkinson. New York: G. P. Putnam's Sons, 1908.

Thoughts on the Present Position of Protestantism. Translated by Thomas Bailey Saunders. London: A. & C. Black, 1899.

What Is Christianity? Translated by Thomas Bailey Saunders. New York: Harper and Row Publishers, 1957.

Harnack, Adolf, et al. *The Atonement in Modern Religious Thought.* London: James Clarke and Company, 1900.

Harnack, Adolf, and Wilhelm Herrmann. *Essays on the Social Gospel.* Edited by Maurice A. Canney and translated by G. M. Craik. New York: G. P. Putnam's Sons, 1907.

SECONDARY SOURCES

Cremer, Hermann. *A Reply to Harnack on the Essence of Christianity.* Translated by Bernhard Pick. New York: Funk and Wagnalls Co., 1903.

Garvie, A. E. *The Ritschlian Theology.* Edinburgh: T. and T. Clark, 1899.

Glick, G. Wayne. *The Reality of Christianity: A Study of Adolf von Harnack as Historian and Theologian.* New York: Harper and Row Publishers, 1967.

Hirsch, E. Felix. "The Scholar as Librarian: To the Memory of Adolf von Harnack." *The Library Quarterly* 9 (1939): 299–320.

Pauck, Wilhelm. *Harnack and Troeltsch: Two Historical Theologians.* New York: Oxford University Press, 1968.

Pauck, Wilhelm, "The Significance of Adolf von Harnack Among Church Historians." *Union Theological Seminary Quarterly Review,* "Special Issue" (Jan. 1954): 13–24.

Rumscheidt, H. Martin. *Revelation and Theology: An Analysis of the Barth-Harnack Correspondence of 1923*. Edinburgh: Scottish Academic Press, 1972.

NOTES

1. Quoted in S. W. Sykes, "The Essence of Christianity," *Religious Studies*, 7, no. 4 (1971): 294.

2. George Tyrrell, *Christianity at the Crossroads* (London, 1909), 44.

3. Quoted in *Adolf von Harnack: Liberal Theology at Its Height*, ed. Martin Rumscheidt (San Francisco: Harper & Row, 1989), 10–11.

4. Cf. D. L. Deegan, "The Ritschlian School, the Essence of Christianity, and Karl Barth," *Scottish Journal of Theology* 16 (1963): 404.

5. Colin Brown, "Adolf Harnack," *The New International Dictionary of the Christian Church*, ed. J. D. Douglas (Grand Rapids: Zondervan, 1978): 452.

6. Floyd V. Filson, "Adolf von Harnack and His 'What Is Christianity?'" *Interpretation* 6 (January 1952): 57.

7. Ibid., 52.

8. Ibid.

9. Cf. F. F. Bruce, "Adolf Harnack," *New Dictionary of Theology*, ed. Sinclair B. Ferguson and David F. Wright (Leisester, England: IVP, 1988), 286.

10. Cf. Rumscheidt, *Adolf von Harnack*, 9.

11. Adolf Harnack, *What Is Christianity?* trans. Thomas Bailey Saunders, 5th ed. (London: Ernest Benn Limited, 1958), 16.

12. Rumscheidt, *Adolf von Harnack*, 46, quoting from Harnack's lecture "What Has History to Offer as Certain Knowledge Concerning the Meaning of World Events?".

13. Ibid., 55.

14. Ibid., 54.

15. Ibid., 56–57.

16. Ibid., 57–58.

17. Ibid., 61–62.

18. Ibid.

19. Ibid., 62–63.

20. Ibid., 65.

21. Ibid., 73.

22. Ibid.

23. Ibid., 74–75.

24. Ibid., 75.

25. Ibid., 75–76.

26. Ibid., 76.

27. Ibid., 44–45.

28. Richard Klann, review of *Adolf von Harnack: An Anthology of Harnack's Writings*, ed. Martin Rumscheidt, *Concordia Journal* 16 (October 1990): 408.

29. Jaroslav Pelikan, editor's preface to *The Reality of Christianity: A Study of Adolf von Harnack as Historian and Theologian*, by G. Wayne Glick (New York: Harper & Row, 1967), xi.

30. H. Martin Rumscheidt, *Revelation and Theology: An Analysis of the Barth-Harnack Correspondence of 1923*, (Cambridge: The University Press, 1972), 3.

31. Quoted in ibid., 38.

32. Quoted in ibid., 39.

33. Quoted in ibid., 53.

34. Quoted in ibid., 46.

35. Quoted in ibid., 49.

36. Cf. Ibid., 191.

37. Glick, *Reality of Christianity*, 36.

38. Quoted in ibid., 53 from Agnes von Zahn-Harnack, *Adolf von Harnack* (Berlin: Hans Bott, 1936), 135.

39. Quoted in ibid., 53 from von Zahn-Harnack, *Adolf von Harnack*, 129.

40. Quoted in ibid., 40 from von Zahn-Harnack, *Adolf von Harnack*, 97-98.

41. Harnack, *What Is Christianity?* 30.

42. Ibid., 31.

43. Ibid., 32–33.

44. Ibid., 50.

45. Carl-Jurgen Kaltenborn, "Adolf von Harnack and Bonhoeffer," in *A Bonhoeffer Legacy: Essays in Understanding*, ed. A. J. Klassen (Grand Rapids: Eerdmans, 1981), 49.

46. Quoted in Glick, Reality of Christianity, 53 from von Zahn-Harnack, Adolf von Harnack, 93–94.

47. Harnack, *What Is Christianity?* 95–96.

48. Ibid., 96.

49. Ibid., 110.

50. Ibid., 135.

51. Ibid., 108.

52. Ibid., 97.

53. Ernst Bammel, "The Jesus of History in the Theology of Adolf von Harnack," *Modern Churchman* 19 (spring 1976): 92.

54. Harnack, *What Is Christianity?* 135.

55. Ibid., 119.

56. Ibid., 120.

57. Quoted in Glick, *Reality of Christianity*, 27 from von Zahn-Harnack, *Adolf von Harnack*, 143.

58. Ibid., 26 from Agnes von Zahn-Harnack, *Adolf von Harnack*, 106–107.

59. Quoted in Hemchand Gossai, "The Old Testament: A Heresy Continued?" *Word & World* 8, no. 2 (spring 1988): 151, from Harnack's *Marcion*, 127, 222. See also Harnack's comments in *What Is Christianity?* 136–137.

60. Filson, "Adolf von Harnack," 61.

61. Ibid., 62. Harnack states in *What Is Christianity?* that the Gospel of John "cannot be taken as an historical authority . . . The author of it acted with sovereign freedom, transposed events and put them in a strange light, drew up the discourses himself, and illustrated great thoughts by imaginary situations." (26) The Fourth Gospel ". . . can hardly make any claim to be considered an authority for Jesus' history; only little of what he says can be accepted, and that little with caution." (Ibid.)

62. Op. cit., Gossai, "Old Testament," 151.

63. Cf., Filson, "Adolf von Harnack," 58.

64. Ibid., 58–59.

65. Harnack, *What Is Christianity?* 111–17.

66. Filson, "Adolf von Harnack," 59. See also Harnack's comments in *What Is Christianity?* 167–68.

67. Quoted in Glick, *Reality of Christianity*, 162.

68. Harnack, *What Is Christianity?* 145.

69. R. V. Pierard, "Adolf Harnack," *Evangelical Dictionary of Theology*, ed. Walter A. Elwell (Grand Rapids: Baker 1984), 495.

70. Adolf Harnack, *History of Dogma* (New York: Dover Publications, 1961), 180.

71. David L. Balas, "Marcion Revisited: A 'Post-Harnackian' Perspective," *Texts and Testaments: Critical Essays on the Bible and Early Church Fathers*, ed. W. Eugene March (San Antonio: Trinity University Press, 1980), 96, 105.

72. Rumscheidt, *Adolf von Harnack*, 151.

73. Klann, review of *Adolf von Harnack*, 409.

19

KENNETH SCOTT
LATOURETTE

RICHARD W. POINTER

When David Brainerd arrived at Yale College in 1740, his heart was set on scholarship. That dream ended abruptly two years later when Brainerd was expelled from Yale for his New Light sympathies and ill-advised remark that one of his tutors possessed no more Christian grace than a chair. Reluctantly, he altered his life plans and eventually resigned himself to the overwhelming task of evangelizing Native Americans on the colonial frontier. Two centuries later when Kenneth Latourette arrived at Yale College in 1905, he had already dedicated his life to becoming a missionary. After graduate school, he headed off to the Far East to serve with the Yale-in-China missionary program. Unfortunately, ill health forced Latourette's return to the United States after two brief years. Amid a lengthy convalescence he gradually accepted a new life's calling—academic scholar.

As divine providence would have it, David Brainerd went on to become a profoundly influential missionary, although moreso after his death than before it, thanks to the posthumous publication of his diary. Kenneth Latourette developed into one of the most prolific and important church historians of the twentieth century. Like his Yale colleague,

Latourette left a substantial legacy upon his "second" profession, a legacy increasingly evident twenty-five years after his death.

THE FOUNDATION LAID

Beyond Yale and altered careers, Latourette and Brainerd shared a deep evangelical Christian piety. For Latourette, that piety was nurtured by his well-educated and devout parents, Dewitt and Rhoda, and by the local Baptist congregation in Oregon City, Oregon. Born there August 9, 1884, Latourette grew up in a family that took learning and Christianity seriously. He followed that example throughout his life. Both his parents received bachelor's and master's degrees from Pacific University and taught college briefly. His father became a successful lawyer and banker, and anticipated that his son would follow in his footsteps. Kenneth seemed well on his way to fulfilling those expectations after graduating from high school at age fifteen and becoming valedictorian of his small class at McMinnville (later Linfield) College. But his active involvement in the college's Young Men's Christian Association and the summer conferences presented him with a challenge and a duty he could not escape, foreign missionary service. The urgent plea to college students to help evangelize the world in their generation resonated with Latourette's pietistic faith. He headed to Yale for more education in preparation for a missionary career.[1]

What began as a one-year venture in New Haven to earn a second bachelor's degree at a better-known and more prestigious eastern university turned into a four-year sojourn to earn M.A. and Ph.D. degrees, and ultimately into a lifelong association with Yale. While finishing his one year of undergraduate work majoring in history, Latourette was invited to become part of the staff of Yale-in-China, a missions outreach begun by Yale students in 1901. The job required that Latourette first get a doctorate, a task he dutifully pursued at Yale from 1906 to 1909. Choosing history over economics and geology (two of his other strong interests), he took almost every available history class, although only one in church history, a survey course from Williston Walker. His dissertation studied U.S.-China relations from 1784 to 1844 and was supervised by sinologist Frederick Wells Williams. Apart from his formal studies, Latourette helped prepare for his work overseas by organizing and leading numerous student Bible study groups through Dwight Hall, the home of the Yale YMCA. Following graduation, Latourette spent a year working as a traveling secretary for the Student Volunteer Movement for Foreign Missions, and then left for China.[2]

The Yale mission in Changsha seemed ideally suited for a person of Latourette's intellectual abilities and spiritual commitments. He threw himself into learning the Chinese language and culture in hopes of soon teaching Chinese students, but in the process he fell victim to a severe case of dysentery. Unable to recover fully there, he made the long trip home to Oregon City. What had seemed promising turned into one of his life's greatest disappointments. Yet his short time in China (1910–1912) solidified his belief in the value of Christian expansion and confirmed his suspicion that Americans, and the West in general, were woefully ignorant of the Orient. Both convictions would greatly influence his future work as a historian.[3]

Latourette's return to academia came piecemeal, but he soon developed an impressive reputation. Plagued by physical weakness and emotional depression, he was unable to take on any new assignments until the fall of 1914, when he was hired as a part-time history instructor at Reed College. His two years there proved a turning point. He began writing scholarly articles and produced his first book, *The Development of China*. More importantly, he decided against returning to China and embraced college teaching as his vocation. He spent the next five years (1916–1921) as a professor at Denison University in Ohio, where he wrote a companion volume on the history of Japan and became an outspoken voice within the American Historical Association for greater study of the Far East.[4]

A rising scholarly star, Latourette received several job offers at major universities, but only one he could not refuse—the chance to return to Yale.[5] He became the D. Willis James Professor of Missions at the Divinity School, succeeding Harlan Page Beach. Thus began a more than thirty-year stay on the faculty. The first ten years proved the most difficult as Latourette found himself adjusting to a host of new circumstances: colleagues with far more theological training; a more secular student body and university than in his student days; a faculty at large that doubted the academic credibility of mission studies; and a personal crisis of faith. Latourette weathered each storm and soon took on additional responsibilities within and outside Yale. He began teaching courses on East Asia for the History Department, joined the Department of Religion in the Graduate School, was named a Fellow of Berkeley College, and in 1949 received one of the university's distinguished Sterling professorships. Throughout his long teaching career (he retired in 1953) and beyond, he lived, worked, and worshiped with Yale students and was a fixture within the Divinity School community.[6]

Latourette was also a fixture within those religious circles responsible for the emergence and development of the Ecumenical Movement. From the 1920s on, he brought rare expertise on the history of Christian movements around the world to countless boards and committees concerned with Christian unity and global mission. Unlike many American evangelicals, Latourette enthusiastically embraced ecumenical efforts and saw them as an important sign of Jesus' ever-widening influence in the world.[7]

Remarkably, amid all these activities, Latourette maintained a disciplined writing regimen that produced three dozen books and hundreds of articles and reviews. After his early concentration on the Far East, he shifted attention to the history of Christianity and especially its expansion in the last two centuries. His two largest and greatest works addressed these topics in monumental fashion: *A History of the Expansion of Christianity* (7 volumes, 1937–1945) and *Christianity in a Revolutionary Age* (5 volumes, 1958–1962). His impressive scholarship brought him a host of honorary doctorates and the presidencies of the American Baptist Convention, the American Society of Church History, and the American Historical Association. He continued writing throughout his emeritus years, culminating with his autobiography, *Beyond the Ranges*, published shortly before his death in 1968.[8]

TRAILBLAZER

As Kenneth Latourette wrote about the eight decades of his life, he portrayed himself principally as a trailblazer.[9] In the spirit of pioneering missionaries reaching unevangelized peoples, he saw his scholarly and personal pursuits as carving out new paths for inquiry and opening up new vistas for understanding. His hope naturally was that other historians would follow his lead. Now, a generation after his death and two generations after the publication of his central work, it is possible to see that many of the trails he blazed have indeed been followed by other historians who, whether aware of Latourette or not, have chosen to keep company with him.

Understanding where Latourette wished to take his discipline, and specifically church history, requires probing more deeply into the character of the man. Four qualities stand out as responsible for shaping his agenda. Put simply, Latourette was a man of evangelical piety, ecumenical vision, enlightened optimism, and enthusiastic missionary-mindedness. As a typical scholar, he displayed those qualities even more powerfully in print than in person. Yet each was securely rooted in his own life experiences.

Latourette acknowledged his strong religious convictions in writing numerous times, once describing his belief system as the "historic Christian faith as held by fairly conservative Protestant evangelicals."[10] Holding on to his parents' faith and making it his own as an adult were never easy, especially in the midst of an increasingly hostile academic world. But as the years went on, he found himself more rather than less convinced of the truth claims of Christianity and remained actively involved in leading Bible studies, teaching Sunday school, organizing prayer groups, and maintaining a conservative Protestant lifestyle. His faith centered on the love of God as chiefly manifested in the incarnation, death, and resurrection of Jesus. These were the crucial facts of human history and all else had to been seen in their light.[11]

Presenting the good news of those facts to others around the globe compelled Latourette from adolescence on. His concern for missions grew naturally amid an evangelical Protestantism excited about the possibilities of American and Christian overseas expansion in the late nineteenth and early twentieth centuries. While his missionary career was short-lived, he maintained an active interest and involvement in the movement through serving on various mission boards, training graduate students headed to the mission field, travelling to and speaking at mission conferences around the world, and perhaps most importantly, researching and writing about the history of missions for scholarly and popular audiences. Few individuals did more to further the cause of Christian missions in the twentieth century.[12]

That something similar may be said of Latourette's contribution to Christian ecumenism comes as no coincidence. For as his missionary-mindedness sprang from his evangelical piety, so did his ecumenical vision spring from his passion for missions. At a practical level, his participation in organizations such as the Student Volunteer Movement, the International Missionary Council, and the World's Student Christian Federation brought him into contact and friendship with key people in the birth and growth of the Ecumenical Movement, including John R. Mott, William Temple, J. H. Oldham, and William Paton.[13] At a theoretical level, Latourette saw Christian unity as not only the urgent prayer of Christ (John 17), but as the best means for advancing the gospel's cause worldwide. As one recent analysis of Latourette's thought puts it, "[for Latourette] ecumenical cooperation was born out of mission, the motive being not a theological reflection on unity but a practical concern for carrying out the Great Commission."[14] In other words, a united Church had a much better chance of winning the world to Christ than a divided one. And if anybody wanted proof, Latourette was ready to cite lots of historical examples.

Latourette was also persuaded that there was plenty of scriptural and historical proof underlying his essential optimism.[15] The disillusionment and pessimistic realism that infected so many Western intellectuals following World War I made little impression on his historical perspective. Critics have charged that that reflects how deeply he had drunk at the waters of late nineteenth-century progressive views of history.[16] Inspired by Williston Walker's understanding of church history as a "divinely guided process . . . moving forward to a larger realization of the kingdom of God," Latourette may have embraced a philosophy of history that predisposed him to find positive signs of Christianity's and humanity's advance.[17] But fairness demands that Latourette's retention of that view be seen as much as a by-product of continuous study and reflection than as an *a priori* assumption about the nature of history. Latourette convinced himself, if few others, that the historical record genuinely revealed a growing worldwide Christian influence and concluded that "unless a long-term trend, a trend now more than nineteen centuries long, is to be reversed, that influence will continue to grow."[18] Perhaps it is safest to say that his optimism was both a cause and an effect of his historical interpretation.

Evangelically pious, ecumenical, evangelistic, optimistic—these qualities colored most of Latourette's life and collectively pushed his scholarship "beyond the ranges," outward from traditional approaches, conventional subjects, and parochial viewpoints. Nowhere was this more evident than in his efforts to globalize church history. The same narrow concentration on Europe and to a lesser extent the United States that plagued the historical discipline as a whole afflicted the study of the history of Christianity in the early twentieth century. European-trained scholars on both sides of the Atlantic riveted their attention on the Western Church's internal development. Everything about Kenneth Latourette prompted him to break away from that mold. Most fundamentally, his missions-consciousness gave him an intrinsic interest in the expansion of Christianity at a time when that expansion was occurring most dramatically outside of the West. His firsthand experience in China left a lasting impression of the reality and vitality of the Christian faith in non-Western cultures. And his teaching of the history of missions and preparation of foreign missionaries inevitably widened his vision of where the Holy Spirit had been and still was at work around the globe.[19]

For these and other reasons, Latourette sought to make his own church history writings and that of others more global in at least two senses. On the one hand, he wanted a straightforward expansion of the discipline's subject matter to include the stories of Christians living everywhere in the world. His first major work on the history of Christianity, *A History of Christian Missions in China* (1929), gave witness to that aim.[20] Eight years later the introduction to the first volume of his *magnum opus* made clear the unprecedented task he had chosen and why it was worth it: "Never has anyone undertaken in an inclusive and thorough fashion to tell the story of the expansion of Christianity. . . . The value of such a work must lie largely in the . . . propounding of questions and the suggestion of answers and generalizations for which a work of lesser scope would be an inadequate background or provide a distorted perspective." Volumes four, five, and six testified clearly to his global focus. All dedicated to the "Great Century" (the 19th), two of the three examined developments outside the United States and Europe.[21] A similar concern for inclusiveness characterized his later multi-volume work, *Christianity in a Revolutionary Age*, as well as his massive one-volume *History of Christianity*, published in 1953.[22]

Broadening church historians' spatial horizons was only one part of Latourette's "globalizing" agenda. Equally important, he wanted them to break away from traditional Eurocentric views of other peoples and their histories, and embrace a more universal perspective. That call was especially incumbent upon historians who were Christians, given the universal character of the gospel.[23] Seeing movements and events in the broadest possible contexts (and for Latourette all events were ultimately a part of one grand context, salvation history) would allow for fruitful comparisons and deter historians from universalizing the experience of particular groups.[24] He readily admitted how difficult it was to acquire such a global stance and often confessed the sources of his own biases: his Americanness; his evangelical Protestantism; his commitment to missions; and his training as a modern historian.[25] Critics of his work have agreed with his self-assessment, suggesting that he was too greatly influenced by the success of the Church in America.[26] Nevertheless, by setting forth the goal of writing about the history of world Christianity from a world Christian perspective, Latourette presented an important challenge to historians of the Church.

That challenge actually included far more than just a call for greater geographical coverage. Throughout his career, Latourette also insisted that "the study of the history of Christianity must be ecumenical in its outlook and scope."[27] Too much church history had been written and taught from strictly Protestant, Catholic, or Orthodox points of view. Historians needed to give all Christian traditions their due and avoid denominational provincialism both in the choice of their topics and in the tone of their treatments. To that end, Latourette took great pains in all of his major books to write substantially and irenically about non-Protestant groups. Favorable reviews by Catholic and Orthodox scholars became not only a source of justifiable pride but confirmation that his approach produced a more balanced and useful church history.[28]

Latourette's desire for an ecumenical history of Christianity naturally went hand in hand with his own ecumenism. Fairer, less partial accounts of past events might facilitate greater harmony and cooperation in the present. Meanwhile, the quest for a unity of spirit compelled him to put the best face on earlier disputes and to downplay those aspects of Christian history that had more often caused division than union.[29] In particular, the history of doctrine received far less attention in Latourette's writings than in comparable studies. As an ecumenist, his historical research convinced him that doctrinal agreement, apart from a few bare essentials, could not and should not be a precondition or basis for unity among Christians. As an historian, his reading of the existing literature persuaded him that church historians had been too long preoccupied by doctrine and now needed to turn their eyes elsewhere. Furthermore, Latourette's academic training as an historian equipped him to deal far more effectively with the social and cultural history of Christianity than with the complexities of doctrinal controversies.[30] Friend and foe alike have noted his lack of theological sophistication and this, too, may have contributed to his choice of topics.[31]

Whatever the causes, Latourette's decision to break away from the standard focus upon doctrine prompted him to take his church history writings in several additional new directions beyond his global and ecumenical emphases. For both substantive and symbolic reasons, he wanted first of all to rename his discipline or at least to label his own work differently. "Church history" for him conveyed too narrow a sense of what needed to be studied. It implied an exclusive concern for the internal history of an institution, an exclusivity amply demonstrated by the bulk of the existing historiography. Latourette's interest was much broader. He wanted to investigate wherever and whenever the Christian impulse had made a difference in people's lives or, as he more often put it, he wanted to study "the influence of Jesus in history."[32] Since that influence sometimes "came outside of the channel of the Church," he preferred to speak and write about the history of Christianity rather than church history.[33]

A History of the Expansion of Christianity exemplified what Latourette had in mind. Seven questions defined his research agenda and reflected the wider bounds of his inquiry: What was the Christianity which spread? Why did Christianity spread? Why has Christianity suffered reverses and at times met only partial successes? By what processes did Christianity spread? What effect has Christianity had upon its environment? What effect has the environment had on Christianity? And what bearing do the processes by which Christianity spread have upon the effect of Christianity on its environment, and of the environment upon Christianity?[34] The last three questions especially pointed up his commitment to analyzing the external relationships between Christian peoples, movements, and ideas, and their surrounding cultures.

Latourette's painstaking efforts to answer these questions for virtually all times and places illustrated what social and cultural history approaches to Christianity's past could reveal. Following the leads of James Harvey Robinson's "new history," and the Chicago School of Religious History, he stressed social factors in his interpretations of Christianity's fortunes and misfortunes.[35] In place of what he considered narrow institutional history, he introduced readers to the sometimes inspiring, sometimes disheartening stories of dozens of groups of people claiming to be Christian. How believers came to and practiced their faith took center stage in the narrative.[36] All manifestations or expressions of Christianity were presented as culturally conditioned and none were equated with the gospel. Human responses to Christ were just that.[37] At the same time, however, a pattern of overall progress was evident to Latourette in the quality and quantity of those responses. World history revealed that the influence of Jesus was growing stronger as the centuries passed. That influence could be measured on the basis of the number of Christian adherents, the emergence of new Christian movements, and the geographical spread of the faith. All three criteria showed that Christianity had progressed in a wave-like pattern, with each advance gaining greater ground before a new retreat set in.[38]

Dismissed by some as mere head-counting, Latourette's quasi-quantitative approach put a very different slant on the overall trajectory of Christianity's history. Far from seeing the Middle Ages or the Protestant Reformation as the high point of Christian influence (as many of his peers did), he set out an interpretation stressing the remarkable gains of the last 150 years and claiming that the best was yet to come. He encouraged other church historians to follow his lead and pay more attention to recent centuries.[39] Moreover, he repeatedly rejected the idea that the West had become "post-Christian" in the twentieth century.[40] He preferred instead to talk about Christianity's "advance through storm" in the 1900s.[41] Latourette developed that theme most fully in the five volumes of *Christianity in a Revolutionary Age*. There he acknowledged the difficult challenges to the faith from both within and without, but insisted on its eventual triumph.[42] Salvation history would culminate in cosmic redemption beyond human history; but until then, the cause of Christ would continue to go forward.[43]

Whether such conclusions owed more to Latourette's scientific research or to his Christian faith is hard to discern. What is clear is that he sought to bring the ideals of both to bear upon his work as an historian. His Yale teachers trained him in the Leopold von Ranke school of "scientific" history where the goal was pure objectivity and the historian ideally let the facts speak for themselves.[44] Latourette imbibed those lessons and became committed to "dispassionate reporting in his historical studies."[45] Early on in his career he established "carefulness of statement," "catholicity of mind," "judgement and balance," and "an absolute fearlessness in facing facts" as appropriate guidelines for writing and teaching history.[46] Like any good historian, he wanted to get the facts right and to produce dependable accounts. In the spirit of von Ranke, as W. A. Speck has put it, "He set out to discover what actually happened in the past."[47]

At the same time, however, Latourette was very un-Rankian in his frank acknowledgment that his Christian values not only would but should have an impact on his work as a historian. He saw being a historian as a Christian vocation and sought to think and act Christianly within it. Among other things, that meant that his Christian convictions informed his choice of topics, organization of materials, and interpretation of events.[48] Like Carl Becker and Charles Beard, Latourette recognized the inevitable subjective element in the doing of history and did not back away from it. While on the one hand that put him on the philosophical cutting edge, on the other his defense of a traditional Christian understanding of history placed him on the margins of an increasingly secular-minded discipline.[49]

That he boldly advocated such an understanding of history to scholarly and popular audiences alike reflects the depth and power of his beliefs. Nowhere was that more evident than in his 1948 presidential address to the American Historical Association. His election as president was an honor few other historians of religion had received and symbolized his having reached the pinnacle of his profession. Under the circumstances, he might have been expected to speak to his fellow historians about the importance of religion in history or about some specific aspect of his own work. Latourette chose instead to use his presidential speech (and its subsequent publication in *The American Historical Review*) to explain and promote a Christian view of history. He began by noting how the variety of philosophies of history made most modern historians leery of believing any of them. Yet because "history cannot be written without some basis of selection," some kind of framework of understanding inherently lay behind all studies of the past.[50] Latourette then set out to show that the Christian framework of understanding conformed most closely with historical reality. He first reviewed the core doctrines of the faith; next, he highlighted unique features of the Christian view, particularly the quest to gain God's perspective on history; then he pointed out that no philosophy of history could be absolutely proved. Hence, "the historian as historian can neither refute nor demonstrate the Christian thesis, but," Latourette continued, "he can detect evidence which suggests a strong probability for the truth of the Christian understanding."[51] Modern thinking about the nature of the universe and the human condition, for example, increasingly squared with Christian insights. Even clearer evidence, according to Latourette, could be seen in the march of history itself. Nothing stood out more than the mounting influence of Jesus around the globe in the past two centuries. Echoing arguments he made elsewhere, he rehearsed how through "pulsations of advance, retreat, and advance" Christian influence had gone forward, transforming the character of individuals, groups, and society as a whole. These developments were signs of divine initiative in the historical process; the Holy Spirit was at work. A loving and sovereign God, while allowing for human freedom, was nevertheless moving history in the direction he intended it to go.[52]

In inviting his academic peers to consider the reasonableness of the Christian view of history, Latourette was no doubt still aware that he really was asking them to put on the eyes of faith. To affirm God's active intervention in history and to offer supernatural explanations of particular events was hardly within the normal purview of the average historian. Latourette himself avoided mention of the divine role in history in his East Asian studies. But writing about the history of the Church was a different matter.[53] For there, and especially in the expansion of Christianity, God's hand was too plain to ignore. Certain facts simply could not be explained through purely "natural" interpretations. Christian belief helped the historian to unlock the mysteries of these events and opened "the mind towards the true understanding of history."[54] Reason and faith each brought illumination and were legitimate means to truth. Both should be employed in making sense of the past.[55]

At first glance, Latourette's attempt to blend scientific history and a Christian world view in his writings would appear out of step with prevailing notions of historical method then and now. As a discipline, church history in the past half century has become less and less tolerant of anything that smacks of "providential history" and embraced more and more of the values and methods of scholars studying the history of religions, where critical skepticism and "outsider" detachment are highly prized. Latourette might well have welcomed some of the emphasis upon a "scientific study of religion" but would certainly have balked at any suggestion that religious commitments of any kind are an impediment to the student of religion. He was too much aware of the inescapability of one's own biases to suppose that any historian was free of "religious commitments." In his mind, the fair thing to do was let your readers know up front your own presuppositions and admit the difference they made in how you saw things. In other words, history was necessarily perspectival.[56] For Latourette, that did not mean that historians couldn't arrive at truth. Nor did it mean that an "insider" couldn't effectively and fairly evaluate his or her own tradition. It only meant that the validity of scholars' assumptions about the nature of reality would invariably affect the soundness of their interpretations.

Ironically, parts of what Latourette argued for here in the 1940s and 1950s approach modern, or perhaps more accurately postmodern, views of historical study. As more historians consider postmodern notions of what their discipline can and cannot do, Latourette's method may not seem so foreign. At the very least, his call for open declarations of allegiances fits right in. Beyond that, few contemporary scholars would agree with his reading of Christianity's history or with his belief in absolute truth, but a growing number might be ready to acknowledge the inevitability, if not the legitimacy, of what he did in consciously (as well as unconsciously) bringing together historical study and Christian faith.[57]

To suggest that today's historians may be more willing to accept parts of what Latourette argued for and embodied than his peers were fifty years ago is only to re-confirm the accuracy of his self-image as a pioneer. He no doubt would wish that more of them would agree with him on not only the role of presuppositions but the adequacy of the Christian understanding of history. Still, he could take heart in the fact that since his death the issue of how best to integrate Christian faith and history has become of more vital concern to Christian historians in this country and abroad. And indeed, his own contributions on that question remain a part of the dialogue.[58]

CONCLUSION

In retrospect, it is now possible to see that Latourette's other pathbreaking contributions highlighted here also remain as important parts of the discipline to which he devoted most of his life. Recent general accounts of the history of Christianity have almost invariably embraced his global emphasis and perspective, and the pages of *Church History* and other journals devoted to religious history have slowly but surely included more material relating to Christianity's fortunes outside of the Western world.[59] Similarly, an ecumenical, or at least non-sectarian, tone characterizes the vast majority of scholarship being done today on the history of the church. Less and less of that scholarship would see itself as having any apologetic intent, as Latourette saw in his work; he thought that a more ecumenical history of Christianity would provide a stronger defense of the faith.[60] Nevertheless, in becoming more inclusive and less partisan, the study of church history has moved in the direction Latourette hoped it would go. It has also moved towards paying greater attention to the social and cultural dimensions of Christianity as believers tried to live out their faith, topics central to Latourette's historiographic agenda. Lay men and women are beginning to get the scrutiny they require if the full story of Christianity's past is going to be told. Latourette's writings surely pointed to this trend even if they only took minimal steps towards accomplishing it.[61] His work did more than point to another recent trend—the concentration upon post-Reformation church history and especially the last two hundred years. Latourette must be seen as a major contributor to the discipline's relative shift (at least in North America) away from ancient and medieval studies to a primary focus on modern church history. The fact that he geared much of his writing for a popular audience also served to broaden the Christian public's interest in the recent history of Christianity. Of course, within that recent history, no subject fascinated Latourette (and much of the public) more than the spread of Christianity through missionary endeavor. He more than anyone else made the history of missions an integral part of the history of Christianity and brought together the disciplines of missiology and church history. Here stands perhaps Latourette's central legacy.[62] That seems only fitting for a man who was as much a scholarly missionary as he was a missionary scholar.

Whether all the changes that Latourette helped to initiate have been positive or whether all the interpretations he offered were accurate are issues naturally open to debate. Historians, theologians, missiologists, and church leaders both during and after his life have levelled sharp attacks on much of his scholarship. Some of that criticism he expected. The broad scope of most of his writings demanded that he rely on existing (and often inadequate) secondary accounts. He knew that if and when the monographic studies he hoped to stimulate were done, many of his conclusions about particular times and places would have to be revised.[63] But more than those conclusions have come under siege. His overall interpretive framework regarding the advance of Christianity has been dismissed as inadequate, overly idealistic, unsophisticated, naive, ludicrous, wishful thinking, and even un-scriptural.[64] Reinhold Niebuhr, one of Latourette's most persistent critics, characterized it as "open to doubt" and "dubious."[65] The magnitude of modern evil and the pace of secularization have simply been too great for most scholars to accept Latourette's optimistic thesis. Furthermore, his tendencies to identify closely, on the one hand, the history of the Church with salvation history, and on the other hand the spread of Christian influence with modern progress, have been seen as historically questionable and theologically unsound.[66] If Latourette had paid more attention to the history of doctrine and been better trained theologically, so the argument goes, his writings might have been less misguided and ultimately more useful. As is, his "ethical interpretation of Christianity" and preoccupation with Christian practice is too one-dimensional.[67] Perhaps most damning of all has been the suggestion that Latourette allowed his particular Christian presuppositions to dictate the results of his historical inquiries.[68] To be guilty of that sin is to violate the most basic rule of historical scholarship and to cast a shadow over the integrity and validity of all of one's work.

It is largely for that reason that such a suggestion seems ill applied to Kenneth Latourette. As a man and as a scholar, integrity was high on the list of his personal attributes. He was uncompromising in his religious faith, dedication to students, daily writing, and professional standards. His Christian values were equally evident in the classroom, chapel, dormitory, and library. Respected and loved by an immense array of Christians around the globe, Latourette managed to live out the kind of ecumenically-oriented evangelical Christianity that he believed Jesus taught. All of his life's activities were devoted to seeing the Kingdom of God go forward. That was his central wish for his church history writings, that they might somehow advance the cause of Christ. There is little doubt that they have already done and will continue to do precisely that.

SELECT BIBLIOGRAPHY

PRIMARY SOURCES

Anno Domini: Jesus, History, and God. New York: Harper & Brothers, 1940.

Beyond the Ranges, An Autobiography. Grand Rapids, Mich.: Eerdmans, 1967.

The Chinese: Their History and Culture. New York: Macmillan, 1934.

Christianity in a Revolutionary Age: A History of Christianity in the Nineteenth and Twentieth Centuries. 5 vols. New York: Harper & Row, 1958–1962.

"The Christian Understanding of History." *American Historical Review* 54 (1949): 259–76.

The Development of China. Boston/New York: Houghton Mifflin Co., 1917.

The Development of Japan. New York: Macmillan, 1918.

"A Historian Looks Ahead; the Future of Christianity in the Light of Its Past." *Church History* 15 (1946): 3–16.

A History of Christian Missions in China. New York: Macmillan, 1929.

A History of Christianity. New York: Harper & Row, 1953.

A History of the Expansion of Christianity. 7 vols. New York: Harper & Brothers, 1937–1945.

"New Perspectives in Church History." *Journal of Religion,* 21 (1941): 432–43.

A Short History of the Far East. New York: Macmillan, 1946.

The Unquenchable Light. New York: Harper & Brothers, 1941.

SECONDARY SOURCES

Bates, Searle. "Christian Historian, Doer of Christian History: In Memory of Kenneth Scott Latourette, 1884–1968." *International Review of Mission* 58 (1969): 317–26.

Hannah, John D. "Kenneth Scott Latourette, a Trail Blazer—A Critical Evaluation of Latourette's Theory of Religious History." *Grace Theological Journal* 2 (1981): 3–22.

Harr, Wilber C., ed. *Frontiers of the Christian World Mission Since 1938: Essays in Honor of Kenneth Scott Latourette.* New York: Harper & Brothers, 1962.

Hogg, William Richey. "The Legacy of Kenneth Scott Latourette." *Occasional Bulletin of Missionary Research* 2 (1978): 74–80.

Lindgren, Juhani. *Unity of All Christians in Love and Mission: The Ecumenical Method of Kenneth Scott Latourette.* Helsinki: Suomalainea Tiedeakatemia, 1990.

Pitts, William L. "World Christianity: The Church History Writing of Kenneth Scott Latourette." Diss., Vanderbilt University, 1969.

Sella, Domenico. *Gli studi di storia religiosa negli Stati Uniti e l'opera di K.S. Latourette.* Milan: Facoltá di lettere e filosofia dell' universitá di Milano, 1958.

Speck, William A. "Kenneth Scott Latourette's Vocation as Christian Historian." *Christian Scholar's Review* 4 (1975): 285–99.

———. "The Role of the Christian Historian in the Twentieth Century as Seen in the Writings of Kenneth Scott Latourette, Christopher Dawson, and Herbert Butterfield." Diss., Florida State University, 1965.

NOTES

1. Latourette described his early life in his autobiography, *Beyond the Ranges* (Grand Rapids, Mich.: Eerdmans, 1967), 9–24, and in "My Guided Life," in *Frontiers of the Christian World Mission Since 1938: Essays in Honor of Kenneth Scott Latourette,* ed. Wilber C. Harr (New York: Harper & Brothers, 1962), 282–85. In the latter volume, a biographical sketch is also provided in E. Theodore Bachmann, "Kenneth Scott Latourette: Historian and Friend," 231–74. Latourette's life still awaits a full-scale biography.

2. Latourette, *Beyond the Ranges,* 26–37; Bachmann, "Kenneth Scott Latourette," 234–37.

3. Latourette, *Beyond the Ranges,* 39–46, 50–51.

4. Ibid., 48–62; Latourette, "My Guided Life," 289–91. Latourette published these first books with major commercial presses, setting a pattern for his later works. Kenneth Scott Latourette, *The Development of China* (Boston/New York: Houghton Mifflin Co., 1917); Kenneth Scott Latourette, *The Development of Japan* (New York: Macmillan, 1918). One example of his call for greater study of the Orient is "American Scholarship and Chinese History," *Journal of the American Oriental Society* 38 (1918): 97–106.

5. Latourette remembered being approached by the University of Wisconsin, the University of Chicago, and Northwestern. See Latourette, *Beyond the Ranges,* 60–61.

6. Ibid., 63–139. When Latourette entered the field in the 1920s, missiology was yet in its infancy.

7. Ibid., 65–71, 75–78, 95–109. For a brief statement of his ecumenical views, see Kenneth Scott Latourette, "How Should Baptists Look at the World Council of Churches?" *The Watchman Examiner* 27 (March 16, 1939): 273–74.

8. Bachmann, "Kenneth Scott Latourette," 245–76. The bulk of Latourette's periodical writing was for the religious press. His four major areas of concentration were East Asian history, the history of missions, the history of Christianity, and Christian higher education. He also devoted considerable attention to contemporary international relations. Published bibliographies of his writings are contained in Helen B. Uhrich, Ralph Norman, and Raymond P. Morris, "Select Bibliography of Kenneth Scott Latourette" in *Frontiers of the Christian World Mission*, and Juhani Lindgren, *Unity of All Christians in Love and Mission: The Ecumenical Method of Kenneth Scott Latourette* (Helsinki: Suomalainea Tiedeakatemia, 1990) 353–60.

9. Latourette, *Beyond the Ranges*, 9, 51, 129, 143, 155. John D. Hannah, "Kenneth Scott Latourette, a Trail Blazer—A Critical Evaluation of Latourette's Theory of Religious History," *Grace Theological Journal* 2 (1981): 3–4, 21–22, discusses the impact of this self-image on Latourette's work.

10. Kenneth Scott Latourette, "This I Believe," 1, Kenneth Scott Latourette Papers, Manuscript Group No. 3, Box 168, Folder 78, Special Collections, Yale Divinity School Library. Student and friend William Richey Hogg characterized Latourette as "a catholic evangelical steeped in the Bible and of ecumenical conviction" (William Richey Hogg, "The Legacy of Kenneth Scott Latourette," *Occasional Bulletin of Missionary Research* 2 (1978): 76). Many of Latourette's essential beliefs are revealed in "My Guided Life," 281–93.

11. Latourette, *Beyond the Ranges*, 71–74, 128–29, 152–55. Latourette became an ordained Baptist minister while teaching at Denison and preached occasionally over the years. In the 1940s he became Honorary Pastor of Calvary Baptist Church in New Haven, where he was a long-time member. His warm ministry to students at the Divinity School earned him the nickname, "Uncle Ken."

12. Ibid., 95–106. A brief estimation of Latourette's importance for world missions is given in Ralph D. Winter, "The Reluctant Missionary," *World Vision Magazine* 13 (July–August 1969): 4–5. Latourette's missionary-mindedness is nowhere better illustrated than in his brief article, "Every Christian A Missionary" in *Criterion* 111 (May 1955): 3.

13. Latourette, *Beyond the Ranges*, 65–70, 77–78, 106–9.

14. Lindgren, *Unity of All Christians*, 333.

15. Two Latourette books that particularly express his optimism are *Anno Domini: Jesus, History, and God* (New York: Harper & Brothers, 1940) and *The Unquenchable Light* (New York: Harper & Brothers, 1941).

16. Cf. the responses to Latourette's views on "Christ the Hope of the World" from Reinhold Niebuhr and F. Ernest Stoeffler in *Religion in Life* 23 (1954): 334–51.

17. This was Yale historian Roland Bainton's apt phrase for Walker's approach and is quoted in Lindgren, *Unity of All Christians*, 63. Bachmann, "Kenneth Scott Latourette," 234–37, and Hannah, "Latourette, a Trail Blazer," 6, 9–10, emphasize Walker's influence.

18. Kenneth Scott Latourette, "The Christian Future," 5, Latourette Papers, Manuscript Group No. 3, Box 167, Folder 70. Latourette laid out his views of Christianity's future to fellow church historians in "A Historian Looks Ahead; the Future of Christianity in the Light of Its Past," *Church History* 15 (1946): 3–16.

19. William L. Pitts, Jr., "World Christianity: The Church History Writing of Kenneth Scott Latourette" (diss., Vanderbilt University, 1969), 63–71, 216–19.

20. Kenneth Scott Latourette, *A History of Christian Missions in China* (New York: Macmillan, 1929). This early work was more of a monograph than his later books. It exhaustively covered its topic, running over 900 pages and containing thousands of footnotes.

21. Kenneth Scott Latourette, *A History of the Expansion of Christianity* (7 vols.; 1939–1945; reprint ed., Grand Rapids, Mich.: Zondervan, 1970) 1: ix–x, xxii. Latourette stated his case for a global church history plainly in "New Perspectives in Church History," *Journal of Religion* 21 (1941): 434–38.

22. Volumes three and five of *Christianity in a Revolutionary Age: A History of Christianity in the Nineteenth and Twentieth Centuries* (5 vols.; 1958–1962; reprint ed., Grand Rapids, Mich.: Zondervan, 1969) were devoted to developments outside of Europe. Similarly, non-Western events take up much of Latourette's coverage of the last two centuries in *A History of Christianity* (2 vols.; revised ed., New York: Harper & Row, 1975).

23. Latourette, "New Perspectives," 434–38; Latourette, *Beyond the Ranges*, 109–10, 114; Latourette, *History of Christianity*, 2: xv–xvi; Latourette, *Christianity in a Revolutionary Age*, 2: 58–59; William A. Speck, "Kenneth Scott Latourette's Vocation as Christian Historian," *Christian Scholar's Review* 4 (1975): 289–90.

24. Kenneth Scott Latourette, "The Christian Understanding of History," *American Historical Review* 54 (1949): 263; Latourette, *Christianity in a Revolutionary Age*, 5: 515–16; Hogg, "Legacy of Latourette," 76.

25. Latourette, *History of the Expansion of Christianity*, 1: xvii; Latourette, *History of Christianity*, 1: xix–xx; Latourette, *Christianity in a Revolutionary Age*, 1: xiii.

26. Niebuhr, "Christ the Hope of the World," 334; Ernest A. Payne, "The Modern Expansion of the Church: Some Reflections on Dr. Latourette's Conclusions," *Journal of Theological Studies* 47 (1946): 149.

27. Kenneth Scott Latourette, "The Place of Church History in the Training of Missionaries," in *The Madras Series* (7 vols.; New York/London: International Missionary Council, 1939) 4: 256.

28. Latourette, *Beyond the Ranges*, 78–79, 111–12, 116–20; Bachmann, "Kenneth Scott Latourette," 247. European analysts of Latourette's work have especially warmed to his ecumenical emphasis. See summaries of the interpretations of Italian Domenico Sella and German Ernst Benz in Lindgren, *Unity of All Christians*, 20–22. Lindgren's study itself is devoted to analyzing Latourette's ecumenical method.

29. One example would be his comparatively brief discussions of the early Ecumenical Councils in *History of Christianity*, 1: 153–57, 164, 167, 171–72, which he saw as causing as much tension and disunity as their opposite.

30. Lindgren, *Unity of All Christians*, 331–35; James E. Wood, Jr., "Kenneth Scott Latourette (1884–1968): Historian, Ecumenist, and Friend," *Journal of Church and State* 11 (1969): 10–12.

31. Hannah, "Latourette, a Trail Blazer," 15–18, describes the various criticisms that have been made of Latourette's theology and lack of theological acumen.

32. Latourette, "The Place of Church History," 255–56; Latourette, "New Perspectives," 432–34; Searle Bates, "Christian Historian, Doer of Christian History: In Memory of Kenneth Scott Latourette, 1884–1968," *International Review of Mission* 58 (1969): 319. The theme of Jesus' influence in history pervades all of Latourette's writings on the history of Christianity. For one example, see Latourette, *Anno Domini*. Lindgren, *Unity of All Christians*, 75, suggests that the "idea of the ever-growing influence of Jesus in the world" was the "all-absorbing idea in Latourette's historical writing."

33. Pitts, "World Christianity," 74.

34. Latourette, *History of the Expansion of Christianity*, 1: x–xv.

35. Pitts, "World Christianity," 159–60.

36. Latourette's emphasis on Christian practice has been widely noted. Some sense of his own view of what his writings would concentrate upon may be gained from the preface to *History of Christianity*, 1: xiv–xv, and in "New Perspectives," 433.

37. Kenneth Scott Latourette, *Challenge and Conformity* (New York: Harper & Brothers, 1955), 22–23; Latourette, *Christianity in a Revolutionary Age*, 5: 518–19, 533–34. Latourette believed that the historian of Christianity had to study all groups who claimed that name and that the test of their "Christianness" lay in the quality of their Christian practice, not in the quality of their Christian dogma. Pitts, "World Christianity," 72–73, critiques Latourette on this point, arguing that Latourette's work lacks a concept of heresy and "does not include sufficient theological criteria by which to judge whether a movement is Christian."

38. Latourette advanced this thesis numerous times. For a sampling, see Latourette, "Christ the Hope of the World," 323–33; Latourette, "Christian Understanding of History," 272–75; Latourette, *Unquenchable Light*; Latourette, *History of Christianity*, 1: xxi–xxiv; Kenneth Scott Latourette, "Do We Live in a Post-Christian Age?" *Religion in Life* 33 (1964): 170–79; Kenneth Scott Latourette, "Jesus in History," Latourette Papers, Manuscript Group No. 3, Box 147.

39. Latourette, *History of the Expansion of Christianity*, 1: xix–xxi; Latourette, *Christianity in a Revolutionary Age*, 1: viii–x; Latourette, "New Perspectives," 436–43; Latourette, "The Place of Church History," 257.

40. Latourette, "Do We Live in a Post-Christian Age?" 170–79; Kenneth Scott Latourette, "The Christian Church in the Last Seventy Years," *Annual Report of the American Historical Association* 3 (1942): 67–72. Part of Latourette's argument was the claim that Christianity was young, not old, in light of the age of the earth, and that, if anything, modern times continued to represent a "pre-Christian" era, not a "post-Christian" one. He began the first chapter of his *History of Christianity* (1:3) by writing, "Christianity is relatively young. Compared with the course of mankind on the earth, it began only a few moments ago." The last chapter of *Christianity in a Revolutionary Age* (5:516) made the same point.

41. He used the phrase as the title of the final volume of his *History of the Expansion of Christianity*.

42. Pitts, "World Christianity," 122, characterizes Latourette's thesis as Christianity "challenged but triumphant."

43. Latourette, *Christianity in a Revolutionary Age*, 5:533–34. Latourette's views on the relationship of history and eschatology have received considerable attention. In a series of reviews of *A History of the Expansion of Christianity*, Englishman J. S. Whale repeatedly assailed Latourette's perspective, finally claiming that "the philosophy of history with which Dr. Latourette is working is not that of the Hebraic-Christian eschatology of the New Testament but rather the evolutionary perfectionism which dreams of a Utopia achieved by human efforts within the time process" (*International Review of Missions* 34 [1945]: 429). Bachmann, "Kenneth Scott Latourette," 266–67, argues that Latourette became more realistic in his views of the end of history later in life, particularly as reflected in his book *The Christian Mission in Our Day* (New York: Harper & Brothers, 1954). Lindgren, *Unity of All Christians*, 28 n. 60, suggests that Latourette rejected "the notion that he ever intended a this-worldly utopia in his historical interpretation." On this topic, also see Hogg, "Legacy of Latourette," 76.

44. William A. Speck, "The Role of the Christian Historian in the Twentieth Century as Seen in the Writings of Kenneth Scott Latourette, Christopher Dawson, and Herbert Butterfield" (diss., Florida State University, 1965), 6–18; Hannah, "Latourette, a Trail Blazer," 17–18.

45. Pitts, "World Christianity," 28.

46. Kenneth Scott Latourette, "A History Teacher's Confession of Faith," *The Ohio History Teacher's Journal* No. 19 (1920): 182.

47. Speck, "Latourette's Vocation," 289.

48. Ibid., 287–92; Speck, "Role of the Christian Historian," 6, 13–15.

49. While agreeing with Becker and Beard on this point, it does not appear that Latourette accepted other aspects of their historical relativism. Cf. Lindgren, *Unity of All Christians*, 65–66.

50. Latourette, "Christian Understanding of History," 259–61. Latourette would re-state much of this same case in the preface to his *History of Christianity*, 1: xix–xx.

51. Latourette, "Christian Understanding of History," 262–71 (quote on 271).

52. Ibid., 272–76. Latourette's "attempt to discern the meaning of the story" at the end of his *Christianity in a Revolutionary Age*, 5: 531–34, affirmed several times that the course of history confirmed Christian belief. For him, history was a powerful testimony to Christianity's validity.

53. Speck, "Latourette's Vocation," 288–89, 293.

54. Latourette, *History of Christianity*, 1: xx. Also see Latourette, *History of the Expansion of Christianity*, 1: xvii.

55. Latourette, *History of Christianity*, 1: xx.

56. Ibid., 1: xix–xx; Latourette, *Christianity in a Revolutionary Age*, 1: xiii; Latourette, *History of the Expansion of Christianity*, 1: xvi–xvii; Kenneth Scott Latourette, "The Relation of Christian Faith to History and the Social Sciences," 3–4, 8–11, Latourette Papers, Manuscript Group No. 3, Box 167, Folder 77.

57. In a speech in 1953 ("Relation of Christian Faith to History"), Latourette sharply attacked non-theistic humanism which he saw as dominating his profession and American higher education. Its "alleged 'objectivity' . . . professes to be free from bias and from presuppositions [but] is as dogmatic as the Christian 'bias' which it endeavors to shun." For the history of the ideal of objectivity among historians in America, see Peter Novick, *That Noble Dream: The "Objectivity Question" and the American Historical Profession* (Cambridge: Cambridge University Press, 1988). For one dialogue about postmodernist theory and history, see David Harlan, "Intellectual History and the Return to Literature," *American Historical Review* 94 (1989): 581–609; David Hollinger, "The Return of the Prodigal: The Persistence of Historical Knowing," ibid., 610–21; and David Harlan, "Reply to David Hollinger," ibid., 622–26.

58. The inclusion of work by or about Latourette in two important collections of essays on Christian philosophies of history in the 1970s indicated his ongoing importance. His AHA address was reprinted in *God, History and Historians* (ed. C. T. McIntire; New York: Oxford University Press, 1977), 45–67, and William Speck's insightful article ("Latourette's Vocation") was also printed in *A Christian View of History?* ed. Frank Roberts and George Marsden (Grand Rapids, Mich.: Eerdmans, 1975), 119–37.

59. Recent surveys of the history of Christianity that take a more global approach include Justo L. González, *The Story of Christianity* (2 vols.; San Francisco: Harper & Row, 1984), *The Oxford Illustrated History of Christianity* ed. John McManners (Oxford/ New York: Oxford University Press, 1990), and Robert G. Clouse, Richard V. Pierard, and Edwin M. Yamauchi, *Two Kingdoms: The Church and Culture Through the Ages* (Chicago: Moody Press, 1993). Lindgren, *Unity of All Christians*, 50, discusses the "global" trend within German church history scholarship.

60. Pitts, "World Christianity," 171, 182–95.

61. In the preface to his *History of Christianity*, 1: xv, Latourette emphasized the need to study the laity: "A well-balanced narrative of the course of Christianity must also seek to disclose what the faith has meant to the rank and file of those who bear the Christian name and of those, unknown to wide fame, who in communities, most of them small and obscure, have been radiating centres of the faith." Recent surveys of the history of Christianity which emphasize social and cultural history include González, *Story of Christianity*, and Roland Bainton, *Christendom: A Short History of Christianity and Its Impact on Western Civilization* (2 vols; New York: Harper & Row, 1966).

62. Bates, "Christian Historian," 319, 326; Pitts, "World Christianity," 140–44, 216–17; Bachmann, "Kenneth Scott Latourette," 279–80; Hogg, "Legacy of Latourette," 74, 78–79.

63. Hogg, "Legacy of Latourette," 77; Pitts, "World Christianity," 178–81.

64. Speck, "Latourette's Vocation," 299; Bates, "Christian Historian," 322; Hogg, "Legacy of Latourette," 78; Payne, "Modern Expansion," 148; Hannah, "Latourette, a Trail Blazer," 18–22.

65. Niebuhr, "Christ the Hope of the World," 336.

66. Speck, "Latourette's Vocation," 297–99; Hannah, "Latourette, a Trail Blazer," 4, 12–15; Pitts, "World Christianity," 167–70.

67. Hannah, "Latourette, a Trail Blazer," 15–17, 22; Lindgren, *Unity of All Christians*, 28; Leroy Moore, Jr., review of *Beyond the Ranges*, by Kenneth Scott Latourette, in *The Hartford Quarterly* 8 (1968): 90.

68. Winthrop S. Hudson, review of *Christianity in a Revolutionary Age* by Kenneth Scott Latourette, in *Journal of Bible and Religion* 27 (1959): 248; Pitts, "World Christianity," 124–27; Hannah, "Latourette, a Trail Blazer," 20.

20

CHRISTOPHER DAWSON

CAROLINE MARSHALL

Henry Christopher Dawson was born at Hay Castle, Herefordshire, October 12, 1889. He was the second child and only son of Colonel Henry Dawson and Louisa Mary Beven of Harlington Hall, Burnsall, in Yorkshire. He was born into a landholding family of some piety and learning. His mother was the daughter of an Anglican archdeacon, and his father had Anglo-Catholic sympathies. Dawson was, in brief, the child of an impeccably establishment background. He belonged to the gentry, the Church of England and to the secure world of Victorian values of which his family was representative. [1]

He grew up at the Dawson estate in Yorkshire. From his mother, a low-church Anglican of profound Protestant sensibilities, he learned about the mystical saints of her Welch ancestry. All his life he maintained an affinity for the mixture of poetry and faith that was the bedrock of his childhood.

Dawson was a shy boy brought up in a learned and sheltered atmosphere. His people were not the unintellectual, hunting gentry of legend but graceful, sensitive people with serious religious preoccupations. His world was upset when, in 1904, he was sent to Bilton Grange, a preparatory school near Rugby. We have no reason to believe that Bilton Grange was an unusually cruel or uncouth place, though Dawson despised it. He was not accustomed to the rough-and-tumble life of most adolescent boys. He found the experience at Bilton Grange devastating. In 1904, he was sent to Winchester, the famous public school, where he passed through a brief agnostic phase. He was removed from Winchester because of serious illness, episodes of the bronchial troubles that were periodically to disrupt his life thereafter. He went to Bletsoe in Bedfordshire to continue his preparations for Oxford with an Anglican parson. While at Bletsoe, he formed the most important friendship of his life with Edward Watkin, also a boy of intellectual Anglo-Catholic tradition.

In 1908, Dawson went up to Trinity College, Oxford. He was not a part of either the wild and eccentric social life or of the most serious intellectual circles of the university. He did, however, have an excellent tutor, Ernest Barker, a classical scholar with medieval interests as well and a nonconformist background. During his Oxford years, Dawson regularly attended the Anglo-Catholic services at the university, though he did not especially fraternize with the "spikes," local slang for high churchmen. While a student, he made his first trip to Italy and was touched by the Baroque culture of ecclesiastical Rome. Increasingly he moved within a circle of Roman Catholic friends and their families. By this time Watkins had, in the phrase of the time, "gone over to Rome." Dawson and Watkins shared lodgings and were best friends.

On Easter Day, 1909, Dawson was in Rome and visited the church of the Ara Coeli, where Gibbon had his vision of writing a great (and anti-Christian) history of the end of the Roman Empire. Here Dawson himself first conceived the idea of writing a history of culture. In the meanwhile, he met and fell in love with Valery Mills, a Roman Catholic. Thus, his conservative nature and the circumstances of his personal life conspired to bring him to a Roman conversion. He was concerned about a variety of problems in the Protestant tradition: the absence of well-defined authority, the abolition of the liturgy and the saints, and the end of voluntary asceticism at the closure of the monasteries. In other words, Dawson missed what he conceived of as historic Christian culture. Although the Anglo-Catholic movement had done much to restore the missing elements, for Dawson it was not enough. Anglicanism, he believed, was part of the great schism that had wounded the church and had made a fissure in Europe from which had flowed the heresies and evils of contemporary social life.

In 1911, Dawson went to Sweden, where he studied briefly under Professor Gustav Cassel, an economist. The next year he studied at the Oxford School of Rural Economy, and, for a time, worked for the Conservative Party's Central Office. On January 5, 1914, he was received into the Roman communion at St. Aloysius Church, Oxford. He was not strong enough to meet the military's requirement to participate in World War I. In 1916, he married Valery Mills. They had three children, a son and two daughters. He supported his new family through an allowance from his father which he supplemented through writing.

Dawson believed that he was destined to be a writer. From 1917 to 1918, he worked for the Admiralty Intelligence Division, and in 1920 began his writing career. His first publication was an essay, "The Nature and Destiny of Man," which was given at a symposium on *God and the Supernatural* and was later published in *Enquiries into Religion and Culture* (1933) by the Catholic publishers Sheed and Ward, with whom Dawson had a long and sympathetic relationship. He also began to contribute to *The Sociological Review*. From 1925 till 1933, he worked, on and off, as a lecturer at the University of Exeter.

In 1928, he fulfilled the pledge he had made on Easter, 1909, with the publication of *The Age of the Gods*, published by John Murray. *Progress and Religion* (1929) was published by Sheed and Ward. Frank Sheed became Dawson's friend and advisor for the next thirty years. Because he had not pursued advanced studies, Dawson had difficulty finding an academic appointment. He continued to lecture and publish quite consistently during the interwar period, however, always in the area of the religious basis of culture, which was his primary thesis. Between 1930 and 1939, Dawson published: *St. Augustine and His Age* (1930), *Christianity and the New Age* (1931), *The Making of Europe* (1932), *The Modern Dilemma* (1932), *Enquiries into Religion and Culture* (1933), *Medieval Religion and Other Essays* (1934), *The Spirit of the Oxford Movement* (1934), *Religion and the Modern State* (1936), and *Beyond Politics* (1939).[2]

Throughout the 1940s Dawson sold articles to a variety of journals and papers, including *The Dublin Review*, *The Criterion* (edited by T. S. Eliot), *The Colosseum*, and *The Tablet*. During the Second World War, he edited *The Dublin Review*. In 1943, he published *The Judgment of the Nations*, a book in which he reflected upon Europe's darkest hour in terms reminiscent of the Old Testament prophets. Though criticized by the Catholic right and the Liberal left as well, this book was highly praised by many Anglicans. Following the war, one of his Anglican admirers, George Beck, the Bishop of Chichester, put Dawson's name forward as Gifford Lecturer at the University of Edinburgh. Dawson was thrilled, but as the time approached, he grew nervous about the prospect of going into the heart of Calvinism to give lecture in Natural Theology. With encouragement, however, he gave two brilliant series of lectures in 1947 and 1948 which were later published as *Religion and Culture* (1948) *and Religion and the Rise of Western Culture* (1950).

During the fifties, Dawson lectured in Spain and at Dublin University. He published two books: *Understanding Europe* (1952) and *The Dynamics of World History* (1957). In 1958, he was invited to become the first Stillman Guest Lecturer of Roman Catholic Studies at Harvard University. This appointment was the crowning achievement of Dawson's career. As at Edinburgh, he felt he was going into the heartland of Protestantism to bring the Catholic perspective. As a lecturer, he was not a complete success. His voice did not carry well, and he was shy in public. He had some difficulty with the seminars as well and required a helper or interpreter to deal with the students. The published lectures, however, *The Dividing of Christendom* (1965) and *The Formation of Christendom* (1967), were among his most interesting.

While in America, Dawson inaugurated a course in Christian culture at St. Mary's College, Notre Dame University. Dawson dreamed of a Christian-based education in which the scattered topics of liberal arts learning could be bound together in one unified whole as manifestations of Christianity. His ideas for such a program were included in *The Crisis of Western Education* (1961). In 1959, he published *The Movement of World Revolutions*, followed in 1960 by *The Historic Reality of Christian Culture*.

While in America, Dawson's health declined. He suffered a stroke and returned to England in 1962. He died at Budleigh Salterton, Devonshire, May 25, 1970. It was the feast day of St. Bede who was Dawson's model of the Christian historian. In 1972, Dawson's estate published *Religion and World History*. It included some unpublished work and selections from *The Formation of Christendom*, *The Gods of Revolution*, and *The Movement of World Revolution*. It also included a brief essay on "The Future Life," which first appeared in *The Spectator*.

From the beginning of his academic life, Christopher Dawson was a historian of culture. He rejected the narrow political and national history of his age, and was, instead, drawn to the social sciences and to psychology. Above all, he believed the human being to be a social creature whose life was broader and more complex than traditional historians understood. Somehow, in their endless preoccupation with politics and nation-building, those historians missed the essence, the meaning of human life in time.

Dawson believed that culture is the "common way of life" that represents a people's adjustment to the genetics, environment, economics, and psychology current in their age, circumstance, and place. [3] Cultures take their character from the interaction of these factors. In a way, this process corresponds to the purely biological and material adaptation of the animal kingdom in the evolutionary process. There is, however, an absolute boundary and differentiation between mankind and the animal kingdom. While it may not be easy to see the demarcation line between humans and animals because humanity is still stumbling along its way, history is urging us toward a kind of perfection, which shall, in the end, make us as remote from our spiritual descendants as the animals are from us.[4]

The faith that modern people have in rationalism, Dawson thought, was inadequate both as "a philosophy of life and a means of education."[5] The history of Europeans since the Enlightenment did not demonstrate the triumph of reason. As a member of the generation of World War I, in which Western civilization seemed to attempt mass suicide, Dawson felt keenly the failure of the rationalist tradition to explain or even to illumine the events of his time. This drove him outside the traditional methods of historical study to the social sciences.

Above all, Dawson was interested in the missing links that psychology seemed to provide. He accepted the three-strata complex of the human mind: the subconscious or sub-rational layer of instinct and emotion; the conscious rational level that is the obvious sphere of culture; and the "super-rational level of spiritual experience, which is the sphere not only of religion but of the highest creative forces of cultural achievement—the intuition of the artist, the poet and the philosopher"[6]

To acquire its prosperity and happiness, every civilization must call upon "the spiritual vision of its greatest minds and the way in which this is transmitted to the community by faith, tradition and education."[7]

The greatest factor in cultural progress, according to Dawson, is religion. The religious teacher or prophet is the most important agent of social change. Even though the prophet is himself the product of the culture, he is able to see a new revelation, a way of looking at life, which can alter the reality of his civilization. Under divine prophecy everything can change, and "all things can be made new again." This does not mean that all the old circumstances disappear, only that they are so altered by the new revelation that they are, in fact, unique.

In his Gifford lectures, Dawson developed his theme of religion as the key to history and culture. Above all, he asserted, mankind, through time, has identified a great *transcendent order* outside ourselves that controls the world. Humanity has within itself the intuitive recognition of this power and a profound desire to associate itself with it. To this end, there are sacred places and ceremonies as well as a priestly class to facilitate communication between the merely human and the divine. Throughout his life, Dawson had a profound regard for ritual and liturgy, which he saw as more vital in popular religious culture than are the Scriptures. He gives full value always to the sacred *word*, but for the bonding of the people and their God, the ritual of sacrifice is indispensable, as is the sacerdotal class presiding at the altar.

When the Gifford lectures were published, the English public had an opportunity to read Dawson's humane and lively views on primitive religion as well as the "higher religion" of the Orient and the West. He defends the dignity and integrity of primitive religions, and sees in them a religious intent—the intent to commune with the divine. In addition, he insists that they have a belief in a transcendent, divine order upon which their material world depends, which is as complete as anything apprehended by the higher religions of more sophisticated civilizations.[8]

In the non-Christian "higher religions" of the Far East, Dawson speculates that an intense preoccupation with the spiritual, the *Transcendent*, led Hindus and Buddhists to search for pure Being and to abandon the ethical, social, or worldly obligations of faith. He further insists that, "it is impossible to construct a dynamic religion on metaphysical principles alone, since pure intuition affords no real basis for social action."[9] Although classical Hinduism teaches a profound obligation toward one's social duties, its disregard for material reality encourages a "fatalistic acceptance of the established order of things."[10] The true dynamic of history is the communion between the spiritual world and human life on earth, the coming together of God's order and human society.

Dawson finds this interaction only in Christianity. He finds the meaning of history first in theistic societies, then in Christianity and, finally, in the Roman Catholicism to which he was an adult convert. His themes are faith, unity, Christendom. Because it is the culture that most nearly fits his definitions, the medieval West occupies much of Dawson's interest and effort. To Dawson, history is, in the classic sense, the working out of God's will in time. Human progress is possible in this context, although it is most likely only within the confines of Catholic Christendom.

In *A Monument to St. Augustine*, *The Making of Europe* and *Medieval Religion and Other Essays*, Dawson introduced the themes of medieval Christendom that he believed were more than issues of Christian history. In these volumes, he argued that the social, intellectual, and institutional foundations of Europe were medieval and Christian and that the church had created European civilization during the thousand years between the classical age and the era of Renaissance and Reformation. With Europe as the dynamic hub, the Christian West spread not only to the New World, but, in reverse historical fashion, back again to its Middle Eastern and African origins during the imperial centuries.[11] No one has written so movingly of the remarkable evolution of medieval civilization as has Christopher Dawson. He takes his theme from Saint Augustine of Hippo's image of the two cities. Clearly Augustine is Dawson's greatest teacher among the church fathers. Dawson, nevertheless, also spends considerable effort exploring the idea of the divine community, as it is found in ancient Israel and in the Gospels. For all his preoccupation with the early Middle Ages, Dawson always claimed that his conversion to Roman Catholicism and its general view of history were first a result of reading the Scriptures, especially the Gospels. "It was by the study of St. Paul and St. John that I first came to understand the unity of Catholic theology and Catholic life. I realized that the Incarnation, the sacraments, the external order of the Church and the internal work of sanctifying grace, were all parts of one organic unity, a living tree whose roots are in the Divine nature and whose fruit is the perfection of the saints."[12]

From their Hebrew past, Dawson asserted, the early Christians inherited a quite remarkable idea, one at which modern people often balk. The Christian of any age must begin by accepting that his history is a *sacred* history. This history reaches back beyond the Fathers, beyond the Gospels, to a minor tribe in ancient Palestine. The Christian must accept that in God's adoption of the Hebrews and His covenant with them, the stage is set for the *Kingdom*, not a kingdom like other ancient nations, but one which is both eternal and universal. These ancient people were the bearers of divine revelation: from them would come the Son of Man, whose messianic fulfillment would itself be a new nation, catholic rather than tribal, and triumphant over the empires of the world. This vision was apocalyptic; it called for a new Jerusalem which will descend out of heaven in God's good time by way of cosmic revolution.[13] What Dawson defines as the Catholic view of history rejects both a literal millenarian view and the escapism of the Gnostics by concentrating on the principle of *Incarnation*, which taught that God has entered history. The way to salvation is now open to all. In this tradition the crucifixion initiated a new order in the world, an order in which "a real leaven of spiritual progress is at work in mankind and the life of the world to come is already stirring in the womb of the present."[14] Christendom is not the Kingdom of God, and the best the Christian can say of a relatively Christian culture is that it should be more open to the progress of the Spirit than would a purely material culture. But one can never say this for certain, because in its moments of apparent institutional success Christianity is sometimes most at risk, while in time of hideous trial it may be secretly triumphant. Nothing characterizes Dawson's view of Christian history so much as his commitment to the secret working of the *Spirit*. While Dawson recognizes that one really never knows the future or the coming of the *Kingdom*, along with Augustine he asserts that one can recognize that "the principle of charity, inspired by divine grace is at work throughout the ages, building the new social order that is the city of God and the kingdom of Christ, whereas the principle of self-love is inevitably a divisive and destructive one, which creates the city of confusion—Babylon—which is the kingdom of the devil."[15]

Clearly no age so pleased Dawson as did the Middle Ages, in which he believed one could witness the unambiguous working of the *Spirit* in the birth of Europe through the Christian integration of classical civilization with the barbarian West. He noted with some justice the reluctance of modern historians to give medievalism its due, a tendency he traces back to the Renaissance and its renewed humanism, to the Reformation and its sectarianism, to the Enlightenment and its Deism, and to the nineteenth century and its secular liberalism.

Some of Dawson's best historical writing can be found in his *Religion and the Rise of Western Culture*. Here his Roman convictions are free to luxuriate in the light of a triumphant Catholic order and in one of the most brilliant epochs of human history. Although his career lay on the edge of a great renewal of medieval studies, Professor Dawson was heir to their neglect in the English-speaking world, whose historians tended to be both bourgeois and Protestant in heritage and liberal and secular in training. The great preoccupation with nationalism, which he saw as a tragedy of particularism, absorbed much of the historian's energy. The Christian culture of the Middle Ages had been neglected.

The pervasive theme of Dawson's Medieval studies is the impressive integration of Christian society and the Catholic faith. In arguing this theme, he gives us a refreshing portrait of a religion reflected in the total life of its people rather than a world in which religion stands simply as a part of a multi-institutional structure: "Christianity was not merely a doctrine and a life; it was above all a society, and it was the organic unity of the Christian society which preserved the spiritual identity of the Christian religion."[16]

The creation of this Christian society was not easy. Having survived the ordeal of Roman persecution and the threat of early heresies, early medieval Christendom was faced with the barbarian invasions of the fifth century. The collapse of the Christian Roman Empire meant the reconstruction of society and all its institutions. Only the ecclesiastical orders, sustained by the unity of faith and social purpose that had been refined in the previous catastrophes, could have accomplished the task. "The rise of the new Western European culture is dominated by this sharp dualism between two cultures, two social traditions and two spiritual worlds—the war society of the barbarian kingdom with its cult of heroism and aggression and the peace society of the Christian Church with its ideals of asceticism and renunciation and its high theological culture."[17]

In Dawson's historical chronology, this is the "Second Age of the Church," a period following the era of Christ, the apostles, and the Fathers. The second phase of European development begins with Constantine and ends with the rise of Islam. This period's most significant achievement is the development of monasticism, which preserved for the church the pure Christian life in a form that "renounced the sexual instinct, the economic instinct and the desire for individual power."[18] In the ordinary way of things in the modern materialist world, we see this as, at the very least, a neurotic or "life-denying" movement. The monks and nuns, however, proved to be living replacements for the martyrs of the Roman persecution in a post-apocalyptic time. They gave the newly challenged Christian society "living witnesses to the inescapable demands of Christ's kingdom on earth."[19] Again, we notice Dawson's persistent theme that in history what seems to ordinary human reason to be useless or inappropriate is, in the Kingdom of God, the prescription for progress. Instead of the traditional secular themes of monasticism as "flight" from the world of the barbarians or from the world of reality, we see a new perspective. From Christian historians like Dawson, who is alert to the possibility of God's working in time, we expect fresh views and a new understanding. We get them.

Dawson's next medieval era, or "Third Age of the Church," begins with the collapse of Byzantium into constituent national, often sectarian, units and the first incursions of Islam into Christendom. It closes with the crisis precipitated by the new barbarian (Viking, Magyar, and Saracen) attacks and the collapse of the Frankish imperial order. The great achievement of the period was the salvation of literary culture during the Carolingian Renaissance. More than ever, this reform of education solidified the connection between high culture and the church so that the clergy came to have a monopoly on medieval education.

The last medieval era, according to Dawson, begins with the reform of medieval society as the church attempted to free itself from absorption by the emerging feudal order. Bishops, abbots, and other great churchmen had become a part of the feudal caste of power and landed wealth, of government and military defense. A society *in extremis* required much of its most capable members, and the church was rich with the best and the brightest. In Dawson's view, the two great vehicles of reform were the papacy, represented by Gregory VII, and the monastic reformers beginning with the Cluniacs and culminating in the Franciscans. Dawson believes that Christian society was preserved by the interaction of these two movements which freed the church from a crude and brutal feudal order.[20] Dawson's view of the High Middle Ages is thus deeply colored by his commitment to the papacy as the central and necessary hierarchial feature of a united Christendom. He sees Innocent III, the most worldly and powerful of all medieval popes, as a spiritual reformer, responsible for the universal element in the success of the Dominicans and the Franciscans.

In the fourth and final Medieval age of the church, Francis of Assisi emerges to reconcile the order of the church and the new urban society. In Francis, Dawson believes we find the perfection of the Catholic idea of the saint as Christian hero, one who incorporates the three saintly elements of the democratic or the popular, the moral, and the supernatural.[21]

Francis rises from the people with an enormous mystical understanding of their dilemma. His cult among the laity precedes his recognition by church "authority," and by his life and his work he revives and rescues the age.

The next period in European history (or "Age of the Church") is very difficult for Dawson because it features the era of Renaissance and Reformation, when schism split Christian society. Historically, Dawson holds accountable the rise of that element of medieval civilization that he found most dangerous and destructive—the nation-state. Here, he believes, the definition of society fundamentally changes, because the Protestants conceive of a new church, composed of the elect, present through time struggling against that great harlot, Babylon, which in their theology, is the medieval Catholic Church. Thus, concludes Dawson, there appears a permanent warp in the planks of European history, namely the rejection of the thousand years of medieval Christian history. The end result of this rejection is a schism more profound than a simple religious dispute, because Europeans have lost connection with their roots in the culture that gave them birth.[22]

The Renaissance is a difficult topic for Dawson because it is a movement shared by the Protestant and Catholic cultures, and because both lay claim to its good offices. Humanism, the rediscovery of classical sources and their emphasis on human or worldly ideals, gave birth to the spirit of criticism that was vital to the Protestants. The glorious visual arts of the Italian Renaissance, however, were the very lifeblood of the Catholic recovery and the Catholic or Counter-Reformation. Dawson said of the Renaissance: "It has a peculiar and tragic interest for Christians, it was the age which saw the division of Christendom, when the Catholic and Protestant worlds assumed their existing forms and when Western culture began to undergo that process of secularization which has been completed in our own day."[23]

In substance, Dawson sees the Protestant Reformation as a response to the failure of the church to extricate itself from the corrupting influences of the national monarchies and the new capitalist economy. The church entered into the new economy, but did not comprehend its destructive influence on the medieval order. In "The Vision of Piers Plowman," Dawson finds the definitive portrait of late medieval common man. William Langland, the English poet, is not simply initiating us into the profound suffering of an individual; he is also instructing the reader in the collapse of the old society based on service, custom, and loyalty.[24]

The power of money is embodied in the terrible image of Lady Meed:

Trust in her treasure . betrayeth full many,
She hath poisoned Popes . and impaired Holy Church.
Monks and minstrels . are among her lovers,
Both learned men . and lepers in hedges.
Summoners and jurymen . are such as prize her,
She is with the sheriffs . who rule the shires;
For she robs men of their lands . and their life as well.[25]

In his painful exploration of the collapse of unified Christendom, Dawson returns often to the image of Piers Plowman: "Thus the figure of Piers Plowman has both theological and economic implications and stands for an ideal of social and spiritual renewal—a drastic reformation of both Church and State.[26]

The appeal of the poem and Dawson's preoccupation with it can probably be attributed to his conclusion that in Piers Plowman we do not have the forerunner of Wycliffe but rather a prototype of the poor man who would follow "Holy Church" to the end while the rich and the intellectual would become apostate and follow the Antichrist, which is, one suspects, what Dawson thought the Protestant Reformers truly represented. Piers Plowman is Dawson's ideal representative of the common Christian culture then under attack.

Although Dawson is far too sophisticated and too inherently fair to dismiss the earliest Protestants as know-nothing savages, his Roman Catholic orientation is quite apparent in his treatment of their Reformation. He tends to dismiss Luther as a crank and a creature of the German princes. Luther, he thought, simply abandoned the church to the authority of the state.[27] Dawson has far greater regard for Calvin, whom he recognizes as a brilliant intellect with a genuine, though misguided, theology. Dawson says of Calvin: "He seems never to have experienced doubt or fears or psychological crisis, but followed one undeviating line with absolute conviction and certitude; an austere, self-controlled man with a powerful and logical mind and a strong sense of authority and order."[28]

In addition, Dawson sees Calvin as the author of a real culture, perhaps, even, of a real church, although a heretical one:

> Unlike Luther he (Calvin) was essentially an intellectual, a scholar and a man of letters. But he was an intellectual who had the gift of ruling men, and from his study he was able at once to govern a state and to direct a world-wide movement of religious propaganda and ecclesiastical organization. In place of the somewhat shapeless and incoherent mass of doctrines and tendencies represented by Luther and the German reformers, he represented a coherent logical body of doctrine and an iron discipline . . .[29]

This new culture is genuine, though flawed: "The sermon took the place of the liturgy. Bible reading took the place of religious art and symbolism; the communal character of the medieval festivals and pilgrimages was repacked by an individualistic type of piety, which was, however, very different from that of the medieval hermit and ascetic . . . ."[30]

Despite his understanding of the importance of *Bible* reading and the sermon, Dawson appears not to recognize the importance in the new Protestant culture of literacy. He acknowledges the profound effect of humanism on the reformers, but he believes it was something confined to an educated elite. He believes that the leaders of the new Protestant and Catholic Europe, who shared in the humanistic learning of the Renaissance, might understand one another, but the ordinary people were left out of their discussions. He believes a virtual "Iron Curtain" descended between the two groups of Western Europeans, leaving two peoples separated by common culture and understanding.[31]

At the heart of this wreckage, Dawson finds the full-blown horror of nationalism, of the political order that competed with the reform papacy of the Middle Ages. In the bright reflection of Renaissance humanism, the reform impulse went awry. Instead of Francis of Assisi, we see Luther and the schism of Western Christendom. The tragedy of the schism Dawson describes most knowingly in the context of the English Reformation: "It was to a great extent a movement of the State against the Church, and the driving force behind it was the awakening of national consciousness and the self-assertion of national culture. Hence the religious issue became so identified with the national cause that Catholicism became the representative of all the forces that were hostile to nationality, and every Catholic was regarded as a bad Englishman and disloyal subject."[32]

So profound was the popular anti-Catholic feeling that the typical English Catholic was not identified as Sir Thomas More but as Guy Fawkes, who was burnt in effigy each year in a national ritual of expulsion. The schism, then, was national and cultural, and humanism, rather than providing a new unity, was buried in nationalistic tribalism. The Roman Catholic revival that faced off against the Protestants, Dawson sees coming first from the Italian reforming movement, a new phase of the old mysticism which lay at the core of Christian renewal. He is particularly impressed with the work of Catherine of Genoa and of Philip Neri. The latter's Oratory was typical of the new effort on the part of the Roman priesthood to combine pastoral care with a monastic rule. Dawson, however, acknowledges the difficulties in overcoming Protestantism. In a rare moment of chauvinism, he concludes that the Roman humanists were simply "too civilized to cope with the titanic forces which had been loosed against them by Martin Luther."[33]

It remained for the Spanish "crusading spirit" to turn the tables on the Protestant rebellion and to become the vanguard of the Catholic Reformation in the success of Ignatius Loyola and the Society of Jesus with their great dedication and missionary energy, an energy not spent merely on reclaiming Protestants but on spreading Roman Catholicism to the New World and to Asia.

In Spain, as well as in Italy, came a wonderful revival of mysticism in the spectacular works of Theresa of Avila and John of the Cross. These new currents of Catholicism spread throughout Europe and provoked the rise of the great seventh-century Baroque, which Dawson sees as the most successful phase of the Catholic renewal in its emotional appeal to the common culture of Europe. The Baroque, however, failed to achieve the reunification of Christian Europe because it could not overcome with art and feeling the hideous destruction of the religious wars and the cynical political settlements that followed them.

In essence, the rise of Rationalism came in response to what Europeans saw as the frightful price of doctrinal dispute and to the increased power and centralization of the European states, particularly France. The huge bloodletting in the Wars of Religion turned many away from what came to be known in the English tradition as "enthusiasm." The centralizing national monarchy in France, although directed by a Roman Catholic cardinal, was the archetype of the new rational state in which the quasi-pagan worship of the monarchy undermined the traditional Catholic order. The intelligentsia and the monarchy glorified in the way reason replaced faith as the *modus vivendi* of the nation. Thus an ancient Catholic kingdom led the way to the Enlightenment with its profound secularity.[34]

The Enlightenment was the initial phase of the French Revolution, which, along with its successor revolutions, destroyed the institutional structure of the religious community in Europe. The bourgeois capitalists who became the backbone of the new rationalist society were persons whose public life was essentially business life. Dawson sees their advent as deeply destructive of the old public culture of faith. They were not the conscious enemies of religion. They lived strict and careful lives. But they saw religion as a personal and individual matter, and this contributed largely to the secularization of society. Dawson was always deeply suspicious of the new culture of cities, capitalism, and the bourgeoisie: "For it is difficult to deny that there is a fundamental disharmony between bourgeois and Christian civilization and between the mind of the bourgeois and the mind of Christ."[35]

The latter theme is repeated often in Dawson's work. Although he had no sympathy for the crude materialism of the Marxist rebellion against the bourgeoisie, he remained deeply affected by the essentially un-Christian, if not actually anti-Christian, nature of bourgeois culture. At the heart of the matter, he says, is the value system of money and profit in which wealth is detached from anything other than itself. The spirit of the Christian, by contrast, is open, full of desire. The Christian ethos is an ethos of love; it gives and spends itself for others. In the Gospels, the sinner who is open and giving is far closer to God's saving grace than the careful Pharisee who obeys the rules. Thus, Dawson is really as concerned about the "free" bourgeois society in which religion is technically free, as he is in the societies in which the faith is actively persecuted. In a way, things are at their most dangerous when religion tries to make common cause with the triumphant bourgeois order because it becomes fearful of the more frightening alternatives.[36]

The rational bourgeois order of the eighteenth century, Dawson believed, was terribly destructive of Christian culture, and it denied the open and emotional nature of humans, which Christianity has always nourished. The response to this was the new "secular" faith of Rousseau, and its idealogy of *the rights of man* and *the general will*, which inspired the development of the political and social philosophies that have dominated the modern world.[37]

In Rousseau's vision, the troubles of humanity did not derive from sin or from a badly constructed social order, but from an incorrect understanding of the corrupting influences of civilization on the individual. The honest savage in a state of nature was closer to truth and was far happier following native instinct than the sophisticated human weighted down by the artificial arts of life in a wicked society. Rousseau's ideas enraged the philosophes and "came into the brilliant artificial world of the Enlightenment like a warm west wind from the fields into a lighted salon, extinguishing the tapers and filling the air with the scent of damp earth and rain-soaked vegetation."[38] Here, in Dawson's view, is the origin of the new religion of social justice and brotherhood, which for modern man will come to represent "the kingdom of God on earth."[39]

With the destruction of the ancien régime, Dawson comes to his sixth and last Age of the Church. He sees the revival of faith in the very "shadow of the guillotine," an image which reinforces his theory that the great works of the faith are usually off-stage, as it were, so that the triumph of Christianity is often a surprise, occurring, as Christ hinted, in the underappreciated moments of life. One of the great aspects of this contemporary age is found in the success of Roman Catholicism in the United States in the past two centuries. Dawson had great hopes for the reorientation of Catholic education in America. To this movement he gave the last great effort of his life. He believed that in new soil there might be a freeing up of Catholic education from its Thomist domination and that some place might be made for the mystical, spiritual revival which, he believed, had always lain at the heart of reform.[40]

Thus, at the time of his death in 1970, Dawson believed that he was living in the sixth, but certainly not the final, Age of the Church. Some of his most important writing dealt with issues of his own time, which he interpreted in light of his understanding of historical and contemporary Christianity. Among the most serious contemporary issues he explored were the expansion of Western culture, especially Western religion, ideology, and politics. Because his analysis of the events and movements of his own time were seen through a prism unlike that of most modern historians and critics, they provided a unique view for his fellow intellectuals, as well as the more obvious community of self-conscious Christians for whom his work had special meaning. It was always clear to Dawson that, unlike the majority of his colleagues, he was not a traditional *historian* but a *Christian historian*. Nowhere is the difference between the two clearer than in his essays on Marx and the Marxist theory of history.

Dawson begins by describing the similarities between Marxist ideology and the Christian view of history, and what he finds significant here is their shared determinism featuring an apocalyptic end of ordinary historical time. By no means could all Christians sympathize with the Marxist view that "it is the material element in bourgeois culture that is the permanent one and that the idealist liberal element is incapable of maintaining itself by its own inherent resources."[41] What might be even more disturbing to Christians, Dawson points out, is that Marx did not see them as interesting rivals because he believed that they belonged to the dead world of the *ancien régime*, which had, in the proper order of the dialectic, been overthrown by the liberal capitalist order of the bourgeoisie. Marx, Dawson says, was correct not to confuse the capitalist bourgeoisie with anything Christian. Capitalism was merely the strongly materialist phase of Liberalism, and on the importance of materialism, Marx and the Liberals agreed.

Liberalism, Dawson concludes, is the quasi-religious replacement that the twentieth century inherited from the nineteenth. Christians can appreciate the moral standards and the regard for the individual that Liberalism inherited from Christianity, but they cannot much approve the secularity and materialism that are Liberalism's gift to Marx.

Dawson believes that religious fervor drove people to Communism, a fervor which, in the absence of true religion, has no appropriate outlet. The secular promises of the Liberal tradition failed to satisfy the longing of humanity for the meaning and direction, the satisfaction of soul that modern Western society failed to provide. Thus, the true rival of Communism is not bourgeois capitalism, but the Christian religion.[42]

The political and ideological excesses of the twentieth century filled Dawson with distress. He despised and feared the modern absolutist state, which he saw as the ultimate horror of the nationalism that had split Christendom apart. Whether Fascist or Communist, the state had the same terrible ambition: to crush the individual under its power. Dawson feared that the Liberal democratic state would acquire the same destructive power. The modern secular state has no competitive power to check it as it had in the medieval era, when a powerful ecclesiastical authority also laid claim to human's loyalties. Standing alone, with all the power of the nation-state behind it, the modern state was fearful to behold.

No one understood better than Dawson the impact of the West on the world. He saw clearly the ravages wrought on other societies by the spread of Western Empire. Although he supported the missionary efforts of Christianity, he well understood the destructive element of the West, the horrors of technology insinuated into the life of the Third World.

Dawson was an English gentleman of the old school. He understood better perhaps than anyone in the twentieth century the wreckage of his civilization and the pain it inflicted on others. But he believed the civilization of the West, kept mindful of its Christian roots, had much to offer. Above all, he was a Christian, a Roman Catholic. He was also a man of truly catholic dimensions. He loved Western society, but spent much of his career studying other civilizations, for which he not only had understanding but also feeling and admiration. The key to this man may be his belief in the "communion of saints," not the elect or the few of one time and place, but all those who, in faith, have populated the Christian world—yesterday, today, and tomorrow—in this world and in heaven, a real community with mission not yet fulfilled.

BIBLIOGRAPHY

PRIMARY SOURCES

Age of the Gods. New York: Howard Fertig, 1970.
The Dividing of Christendom. New York: Sheed and Ward, 1965.
The Dynamics of World History. New York: Mentor, 1962.
Education and the Crisis of Christian Culture. Chicago: Henry Regency Co., 1949.
The Historic Reality of Christian Culture. Westport, Conn.: Greenwood Press, 1976.
The Judgment of the Nations. New York: Sheed and Ward, 1942.
Medieval Essays. New York: Sheed and Ward, 1953.
The Movement of World Revolutions. New York: Sheed and Ward, 1959.
Religion and Culture. New York: Sheed and Ward, 1948.
Religion and the Rise of Western Culture. New York: AMS Press, 1979.
Religion and World History. New York: Image Books, 1975.

SECONDARY SOURCES

Beliese, John. "Christopher Dawson: His Interpretation of History." *Modern Age* 23 (Summer 1979): 259–65.
Hitchcock, James. "Christopher Dawson," *The American Scholar* 62 (winter 1983): 111–18.
Scott, Christina. *Christopher Dawson: A Historian and His World.* New Brunswick, N. J.: Transaction Publishers, 1992.

NOTES

1. The details of Dawson's life are found in a sympathetic biography written by his daughter. See Christina Scott, *Christopher Dawson: A Historian and His World* (New Brunswick, N.J.: Transaction Publishers, 1992).

2. A complete chronology of Dawson's writing has been prepared by James Oliver and Christina Scott in Christopher Dawson, *Religion and World History: Selections from the Works of Christopher Dawson* (Garden City, N.Y.: Image Books, 1975), 15-18.

3. Christopher Dawson, *The Age of the Gods* (New York: Howard Fertig, 1970), xiii.

4. Christopher Dawson, *The Dynamics of World History* (New York: Mentor Omega Books, 1962), 246.

5. Christopher Dawson, *The Historic Reality of Christian Culture* (Westport Conn.: Greenwood Press, 1976), 91.

6. Ibid., 92.

7. Ibid., 93.

8. Dawson, *Dynamics of World History*, 178.

9. Ibid., 184.

10. Ibid., 183.

11. Dawson, *Historic Reality of Christian Culture*, 117.

12. Christopher Dawson, "Why I Am a Catholic," *The Catholic Times* (21 May 1962), quoted in Scott, *Christopher Dawson*, 64.

13. Dawson, *Dynamics of World History*, 252.

14. Ibid., 257.

15. Dawson, *Religion and World History*, 165.

16. Christopher Dawson, *Medieval Essays* (London: Sheed and Ward, 1953), 57.

17. Christopher Dawson, *Religion and the Rise of Western Culture* (New York: AMS Press, 1979), 17.

18. Dawson, *Religion and World History*, 184.

19. Ibid., 163.

20. Dawson, *Religion and the Rise of Western Culture*, 163.

21. Dawson, *Religion and World History*, 333.

22. Dawson, *The Dynamics of World History*, 347

23. Christopher Dawson, *The Movement of World Revolution* (New York: Sheed and Ward, 1959), 28.

24. Dawson, *Medieval Essays*, 240.

25. Ibid., 252. In his use of William Langland's *Piers Plowman*, Dawson does his own translation and combination of lines from the B text of the poem. Here he is using material from the B text, part 14.

26. Ibid., 259.

27. Christopher Dawson, *The Division of Christianity* (New York: Sheed and Ward, 1965), 129.

28. Ibid., 128.

29. Dawson, *Movement of World Revolution*, 36.

30. Dawson, *Division of Christianity*, 210.

31. Ibid., 140.

32. Dawson, *The Dynamics of World History*, 94.

33. Dawson, *Movement of World Revolution*, 39–40.

34. Dawson, *Revolution and World History*, 215.

35. Dawson, *The Dynamics of World History*, 199.

36. Ibid., 204.

37. Dawson, *Movement of World Revolution*, 62.

38. Dawson, *Religion and World History*, 221.

39. Ibid.

40. Christopher Dawson, *Education and the Crisis of Culture* (Chicago: Henry Regency Co., 1949), 19.

41. Dawson, *Religion and World History*, 243.

42. Ibid., 245.

21

GEORGES FLOROVSKY

BRADLEY NASSIF

Some mention Georges Florovsky in the same breath as Karl Barth; others consider him a church father of the twentieth century; to many younger theologians, however, his name remains largely unknown. Florovsky was a churchman, ecumenist, and scholar of the Eastern Orthodox Church, one who maintained a love/hate relationship with his church. Even though he publicly deplored the quality of church life from time to time, he was no less convinced that the Orthodox Church had faithfully preserved the apostolic tradition through its theology and liturgy. As a Russian émigré living in America, he built a bridge between the Orthodox East and the Catholic and Protestant West. Few have attracted the attention of such a broad range of Christian scholars, such as Eastern Orthodox thinkers John Meyendorff, George Dragas, and John Romanides; post-Vatican II Catholics like Henri de Lubac, and Yves Congar; and even Protestant evangelicals such as Mark Noll, Thomas Oden, and Harold O. J. Brown. All in their own ways have borrowed a flame from the fire of Florovsky's creativity.

Until recently, the vast majority of Americans have viewed the Orthodox Church as a marginal, exotic, and mysterious relic of antiquity. The fall of communism in Russia and Eastern Europe, however, no longer permits that perspective to prevail. Seminaries and university religion departments can regard the study of Eastern Orthodoxy as an optional extra in their curriculum only if they minimize the spiritual significance of developments in that vast region of the world today. New political developments have created an unprecedented encounter between the Orthodox Church and Protestant and Catholic bodies. Possibly the most urgent need of Christians who work in those countries today is to acquire a knowledge of the history and theology of the Orthodox Church, in general, and of Georges Florovsky, in particular. Now more than ever, his works serve as an essential guide through the rich complexities of the Christian East.

The goal of this chapter, therefore, is to introduce readers to the life and work of Georges Florovsky and to assess his impact on historiography. I shall do this by outlining his life, his theology of history, his historiographical method, and his impact on Western thought.

BIOGRAPHY

Florovsky's contributions to the study of history are best understood in their historical context. The career of Georges Vasilievich Florovsky can be divided into two parts: his life and work in Europe (1893–1948) and in America (1948–1979).[1] Florovsky was born in 1893 near Odessa in Southern Russia, where his father, Archpriest Basil, served as rector of the Orthodox seminary and gymnasium in Odessa. Seminaries in nineteenth century Russia were not institutions of high academic or social repute.[2] For example, in 1836 the *Oberprocurator*, or head of the "Holy Synod" (the country's department of religious affairs), had to enact reforms in the curriculum that introduced the study of "neglected" subjects such as early church history, patristics, and Russian church history. Despite numerous efforts to improve the seminaries by both secular and ecclesiastical leaders, the educational level of the clergy remained low. This deficiency doubtless provided the motivation behind Florovsky's efforts to raise the academic standards of clerical training during his tenures later at the Orthodox Theological Institute of St. Sergius in Paris and St. Vladimir's Orthodox Seminary in New York. In America, he lamented that even though the situation was bad in Russia, materials once used as textbooks for children in prerevolutionary times were now regarded as too heavy even for seminarians![3]

As one who stood in a long line of pastoral ancestors belonging to clerical estates, Florovsky was keenly aware of his family's multigenerational service to the church. (Clerical estates were lands that belonged to the church which, in turn, were subject to the regulations of the Tsar and his *Oberprocurator*.) Russian clergymen and their families developed a religious caste of their own with distinct sociological patterns. They enjoyed close personal friendships, shared a common ecclesiastical and secular education, and were deeply loyal to one another. Inter-family marriages were common. Although Father Georges faithfully sought to distinguish the gospel from Slavophile encrustations, his heritage, and that of the woman whom he would eventually marry, influenced virtually every major aspect of their lives.

The beginning of young Florovsky's academic career was marked by a passionate interest in the physical sciences, not theology. He studied at the secular state Gymnasium modeled after the German rationalist system of the post-Enlightenment era. There he learned the literature and languages of Greek and Roman antiquity. He graduated valedictorian in 1911 with a distinction in history. In 1912, Florovsky entered the University of Novo Rossia in Odessa, where he studied philosophy, philology, history, mathematics, and the natural sciences. During those years he demonstrated a propensity towards logic and intellectual precision that later governed his study of Christian history and theology. In 1916 he passed the state examination (Baccalaureate) in the Historical Philological Faculty. He soon assumed a teaching post in history at a high school, continuing to read theology only as a peripheral interest. In 1917 he published a paper entitled, "On the Mechanism of Reflex Salivary Secretion," which later was presented to the Imperial Academy of Sciences by the famous Russian physiologist, Ivan P. Pavlov. In 1919 Florovsky was awarded the *Philosophia Magister* from the university and was invited to teach philosophy on its faculty. His tenure, however, was short-lived because the following year he and most of his family fled to Sophia, Bulgaria in the wake of the communist revolution.

During his stay in Bulgaria, Florovsky's career took a new direction. He began cultivating his interest in ecclesiastical history and theology. He temporarily joined a group of Russian intelligentsia who called themselves the "Eurasianists." The Eurasianists attempted to interpret the Russian Revolution in historically and culturally significant ways. They viewed Russia as belonging neither to Europe nor Asia, but to a geographically distinct "Euroasia." The Eurasianists placed special emphasis on the importance of the Mongol period in Russian history. In this context Florovsky began to make a public literary declaration of his Christian convictions to other intellectuals. Repelled by the Euroasians' narrow focus, he took an anti-Slavophile stance by emphasizing Russia's Byzantine-Orthodox heritage. He grappled with the truth of philosophy and the meaning of history, declaring that Russia's troubles were spiritual, not ethnic. The revolution was a "judgment of God" on a Russia in need of exorcism. Partly reflecting the work of Charles Renouvier, Florovsky argued that the universe is not a predetermined system, but a contingent cosmic reality. Clearly, Florovsky had come to basic convictions about the world, convictions that would influence all his subsequent thinking. Those convictions centered on his concept of creation, the creatureliness of the universe, and freedom of the will.

After leaving Bulgaria, Florovsky moved to Prague, where he taught Philosophy of Law at the Russian Faculty of Law from 1922 until 1926. There he married Xenia Ivanovna Simonova, the daughter of a Russian priest. Later, they took up residence in France where he worked at St. Serge Orthodox Theological Institute.

St. Serge was founded in Paris by a small group of Russian émigrés. In 1926 its Dean, Sergei Bulgakov, invited Florovsky to serve as the Professor of Patristics and later of Systematic Theology. Florovsky accepted, and shortly after was ordained a priest in 1932. Because of the ecclesiastical confusion resulting from the Russian Revolution, the faculty placed themselves under the Ecumenical Patriarch of Constantinople rather than under the Patriarch of Moscow. Soon Florovsky found himself at odds with Bulgakov and the majority of the faculty over the matter of "sophiology" (a system of thought seeking to understand the relationship between God and the world by means of the concept of Divine Wisdom or *sophia*). Sophiology was developed in the late nineteenth and early twentieth centuries by Vladimir Soloviev, Pavel Florensky, and Sergei Bulgakov. Bulgakov was a Marxist economist turned theologian, and one of the most controversial Orthodox theologians in the twentieth century. The sophiologists attempted to explain the relationship between God, creation, and the Virgin Mary in terms of modern science. They interpreted Wisdom (Sophia) in the Old Testament book of Proverbs as a fourth principle (*hypostasis*) distinguishable from the Trinity and symbolized by Mary. Drawing upon his grasp of the historical process, Scripture, and patristics, Florovsky respectfully claimed that this was nothing less than Origenism all over again and, thus, heretical. He published his critiques of sophiology in a two-volume work entitled *Ways of Russian Theology* (1937), which became one of his greatest literary achievements. Other major works of this period included two patrologies, the *Eastern Fathers of the Fourth Century* (1931) and *Byzantine Fathers of the Fifth Through the Eighth Centuries* (1933). These reflect Florovsky's efforts to articulate a "neopatristic synthesis" (to be discussed below). The chapters were originally class lectures that provided a straightforward account of the history of Christian doctrine. Some parts, however, were implicitly aimed at refuting the sophiologists.

Florovsky believed that Russia's most significant contributions lay in its rich spirituality and iconography, not in its theological creativity. *Ways of Russian Theology* was at times severe in its judgments. It combated the influence of Slavophile mystique in Russian theology and tried to rescue the doctrine of the church's catholicity from edifying rhetoric about Slavic *sobornost* (catholicity). A brilliant history of Christian thought in Russia, it included a hostile account of Slavophile Christianity and ended with a call to return to the church fathers. Some students found it liberating, others distressing. His colleagues regarded it negatively and attempted to curtail his influence on the student body, which pushed Florovsky to assume a more active role in ecumenical and pan-Orthodox discussions. He sought to strengthen Orthodoxy from within by purifying its testimony of nationalist, scholastic, philosophic, and doctrinal contaminations.

In 1936 Florovsky participated in the first Congress of Orthodox Theological Professors in Athens. He traced what he called the "pseudomorphosis" of Orthodox theology under both Catholic and Protestant influences in the seventeenth and eighteenth centuries. By this he meant the "Latinization" of Orthodox theology that occurred in the seminary of Kiev under Peter Mogilia, and the "Protestantization" of Orthodox theology that occurred under Peter the Great. In order to be true to itself, the Orthodox Church needed to free itself from these alien approaches to theology and return to what he called a "re-Hellenization" of Orthodoxy. This meant not only a "return to the Fathers" such as Irenaeus, Athanasius, the Cappadocians, Gregory Palamas and other Byzantines; it also meant the acceptance of Hellenism as "a standing category of the Christian experience" which included the church, worship, doctrinal formulae, and icons.

In 1948 Florovsky attended the first Assembly of the World Council of Churches (WCC) in Amsterdam. During the meeting he began to articulate Orthodox ecclesiology with an emphasis on the church's belief that while bishops are "the principle of unity," the Christian community as a whole confirms the apostolic tradition—a hierarchical yet charismatic organism. In the drafting of Section 1, Florovsky worked with other notables such as Karl Barth, Anders Nygren, and Donald M. Baillie. Florovsky was not satisfied with the final wording of the Section and proposed that the following statement be inserted into the document: "Even the name of the World Council of Churches implies a situation which should not be; we agree to call our denominations 'Churches' in a sense which the New Testament could never allow." He also explained that the presence of the

Orthodox in the meetings was a kind of "missionary activity" to the World Council of Churches, which resulted in widespread resentment among its members.

In 1948 the second phase of Florovsky's career began when he moved to America to become Professor of Patristics and Dogmatic Theology at St. Vladimir's Orthodox Seminary in Crestwood, New York. Florovsky was dean of the seminary from 1951 to 1955. While remaining under the Ecumenical Patriarch of Constantinople, he associated himself, for academic reasons, with the Russian Orthodox in America (now the "Orthodox Church in America"). He withdrew from it in 1955, due to differences over administration and the questionable quality of academic standards then practiced at St. Vladimir's. During his tenure as dean, Florovsky taught as Adjunct Professor of Eastern Orthodoxy at Columbia University, Union Seminary, and Boston University. He was also chaplain to Orthodox students at Columbia, and chairman of both the Sunday School Committee of the Russian Archdiocese and the Pan Orthodox Student Christian Movement. In 1952 he founded *St. Vladimir's Seminary Quarterly*.

Florovsky's perspective on his mission in America was controlled by the needs and witness of the wider community of world Orthodoxy. Orthodox ecclesiastical history in early twentieth-century America was marked by a series of emigrant communities of Russians, Greeks, Syrians, Lebanese, and other Orthodox peoples of Middle Eastern and Eastern European ancestry. He envisioned a single "American Orthodox Church" in the United States and Canada that would accommodate the various cultures and separated ecclesiastical jurisdictions. Remaining as he did under the See of Constantinople, Florovsky believed that the Greek branch, under the leadership of the Archbishop of North and South America, would be the most likely jurisdiction under which to unite the different Orthodox communities. Florovsky accepted the formal separation of church and state in the American constitution. His vision for the American church, however, was for the Orthodox to fulfill an "eschatological" calling by influencing all segments of society with the leaven of the gospel, while resisting the temptation to regard America as its eternal abode.[4]

Throughout his years in the United States, Florovsky was a major spokesman for world Orthodoxy. He served on numerous committees of the WCC's Faith and Order Commission (including work with Albert Outler), and other academic societies and congresses. After leaving St. Vladimir's in 1955, he accepted an appointment as Associate Professor of Patristics and Dogmatic Theology at Holy Cross Greek Orthodox Theological School in Brookline, Massachusetts. (Students occasionally found his class lectures "rhapsodic," if not altogether confusing due to the broad jaunts across the centuries he would make when jumping from Origen to Bulgakov and authors in between.) In 1956 Florovsky went to Harvard Divinity School, where he became professor of Eastern Church History the following year. There he taught church history, liturgics, spirituality, and patristics. In 1964 he became an associate of the Slavic Department at Harvard, where he taught Russian religious and intellectual history. Some of his most important articles written during those years include "Predicament of the Christian Historian," "Origen, Eusebius, and the Iconoclastic Controversy," "Eschatology in the Patristic Age," "Patristic Theology of the Church," "The Concept of Creation in Saint Athanasius," and "St. Gregory Palamas and the Tradition of the Fathers."[5] Upon his retirement from Harvard in 1964, Florovsky became Visiting Professor in the departments of History and Slavics at Princeton University. Later he was elected to the American Academy of Arts and Sciences and became an honorary member of the Academy of Athens (along with Cardinal Bea and Albert Schweitzer). Between 1948 and 1979 Florovsky produced well over 200 titles. His articles alone appeared in over a hundred journals in some ten languages and twenty countries. Yet, the scope of Florovsky's intellectual interests and knowledge was much broader than the fields in which he published. His unquenchable passion for books, coupled with his multilingual abilities, made him a voracious reader of philosophy, science, psychology, history, literature, theology and virtually anything else that he could get his hands on! He was highly accomplished in every field he set out to master. He was a scholar's scholar.

In the final decade of his life, creative scholarship declined due to the restrictions of old age and limited finances. But by then his fame had spread throughout the world. Among the Orthodox, he was hailed as one of the most profound Orthodox theologians of the twentieth century; in Protestant and Catholic circles, he was viewed as a forceful and creative leader in the WCC; and to secular academicians, he was recognized as a distinguished authority on Russian philosophy and intellectual history. A gifted and rare individual, Father Georges Florovsky was a leading figure among scholars and church leaders of both the academy and the church. His most insightful biographer, George Williams, characterized him as a "Preeminent theologian of Orthodoxy and historian of Christian thought, ecumenical leader and interpreter of Russian literature of the 19th century."[6]

THEOLOGY OF HISTORY

Father Georges believed that history has *meaning*, and this meaning is not properly historical, but *theological*. Consequently, one must describe his approach as a "theology of history" rather than a "philosophy of history." Florovsky observed the "philosophy of history" of modern thinkers like Hegel, Comte, Marx, and Nietzche is nothing else than a "pseudo-theology of history," more or less disguised. He articulated his position most systematically in a 1959 essay entitled, "The Predicament of the Christian Historian."[7]

In that essay Florovsky observed that the majority of social historians of his day took a hostile or indifferent attitude towards the notion of meaning in history. Few thought deeply about the ultimate nature of historical reality, the process of gaining historical knowledge, or the moral assumptions underlying historical judgments. Because of his own theological predelictions, and his belief that Christianity has a unique relationship to history, Florovsky assigned priority to this feature of his scholarship. He believed that the most important questions about the past concerned its *ultimate significance*. When a historian searches for that, he or she moves beyond the realm of historian to the higher plateau of theologian.

In this seminal study, Florovsky explained that "one has to define the aim and purpose of historical study and then to design methods by which this aim, or these aims, can be properly achieved."[8] The object of historical inquiry, however, is ambiguous by its very nature. One must narrow the scope at the outset.

> History is indeed the study of the *human* past [emphasis his, here and throughout]. An equation of human history and natural history would be an unwarranted presupposition or option. Much harm has been done to the study of history by such naturalistic presuppositions, which amount, in the last resort, to the denial of any specific character of human existence. . . . Historical knowledge is not a knowledge of *objects*, but precisely a knowledge of *subjects*—of "co-persons," of "co-partners" in the quest of life. In this sense, historical knowledge is, and must be *an existential knowledge*. This constitutes a radical cleavage between the "study of Spirit" and the "study of Nature," between *die Geisteswissenschaften* and *die Naturwissenschaft*.[9]

The starting point for historical research is always the present to which the historian himself belongs. Virtually anything from the past can serve as an historical source so long as the historian knows how to understand it. But no collection of factual statements such as news, dates, letters, and documents are, by themselves, history. A catalog of an art museum, for instance, is not a history of art; no chronicle is history. All such data must be interpreted from a certain perspective. This implies the absence of neutrality on the part of the knower. The so-called "objective observer" of the past simply does not exist. Indifference, neutrality, and indecision are not academic virtues, but vices. "It has been often contended, especially by the historians of the old school, that historians are led, in the last resort, in their study, by the desire 'to know the past as an eyewitness may know it,' that is, to become, in some way, just a 'witness' of the past events. In fact, this is precisely what the historian cannot do, and never does, and never should attempt to do, if he really wants to be a historian."[10]

Florovsky maintained that "the art of hermeneutics is the core of the historical craft."[11] The interpreter belongs to the process of interpretation, as does the data to be analyzed. Both function as dialogue partners in conversation. The first objective for which the interpreter should strive is exegetical: to grasp the mind of an author in order to discover exactly what he intended to say. The historian should not read his or her own ideas into the text. Admittedly, this involves an element of guesswork in the process of textual understanding, just as uncertainty enters into every attempt to understand another person. Understanding requires interpretation. Hence, the personal characteristics of the interpreter play a crucial role. "Now, the kind of questions a particular historian is actually asking depends ultimately upon his stature, upon his total personality, upon his dispositions and concerns, upon the amplitude of his vision, even upon his likes and dislikes."[12]

The ultimate goal of historical inquiry is to encounter living people. What are called "facts" are really "actions" that express human "intentions." The historian's business is to identify the intelligent and purposeful character of human life reflected in the relevant documents. Thus, the task of the historian is defined as follows: "The ultimate purpose of a historical inquiry is not in the establishment of certain objective facts, such as dates, places, numbers, names, and the like, as much as all this is an indispensable preliminary, but in *the encounter with living beings*."[13]

Is, then, the search for "meaning" in history ultimately an historical quest? "In fact, the term 'meaning' is used in different senses when we speak of the meaning of particular events or of the sets of actions and events, and when we speak of the Meaning of History [sic], taken as an all-inclusive whole, that is in its entirety and universality. In the latter case, indeed, we are speaking actually of the ultimate meaning of human existence, of its ultimate destiny. And this, obviously, is not a historical question."

The rise of Christianity was a turning point in the meaning of history. Unlike the classical historians of Greek and Roman antiquity, who stressed rotational cycles of human events, Christianity offered a revolutionary perspective on the course of human life. Biblical revelation revealed that all history was moving towards a goal. The starting point of the

Christian faith is the acknowledgement of certain actual events in which God has decisively acted for human salvation. These events include Christ's incarnation, death, resurrection, and the descent of the Holy Spirit. These events are both *eschatological* and *final* events in salvation history. In light of eschatology, and the nature of the human person as a unique and unfathomable being, historical research is unfinished and unfinishable. "This entire pattern of interpretation is definitely *linear*, running from the beginning to the end, from Creation to Consummation, *but the line is broken, or rather 'bent,'* at a particular 'crucial' or 'turning' point. *This point is the center of history*, of the 'history of salvation,' *die Heilsgeschichte*."[14]

The Bible reveals God's rule in history. History is not really a history of humanity, but rather, the history of God! Here the Christian tradition makes a unique contribution to our proper understanding of world history.

> But *precisely because history was apprehended as "God's history," the "history of man" was made possible*. Man's history was then apprehended as *a meaningful story* and no longer as a reiteration of the cosmic pattern, nor as a chaotic flux of happenings. The history of men was understood in the perspective of their salvation. . . . The decisive contribution of the Christian faith to the understanding of history was . . . precisely in *the discovery of perspective in history*, in which man's historical existence acquires relevance and meaning. Therefore, the modern existentialist emphasis on "man's historicity" is, in fact, neither historical nor distinctively Christian. It is, in many instances, rather *a relapse into Hellenism*.[15]

Father Florovsky did not construct such views in an ecclesiastical vacuum, one isolated from the broader fields of the social sciences. In addition to theological premises, he based the discovery of meaning in history on anthropological, psychological, and epistemological grounds. We previously observed that he was not exclusively a Christian historian, but also, among other competencies, a philosopher. Lewis Shaw explains the impact of non-theological factors on Florovsky's view of history: "Florovsky's concern with the fate of man in society and history evolved from his early study of psychology, and his psychological and philosophical-historical concerns were mutually interpretative. . . . Florovsky's philosophy has as its constant aim the affirmation of the decisive value of personal freedom in human history, a freedom highlighted by ascetical achievement."[16]

Human freedom played an important role in Florovsky's interpretation of history. He believed that humans are not determined, but free to make their own moral choices. His definition of freedom was developed in the context of German and Russian neo-Kantianism, and resulted from a synthesis of Charles Renouvier, William James, and the Scottish "Common Sense Realism" school of philosophy. The general platform upon which Florovsky built his views included the belief that human nature is rational, and that people believe themselves to be free. He rejected any moral determinism that denied human freedom (including predestination or dialectical materialism). Evidence for freedom in history came from the monastic tradition of the desert Fathers: "Ascetical achievement" testifies to the potential for growth and human change, depending upon the spiritual choices one makes in this life. An emphasis on ascetical achievement became a recurring theme throughout his writings.[17]

While he accepted the importance of reason, he rejected the belief that reason alone is sufficient for faith and morals. Common Sense Realism, for example, did not explain such traditional theological tensions as how divine sovereignty and human freedom could co-exist. This caused Florovsky to move beyond philosophical and psychological premises to the church's patristic theology in order to understand the relationship between personal freedom and meaning in history. The patristic analogies that had influenced him were found in John Chrysostom's anthropology, Athanasius' trinitarian theology,[18] and Maximus the Confessor's distinction between the natural and gnomic wills.[19] These Fathers were adopted as representatives of the church's tradition, and not as isolated individuals in the history of Christian thought.

Florovsky did not provide a detailed explanation of the relationship between grace and freedom when developing his theology of history. We are left to speculate that, because he adopted a Greek patristic view of human nature, which rejected both Pelagian and Augustinian theories of original sin, he most likely applied that same patristic model to his interpretation of historical causation. Following Chrysostom, Florovsky maintained that by God's grace, despite the results of the Fall, humans remain free to accept or reject Christ. To be sure, sin has darkened the mind so that it is unable to understand the fullness of salvific realities apart from divine revelation given in Scripture. Yet, because of God's grace, people are still free and responsible for their own moral actions. Florovsky's main emphasis on historical causation was decidedly anthropocentric: the constant goal of the Christian life was to engage in a militant *askesis* (ascetic self-denial) by imitating the life of Christ. Florovsky so emphasized asceticism as the Christian's calling that he laid himself open to the charge of minimizing God's grace and forgiveness. To that he replied, "Once the synergism of the redemptive process takes place in the human heart, then the existential reciprocity of grace and response is so dynamic that one can, as it were, use such expressions, precisely because it is assumed that God has initiated that grace is always at work in the human heart, in all the depths of the interior of man as well as in external life."[20]

Because of human freedom, historians in all branches of knowledge (art, music, philosophy, politics, science, psychology, etc.) are obligated to seek an answer to the question of meaning in history, which is the ultimate predicament of the historian: *"Here lies the major predicament of all historical study*—no historian can, even in his limited and particular field, within his own competence, avoid raising ultimate problems of human nature and destiny, unless he reduces himself to the role of a registrar of empirical happenings and forfeits his proper task of 'understanding.'"[21] The way to resolve the predicament was not through the neo-orthodoxy of Barthian and Neibuhrian Protestantism, nor through a return to Roman primacy, but by what Florovsky ingeniously called a "neo-patristic synthesis."

HISTORIOGRAPHIC METHOD:
THE "NEO-PATRISTIC SYNTHESIS"

Florovsky's methodology governed not only his theological writings, but also lectures, sermons, ecumenical dialogue, personal correspondence, and conversations with students and colleagues. It affected his approach to research, the collecting and analyzing of data, literary style—in short, his entire worldview. He described his methodology with a coining of the phrase, "neo-patristic synthesis."[22]

The neo-patristic synthesis can be described as "a return to the Fathers," or a return to the classics of Christian antiquity, including their Hellenistic thought forms and Christian theology. Augustine and Cyprian, but especially Greek church fathers such as Irenaeus, Athanasius, the Cappadocians, Maximus the Confessor, and Gregory Palamas, provided a synthesis of Christian truth which is indispensable for Christian identity, past and present.[23] Only through a "return to the common sources" can the future of Eastern Orthodoxy have hope and authentic Christian reunification take place.[24] The neo-patristic synthesis was, in short, a plea to recover the "catholicity" of the church in all the fullness of her biblical and ecclesial tradition.

Such an expression of catholicity was at odds with German-Russian Idealism and the heresy of "Sophiology." It also revealed the decay of Protestant and Catholic liberalism, and Russian Orthodoxy's own "Latin captivity" to its scholastic ways of doing theology.

Father Georges was convinced that modern theology had forgotten its patristic roots. There was a "common mind," a "universal tradition" in

Christian antiquity that needed to be recovered, especially from the fourth to eighth centuries, the age of the great ecumenical councils. Contrary to the approach to patristics usually taken by Protestant and Catholic theologians, the "end of the patristic age" did not occur in the fifth century (with Gregory the Great in the West) or eighth century (with John of Damascus in the East). Though one can and should recognize the first eight centuries as a formative age, it is a mistake to freeze the Fathers in a period of church history. Their formative work was adapted and further developed in the Byzantine Orthodox Church well into the fourteenth century. Yet, the common mind of the Fathers did not end even with the fourteenth century. It is not limited to any given period in history. It is a Spirit-inspired tradition that continues to live on through the life of the church. The ethos of this approach can be illustrated through the story of a reply that Florovsky once gave at an ecumenical gathering. A participant noted that the age of the church fathers had ended and was no longer relevant to the modern world. To that Florovsky replied, "The Fathers are not dead. I am still alive!"

That conviction permeated Florovsky's work as an historian and theologian. He gratefully acknowledged his indebtedness to western European scholarship when working with the primary sources. Catholic and Protestant scholars had made available critical editions of biblical, patristic, and historical texts. But it was not enough merely to know what the Fathers said; one must also adopt their way of thinking. Textual criticism was a necessary prerequisite to understanding the Fathers, but Christians must go beyond their texts and make them their teachers as well. "Patristic writings are respected indeed," lamented Florovsky, "but more as historical documents than as books of authority."[25]

The problem to which Florovsky was responding was a dichotomy scholars had made between quoting the Fathers as past thinkers and relying on them as witnesses to the apostolic tradition. For him, the Eastern Orthodox Church was the heir apparent to that tradition and had most faithfully preserved it in its theological history and liturgical life. "It is a dangerous habit just to handle 'quotations' from the Fathers and even from Scripture, outside of the total structure of faith, in which only they are truly alive. 'To follow the Fathers' does not mean simply to quote their sentences. *It means to acquire their mind*, their *phronema*: The Orthodox Church claims to have preserved this mind (*phronema*) and to have theologized *ad mentem Patrum*."[26]

Because the mind of the Fathers was embedded in the church's past, Florovsky needed to explain the Orthodox view of the relationship between Scripture and tradition. He rejected attempts by some of his own churchmen, who thought it their calling simply to restate the past, as if a "theology of repetition" was all that was needed to be a good Orthodox believer. He argued that tradition must be faithful to the past and yet be creatively appropriated to meet the needs of the contemporary world. Faithfulness to tradition is not loyalty to antiquity, but a living relationship with the fullness of the church's life. Tradition must not be viewed as oral revelation versus written revelation. Neither should the canon of Vincent of Érins be misunderstood when it describes the catholic faith as "that which is believed everywhere, always, and by all." The formula is based on a tautology. Universality is not external but internal. It is not a quantitative reality but a qualitative criterion. The Orthodox Church might actually turn out to be a small flock of faithful believers. True catholicity is the inner, mystical memory of the church, a unity in the Spirit that began on the day of Pentecost. "Tradition is a *charismatic* principle, not a historical principle," he declared.[27] Thus, tradition is nothing less than "Scripture rightly understood."[28] Scripture is the inspired Word of God, totally truthful in all its affirmations. Scripture is both a record of revelation and revelation itself. The councils, creeds, liturgies, Fathers, and ecclesiastical canons are nothing more than commentaries on Scripture and witnesses to its divine message. The hermeneutical problem, however, goes deeper than that. There is *continuity* between the Old and New Testaments and the people of God.[29] The Fathers were all agreed that Scripture had to be interpreted comprehensively according to the church's *regula fidei* (rule of faith). The Word of God and the people of God are inseparably united. The Protestant principle of *sola Scriptura* does not require the *regula fidei*, which has led to denominational divisions and interpretive anarchy. The church existed before the completion of the canon, and therefore the New Testament could not be the sole source of knowledge. Consequently, Florovsky claimed that the Bible is the *final* authority, but not the *sole* authority of Christian truth.

> The Bible, as a book, has been composed in the community and was meant primarily for its edification. The book and the Church cannot be separated. The book and the Covenant belong together, and Covenant implies people. . . . The Bible is the Word of God indeed, but the book stands by the testimony of the Church. The canon of the Bible is obviously established and authorized by the Church. . . . If we declare Scripture to be self-sufficient, we only expose it to subjective, arbitrary interpretation, thus cutting it away from its sacred source. Scripture is given to us in tradition. . . . In the times of the early Christians the Gospels were not yet written and could not be the sole source of knowledge.[30]

As a historian of Christian thought, Florovsky strongly rejected the idea of "the development of dogmas" in the course of history, especially if that meant the church changed or altered the biblical message. (He rejected a Roman Catholic argument that the pope's authority started from a "seed" in the New Testament, one that later grew into the "tree" of the medieval papacy.) Dogmas do not change or grow. They arise and are established as expressions of divine revelation. Father Georges also rejected Adolf von Harnack's thesis that dogmas such as the Nicene Creed and Chalcedonian Definition transformed the original Gospel into a Hellenized form of Christianity. According to Harnack, classical Christianity was not part of the original apostolic faith, but a later development: "[Dogma] in its conception and development is a work of the Greek spirit on the soil of the gospel."[31] Dogmatic formulations represent a thoroughgoing "hellenization of Christianity" which transpired in the fourth and fifth centuries. Florovsky countered this by turning around Harnack's scheme by proposing a "Christianization of hellenism."[32] He urged that creedal terms such as *phusis*, *hupostasis*, *ousia*, and *prosopon* not be seen simply as temporary formulations without continuing significance. The Greek language remains a permanent part of the Christian heritage and should be used in contemporary formulations of the faith because it was the language of the New Testament and of later patristic tradition. He castigated the barrenness of modern theology and the bondage of Russian theology to post-Enlightenment philosophy. Instead, he proposed a program of "re-hellenizing" the Christian faith by arguing that theology could only recover itself by deepening its commitment to the baptized Hellenism of the Byzantine Fathers. Florovsky's near slavish devotion to "things Greek" caused his detractors to accuse him of limiting the work of God to Hellenistic cultural norms. He took pains to deny this by pointing to the Syriac and Latin Fathers. But the rebuttal lost force in the face of his exposition. Although Florovsky recognized non-Greek Fathers as part of the universal mind of the church, they had a limited effect on his theologizing. He seldom incorporated their thought into his neo-patristic scheme. Moreover, by rejecting Harnack's "hellenization of Christianity" Florovsky ironically ended up advocating Hellenism as a permanent vehicle for expressing Christian truth! This could be seen often when Father Georges carried patristic language into discussions of modern philosophy and theology without translating that language into contemporary idioms. In his emphasis on Greek culture, Florovsky was a child of his age. His interest must be understood within the broader context of nineteenth century German historiography and philosophy, which stressed the abiding cultural values of ancient Greece. Florovsky seems to have followed that same emphasis on "things Greek," but he did so with a Christian twist. Nevertheless, if his neo-patristic synthesis led him into an inordinate emphasis on the abiding values of Hellenism, it remains a most creative method for interpreting the sources of Christian theology.

FLOROVSKY'S IMPACT ON WESTERN THOUGHT

More than anything else, Florovsky was a missionary statesman of Orthodoxy to America. He introduced Protestants to the church fathers in a way that had not previously been done.[33] Through his publications and oral discourses at Harvard, Princeton, Columbia and other Ivy League schools, Father Georges lived out the "neo-patristic synthesis" he so earnestly advocated. He demonstrated that Orthodoxy is a living tradition, not a dead acceptance of the past. The church fathers were revered as contemporary witnesses to the unchanging truth of the gospel in an ever-changing world. Hence, Father Georges emphasized the priority of patristic methods and themes as the starting point for doing theology today.

Florovsky's insistence on "ascetical achievement" and its implied synergism also led him to stress ultimate questions in historical inquiry. The search for "meaning in history" became the noblest quest of the historian. Due to Christian convictions about eschatology and the ever-changing nature of the human person, historical knowledge is an unfinished and unfinishable task. No historian or historical source can escape being a personal point of view because historical events are acts that are mediated by further acts of interpretation. The meaning of history can make sense only in the framework of an eschatological overlapping of "this age" with "the age to come."

More than any other thinker, Florovsky brought Greek patristic theology to bear on the problems of modern philosophy. He combined the best of German, French, and Russian philosophy with Orthodox theology. But it is here that Florovsky himself was tainted in his perspective by his Russian interests. Some of his work pales when compared to, for instance, that of Vladimir Lossky, an Orthodox philosopher of the last generation, who sought to achieve the same synthesis. Of the two, however, Florovsky remained more faithful to the distinction the church fathers made between Greek philosophy and the gospel. He knew where the gospel ended and Hellenism began.

In Slavic studies, his range of skill and erudition enabled him to impact the fields of linguistics and literature. Russian religious history became one of his special contributions to American theology. Critical as he was of Russia's lack of theological creativity, he believed the Russian Orthodox Church still bequeathed to western civilization a rich heritage of spirituality and iconography. His essays on the meaning of icons and of spiritual elders are masterpieces that have not yet been given the serious attention they deserve.

Perhaps the most lasting of his legacies was the English translation of a fourteen-volume series entitled *The Collected Works of George Florovsky*, begun in 1972. Because of its accessibility and format, most readers will be inclined to use this collection as a standard reference work for the subjects discussed and as a compendium of Florovsky's own thought. The circumstances surrounding the publication of these volumes, however, are controversial, if not tragic. Andrew Blane explains:

> Nordland Press, in an ambitious undertaking, set out in the 1970's to publish Florovsky's collected works in English. He was pleased by the plan, and welcomed the first two volumes to reach print in 1972 and 1974. But disenchantment followed. He voiced strong displeasure with changes in the next two volumes, particularly volume three, saying they were not to his liking and he had not been consulted. In 1979, when the next volume was in prospect, he took the unusual step of insisting through a lawyer that he be sent a proposed contract as well as all aspects of the planned text not already posted for his personal checking and correcting. Until these conditions were met, publication could not go forward.[34]

Nordland continued publishing the works, but in a few years filed for bankruptcy. Modern English readers of the *Collected Works* must therefore consult them with discretion. The best of the *Collected Works* are *Bible, Church and Tradition: An Eastern Orthodox View* (vol. 1), and *Christianity and Culture* (vol. 2); some of lesser quality, which contain mistranslations or unauthorized revisions, are *Creation and Redemption* (vol. 3) and *Aspects of Church History* (vol. 4). None of the *Collected Works*, however, should be disregarded because of these shortcomings. They remain indispensable for all those who wish to acquire the same spirit of the Fathers which Georges Florovsky still imparts to the contemporary world.

SELECT BIBLIOGRAPHY

Not all references cited in the footnotes are repeated here. See notes for additional studies.

PRIMARY SOURCES

Volumes 1–5 published by Nordland Publishing Company, Belmont, Mass.; volumes 6–14 edited by Richard Haugh, Buchervertriebsanstalt, Notable & Academic Books, Belmont, Mass.

Volume 1 *Bible, Church, Tradition: An Eastern Orthodox View*
Volume 2 *Christianity and Culture*
Volume 3 *Creation and Redemption*
Volume 4 *Aspects of Church History*
Volume 5 *Ways of Russian Theology* (part 1)
Volume 6 *Ways of Russian Theology* (part 2)
Volume 7 *The Eastern Fathers of the Fourth Century*
Volume 8 *The Byzantine Fathers of the Fifth Century*
Volume 9 *The Byzantine Fathers of the Sixth to Eighth Century*
Volume 10 *The Byzantine Ascetic and Spiritual Fathers*
Volume 11 *Theology and Literature*
Volume 12 *Philosophy. Philosophical Problems and Movements*
Volume 13 *Ecumenism I. A Doctrinal Approach*
Volume 14 *Ecumenism II. A Historical Approach*

SECONDARY SOURCES

Blane, Andrew, ed. *Georges Florovsky: Russian Intellectual, Orthodox Churchman* (Crestwood, New York: St. Vladimir's Seminary Press, 1993). Blane's chapter should be read in conjunction with George Williams' biography below. Includes a comprehensive bibliography of Florovsky's published writings through August, 1979.

Kunkel, Christoph. *Totus Christus, die Theologie Georges Florovskys*. Gottingen: Vandenhoeck & Ruprecht, 1991.

———. "The True Church Is Not Yet the Perfect Church." In *Tausend Jahre Christentum in Russland: Zum Millenium der Taufe der Kiever Rus'*, ed. K. C. Felmy et al., 583–90. Vandenhoeck und Ruprecht, Gottingen, 1988. The latter entry offers a balanced appraisal of Florovsky's ecumenism in light of his claim that Orthodoxy represents the "one true church." Dispels ultra-Orthodox caricatures.

Neiman, David, and Margaret Schatkin, eds. *The Heritage of the Early Church. Orientalia Christiana Analecta* 195. Roma: Pontifical Institutum Studiorum Orientalium, 1973. A *Festschrift* by eminent scholars in honor of Florovsky.

Shaw, Lewis. "An Introduction to the Study of Georges Florovsky." Unpublished doctoral dissertation, Cambridge University, 1990. An introduction to Florovsky's life and thought with special attention to Russian intellectual history.

Williams, George. "Georges Vasilievich Florovsky." *Greek Orthodox Theological Review* 11:1 (1965): 7–107. Revised with a new introduction and in an abbreviated form as "The Neo-Patristic Synthesis of Georges Florovsky." In *Georges Florovsky: Russian Intellectual, Orthodox Churchman* Andrew Blane, ed., 287–340. New York: St. Vladimir's Seminary Press, 1993.

———. "Father Georges Florovsky's Vision of Ecumenism." In the *Greek Orthodox Theological Review* (1994). Williams is Florovsky's best biographer: judicious, sympathetic, and balanced.

NOTES

1. Credit belongs to George Williams for much of the biographical account which follows, taken from his still unsurpassed, "Georges Vasilievich Florovsky: His American Career (1948–1965)," *Greek Orthodoxy Theological Review* 11, no. 1 (1965): 7–107.

2. G. L. Freeze, *The Parish Clergy in Nineteenth Century Russia: Crisis, Reform, Counter-Reform* (Princeton: Princeton University Press, 1983), chap. 3.

3. Georges Florovsky, "The Duty to Learn," *St. Vladimir's Seminary Quarterly* 1 (1952–53): 2–4.

4. This was given as his first major discourse in America when invited for the Hewett Lecture at Union Theological Seminary in February, 1949. It was later printed as "Empire and Desert: Antinomies of Christian History," now available in the *Collected Works*, vol. 4.

5. Many are now assembled in the *Collected Works*.

6. George H. Williams, "Georges Florovsky Memorial Minutes Adopted by the Faculty of Divinity Harvard University (September 16, 1982)," *Harvard University Gazette* 78:5 (October 1, 1982).

7. Georges Florovsky, "The Predicament of the Christian Historian," reprinted in *God, History, and Historians*, ed. C. T. McIntire (New York: Oxford, 1977), 406–42.

8. Ibid., 411.

9. Ibid., 414, following R. G. Collingwood. The difference between evolution and human history is in man's freedom to choose his own path within the context of divine providence. The dichotomy between natural and human history makes him vulnerable to the charge of crypto-Gnosticism or Manichaeism.

10. Ibid., 419.

11. Ibid., 417.

12. Ibid.

13. Ibid., 418.

14. Ibid., 432.

15. Ibid., 433–34, against Rudolf Bultmann, *History and Eschatology*, the Gifford Lectures at Edinburgh in 1955.

16. F. Lewis Shaw, "The Philosophical Evolution of Georges Florovsky: Philosophical Psychology and the Philosophy of History," *St. Fladimir's Seminary Quarterly* 36 (1992):237.

17. Ibid., 243–47.

18. *Collected Works*, 4:53.

19. Ibid., 2:69.

20. Ibid., 10:58.

21. Florovsky, "Predicament of the Christian Historian," 425.

22. It is not possible to cover the main emphases of his theology in this chapter. If space permitted, we would need to examine his doctrines of ecclesiology (extremely important), creation, Christology, Salvation (*theosis*), and eschatology. Along with the primary sources, the best secondary treatments of Florovsky's theology are by George Hunston Williams, "Georges Vasilievich Florovsky: His American Career (1948–1965)," *Greek Orthodox Theological Review*, 9 (1965):7–107; Ibid., "Father Georges Florovsky's Vision of Ecumenism," *Greek Orthodox Theological Review*," *(forthcoming)*; Lewis Shaw, *"An Introduction to the Study of Georges Florovsky"* (unpublished dissertation, Cambridge University, 1990); Andrew Blane, ed., *George Florovsky: Russian Intellectual, Orthodox Churchman* (New York: St. Vladimir's Seminary Press, 1993).

23. Florovsky held Chrysostom, Maximus, and Palamas in particularly high regard along with Augustine and Cyprian. His creative appropriation of Augustine into the

Greek patristic tradition argues against some contemporary Orthodox extremists from the Old Calandarists of the Church of Greece and the Russian Church in Exile who attempt to depict Florovsky as ecclesiologically exclusionary toward non-Orthodox Christians.

24. "The renaissance of the Orthodox world is the necessary precondition for solution to the ecumenical problem." *Collected Works*, 5:56.

25. Georges Florovsky, "Patristics and Modern Theology," in *Proces-Verbaux du Premier Congres du Theologie à Athenes 29 Novembre—6 Decembre 1936*, ed. Hamilcar A. Alivasatos (Athens: Pyrsos, 1939), 238. His use of the word *authority* in this sentence should not be construed to indicate a replacement of the Bible with the Fathers. For his "charismatic" view of church authority, see *Collected Works*, vol. 1, especially chap. 6, "The Authority of the Ancient Councils and the Tradition of the Fathers," 93–104, and chap. 2, "Revelation and Interpretation," 17–36.

26. *Collected Works*, 4:18.

27. Ibid., 1:47. Volume 1 of the *Collected Works*, entitled *Bible, Church, and Tradition: An Eastern Orthodox View*, is still one of the best treatments to be found anywhere in Orthodox literature today. See also John Meyerdorff, "Light from the East? 'Doing Theology' in an Eastern Orthodox Perspective," in *Doing Theology in Today's World: Essays in Honor of Kenneth S. Kantzer*, eds. John D. Woodbridge and Thomas E. McComiskey (Grand Rapids: Zondervan, 1991), 339–58; "Scripture, Tradition, and Authority: Conceptions of Orthodoxy," Emmanuel Clapsis (unpublished paper delivered to the Society for the Study of Eastern Orthodoxy and Evangelicalism, Billy Graham Center, Wheaton College, September, 1992).

28. *Collected Works*, 1:75.

29. Ibid., 1:29–30.

30. Ibid., 1:18, 48.

31. Adolf von Harnack, *History of Dogma*, trans. Neil Buchanan (London: Williams and Norgate, 1899) 1:60.

32. *Collected Works*, 2:123.

33. Before his death, he began to view Orthodox dialogue with liberal Protestants as a dead end. A ground-breaking article that compares Orthodoxy with conservative Protestantism can be found in "The Many and the One: The Interface Between Orthodox and Evangelical Protestant Hermeneutics" (forthcoming, *St. Vladimir's Theological Quarterly*, 1995); and the author's "New Dimensions in Orthodox Theology," in *New Dimensions in Evangelical Theology*, ed. David S. Dockery (forthcoming, 1996).

34. Andrew Blane, ed., *Georges Florovsky: Russian Intellectual, Orthodox Churchman* (New York: St. Vladimir's Seminary Press, 1993), 150.

22

ROLAND BAINTON

MARTIN KLAUBER

Roland Herbert Bainton (1894-1984) is most famous for his *Here I Stand: A Life of Martin Luther*.[1] He was one of the most important Reformation historians of his era. Bainton spent his entire professional career at Yale University, where he held the endowed Titus Street Chair of Church History from 1936 until he retired in 1962. As a prolific author he published a wide array of works; most relating to the Reformation and general church history, with others covering topics from marriage and family life to contemporary ecumenical theology.

Bainton was born in Ilkestos, England, on March 30, 1894, the only son of the Congregationalist minister, James Herbert Bainton. In 1898, the Bainton family emigrated to Vancouver, British Columbia, where the Rev. Bainton served as the minister of a small congregation. In 1902, after the church split over James Bainton's opposition to the British participation in the Boer War in South Africa, the family moved to Colfax, Washington, and a new parish. The elder Bainton thereby expressed his adherence pacifism, a position his son also adopted.

Bainton later authored a biography of his father, entitled *Pilgrim Parson: The Life of James Herbert Bainton*,[2] in which he outlined his own intellectual and spiritual pilgrimage and noted the strong positive influence his father exerted over him. From his father, young Roland gained a love for learning and a deep sense of personal piety. He reminisced that his father would often have long discussions with him over the books that the young Bainton read out of his father's library. This love for study carried him to Whitman College in Walla Walla, Washington, where he received his B. A. in classics in 1914. While there he often wrote to his father about his intellectual discoveries. He continued his studies at Yale Divinity school, earning his Bachelor of Divinity degree in 1917 and his Ph.D. in Semitic and Hellenistic Greek in 1921.

As a pacifist, Bainton refused to serve in the military in World War I, but he did serve with the American Friends Service Committee under the Red Cross in France. After his return he was made Instructor of Church History and New Testament at Yale Divinity School in 1920 and then Assistant Professor in 1923. In 1932, he was named to the Titus Street Chair in Church History, succeeding George P. Fisher and Williston Walker. Bainton retired in 1962 and spent the rest of his life as a world renowned lecturer and author. He received honorary D.D. degrees from Meadville Theological Seminary, Oberlin College, and Whitman College. Other honorary degrees included the Litt.D. degree from Gettysburg College and the D.Theol. degree from the University of Marburg. Bainton was also an ordained minister with the Congregational Church and held affiliate membership in the Society of Friends.

Bainton was both a gifted teacher and scholar and proved that careful research can certainly enliven the classroom experience. He guided many young Reformation scholars through their doctoral studies and helped them lay the foundation for academic careers. Fifteen of these former students paid tribute to their mentor by publishing a *Festschrift* in 1963.[3] Bainton published thirty-two books and a long list of journal articles. Part of his genius was his ability to write for the specialist and layman alike without sacrificing academic integrity. He even wrote a survey of church history designed specifically for teens entitled *The Church of Our Fathers* (1941).

Bainton was a liberal Protestant during that era of rapprochement between Protestants and Roman Catholics that culminated in Vatican II. Scholars such as Bainton attempted to bridge the long-standing animosity between Catholic and Protestant camps. Bainton did not exaggerate the accomplishments of the Protestant reformers, nor did he criticize the medieval Catholic church as so corrupt that the Reformation was inevitable. He devoted much of his work to biographical studies of individuals involved in the struggle for religious freedom.

Of particular interest to Bainton were the issues of war and peace and religious toleration. In *Christian Attitudes Toward War and Peace*, he argued that pacifism was the most logical position for the Christian.[4] He listed three alternatives: pacifism, the just war, and the crusade. The early church chose pacifism. It was not until the Constantinian era, when the church became coterminous with the state, that the other two options became viable. Bainton argued that Christian pacifism was not a strategy to stop a war, but a witness to the world. Because Bainton was writing in the nuclear age, when even a just war could possibly annihilate humankind, his pacifism had particular relevance.[5] In addition, religious toleration was a major theme of his analyses of key figures of the Reformation. He argued that cries for freedom of belief in the sixteenth century were rare and were in keeping with his interest in religious liberty; not followed by western society until the nineteenth century. Most of Bainton's reformation works were biographies of those involved in the fight for religious freedom.

Bainton's other works reflect his concern for the downtrodden throughout history. He was particularly interested in the role of women in history and composed three separate volumes on women in the Reformation: *Women of the Reformation: In Germany and Italy* (Minneapolis: Augsburg, 1971) *Women of the Reformation: In France and England* (Minneapolis: Augsburg, 1973), and *Women of the Reformation: From Spain to Scandanavia* (Minneapolis: Augsburg, 1977). Bainton's work on women was primarily biographical and focused on both women of prominence and women of lower social position, primarily those discussed in Fox's *Book of Martyrs*. A. G. Dickens and John Tonkin note that Bainton did not attempt the kind of social analysis popularized more recently by Miriam Chrisman and others to discover more about the role of women in society as a whole.[6]

Bainton's area of specialization was Renaissance and Reformation history and he composed several works on the Renaissance with particular attention to northern Europe. Most importantly, he wrote a biography of Erasmus, in part, as a celebration of the 500th anniversary of Erasmus's birth.[7] Bainton was, above all, a Reformation historian with emphasis on Luther and the persecuted minority of what he called the "left wing" of the Reformation. In his analysis of both, Bainton stressed religion as a motivating force in history, and argued that religion often serves as a primary and legitimate basis for human action.

PHILOSOPHY OF HISTORY

Bainton expressed his philosophy of history in an essay entitled "Interpretations of the Reformation."[8] In this piece, he explained that the historian is a product of his own era as well as of his own personal experience.

Hence, he argued that attempts by such historians as Leopold von Ranke to gain full objectivity are impossible. The modern historian is well aware of such biases and seeks to correct them, but often overcompensates and ends up being even more non-objective. The historian is a product of his or her own era, and this injects a subtle bias of which it is often difficult to be aware.[9]

Bainton explained that historians of the eighteenth century tried to look impartially at the Reformation and either disassociated themselves from Catholic and Protestant alike or else looked sympathetically at both groups. The latter was the case with Gottfried Arnold, who "responded with equal warmth to every vital religious movement of the past whether orthodox or heretical, Catholic or Protestant."[10]

In the late nineteenth and early twentieth centuries, liberal Protestant historians "associated the Renaissance and the Reformation as conjoint phases of a movement of emancipation away from the authority of the Church."[11] German nationalists saw the Reformation as the beginning of the rise of the German spirit. In the early twentieth century, Ernst Troeltsch approached the Reformation from the perspective of the relationship between Christianity and culture, in which he saw Christianity as a form of religion that met the cultural needs of the people at that particular time.

Bainton took particular interest in the approach of Karl Holl, who in 1917 argued that religion was the most important factor in the Reformation. Bainton explained: "Holl rediscovered the core of Luther's piety, his overpowering sense of moral obligation, his feeling of utter impotence before the demands of God, his terror of the divine wrath. . . . Luther was afflicted with the *malaise de l'univers* and found surcease only through a new view of God and the Scriptures. Neither philosophy, sociology, nationalism nor economics can explain Luther. Only religion can provide the explanation."[12]

Bainton agreed with Holl's approach that religion was the primary motivation for Luther and argued that the importance of religion was a major reason that Luther was able to gain such a strong following. Luther's religious beliefs were not completely new, but he presented them within an era of religious crisis that made the people ready to follow him.

In arguing for religion as the primary interpretative vehicle for understanding the Reformation, Bainton rejected other approaches that stressed economics, politics, or psychoanalysis. The psychoanalytic approach was particular distressing for Bainton because it attempted to come to conclusions about an individual's inner life without sufficient evidence.[13] Bainton explained: "In the case of Luther, we know much, and for some thirty days of his life we know something that he did on twenty days out of every month. What we know, however, is not what, for this purpose, we need to know. The result is that the psychiatrist fastens on three or four remarks of the aged Luther about his boyhood, remarks transmitted to us only at second hand. Then on the basis of such sparse material the psychiatrist reconstructs all the turmoil of Luther's inner life."[14]

LUTHER WRITINGS

Studies of the life of Luther have served as the basis of religious controversy since the sixteenth century. Biographers of that era typically carried their own religious prejudices into their analysis, which resulted in a caricature of the Saxon reformer that made him look as pristine as the Lord himself if the biographer were Lutheran, or the devil himself if the biographer were Roman Catholic.

Bainton sought to interpret Luther in the light of his own religious convictions: "Luther's principles in religion and ethics alike must constantly be borne in mind if he is not at times to appear unintelligible and even petty. The primary consideration with him was always the pre-eminence of religion." Of paramount concern to Luther was the relationship between God and man. Any other matter was of relatively minor importance, even matters of the state. The bottom line for Luther was man's reconciliation to God and obedience to the Word of God.[15] Bainton summarized this interpretative principle as follows: "These were Luther's religious principles: that religion is paramount, that Christianity is the sole true religion to be apprehended by faith channeled through Scripture, preaching, and sacrament."[16]

Bainton contended that all of Luther's actions must be seen in light of his exclusive commitment to the Christian faith. All institutions, including the state, must follow the principles of the Christian faith. This would include proper instruction in the rudiments of the faith in schools. Furthermore, every relationship must be seen in light of such exclusiveness. Luther would not hesitate to break the bonds of friendship over a point of doctrinal disagreement. Such was the case with Carlstadt, Zwingli, and the Anabaptists.

For Luther, the quest for personal salvation and assurance was of major importance. A key term for understanding Luther's religious motivation was his experience of *Anfechtung*, which Bainton describes as "all the doubt, turmoil, pang, tremor, panic, despair, desolation, and the desperation which invade the spirit of man."[17] Bainton argued that this despair totally pervaded Luther's psyche and was a major factor in Luther's search for assurance of salvation. Prior to his discovery of the doctrine of justification by faith, Luther was in a state of depression and was riddled with doubt to the point that prayer was of little help. After all, what help could prayer be to a sinful man who is the dust of the earth, when God is holy, all-knowing, and all-powerful.[18]

Luther himself was quite conscious of *Anfechtung*. Late in his life, in *Table Talk*, a book edited by Luther's students as they recalled conversations with him over the years, Luther stated: "If I should live a little while longer, I would like to write a book about *Anfechtung*. Without it no man can rightly understand the Holy Scriptures or know what the fear and love of God is all about. In fact, without *Anfechtung* one does not really know what the spiritual life is."[19]

Luther viewed *Anfechtung* as a healthy fear of God, which was a driving force to lead him on the path to true righteousness. Luther described two types of *Anfechtung*: one of vocation and one of belief. Luther had the strong sense of terror in God's presence because he realized that his eternal destiny was at stake. This sense of terror led him initially to choose the monastery over a degree in law. It was *Anfechtung* that made Luther different from other men of his era. Bainton explained that Luther was highly sensitive and subject to extreme swings of mood from despair to exaltation. However, he disagreed with psychoanalysts, such as Erik Erickson, who argued that Luther suffered from a delayed identity crisis caused by an overbearing father. One of Bainton's primary points in this regard is that Luther's mood swings continued throughout his life and cannot be dismissed as mere delayed adolescent crisis. Furthermore, Luther cannot be called a manic-depressive because he was extremely productive throughout his life, a characteristic not typical of those who suffer from such a mental disorder.[20]

Bainton argued further that Luther's anxiety was caused largely by the deceitfulness of medieval religion, which threatened the terror of hell in order to bring individuals to the sacraments and hence into the Church. Bainton explained: "Even more disconcerting than the fluctuation of the temperature of the afterlife was the oscillation between wrath and mercy on the part of the members of the divine hierarchy. God was portrayed now as the Father, now as the wielder of his kindlier Son, who again was delineated as an implacable judge unless mollified by his mother, who, being a woman, was not above cheating alike God and the devil on behalf of her suppliants; and if she were remote, one could enlist her mother, St. Anne."[21]

Luther's struggle of *Anfechtung*, therefore, had everything to do with the lack of assurance of salvation. This lack of assurance was directly related to the major crises of Luther's early career.

Luther personalized and internalized his faith and continually wrestled with God for acceptance. According to Bainton, three events were critical in Luther's pilgrimage, each of which involved an encounter with *Anfechtung*: (1) Luther's decision to enter the monastery; (2) Luther's celebration of his first Mass; and (3) Luther's "Tower experience," by which he discovered the doctrine of justification by faith. In each event, Luther struggled with *Anfechtung*. According to Steven Simpler, these crises were essential for Luther's progress toward the break with the Roman Church and the establishment of the Lutheran movement.[22]

Luther's decision to enter the monastery was the most famous of his personal crises and was precipitated by a lightening storm as Luther was returning home from his first term of law school at the University of Erfurt. Afraid of being struck by lightening, he cried out to the patron saint of miners (his father was a miner) for aid: "St. Anne, I will become a monk." The cry itself was not that unusual; what was unusual was that Luther carried out his promise. Bainton argued that in the storm, Luther saw the lightening as the demonstration of the power of God, the all-powerful judge. Bainton also contended that this decision was not made in a vacuum while Luther was caught in a storm, but was the culmination of a series of events in Luther's life that led him to a state of mind to make such a decision.[23]

Luther's decision to enter the monastery has been the source of considerable criticism because he later abandoned the cowl. His decision, some argue, must have been the result of an inner conflict rather than a true call from God. Bainton dismissed this argument primarily because of its lack of historical data. Many of Luther's comments concerning his youth and his decision to enter the monastery came later in his life and were recorded in the *Table Talk*, which is not a completely reliable source in terms of accuracy because Luther's students wrote it based on Luther's comments. Bainton argued, as well, that Luther was so committed to the Protestant cause that he could no longer recall his Roman Catholic period with significant objectivity.[24] Such information includes two incidents of harsh discipline at home and at school. Bainton noted that Luther may have been exaggerating in such cases in order to argue for more humane discipline of children. Furthermore, Luther's comments did not reflect any resentment toward his parents.[25] Bainton has argued on this score that Luther was not some maladjusted child with a delayed identity crisis, but a normal, well adjusted individual with personal crises similar to other people of his generation.

The second major crisis that revealed this experience of *Anfechtung* was Luther's celebration of his first Mass. This was an especially difficult experience for Luther because of his sense of his utter sinfulness before an almighty God. Bainton wrote that Luther possessed a graphic sense of his own unworthiness before God and desperately sought divine favor. However, he felt so utterly sinful that any true reconciliation with God seemed impossible. Here Luther felt extreme pangs of *Anfechtung*.[26]

Luther experienced *Anfechtung* not only because of his sense of awe at the ceremony but also because his father was present. Luther was afraid of his father, who had ardently opposed his decision to enter the monastery. The occasion of the first Mass was an opportunity for Luther and his father to make amends and after his personal terror during the sacrament, Luther looked to his father for approval. He was greeted instead with a question: "You learned scholar, have you never read in the Bible that you should honor your father and your mother? And here you have left me and your dear mother to look after ourselves in our old age."[27]

A final crisis point in Luther's early career was his discovery of the doctrine of justification by faith, which, according to Bainton, occurred sometime between 1516 and 1517, while Luther was lecturing on the Psalms. Bainton pointed out that this discovery was different from the earlier crises because it did not occur in the midst of a blinding storm or the holy altar, but in the study-room of the Augustinian monastery. Luther viewed the Psalms as a book prophetic of the life and ministry of Christ. Bainton explained that Luther's use of Psalm 22 was especially important because Christ quoted a section of it while on the cross: "My God, my God, why hast thou forsaken me?" Luther realized in reading this passage that Christ felt abandoned by God and also experienced *Anfechtung* in the process. Christ had gone through the same type of experience that Luther had felt. Luther thereby identified with Christ and recognized the severity of the Lord's suffering. Christ's work upon the cross was therefore a truly atoning work that accomplished once and for all the forgiveness of sins. It made redemption possible.[28]

Bainton argued that Luther discovered justification by faith in the study, not on the toilet, as Erikson argued.[29] Luther based his theology upon careful exegetical study of Scripture, following the humanist emphasis on the use of the original biblical languages. Bainton did not place much credence in Erikson's approach mainly due to methodological deficiencies. The historian is limited because he or she depends on written records. Erikson based most of his conjectures about the young Luther on Luther's reminiscences in the *Table Talk*, written by Luther's students, in which they recalled his statements about his youth.

These statements were made over thirty years after the fact and could easily have been distorted or exaggerated. In addition, these statements were recorded secondhand and might not have been totally accurate. The methodological problem with constructing a psychoanalysis of a historical figure is the lack of evidence. Proper psychoanalysis requires series of in-depth interviews with the subject, which would obviously be impossible to do with someone who has been dead for several hundred years.[30]

Bainton argued that Luther's depressions were religiously, not psychologically, motivated. Luther's moods never led him to escapism: they only reflected his intense commitment to the issues at hand.[31]

Bainton argued that Luther suffered from *Anfechtung* throughout his life. This religious motivation serves as the lens for interpreting some of Luther's statements and actions that seem unduly harsh to contemporary readers. Bainton pointed out that, from 1525 until the end of his life, Luther became more irascible toward his opponents. Several controversial episodes such as his condoning of the bigamous relationship of Philip of Hesse and his condemnation of the Jews have sullied Luther's reputation. Early Roman Catholic critics of Luther, like Cochlaeus, condemned such statements as evidence of Luther's unbalanced condition. Bainton interpreted these events in purely religious terms.

For example, in 1525, Luther condemned the peasants' revolt in his tract *Against the Murdering and Thieving Hordes of Peasants*, which was published just at the time that the peasants were being routed. This tract contributed to the virulent attack against the peasants, who felt betrayed by Luther. This incident has been the source of considerable criticism against Luther, although some historians, such as Karl Holl, agreed with Luther's stance arguing that radicals such as Thomas Müntzer undermined social order.[32] Bainton, however, did not agree with Luther's position, but explained how Luther was really against violence of any sort. Bainton explained that Luther "tried to counteract the effect by another pamphlet in which he still said that the ears of the rebels must be unbuttoned with bullets, but he had no mind to decry mercy to captives. All the devils, he declared, instead of leaving the peasants and returning to hell, had now entered the victors who were simply venting their vengeance."[33]

Bainton noted that most of the content of this tract was ignored except the phrase "smite, slay, and stab," which brought Luther under intense criticism by the peasants. Ironically, the peasants blamed Luther for starting the slaughter while the Roman Catholic princes blamed him for instigating the rebellion.

Furthermore, Bainton argued that Luther called for the destruction of the revolt precisely because he hated violence. He did not believe that Christians should take up the sword in defense of the faith. After the revolt was put down, he called for mercy on the survivors as well as legitimate consideration of their grievances.[34] Bainton wrote: "His [Luther's] very pacifism drove him to persecute. The sword he recognized as of divine ordination when wielded by the magistrate to protect the good and punish the bad, but the sword in the hands of the minister for the furtherance of the gospel is simple monstrous."[35]

Bainton criticized Luther's lack of religious tolerance, arguing that Luther's criticism of the Jews in *On the Jews and Their Lies* was grounded in such a conviction. Luther hoped and worked for the salvation of the Jews, but when they refused to believe in Christ, he stated that they should be condemned. Bainton did comment, however, that "one could wish that Luther had died before this tract was written." But Bainton also downplayed the racist nature of the work: "He [Luther] might or he might not be charitable to the worshipers of false gods, but their error he could never condone. Neither could he feel leniently disposed toward those who disparaged or in his judgment misinterpreted the Scripture and the sacraments." Furthermore, Luther was not motivated by anti-Semitism in his remarks, but was frustrated with his inability to win Jews over to the Christian faith.[36] On this score, Bainton's analysis overstates Luther's religious motivations and, according to Robert Michael, overlooks some of Luther's more severe comments about the Jews. Bainton also ignored comments made by Luther in sermons and other works.[37] In any case, Bainton's analysis on this issue shows how rigorously Bainton applied his method of interpreting Luther in light of religious motivations.

ERASMUS

A second class of Bainton's writings falls into the category of Renaissance writings, which includes his biography of Desiderius Erasmus, although a good case can be made that Erasmus's work had tremendous implications for the Reformation. Erasmus was a key subject for Bainton because of his emphasis on religious toleration. Bainton begins his biography by noting that Erasmus has never truly received his due as a seminal scholar of the period because he did not found a new religious movement as Luther had done and thereby have his followers carve out his significance in history.

In a manner consistent with his approach to Luther and the left wing of the Reformation, Bainton argued that Erasmus was both a religious man desirous of true reform in the church and one who was thoroughly schooled as a man of letters in the Renaissance tradition. Erasmus thereby attempted to synthesize the classical tradition with Christian beliefs. True reform of the church and of society should follow the humanist model based on the *studia humanitatis* and on personal piety. In such a system the

Christian is to be educated by a thorough study of classical and Christian sources. Furthermore, Erasmus advocated training in rhetoric or the art of persuasion.[38] Erasmus was, therefore, not just a humanist, but a Christian humanist, one who sought to harmonize both traditions.

Bainton argued that this combination of the two traditions allowed Erasmus to make a unique contribution to the Christian tradition. Certainly, the cry *ad fontes*, or the return to original sources, was at the heart of Erasmus' edition of the Greek New Testament, which served as the basis for Luther's translation into German. However, Bainton did not agree that Erasmus laid the egg that Luther hatched.

Although Erasmus never joined the Protestant movement, he had much affinity with Luther. Erasmus's personal piety was a major reason for his disdain for the superfluous ritual of the ecclesiastical hierarchy. In the *Enchiridion*, Erasmus argued that the true Christian soldier should emphasize true faith. Simpler writes: "One of Erasmus's three great aversions was 'Pharasaism' or legalism, i.e., the effort to secure salvation through meticulous observance of rules. The piety of Erasmus easily transcended such externalism and placed him in conflict with many of the religious practices of his day. The monks in particular became the focus of many of Erasmus's attacks against legalism."[39]

According to Simpler, Bainton believed that the piety of Erasmus was the key to understanding his thought. "One can find in this theme of piety a key not only to Bainton's interpretation of Erasmus but also to Bainton's own religious presuppositions."[40] Erasmus's piety was based on his education under the tutelage of the Brethren of the Common Life; he saw as a brother anyone with a "warm faith and an upright life."[41]

Why, then, did Erasmus refuse to join the Lutheran movement? Some scholars have argued that it was because he was a shy, academic type who was afraid to mix it up in the non-academic arena. Bainton argued that Erasmus hated schism to such a great extent that he could not leave the Catholic Church.[42] In addition, because he lived in so many different parts of Europe, he could never really call any one country his home. The Catholic Church, in which he had so many friends and colleagues, served as his source of refuge. He could not conceive of leaving it.[43] Furthermore, Erasmus was very much involved in attempting to mediate disputes between various religious groups such as the Lutherans, Hussites, and Anabaptists. According to Bainton, Erasmus was not the shy recluse as many historians have described him, but an activist scholar who was very much involved in the events of his era.[44]

Although he remained a Catholic, Erasmus advocated tolerance for Luther. Erasmus was the first scholar to argue for religious toleration based on the fundamental articles of the faith, stating that one should allow some latitude on secondary or *adiaphoric* points of doctrine and refuse to persecute those who would still remain within the faith, at least according to Erasmus's parameters. His list of fundamentals was indeed short and he deliberately omitted such doctrines as the Trinity and papal authority. As a result, persecution would be possible, but only within the narrow band of fundamental articles. Erasmus did not regard Luther a heretic because Luther agreed on the essentials of the faith, at least as Erasmus defined them.[45]

If Protestant and Roman Catholic camps had adopted Erasmus's theory, religious persecution would virtually have ceased in the sixteenth century. For example, Sebastien Castellio adopted many of Erasmus's ideas on religious freedom in his condemnation of the execution of Servetus over the rejection of the doctrine of the Trinity.[46]

Furthermore, Bainton pointed out that the geographical areas where Erasmus had the most influence were the areas that advocated the greatest degree of religious freedom. Bainton wrote:

> The low Countries were presumably the area where Erasmus had the most unbroken influence, despite the readiness the Louvain to follow the lead of the Soronne and Trent. The liberals were Erasmian Coornhert, Arminius, Grotius. The Socinian Leclerc in the eighteenth century brought out a complete, though not a critical, edition of the *Opera Omnia* at Louvain. Significantly Holland was the first country to grant toleration to the Mennonites. The reason for the continuous hold of Erasmus on this area may be that the temper of the land had long since been formed by that tradition in which Erasmus himself stood, the piety of the *Devotio Moderna*.[47]

Likewise, Erasmus's writings remained extremely popular in England through the Elizabethan era. Erasmus's works were quite useful there for their critique of the papacy and the emphasis on a *via media*, or middle way, which attempted to "achieve comprehension through minimal doctrinal demands."[48]

In light of Erasmus stance on religious toleration and the extent of his influence, it is not surprising that Bainton painted a very favorable portrait of him. Bainton argued that Erasmus was ahead of his time and provided an important basis upon which theologians and scholars of later generations could build.

In the twentieth century, Erasmian studies have experienced somewhat of a revival because of the ecumenical spirit between Catholic and Protestant. Furthermore, the current era is one of social flux in which Erasmus serves as the model of change without the need for violence.[49] It is no wonder that Bainton called himself an Erasmian.[50]

THE LEFT WING OF THE REFORMATION

Bainton described the non-magisterial Reformation as the "left wing" of the Reformation. Bainton's left wing includes roughly the same groups as George H. Williams, "radical" Reformation. Both terms denote some aspect of political protest, and Bainton used the terms "left wing" and "radical" interchangeably. Bainton defined the left wing of the Reformation as follows: "The left wing is composed of those who separated Church and state and rejected the civil arm in matters of religion. These groups were commonly on the left also with regard to Church organization, sacraments and creeds."[51] Bainton realized that the Reformation was far too complex to fit into simple, neatly defined categories. He included under the left wing heading groups such as the Zwickau prophets, Thomas Müntzer and his followers, the Swiss Anabaptists, the Melchiorites, the Mennonites, the Hutterite Brethren, the Schwenckfelders, and the Socinians.

The key issue uniting these various groups, according to Bainton, was their common allegiance to the separation of church and state. They argued that the church should not be coterminous with the state; a person's life should be the true test for membership in the body of believers. They typically criticized the magisterial reformers on this score for their lack of insistence on a change in moral character for church membership. The radicals also attempted to reconstitute the pre-Constantinian church. They believed the ancient church lost vitality after the Roman Empire adopted the Christian faith as its own. Along with this form of "primitism" was a strict biblicism that the radicals believed was in stark contrast to the Lutherans, whom they described as well-versed in Scripture but not following its provisions. The radicals had a heightened sense of eschatology, believing Christ's return was imminent. The example of the Anabaptists' rebellion in Munster was an exception to the typical response to this view because violent revolt presumes the desire to change society. If the present world is merely transitory, the true radical will wait for Christ's appearance rather than engage in violent revolt. Lastly, Bainton pointed to an anti-scholastic bias among the left wing groups; they rejected the medieval approach to theology that made the faith almost incomprehensible to the masses.[52]

Bainton wrote his most creative works on subjects of the left wing of the Reformation. He viewed the Anabaptists as making a positive contribution to the development of western culture because of their interest in religious toleration. Under the auspices of a Guggenheim fellowship in 1926,

Bainton spent the entire year in European archives doing research on the radicals. This resulted in biographical studies of four major radical figures: Bernardino Ochino, Michael Servetus, Sebastien Castellio, and David Joris. All were important to Bainton for their role in the quest for religious freedom. For the purposes of this essay, I will focus on Bainton's writings on Servetus and Castellio.

SERVETUS

Bainton's interest in Michael Servetus stemmed from his commitment to religious toleration. Servetus's denial of the Trinity led to his execution as a heretic at the hands of the Genevan city council, with the approval of John Calvin. Bainton devoted an entire monograph to Servetus, entitled *Hunted Heretic*, which dealt largely with religious toleration. Bainton argues that the martyrdom of Servetus was significant "because it served as the occasion for the rise in volume and intensity of the toleration controversy within Protestantism."[53] Although there were thousands of religious martyrs during the Reformation era, Servetus was important in the history of religious toleration because of the controversy surrounding his execution.

Bainton argued that religious intolerance is, in part, a problem of the mind. Sixteenth-century society believed that freedom of religion would lead to the destruction of the social order. Protestants and Roman Catholics alike never understood that diversity of opinion on theological issues could be resolved without significant social dislocation. Both sides could co-exist peacefully, if only they believed it possible.

Bainton summed up the case against Servetus: Heresy is the supreme crime against God; it is actually worse than murder because it destroys souls for eternity rather than just for this lifetime. Heresy also qualifies for matricide because it amounts to severing part of the church, the bride of Christ. Furthermore, within the civil sphere, heresy violates the divine covenant between God and the people.[54]

Historians basically have taken one of two views in evaluating Calvin's role in the execution of Servetus: (1) Calvin acted responsibly and humanely; (2) Calvin was wrongly intolerant. Bainton takes the latter position, which is consistent with his emphasis on religious toleration. Bainton concludes his study of Servetus with the warning that we should be continually reevaluating our position of human freedom. Calvin made the mistake of elevating what he considered to be truth over the welfare of the individual. In doing so, he was hating both sinner and sin, a position that makes little sense to the contemporary stance of loving the sinner but hating the sin. However, Bainton, writing in the wake of the Second World

War and in the midst of the Cold War, points out that his own society possessed its own areas of intolerance by which devastation of entire cities was justifiable for the preservation of a particular way of life.[55]

Bainton argued that Servetus was executed solely for his religious beliefs and not for sedition against the state. There were two religious grounds for his condemnation: his anti-Trinitarianism and his rejection of infant baptistism.[56] Simpler points out that the only other possible motive for Calvin was political. According to this position, Calvin believed that Servetus allied with the Libertines in an attempt to undermine the city council, which supported Calvin. Since this amounted to a form of civil insurrection, Calvin might well have argued for Servetus's condemnation on the grounds of high crimes against the state. Bainton, however, totally rejects this argument because it is pure speculation without any form of historical documentation.[57]

Bainton did not spare Calvin from criticism for his participation in the affair, explaining that Calvin merely repeated familiar arguments against heresy expressed by Roman Catholics and Protestants alike. Calvin, however, was more intense in his condemnation of heretics than any of his fellow Protestant reformers. For example, Luther distinguished between heresy and blasphemy and argued that the blasphemer should be punished while the heretic should be converted. Luther believed that both individuals had incurred God's wrath and should pay the consequences. Furthermore, Bainton linked Calvin's strong intoleration to his stance on predestination. Since the heretic and the blasphemer are not among the elect, they should both be punished to vindicate the honor of God.[58]

Calvin believed that he was acting as the representative of all of Christendom and not merely for the city of Geneva. The Justinian Code, which served as the basic law of the Holy Roman Empire, clearly prescribed death as the penalty for denial of the Trinity. Calvin was acting within the law in supporting such action against Servetus. Nevertheless, Bainton argued that this legal code shows the problems of unification of church and state in which ecclesiastical law, however unjust, rules the land.[59]

Calvin's motivation for persecuting Servetus stemmed from his concept of God, which was markedly different from that of Servetus. Servetus argued that God is so immanent that man can, indeed, achieve union with the divine. Calvin contrasted God's glory and holiness with humanity's sinful nature. Servetus's argument that the Eternal Logos was combined temporally with the human Jesus undercut for Calvin the basis of soteriology. Furthermore, Servetus believed that we are not born with a sin nature and are free to choose our own destiny and even our own salvation. This conflicted directly with Calvin's positions on the sinful nature of humanity and on the sovereignty of God, which served as the basis for the predestination of individuals to eternal bliss or eternal judgement. In addition, because Servetus did not believe in the corruption of the nature of humans through original sin, there was no need for infant baptism. This rejection of infant baptism destroyed the covenant relationship between God and His people, which served as the basis for a Christian society. Lastly, Servetus was not content to keep his heretical ideas private. He sought to convert others and thereby to destroy the community of the faithful. As a result, Calvin had no choice but to support the execution of the heretic to protect the lives of the faithful.[60]

Bainton severely criticized Calvin's role in the Servetus affair. This is not surprising considering Bainton's strong advocacy of religious toleration. Bainton stated that if Calvin ever wrote anything in favor of freedom of religion, it was a "typographical error." Furthermore, Calvin's use of the Old Testament in support of the execution of Servetus stemmed from a concept of God as "ruthless and arbitrary." Bainton explained that according to Calvin:

> In the service of God we must crush all considerations of humanity. He does not feel them. God is not a father in the ordinary sense. What father would suffer his children to be eaten by lions and tigers or to be born morons? The God who permits the inequalities of creation is bound by no law, not even by the law of nature. . . . He is just, and some day we shall understand His justice, but for the present we can only sit like Job upon his dungheap and confess that God does well when He disposes of us according to His will. Zeal for His glory must almost denude us of our nature and make us ready to repudiate the love of wife and child. This was no idle talk. Calvin was not devoid of human feeling, he could be tender and moving; but his ideal was Abraham sacrificing Isaac, save that for Calvin all too often no ram was caught in the thicket.[61]

In his critique of Calvin in the Servetus affair, Bainton allowed his own bias in favor of religious toleration to color his interpretation. This illustrates that the historian is a product of his or her own era and personal experience.

CASTELLIO

Sebastien Castellio was an important subject for Bainton because of his authorship of *Concerning Heretics; Whether They Ought to Be Persecuted*, one of the most important works on religious toleration in the Reformation era. Bainton wrote three articles on Castellio and translated his *Concerning Heretics* into English.

Castellio had been a school teacher in Geneva under Calvin and hoped to rise to the office of minister. However, Calvin refused to recommend him to the city council because of Castellio's rejection of Calvin's interpretation on Christ's descent into hell and for Castellio's belief that the Song of Solomon was a secular love poem. This rejection was a crushing blow for Castellio, who could not afford to support his family on his teacher's salary. He then moved to Basel, where he eventually was appointed a professor of Greek at the university. When he heard of the Servetus affair, he saw an opportunity to express his views and to express his resentment toward Calvin.

Bainton portrayed Castellio as an early voice calling for toleration. He helped lay the foundation for the modern view on religious freedom. Although Castellio was not rewarded for his prophetic vision in his own era, his ideas were vindicated by the progress of history.[62] Castellio gained notoriety in *Concerning Heretics* by championing the cause of Servetus and by criticizing Calvin for his lack of Christian charity. Servetus was by no means the only individual executed for heresy in the sixteenth century, but Castellio ensured that his case would gain significant attention. Religious liberty thereby became a topic of discussion.[63]

Castellio's writings on toleration built a strong case against Calvin's role in the execution of Servetus. Castellio's first point was that executing a heretic only advertises his ideas and makes them more popular. It would be far better to leave the heretic alone and allow his ideas to languish. Second, persecution never leads unbelievers to faith but rather leads them away from belief in Christ. Third, persecution often leads individuals to hypocrisy because they fear reprisal; in extreme forms, persecution can lead to popular rebellion.[64]

Bainton recognized the major philosophical influences on Castellio as humanism and mysticism, both of which were highly individualistic and required little commitment to the church as an institution. According to Simpler, Bainton argued that "Castellio imbibed the ethical relativism of Erasmus and the mystical piety of Sebastian Franck. Bainton states that 'the ability to effect a combination [of these two movements] is itself an instance of breadth and balance.' Some scholars argue that Castellio was definitely no mystic, yet Bainton claims that through Franck's influence Castellio 'had been warmed to the core.'"[65]

Castellio was especially critical of Calvin's use of the doctrine of predestination as a basis for persecution. According to this theory, the heretic is already reprobate and has no chance for salvation. Therefore, execution would not cause one of the elect to perish unjustly. Because the goal of such persecution is ultimately to save souls for eternity, the execution of

Servetus did not change God's decree. Simpler points out that, on this score, "Bainton compares the theological alignments of Calvin and Castellio. For Calvin God was arbitrary and sovereign, a law unto Himself. Castellio held that God was merciful and forgiving. Calvin contended that man was a worm; Castellio proposed that man was a worm 'with great expectations, capable of perfectly obeying God.'"[66]

In his argument against such religious persecution, Castellio echoed the argument of Erasmus on the distinction between the essentials and non-essentials of the faith. If one eliminates all controversial doctrines from the list of essentials, religious persecution would be unnecessary. Such topics would include predestination, the nature of Christ's presence in the Eucharist, and the Trinity—all doctrines in which he believed that Scripture was unclear.[67] Castellio's argument on the essentials of the faith was rationalistic and emphasized that Scripture was unclear on many topics. Reason, therefore, must determine which dogmas should be included among the essentials.

Castellio also argued that behavior is a better test of one's true faith than adherence to creeds. Furthermore, one should respect the conscience of the individual even if the person's beliefs are incorrect. Bainton obviously agreed with Castellio on such arguments and commented that Castellio anticipated many of the themes of the Enlightment.[68]

CONCLUSION

In all the works discussed, the themes of religious toleration, pacifism, and the fact that religion is a legitimate factor for human action stand out. In his *Travail of Religious Liberty*, Bainton outlined his personal views on such topics. Writing in the era of the Cold War, he feared the threat of impending nuclear holocaust and argued that the contemporary world needs to avoid the mistakes of sixteenth-century society.[69]

Bainton asserted that the state must respect the conscience of the individual, such as in the case of one who refuses to serve in the military as a concientious objector. One who refuses to serve today might well be an excellent public servant under different circumstances.[70]

In the area of religious discord, Bainton agreed with Erasmus and Castellio that one should distinguish between the essentials and non-essentials of the Christian faith in such a way as to be as inclusive as possible. Dialogue on such topics can serve to bridge the gap between faiths whose histories have been full of strife.

However, he cautioned that one should not go so far in limiting the essentials that one falls into complete relativism by which all religions of the world would lose their distinctiveness.[71]

Bainton also agreed with the left wing of the Reformation in the appropriateness of the separation of church and state. However, in the area of education, he saw a legitimate place for religious instruction whether it be in parochial schools or in Sunday School. Furthermore, Christians should play a vital role in the state and thereby influence public policy in furthering the conscience of an entire society. He especially saw the church as maintaining a vital role in preventing the spread of totalitarian movements, such as Fascism and Communism, that seek to erase all religion from society.[72]

Bainton concluded that tolerance and religious freedom are among the most important achievements of contemporary society. He wrote: "The noblest achievement of the western world has been the conduct of controversy without acrimony, of strife without bitterness, of criticism without loss of respect. . . . Only those who believe in universal right, in integrity, law, and humanity, if not in the Christian God, are in a position to clash on higher levels and retain personal friendship."[73]

There is no doubt that Bainton made a major contribution to this spirit of liberality and religious freedom.

SELECTED BIBLIOGRAPHY

PRIMARY SOURCES

The Age of the Reformation. Princeton: Van Nostrand, 1956.

Bernardino Ochino: Esule E. Riformatore Senese Del Cinquecento, 1487-1563. Translated by Elio Gianturco. Florence: G. C. Sansoni, 1940.

Bibliography of the Continental Reformation. Monographs in Church History, no. 1. Chicago: American Society of Church History, 1935; reprint ed., Hamden, Conn.: Archon Books, 1972.

Christendom: A Short History of Christianity and Its Impact on Western Civilization. 2 vols. New York: Harper & Row, 1966.

Christian Attitudes Toward War and Peace: A Historical Survey and Critical Re-evaluation. New York: Abingdon, 1960.

Christian Unity and Religion in New England. The Collected Papers in Church History, series 3. Boston: Beacon Press, 1964.

Erasmus of Christendom. New York: Charles Scribner, 1969.

Here I Stand: A Life of Martin Luther. New York: Abingdon- Cokesbury Press, 1950.

Hunted Heretic: The Life and Death of Michael Servetus, 1511-1553. Boston: Beacon Press, 1953; reprint ed., Gloucester, Mass.: Peter Smith, 1978.

Pilgrim Parson: The Life of James Herbert Bainton. New York: Thomas Nelson, 1958.

The Reformation of the Sixteenth Century. Boston: Beacon Press, 1952.

Studies on the Reformation. Collected Papers in Church History. Boston: Beacon Press, 1963.

The Travail of Religious Liberty: Nine Biographical Studies. Philadelphia: Westminster Press, 1952; reprint ed., Hamden, Conn.: Shoe String Press, 1971.

Women of the Reformation: In France and England. Minneapolis: Augsburg, 1973.
Women of the Reformation: From Spain to Scandanavia. Minneapolis: Augsburg, 1977.
Women of the Reformation: In Germany and Italy. Minneapolis: Augsburg, 1971.
Yesterday, Today, and What Next? Minneapolis: Augsburg, 1978.

NOTES

1. Roland H. Bainton, *Here I Stand: A Life of Martin Luther* (Abingdon, 1950).
2. Bainton, *Pilgrim Parson: The Life of James Herbert Bainton* (New York: Thomas Nelson, 1958).
3. Franklin Littell, ed., *Reformation Studies: Essays in Honor of Roland H. Bainton* (Richmond, Va., John Knox Press, 1963).
4. Bainton, *Christian Attitudes Toward War and Peace: An Historical Survey and Critical Evaluation* (New York: Abingdon Press, 1960).
5. Ibid., 248–51.
6. A. G. Dickens and John Tonkin, *The Reformation in Historical Thought* (Cambridge, Mass.: Harvard University Press, 1985), 308.
7. Bainton, *Erasmus of Christendom* (New York: Charles Scribner, 1969).
8. Bainton, "Interpretations of the Reformation," *American Historical Review* 66 (October, 1960): 74–84. This article was later reprinted in Bainton's series of essays entitled *Studies on the Reformation* (Boston: Beacon Press, 1963) 104–16. My citations are from the latter source. See also Bainton, *Yesterday, Today, and What Next?* (Minneapolis: Augsburg, 1978). Here, Bainton argued that the work of the historian has valid applications to the present era. In Bainton's own case his work on the history of religious toleration has particular relevance.
9. Bainton, "Interpretations of the Reformation," 104.
10. Ibid., 105.
11. Ibid., 106.
12. Ibid., 107.
13. Bainton was particularly concerned with Erik Erikson's biography of Luther that employed such a psychoanalytic approach. See Erikson, *Young Man Luther: A Study in Psychoanalysis and History* (New York: W. W. Norton, 1958).
14. Bainton, "Interpretations of the Reformation," 112.
15. Bainton, *Here I Stand*, 167.
16. Ibid., 174.
17. Ibid., 42.
18. Bainton, *The Reformation of the Sixteenth Century* (Boston: Beacon Press, 1952), 33.
19. Luther, *Tischreden*, 47777 (1530–40) in Luther's Works, Weimar edition.
20. Bainton, *Here I Stand*, 20.
21. Ibid., 21.
22. Steven H. Simpler, *Roland H. Bainton: An Examination of His Reformation Historiography* (Lewiston, N. Y. and Queenston, Ontario: Edwin Mellen Press), 79–80.
23. Bainton, *Here I Stand*, 25.
24. Ibid., 16.
25. Ibid., 17.
26. Ibid., 31.
27. Ibid.
28. Ibid., 47.
29. Erikson argued that Luther's later reference in the *Table Talk* to the location of his discovery of the doctrine of justification by faith in the *cloaca* could legitimately be

translated as "toilet" rather than as the "tower." This would fit into his argument that Luther suffered from a delayed identity crisis manifested physically in severe constipation. Once Luther experienced physical relief, he was able to overcome the dominance of his father and be freed to express himself in a powerful manner. See Erikson, *Young Man Luther*, 204-206.

30. Bainton, "Psychiatry and History: An Examination of Erikson's *Young Man Luther*," in *Psychohistory and Religion: The Case of Young Man Luther* ed. Vilmas Vajta (Berlin Lutherisches Verlagshans, 1958) 23–25.

31. Ibid., 36; Bainton, *Studies on the Reformation* (Boston: Beacon Press, 1963), 18.

32. Dickins and Tonkin, *Reformation in Historical Thought*, 223.

33. Ibid., 220.

34. Bainton, *The Travail of Religious Liberty: Nine Biographical Studies* (Philadelphia: Westminster Press, 1952), 280–81.

35. Bainton, Introduction to *Concerning Heretics; Whether They Are to Be Persecuted and How They Are to Be Trusted* by Sebastian Castellio (New York: Columbia University Press, 1935) 47.

36. Ibid., 174.

37. Robert Michael, "Luther, Luther Scholars, and the Jew," *Encounter* 46 (autumn 1985): 344.

38. Bainton, *Erasmus*, 41–43.

39. Simpler, *Reformation Historiography*, 39.

40. Ibid., 41.

41. Bainton, *Erasmus*, 194.

42. Ibid., 52.

43. Ibid., 196.

44. Ibid., 54.

45. Ibid., 186.

46. Bainton, *Erasmus*, 185.

47. Ibid., 280.

48. Ibid., 279.

49. Ibid., 280.

50. Ibid., 7.

51. Bainton, *Studies on the Reformation*, 121.

52. Ibid., 119–29.

53. Bainton, *Hunted Heretic: The Life and Death of Michael Servetus, 1511–1553* (Boston: Beacon Press, 1953), 1.

54. Bainton, *Hunted Heretic*, 77.

55. Ibid. 214.

56. Simpler, *Reformation Historiography*, 134.

57. Ibid. 137–38.

58. Bainton, *Hunted Heretic*, 70.

59. Ibid., 210.

60. Ibid., 272.

61. Bainton, Introduction to *Concerning Heretics*, 73–4.

62. Simpler, *Reformation Historiography*, 141.

63. Bainton, *The Travail of Religious Liberty: Nine Biographical Studies* (London: Lutterworth Press, 1953), 91.

64. Simpler, *Reformation Historiography*, 145; Bainton, *Studies on the Reformation*, 177.

65. Simpler, *Reformation Historiography*, 141.

66. Ibid., 144-45.

67. Bainton, *Travail*, 109.

68. Ibid. 114–16.
69. Ibid. 247.
70. Ibid., 250–51.
71. Ibid., 251.
72. Ibid., 252.
73. Ibid., 253.

23

HUBERT JEDIN

FRANCESCO C. CESAREO

Church historian Hubert Jedin (1900–1980) has contributed significantly to our knowledge and understanding of the religious history of sixteenth-century Europe. Author of numerous books and articles, Jedin studied many of the leading personalities and events central to the unfolding of the religious history of the sixteenth century. In the course of these studies, Jedin discovered, edited, and evaluated new source material, analyzed the literary production of the age, and discussed the various aspects of its reformatory work. Best known for his work on the Council of Trent, Jedin provided scholars with careful studies on fundamental problems relating to the council and the Catholic reform movement, as well as investigations into conciliar historiography.

In order to assess Hubert Jedin's place among church historians, this chapter highlights his contributions to the study of the church during the sixteenth century. Beginning with an overview of his life, the chapter will then examine his understanding of the historian's task, in particular the church historian. From there, it will examine Jedin's understanding of church history as a theological discipline. This will be followed by an analysis of his key works and an assessment of Jedin's contribution to historiography.

OVERVIEW OF HUBERT JEDIN'S LIFE

Hubert Jedin was born on June 17, 1900, in Grossbriesen, Silesia. He received his higher education at the universities of Munich, Frieburg, and Breslau, graduating from the latter with a degree in theology. On March 2, 1924, Jedin was ordained to the priesthood.[1] These formative years took place in the midst of a spiritual and cultural Catholic tradition which was stimulated and enriched by its confrontation with a similar Protestant tradition. Additionally, Jedin was exposed to a rich and vital historical tradition under lay auspices.[2] This intellectual environment was the foundation of Jedin's own historical outlook.

Jedin's career as a historian began with his acceptance of a position in Rome at the Collegio Teutonico in 1926. This post, which he held until 1930, allowed him to conduct research in the Vatican Archives and the Vatican Library. He also gathered the sources for a later biography of the Augustinian General and Legate at the Council of Trent, Girolamo Seripando, sources which were held in the archives of the Augustinian Order and the Biblioteca Nazionale in Naples.[3] The immediate result of his early archival work was the publication in 1927 of *Des Johannes Cochlaeus Streitschrift De Libero Arbitrio Hominis*. This study of Martin Luther's first biographer and one of his earliest adversaries, "opened a long-neglected field of Reformation studies—the Catholic opponents of Luther."[4] This would later result in Jedin's assuming direction of the *Corpus Catholicorum* and the *Reformationsgeschichtliche Studien und Texte*, the vehicles for the publication of critical editions of Catholic reform writers.[5]

In 1930, Jedin left Rome to become *Privatdozent* at the University of Breslau, lecturing in ecclesiastical history.[6] One year after his arrival in Breslau, Jedin published one of his most influential works in the field of Reformation studies, *Die Erforschung der kirchlichen Reformationsgeschichte seit 1876*. In this study, Jedin assesses the strengths and weaknesses of nineteenth-century historical scholarship. He not only exhibits a critical awareness of the German religious historiographical tradition, but also presents a study that anticipates his contribution to that tradition. The essay, which begins with the views of J. A. Mohler, the most significant of the adherents of German Romantic theology, goes on to criticize the research and methods of an uninterrupted line of German ecclesiastical historians, such as Dollinger, Janssen, and Pastor. Jedin's aim was to uncover the underlying notion operative in German religious history, the schism that took place in the sixteenth century. His point is clear—the need to break away from confessionalism in the writing of history. Jedin argues that such an approach must give way to a religious history based on a knowledge and awareness of the documents and sources available. Herein one gains a first glimpse at Jedin's contribution to the study of the sixteenth century, the application of a critical historical method. This shall transform the study of sixteenth-century religious events from one dominated by confessionalism and apologetics to one that is more purely historical, based on the analysis of documentary evidence.

The rise of Adolf Hitler to power in 1933 had a direct impact on Jedin's career and placed his future in uncertainty. Jedin's license to teach was revoked by the Minister of Public Instruction because his mother was a convert to Catholicism from Jewish ancestry. Compelled to leave his post at the University of Breslau, he accepted the invitation of the president of the Gorres-Gesellschaft, Heinrich Finke, to assume the editorship of the *Concilium Tridentinum*. Jedin had assisted the former editor, Vincenz Schweitzer, who died in 1931, with the completion of the twelfth volume in the series[7] and was able to dedicate the years 1933–36 to this project. The events of 1933 marked a significant crossroad for Hubert Jedin, as he himself indicates: "I understood that the critical year for Europe, 1933, was also a difficult year in my life. Looking back on it now, I see it in a different light. I see, in fact, the ancient truth confirmed that the ways of the Lord are different from the ways of men. I can confirm with certainty that without that catastrophe which then hit me, I would never have decided to write a history of the Council of Trent."[8]

At the request of Cardinal Bertram, Jedin beame archivist for the archdiocese of Breslau in 1936. The following year his biography of Girolamo Seripando, *Papal Legate at the Council of Trent: Cardinal Seripando*, was published. Despite his continued productivity, his life was still very much determined by the unfolding political events in the Third Reich. On November 10, 1938, the morning after the famous "Crystal Night," two members of the Gestapo went to the archdiocesan archives and escorted Jedin to the nearest police station, where those who were to be transported to the concentration camp in Buchenwald were being registered. After providing the necessary information, Jedin was let go.[9] From that moment, he knew that in Hitler's Germany his life would be in constant danger. As a result, in May 1939, Jedin went to Rome to speak with Cardinal Giovanni Mercati, who was familiar with his scholarly works. Informing Mercati of the situation in Germany, he asked if he could arrange for his transfer to Rome for the purpose of writing a history of the Council of Trent. With the agreement of Mercati, Jedin returned to Breslau to seek release from his duties as archivist from Cardinal Bertram. Bertram consented and Mercati arranged his transfer to Rome on September 1, 1939.[10] Once again, political events intervened. Germany's invasion of Poland on September 1, 1939, and the outbreak of World War II prevented Jedin from leaving Germany. Furthermore, at age 39 he was still obliged to render military service, reason enough to be denied a visa to travel to Italy.

Given the turn of events, Jedin went to the dean of the archdiocese of Breslau, Ferdinand Piontek, who encouraged him to submit a new request for a visa. In mid-October 1939 Jedin went to the Ministry of Foreign Affairs and the Ministry of Worship in Berlin to renew his request. On November 8, 1939, he was granted a visa for Italy and left Breslau thirty-six hours later, arriving in Vienna on November 10, where he caught a train for Italy. Upon his arrival in Rome, he resided at the Collegio di Sacerdoti al Camposanto Teutonico.[11]

Jedin spent the next decade gathering and reading materials for his work on the history of the Council of Trent, the first volume of which was published in 1949. Focusing first on the "history of the history" of the Council of Trent, Jedin examined how the Council became an object of theological controversy, then an object reflecting different religious views, and finally, an object of modern historical research. His approach was to examine the sources of the council, those that had been assembled in the *Concilium Tridentinum* and those that he had gathered personally in various archives, to determine to what extent they had been used in past histories of the Council of Trent. Jedin's main objective was to counter the interpretation of the Council by Paolo Sarpi and Sforza Pallavicino, which dominated history for more than two centuries.

In 1949 Jedin left Rome to accept the post of Professor Ordinarius of Church History at the University of Bonn, a position he held until his retirement in 1965. In this period he continued to work on his history of the Council of Trent, as well as numerous related articles and books. When Pope John XXIII convoked the Second Vatican Council in 1961, Jedin was called to Rome to be a member of the preparatory commission examining studies and schools. With the opening of the Council, Jedin was named a *peritus* and assigned to the conciliar commission on studies and the conciliar commission on the episcopacy.[12] His participation at the Second Vatican Council had a profound impact on his understanding of the Council of Trent, as seen in the final volumes of his history and his other writings on Trent from this period.

Throughout his life, Jedin received awards and honorary degrees from many nations in Western Europe. "He held the *Grosses Verdienstkreuz mit Stern des Verdienstordens der Bundesrepublik Deutschland*. He was named a prothonotary apostolic, an honorary canon of the Cathedral of Trent, an honorary citizen of the City of Trent, and a member of many learned academies. He was a visiting professor at the University of Wisconsin in

1965 and a frequent lecturer at the Pontifical Gregorian University, the Catholic University of Louvain, the University of Salamanca, and many other institutions of higher learning in Europe."[13] Jedin died on July 16, 1980, in Bonn, bringing an end to an illustrious career that contributed greatly to the revival of Catholic historical scholarship and interest in the religious history of the sixteenth century.

THE TASK OF THE CHURCH HISTORIAN

Jedin gives us a glimpse into his understanding of the historian's task in a self-reflective article entitled "Esame di coscienza di uno storico."[14] Written in light of the collapse of Nazism and Fascism, he poses the question of the nature of historical inquiry: Does the historian narrate the facts from a philosophical point of view? In answering this question for himself, he indicates that he believes that the historian must focus primarily upon the sources. By approaching history in this way, the historian deduces the facts from the sources, while attempting to remain outside of the narration itself.[15] The application of dry philosophical categories to the facts repulses the historian. The historian must limit himself to the concrete facts of which he is certain.[16] History, for Jedin, whether secular or religious, must always remain in direct contact with its sources.

The same holds true for the church historian. The professor of dogma, focusing on the definitions of popes and councils and upon the sources of revelation, expounds the doctrine of the essence of the church. Yet, in doing this, the professor of dogmatic theology is obliged to place himself in contact with the historical reality and to study the activity of the church as mediator of grace and truth in the course of history. The church historian, however, begins with the study of the church's activity in the course of history, always in concert with dogma. Jedin contends that even the church historian, through varied approaches, through the events developed in the course of time and space, seeks to manifest the supernatural essence of the church.[17] Thus, the history of the Church also becomes *aedificatio corporis Christi*.

Given this fact, Jedin contends that church history is, above all, theology. More precisely, it is historical theology, having as its object the Church of Christ.[18] However, in attempting to follow the development of the church in time and space, church history is history, and makes use of the historical method. In this regard, the historian of the church is not substantially different from secular historians.[19]

While Jedin accepts the theological nature of church history, he is also cautious as to the character of theological history. He indicates that many consider the church from the point of view of the history of salvation, leading to the creation of a theology of history and a theological historiography.[20] The significance of church history is considered from the position that the church assumes in the history of salvation. Consequently, church history from this perspective focuses more on the immutable and permanent aspects of the Church, the continued presence of the living Christ, than on the changeable and transitory nature of the church, which is the proper object of church history.[21] The modifications in the church's structure, the decline of its institutions, the changes in leadership assume importance only as a reflection of the eternal and the divine in the Church. A new pragmatism emerges, which contends that church history is only needed to demonstrate the supernatural essence of the Church itself.[22]

Jedin is not comfortable with this approach to church history, because it is difficult to reconcile with a critical historical method. He poses two questions to the adherents of this viewpoint. In the first place, how can one apply this concept of the history of salvation to the research and exposition of the history of the church? Second, how can a theological historiography satisfy the requirements of a scientific historical approach?[23] Jedin reminds the adherents of this approach that while it is justifiable to explain history as an integral part of our spiritual essence, one must not forget that the most significant justification for history consists in acquainting people with the basic facts.[24]

Another problem church historians face is the criteria for evaluation that must be applied in choosing an argument and in the judgment made on individuals and facts. Jedin indicates that in the past the common belief was that the historian should not attempt to evaluate the evidence, but merely establish the facts. However, Jedin states that most agree that the historian, who must strive for maximum objectivity, makes a judgment in the choice of criteria used to evaluate the facts. The church historian, knowingly or not, always views the history of the church by the ideal of the church which he longs. He judges the positive or negative efforts of humans in history according to the duties which were entrusted to him in a particular situation. He confronts the rise and fall of institutions according to the functions they themselves assumed or which were entrusted to them. He seeks to understand the significance and importance of single episodes or entire periods of the history of the church from their ultimate end, which is the realization of the reign of God in time and space.[25] This last point is important for Jedin. He believes that every church historian must be convinced that the definitive judgment on the positive or negative value of a phenomenon of the history of the church can only be made when this history is joined to its end, namely after the parousia of the Lord. Only then can the events be manifested in their reciprocal relations and in their ultimate significance, as intended by God. Only then will the church historian find the answer to the many difficult questions that surfaced in the midst of his research.[26]

For Jedin, then, the history of the church is a science based on facts. Consequently, Jedin considers the pure and simple assessment of the facts the principal aim of church history. The history of the church should not be reduced to a spiritual history of ideas, because the church itself is not an idea but a reality.[27] The task of the church historian for Jedin is simple—to recount the events which took place as expressed in the documentary sources.

While Jedin emphasizes the necessity of grounding church history in the facts, he views church history as a theological discipline because its subject matter is derived from and rooted in faith. This differentiates church history from the history of Christianity.[28] Yet, this theological element must in no way compromise the critical approach to church history. Jedin states:

> Its theological point of departure, the idea of the Church, must not however be understood as though it were based on the structure of the Church as revealed in her dogma: a kind of preconceived pattern which history must follow and demonstrate, limiting or hindering the empirical establishment of facts based on historical sources. It refers solely to the Church's divine origin through Jesus Christ, to the hierarchic and sacramental order founded by Him, to the promised assistance of the Holy Spirit and to the eschatological consummation at the end of the world: the very elements, in fact, in which her essential identity consists, namely her continuity in spite of changing outward forms.[29]

This last point is significant. Jedin does not accept the image of the "ship of the Church" sailing unchanged for centuries. He contends that the church's nature manifests itself in changing forms during the course of history, but remains always true to itself.

The historical character of the church rests ultimately, for Jedin, on the Incarnation of the Word and its entry into human history. Above all, the church's historical character rests on the fact that Christ willed His Church to be a society of human beings, the "people of God" under the leadership of men: the apostolic college, the episcopate, and the papacy. Jedin writes:

> Thus He made her dependent on human actions and human weakness; but He has not left her entirely to her own devices. Her suprahistorical, transcendent entelechy is the Holy Spirit, who preserves her from error, produces and maintains holiness within her, and can testify to His presence by the performance of miracles. His presence and

working in the Church, like those of grace in the individual soul, can be inferred from historically comprehensible effects, but belief in them is also necessary; and it is in the cooperation of these divine and human factors in time and space that Church history has its origin.[30]

One's conception of the church impacts one's interpretation and understanding of church history. Jedin makes this clear by comparing the notions of the church as defined by non-Catholic ecclesiastical historians. Church history cannot be conceived, for Jedin, in "the Hegelian sense as the dialectical movement of an idea (F. C. Baur), for the Church is not only a divine idea but an historical fact. Its subject is not merely the 'Church of the Word' (W. von Loewenich), the 'history of the interpretation of Holy Scripture' (G. Ebeling), the 'history of the Gospel and its effects in the world' (H. Bornkamm), or the Church as we find it in the New Testament (W. Delius): all these definitions being derived from the Protestant idea of the Church."[31] For Jedin, these definitions fail to safeguard the theological nature of church history.

Church history is theology because of its object, the Church. The Church is an object of faith, as indicated in the Apostles' Creed—"I believe in one holy catholic and apostolic Church." Faith in the Church consists of two diverse aspects: in the first place, her foundation by Christ, and in the second, the fact that she, constituted precisely as a community of men and women, as the people of God, will not be abandoned, but will be sustained by the Spirit of Christ.[32] This Church is not an invisible community, composed of the true believers or predestined, but a visible community and consequently an historical entity, which does not merely have a soul, the Holy Spirit, but also a body. Thus we must place our faith in the Church because it is founded by Christ and guided by the Holy Spirit: But the Church is also historic and has a history because it is visible, made up of humans and guided by humans.[33] For Jedin, it is a Church of faith and a Church of history.

Among the concerns of the church historian is the development of the church. Because of the church's divine foundation, Jedin believes that the church historian must realize that the church does not evolve merely as a human institution situated in history. The church historian must be aware that the church develops also under the guidance of the Holy Spirit, as it penetrates the world.[34] Thus, the development of the church is not exclusively human, but is also divine.

This interplay between the human and the divine leads Jedin to view church history as ecclesiology or historical ecclesiology.[35] Its starting point is the human, the visible church, in which one seeks the divine. Furthermore, Jedin indicates that church history not only must take into account the human element, but also sin and the faults of its members. Any account of the history of the church that passes over these faults in silence or minimizes them is not history but apologetics.[36] Jedin is fully aware that there have always been corrupt priests, bishops, and popes, but they have not been able to destroy the church. The church weathered these stormy periods of corruption and decadence, emerging renewed and reformed. These periods in the church's history reflect the image of the pilgrim church making its way through time, struggling with its problems, eliminating its abuses, reforming its structure and renewing its spiritual life. A history of the church that merely highlights its accomplishments and positive character and neglects to account for its darker side is not a true history of the church for Jedin and does not fulfill its task.[37]

In fulfilling its task, church history employs the historical method. This can sometimes lead to tensions between faith or theological postulates, on the one hand, and established historical fact, on the other.[38] The application of the historical method to church history is carried out in various stages. Like all forms of history, church history is bound by its sources, whether written or otherwise. Once these sources have been uncovered, the church historian, like any historian, must evaluate their authenticity. This done, the church historian reconstructs the facts based on the sources. Finally, the church historian assesses the factual information, recognizing that the ultimate meaning of church history can be apprehended only by the eye of faith.

According to Jedin, no science exists, above all no historical science, without presuppositions. There is no such thing as a purely objective history; there is merely an impartial history.[39] The historian must judge according to the reality of the situation, that is, according to the information in the sources.[40] The historian must attempt to understand particular events or personalities from their own perspective.

The views and ideas of Jedin concerning church history and the task of the church historian all find expression in his scholarship, to which we now turn. While Jedin was a prolific writer, the majority of his work remains unavailable in English.[41] Given this fact, the analysis of his works will be limited to those key studies that have been translated into English, with the exception of an important essay published in 1946. In examining these works, the aim will be not merely to summarize its content, but to indicate how this work contributes to our historical understanding of religious history in the sixteenth century.

Analysis of Hubert Jedin's Scholarship

Historians have always struggled with the proper terms to designate the Catholic Church's response to the changes and movements that characterized the sixteenth century. Jedin entered this debate with the publication of an essay in 1946 entitled *Katholische Reformation oder Gegenreformation?* in which he made a distinction between the Catholic Reform movement, characterized by a continuation of healthy impulses within the church of the late Middle Ages, and the Counter-Reformation, characterized by the new anti-Protestant institutions and mentality.[42] Jedin's essay did not end the uneasiness about terminology because one's conception of the historical facts determined how one described the events and reactions of the period.

Many Catholic historians see the renewal of the church in the sixteenth century as a phenomenon caused from within the church itself, completely independent of the emerging Protestant movement. For these historians, the Catholic Reformation represents an honest attempt on the part of the church to reform itself. These historians consider the Catholic reform movement the true renewal. They do not accept the notion of a Counter-Reformation because this term considers the renewal of the church merely a reaction to the religious schism. By contrast, non-Catholic historians understand the Protestant Reformation as the true movement for renewal because it sought to return to the primitive apostolic church. From this perspective, the notion of the Catholic Reformation makes no sense; there is only room for a Counter-Reformation understood simply as a reaction against Protestantism.

In light of this situation, Jedin's aim in this essay was to clarify the meaning and use of each term. Jedin begins his essay with well-known historical facts as a means of opening the way for an intelligent link between the two concepts in question and to free the historical use of these terms from misunderstanding.

Jedin indicates that the term "Counter-Reformation" is older than the term "Catholic Reformation." It was first employed in the eighteenth century to describe the forceful return to Catholicism of those areas of Europe that had embraced the Protestant faith. The term was used in the plural, however, indicating that historians did not understand this return as a unified movement.[43] Jedin contends that at the base of this movement was the internal regeneration of the Church.[44] The term "Catholic Reformation," coined by the Protestant Maurenbrecher and popularized by Pastor, began to be employed by historians who recognized that the church's response to the changes taking place were not all reactionary.[45] Jedin indicates that historians became aware of a reform movement that stretched back to the late Middle Ages and continued uninterrupted into the sixteenth century.

Jedin believes that both terms are needed if one is to understand the church in the sixteenth century. The Catholic Reformation, concerned with the inner renewal of the church and its members, has its roots in the fifteenth century. However, because these reform efforts were scattered throughout Europe and did not enjoy the support and direction of the papacy, the effects of these movements on the church as a whole were minimal. This situation changed with the pontificate of Paul III, who united the various forces of reform and gave them direction.

The continuity of reform between the fifteenth and sixteenth centuries is evident in the various reform proposals drawn up throughout these centuries. The reform principles that inspired the earlier petitions are identical to the later ones; the problems and abuses afflicting the church in the fifteenth century were the same in the sixteenth. The noticeable difference between these centuries was the involvement of the papacy and the efforts of an ecumenical council. The Council of Trent not only drew up solutions for the problems but, more importantly, implemented the decrees under papal auspices. This entire movement is characterized as the Catholic Reformation, yet indirectly it is also the premise of the church's defense against the new Protestant teachings. In order to defend itself from heresy and to regain lost territory, the church created new methods and new weapons, such as the Index and the Inquisition, which the papacy utilized in its battle against Protestantism. These efforts are often characterized as aspects of the Counter-Reformation. However, Jedin indicates that a clear link exists between the Catholic Reformation and the Counter-Reformation in the functions of the papacy, where these movements are both joined and separated.

Jedin uses the phrase "Catholic Reformation" to describe a singular movement encompassing all efforts aimed at renewing the church. But, some historians prefer to speak not of a single movement, but of a plurality of movements sharing a common aim. Jedin acknowledges that in its early stages one can speak of a variety of Catholic reform movements because they had not been organized into a united whole. However, he believes one must speak of a singular Catholic reform movement because only in this way is the continuity of reform from the fifteenth to the sixteenth centuries clearly understood.[46]

The foundation of the Counter-Reformation for Jedin is the Catholic Reformation. From this perspective, the Counter-Reformation is not merely a defense, but the development of the vital laws of the Church itself.[47] To defend itself from new teachings, the Church used new methods to recover what it had lost. The Counter-Reformation also includes for Jedin doctrinal discussions with Protestantism. While this resulted in polemics against erroneous teachings, Jedin contends that it also resulted in the positive exposition of Catholic doctrine, which proved to be an effective defense against Protestantism. While acknowledging the use of repressive measures such as the Index and the Inquisition, Jedin indicates that their effect was only truly felt when the Catholic Reformation controlled the papacy, which subsequently assumed direction of the struggle.[48]

For Jedin, an inner connection exists between the Catholic Reformation and the Counter-Reformation, namely the papacy. The papacy, having experienced inner renewal, became the promoter of the Counter-Reformation and pushed the religious forces to respond against Protestant innovations. Given this intimate link between both movements, Jedin contends that historians must acknowledge two separate movements dissimilar in their origin and in their essence—one, spontaneous, based on the continuity of the church's inner life; the other, dialectical, provoked by the church's reaction against Protestantism. If one wants to understand the development of the history of the church in the sixteenth century, one must retain these two fundamental elements—the element of continuity expressed in the concept "Catholic Reformation," the element of reaction expressed in the concept "Counter Reformation."[49] For Jedin, the Catholic Reformation is the church's reflection upon itself as it attempted to restore and renew its inner life; the Counter-Reformation is the church's self-affirmation in the fight against Protestantism. The Catholic Reformation is based on the reform of the individual members of the church begun in the late Middle Ages, developed under the impetus of Protestantism, and joined to the efforts of the papacy in combating the new religious teachings. In the Catholic Reformation are stored the forces used in the Counter-Reformation.[50] The Catholic Reformation, then, precedes and flanks the Counter-Reformation.

One important figure in the religious drama of the sixteenth century was the Augustinian Girolamo Seripando. Jedin began gathering material relevant to Seripando during his first years in Italy, which resulted in 1937 with the publication of a biography of Seripando. The English translation, *Papal Legate at the Council of Trent: Cardinal Seripando*, was published in 1947. Jedin's purpose was to determine the historical place of Seripando in the spiritual struggles of this era of religious revolt. This study is not a simple biographical sketch of Seripando. Rather, Seripando's life is interwoven with a running commentary of his theological work and broadens into a full-fledged historical study of those movements and events in the unfolding of the sixteenth century in which Seripando played a role.

The chapters dealing with Seripando's activities at Trent—as one of the voting mendicant generals and an adviser to Marcello Cervini during the first convocation, and as one of the presiding legates during the third convocation—provide a concise yet comprehensive examination of this period of the Council of Trent. Jedin integrates objectively Seripando's contributions to the religious happenings of the sixteenth century into the greater context of conciliar history.

Jedin's study is theologically inflected, making it of greater interest because Seripando, an Augustinian, was a member of an order that played a unique part in the Protestant Reformation. While Seripando was not a member of the nine-man commission appointed by Paul III in 1536, he spoke out against ecclesiastical abuses.[51] As general of the Augustinian Order, he inaugurated a reform of his own by a visitation to Augustinian monasteries in Italy, France, and Spain.

Seripando's greatest contributions to the Council of Trent ended in failure. In the doctrines of original sin and justification, as defined in the fifth and sixth sessions, most of the views for which he had fought over several years in treatises, opinions, and drafts suffered defeat.[52] Yet, Jedin indicates that had it not been for Seripando's strenuous defense of the theological traditions of the Augustinian school and for the discussions prompted by the drafts he had prepared at the request of the legates, Trent would hardly have been successful in determining the crucial difference between the Catholic thought of Augustine and its Lutheran interpretation.[53]

Much of Jedin's scholarly life was spent studying the Council of Trent, and for it he is most noted. No other council, with the exception of the Second Vatican Council, has had such a profound impact on the history of the church as the Council of Trent. Of the twenty-one ecumenical councils held to date, Trent is, without doubt, one of the most memorable, largely because no other previous council had such profound effect in all aspects of ecclesiastical life.[54]

Jedin's multivolume history of the Council of Trent, published between 1948 and 1975, reveals the inner workings of the council as well as its ecclesiastical and political context. From this perspective, Jedin's history has finally overcome the subjective interpretation of the Council, such as the negative assessment of Paolo Sarpi and the positive assessment of Sforza Pallavicino.[55] As Jedin writes in the preface, "Ever since the days of Sarpi and Pallavicino, that is, for some three hundred years, the world has been waiting for a history of the Council of Trent that would be other than an accusation or a defence."[56] Jedin met that need by removing the council as an object of religious controversy and placing it within a historical context. Based on extensive analysis of the sources, Jedin's aim was to recount the history of the Council of Trent as it unfolded amidst the realities of sixteenth-century Europe.

Jedin's study has destroyed the monolithic image of the Council of Trent. Jedin portrayed Trent as an everchanging body of personalities with diverse experiences and perspectives. More importantly, each period of the Council confronted different political and religious situations which had to be taken into account. The final period of Trent was attended by more than two hundred bishops, representing diverse attitudes and theologies prevalent in sixteenth-century Catholicism. "This polyhedral quality of Trent is one of the discoveries for which we are indebted to Jedin. The Council was, in other words, anything but monochromatic, single-minded, or docile and submissive to Rome, as the popes would probably have preferred."[57] In order to appreciate this contribution fully, we must briefly examine the view of the Council of Trent presented by Paolo Sarpi and Sforza Pallavicino.

The Venetian Servite, Paolo Sarpi, was a court theologian to the duke of Mantua and a member of the Roman Curia. In 1606, Pope Paul V placed Venice under interdict. The republic searched for a theological consultant to respond to Rome's action and appointed Sarpi state theologian and canonist. In numerous polemical writings, he defended Venice's ancient tradition of ecclesiastical independence and claimed that the papal interdict was invalid.[58] Sarpi became the spokesman of antipapal sentiment in Venice. His harsh criticisms resulted in his excommunication for a short time in 1607. After the excommunication was lifted, Sarpi decided that he would inflict a mortal wound on the papacy by writing a history of the Council of Trent.[59]

Sarpi's *Istoria del Concilio Tridentino* was based not only on documentary sources available in the state archives of Venice and those in the possession of Venetian noble families, but also on the recollections of actual participants, some of whom were Protestant. During his time in Mantua, Sarpi came to know the former secretary of Cardinal Ercole Gonzaga, Camillo Olivo, who had witnessed the first crisis of the Council in the spring of 1562. In Venice, Sarpi became acquainted with the former French ambassador to the Council, Arnauld du Ferrier, who had been a vocal critic of the Roman Curia during the conciliar sessions and eventually embraced Calvinism.[60] Undoubtedly the recollections of these participants were one-sided and perhaps raised Sarpi's suspicions as to the aim of the Council.

To Sarpi, the Council of Trent was an instrument to strengthen papal influence on ecclesiastical life, especially the bishops. The Congregation of the Council entrusted with the task of interpreting conciliar decrees possessed jurisdiction unlike any other curial authority. Sarpi was convinced that at the Council of Trent, the Roman Curia had dealt a masterstroke against an anti-curial movement, thereby asserting its influence in the church. If Sarpi could unveil this process, he believed that he could significantly injure the papacy.[61] This prospect moved him to write a history of the Council of Trent, which was published in 1619.

On the first page of his *Istoria del Concilio Tridentino*, Sarpi sets down three questions:

> How did it come about that the Council which men had longed for and promoted as a means for restoring the crumbling unity of the Church, actually consolidated the cleavage and so embittered the parties as to render a reconciliation impossible? How was it possible that the princes' plan to reform the clergy by its instrumentality, was frustrated, and that the bishops' attempt to recover their authority, which had largely devolved on the Pope, not only ended in the complete forfeiture of that authority, but that they themselves contributed to their enslavement? Lastly, what is the explanation of the fact that the Council, dreaded and shunned by the Roman Curia, which saw in it the most effective means by which its supremacy could be curtailed, so consolidated and secured that supremacy—at least in that part of the Church which had remained faithful—as to enable it to strike even deeper roots than ever before?[62]

According to Jedin, with these questions Sarpi forestalls the answers which his history was supposed to supply. Sarpi believed that the schism was still in the opening stages when the council met. From Sarpi's perspective, the obstacle to reunion between the Protestants and the church was not the teachings of the reformers or the ecclesiastical structures they set up, but the dogmatic definitions issued by Trent.[63] Thus, according to Jedin, Sarpi believed there was no religious schism before Trent.

Sarpi's questions, especially the second, derive ultimately, according to Jedin, from his notion of the church. As far as Sarpi was concerned, the Tridentine reform was a misnomer because it resulted not in reformation, but in deformation. Jedin argues that Sarpi's view derived from two preconceived notions:

> The secular arm ... had not succeeded in using the council for the purpose of effecting the kind of reform of the clergy which, in Sarpi's opinion would alone have guaranteed a lasting improvement, namely a reform of State-Church lines. . . . Episcopalism, from which [Sarpi]

hoped for a genuine reform of the Church . . . had not prevailed at Trent; on the contrary, the Council had left the Pope's supremacy intact and left its own guidance and the execution of its decrees in his hands. The Tridentine decrees about Church reform and their subsequent execution he made nothing of because not only had Erastianism and episcopalism not triumphed at Trent, but the Papacy had made of the Tridentine decrees the palladium of the Catholic reform as well as the Counter reform. By this means it had won for itself fresh influence and renewed prestige.[64]

Despite the limitations of Sarpi's questions, Jedin contends that they must be considered by the historian of the Council of Trent. Thus, Jedin gives this as the reason for following up the struggle for the Council from 1520–1545: "So as to show that the course of the schism was no longer in an early stage, as Sarpi thought, but that it had already made considerable progress."[65] While the process had not yet reached its completion, many influential voices in Rome believed that Germany could not be restored to Rome. Thus, it was more important to concentrate on preserving those nations that remained Catholic, by providing them with unambiguous doctrine and effective reform.[66]

Jedin questions the sources upon which Sarpi bases his view of the Council. In his description of the first period of the Council, Jedin believes that Sarpi fills the gaps in his narrative with conjectures and even with outright inventions: "Suspicion is raised when in the first congregation of theologians, on 20 February, [Sarpi] puts into the mouths of Lunello and Marinarius discourses on the problem of the faith of which no protocol, no diary, no letter tells us anything, but the content is remarkably in agreement with known discourses of Alfonso de Castro and the Bishop of Chioggia."[67] Jedin also points out inconsistencies in Sarpi's discussion of the debate on original sin and justification. Jedin concludes his assessment of Sarpi's history of the Council of Trent in a critical tone: "The arbitrary way in which Sarpi uses his sources in cases where we are in a position to check his statements makes it impossible to rely on the information he supplies and deprives it of all value. Sarpi had political talent; he could question history. He was a gifted writer and a master of the Italian language—as a historian he cannot be relied upon."[68]

The success of Sarpi's work led the Church to seek out someone who could refute his view. This task was undertaken by a professor at the Roman College, Terenzio Alciati. He knew that only a new history of the Council, based on better and authentic sources, could counter Sarpi's work.[69] However, Alciati died before completing his work and was succeeded in this task by Cardinal Sforza Pallavicino, who published his *Istoria del Concilio di Trento* in 1656. Pallavicino based his study on the numerous documentary sources available to him in Rome, allowing him to point out the errors in Sarpi's study.[70] However, while Pallavicino based his work on the sources, it is guided by a specific purpose. His intention was to provide an *apologia* mixed with history, rather than an impartial history.[71] Consequently, an overly positive picture of the Council of Trent emerges in contrast to Sarpi's excessively negative portrayal.

Jedin corrects those two extremes in his monumental history, based on vast documentary sources gathered from various European archives and those already published in the *Concilium Tridentinum*. While only the first two volumes of Jedin's work have been translated into English, to appreciate the significance of this work, one must consider it in its entirety.

Jedin's *A History of the Council of Trent* begins by discussing the notion of council and reform, starting with the Council of Basel and ending with the Fifth Lateran Council. The chapters comprising this section demonstrate that the work of the Council of Trent must be understood not merely as a reaction against Luther's challenge to Catholicism and as an instrument of the Counter-Reformation, but also as the result of historical realities within the church in the preceding century.

At the beginning of the sixteenth century, the church experienced a weakening of genuine reform movements, a papacy which failed to take an aggressive leadership role in reform efforts, and doctrinal ambiguity and confusion, all of which contributed to the success of Luther's movement. Perhaps most important in trying to understand these critical years before Trent was the notion of conciliarism. In its extreme form, as a doctrine of conciliar supremacy, it paved the way for the denial of the hierarchical structure of the church, which is found in the Lutheran conception of a "free Christian council." Equally important are the more moderate expressions of conciliarism, which postulate, within the doctrinal system of papal supremacy, the general council as the ultimate remedy in a "case of necessity."[72]

In retracing the development and consequences of conciliarism, Jedin indicates how the desire for reform became identified in the minds of many with the need for a council.[73] Yet fear of reform under the leadership of a council was largely responsible for the failure of the papacy in Luther's day to assemble an ecumenical council when it was perhaps more urgently needed than ever. Moreover, the uncertainty resulting from conflicting views of the foundations of ecclesiastical authority overshadowed the Council of Trent itself to the end.

Jedin postulates that a Council along traditional lines convened by the pope in the middle 1520s in response to the German appeal might have possessed sufficient authority to curtail the spread of Protestantism and to prevent the establishment of territorial churches, by condemning Lutheranism as theologically unsound and by carrying through suitable and effective reforms.[74] Jedin holds this position because he recognizes a truly Catholic nature in Luther's first aspirations. Yet, no council was convened.

One of the central questions emerging from the first volume of Jedin's history revolves around the reasons for convoking the Council of Trent so late. Jedin presents a balanced picture of the complicated situation that prevented an earlier summoning of the council. Throughout the book, Jedin provides excellent interpretations of the antagonism between Pope Paul III and Emperor Charles V, both of whom share responsibility for the council's belated opening. Charles' greatest shortcoming, according to Jedin, was his lack of understanding for the primacy of theological truth. Jedin's judgment of Paul III is clearly expressed in the following description: "He was not the first pope of the Catholic Reform, but it was he who prepared its way. The sensitive ear of this superior mind heard the call of the times for Council and Reform, but the delicate, aristocratic hand of the old man was not rigorous enough to cut the threads that held his entire personality and the interests of the Curia tied to the Renaissance period of the papacy."[75]

Jedin stresses that among the reasons for the council's delay was Paul III's refusal to abandon political neutrality and to ally himself with Charles V against the king of France, even though the latter did all in his power to obstruct a council.[76] This situation prevented harmony between pope and emperor in the conciliar endeavor. Jedin emphasizes the tendency of ecclesiastical and secular statesmen to continue to pursue the political policies of the Renaissance, failing to grasp that a radically new situation was being created by events in Germany.

Jedin's first volume concludes with the opening of the Council of Trent, December 13, 1545. Because the events between 1517 and 1545, as well as earlier, significantly influenced the Council of Trent, they must be recounted. Jedin contends that the Council's history cannot be properly understood in isolation from the events and theories of the preceding century.

Three main points emerge from this volume: First, the Council of Trent can only be understood against the long background, not merely of the events of its own age but also of a full century before. Second, a council in the earliest days of the Lutheran movement might have been powerful enough to confine the latter within small limits and to preserve the unity of Christendom. Third, this early council not having taken place, and the religious breach having become unbridgeable, the Catholic Reform as it historically developed needed several decades after Luther's emergence to reach maturity.

The second volume of Jedin's history of Trent covers the period from the opening of the first session of the council to its translation to Bologna in March 1547. Jedin's balanced account of this period demonstrates his command of the documentary sources, as he presents a chronological discussion of the development of dogmatic and reform decrees. One notes an interplay between two themes running through this volume: (1) the desire of the council to issue authoritative decrees settling dogmatic controversies and restoring ecclesiastical discipline, and (2) the external influences upon the council growing out of the emperor's plan to crush the military and political power of the Schmalkaldic League, thereby forcing the German Protestants to attend the council. To achieve this result, the emperor had to delay the council in its definition of dogma until the Protestants were represented and to prevent its either being suspended or translated to a location outside the empire, an act unacceptable to the Protestants. In regard to this plan, the pope, though anxious to have the German religious dissidents suppressed, feared the growing power of the emperor. Jedin expresses regret at the dissension between pope and emperor, which allowed the council to be translated to Bologna, a dissension which saved German Protestantism in the hour of its greatest danger. Jedin writes: "We do not lose ourselves in a labyrinth of speculations about historical possibilities, but start from assured facts, when we maintain that if there had been no translation of the Council of Trent to Bologna, the German schism might have had a different issue."[77]

The remaining volumes, not yet available in English, continue the story of Trent. As in the previous volumes, Jedin handles the intricate detail of sixteenth-century politics, the workings of church institutions, and the controversial issues in theology and canon law. Volume three covers the period from the translation of the council to Bologna in 1547 to its suspension in 1552. The history of these years weaves together the political maneuvering, the efforts at reform, and the making of dogmatic decrees. According to Jedin, "The transfer to Bologna was an embarrassing mistake, nor did the second convocation at Trent achieve what the emperor had hoped—a true synodal dialogue between Catholics and Protestants. The reform work of the period 1547–52 is meager and Jedin questions whether they actually addressed the spiritual concerns that were at the heart of the Protestant dissent. Jedin quite impartially sees that responsibility and blame must be shared by all concerned: by pope and emperor, legates and bishops, Protestant estates and divines."[78]

In the final volume, Jedin continues his account of all affairs bearing on the council from its suspension in the spring of 1552 to its completion, under papal auspices in the years following its solemn closing on December 4, 1563, of its undertakings still in progress at that date—the revision of the Index of Forbidden Books, the revision of the missal and breviary, and the compilation of a catechism.[79] Jedin maintains a balance in his exposition between external and internal developments, between ensuring the cooperation of the secular powers and effecting a consensus among the council fathers. He illustrates how the different conditions within the Catholic countries affected the roles played by their bishops and ambassadors at the council. Jedin presents a careful analysis of the conciliar decrees, explaining why certain things were either included or omitted in the decrees and why certain words were selected in preference to others.[80] Jedin not only makes comparisons between the final period of Trent and the first two periods, "but he also makes references to the First and Second Vatican Councils when he examines matters that were discussed but left undecided at Trent and then taken up again at the last two ecumenical councils, such as the relationship between pope and bishops."[81] Proceeding along these lines, Jedin leaves no doubt about the relevance of the Tridentine decrees to contemporary concerns in both doctrine and reform.

After concentrating on the theological, canonical, and diplomatic aspects of Trent up to its closing, Jedin reviews the two years in terms of its social and economic structure. The final chapter examines how the council fulfilled the obligations imposed on it by Paul III at its inception.[82]

According to Jedin, the Council of Trent did not condemn the leaders of the Protestant movement; it did more than that: it gave to the church the necessary clarity and confidence to repel the errors of the Protestants. But if one were to ask why this council penetrated the historical consciousness so profoundly, the response which history would provide, either political or ecclesiastical, would always be the same: The reforms of the Council of Trent renewed from its foundations the religious life and dignified the church.

Because Jedin does not allow his theological presuppositions to influence his historical judgments or personalities and motives, his history of the Council of Trent has been praised for its impartiality. Jedin downplays sympathy for the aspirations of conciliarists who were genuinely concerned to reform the state of the church, while recognizing that they were doctrinally at fault. By contrast, Jedin has sharp words for those Renaissance pontiffs who, while adhering to the orthodox doctrine of papal power, used that doctrine only to defend a crudely arbitrary and selfish form of personal despotism. The essence of Jedin's achievement is his ability to fuse intellectual, diplomatic, and institutional history into a complete picture of the Council of Trent.

While Jedin's history of Trent remains his masterpiece, he has written other works on the subject, which view the council in light of contemporary criticisms of its work. One criticism of the Council of Trent is the one-sided prominence it accorded to the church's hierarchical structure, thereby neglecting the laity. In his *Crisis and Closure in the Council of Trent*, Jedin contends that this criticism is unjustified because it applies more to post-Tridentine theology than to the council itself. Jedin states:

> Theology was not compelled to forget the universal priesthood of all believers and the position of the laity with regard to the church's hierarchical structure. But the council's task had been to work out, and as far as possible to define, this hierarchical structure according to the Church's official teaching. To work out an ecclesiology was the theologians' not the council's task. To demand more than the demarcation of the church's teaching against error would be asking too much of the council.[83]

Thus, according to Jedin, the council's primary goal was to distinguish Catholic doctrine from the teaching of the reformers and to define what was Catholic faith and what was error.

In fulfilling this task, the Council of Trent has been criticized for solidifying the schism. Jedin responds that such criticism results from "unhistorical thinking," that is, from not having a clear understanding of the council's aims.[84] The council's aim in demarcating the boundaries of the church's teaching was to provide certainty in faith. "They were boundary stones set up by the council in an attempt to put an end to the widespread uncertainty about what was still Catholic and what was already Protestant, and they should be seen as such—as boundary stones, and not as barbed wire acting as a barrier to all free movement."[85] Futhermore, according to Jedin, Trent could not have been a council of union. Even during the first period which began in 1545, the division between the churches was a settled historical fact: national churches along Lutheran lines had already been established, and despite the defeat of the Schmalkaldic League, they continued to survive. In addition, Calvinism was already developing. Given these historical realities, Jedin concludes that there "was scarcely a single responsible person on the Catholic side who at that time believed that the gap between the Protestants and the Catholics could be bridged. The aim at the council was to strengthen those who had remained faithful to the Catholic Church and to clarify and reaffirm their faith, not to win the Protestants over."[86] Thus, the Tridentine reform was in essence the inner renewal of the spiritual life of the Church, a renewal which had begun in the late Middle Ages.

Because the council's aim was to delineate Catholic teaching from Protestantism, some historians blame the split on the council itself. In an article entitled "Is the Council of Trent an Obstacle to Reunion?" Jedin responds to this interpretation. He indicates that when discussing the council in terms of the religious schism, one must proceed from the historical fact that the "Council of Trent was not the cause of the division between Catholics and Protestants, but it set the seal on an already existing division."[87] The definitions of the Council of Trent confirmed rather than brought about a separation that had already come into being. The division in the church had become an historical fact once the civil visitations initiated by the princes of Electoral Saxony and Hesse had eliminated the jurisdiction of the Catholic bishops and created Protestant regional churches. In 1530, the Augsburg Confession gave a dogmatic backbone to the Lutheran ecclesiastical communities which had been organized. Jedin contends that the continual postponement of a General Council since 1521, along with various political events that prevented the carrying out of the Edict of Worms, made the inner development of the Protestant regional churches possible and with this, the consolidation and expansion of the Lutheran movement.[88]

While Jedin believes that the division in the Church was already an accomplished fact long before the opening session of the Council of Trent, he does so with some qualifications. Jedin states that as far as Protestants were concerned, they still belonged to Christendom. Furthermore, at the head of the Augsburg Confession stood the three creeds of the early church and a confession of the Trinitarian and Christological dogmas of the ancient church. "The differences between Catholics and Protestants were in many places effaced, and that a sharper division between the confessions only opened up after Trent, and because of Trent."[89] Jedin does not mean by this that the separation was caused by the council, but that it confirmed the division by forcing both positions to be formulated with decisive clarity.

Jedin highlights three reasons for the Protestant refusal to participate at Trent. In the first place, Protestants rejected Trent because it was convoked and directed by the pope rather than the emperor. This meant that the council could not be free. Jedin acknowledges that earlier ecumenical councils had been summoned and supervised by the emperor. However, since the Middle Ages, councils were convoked, directed, and confirmed by the pope. Jedin states that the "Protestant notion of a council was thus determined by historical reminiscences, and by the ever-present conciliar theory. It also depended on a false notion of the Church. They denied not only the *ius divinum* of the papal primacy and of the hierarchy, but also the very notion of an official priesthood, and of the councils as being the bearers of the highest teaching office in the Church, the Magisterium."[90] Second, the Protestants demanded the participation of the laity in the consultations and discussions of the council. Jedin indicates that while lay powers were present at earlier councils, they never took part in the elaboration of truths of the faith. Jedin argues that "had the Protestant states accepted the invitation to Trent they would have had, through their theologians, a good opportunity of expounding their standpoint and defending it, but judgment upon it would always have rested with the pope and bishops in unison, who as possessors of the supreme ecclesiastical authority have the duty of judging matters of faith."[91] Third, the Council was rejected because it did not accept the Protestant scriptural principle. Protestants desired that Scripture alone be the sole judge in the council, thereby excluding both tradition as a source of faith and the Magisterium of the church as the bearer of that tradition.[92]

Given these arguments, the Council of Trent, according to Jedin, could not have restored unity in the church. "There was no bridge. For both parties there was a clear question of principle involved, in which a concession would have meant surrender. Given these principles the Protestants could not have acted in any other way, and the council was equally restricted."[93] The reasons for not participating at the Council of Trent came from a notion of the Church fundamentally different from the Catholic concept of church. The Protestants of the sixteenth century rejected Trent because it was truly contrary to their idea of the church. They rejected the claim of a living Magisterium for deciding controversies of faith because this authority rested on the notion of a hierarchical church, which contradicted their scriptural principle and their own ecclesiastical order. This in Jedin's opinion, was the greatest obstacle to reunion. "In the forty years in which I have been studying Reformation history I have built up the conviction with ever greater assurance, that the deepest gulf which divides Catholics and Protestants from each other is not Justification and the teaching on salvation, but the teaching on the Church itself."[94]

CONCLUSION

Jedin's significance for church history lies in his application of a critical historical method to the study of an age that was always an object of controversy. This resulted in the historiographical transformation of Reformation era history, raising it from the apologetic to the historical plane. Jedin's historical scholarship fostered the abandonment of confessionalism that characterized church history, particularly in the recounting of the events of the sixteenth century. At the same time, Jedin emphasized the broader European context of religious history.

Jedin rejects confessionalism as a valid historiographical criterion and substitutes extensive research in attempting to recount the details of a particular event. Consequently, Jedin's works differ from earlier polemical religious histories, as he presents the facts in a more impartial manner. Similarly, Jedin goes beyond the narrow limits of nationality common in the historical works of his predecessors, who presented the Reformation era as inherently German.[95] It was perhaps Jedin's ten-year sojourn in Rome that gave him a broad European vision and understanding of the religious happenings of the sixteenth century. This is evident in the first volume of his history of Trent, which presents a rich and suggestive panorama of the religious and ecclesiastical conditions of Europe prior to the emergence of Luther.

Jedin's ability to move church history away from confessionalism rests on his insistence that the study of religious history be approached in the same manner as secular history. Jedin was guided by a critical analysis of the documentary sources. This important contribution to the study of the Reformation era resulted from the rigorous application of the methods of historical research to religious history.

In recent years, the study of sixteenth- and seventeenth-century Catholicism has witnessed a renewed interest on the part of scholars. This is in no small measure due to Jedin's scholarship, in particular his study of the Council of Trent. Much of Jedin's own studies focused essentially on the pre-history and history of the Council of Trent. In so doing, he laid the foundation for the future research in this area. Through his mastery of source material, his vast erudition even on marginal questions, his sympathetic understanding of his subject, and his impartiality, Hubert Jedin redirected the approach to the contemporary study of church history.

BIBLIOGRAPHY

PRIMARY SOURCES

Jedin, Hubert, "Il significato del Concilio di Trento nella storia della Chiesa." *Gregorianum* 26 (1945): 117–136.
Katholische Reformation oder Gegenreformation? Lucern, 1946.
Papal Legate at the Council of Trent: Cardinal Seripando. Translated by Frederic C. Eckhoff. St. Louis: Herder, 1947.
"Esame di coscienza di uno storico." *Quaderni di Roma* 1 (1947): 206–17.
"La riforma ecclesiastica e l'umanesimo." *Humanitas* 3 (1948): 817–23.
"Riforma e concilio nel pensiero di Lutero." *Humanitas* 4 (1949): 276–92.
Il tipo ideale di vescovo secondo la riforma cattolica. Brescia: Morcelliana, 1950.

"The Blind 'Doctor Scotus.' *The Journal of Ecclesiastical History* 1 (1950): 76–84.

"Il Sarpi storico del Concilio di Trento." *Humanitas* 7 (1952): 495–504.

A History of the Council of Trent. 2 vols. Translated by Ernest Graf. St. Louis: B. Herder Book Co., 1957–1961.

Ecumenical Councils of the Catholic Church: A Historical Outline. Translated by Ernest Graf. New York: Herder, 1959.

"Is the Council of Trent an Obstacle to Reunion?" *The Eastern Churches Quarterly* 15 (1962–63): 209–23.

"The Council of Trent and Reunion: Historical Notes." *Heythrop Journal* 3 (1962): 3–14.

"Luther: A New View." *Chicago Studies* 5 (1966): 53–63.

Crisis and Closure of the Council of Trent: A Retrospective View from the Second Vatican Council. London: Sheed and Ward, 1967.

Chiesa della Fede Chiesa della Storia. Saggi scelti. edited by Giuseppe Alberigo. Brescia: Morcelliana, 1972.

"Come e perche ho scritto una storia del Concilio di Trento." *Humanitas* 31 (1976): 90–105.

Jedin, Hubert, and John Dolan, eds. *Handbook of Church History.* 7 vols. New York: Herder and Herder, 1965.

SECONDARY SOURCES

Alberigo, Giuseppe. "Hubert Jedin (1900–1980)." *Cristianesimo nella storia* 1 (1980): 273–278.

Samulski, Robert. "Bibliographie Hubert Jedin." *Annali dell'Istituto storico italo-germanico in Trento* 6 (1980): 287–367.

NOTES

1. John P. Dolan, "Obituary," *The Catholic Historical Review* 66 (1980): 701.

2. Giuseppe Alberigo, "Hubert Jedin (1900–1980)," *Cristianesimo nella storia* 1 (1980):273.

3. Hubert Jedin, "Come e perche ho scritto una storia del Concilio di Trento," *Humanitas* 31 (1976):90.

4. Dolan, "Obituary," 701.

5. Ibid., 701–702.

6. Jedin, "Come e perche," 91.

7. Ibid., 92.

8. Ibid.

9. Ibid., 93.

10. Ibid., 94.

11. Ibid., 94–95.

12. Ibid., 100.

13. Dolan, "Obituary," 703.

14. Hubert Jedin, "Esame di coscienza di uno storico," *Quaderni di Roma* 1 (1947): 206–17.

15. Ibid., 208.

16. Ibid.

17. Ibid., 209.

18. Hubert Jedin, "Considerazioni sul compito dello storico della chiesa," *Chiesa della Fede Chiesa della Storia*, ed. Giuseppe Alberigo (Brescia: Morcelliana, 1972), 18.

19. Ibid., 19.

20. Ibid.

21. Ibid., 20.

22. Ibid.

23. Ibid.

24. Ibid., 21.

25. Ibid., 22.

26. Ibid., 24.

27. Ibid., 26.

28. Hubert Jedin, "General Introduction to Church History," *Handbook of Church History*, eds. Hubert Jedin and John Dolan (New York: Herder and Herder, 1965), 1:1.

29. Ibid.

30. Ibid., 2.

31. Ibid., 3.

32. Hubert Jedin, "La storia della chiesa e teologia e storia," *Chiesa della Fede*, 52.

33. Ibid.

34. Ibid., 53.

35. Ibid., 54.

36. Ibid.

37. Ibid.

38. Jedin, "General Introduction to Church History," 3.

39. Jedin, "La storia della chiesa e teologia e storia," 58.

40. Ibid.

41. Robert Samulski, "Bibliographie Hubert Jedin," *Annali dell'Istituto storico italogermanico in Trento* 6 (1980): 287–367.

42. Hubert Jedin, *Katholische Reformation oder Gegenreformation?* (Lucerne, 1946). While no English translation is available of this work, there is an Italian translation by Marola Guarducci, *Riforma Cattolica o Controriforma?* (Brescia: Morcelliana, 1967). The Italian edition will be utilized in this chapter.

43. Jedin, *Riforma Cattolica o Controriforma?* 13.

44. Ibid., 14.

45. Ibid., 18.

46. Ibid., 44–45.

47. Ibid., 49.

48. Ibid., 49.

49. Ibid., 52.

50. Ibid., 53.

51. Hubert Jedin, *Papal Legate at the Council of Trent: Cardinal Seripando*, trans. Frederic C. Eckhoff (St. Louis: B. Herder Book Co., 1947), 113.

52. Ibid., 325.

53. Ibid., 391.

54. Hubert Jedin, "Il significato del Concilio di Trento nella storia della Chiesa," *Gregorianum* 26 (1945): 118.

55. Paolo Sarpi, *Istoria del Concilio Tridentino* (London, 1619) and Sforza Pallavicino, *Istoria del Concilio di Trento*, 3 vols. (Rome, 1656–57).

56. Hubert Jedin, *A History of the Council of Trent*, trans. Ernest Graf (St. Louis: B. Herder Book Co., 1957), 1:1. Subsequent references to this work will appear as *HCT*.

57. Giuseppe Alberigo, "The Council of Trent," *Catholicism in Early Modern History: A Guide to Research*, ed. John O'Malley (St. Louis: Center for Reformation Research, 1988), 217–18.

58. Hubert Jedin, "Il Sarpi storico del Concilio di Trento," *Humanitas* 8 (1952): 499.

59. Ibid.

60. Ibid.

61. Ibid., 500.

62. *HCT*, 2:7.

63. Ibid.

64. Ibid., 2:7–8.

65. Ibid., 2:8.

66. Ibid., 2:9.

67. Ibid., 2:518.

68. Ibid., 2:520.

69. Jedin, "Il Sarpi storico del Concilio di Trento," 503.

70. Ibid.

71. *HCT*, 2:521.

72. Ibid., 1:32–61.

73. Ibid., 1:200–201.

74. Ibid., 1:218.

75. Ibid., 1:355.

76. Ibid., 1:310.

77. Ibid., 2:443.

78. Stephan Kuttner, review of *Geschichte des Konzils von Trient. Band 3: Bologneses Tagung Zweite Trienter Tagungsperiode*, by Hubert Jedin, in *The American Historical Review* 78 (1973): 91–92.

79. Robert Trisco, review of *Geschichte des Konzils von Trient. Band 4: Dritte Tagungsperiode und Abschluss*, by Hubert Jedin, in *The Catholic Historical Review* 64 (1978): 502.

80. Ibid.

81. Ibid.

82. Ibid., 505.

83. Hubert Jedin, *Crisis and Closure of the Council of Trent: A Retrospective View from the Second Vatican Council* (London: Sheed and Ward, 1967), 163.

84. Ibid., 164.

85. Ibid.

86. Ibid., 165.

87. Hubert Jedin, "Is the Council of Trent an Obstacle to Reunion?" *The Eastern Churches Quarterly*, 15 (1962–63): 210.

88. Ibid., 210–11.

89. Ibid., 211.

90. Ibid., 214.

91. Ibid., 215.

92. Ibid., 216.

93. Ibid.

94. Ibid., 217.

95. Alberigo, "Hubert Jedin," 275.

24

HERBERT BUTTERFIELD

ROBERT CLOUSE

Herbert Butterfield (1900–1979) was born in the village of Oxenhope in Yorkshire. His mother was a member of the Plymouth Brethren and his father, Albert, was a staunch Methodist. A number of textile mills provided employment in this area of England and Albert Butterfield worked as a bookkeeper in one of the mills. He had wanted to be a minister, but financial problems had forced him to leave school at age ten. Despite this disappointment he worked part-time at a religious vocation, becoming the leader of a Wesleyan class meeting consisting of about twelve to sixteen young mill workers. He also insisted that his family attend the Methodist church several times each Sunday.

Herbert respected his father and the most important religious influence on him did not seem to be these organized religious meetings, but rather the frequent walks that they took. From the age of seven until the age of fourteen Herbert with his father walked in the evening, discussing nature, faith, God, or similar topics. The Butterfield family was fortunate because the father's employer gave them magazines, books, and music, and even helped them to buy a piano. These early years set the pattern for Herbert's later development as a Christian scholar.

The faith that Butterfield was reared in has been "described as a liberal version of evangelical Methodism." There was no great emphasis on doctrine, but the church and his father believed in the main teachings of orthodoxy—God and Providence; the redeemer, Christ, born divine and human; the resurrection of Christ; the reality of sin in the human heart; the need for personal salvation; and the ultimate authority of the Bible.[1] More crucial than these doctrinal beliefs, however, was the need for a genuine religious experience which resulted in a deep spirituality and an attitude of humility, love, and kindness toward others.

THE MAKING OF A HISTORIAN

Herbert attended a grammar school in the neighboring town of Keighly. In addition to his studies he began preaching in Methodist chapels when he was seventeen. He passed the advanced level examinations in history, English, and French at age eighteen and was given a scholarship in history at Peterhouse, Cambridge. By this time he wanted to become a writer but consoled himself by thinking that historical studies would be an excellent preparation for such a career.

When Butterfield arrived at Cambridge University in 1919, he was in a very different world from his familiar Yorkshire surroundings. The prevailing atmosphere was sophisticated, upper-class, and Anglican whereas he had a simpler, working class or lower middle class, and Nonconformist background. He related these two worlds in his own personality by maintaining an inner personal religious life along with an outer academic career which resulted in some outstanding technical historical studies. At first he made no attempt to link these two worlds. Even when he did in his 1948 lectures on "Christianity and History," many would question his success in the project.

Butterfield carried on his religious life through prayer, daily Bible reading, and regular attendance at worship services. He was active in the Wesley Methodist Church and preached in several chapels in the Cambridge area. Even after he stopped preaching in 1936, he continued to teach Church History at Wesley House, Cambridge. In the 1920s, when liberalism was gaining ground, he took a stand against the movement, but he never became an Evangelical. He felt that the flexibility of liberals in the matters of biblical criticism and theological thought was too helpful to give up. When he arrived at his mature faith, it was neither liberal nor evangelical. His diary entry of August 27, 1932, explains:

> To live a life of piety is inwardly to trust God and often to have communion with him and also to place one's treasure in heaven. The fruits

of this are contentment and reconciliation within the self, and the acquisition of inner life—the building up of a fund of spiritual resources, and the deepening of personality. The blossom is in charity that overflows to all men, and in a life that is lived humbly in the world. In all this there is something very difficult for sophisticated men. And it is utter foolishness to those who are worldly wise.[2]

In his outer vocational world Butterfield abandoned his earlier desire to be a writer or a minister and, carried along by the influences at Cambridge, became a historian. He studied under Paul Vellacott and Harold Temperley, the diplomatic historian known for his research on George Canning. From Temperley he learned history in the Rankean tradition, employing the careful use of evidence, the critical method, and a belief that finality and precision are possible in diplomatic history. Despite this emphasis on technical history, he continued to read novels, poetry, plays, and detective stories. In 1923, he won a prize for his essay on the historical novel.[3]

Another influence on Butterfield was the work of Lord John Acton (1834–1902), Regius Professor of Modern History at Cambridge from 1892–1902. Acton was an individual to whom Christian faith was important in his studies. He stressed the value of individual liberty and believed that a scholar had a right to judge historical figures. Despite his profound respect for Acton, Butterfield could not accept his idea of judging earlier generations by contemporary standards. Rather Butterfield taught that historians have no right to bring moral judgment to bear on other times.

HISTORICAL WRITINGS

Butterfield presented these ideas in *The Whig Interpretation of History* (1931), where he warned against "textbook history," that is, the tendency to trace a straight line from the past to whatever the writer found favorable about the present. The particular case that he used to illustrate this was the habit of crediting the Protestant Whigs as the force behind English political and religious liberty. In reality, freedom developed from a strange dialectic of clashing circumstances and wills. Butterfield argued, "It is not by a line but by a labyrinthine piece of network that one would have to make the diagram of the course by which religious liberty has come down to us, for this liberty comes by devious tricks and is born of strange conjunctures, it represents purposes marred perhaps more than purposes achieved, and it owes more than we can tell to many agencies that had little to do with either religion or liberty."[4]

Despite his strictures, in a later work, *The Englishman and His History* (1944), Butterfield celebrated the Whig interpretation and stated that, in its initial stages, it had been an advance in historical interpretation. The moderation of the Whigs caused the situation in eighteenth-century England to contrast sharply with that in France. The philosophes on the continent, he argued, produced a cleavage between Roman Catholicism and secular liberalism. In England there had been no similar rupture with the Christian tradition; for this reason, both English individualism and patriotism were less dangerous. English society was not torn by the pagan hatred generated by secular liberalism because Whigs were never forced into an anti-Christian stance and the churches did not need to take a reactionary position. The line between Christian and non-Christian elements was vague, and "even those who would have claimed to have jettisoned Christian dogma" were still influenced by it. "So the new and the old were allowed to mingle and frontiers were blurred, producing another piece of that English history which, like a weed, grows over the fences, chokes and smothers the boundaries—luxurious and wanton as life itself—to drive the geometers and the heavy logicians to despair."[5] These frontiers combined in such a way that the whole nation "could appropriate the traditions of monarchy, aristocracy, bourgeoisie, and church."[6]

In addition to historiography, Butterfield maintained his interest in diplomatic history and narrative and, in 1929, produced his most detailed monograph, *The Peace Tactics of Napoleon, 1806–1808*. This book explores the relationship between Napoleon and Czar Alexander, a relationship that led the Russian ruler to desert his Prussian ally and agree to the Treaty of Tilsit (1807). Another important monograph, *George III, Lord North, and the People (1779–80)*, concentrated on the history of politics, particularly the influence of public opinion on the King, his ministers and Parliament. This book developed from Butterfield's interest in Charles James Fox, whose papers had been given to him by George M. Trevelyan in the early 1930s.

The year 1949 was crucial in Butterfield's career because in that brief period his second major monograph appeared and his two most widely known books, *The Origins of Modern Science, 1300–1800* and *Christianity and History* were published. Both of these were the result of invitations to deliver lecture series on areas that were new to him. In the first instance, a Cambridge committee on the history of modern science led by Joseph Needham invited him to speak in order to bridge the gap between the sciences and the humanities. His study begins during the Middle Ages, when the outlook of Aristotle was accepted; it traces the gradual emergence of the new views in dynamics with individuals such as Galileo, in celestial mechanics through the work of Copernicus, Kepler, and Newton, in anatomy and physiology with Vesalius and Harvey, and in methodology through Bacon and Descartes. He also discusses the philosophes, the revolution in chemistry and eighteenth-century evolutionary ideas. The book emphasizes the thesis that the Scientific Revolution "outshines everything since the rise of Christianity and reduces the Renaissance and Reformation to the rank of mere episodes."[7] Butterfield's discussion was unique in the sympathy that he demonstrated with theories that failed as well as those that triumphed. He did this in the context of focusing on certain intellectual problems which puzzled previous generations and whose solution involved a change in humankind's ideas about the world. The result was a depth and subtlety of interpretation never before achieved in a work on the origins of science.

Christianity and History, Butterfield's other major contribution, developed from a request by the Cambridge Faculty of Divinity to deliver a lecture series. Although not a philosopher or theologian, Butterfield shared with his audience a lifetime of Bible study, a deep personal commitment to Christ, and a profound understanding of narrative history. "The lectures were a wild success. For seven Saturday mornings during October and November, 1948, perhaps eight hundred dons and students listened to Butterfield talk about the limits of historical study, human personality, sin and cupidity, judgment, cataclysm, Providence, Christianity, the Promise, and Jesus. The BBC broadcast six of his lectures during the spring of 1949, and in October 1949 Butterfield published the lectures, revised, in the book *Christianity and History*."[8]

These opportunities indicate the wide respect that was accorded to Butterfield at his university. In 1955, he was chosen Master of Peterhouse. He presided over a college eminent in many academic disciplines, but especially distinguished in history. In 1959 he was elected Vice-chancellor of the university. During his tenure in this position he successfully defended the tutorial approach against government officials who were determined to change the teaching method of the university in the direction of the newer British Institutions which operated along the lines of American state universities.

For outstanding service to his profession, college and university he was knighted in 1968. During his thirteen years in administrative work, Butterfield found it difficult to continue his research activities. Consequently he resigned from his mastership in 1968 and moved to a village outside Cambridge intending to resume his research and writing. Whether it was due to physical problems or the habits of many years he could not regain his former intensity and thus never finished his projected study of Charles James Fox.

Undoubtedly one of the reasons for this was his popularity as a speaker. He lectured in Germany in 1938, 1948, 1949 and 1950, delivered the Riddell Memorial Lectures at Durham University in 1951; the David Murray Lecture at Glasgow University in 1951; and the Wiles at the Queen's University in Belfast in 1954. In fact, the last lectures were established by a private donor who admired his writings, and Butterfield continued to serve on the management board of the Wiles Trust. He also served as the editor of the *Cambridge Historical Journal* from 1938 to 1952 and in his later years acted as the founding-chairperson of the British Committee for the Theory of International Politics.

FAITH AND HISTORY

Butterfield's writings on Christianity appeared at an opportune time because they became part of the spiritual and intellectual movement that spread through the Western World during and after World War II. Writers such as C. S. Lewis, T. S. Eliot, Dorothy Sayers, Christopher Dawson, David Knowles, Gordon Rupp, Reinhold Niebuhr, Kenneth Scott Latourette, Jacques Ellul, Hendrickson Berkhof, and Jacques Maritain figure in this renewal of a predominately Augustinian view of man and God.[9] An entire generation that had fought in the war, experienced the tension of the East-West conflict and the threat of nuclear destruction, appeared to have been influenced by what has been termed "foxhole" religion. To put it another way, there was a renewal of Christianity that touched every level of Western society. Butterfield was important to this movement through his example and his teaching, which he expressed in both oral and written form. Perhaps his greatest significance lay in the part he played in making the Christian historian respectable. His prestigious position in one of the world's greatest intellectual centers and his popularity as a leader at Cambridge demonstrated that a Christian could make his faith relevant to the twentieth century. A "world come of age" still needed the insights of one whose life was deeply influenced by the Christian gospel.

In addition to his personal example, he also attempted to relate faith and history in many of his lectures and writings. These ideas are presented in a rather different form than one would expect because they involve political narration, technical studies of historiography and the history of diplomacy rather than work focusing on the incarnation and the life of the church. Much of his thought centers on two major themes: humankind and providence.

Butterfield regarded the human personality as supremely important and emphasized the dignity and value of each individual. This outlook runs throughout his writing and contrasts sharply with the quantitative, Marxist, or Behaviorist emphases of many of his contemporaries. However, his humanistic viewpoint was not of the liberal, utopian, and optimistic kind, for he regarded humans as limited by sin. This was manifested in several characteristics including cupidity, self-righteousness, willfulness and sloth. Cupidity or avarice (a strong desire for gain), he believed, is common to everyone at all social levels. This desire of each individual to improve his condition of existence, while responsible for much achievement, has also led to friction and struggle because the welfare of others is forgotten. Humans are also self-righteous as they believe that virtue and progress lie with their class, race, or nation. Unreasonableness and troublemaking are always the result of those who represent the "other." The indictment of the human condition continues by pointing out that people are self-righteous and presumptuos because they try to master the course of history through war and violence. Finally, Butterfield states that the catastrophes of history do not occur because of some particular evil deeds, but are due to the fact that many do not perform their duties in an acceptable manner. As he puts it: "A civilization may be wrecked without any spectacular crimes or criminals but by constant petty breaches of faith and minor complicities on the part of men generally considered very nice people."[10]

Although people follow their own inclinations and desires, their efforts are still harmonized by divine providence. Butterfield often used the analogy of a symphony in which each individual plays his part in the orchestra and does not realize how it fits into the whole, while God, the composer blends them together to make a harmony. "There is a Providence that we must regard as lying in the very constitution of things."[11] This conception of providence puts less emphasis on supporting and providing for humankind and more on judgment and grace. He illustrates these ideas by referring to Napoleon and Hitler, who were punished for their selfishness and presumption by being destroyed, while others, including Frederick the Great and Bismarck, although proud, were more moderate in action; consequently, retribution on the Prussian system came later with the destruction of its successor, the Third Reich. Some political units such as ancient Rome and the British Empire began through the plundering of other lands and changed to a great extent into more lawful entities, but they still collapsed because of their sin. Thus a divine historical order operates through judgment on all human systems.

Providence has a brighter side, however, and through grace it can bring good from evil. The London fire of 1666 cleared the dingy old town and led to the construction of a finer city. The British arrogance that provoked the American colonists to rebel led to a better system of empire. Butterfield often cites the operation of grace in history, returning to the example of the Reformation and the rise of toleration. The Protestant movement led to a period of bitter religious wars. Rather then crediting any of the various churches or sects with the growth of the idea of religious liberty, he believes that the resulting cynicism and war weariness led to a new method of handling religious dissent. As Adam Watson, one of his close friends, summarized his views: "So toleration comes, not through any belief in freedom of religion, and certainly not from thinking that religion doesn't matter, not even from a positive belief in peace. It comes in spite of a nagging sense among weary believers that they were failing in their duty, that they were craven, or worldly wise. Their consciences were pulled by preachers like John Bunyan who exhorted them to continue the good fight and to be valiant against all disaster. But they could not go on. Religious toleration came in the end through exhaustion: spiritual as well as material."[12]

Butterfield even goes farther in applying his idea of providence and states that even examples of undeserved suffering such as the case of Israel or the treatment of Christ may call people to repentance and to a deeper understanding of God's purposes in history. In fact: "It is hard to rid oneself of the impression that in general the highest vision and the rarest creative achievements of the mind must come from great internal pressure, and are born of a high degree of distress. In other words, the world is not merely to be enjoyed but is an arena for moral striving."[13]

Butterfield also emphasizes the need for sympathetic imagination in studying individuals from the past. The historian must try to "walk alongside" those from another age. This involves the exercise of something like charity or love as one begins to understand someone unlike oneself and tries to interpret contrasting personalities fairly. In a thoughtful essay, "God in History," he brings together various historical approaches. This is done by looking at events from three levels and with three types of analysis. At the first level one may say "that men's actions make history—and men have free will—they are responsible for the kind of history that they make. But, then, secondly, at a different level, we find that history, like nature itself, represents a realm of law—its events are in a certain sense reducible to laws. However unpredictable history may be before it has happened it is capable of rational explanation once it has happened. . . . Now these two things are difficult enough to reconcile in themselves—

first of all the free will of human beings and secondly the reign of law in history. . . . But there is a further factor that is operative in life and in the story of the centuries—one which in a sense includes these two other things—namely the Providence of God, in whom we live and move and have our being. And in part the Providence of God works through these two other things—it is Providence which puts us in a world where we run all the risks that follow from free will and responsibility. It is Providence which puts us into a world that has its regularities and laws—a world therefore that we can do something with, provided we learn about the laws and the regularities of it."[14]

Butterfield also believes that the historian and the Christian can agree on the uniqueness of individuals and events. Some of his comments defend both his faith and his discipline in a masterful way, as he states that "in the long run it is always of great significance, however, that Christianity sees human beings as souls meant for eternity, unlike anything else in creation; and it is possible that the greatest of future conflicts between Christian and pagan will concern the question whether the individual personality is regarded as an absolute or man is envisaged as merely part of nature; part of the animal kingdom. Now the thing which we have come to regard as history would disappear if students of the past ceased to regard the world of men as a thing apart—ceased to envisage a world of human relations set up against nature and the animal kingdom. Because in man the spiritual and the temporal intersect, every moment, every individual, matters, every human soul is worth befriending."[15]

So Butterfield emphasizes the spiritual aspect of humanity. Although we are sinners, the way is open to eternal life though the New Testament teaching of redemption. As Christians communicate these truths, they perform a task that contributes by-products, including the major elements of contemporary Western liberal culture. Those who serve Christ, Butterfield believes, have always helped the world more than they realized—indeed, probably more than they would have wished if they could have foreseen the consequences, because "spiritual forces have an extraordinary spontaneity and originality so that we can never tell what a man may not do when he says to himself 'How shall I worship God?', and we can never tell what he may not do just for love. . . . Our religion as it mixes with the events of the world, generates new things—now a kind of art, now a form of science, now humanism, now liberty, now a theory of egalitarianism."[16]

AN EVANGELICAL ASSESSMENT

It is difficult to assess the work of such a versatile, gifted scholar as Butterfield. Every Christian should appreciate the major apologetic role that he performed in one of the great centers of modern culture. Yet an Evangelical must raise some questions about his work. Perhaps the major concern is his lack of trust in the God who reveals Himself through Scripture. Humans through reason cannot find God, and Butterfield's explanation of Providence in another person's hands could come out quite differently. He believed that the Old Testament prophets were not inspired by God but rather spoke in reaction to contemporary historical events. With a similar attitude he compares the Gospel accounts to stories about Winston Churchill. Many of these anecdotes he believed "that ultimately proved to be apocryphal might well be more true in a sense, more typical of the man, than another which could be established as absolutely correct. The person who invents such a story, or rounds it off in order to give it the Churchillian ring, is just the one who struggles to produce what contemporaries will accept as typical. It might even be true that the anecdotes in the mass can bring us nearer to the man than an historical work which absolutely restricts itself to the things that can be documentarily demonstrated. At the first level of analysis the historian is in a somewhat analogous position in respect to the man Jesus. It is more possible for us to form a general picture of him than to distinguish which of the detailed anecdotes are authentic."[17]

Butterfield's concept of God as expressed through the metaphor of a composer who improvises his work to repair human mistakes does not harmonize with the Christian teaching of the Almighty Creator, Sustainer and Redeemer of the universe. As historian William Speck has pointed out, "We can welcome Sir Herbert's revival of a doctrine of providence, too frequently ignored in our time. Yet, is that doctrine, unaccompanied by a doctrine of Christ, the church, and the parousia an adequate basis for a Christian interpretation of history?"[18]

There is also a problem in much of Butterfield's approach for those who feel that they must share the gospel of Christ with others. His emphasis on a spiritual life that demonstrates itself in "humble charity" is not clear enough to win others to the Lord. The way of salvation must be made more explicit for those who live in the tumultuous modern technological era. For Evangelicals, two other outstanding twentieth-century Cambridge graduates, J. N. D. Anderson and John R. W. Stott, are more reliable guides to a Christian interpretation of life and history.[19] Although Butterfield misses many important matters in his attempt to bring Christianity and history together, his work has helped believers. His oft-quoted advice at the conclusion of *Christianity and History* suggests "the elasticity" that more Christians should follow rather than bickering over political and social matters: "Hold to Christ and for the rest be totally uncommitted."[20]

NOTES

1. C.T. McIntire, *Herbert Butterfield, Writings on Christianity and History* (New York: Oxford University Press, 1979), xxi. For further biographical information on Butterfield, see Maurice Cowling, "Herbert Butterfield: 1900–1979," *Proceedings of the British Academy*, vol. 65, *1970* (London: Oxford University Press, 1981), 595–609. See also the memorial address by Owen Chadwick and comments by Brian Wormald, "Obituaries: Sir Herbert Butterfield," *The Cambridge Review* (November 16, 1979): 6–9; and Patrick Cosgrave, "An Englishman and His History," *Spectator* 243 (July 28, 1979): 22–23. For a bibliography of Butterfield see: R. W. K Hinton in *The Diversity of History: Essays in Honor of Herbert Butterfield*, ed. J. H. Elliott and H. G. Koenigsberger (London: Routledge and Kegan Paul, 1970), 315–25.

2. Butterfield as quoted in McIntire, *Herbert Butterfield*, xxvvi.

3. Herbert Butterfield, *The Historical Novel: An Essay* (Cambridge: Cambridge University Press, 1965), 45.

4. Herbert Butterfield, *The Whig Interpretation of History* (New York: Norton, 1965), 45.

5. Herbert Butterfield, *The Englishman and His History* (Cambridge: Cambridge University Press, 1944), 122F.

6. Ibid., 139.

7. Herbert Butterfield, *The Origins of Modern Science 1300–1800* , revised edition (New York: Free Press, 1957).

8. McIntire, *Herbert Butterfield*, xv.

9. C. T. McIntire, ed., *God, History, and Historians: Modern Christian Views of History* (N.Y.: Oxford University Press, 1977).

10. Ibid.

11. Ibid, 95.

12. Adam Watson, "Toleration in Religion and Politics," in *Herbert Butterfield: The Ethics of History and Politics*, ed. Kenneth W. Thompson (Washington, D.C.: University Press of America, 1980), 73f.

13. Butterfield, *Christianity and History*, 76.

14. Ibid, 5ff.

15. Herbert Butterfield, "The Christian and Academic History" in McIntire, *Herbert Butterfield*, 181.

16. Herbert Butterfield, *Christianity in European History* (London: Collins, 1952), 55.

17. Herbert Butterfield, *The Origins of History* (N.Y.: Basic Books, 1981), 165.

18. William Speck, "Herbert Butterfield: The Legacy of a Christian Historian," in *A Christian View of History?* ed. G. Marsden and F. Roberts (Grand Rapids: Eerdmans, 1975), 116.

19. For Stott, see Christopher Catherwood, *Five Evangelical Leaders* (Wheaton, Ill.: Harold Shaw, 1985), 13ff. Also the *Festschrift* ed. M. Eden and D. F. Wells, *The Gospel in the Modern World, A Tribute to John Stott* (Leicester, England: Intervarsity Press, 1991). For Norman Anderson, notice his autobiography, *An Adopted Son: The Story of My Life* (Leicester, England: InterVarsity Press, 1985).

20. Herbert Butterfield, *Christianity and History*, 146.

25

STEPHEN NEILL

RICHARD V. PIERARD

Stephen Neill distinguished himself as an Anglican churchman, biblical scholar, missionary theorist, ecumenical leader, and historian. Born on the last day of the nineteenth century, December 31, 1900, his life spanned much of the twentieth, and he labored indefatigably almost to the day of his death, July 20, 1984. He possessed competence in biblical and classical languages as well as several modern European and Indian languages, and was the author, co-author, or editor of at least sixty-five books, as well as innumerable essays, reviews, addresses, and sermons. Because he never held a professorial appointment in his native Britain, it is easy to overlook his work, but his contributions to church history, or what he preferred to call "the church in history," are substantial.[1]

NEILL THE MANN

Stephen Charles Neill lived a long and full life, but details about some aspects of it are obscure. In 1973 he penned a rambling anecdotal autobiography, but he passed over some conflict situations and minimized some important events in his life. In fact, the thousand-page manuscript remained in typescript until Eleanor M. Jackson, a well-known scholar of modern Christianity in India and personal acquaintance of Neill, pared it down drastically and made it available to the reading public.[2] As yet, nobody has written a full-length, critical biography of him, but a few shorter essays and encyclopedia entries have been published.[3]

Neill was born in Edinburgh, the third child of a husband-and-wife team of missionary doctors. His Scottish maternal grandfather, James Monro, first served in the Bengal Civil Service, then returned home to become a police commissioner in London. After resigning that post he studied medicine and returned to Bengal to create his own medical mission. His daughter Margaret Penelope (known by her nickname Daisy), who had decided to study medicine herself, fell in love with an Ulster medical student at Cambridge, Charles Neill. The son of a wealthy wine merchant, Charles had come under the influence of the late nineteenth-century evangelical revivals and was converted while at Cambridge. The two were married after completing their studies and went to India, but they were home on furlough when their son was born. Although Stephen spent his first two years in India, this experience had no apparent impact on him. The Neills returned to Britain in 1903 because of health problems. Charles then received some theological training and was ordained an Anglican priest, and he spent the next four decades alternating between serving parishes in southern England and working in India. The pair eventually retired in India and died at Coonoor.

Stephen was raised in a family environment marked by evangelical and Keswick piety and a Victorian sense of duty and discipline. Thus it is not surprising that in 1912 his father placed him in the Dean Close School at Cheltenham, an unabashedly evangelical boarding school for boys, where he proved to be a precocious youth. He received a first-rate classical education and demonstrated a love of reading and facility for languages that would be a hallmark of his life. He taught himself Hebrew at night by flashlight while under the bedcovers. In 1914 while recovering from mumps, he had a distinct conversion experience in which he suddenly "just knew" the reality of the atonement. He regarded his confirmation the following year as particularly memorable because he was already a convinced Christian. As a teenager he began to display the psychological symptoms that would plague him throughout his life—insomnia, deep depression, and outbursts of temper—all products of unmixed laterality, a condition in which one is neither right handed nor left handed. Others have suggested he suffered from repressed sexuality (one even said homosexuality), since he never married and had a negative attitude toward women involved professionally in Christian work.[4]

In December 1918 he won a scholarship to Trinity College, Cambridge, and his brilliance and diligence resulted in numerous awards and prizes and "firsts" in classical and theological studies. Neill became interested in the New Testament as well, mastering German in the process. Laboring in the wider world of a more liberal divinity school, he began breaking away from his strongly conservative upbringing and moving to a centrist evangelicalism.

Intensely desirous of winning a fellowship at Trinity College, he wrote a dissertation comparing the writings of the mystical neo-Platonist Plotinus with those of the Greek Cappadocian Fathers—Basil the Great, Gregory of Nyssa and Gregory of Nazianzus; he demonstrated that all three were under the philosophical influence of neo-Platonism.[5] Although he was successful and thereafter deeply treasured the relationship with Cambridge which the status of being a Fellow of Trinity College from 1924 to 1928 bestowed, he was unable to gain a suitable position in the academic community. His disappointment at being passed over for the post of Regius Professor of Divinity at Cambridge in 1950 was indeed great, and the academic appointments he did receive in later life were in universities abroad—Professor of Christian Missions and Ecumenical Theology at Hamburg (1962–67), Professor of Philosophy and Religious Studies at the University of Nairobi (1969–73), and short-term visiting professorships.

Neill's university years shaped him in two important ways. First, his studies, which focused on the interaction between Christianity and Hellenism in the European intellectual tradition, prepared him well for his future work as a missionary. The mysticism of Plotinus enabled him to understand Hindu monism and served as a foundation for his later writing on Christianity and other faiths. The emphasis on the classical writers and church fathers (rather than the Reformation) gave him a catholicity of mind not usually seen in an evangelical Anglican, and this comprehensiveness would orient him toward ecumenism.

The second influence was his involvement in Christian student work. Being an evangelical, Neill joined the Cambridge Inter-Collegiate Christian Union (CICCU), the forerunner of the Inter-Varsity Fellowship. Then, as his reputation in student ministry grew, he was asked, to his great surprise, to chair the Cambridge Student Christian Movement (SCM), the more liberal group. His work in the latter was his first real exposure to ecumenism on a national scale, and he spent considerable time in organizing university missions, student missions to towns and villages, and Bible study programs. He was not fully happy with either group, as he saw an empty liberalism on the SCM side and unthinking spiritual intransigence among the CICCU adherents. In April 1924 he participated in his first ecumenical gathering, the Conference on Christian Politics, Economics and Citizenship in Birmingham, and many years later he observed that from that point on he had "lived ecumenically."[6]

After finishing his studies in 1924, Neill decided to delay assuming his Trinity College fellowship and go with his parents and sister to South India to take up the life of a missionary (for a time with the Bible Churchmen's Missionary Society, which had split from the Anglican Church Missionary Society [CMS] in 1922). Reaching India in late 1924, they settled in the Tirunelveli (known to Europeans as Tinnevelly) region. Although he later claimed he had gone out under the CMS, in fact he did not join this group until four years later. The Neill family went to Dohnavur and resided in the compound of the celebrated Amy Carmichael. Almost at once tensions arose between the strong-willed Carmichael and the newcomers, who wanted to work more closely with the Indian villagers. The Drs. Neill departed within six months and Stephen stayed on until November 1925, when the final break between him and Carmichael occurred and he too left Dohnavur. The differences between them have never been clarified, and Neill himself completely omits any mention of this phase of his life from the autobiography. Jackson points out that the animosities were so deep that she severed her mission's connection with the Diocese of Tinnevelly when Neill was chosen as its bishop thirteen years later.[7]

Within a few months after arriving, he had mastered Tamil and began itinerant work on his own. He established a pattern that he would follow for the next two decades as a missionary in India—learning the language of the region in which he was laboring; placing heavy emphasis upon evangelism, literature work (providing catechists, teachers, and lay workers with notes and simple books in their language), theological education in the vernacular, and spiritual development of both the Christian workers and ordinary believers; manifesting an ecumenical spirit in all his endeavors. He clearly perceived a basic coherence of gospel, mission, and church. He also became known for his organizational efficiency, prodigious literary efforts, deep theological acumen, readiness to say unpopular things, and ability to discern an idea whose time had come.[8]

In all probability CMS/Anglican contacts in South India which he had made at Cambridge helped him find work after the break with Carmichael, and in 1926 he was ordained a deacon in the (Anglican) Church of India, Burma, and Ceylon. The following year he went home to take up his fellowship at Trinity College, Cambridge, after ordination as a priest in 1928, he returned to India. He now served under the auspices of the CMS, and became principal of Alwaye Christian College in Travancore state. After a brief term in this place, he relocated in Tirunelveli to engage in direct evangelism and in 1930 was appointed warden of Tirumaraiyur, a theological college just founded to train an Indian ministry. He set for himself and his clergy exacting standards of pastoral energy and published numerous works to guide their spiritual development. His great breadth of knowledge was reflected in the courses he taught—Old and New Testament, Christian Doctrine, Church History, Pastoral Theology, Religions of India, and Greek. In 1935 he was appointed to the General Council of the Church of India, Burma, and Ceylon, and here he learned the skills of working in a large-scale church organization. Through his involvement in the Madras conference of the International Missionary Council (1938), where he chaired a section "On the Training of the Ministry," and service as an Anglican delegate to the Joint Committee on Church Union in South India, Neill enhanced the ecumenical vision that was becoming the distingishing feature of his life.[9]

As his talents became increasing known and appreciated, it was only a matter of time until he would be named to a vacant diocese, and in January, 1939, he was consecrated Bishop of Tinnevelly, thus remaining in the area where he had been ministering for over a decade. As the youngest bishop in the Anglican communion, Neill was a hard-working, driven person who brooked no opposition from the British authorities or indigenous churchmen. Through his incessant labors he overextended himself, resulting in a health crisis in 1944, and he returned to England for medical treatment under circumstances that have never been explained precisely.

This reflects the point mentioned earlier that there was a darker side to Neill's life, the "thorn in the flesh," as Archbishop of Canterbury Donald Coggan aptly labeled it.[10] Richard Holloway, Bishop of Edinburgh, who knew Neill quite well, maintained in an essay in the *Church Times* that he had an obsessive concern with pain and punishment. He struggled constantly with God about these fantasies, which resulted in the bouts of deep depression and insomnia, a violent temper, and an almost insatiable appetite for praise. These problems were evident during his two decades of missionary service, and something definitely went wrong in 1944 that forced him to leave his post. Neill explained it in the autobiography as a breakdown in health. However, rumors circulated in India that during these outbursts of rage he had actually struck some indigenous clergy whose actions had met with his disapproval, and Archbishop Foss Westcott ordered him sent home for treatment.[11]

This would explain why Neill recognized there was little chance of further advancement in the Anglican Church and resigned his position in

Tinnevelly in 1946, but he never gave up his title as bishop. Reappearing in Cambridge, he was named chaplain of Trinity College and the Faculty of Divinity appointed him to a lectureship, and at once he became a popular lecturer and preacher. Because he showed such enthusiasm for ecumenism in his public addresses, the Archbishop of Canterbury appointed him Assistant Bishop in January 1947 with responsibility to represent the archdiocese in church matters in northern and central Europe and to act as liaison officer with the developing World Council of Churches. He now found a new calling in the ecumenical movement and in effect spent the rest of his life "wandering the earth as a theological mercenary," as Bishop Holloway so colorfully put it.

In June 1947 he gave up his Trinity chaplainship and moved to Geneva. The following month he took part in the Whitby (Ontario, Canada) meeting of the International Missionary Council (IMC), the first post-war ecumenical gathering. He wrote its main report, in which he launched the idea of "partnership in mission," and after this was named co-director of the Study Department of the IMC. In 1948 he drafted the crucial resolutions on the Church of South India at the Anglican Lambeth Conference in London, and at the founding assembly of the World Council of Churches (WCC) in Amsterdam he wrote the paper "The Church's Failure to Be Christian."[12] From 1948 to 1951 he served as the WCC's Associate General Secretary with responsibility for study and evangelism. He soon became a strong critic of the WCC's centralization, bureaucratization, and clericalization. In 1950 and 1951 he suffered from health problems again and had to resign both the assistant bishop and WCC posts. The following year with the help of friends he started a publishing venture, World Christian Books, which had financial support from the IMC. It was designed to educate the English-speaking church about theological concerns, including those raised by the emerging "younger" or Third World churches. He served as general editor, 1952–62, and as director until 1970. During its lifespan sixty-four books were published, including six which Neill authored himself and two others which he translated.

At the same time he lectured in Britain and throughout the world and was awarded several honorary doctorates, and the books flowed from his pen. Then in 1962 he was able to revive the career which he had essentially given up fifteen years earlier when he was named to the chair of missions at the University of Hamburg (Germany), succeeding the respected missiologist Walter Freytag, who had just died. Neill remained there until reaching retirement age in 1967. Since some years earlier he had conducted a study on theological education in Africa for the IMC[13] and was well-regarded there, the University College at Nairobi (Kenya) requested him in 1969 to help organize a department of religious studies. He remained at this post for four years and then retired again.

Honors continued to come, including election to the British Academy and an honorary D.D. from his beloved Cambridge. From 1979, when he was not traveling, Neill lived at Wycliffe Hall, Oxford, and served as an assistant bishop in the diocese and a mentor to ordinands. He resumed work on his first love, Indian history, and had completed two volumes of his magnum opus, *A History of Christianity in India*, when he died in Oxford at the age of 83. At his memorial service on October 31, 1984, in St. Margaret's, Westminster (London), various dignitaries of the Anglican church, including the Archbishop of Canterbury, paid their respects.[14]

NEILL THE SCHOLAR

BIBLICAL STUDIES AND APOLOGETICS

Stephen Neill wore many hats. He was a missionary, evangelist, teacher, church official, editor, lecturer, and above all a scholar. He was not a theologian, and it is debatable whether he was an original thinker in the areas where he published, but he was diligent in his research and his interests were catholic. In fact, his writings reflected on the church in its manifold expressions. In a brief essay it is impossible to discuss Neill's entire literary corpus. The excellent classical education he received guaranteed that he would be more than a run-of-the-mill scholar in biblical studies and apologetics.

Although Neill is generally remembered for his studies on mission history, many regard his most thoughtful and useful work to be a historical account of the trends in New Testament studies during modern times, *The Interpretation of the New Testament 1861–1961*. This was a lecture series given at the University of Nottingham which Oxford University Press published in 1964 and reissued in 1988 with an update by Tom Wright that covered the period 1961–88. It is one of the most informative one-volume surveys of the topic available. It reflects a commitment to the inspiration of the New Testament, an evangelical understanding of its meaning (including the existence of a historical Jesus and the need for personal salvation), and a willingness to deal critically with the various interpreters. Neill's focus on the personalities of the scholars involved in the debates over New Testament criticism, depth of knowledge of their works in the major European languages, and balanced assessment of their contributions make the book absorbing reading.

Other noteworthy contributions to biblical studies included paraphrases of Paul's letters to the Galatians (1958) and Colossians (1963), a study of

The Gospel According to St. John (Cambridge: Cambridge University Press, 1930; 2nd ed., 1950), *Jesus Through Many Eyes: Introduction to the Theology of the New Testament* (Philadelphia: Fortress, 1976), *Bible Words and Christian Meanings* (London: SPCK, 1970), two chapters in Michael Green, ed., *The Truth of God Incarnate* (Grand Rapids: Eerdmans, 1977), and the *Concise Dictionary of the Bible* (American title, *Modern Reader's Dictionary of the Bible*) which he co-edited with John Goodwin and Arthur Dowle (London: Lutterworth; New York, Association, 1966).

In the field of apologetics Neill's best-known work is *Christian Faith and Other Faiths: The Christian Dialogue with Other Religions*, first published in 1961 by Oxford University Press and most recently by InterVarsity Press in 1984. He contended that no general concept of religion exists under which all the particular forms of religion my be subsumed; comparison can only be made of ideas, not living traditions in their totality, and a faith may be experienced only as a whole, thus making the world faiths essentially incommensurable with one another. However, a Christian who is confident in his or her own beliefs is able to examine those of someone else. This does not involve indifference to truth or the abandonment of all objective criteria of judgment, because another religion may be evaluated with regard to its adequacy in the context of the total human situation. Even as we question the beliefs of others, we must reckon with their questioning of us, but if we stand within the truth, we have everything to gain by exposing ourselves to such investigation. This will help to elucidate our faith, open up aspects of it that were hidden from us, rid us of illusions, and strengthen our hold on that which we believe.

In approaching other faiths, one must acknowledge three categories in which Christians think. First is contingency—the world and people within it have reality and existence. But this is wholly dependent on forces and principles in that which is beyond us, on which the world exists and man can find his freedom. Second, people think in terms of purpose. There is a divine purpose in the universe, and individual persons operate in the realm of their own purposes. Third, events really do happen, and history is the medium in which we operate and God is prepared to operate. Human decisions count and do affect the future. For the Christian the future is a world of glorious possibilities, influenced but not predetermined by the past.

Thus, Christianity is the religion of a Man, and the relation that exists between the adherents of this religion and its founder is unlike that in any other faith. The historical figure of Jesus of Nazareth is the criterion by which every Christian affirmation must be judged. Through Jesus it is possible for one to be free, but this requires an understanding that structures exist which limit absolute freedom, one must live in total dependence upon God, and freedom can be exercised only in a context of suffering where the free individual criticizes all things by standards external to himself, standards established by a Man who died on the cross to make all people free. In other words, Jesus Christ is a figure of history in whom God's action is seen at a particular point in space and time. But this action occurs in a historical context that sees the love of God as operative throughout all time, from eternity past to eternity future. In Christianity the individual exists in relationship with God and with others, not in some sort of mystical absorption of self into God so that there is no longer any distinction between the two.

Moreover, the Christian gospel is unique because it is rooted in an event, not just an idea. In Jesus the one thing that needed to happen has happened, and it never needs to happen again. The universe has been reconciled to its God. Through the perfect obedience of Christ a new and permanent relationship has been established between God and the whole human race. No situation can ever arise in the future which cannot be interpreted in the light of this central event of human history.

Christians affirm that all people need the gospel. For the human sickness there is one specific remedy, and this is it. There is no other, and thus the gospel must be proclaimed to the ends of the earth and to the end of time. The church cannot compromise on its missionary task without ceasing to be the church. If it fails to take up this responsibility, it changes the gospel into something other than itself. The truth claim of Christ is not something set forth in propositions to which one must give intellectual assent, but in a person who demands surrender and self-commitment. Christians cannot compromise on this, but they must approach the other forms of human faith with deepest humility. If the Christian has really trusted in Christ, he can open himself without fear to any wind that blows from any quarter.[15]

This understanding of the Christian faith permeated all of Neill's writings on the interaction between Christianity and other religions and was the cornerstone of his philosophy of history. As for missionary work and the cross-cultural communication so vital to it, its task was making the Lordship of Christ known throughout the world and bringing to all people the benefits of eternal life in him. Although Neill was convinced of the validity of the universal claims of the Christian message, his approach to other faiths was that of dialogue rather than simply scoring debating points. He believed it was possible to learn from others and deepen one's own faith in the process. Other apologetic works reflecting this outlook included *Foundation Beliefs* (Madras: Christian Literature Society, 1937,

1941), *The Christians' God* (London: Lutterworth, 1948), *The Unfinished Task* (London: Lutterworth, 1957), *Creative Tension* (London: Edinburgh House, 1959), *What Is Man?* (London: Lutterworth, 1960), *The Eternal Dimension* (London: Epworth, 1963), *Salvation Tomorrow: The Originality of Jesus Christ and the World's Religions* (Nashville: Abingdon, 1976), and *The Supremacy of Jesus* (Downers Grove, Ill.: InterVarsity, 1984).

CHURCH HISTORY

Neill's most important general work in church history was *The Christian Society* (London: James Nisbet, 1952). It is a one-volume survey that focuses on the continuity of Christian society in the face of centuries of internal division and external conflict, but it pays little attention to dogmatic and theological matters. He believed Christianity is shaped by its environment and constantly regenerated by its readiness to adapt to new conditions and ideas. The book includes Neill's customary emphases: Christianity's leavening impact in the classical world,[16] the church's survival due to its continuing contact with Jesus Christ and resulting times of renewal, and its world-wide missionary expansion.

Neill also wrote a popular history of his church, *Anglicanism* (Harmondsworth: Penguin Books, 1958; 2nd ed., London: Mowbrays, 1977). This useful book examines the Church of England's Catholic roots, theological development, spiritual life, organizational structure, and worldwide expansion within the larger picture of the ecumenical movement. Anglican scholar Stephen Green points out that the book expressed Neill's own understanding of the church from the perspective of a "liberal Evangelical" and that it contained "his spiritual autobiography."[17] Neill's other noteworthy contributions to Anglican history include *The Ministry of the Church* (London: Canterbury Press, 1947), an exposition of the role of the episcopate in the church, *On the Ministry* (London: SCM, 1952), which deals with pastoral theology from an Anglican perspective, and his chapter "Liturgical Continuity and Change in Anglican Churches," in *No Alternative: The Prayer Book Controversy*, ed. David Martin and Peter Mullen (Oxford: Basil Blackwell, 1981), which surveys the historical evolution of its liturgy.

Neill was an evangelical committed to ecumenism in the tradition of evangelical ecumenists such as John R. Mott (1865–1955), Robert P. Wilder (1863–1938), and Kenneth Scott Latourette (1884–1968). Biographer Christopher Lamb notes that Neill wished to be a "reconciler" in the evangelical-ecumenical debate. He had confidence in "the general direction in which the evidence was moving" that came from a deeply held faith in God as the creator of all available evidence. His faith was not immune to advances in human knowledge and he asked ultimate questions. He admitted that if the bones of Jesus were to be found in a Palestinian grave, he would cease being a worshipping Christian, but no evidence of this had been found. Thus for him, a personal faith in the crucified and risen Jesus and the new life resulting from this was central, and personal conversion was at the heart of the Christian mission.

Accordingly, Neill discovered the necessity for ecumenism from missions. As he pointed out to an American theologian, "in a missionary environment one feels the shame of Christian divisions much more than in a Western country." There one sees more sharply the realities of the gospel. Speaking of his experiences in South India: "It was basically the need for unity in evangelism that drove us on to seek unity in the church."[18] Still, his misgivings about the growing emphasis on social justice by the World Council of Churches were evident in this statement: "Those who start at the social end never seem to get to the Gospel, whereas those who start with the Gospel sometimes accomplish, without knowing or intending it, the social revolution."[19]

Neill wrote often on the theme of church unity. Some were brief historical treatments of ecumenism that had a didactic quality, such as *Christ, His Church and His World* (London: Eyre and Spottiswoode, 1948), and *Christian Partnership* (London: SCM, 1952). Study books like *Towards a United Church, 1913–1947* (London: Edinburgh House, 1947) were intended for those involved in promoting ecumenism. His major work on Christian unity was *A History of the Ecumenical Movement 1517–1948*, which he edited with Ruth Rouse (London: SPCK; Philadelphia: Westminster, 1954). In 1968 Neill produced a second edition that contained some minor corrections and an updated bibliography.[20] Sponsored by the Ecumenical Institute at Bossey, Switzerland, it was not an official publication of the World Council of Churches, but it enjoyed the body's blessing. The volume contained lengthy contributions from thirteen eminent scholars as well as the two editors. It focused on ecumenical trends in Europe and North America since the Reformation, the various endeavors that arose in nineteenth- and early-twentieth-century Protestantism and fed into ecumenism, the attitudes of Eastern Orthodox and Roman Catholic figures toward these developments, and the formation of the WCC as the culminating event. Around half of the material dealt with the twentieth century. Several of the writers were participant-observers in the process and brought firsthand knowledge as well as scholarly research to their essays.

Although impressive in bulk, the book did not deal with all aspects of ecumenism. Essentially, it reflected Neill's own perspective. Most reviews were favorable, but its reception was not universally enthusiastic. Lutheran Hermann Sasse, for one, was quite critical, insisting that it was deficient in treating the matters of unity, schism, and heresy in the early church, lacked understanding of confessional problems in the Reformation and post- Reformation periods, and sidestepped the difficulties of intercommunion, since both the Roman Catholic and the Orthodox churches had refused to acknowledge the validity of Anglican ordination.[21]

Neill provided a personal view of the ecumenical movement in *Brothers of the Faith* (Nashville: Abingdon, 1960), written to commemorate the fiftieth anniversary of the World Missionary Conference at Edinburgh.[22] It is more or less an insider's account of the church unity movement and contains some fascinating vignettes of its luminaries. It is a skillful weaving together of Neill's own reminiscences and historical research that conveys rather pointedly his optimistic approach to ecumenism.

He also produced an edited volume, *Twentieth Century Christianity* (London: Collins, 1961), containing essays by a dozen scholars and churchmen that assessed from a historical approach the denominational developments and theological trends in various parts of the world. Since it appeared on the eve of the WCC's New Delhi Assembly, it was obviously intended to assist the delegates and observers in understanding the current situation. Neill insisted that, although during the previous two generations the Church of Jesus Christ had been torn and shaken, it was still putting forth new flowers and fruit and "the gates of hell shall not prevail against it." Another important edited work, sponsored by the Department on the Laity of the World Council of Churches, was *The Layman in Christian History*, which Neill put together with Hans-Ruedi Weber (Philadelphia: Westminster, 1963). Most of the fifteen contributors were church historians, and they persuasively showed that laypeople occupied significant roles in the church throughout its nineteen-hundred-year history. This was a significant corrective to the clericalism which so prevailed in conciliar circles at the time.

CHRISTIAN MISSIONS

Neill is most widely recognized for his historical work on Christian missions, much of which he completed during the Hamburg years. Yet he wrote in his autobiography that "it was never my intention to write mission history *per se*, which seems to me to be a very dull subject." What he hoped to do in *A History of Christian Missions* was simply deal with one aspect of God's purpose for the whole of the human race.[23] However, this work, the sixth volume in the Pelican History of the Church, proved to be enormously popular and is still used as a standard textbook in history of missions courses in theological schools in the English and German-speaking worlds.[24] It covers the story of the spread of Christianity, starting with its origins in the Roman Empire and moving through medieval times, the age of discovery, Roman Catholic and Protestant work in the early modern era, and into the modern period. Sixty percent of the book covers the last two centuries and is especially strong in its treatment of India and ecumenical developments, but it deals with all parts of the world newly touched by Christianity and does not overlook Roman Catholic and Orthodox contributions to Christian expansion. Neill was especially interested in the process whereby missions became churches, and he looked to the future with optimism even though Christianity was being challenged by secular ideologies and resurgent major religions.

Neill also recognized that missions had made great progress under European colonialism, but now the imperial era was passing. For him the important questions were these: (1) What consequences would the decline of Europe have on Christianity in the non-Western world? (2) To what extent were Christian missions dependent on political power from the West? He addressed these in his history of missions book. A follow-up volume, *Colonialism and Christian Missions* (New York: McGraw-Hill, 1966), treats the cause-and-effect-relationship between missions and colonial forces and shows this was a two-way street. The level of missionary involvement in colonialism varied from place to place and time to time. Sometimes missionaries supported colonialism—even at the leading edge—but almost always they did this for higher motives than those of the colonial regimes. This led frequentlly to differences between them and at times missionaries even opposed colonization or the policies of existing colonial governments. On occasions they served as mediators and brought about understanding and improved conditions between the colonial rulers and the colonized. Neill heavily emphasizes the motives and attitudes of those involved in the process.[25]

In 1970 Neill published three noteworthy missiological works. One was the *Concise Dictionary of the Christian World Mission,* co-edited with Gerald H. Anderson and John Goodwin (London: Lutterworth; Nashville: Abingdon), which contained useful entries on a wide range of topics authored by leading scholars in the field. Another was *Call to Mission* (Philadelphia: Fortress, 1970), which answered the objections to missionary work and affirmed the truth of Christianity. Neill insisted that if a Christian really believes the gospel of Christ is true, then he will be an ambassador for Christ.

To be sure, missionaries made many mistakes—overemphasis on Western culture, financial dominance of the new Christians, sectarian divisions among the sending churches, involvement in politics, and monopolizing positions of authority and responsibility in the new churches. On the other hand, missionaries did some things right: they endeavored to master the languages of the people and learn about their cultures; provided agricultural assistance, modern medicine, and education; and trained indigenous leaders to take over the work of the local churches. The missionary enterprise in the future will surely be carried on in new and different ways, but the gospel will continue to go forth.

In a paper delivered to the Ecclesiastical History Society entitled "The History of Missions: An Academic Discipline" (published in *The Mission of the Church and the Propagation of the Faith*, ed. G. J. Cuming [Cambridge University Press, 1970]), Neill made a strong case for including missions in the program of theological studies. He criticized earlier missionary literature for overemphasizing the internal developments of the mission societies, its hagiographical and edifying character, and failure to set the events recorded in the framework of contemporary history. He called for a reconsideration of how church history is studied and taught and insisted the church should be portrayed as the story of God at work among the nations, a dynamic power in dialogue or conflict with all the religions and cultures on earth. He laid out an agenda for work in mission history which included the following elements: redoing almost all the missionary biographies, producing ecumenically oriented area studies dealing in depth with the impact of the gospel on places and peoples, encouraging converts to write accounts of their experiences, giving serious consideration to studies by those who are hostile to missions, paying more attention to the work of marginal Christian groups and independent churches that developed outside the denominational mainstream, and analyzing the positions of those who came in contact with the Christian faith but did not accept it. Neill also called for greater participation by new scholars in the "younger churches" in the historiographical task. He had a far-seeing, expansive vision of historical scholarship which only now is beginning to be realized.

HISTORY OF CHRISTIANITY IN INDIA

In his last years Neill set out to fulfill his life's ambition—to write a general history of the spread of Christianity in the Indian subcontinent. He had already addressed some aspects of the topic in his first historical work, *Builders of the Indian Church* (London: Edinburgh House, 1934), which traced the development of Christianity beginning with Thomas Christians of Malabar and then focused on the activities of significant individuals—Francis Xavier, Robert de Nobili, C. F. Schwartz, William Carey, Alexander Duff, Pandita Ramabai, and others. He viewed with hope the transition from mission to church in India and with it the development of church union. He related the account of Christian development in more detail in *The Story of the Christian Church in India and Pakistan* (Grand Rapids: Eerdmans, 1970), a book in the "Discipling the Nations" series on the planting and development of churches throughout the world. This flowed from his deep feeling about the need for unity because the numbers of Christians are so small and from his conviction that missionaries should work in partnership with the Asian church and serve under its leadership, views which he had eloquently expressed in an earlier book about developments in India, Pakistan, and Sri Lanka after independence, *Under Three Flags* (New York: Friendship, 1954).

After he had returned from Nairobi and was ensconced in Oxford, where he had access to the incomparable resources of the Bodleian Library, Neill labored in earnest on his monumental venture. He was able to complete the first two volumes and deliver the manuscript to Cambridge University Press before death overtook him (*A History of Christianity in India*, vol. 1, "The Beginnings to A.D. 1707" [1984], and vol. 2, "1707–1858" [1985]). This is a work of great erudition, with dozens of pages of notes and bibliographies in many languages, marked by fairness and generosity to individuals and points of view, both Christian and non-Christian.

Neill portrayed the Christian faith, the third largest religious community in the nation, as an institution firmly rooted in the soil of India. It was not a history of missions as such, but instead an effort to place Christianity in the social, political, and religious context of the Indian peoples and to assess their responses to the Christian presence. He also attempted to deal with all forms of Christianity present in the subcontinent, from that which arrived in the Roman era down to the varieties that came in the nineteenth century. The first volume traces the sketchy record of Christian origins and spread in the middles ages, the coming of the Portuguese and their missionary work, and the expansion of European contacts in the seventeenth century. The Portuguese expansion is portrayed in terms of crusade, curiosity, commerce, conversion, conquest, and colonization, and the papal grant of patronage (the *padroado*) to the country's kings meant the work of evangelization as well as conquest would be in the hands of secular rulers. Since this gave the Portuguese a monopoly over the conversion of the peoples of the East, other European powers did what they could to evade this and penetrate their sphere of influence.

The second volume focuses on political changes in India and the beginning of Protestant missions in 1707 with the arrival of Bartholomäus Ziegenbalg at Tranquebar. Neill deals with the German Lutherans who served under the British East India Company, the renewal of Roman

Catholic mission efforts, the ongoing Thomas church, the enormous expansion of Protestant efforts after William Carey's arrival in 1793, and the subsequent development of an Anglican church structure. Other themes include the role of education and the Indian renaissance, the government and missions, and the development of an indigenous Indian church. The book concludes with the great uprising against British rule in 1857–58.

The book received favorable treatment in the Western press,[26] but the response in India was less enthusiastic. The time had passed when one lone individual could carry out a task so massive as writing the full story of Christianity in the subcontinent. A new breed of Indian scholars had emerged, such as the Jesuit E. R. Hambye, who produced important works on the Eastern rite churches in India,[27] and the Anglican layman Rajaiah D. Paul (1895–1975), a contemporary of Neill. After retiring from the Indian civil service, Paul served ten years as Secretary of the Synod of the Church of South India, and during his life wrote nine books and over three hundred articles on Indian Christianity, the best-known of which are *Chosen Vessels* (1961) and *Triumphs of His Grace* (1967), published by the Christian Literature Society in Madras.[28] The Church History Association of India, headquartered in Bangalore, began publishing the journal *Indian Church History Review* in 1967, and in the 1980s it launched a comprehensive, multivolume *History of Christianity in India* project that is still far from completion. Since the 1960s numerous scholars from the West and India have engaged in a far-reaching reinterpretation of the subcontinent's history, both secular and religious. Much of this research was unknown to Neill, who relied heavily on traditional primary and secondary sources for his work.

Thus, the *Indian Church History Review* was extremely critical and said the two volumes would disappoint one who was looking for the contemporary perspective in Indian historiography. Neill had made many errors and anachronisms, overlooked important scholarly studies that had appeared in the previous two decades, and lacked coherence, movement, and direction. After reading the book, one carries away the impression that it is a history written in "the traditional, somewhat paternalistic, missionary style." In fact, it can be seen as an "apologia" both for Western missionaries and British rule in India. The reviewer feared that the names of Bishop Neill and Cambridge University Press "may give the book an unwarranted scholarly legitimacy among western readers which will not serve the cause of Indian church history well."[29]

The work of Neill was the result of lifelong study and reflection, and it did much to inform people in the West about the spread of Christianity in that far-away land. Neill's language and interpretations became dated, but this did not keep the churches from disentangling themselves from the colonial regime and taking their place in an independent India. With his ecumenical vision and deep commitment to an indigenous church, Neill contributed in no small way to this development.

NEIL THE GLOBAL CHRISTIAN

Probably more than any other Christian historian in the twentieth century, Neill captured the vision of a global faith and sought to communicate this to his fellow believers. Both as a participant-observer and a scholar of the Scriptures, he encouraged Christians everywhere to find one another and to work together in proclaiming the gospel message. Although he spent much time in the libraries, his real workshop was in the world. He was more than an intellectual: he was an equipper of the saints. He was truly a striking and gifted personality with a versatile mind, a prolific pen, and a compassionate heart.

After confronting the life and works of Stephen Neill, no one can dare say that Christianity is merely a Western religion. He has ensured that we will understand Christianity as a faith which is at home in all cultures and all lands. As a global Christian he has modeled a global faith, and that will surely be the hallmark of the church in the twenty-first century.

NOTES

1. Christopher Lamb, "The Legacy of Stephen Neill," *International Bulletin of Missionary Research* 11 (April 1987): 65.

2. *God's Apprentice: The Autobiography of Bishop Stephen Neill*, ed. Eleanor M. Jackson (London: Hodder & Stoughton, 1991). Jackson's most significant work is *Red Tape and the Gospel: A Study of the Significance of the Ecumenical Missionary Struggle of William Paton 1886–1943* (Birmingham: Phlogiston Press, 1980). See the review of *God's Apprentice* by Jocelyn Murray in the *International Bulletin of Missionary Research* 17 (July 1993): 142, which calls attention to some omissions in Neill's manuscript. Another insightful review is by Cyril S. Rodd in *The Expository Times* 103 (April 1992): 224.

3. The Lamb article cited above ("Legacy of Stephen Neill," April 1987, 62–66), and Eleanor M. Jackson, "The Continuing Legacy of Stephen Neill," *International Bulletin of Missionary Research* 19 (April 1995): 77–80, are the most readily accessible treatments. I wish to express my appreciation to Dr. Jackson for having shared her manuscript with me prior to its publication in the *IBMR*. Other accounts include Anneliese Vahl, "Stephen C. Neill: Im Einsatz für die Ökumene," in *Ökumenische Gestalten: Brückenbauer der Einen Kirche*, ed. Günter Gloede (Berlin: Evangelische Verlagsanstalt, 1974), 275–83; "Stephen Neill: Equipper of Saints," in *Between Peril and Promise*, ed. James R. and Elizabeth Newby (Nashville: Thomas Nelson, 1984), 100–109; the obituary in *The Times* (London, July 24, 1984): 12; Kenneth Cragg and Owen Chadwick, "Stephen Charles Neill 1900–1984," *Proceedings of the British Academy* 71 (1985): 602–14; and the entries in *Dictionary of the Ecumenical Movement* (1991), 720 and *The New 20th-Century Encyclopedia of Religious Knowledge* (1991), 588–89.

Jolyon Mitchell submitted an M.Litt. thesis in 1993 at the University of Durham, "A Traditional Communicator in a World of Revolutionary Change," which is a study of Neill's methodology and theology and contains an exhaustive bibliography of his works.

4. With respect to his attitude toward women, Jackson points out that his books "bristle with sexist statements" and that three women missionaries in South India whom she had interviewed "felt he was both patronising and dismissive of their work" (Jackson, "Continuing Legacy," 79). This negativity is well–illustrated in a passage about women missionaries in Neill's *A History of Christian Missions* (Baltimore: Penguin Books, 1964), 256.

5. Cragg and Chadwick point out that modern technical scholarship has confirmed Neill's contentions ("Stephen Charles Neill," 604).

6. Stephen C. Neill, *Brothers of the Faith* (Nashville: Abingdon, 1960), 5.

7. See Elisabeth Elliott, *A Chance to Die: The Life and Legacy of Amy Carmichael* (Old Tappan, N. J.: Revell, 1987), 267–70. Murray calls attention to this incident in her above-mentioned review of *God's Apprentice*, as does Jackson in "Continuing Legacy," 77–78.

8. Jackson, "Continuing Legacy," 79–80, discusses his personal qualities at some length.

9. The role he played in helping to form the United Church in South India is mentioned in Bengt Sundkler, *Church of South India: The Movement Towards Union 1900–1947* (London: Lutterworth, 1954), 269, 293–94. Neill's own account of the endeavor is a chapter, "Church Union in South India," in the collective work *Towards a United Church, 1913–1947* (London: Edinburgh House, 1947), 75–148.

10. *Church Times*, no. 6718 (Nov. 15, 1991): 11.

11. Richard Holloway, "The Mystery in Stephen Neill," *Church Times*, No. 6717 (Nov. 8, 1991): 13. Jackson mentions that he later was receiving treatment from a Swiss psychotherapist for "manic depression," but this diagnosis was leaked to the public in 1958 and ended what seemed to be a promising treatment (Jackson, "Continuing Legacy," 79). In a way, he revealed his own inner tensions in *A Genuinely Human Existence: Towards a Christian Psychology* (London: Constable, 1959), a book which Cragg and Chadwick labeled "as thorough and competent a piece of writing as any in his immediate academic fields" (Cragg and Chadwick, "Stephen Charles Neil," 606–7).

12. *Man's Disorder and God's Design: The Amsterdam Assembly Series* (New York: Harper, 1948), 2:72–79.

13. Stephen C. Neill, *Survey of the Training of the Ministry in Africa, Part I: Report of a Survey of Theological Education in East and West Africa with Special Reference to the Training of the Ordained Ministry, Undertaken in April to July, 1950, under the Auspices of the International Missionary Council* (London: IMC, 1950). Neill visited theological schools in the British-ruled territories of tropical Africa. Two subsequent studies by other scholars focused on the French-and Portuguese-speaking areas and those under British control in central and southern Africa.

14. *The Times* (London, Nov. 1, 1984): 18.

15. Stephen Neill, *Christian Faiths and Other Faiths: The Christian Dialogue with Other Religions*, 2nd. ed. (New York: Oxford University Press, 1970), 3–19.

16. Neill's lifelong interest in Greek Christianity was reflected in the sermons he translated for the World Christian Books series, *Chrysostom and His Message* (London: Lutterworth, 1962).

17. *Church Times*, no. 6339 (Aug. 10, 1984): 14.

18. John E. Groh, "Ecumenism's Past and Future: Shifting Perspectives. An Interview with Bishop Stephen C. Neill," *Christian Century* 92 (June 4, 1975): 569.

19. Lamb, "Legacy of Stephen Neill," 65. See also Stephen Neill, "Conversion," *Scottish Journal of Theology* 3 (No. 4, 1950): 352–62; and Timothy Yates, "Anglican Evangelical Missiology," *Missiology* 14 (April 1986): 148–49, 156.

20. Ruth Rouse (1872–1956) spent forty years in leadership roles in the YWCA as well as nineteen years as a traveling secretary for the World's Student Christian Federation. She was a prolific writer and indefatigable organizer. See Ruth Franzén, "The Legacy of Ruth Rouse," *International Bulletin of Missionary Research* 17 (October 1993): 154–58. A second volume of the history was edited by Harold E. Fey in 1968 which covered the period 1948–1968, and Fey updated his own bibliography in a third edition published in 1986 by the WCC.

21. Hermann Sasse, "A History of the Ecumenical Movement 1517–1948," *Reformed Theological Review* 14 (February 1955): 1–9.

22. The English edition, *Men of Unity* (London: SCM, 1960), is somewhat shorter.

23. Neill, *God's Apprentice*, 327.

24. The Pelican series was a six-volume survey of church history by distinguished British scholars published between 1961 and 1970 by Penguin Books (Harmondsworth, Middlesex, England, and Baltimore, Md., U.S.A.). In 1992 Owen Chadwick brought out a seventh volume on the church after World War II. Penguin released a second edition of Neill's book in 1986 with the last two chapters thoroughly rewritten by Chadwick. The German edition, *Geschichte der christlichen Mission* (Erlangen: Verlag der Ev.-Luth. Mission, 1974), contains a supplementary chapter by missiologist Niels-Peter Moritzen that excellently sketches the history of German Protestant missions.

25. A particularly useful review of the book is Sigurd F. Westberg, "An Evaluation of Stephen Neill's Colonialism and Christian Missions," *Covenant Quarterly* 27 (August 1969): 37–41.

26. Examples of favorable reviews include those of P. J. Marshall in the *Times Literary Supplement* (May 4, 1984): 501, and (April 18, 1986): 426; G. Ernest Long, *The Expository Times*, 96 (Nov. 1984): 60; John Pollock, *The Churchman* 98, no. 3 (1984): 266–67; and Klaus K. Klostermaier, *Pacific Affairs* 58 (summer 1985): 352–53.

27. For example, *The St. Thomas Christian Encyclopedia of India* (Trichur, India: St. Thomas Christian Encyclopedia, 1973); *Dimensions of Eastern Christianity* (Vadavathoor, India: Pontifical Institute for Religious Studies, 1983); and a 183-page *Bibliography on Christianity in India*, published by the Church History Association of India.

28. See the biography by Chandran D. S. Devansen, *Rajaiah D. Paul: Layman Extraordinary* (Madras: Christianity Literature Society, 1982).

29. M. Mundadan, C. M. I., in *Indian Church History Review* 24 (June 1990): 87–90.

26

JAROSLAV PELIKAN

W. DAVID BUSCHART

BIOGRAPHICAL INTRODUCTION

In the introduction to a *Festschrift* honoring Jaroslav Pelikan, Patrick Henry suggests that "no one in the late twentieth century has attempted a more comprehensive address to the problem of Christian tradition than Jaroslav Pelikan."[1] The scholar with whom Pelikan is most often compared is a scholar of the late nineteenth century, Adolf von Harnack.[2] Harnack once made the suggestion, noted more than once by Pelikan, that to be a scholar one must "get an early start." Jaroslav Pelikan got an early start and has pursued his "comprehensive address" to the Christian tradition ever since.

Anna and Jaroslav Jan Pelikan, Sr., did not abandon the Slavic world when they immigrated to the United States from Czechoslovakia, shortly before Jaroslav Jan Pelikan, Jr., was born on December 17, 1923. Jaroslav Pelikan, Jr., indicates that as a young person he was "very conscious of Europe and European ways."[3] One of the most significant conveyors of that consciousness was language—or, more accurately, languages. From his parents Pelikan learned Slovak, Serbian, Czech, and German. In addition to being marked by a Slavic heritage and polylingual skills, there are indications that the Pelikan household was one in which "the notae of culture flourished."[4] Pelikan describes his parents' home as one "where both the theological tradition and humanistic culture were so much my daily bread that I still find the present antithesis between them quite incomprehensible."[5] He periodically makes references to childhood encounters with literature such as Shakespeare's *The Tempest* and Goethe's *Faust*, and music such as Mozart's *The Magic Flute* and Bach's chorales. Moreover, he indicates that his resolve to become a historian was prompted through reading, early in life, the "unlikely combination" of Ralph Waldo Emerson's *Representative Men* and Edward Gibbon's *Decline and Fall of the Roman Empire*.[6]

The language and concepts of the Christian tradition also were a part of Pelikan's life from his early years. His father and paternal grandfather were Lutheran churchmen, and the life and thought of the church were part of the atmosphere of his home. In the preface to an intellectual autobiography, *The Melody of Theology*, he writes that his father taught him "to sing 'the melody of theology'."[7] Indeed, Pelikan credits both of his parents as being among his most influential teachers.[8] As will be seen, Pelikan's work bears the marks of a number of these early formative influences.

Having manifested what was apparently a certain precociousness in childhood, Pelikan went on to attend Concordia (Junior) College in Ft. Wayne, Indiana. He then simultaneously pursued the B.D. at Concordia Theological Seminary, St. Louis, and the Ph.D., in historical theology, at the University of Chicago, receiving both degrees in 1946. At Chicago he studied under the one whom he regards as his *Doktorvater*, Wilhelm Pauck.

In 1946, in addition to receiving both his B.D. and Ph.D., Pelikan was ordained into the ministry of the Lutheran Church-Missouri Synod. He subsequently served for three years as an assistant pastor of Holy Trinity Lutheran Church, Chicago, where his father was pastor. He also accepted an appointment as an assistant professor in the department of history and philosophy at Valparaiso University, Valparaiso, Indiana, and began teaching there in the summer of 1946. In addition to teaching, editorial work on a denominational journal, special projects for the President of Valparaiso, and assisting his father at the church in Chicago, Pelikan published a number of journal articles and worked on his first book, *From Luther to Kierkegaard*.[9] He also continued to develop his précis of *The Christian Tradition*,[10] which he had begun during his graduate study at the University of Chicago.

After three years at Valparaiso, Pelikan accepted a position teaching dogmatics at Concordia Theological Seminary, St. Louis. In January 1951, he was elected to a professorship in historical theology at Concordia, effective with the fall term of that year. During that next academic year, however, Pelikan received and accepted an invitation to join the faculty of his other alma mater, the University of Chicago.

Pelikan was called to succeed Wilhelm Pauck on the Federated Theological Faculty at the University of Chicago, assuming his responsibilities in the fall of 1953. The Federated Theological Faculty was an explicitly ecumenical endeavor, and Pelikan pursued a number of ecumenical involvements, including service as a member of the Commission on Faith and Order of the World Council of Churches. Pelikan regards himself as being essentially self-taught in the area of early church doctrine, and indicates that while at Chicago he taught seminars on selected patristic figures as a way to teach himself about this period. The fruits of this are found in his books *The Shape of Death: Life, Death, and Immortality in the Early Fathers*, *The Light of the World: A Basic Image in Early Christian Thought*, and *The Finality of Jesus Christ in an Age of Universal History: A Dilemma of the Third Century*.[11] During his years at Chicago he was engaged in editorial and translation work as well. From 1955 through 1968 he served as religion editor for the *Encyclopedia Britannica*, and he worked as a collaborating editor on a 1959 publication of *The Book of Concord*.[12] The most significant editorial and translation work begun during this period continued for almost a decade after he left Chicago, during which time he served as one of two general editors for what many regard as the standard English-language edition of the works of Martin Luther.[13]

On July 1, 1962, Pelikan succeeded Roland H. Bainton as Titus Street Professor of Ecclesiastical History at the Divinity School of Yale University. He has remained on the faculty of Yale from 1962 to the present, occupying a number of faculty positions. In 1972, he moved from the Titus Street chair in the Divinity School to the Sterling chair of history in the Graduate School of Arts and Sciences, a post which he still holds. In 1979 he received the Cross Medal of the Yale Graduate School Association, and in 1984 he was chosen to deliver the William Clyde DeVane Lectures at Yale.[14]

Since going to Yale in 1962, Pelikan has seen the publication of over twenty-five books which he has written or edited. Not least among these are the five volumes of *The Christian Tradition*, which he regards as his "big book." During this same period he has written over one hundred articles and essays, published primarily in reference works, books edited by others, and scholarly journals, but also including popular magazines and newspapers. Over thirty-four colleges and universities have honored Pelikan in the awarding of an honorary doctorate, and he has held leadership positions in a variety of professional organizations and scholarly societies. The year in which Pelikan was chosen William Clyde DeVane Lecturer also saw the publication of a *Festschrift* in honor of his sixtieth birthday. He has twice been honored by the National Endowment for the Humanities, being selected as a Senior Fellow in 1967–68 and chosen for its highest honor in 1983, delivering the Jefferson Lecture in the Humanities.[15] He served as the Gifford Lecturer in the University of Aberdeen, Scotland, for 1992–93.[16] Pelikan is active in ecumenical dialogue, and has served as a member of the Commission on Faith and Order of the World Council of Churches.

PELIKAN AS HISTORIAN

OVERVIEW OF WORK

An interpretive overview of Pelikan's published writings will afford an introduction to his thought. This overview is ordered around several influences and commitments which have shaped his work: the Christian tradition, his Eastern European heritage, his historical consciousness, and humanistic scholarship.

First, the vast majority of Pelikan's writings have as their subject the history and/or teachings of Christianity, and in most of those writings which do not have this as the primary subject he incorporates insights from his study of Christianity. The Lutheran tradition constituted the religious context in which Pelikan was raised and received much of his formal education. Though he devoted more attention to Luther and Lutheranism early in his career, Pelikan has written on the tradition of his childhood throughout his career. These writings include a number of articles on sixteenth- and seventeenth-century Lutheran confessions,[17] a pair of articles delineating a historical outlook cast in a Lutheran Law/Gospel framework,[18] a critique of the object-subject antithesis in Lutheran dogmatic theology[19] a discussion of "Theology and Missions in Lutheran History,"[20] analysis of the American expressions of Lutheranism,[21] and essays on and tributes to a number of scholars with ties to the Lutheran tradition.[22] The first book Pelikan published is *From Luther to Kierkegaard*, the purpose of which is "to analyze the interrelations that have existed between philosophical thought and Lutheran theology since the days of the Reformation."[23] In addition to serving as an editor for *Luther's Works*, he contributed the only companion volume to that collection, *Luther the Expositor*, a study of Luther's exegetical principles and practices.[24] In the decade that followed the publication of *Luther the Exposi-*

tor, he wrote three books[25] and edited one book related to the thought of Martin Luther.

While he has deep roots in the Lutheran tradition, Pelikan sees Lutheranism as "ecumenical to the core."[26] Pelikan's vision of the Christian tradition extends to all of its major communities—Roman Catholic, Orthodox, and Protestant—and to its ties with Judaism. From 1959, the year in which *Riddle of Roman Catholicism* was published, through the time of his most recent publications, Pelikan's writings clearly manifest an ecumenical spirit. The origins of this dimension of his work are not as readily identifiable as the origins of his attention to Luther and Lutheranism. It may well be a combination of his parents and the Federated Theological Faculty at the University of Chicago, particularly Wilhelm Pauck.[27] Whatever its origins may be, Pelikan's ecumenical spirit is reflected in both the form and substance of his writings. In addition to the manifestation of an ecumenical spirit in *The Christian Tradition*, which will be considered below, this spirit is evident throughout his writings. Among his shorter writings, one finds sensitive discussions of topics related to the Jewish, Orthodox, and Roman Catholic communities. In numerous writings, Pelikan encourages Christians to respect the Jews as "those to whom the Covenant of God was first given and those to whom it has been extended—not transferred, merely extended."[28] His sensitivity to Eastern Orthodoxy goes beyond mere respect for the history of this tradition to the conviction that "in the liturgical traditions of the Eastern churches we can find some resources more closely akin to the Reformation and the New Testament than the badly mangled forms of the Mass which were the only Catholic liturgy Luther knew."[29] Pelikan has written more about Roman Catholicism than any Christian tradition other than Lutheranism, and these writings are characterized by a self-consciously "critical reverence" for Roman Catholicism.[30] In recent years, the circle of Pelikan's writings has extended even further, going beyond the perimeters of Christian ecumenicity to include major religions of the world.[31]

Second, Jaroslav Pelikan is very proud of his Eastern European heritage. He includes himself among those "who find our own Christian roots in the evangelical mission of Saints Cyril and Methodius."[32] Speaking of Orthodox theologian Georges Florovsky, Pelikan says, "My own roots in Eastern Europe resonate to his thought."[33] In a similar fashion, he points to his "family roots" as explaining why the existential dimension of Christian thought was first mediated to him through the writings of Fyodor Dostoevsky.[34] Pelikan writes, "The liturgical, political, and doctrinal history of Eastern Christendom is an indispensable component of any responsible research in [the history of Christianity], but ignoring the Christian East has long been characteristic both of the churchmanship and of the scholarship of the West, whether Roman Catholic or Protestant."[35] In addition to many details and nuances woven into his writings, Pelikan's inclusion of this "indispensable component" is evident in both the amount of attention he gives to and the sensitivity he demonstrates toward Eastern Christianity.

Pelikan has written on a number of figures, both well-known and not-so-well-known, of the Eastern Church and the Slavic world. These include John Chrysostom,[36] Gregory of Nyssa,[37] Basil the Great,[38] Maximus Confessor,[39] Gregory Palamas,[40] Clement Mary Hofbauer,[41] Josef Miloslav Hurban[42] Thomas Garrigue Masaryk,[43] and Josyf Slipyj.[44] He has devoted two large-scale lectureships to topics related to Eastern Christianity. As his subject for the 1987 A. W. Mellon Lectures in the Fine Arts, Pelikan chose Byzantine iconography,[45] and his 1992–93 Gifford Lectures were devoted to natural theology in the thought of four Cappadocians.[46] Furthermore, Pelikan has worked with a number of Eastern churchmen, and one of them, Georges Florovsky, is among the scholars who have had the most influence on Pelikan. As recently as 1987, Pelikan identifies Florovsky as becoming "more important to me all the time," and in *The Melody of Theology*, Pelikan writes that Florovsky "more than any other person except my late father, taught me to sing 'the melody of theology. . . .' "[47]

Perhaps the most significant manifestation of the influence of this sensitivity to Eastern Christendom is found in the structure of *The Christian Tradition*. In contrast with the majority of comprehensive church histories and histories of doctrine, Pelikan devotes a major portion, indeed an entire volume, to "The Spirit of Eastern Christendom."[48]

Third, Pelikan's approach to Christianity and its traditions is essentially historical. While the word "theology" must not be overlooked in "historical theology," it is Pelikan's conviction that "the primary requirement of historical theology is that it be good history."[49] And, Pelikan is an untiring advocate on behalf of historical inquiry and the value of its fruits.

Overall, Pelikan's work is characterized by a pervasive and sweeping historical consciousness. In addition to the chronologically comprehensive account set forth in *The Christian Tradition*, publications on persons and topics from every major period of the history of the church are to be found among his writings. This comprehensive historical consciousness is portrayed in Pelikan's intellectual autobiography, *The Melody of Theology*, and embodied in the rest of his writings. *The Melody of Theology* includes entries on most of the major periods in the history of doctrine—Patristics,

Medieval, Renaissance, Reformation, and Enlightenment—and a variety of historical figures from Augustine and Origen to Harnack and Newman, from Dante and Aquinas to Dostoevsky and Söderblom.

Fourth, Pelikan is committed to the advancement of humanistic scholarship. In both the work he has done and the way in which he has done it, Pelikan has sought to advance the cause of humanistic scholarship and the academy in which it is best carried out. As early as 1965, Pelikan wrote a book entitled *The Christian Intellectual*.[50] In this book he offers an apologetic, rooted in the history of the Protestant Reformation, for the value of intellectual pursuit and the necessity for Christians to engage in this pursuit. The intervening years have seen the publication of several books[51] as well as many articles and lectures related to the academy and the scholar's vocation. Pelikan suggests, "The love of learning and the desire for God" is not only a principle of Benedictine monasticism—it is also "the leitmotiv of the dedication to patient historical scholarship that I would define as the genius of 'Christian humanism'."[52]

ANALYSIS

Jaroslav Pelikan is a historian and as such has not attempted to set forth any system of thought. Consequently, it would be ill-advised to posit any particular concept or concepts as the controlling or organizing factor in his work. However, in the context of the overview given above, we may now analyze Pelikan's work as a historian by examining three facets of his historical scholarship: his concept of Christian doctrine, his perspective on the phenomenon of the development of Christian doctrine, and his methodological approach to the historian's craft.

First, Pelikan's distinctive concept of Christian doctrine serves as a cartographic device in the mapping of the history of doctrine. He conceives of Christian doctrine as "What the Church of Jesus Christ believes, teaches and confesses on the basis of the word of God."[53] Of particular significance is his descriptive definition of "the Church" and his inclusion of what the Church "believes" and "teaches."

Following the Nicene Creed, Pelikan describes the church as one, holy, catholic, and apostolic. He believes that all four attributes must be acknowledged in order to have a proper understanding of the church. However, Pelikan places particular emphasis on the oneness and catholicity, the unity and universality, of the church—an emphasis which is an expression of his ecumenical spirit. He does not overlook the holiness and apostolicity of the church, but neither does he employ them in the programmatic way that he does unity and universality.

This emphasis is clearly manifest, for example, in *Obedient Rebels*. "It has been said that there is an ecumenicity in time and an ecumenicity in space."[54] With this statement, Pelikan sets forth the principle which provides the structure for two-thirds of the book. Part One considers Luther's reformation vis-a-vis ecumenicity in time; Part Two considers it with reference to ecumenicity in space. This same ecumenical formulation—ecumenicity in time and space—provides the structure for Pelikan's discussion of "A Theological Consensus on the Church" in Part Three of *Obedient Rebels*. While *The Christian Tradition* will be discussed below, it should be noted here that this ecumenical emphasis on the unity and universality of the church also can be seen in that five-volume history. In *The Christian Tradition*, Pelikan seeks to focus on "the common faith of the church," rather than "the private beliefs of theologians."[55] His commitment to unity and catholicity, to universality in both space and time, leads him to compose a history of doctrine which, in Robert Wilken's words, "offers a vision of a continuous and integrated history of Christian thought embracing both East and West, Latin and Greek, ancient and modern, Slavic and Western European."[56]

Another facet of Pelikan's concept of Christian doctrine is the inclusion of what the church "believes" and "teaches," in addition to what it "confesses." He conceives of doctrine as "more than dogma" (i.e., what the church "confesses"); it also includes "liturgical-devotional" (i.e., what the Church "believes") and "hermeneutical-exegetical" (i.e., what the church "teaches") modalities.[57] For Pelikan, the study of the history of doctrine includes not only creeds and confessions, but also "preaching, instruction, exegesis, liturgy, and spirituality."[58]

Pelikan draws upon what the church believes—sources from the prayer, spirituality, piety and particularly the liturgy of the church. For example, in discussing apocalyptic thought of the third and fourth centuries, Pelikan cites the *Apostolic Constitutions* and a number of other liturgical sources.[59] Pelikan cites hymns, poetry, and liturgical practice during his consideration of the medieval understanding of the doctrine of redemption.[60] There are also references to sources expressive of "what the church . . . believes" in his discussion of modern doctrinal thought pertaining to Mary[61] and to prayer.[62]

Pelikan draws upon what the church teaches—sources from the preaching, instruction and particularly the exegesis of the church.[63] For example, he structures his discussion of the early church's formulation of the divinity of Christ around "four sets of Old Testament passages."[64] Recounting medieval ecclesiological thought, he turns to monastic exegetes and expository preachers.[65] In his discussion of John Calvin, Pelikan's eye for exegetical sources of doctrine manifests itself when he writes, "The theme of the word of God was, of course, dominant in the *Institutes*, but it could be heard perhaps even more resonantly in his *Commentary on Romans*."[66]

Though Pelikan regards the modern era to be "a time when the relation between the three terms 'believe, teach, and confess' . . . was basically revised,"[67] he continues to incorporate into his narrative sources representative of the teaching of the church. The interpretation of Genesis 49:10 and Jeremiah 31:31–34 constitutes part of the history of the doctrine of God, and Eastern Orthodox exegesis has a place in the discussion of eschatological thought.[68] And, the preaching which takes place within the church is often cited,[69] especially in Pelikan's discussion of Wesleyan and Pietist thought.

Second, Pelikan's perspective on the phenomenon of the development of Christian doctrine influences the way in which he recounts the history of that doctrine. The realities of change and continuity occupy a central place in Pelikan's understanding of the phenomenon of development.[70] Pelikan acknowledges the importance of change, and criticizes those who suggest that change is incompatible with Christian orthodoxy.[71] To be historical is to undergo change, and to overlook or deny change is to deny the historical. In Pelikan's estimate, post-Enlightenment historical scholarship there has placed an excessive emphasis on change, and in many instances, upon discontinuity in particular.[72]

Consequently, while acknowledging the fact of change, Pelikan chooses to stress continuity, "the continuity of Christians with one another both within a period of history and between periods."[73] He suggests that "historical theology takes its rise from the question of doctrinal change, but it issues in a quest for doctrinal continuity."[74] Furthermore, the quest for continuity is a quest for orthodoxy, not heresy.[75] For Pelikan, discontinuity is one of the marks of heresy, and the emphasis which historians have placed on change and discontinuity has resulted in an emphasis on heresy, rather than on orthodoxy. Thus, the history of Christian doctrine is the history of orthodoxy.

Third, Pelikan approaches his study of the history of Christian doctrine as a historian of ideas. If his work is analyzed solely in terms of the methods and categories usually associated with "church history," "the history of doctrine" and "historical theology," it will not be properly understood or appreciated. For Pelikan, ". . . *Dogmengeschichte* is part of *Geistesgeschichte*."[76] And, there are some noteworthy commonalities between some of the principles which guide Pelikan and those which guide two historians of ideas, Alfred North Whitehead and Arthur O. Lovejoy.

Pelikan regards philosopher and mathematician Alfred North White-head as "one of the wisest men of the twentieth century."[77] In one of his earliest books, *From Luther to Kierkegaard*, Pelikan indicates that his indebtedness to Whitehead is "more extensive than the specific citations would suggest."[78] And, throughout his writings, he makes a number of references to Whitehead's writings.[79] Pelikan regards Arthur O. Lovejoy as the "founder of the history of ideas as a distinct discipline in modern American scholarship,"[80] and in an introductory bibliography in the first volume of *The Christian Tradition* he lists two essays by Lovejoy on methodology in the history of ideas.[81] Though he makes little mention of Lovejoy by name, Pelikan's statement that at some points Whitehead's influence has been "more extensive than the specific citations would suggest" also appears to be applicable to Lovejoy, as will be seen below. In at least four noteworthy aspects, Pelikan's approach to the history of Christian doctrine is in agreement with the methodology of the history of ideas, particularly as it is articulated by Lovejoy and Whitehead.

Both Lovejoy and Pelikan advocate the need for the exercise of "imagination" in the construction of historical narrative. In addition to the need for "critical documentation" and "analytical discrimination," Lovejoy posits the need for "imagination."[82] The combination of the first two with the latter, Lovejoy suggests, will result in a "fresh perspective" on and a "greater intelligibility" for intellectual history.[83] Pelikan, too, considers "imagination" to be important. In fact, it is "what sets significant research apart from research that is merely competent."[84] According to Pelikan, "information" (analogous to Lovejoy's "critical documentation") and "intelligence" (analogous to Lovejoy's "analytical discrimination") are necessary-but-not-sufficient conditions for great scholarship. To this there must be added the creativity and sensibilities of "imagination."[85]

Both Lovejoy and Pelikan extol the virtues of a "catholicity" of intellect. The exercise of scholarly imagination requires a catholicity of mind. At the conclusion of his introduction to *The Great Chain of Being*, Lovejoy issues the warning that "the history of ideas is . . . no subject for highly departmentalized minds; and it is pursued with some difficulty in an age of departmentalized minds."[86] Thus, "a heavy demand is made upon the catholicity of the intellectual interests" of those who would write and read the history of ideas as envisioned by Lovejoy. Lovejoy advocates greater "collaboration between specialists" within historical studies, and greater cooperation between history and other disciplines. He calls for "more cross-fertilization" between disciplines.[87] In his promotion of general education and an accompanying call for scholarly research which is both interdisciplinary and infradisciplinary, Pelikan, too, values a "universality of interest" in and a non-departmentalized approach to the entire range of academic disciplines.[88] In particular, Pelikan stresses the importance of interaction between theological and non-theological disciplines. He believes that the study of Christian doctrine is best carried out in the context of the university, for it is only in this context that there is the possibility of such mutual exchange of methods, resources, and ideas.[89]

Whitehead, Lovejoy and Pelikan all suggest that one of the keys to a proper understanding of a historical idea or doctrine is to discern the implicit, pervasive assumptions which underlie the ideas or doctrines—indeed, the culture—of an era. Among Whitehead's writings, the book which Pelikan cites more than any other is *Science and the Modern World*, an exercise in "the history of thought."[90] The passage from that work to which Pelikan most often refers is the following:

> When you are criticizing the philosophy of an epoch, do not chiefly direct your attention to those intellectual positions which its exponents feel it necessary explicitly to defend. There will be some *fundamental assumptions which adherents of all the variant systems within the epoch unconsciously presuppose.* Such assumptions appear so obvious that people do not know what they are assuming because no other way of putting things has ever occurred to them. With these assumptions a certain limited number of types of philosophic systems are possible, and this group of systems constitutes the philosophy of an epoch.[91]

As for Lovejoy, he suggests that part of the task of the historian of ideas is to identify "implicit or incompletely explicit *assumptions* or more or less *unconscious mental habits*, operating in the thought of an individual generation." He describes these "intellectual habits," as "the beliefs which are so much a matter of course that they are rather tacitly presupposed than formally expressed or argued for, the ways of thinking which seem so natural and inevitable that they are not scrutinized with the eye of logical self-consciousness, that often are the most decisive character of a philosopher's doctrine, and still oftener of the dominant intellectual tendencies of an age."[92]

Similarly, Pelikan states, "To understand a culture, it is essential to identify those presuppositions in its thought and language that are so obvious to all that they are only rarely raised to the level of formal statement."[93] For Pelikan, these "presuppositions"—these "fundamental assumptions" or "intellectual habits"—are often to be found not in the philosophy of an era but in Christian doctrine, in the life and worship of the church[94] or in "the attempt to come to terms with the meaning of the figure of Jesus of Nazareth."[95] Yet, the method of the history of ideas still pertains. The historian of Christian doctrine needs to include in the narrative the presuppositional doctrines or doctrines assumed from previous eras.

Lastly, Whitehead, Lovejoy and Pelikan each affirm that historical studies are best served by gathering together concepts articulated by disparate groups and individuals. Note in the quotation of Whitehead cited earlier that, the "fundamental assumptions" constitute the key to identifying "a certain limited number" of systems among "all the variant systems within the epoch." As for Lovejoy, he protests the "conventional division" of historical studies along national or linguistic lines, believing that scholars often overlook or deny the fact that "the same idea often appears, sometimes considerably disguised, in the most diverse regions of the intellectual world."[96] Consequently, the history of ideas "aims at interpretation and unification and seeks to correlate things which often are not on the surface connected." Lovejoy recognizes the colossal scale of such an enterprise, and issues the warning that such scholarship "may easily degenerate into a species of merely imaginative historical generalization." However, "in spite of the probability, or perhaps the certainty, of partial failure, the enterprise seems worth attempting."[97] Rooted in his ecumenical ecclesiology, Pelikan adopts this approach in *The Christian Tradition*. In the introduction to the first volume he writes, "Christian doctrine is the business of the church. . . . the historian runs the danger of exaggerating the significance of the idiosyncratic thought of individual theologians at the expense of the common faith of the church. The private beliefs of theologians do belong to the history of doctrine, but not simply on their own terms."[98] In other words, he intends to "listen to the chorus more than to the soloists."[99] He is not content to propose a chronologically serial account of the doctrinal views affirmed by individual persons or documents. Rather, in Lovejoy's words noted above, Pelikan proposes to identify "the manifestations of specific unit-ideas in the collective thought of large groups of persons, not merely in the doctrines or opinions of a small number of profound thinkers or eminent writers." In the preface to volume 1 of *The Christian Tradition*, Pelikan writes:

> "The work as a whole is intended to take on the audacious and yet necessary task of starting at the beginning of the history of Christian doctrine and continuing to the twentieth century. . . . I am acutely aware of the dangers in any such enterprise. But that awareness is outweighed by the conviction, which I share with Sir Steven Runciman, "that the supreme duty of the historian is to write history, that is to say, to attempt to record in one sweeping sequence the greater events and movements that have swayed the destinies of man. The writer rash enough to make the attempt should not be criticized for his ambition,

562

however much he may deserve censure for the inadequacy of his equipment or the inanity of his results.[100]

Toward this end, he seeks to identify, paraphrasing Whitehead, groups of systems of doctrine which constitute the doctrinal history of various epochs; and, reminiscent of Lovejoy, he aims at interpretation and unification, and seeks to correlate things which often are not on the surface connected.

These are some of the principles which guide Pelikan's "audacious" attempt at a "sweeping" account of the history of Christian doctrine. It now remains to consider these principles as they are put into practice by Pelikan. His practice of the historian's craft will be appraised by examining some of the ways in which the influences and commitments described in the overview and the facets of his historical scholarship considered in the analysis above manifest themselves, particularly in the five volumes of *The Christian Tradition*.

APPLICATION AND EVALUATION

Pelikan's practice of the historian's craft is shaped by the influences, commitments, definitions and emphases described above: influences of the Christian faith and a Slavic heritage, commitments to historical research and humanistic scholarship, distinctive definitions of the church and its doctrine, and emphases on continuity and orthodoxy. Furthermore, the methodological principles from the history of ideas facilitate bringing these to bear on the history of doctrine.

It is not difficult to find superlatives in reviews of Pelikan's work, including reviews of the volumes of *The Christian Tradition*, individually and collectively. David Lotz says, "Within present-day historiography . . . [*The Christian Tradition*] commands the field—and rightly so, . . ."[101] David Dawson writes, "All will marvel at the magisterial character of the achievement."[102] Scholars praise the scale and scope, the erudition and clarity of Pelikan's narrative. Yet, serious methodological concerns have been raised by a variety of scholars, including those who employ affirming superlatives. Among the concerns raised are decontextualization, homogenization, and lack of theological evaluation.

David Lotz suggests that *The Christian Tradition* is characterized by a "decontextualization" of the evidence.[103] In a review of volume 1, *Emergence*, Robert Calhoun says that Pelikan recounts the development of doctrine in "isolation" from "the ongoing world," and that this isolation is rooted in the topical ordering of the material.[104] Other readers note a detachment of doctrine and doctrines from discrete times and places.[105] For example, John Drury observes that, in recounting the history of doctrine of the nineteenth and twentieth centuries, Pelikan "expatiates upon history and theology without any of the anxiety injected into such reflections by the cultural self-destruction of two world wars and many more genocides."[106]

A related concern is what Lotz refers to as the "homogenization" of the history of doctrine.[107] Robert Calhoun criticizes Pelikan's "flattening" of the historical landscape.[108] The diversity which characterizes the history of doctrine is minimized, at times lost sight of, due to the pursuit of lines of unity and coherence among diverse figures and movements. Thus, in his narrative of the Medieval period, Pelikan continues to devote so much attention to a figure (i.e., Augustine) from the preceding historical period that one reviewer refers to volume 3, *Medieval* as "Medieval Theology Minus Aquinas."[109]

Pelikan is also criticized for not articulating a distinctly theological evaluation of the doctrinal developments he recounts. It is suggested that he errs in failing to identify and distinguish between legitimate development and illegitimate change. Thus, Ted Peters suggests that volume 5, *Modern* "reads more like a kind of journalism than theology," due to the virtual absence of "evaluations."[110] Linwood Urban suggests that in Pelikan's definition of doctrine, he tells us "more about who decides what Christian doctrine is than about how to judge which is a true and which a false development,"[111] and others find similar fault with a lack of evaluative discussion regarding Pelikan's definition of "the Church."[112]

These criticisms have merit. When viewed in the light of the increased attention given to social, economic and other contextual factors in the writing of church history today, Pelikan does adopt a rather singular focus, at times "decontextualized," on Christian doctrine. In an era in which the history of doctrine is most often structured in strictly chronological ways, Pelikan's synthesis of chronological and thematic factors at times seems "homogenized." And, by and large, Pelikan does refrain from making normative comments, limiting himself to descriptive narrative reflecting his interpretation of the history of development.

Yet, these weaknesses have corollaries in some of the strengths and distinctive contributions of Pelikan's work in general and *The Christian Tradition* in particular. It is true that there is some "homogenization" in *The Christian Tradition*. Pelikan sometimes does overlook points of difference and emphasize commonalities.[113] Yet, *The Christian Tradition* is praised by persons from diverse theological contexts for its ecumenical sensitivity and fairness, and one dimension of this is emphasizing commonalities rather than the often emphasized differences. Albert Outler believes that Pelikan's work constitutes "a landmark in a major paradigm shift" to an "ecumenical consciousness" in the writing of history, and that *The Christian Tradition* is "the most impressive achievement to date" of this ecumenical consciousness in historical theology.[114] This consciousness has enabled Pelikan to describe diverse ecclesiastical and theological traditions in such a way that each tradition, including the Eastern tradition, receives a reasonable hearing.

It is true that there is some "decontextualization" in *The Christian Tradition*. Pelikan rarely discusses the contextual factors, be they cultural or churchly, which might explain "why" particular developments have occurred.[115] This is due in part to Pelikan's focused interest in providing a clear description of the history of *doctrine*, not the history of society or even of the institutional church, and in part to the sheer scale of *The Christian Tradition*. Reviewers from virtually all quarters express some awe at the size of the task that Pelikan has undertaken, and the skill with which he has engaged such a wide range of historical periods and primary sources. As noted earlier, Pelikan himself recognizes the "dangers" associated with such a monumental task, yet he also recognizes the need for historians "to attempt to record in one sweeping sequence the greater events and movements . . ." of history.[116] In the five volumes of *The Christian Tradition*, Pelikan sets forth a remarkably comprehensive and cohesive narrative of the history of doctrine.[117]

It is true that there is a lack of explicitly stated theological evaluation in *The Christian Tradition*. A reader who knows little if anything of Pelikan's background will not readily identify his personal theological commitments. Yet, contrary to Ted Peter's suggestion, this hardly makes *The Christian Tradition* a piece of "journalism," nor is it intended to be a work of "theology."[118] It is intended to be a history, a history guided by an appreciative knowledge of the diverse traditions of Christianity, rather than by a particular tradition. It is creative and interpretive history, but it must be read and evaluated as history, not theology.

Furthermore, as noted earlier, Pelikan's work should be read not as church history or even as historical theology, but as an exercise in the history of ideas which has as its subject the development of Christian doctrine. It is in this methodological approach, in his application of a methodology of the history of ideas, that Pelikan makes one of his most distinctive contributions.[119] Thus, Pelikan attempts to focus on the "chorus" rather than the "soloists," and consciously employs "imagination" in the process. The larger reality of the development of doctrine is not to be neglected due to concentrating exclusively upon commonly studied persons or movements, and imagination has an important role to play in crafting the narrative of this development. In keeping with the history of ideas,

Pelikan also attempts to identify those "fundamental assumptions" which inform the Church's doctrine, and thereby to recognize points of continuity or commonality which often go undetected. Finally, the application of these principles is facilitated by a "catholicity" of intellect. The exercise of imagination, the ability to hear the wide range of the "chorus," and the capacity to perceive "fundamental assumptions" issue from a mind characterized not by narrow specialization but by breadth.

CONCLUSION

Those who agree with Calhoun that "it is not really possible 'to listen to the chorus more than to the soloists' without flattening the result,"[120] think that Pelikan has fallen prey to a danger concerning which Lovejoy issued a warning—the danger of degenerating into "a species of merely imaginative historical generalization."[121] Other scholars, such as Henry Chadwick, are sympathetic with the "audacious and yet necessary task" of composing a "sweeping" portrayal of the history of Christian doctrine.[122] To these readers, Pelikan's work is a tour de force of "interpretation," "unification," and correlation of "things which often are not on the surface connected."[123]

One of the most frequently cited quotations throughout Pelikan's writings is the following line from Goethe's *Faust*: *"Was du ererbt von deinen Vätern hast, Erwirb es, um es zu besitzen."* Pelikan translates this in the following way: "What you have as heritage, Take now as task; For thus you will make it your own!"[124] "If anything is the motto of my life and thought," he says, "that's it."[125] In light of this and the foregoing examination of Pelikan's vocation as a historian of ideas, perhaps Henry Chadwick is correct in reading *The Christian Tradition*, with both its strengths and weaknesses as "a personal view."[126] Pelikan has studied the doctrine of the Christian heritage and, as a historian of ideas, has made it his own.

BIBLIOGRAPHY

Note: Listed here are all books written or edited to date by Jaroslav Pelikan. A considerable number of his shorter writings are identified in the endnotes of the opening section of this chapter. For more comprehensive bibliographies through the mid-1980s, see "Selected Bibliography of the Works of Jaroslav Pelikan," in Patrick Henry, ed., *Schools of Thought in the Christian Tradition* (Philadelphia: Fortress, 1984), 177–188, and W. David Buschart, "Perspectives on Christian Doctrine in the Work of Jaroslav Pelikan" (Ph.D. diss., Drew University, 1988), 416–440.

BOOKS WRITTEN OR EDITED BY JAROSLAV PELIKAN

PRIMARY SOURCES

From Luther to Kierkegaard: A Study in the History of Theology. St. Louis: Concordia, 1950; 2d ed., 1963.

Fools for Christ. Philadelphia: Fortress, 1955. (Also published as *Human Culture and the Holy: Essays on the True, the Good, and the Beautiful.* London: S. C. M., 1959.)

Luther the Expositor: Introduction to the Reformer's Exegetical Writings. St. Louis: Concordia, 1959.

The Riddle of Roman Catholicism: Its History, Its Beliefs, Its Future. Nashville: Abingdon, 1959.

The Shape of Death: Life, Death and Immortality in the Early Fathers. Nashville: Abingdon, 1961.

The Light of the World: A Basic Image in Early Christian Thought. New York: Harper and Brothers, 1962.

Obedient Rebels: Catholic Substance and Protestant Principle in Luther's Reformation. New York: Harper and Row, 1965.

The Christian Intellectual. Religious Perspectives, vol. 14. New York: Harper and Row, 1965.

The Finality of Jesus Christ in an Age of Universal History: A Dilemma of the Third Century. Ecumenical Studies in History, no. 3. London: Lutterworth, 1965; Richmond, Va.: John Knox, 1966.

ed. *Makers of Modern Theology.* 5 vols. Introductions by Jaroslav Pelikan. New York: Harper and Row, 1966-68.

ed. *The Preaching of Chrysostom: Homilies on the Sermon on the Mount.* Introduction by Jaroslav Pelikan. Philadelphia: Fortress, 1967.

Spirit Versus Structure: Luther and the Institutions of the Church. New York: Harper and Row, 1968.

ed. *Interpreters of Luther: Essays in Honor of Wilhelm Pauck.* Philadelphia: Fortress, 1968.

Development of Christian Doctrine: Some Historical Prolegomena. New Haven: Yale University Press, 1969.

ed. *Twentieth Century Theology in the Making.* 3 vols. Introductions by Jaroslav Pelikan. Translated by R. A. Wilson. London: William Collins Sons, 1969–70, and New York: Harper and Row, 1970.

The Christian Tradition: A History of the Development of Doctrine. Vol. 1, *The Emergence of the Catholic Tradition (100–600).* Chicago: University of Chicago Press, 1971.

Historical Theology: Continuity and Change in Christian Doctrine. New York: Corpus Instrumentorum and Philadelphia: Westminster, 1971.

ed. *The Preaching of Augustine: "Our Lord's Sermon on the Mount."* Introduction by Jaroslav Pelikan. Translated by Francine Cardman. Philadelphia: Fortress, 1973.

The Christian Tradition: A History of the Development of Doctrine. Vol. 2: *The Spirit of Eastern Christendom (600–1700).* Chicago: University of Chicago Press, 1974.

The Christian Tradition: A History of the Development of Doctrine. Vol. 3: *The Growth of Medieval Theology (600–1300).* Chicago: University of Chicago Press, 1978.

Scholarship and Its Survival. Princeton, N.J.: Carnegie Foundation for the Advancement of Teaching, 1983.

The Christian Tradition: A History of the Development of Doctrine. Vol. 4, *Reformation of Church and Dogma (1300–1700).* Chicago: University of Chicago Press, 1984.

The Vindication of Tradition: The Jefferson Lecture in the Humanities for 1983. New Haven: Yale University Press, 1984.

Jesus Through the Centuries: His Place in the History of Culture. New Haven: Yale University Press, 1985.

Bach Among the Theologians. Philadelphia: Fortress, 1986.

The Mystery of Continuity: Time and History, Memory and Eternity in the Thought of Saint Augustine. Charlottesville: University Press of Virginia, 1986.

The Excellent Empire: The Fall of Rome and the Triumph of the Church. New York: Harper and Row, 1987.

The Melody of Theology: A Philosophical Dictionary. Cambridge, Mass.: Harvard University Press, 1988.

The Christian Tradition: A History of the Development of Doctrine. Vol. 5, *Christian Doctrine and Modern Culture (Since 1700).* Chicago: University of Chicago Press, 1989.

Confessor Between East and West: A Portrait of Ukrainian Cardinal Josyf Slipyj. Grand Rapids: William B. Eerdmans Publishing Company, 1990.

Eternal Feminines: Three Theological Allegories in Dante's Paradiso New Brunswick: Rutgers Universty Press, 1990.

Imago Dei: The Byzantine Apologia for Icons. Princeton: Princeton University Press, 1990.

ed. *The World Treasury of Modern Religious Thought.* Boston: Little, Brown, 1990.

The Idea of the University: A Reexamination. New Haven: Yale University Press, 1992.

On Searching the Scriptures—Your Own or Someone Else's. New York: Book-of-the-Month Club, 1992.

ed. *Sacred Writings.* 6 vols. New York: Quality Paperback Book Club, 1992.

Christianity and Classical Culture: The Metamorphosis of Natural Theology in the Christian Encounter with Hellenism. New Haven: Yale University Press, 1993.

and Richard R. Caemmerer. *The Cross for Every Day: Sermons and Meditations for Lent.* St. Louis: Concordia, 1952.

and Helmut T. Lehmann, eds. *Luther's Works.* 55 vols. Philadelphia: Muhlenburg and St. Louis: Concordia, 1955–72.

SELECTED SECONDARY SOURCES

Bowden, Henry Warner. *Church History in an Age of Uncertainty.* Carbondale: Southern Illinois University Press, 1991. (Pages 206–18, "Christianity Grasped Entire—Again," are on Pelikan.)

Buschart, W. David. "Jaroslav Pelikan and the Tradition of Christian Humanism." In *Scholarship, Sacraments and Service,* eds. Daniel B. Clendenin and W. David Buschart. Lewiston: Edwin Mellen, 1990.

Duke, James O. Review of *The Christian Tradition: A History of the Development of Doctrines,* 5 vols., by Jaroslav Pelikan. *Religious Studies Review* 18, no. 1 (January 1992): 4–6.

Henry, Patrick, ed. *Schools of Thought in the Christian Tradition.* Philadelphia: Fortress, 1984. (A *Festschrift* in honor of Pelikan's sixtieth birthday.)

Jodock, Darrell. Review essay, *"Christian Doctrine and Modern Culture:* Assessing Its Limits." *Journal of the American Academy of Religion* 61, no. 1 (summer 1993): 321–38.

Lotz, David W. "The Achievement of Jaroslav Pelikan." *First Things* 23 (May 1992): 55–65.

McSorley, Harry. "Pelikan's 'Ambitious Lifework': A High Point of Twentieth-Century Scholarship." *Journal of Religion* 71, no. 3 (July 1991): 404–409.

Wiles, Maurice. Review of *The Christian Tradition: A History of the Development of Doctrines*, 5 vols., by Jaroslav Pelikan. *Religious Studies Review* 18, no. 1 (January 1992): 1–4.

NOTES

1. Patrick Henry, ed., *Schools of Thought in the Christian Tradition* (Philadelphia: Fortress, 1984), 1.

2. E.g., David W. Lotz, "The Achievement of Jaroslav Pelikan," *First Things* 23 (May 1992): 55. Pelikan himself regards Harnack as "probably the most influential historian of Christianity in the modern era" (Introduction to *The World Treasury of Religious Thought*, ed. Jaroslav Pelikan [Boston: Little Brown, 1990], 11). On Harnack, see chapter by Michael Bauman in this volume.

3. Pelikan, quoted in Zoe Ingalls, "Yale's Jaroslav Pelikan: 'Bilingual' Scholar of Christian Tradition," *Chronicle of Higher Education* 26 (4 May 1983): 4.

4. G. Wayne Glick uses this phrase to describe the childhood home of Adolf von Harnack. See *The Reality of Christianity: A Study of Adolf von Harnack as Historian and Theologian* (New York: Harper and Row, 1967), 23–24.

5. Pelikan, "Tradition, Reformation, and Development," in *Frontline Theology*, ed. Dean Peerman (Richmond, Va.: John Knox, 1967), 107. Also see Pelikan's comments about the influence of his mother on his intellectual and vocational development, in his preface to *Nature: A Facsimile of the First Edition*, by Ralph Waldo Emerson (Boston: Beacon, 1985), vii–viii; and W. David Buschart, "Jaroslav Pelikan and the Tradition of Christian Humanism," in *Scholarship, Sacraments and Service: Historical Essays in Protestant Tradition*, eds. Daniel B. Clendenin and W. David Buschart (Lewiston, N.Y.: Edwin Mellen, 1990), 249–82.

6. Pelikan, preface to *Nature*, vii; also see Pelikan's study of Gibbon, *The Excellent Empire: The Fall of Rome and the Triumph of the Church* (San Francisco: Harper and Row, 1987).

7. Pelikan, *The Melody of Theology: A Philosophical Dictionary* (Cambridge: Harvard University Press, 1988).

8. Pelikan, *The Christian Tradition: A History of the Development of Doctrine*, vol. 5, *Christian Doctrine and Modern Culture (since 1700)* (Chicago: University of Chicago Press, 1989), ix; subsequent references, *CT/5: Modern*.

9. Pelikan, *From Luther to Kierkegaard: A Study in the History of Theology* (St. Louis: Concordia, 1950; 2d ed., 1963).

10. Pelikan, *The Christian Tradition*, 5 vols. (Chicago: University of Chicago Press, 1971–89).

11. Pelikan, *Shape of Death* (Nashville: Abingdon, 1961; reprint ed., Westport, Conn.: Greenwood, 1978) and Pelikan, *Light of the World* (Harper and Brothers, 1962) grew out of patristics seminars which Pelikan directed at Chicago. Pelikan, *Finality of Jesus Christ* (Ecumenical Studies in History 3 [London: Lutterworth, 1965; Richmond, Va.: John Knox, 1966]) was published several years after his departure from Chicago,

but also stems from his work in patristics while there. Two other books were published during his years at Chicago: Pelikan, *Fools for Christ* (Philadelphia: Muhlenberg, 1955; also published as *Human Culture and the Holy: Essays on the True, the Good, and the Beautiful* [London: S.C. M., 1959]); and a companion volume to *Luther's Works*, entitled *Luther the Expositor: Introduction to the Reformer's Exegetical Writings* (St. Louis: Concordia, 1959).

12. Pelikan edited and translated "The Apology of the Augsburg Confession" in *The Book of Concord: The Confessions of the Evangelical Lutheran Church*, ed. Theodore G. Tappert (Philadelphia: Fortress, 1959), 97–285.

13. Pelikan and Helmut T. Lehmann, eds., *Luther's Works*, 55 vols. (St. Louis: Concordia, and Philadelphia: Fortress, 1955–72).

14. These lectures are published as Pelikan, *Jesus Through the Centuries: His Place in the History of Culture* (New Haven: Yale University Press, 1985).

15. These lectures are published as Pelikan, *The Vindication of Tradition: The Jefferson Lecture in the Humanities for 1983* (New Haven: Yale University Press, 1984).

16. These lectures as published as Pelikan, *Christianity and Classical Culture: The Metamorphosis of Natural Theology in the Christian Encounter with Hellenism* (New Haven: Yale University Press, 1993).

17. Pelikan, "Tradition in Confessional Lutheranism," *Lutheran World* 3 (1956): 214–22; Pelikan, "The Doctrine of Man in the Lutheran Confessions," *Lutheran Quarterly* 2 (1950): 34–44; Pelikan, "The Relation of Faith and Knowledge in the Lutheran Confessions," *Concordia Theological Monthly* 21 (1950): 321–31; Pelikan, "Church and Church History in the Confessions," *Concordia Theological Monthly* 22 (1951): 305–20; Pelikan, "Some Word Studies in the Apology," " *Concordia Theological Monthly* 24 (1953): 580–96; Pelikan, "The Doctrine of Creation in Lutheran Confessional Theology," *Concordia Theological Monthly* 26 (1955): 569–79; and Pelikan, "Verius Servamus Canones: Church Law and Divine Law in the Apology of the Augsburg Confession," in *Collectanea Stephan Kuttner*, eds. J. Forchielli and Alphons M. Stickler (Bonn: Institutum Gratianum, 1967), 1:367–88. Much of this last essay ("Verius Servamus Canones") was incorporated into Pelikan, *Spirit Versus Structure: Luther and the Institutions of the Church* (New York: Harper and Row, 1968), 98–112.

18. Pelikan, "History as Law and Gospel, 1," *The Cresset* 12, no. 4 (1949): 12–17, and Pelikan, "History as Law and Gospel, 2," *The Cresset* 12, no. 5 (1949): 19–23.

19. "The Origins of the Object-Subject Antithesis in Lutheran Dogmatics: A Study in Terminology," *Concordia Theological Monthly* 21 (1950): 94–104.

20. In *Proceedings of the Thirtieth Convention of the Atlantic District of the Lutheran Church, Missouri Synod*, Atlantic District, Lutheran Church-Missouri Synod (St. Louis: Concordia, 1951), 33–38.

21. Pelikan, "Amerikanisches Luthertum in dogmengeschichtlicher Sicht," *Evangelisch-Lutherische Kirchenzeitung* 14 (25 July 1952): 250–53; and Pelikan, "American Lutheranism: Denomination or Confession," in *What's Ahead for the Churches?* eds. Kyle Haselden and Martin Marty (New York: Sheed and Ward, 1964), 187–95.

22. Pelikan, "Natural Theology in David Hollaz," *Concordia Theological Monthly* 18 (1947): 253–63; Pelikan, "In Memoriam: Joh. Albrecht Bengel, June 24, 1687 to November 2, 1752," *Concordia Theological Monthly* 23 (1952): 785–96; Pelikan, "Ein deutscher lutherischer Theologe in Amerika: Paul Tillich und die dogmatische Tradition," in *Gott ist am Werk: Festschrift fur Landesbischof D. Hanns Lilje zum sechzigsten Geburtstag*, eds. Heinz Brunotte and Erich Ruppel (Hamburg: Furch-Verlag, 1959), 27–36, and Pelikan, "In Memoriam: Paul Tillich," *The Cresset* 28 (1965): 24–25; Pelikan, "The Early Answer to the Question Concerning Jesus Christ: Bonhoeffer's *Christologie* of 1933," in *The Place of Bonhoeffer*, ed. Martin E. Marty (New York: Association, 1962), 145–65; Pelikan, "Paul M. Bretscher, Christian Humanist," *The Cresset* 37, no. 9

(1974): 4; and Pelikan, "Grundtvig's Influence," in *The Rescue of the Danish Jews: Moral Courage Under Stress*, ed. Leo Goldberger (New York University Press, 1987), 173–82.

23. Pelikan, *Luther to Kierkegaard*, v.

24. See note 11 above.

25. Pelikan, *Obedient Rebels: Catholic Substance and Protestant Principle in Luther's Reformation* (New York: Harper and Row, 1965); Pelikan, *The Christian Intellectual*, Religious Perspectives 14 (New York: Harper and Row, 1965); Pelikan, *Spirit Versus Structure* (1968); and Pelikan, ed., *Interpreters of Luther: Essays in Honor of Wilhelm Pauck* (Philadelphia: Fortress, 1968). Over the course of the years he also published over seventeen essays and articles on Martin Luther and nineteen on Lutheran history and thought. The material contained in a number of these articles found its way into some of the books already cited.

26. Pelikan, "Form and Tradition in Worship: A Theological Interpretation," in *The First Liturgical Institute, Valparaiso University* (Valparaiso, Ind.: Valparaiso University Press, 1950), 23.

27. Marion Hausner Pauck, "Wilhelm Pauck: A Biographical Essay," in *Interpreters of Luther: Essays in Honor of Wilhelm Pauck*, ed. Jaroslav Pelikan (Philadelphia: Fortress, 1968), 351. Also see Pelikan's reflections on Pauck in "Wilhelm Pauck" (1981), 25.

28. Pelikan, untitled essay, in *A Sense of Place: St. John's of Collegeville*, ed. Colman J. Barry and Robert L. Spaeth (Collegeville, Minn.: St. John's University Press, 1987), 1. See, for example, Pelikan, "De-Judaization and Hellenization: The Ambiguities of Christian Identity," in *The Dynamic in Christian Thought*, ed. Joseph Papin (Villanova, Pa.: Villanova University Press, 1970), 81–124 (subsequently this essay constituted the basis for the first chapter of *The Christian Tradition: A History of the Development of Doctrine*, vol. 1, *The Emergence of the Catholic Tradition (100–600)* (Chicago: University of Chicago Press, 1971); subsequent references, CT/1: *Emergence*.); Pelikan, "The Pope and the Jews," *New York Times* (28 October 1970): 47; Pelikan, "The Jewish-Christian Dialogue in Historical Perspective," *Bulletin: The American Academy of Arts and Sciences* 32, no. 7 (1979): 18–30; Pelikan, "Commandment or Curse? The Paradox of Work in the Judeo-Christian Tradition," in *Comparative Work Ethics*, Occasional Papers of the Council of Scholars of the Library of Congress 4 (Washington, D.C.: Library of Congress, 1985), 7–23. *Jesus Through the Centuries* (New Haven: Yale University Press, 1985) begins, as Pelikan says it "must," with a consideration of the New Testament picture of Jesus as "The Rabbi" (9–20).

29. Pelikan, "Luther and the Liturgy," in *More About Luther* (Decorah, Iowa: Luther College Press, 1958), 46. In "Luther Comes to the New World," Pelikan speaks of "an intuition that has reappeared from time to time: that some of the solutions to the debates between Luther and Roman Catholicism must come beyond Western Latin Christendom altogether" ("Luther Comes to the New World," in *Luther and the Dawn of the Modern Era*, ed. Heiko A. Oberman [Leiden: E. J. Brill, 1974], 8). This appreciation for Eastern Christendom is also evident in his remarks to a colloquium on "the common roots of the European nations" (Pelikan, "Doctrine of the Image of God" [1982], 54, and 56; see note 32 below), and in his writings on Maximus Confessor (see note 39 below).

30. "Critical reverence" is the term employed by Pelikan in *Obedient Rebels* to describe Luther's attitude toward the thought and life of the church of his day. It denotes a conservative respect and regard for the church, combined with a willingness to critique and to call for change wherever necessary. Pelikan's writings related to Roman Catholicism include *The Riddle of Roman Catholicism: Its History, Its Beliefs, Its Future* (Nashville: Abingdon, 1959); *Obedient Rebels* (1965); "Catholics in America," *New Republic* 142 (21 March 1960): 15; "Catholic and Protestant Americans: What Common Ground?" *Catholic Messenger* 79 (14 September 1961): 5; "Issues That Divide Us: Prot-

estant," in *Christians in Conversation* (Westminster, Md.: Newman, 1962), 3–19; "The American Church in the Church Universal," *The Atlantic* 210, no. 2 (August 1962): 90–94; "That the Church May Be More Fully Catholic," *The Catholic World* 198, no. 1185 (1963): 151–56; "A Scholar Strikes Back," *The Catholic World* 200, no. 1197 (1964), 149–54; "Constitution on the Sacred Liturgy: A Response," in *The Documents of Vatican II*, ed. Walter M. Abbott, trans. Joseph Gallagher (Chicago: Follett, 1966), 179–82; "The Pope and the Jews," *New York Times* (28 October 1970): 47; "Demur to Vatican II," *Saturday Review* 51 (9 March 1968: 30–31; "A New Look at the New Breed," *Priest* 25 (1969): 477–79; "Brother Martin, Pope Martin, and Saint Martin: On the Conditions of Christian Reconciliation," *One in Christ: A Catholic Ecumenical Review* 12 (1976): 142–56; and "Voices of the Church," *Proceedings of the Thirty-third Annual Convention, The Catholic Theological Society of America*, ed. Luke Salm (The Bronx, N.Y.: Catholic Theological Society of America, 1979), 1–12.

31. For example, Pelikan has edited *The World Treasury of Modern Religious Thought* (1990), and a six-volume series entitled *Sacred Writings* (New York: Book-of-the-Month Club, 1992) which includes texts from Judaism, Christianity, Islam, Confucianism, Hinduism, and Buddhism. He has also written a companion volume for this series, *On Searching the Scriptures—Your Own or Someone Else's* (New York: Book-of-the-Month Club, 1992).

32. Pelikan, "The Doctrine of the Image of God," in *The Common Christian Roots of the European Nations, an International Colloquium in the Vatican* (Florence: Le Monnier, 1982), 1:60.

33. Interview by the author, 10 March 1987; also see Pelikan, untitled essay, in *Sense of Place* (1987), [4], and Pelikan, *Melody*, x.

34. Pelikan, preface to *The Triads*, by Gregory Palamas, ed. John Meyendorff, trans. Nicholas Gendle (New York: Paulist, 1983), xii–xiii.

35. Pelikan, foreword to *A Century of Church History: The Legacy of Philip Schaff*, ed. Henry Warner Bowden (Carbondale, Ill.: Southern Illinois University Press, 1988), x.

36. *The Preaching of Chrysostom: Homilies on the Sermon on the Mount*, ed. and intro. Jaroslav Pelikan (Philadelphia: Fortress, 1967).

37. Pelikan, "The Mortality of God and the Immortality of Man in Gregory of Nyssa," in *The Scope of Grace: Essays in Honor of Joseph Sittler*, ed. Philip J. Hefner (Philadelphia: Fortress, 1964), 79–97.

38. Pelikan, "The 'Spiritual Sense' of Scripture: The Exegetical Basis for Saint Basil's Doctrine of the Holy Spirit," in *Basil of Caesarea: Christian, Humanist, Ascetic*, ed. Paul J. Fedwick (Toronto: Pontifical Institute of Mediaeval Studies, 1981), 1:337–60.

39. Pelikan, "'Council or Father or Scripture': The Concept of Authority in the Theology of Maximus Confessor," in *The Heritage of the Early Church: Essays in Honor of the Very Reverend Georges Vasilievich Florovsky*, eds. David Neiman and Margaret Schatkin, Orientalia Christiana Analecta 195 (Rome: Pontificale Institutum Studiorum Orientalium, 1973), 277–88; Pelikan, "The Place of Maximus Confessor in the History of Christian Thought," in *Maximus Confessor: Actes du Symposium sur Maxime le Confesseur*, eds. Felix Heinzer and Christoph Schoenborn, Paradosis: Etudes de Litterature et de theologie anciennes 27 (Friburg: Editions Universitaires, 1982), 387–402; and Pelikan, introduction to *Maximus Confessor: Selected Writings*, trans. George C. Berthold (New York: Paulist, 1985), 1–13.

40. Pelikan, preface to *The Triads*, by Palamas (1983), xi–xiii.

41. Pelikan, "Patron Saint for Christian Unity?" *Ligourian* 54 (September 1966): 15–17.

42. Pelikan, "Josef Miloslav Hurban: A Study in Historicism," in *The Impact of the Church Upon Its Culture*, ed. Jerald C. Brauer (Chicago: University of Chicago Press, 1968), 333–52.

43. Pelikan, *Jesus, Not Caesar: The Religious World View of Thomas Garrigue Masaryk and the Spiritual Foundations of Czech and Slovak Culture*, Westminster Tanner-McMurrin Lectures on the History and Philosophy of Religion, no. 3 (Salt Lake City: Westminster College of Salt Lake City, 1991).

44. Pelikan, *Confessor Between East and West: A Portrait of Ukrainian Cardinal Josyf Slipyj* (Grand Rapids: Eerdsman, 1990).

45. Published as Pelikan, *Imago Dei: The Byzantine Apologia for Icons*, Bollingen Series 35.36 (Princeton: Princeton University Press, 1990).

46. These lectures are published as Pelikan, *Christianity and Classical Culture;* see note 16 above.

47. Pelikan, *Melody*, x; also see 173, and tribute by Pelikan to Florovsky, "Puti Russkogo Bogoslova: When Orthodoxy Comes West," in Neiman and Schatkin, *Heritage of the Early Church*, 11–16.

48. Pelikan, *The Christian Tradition: A History of the Development of Doctrine*, vol. 2, *The Spirit of Eastern Christendom (600–1700)* (Chicago: University of Chicago Press, 1974); subsequent references, *CT/2: Eastern*. See Pelikan's comments on the place of a volume on Eastern Christendom in a multi-volume history of doctrine (*CT/2:* Eastern, 1–2), and Henry Warner Bowden, *Church History in an Age of Uncertainty* (Carbondale, Ill.: Southern Illinois University Press, 1991), 206–207.

49. Pelikan, *Historical Theology: Continuity and Change in Christian Doctrine* (New York: Corpus Instrumentorum, and Philadelphia: Westminster, 1971), 129; also see 94, 97–98.

50. See note 25 above.

51. Pelikan, *Scholarship and Its Survival: Questions on the Idea of Graduate Education* (Princeton: Carnegie Foundation for the Advancement of Teaching, 1983); Pelikan, *The Idea of the University: A Reexamination* (New Haven: Yale University Press, 1992); Pelikan, "Dukedom Large Enough: Reflections on Academic Administration," *Concordia Theological Monthly* 43 (1972): 297-302; Pelikan, "'A Decent Respect to the Opinions of Mankind,'" *Scholarly Publishing* 8 (1976): 11–16; Pelikan, "The Reserach University and the Healing Professions," *Criterion* 15 (Autumn 1976): 25–20; Pelikan, *The Circle of Knowledge in Historical Perspective* (Washington, D.C.: Library of Congress, 1980); Pelikan, "The Research Library, an Outpost of Cultural Continuity," *Imprint of the Stanford Library Associates* 6, no. 2 (1980): 5–10; and Pelikan, "Special Collections: 'A Key into the Language of America,'" *Books at Brown* 29/30(1982–83); and Pelikan, *The Aesthetics of Scholarly Research* (New Orleans: Tulane University, 1984).

52. Pelikan, "Paul M. Bretscher," 4.

53. *CT/1: Emergence*, 1.

54. Pelikan, *Obedient Rebels*, 25.

55. *CT/1: Emergence*, 3.

56. Robert L. Wilken, review of *CT/1: Emergence*, in *Saturday Review* 54 (7 August 1971): 26. Wilken goes on to write, "This conception is kept alive not by a controlling theme or idea, but by the thing itself, the sheer account of what Christians 'believe, teach and confess on the basis of the Word of God.'"

57. Pelikan, "Tradition, Reformation and Development" (1967), 104; also see Pelikan, *Historical Theology*, 98, 109–10.

58. Pelikan, *Historical Theology*, 95. Some scholars have questioned whether or not Pelikan has in fact included this broader range of sources in *The Christian Tradition*. For example, Jack Forstman writes, "It is noteworthy . . . that Pelikan's sources for the most part are identical to those of his predecessors, namely, the writings of theologians and documents related to councils" (review of *CT/1: Emergence*, 97 n. 1). Others, however, have acknowledged what they consider to be his inclusion "not only of seldom quoted theologians but also of often neglected sources such as liturgy, poetry, popular devo-

tion and (to a limited degree) canonical materials." (Walter Principe, review of *The Christian Tradition: A History of the Development of Doctrine*, vol. 3, *The Growth of Medieval Theology (600–1300)* [Chicago: University of Chicago, 1978], in *Speculum* 57 [1982]: 922–26; also see J. S. Preus, review of *CT/1: Emergence*, in *Theology Today* 29 [1972]: 226.)

59. *CT/1: Emergence*, 126–27, 129–30. For other observations about or references to sources expressive of belief, see 133, 142–43, 146, 153, 170–71, 177, 185, 217–18, 229, 238, 241, 270, 342–43.

60. *The Christian Tradition: A History of the Development of Doctrine*, vol. 3, *The Growth of Medieval Theology (600-1300)* (Chicago: University of Chicago, 1978), 132; also see 136, 137, 154, 162, 170–71, 200–201; subsequent references, *CT/3: Medieval*.

61. *The Christian Tradition: a History of the Development of Doctrine*, vol. 4, *The Reformation of Church and Dogma (1300-1700)* (Chicago: University of Chicago, 1984), 42, 50; also see 258, 341; subsequent references, *CT/4: Reformation*.

62. *CT/5: Modern*, 137–38; also see 153–55, 210, 236–37, 264.

63. One reviewer of *CT/2: Eastern* observes, "Professor Pelikan, as his first volume has already shown, has an enviable knack of getting to the point of any controversy, especially by displaying the basic bibical texts involved in contrary interpretations" (R. Butterworth, review of *CT/2*: Eastern, in *Month* 8 [1975]:265).

The importance with which Pelikan regards matters exegetical can also be seen by examining the indexes to *The Christian Tradition*. Each volume contains three to four pages of references to discussions of specific Scripture texts. In addition to the evidence found in *The Christian Tradition*, Pelikan's affirmation of the importance of exegesis and homiletics in the history of doctrine is cleary displayed in "The 'Spiritual Sense' of Scripture" (1981), his editing of *The Preaching of Chrysostom: Homilies on the Sermon on the Mount* (Philadelphia: Fortress, 1967) and *The Preaching of Augustine: "Our Lord's Sermon on the Mount,"* trans. Francine Cardman (Philadelphia: Fortress, 1973), and in his work on *Luther's Works*. The thirty volumes (more than half the collection) for which he was editor are devoted to Luther's exegetical and homiletical writings, and he contributed the companion volume, *Luther the Expositor*, which he describes as "an effort to redress the balance," so that the history of biblical exegesis receives proper attention in the study of the history of doctrine. (Pelikan, *Luther to Kierkegaard*, ix.)

64. *CT/1: Emergence*, 175–84; also see 137, 243, 247; and CT/2: *Eastern*, 51, 106, 108, 158, 205, 218–20, and 236–38.

65. *CT/3: Medieval*, 298; also see references to sermonic material, 28, 29, 124, 128, 131, 162.

66. *CT/4: Reformation*, 188; also see 40, 132, 141–42, 146–47, 151, 160, 195–96, 214, 326–30.

67. *CT/5: Modern*, viii.

68. Ibid. 191–92, and 225. For other illustrations of references to exegetical sources, see 156, 162–63, 166, 193–94, 195, 201–02, 207, 301.

69. Ibid. 118–73 passim; also see 10–11, 73–74, 168, 176, 209–10, 221–22, 223, 240, 264–65, 274, 297.

70. See the entry on "Continuity" in Pelikan, *Melody*, 42–45.

71. Pelikan, *Historical Theology*, 1–3; "Creation and Causality" (1960), 39; Pelikan, *Development of Christian Doctrine: Some Historical Prolegomena* (New Haven: Yale University Press, 1969), 41–42; *CT/1: Emergence*, 10. On this point, as on many others, the work of John Henry Newman is important to Pelikan. See Pelikan, "Darwin's Legacy: Emanation, Evolution, and Development," part of "Darwin's Legacy," sound recording of the 18th Nobel Conference, Gustavus Adolphus College, 5–6 October 1982, cassetes 7 and 8, Archives, Gustavus Adolphus College, St. Peter, Minn.; and Pelikan, forward to *A Century of Church History*, xi.

72. Pelikan, *Vindication of Tradition*, 48; Pelikan, *Historical Theology*, 9; and Pelikan, *Development of Christian Doctrine*, 49.

73. Pelikan, *Historical Theology*, 161. A number of reviewers have recognized Pelikan's concern to portray the continuity within the history of Christian doctrine; e.g., John P. Dolan, review of *Obedient Rebels*, in *Una Sancta* 24 (1967): 101; Franklin Sherman, review of *Obedient Rebels*, in *Heythrop Journal* 6 (1965): 470; Mary Jo Weaver, review of *CT/1: Emergence*, in *Review of Politics* 34 (1972): 237; Robert B. Eno, review of *CT/1: Emergence*, in *American Ecclesiastical Review* 166 (1972): 495; Forstman, review of *CT/1: Emergence*, 106; Wilken, review of *CT/1:Emergence*, 26; and Eileen F. Serene, "Medieval Theology Minus Aquinas," review of *CT/3: Medieval*, in *Religious Studies* 16 (1980): 487. The application of the concept of continuity to the historical narrative is manifest in *CT/5: Modern* also; see, e.g., 84–85, 104–105, 120, 149, 178, 205, 277, 283, 292–93.

74. Pelikan, *Historical Theology*, 156.

75. Pelikan, *Historical Theology*, 155; and *CT/1: Emergence*, 9, 156. Cf., Forstman's criticism of Pelikan with regard to the notion of orthodoxy (vs. heterodoxy) and Pelikan's inclusion/exclusion of specific figures within "the line of developing orthodoxy." (Review of *CT/1: Emergence*, 101.)

76. Pelikan, *Vindication of Tradition*, 68; also see Pelikan, *Historical Theology*, xvii, 114–115.

77. Pelikan, *Historical Theology*, 1; and Pelikan, *Jesus Through the Centuries*, 57.

78. Preface to Pelikan, *Luther to Kierkegaard*, 2d ed., ix. He also indicates that the influence is that of "the Whitehead of *Science and the Modern World* and the *Process and Reality* rather than . . . the thinker who collaborated with Bertrand Russell on *Principia Mathematica*."

79. These include Whitehead's *Process and Reality* (e.g., Pelikan, *Luther to Kierkegaard*, ix; and Pelikan, *Mystery of Continuity*, 140), *Modes of Thought* (e.g., Pelikan, *Human Culture*, 17), *The Aims of Education and Other Essays* (e.g., "Research University and Healing Professions" (1976), 25; and Pelikan, *Scholarship and Its Survival*, 45, 49, 64), *Adventures of Ideas* (e.g., Pelikan, "Theology and Change" (1969), 376; and Pelikan, *Historical Theology*, 1, 10, 95), and *Science and the Modern World* (e.g., Pelikan, *Luther to Kierkegaard*, 160 n. 13; Pelikan, "Beyond Bellarmine and Harnack: The Present Task of the History of Dogma," *Theology Digest* 16 (1968): 307; Pelikan, *Historical Theology*, 80; Pelikan, *Vindication of Tradition*, 75–76; and *Jesus Through the Centuries*, 2–3, 57, 85).

80. Pelikan, *Jesus Through the Centuries*, 4.

81. This (see *CT/1: Emergence*, 361–62) bibliography consists largely of books and essays dealing with the history and development of Christian doctrine . There are also listed, however, four sources which do not deal with the history or development of Christian doctrine per se. Of these four, three specifically deal with the history of ideas, and two of these are by Arthur O. Lovejoy: "The Historiography of Ideas," in *Essays in the History of Ideas* (Baltimore: Johns Hopkins University Press, 1948; reprint ed., Westport, Conn.: Greenwood, 1978), 1–13; and *The Great Chain of Being: A Study of the History of an Idea* (Cambridge: Harvard University Press, 1936). With reference to the latter, Pelikan makes special note of the introductory chapter, "The Study of the History of Ideas." The third essay on the history of ideas is: Richard P. McKeon, "Truth and the History of Ideas," in *Thought, Action, and Passion* (Chicago: University of Chicago Press, 1954), 54–88.

82. Lovejoy, "Historiography of Ideas," 9.

83. Pelikan, *Aesthetics of Scholarly Research* (1984), 3; also see Pelikan, *Scholarship and Its Survival*, 25-26.

84. Pelikan, "A Gentleman and a Scholar," *The Key Reporter* 45, no. 2 (1979-80): 3, 4.

85. Lovejoy, *Great Chain of Being*, 22.

86. *Historiography of Ideas*, 10.

87. Ibid., 6; also 2.

88. Pelikan, "In Defense of Research in Religious Studies at the Secular University," in *Religion and the University*, by Jaroslav Pelikan, et al. (Toronto: University of Toronto Press, 1964), 12; *Christian Intellectual*, 111–112; Pelikan, "A Gentleman and a Scholar" 2–4; and Pelikan, *Aesthetics of Scholarly Research* (1984), 3.

89. Pelikan, *Historical Theology*, xxi, 114-115; Pelikan, *Obedient Rebels*, 191; and Pelikan, "Beyond Bellarmine and Harnack" (1968), 306.

90. Alfred North Whitehead, *Science and the Modern World* (New York: Macmillan, 1925; reprint ed., New York: Free, 1967), 3.

91. Ibid., 49-50; quoted in Pelikan, *Historical Theology*, 80, emphasis mine. This same passage is also quoted in Pelikan, "Beyond Bellarmine and Harnack" (1968), 307; Pelikan, *Vindication of Tradition*, 75-76; and *Jesus Through the Centuries*, 2, and 85.

92. Lovejoy, *Great Chain of Being*, 7.

93. Pelikan, *Historical Theology*, 80.

94. Ibid.

95. Pelikan, *Jesus Through the Centuries*, 2–3.

96. Lovejoy, *Great Chain of Being*, 15. He states that the history of ideas "is especially concerned with the manifestations of specific unit-ideas in the collective thought of large groups of persons, not merely in the doctrines or opinions of a small number of profound thinkers or eminent writers. . . . It is, in short, most interested in ideas which attain a wide diffusion, which become a part of the stock of many minds" (Ibid., 19).

97. Ibid., 21.

98. *CT/1: Emergence*, 3.

99. *CT/1: Emergence*, 122; also see *CT/5: Modern*, 6, 7–8, and 154–55.

100. *CT/1: Emergence*, ix–x, italics mine.

101. Lotz, "Achievement of Jaroslav Pelikan," 64.

102. David Dawson , review of *CT/5: Modern*, in *The Princeton Seminary Bulletin* (1990): 116.

103. Lotz, "Achievement of Jaroslav Pelikan," 61; also 63.

104. Robert L. Calhoun, review of *CT/1: Emergence*, in *Journal of the American Academy of Religion* 40 (1972): 502. Calhoun, review of *CT/1: Emergence*, 502.

105. Forstman, review of *CT/1: Emergence*, 98; George Every, review of *CT/2: Eastern*, in *Heythrop Journal* 16 (1965): 454; Mary Jo Weaver, review of *CT/2: Eastern*, in *Review of Politics* 37 (1975): 401; Principe, review of *CT/3: Medieval*, 925; James M. Kittelson, review of *CT/4: Reformation, in Journal of Modern History* 58 (1986): 261, 263; P. Schaeffer, review of *CT/4: Reformation*, in *Renaissance Quarterly* 39 (1986): 511; Dawson, review of *CT/5: Modern*, 116; Ted Peters, review of *CT/5: Modern*, in *Christian Century* 107 (9 May 1990): 503–504; Lotz, "Achievement of Jaroslav Pelikan," 61; Maurice Wiles, review of *The Christian Tradition*, 5 vols., in *Religious Studies Review* 18, no.1 (1992): 2, 3; and James O. Duke, review of *The Christian Tradition*, 5 vols., in *Religious Studies Review* 18, no. 1 (1992): 6.

106. John Drury, review of *CT/5: Modern*, in *Times Literary Supplement* 4526 (29 December 1989/4 January 1990): 1450.

107. Lotz, "Achievement of Jaroslav Pelikan," 61.

108. Calhoun, review of *CT/1: Emergence*, 503.

109. Serene, "Medieval Theology Minus Aquinas," 487–92.

110. Peters, review of *CT/5: Modern*, 503.

111. Linwood Urban, review of *CT/5: Modern*, in *Anglican Theological Review* 72 (Spring 1990): 230.

112. Lotz, "Achievement of Jaroslav Pelikan," 61; Wiles, review of *CT*, 2; and Duke, review of *CT*, 5.

113. See, for example, Bernard McGinn's comments on developments preceding Anselm's *Why God Became Man* (Review of *CT/3: Medieval*, in *Journal of Religion* 60 [1980]: 203), and John Drury's questioning of the "equanimity" of Pelikan's portrayal of the nineteenth and twentieth centuries which results in the omission of "major" figures and schools of thought (John Drury, review of *CT/5: Modern*, 1450; also Duke, review of *CT*, 6).

114. Albert Outler, "The Idea of 'Development' in the History of Christian Doctrine: A Comment," in *Schools of Thought in the Christian Tradition*, ed. Patrick Henry (Philadelphia: Fortress, 1984), 7, and 12.

115. Darrell Jodock is particularly critical of Pelikan on this point ("Christian Doctrine and Modern Culture: Assessing Its Limits," review essay of *CT/5: Modern*, in *Journal of the American Academy of Religion* 61 [1993]: 321–38).

116. See note 100 above.

117. Many reviewers commend Pelikan for his attempt to compose a unified narrative of the history of Christian doctrine (e.g., Weaver, review of *CT/1: Emergence*, 237; Eno, review of *CT/1: Emergence*, 495; Forstman, review of *CT/1: Emergence*, 106; Wilken, review of *CT/1: Emergence*, 26; and Robert Wilken, review of *CT/2: Eastern*, in *Currents in Theology and Mission* 2 [1975]: 298).

118. See notes 110, 111, and 112 above.

119. Cf. Robert Wilken's suggestion that, ". . . though Pelikan wishes each volume [of *The Christian Tradition*] to stand on its own, it is . . . the conception of the whole, not any individual volume, that is Pelikan's unique contribution" (Wilken, review of *CT/2: Eastern*, 298).

120. Calhoun, review of *CT/1: Emergence*, 503.

121. Lovejoy, *Great Chain of Being*, 21.

122. See notes 100 and 116 above. Chadwick reads *The Christian Tradition* with the attitude that "The learned author is not intending to write a book to help a student through his examinations, but to express a personal view" (Henry Chadwick, review of *CT/1: Emergence*, in *Journal of Religion* 54 [1974]: 315), Cf. Wilken's remark that the work is "more reportorial than interpretive" (Wilken, review of *CT/2: Eastern*, 299).

123. Lovejoy, *Great Chain of Being*, 21.

124. Pelikan, *Vindication of Tradition*, dedication page. See also Pelikan, "Fathers, Brethren, and Distant Relatives" (1962), 718; "Continuity and Creativity" (1975), 197; and *Vindication of Tradition*, dedication page.

125. Pelikan, quoted in Ingalls, "Yale's Jaroslav Pelikan," 5.

126. Chadwick, review of *CT/1: Emergence*, 315.

27

MARTIN E. MARTY

FRED W. BEUTTLER

Christians, as they reflect upon the life of faith, often find favorite biblical texts that reveal their own histories. Menno Simmons used 1 Corinthians 3:11 as the epigram for each of his books. Jonathan Edwards experienced "the Divine Glory" upon reading 1 Timothy 1:17. Sören Kierkegaard clung to James 1:17. Martin E. Marty, the foremost interpreter of American religion in the twentieth century, rests in Colossians 1:15–17: "[Christ] is the image of the invisible God, the first-born of all creation, for in him all things were created . . . and in him all things hold together (RSV)." For Marty, "all things" encompass the curriculum and the library, the newspaper and the phone book, the modern and the secular, the *ecclesia* and the *polis*. They deeply interfuse his work as university professor, religious journalist, and Lutheran pastor. In nearly forty books and roughly four thousand articles, Martin Marty has chronicled a phenomenon that foretells the future shape of Christianity: the problem of religious pluralism. "As an American religious historian in the face of the most jumbled and competitive melange of religiosities the world has ever known," he reflects, "my project [focuses] around the philosophical theme of 'the one and the many' and the political problem of pluralism." A historian of modern Christianity, Marty has sought to chronicle the tension between "the 'many' in the Christian tradition" and the "'one' in Christ," seeking at all times to help people "learn to combine religious commitment with civility, spiritual passion with a public sense."[1]

BIOGRAPHICAL INTRODUCTION

Martin Emil Marty was born in West Point, Nebraska, on February 5, 1928. The son of a Lutheran schoolteacher, Marty grew up in a small Midwestern town, where he sat under the instruction of a Missouri Synod pastor and listened to his father's organ playing. Marty has long felt of his particular heritage that, "the walls were too confining and the ceiling was too low." Early in life he experienced a clear call to the ministry, which came when he was "a four-year old awed by the dark theocratic gloom . . . that emanated from a Nebraska pulpit under which I sat." His education focused on preparation for the pastorate: Concordia High School in Milwaukee; Concordia Seminary in St. Louis, where he received his B.A. in 1949, and a B.D. and ordination in 1952. He earned an S.T.M. at the Lutheran School of Theology in Chicago in 1954, and two years later received the Ph.D. from the University of Chicago Divinity School, writing his dissertation on "The Uses of Infidelity: Changing Images of Freethought Opposition to American Churches."[2]

During his studies Marty was an active contributor to his school papers, and upon receiving the Ph.D. he was invited to write for *The Christian Century*, a liberal Protestant weekly. He became an editor in 1958, a post he has held for over thirty-five years. There he wrote a weekly column, first called "Pen-ultimates," with Dean Peerman, and later his own "M.E.M.O." Since 1969 he has also published a fortnightly newsletter, *Context*, wherein he reviews books and comments on public issues.

After receiving his doctorate, Marty accepted a call as founding pastor of the Church of the Holy Spirit in Elk Grove Village, Illinois, where he served for seven years. Elk Grove was a new middle-class suburb and Marty witnessed great success in reaping the fruits of the religious revival of the 1950s. Marty's first book, *The New Shape of American Religion*, written from the perspective of the parish ministry, was a theological criticism of what he called merely "a revival of interest in religion." Published when he was just thirty-one years old, this work launched Marty's career as a public interpreter of American religion, and he was soon engaged as television panelist, radio personality, and expert on call.

Finding the pressures of pastor and religious journalist too demanding, Marty decided to return to academic life. In 1963 he accepted a professorship in modern Christian history at the University of Chicago's Divinity

School, later becoming the Fairfax M. Cone Distinguished Service Professor in the History of Modern Christianity in 1978. He plans to retire in March, 1998.

While primarily a teacher and interpreter of religion, Marty has not hesitated to act in the public sphere. In 1963 he joined numerous other ministers and academics in Selma, Alabama, marching with the Rev. Martin Luther King. As a leader of Clergy and Laymen Concerned About Vietnam, Marty was one of the first clergymen to speak out against the War. He actively counselled students about selective conscientious objection. In the early 1970s he was a leader of the moderate faction in the Missouri Synod Lutheran Church, leaving the denomination in a schism over biblical authority.

Many of his books fall into the category of interpretive religious essays, rather than church history per se. Throughout his career he has commented on the contemporary state of the church,[3] and, in addition to his continued writings on specifically religious topics such as *Baptism* (1962) and *The Lord's Supper* (1980), Marty has helped shape the field of medical ethics. Following the death of his first wife from a terminal illness, he co-founded the Park Ridge Center, An Institute for the Study of Health, Faith and Ethics, where he has continued his reflections on faith and medicine.[4]

As a university-based historian, Marty has played a major role in shaping the study of modern religious history. Marty's impact stems both from his own research and from his influence as mentor, advisor, and director of other projects, pointing to the emerging role of the academic historian as a manager of scholarship. In addition to co-editing the journal *Church History*, he has edited numerous books and book series, such as *The New Theology*, the "Chicago History of American Religion," and "Modern American Protestantism and Its World."[5]

As one of the preeminent interpreters of American religion, Marty's best works, such as *Righteous Empire* (1970) and his four-volume *magnum opus, Modern American Religion* (1986, 1991, and in progress) are all interpretive synthetic narratives. He does not consider himself a church historian, but rather an historian of American religion, a distinction which is embedded in Marty's work, from his first book on "post-protestant America," to his four-volume history. Yet in all these cases, he retains his primary concern in the story of how the one and the many live in committed civility.

He is not a theologian, though his historical work is infused with a complex theology derived from historical reflection. Admitting that "doubt is the fuel on which faith feeds," he seems remarkably free of the inner hunger and torment that drive much modern religion. As his second wife once commented, "Unlike many Lutherans, he has no guilt. He really believes he has been forgiven."[6] Spiritually, his is a "wintry faith," a "piety for the not naturally pious," one that is "restrained, decorous, cool," which opposes proselytism and feels solidarity with the secular and the unbelieving, yet still affirms hope in a God who is often hidden.[7]

Throughout his career he has sought to mediate between his provincial background, what he calls his "tribe," and his ecumenical vision. Reflecting on his own life, Marty sees it as organized around the term "response." His life project, of conceiving how "the one and the many might live together in civility but with commitment," is rooted in this vision of response, a response not to a "God of Prey" but to a "God of Promise," who is hidden, yet revealed. In his personal beliefs Marty is quite circumscribed; one of the few things he ever admits to being "ardent" about is the ecumenical movement. His anger appears only against those who move from their tribal faith to proclaim exclusive tribalist visions in the civil realm.

Marty's theological heritage also is grounded in deep yet diverse roots. He studied under historians Jerald Brauer, Sidney Mead and Daniel Boorstin, and was deeply influenced by Lutheran theologian Joseph Sittler. He traces his theology back to those whom he regards as "the most creative public religious thinkers" in America, a heritage that runs from Jonathan Edwards through Horace Bushnell, and from Walter Rauschenbush to Reinhold Niebuhr. Yet Marty's emphasis on the public aspect of religion pushes him to include others in his theological lineage, such as two of his favorite theologians, James Madison and Abraham Lincoln.

THE CALLING OF THE CHRISTIAN HISTORIAN

As a historian, Marty has occasionally reflected on his own craft. Often he returns to Martin Luther to describe his sense of calling: "For because histories describe nothing other than God's work—that is grace and wrath—which one must so worthily believe as if they stood in the Bible, they should certainly be written with the greatest diligence, faithfulness, and truth." An academic historian who is also a believer and an ordained minister, Marty mediates between at least two worlds. In his own way, Marty sees himself closer to the secular, seeking what Karl Rahner called "intellectual solidarity with those who have perhaps excluded God from their horizon."[8]

What difference does being a Christian make, in Marty's view, for the writing of history? To be a Christian historian, Marty reflects, "is to construe reality in a particular set of ways through the prism provided by witness to the activity of God, especially as seen in Jesus Christ." In the realm of substantive philosophy of history, this means that there is at least some sense of the future to provide meaning to past and present. Yet, for the ordinary working historian, there is no way out of what he calls "the confining circle of immanence," that is, there is no access to a God's-eye view of the whole. The task of the historian then is to chronicle faithfully people's experience of the divine, rather than the workings of providence itself. In part this restricted vision is necessitated by the limits of the modern academic profession of history, yet for Marty there are also theological constraints.[9]

From his religious commitment comes a critical sensitivity to the presuppositions of others, for the Christian can ask non-believers how one can discern meaning without a vision of the whole of history. Christians insist that "there is no simple, objective, value-free interpretation of history."[10] Christians worship a God whose acts are "always hidden, partly mysterious, and necessarily ambiguous." This frees the Christian historian to "take care for the mundane," that is, ordinary, everyday life. Finally, and most importantly, the Christian historian can help the church "overcome history with history" by demystifying dead traditions and by offering alternative models that can revitalize a forgetful church.

Is there a particularly Christian interpretation of history? For Marty, Christianity is essentially a story, not doctrine, ethics or even belief. As a story, it begins "with the act of a creating God and a created human race that strays from God's ways." Marty sees Christianity as a "syncretistic faith like all others," one that selects from its competitors. A Christian interpretation "affirms *meaning* despite appearances," contenting itself with "seeing traces of God in the human story as clues to meaning," and viewing humans as "co-responsible for creation and preservation." Marty does not claim an absolute perspective, yet he affirms that, despite appearances, "all things cohere in Christ" and thus there is final meaning in history, although it is utterly hidden.[11]

Perhaps the most important theme in his philosophy of history is irony, that is, the paradox of unintended consequences. Christianity introduces realism into historical reflection by viewing humans as sinful. But it also tempers that realism with the promise of redemption. This paradox leads to ironic historical situations, as for example, when an effort at church union leads to schism. Here Marty relies on one of his favorite theologians, Reinhold Niebuhr, who believed that Christianity makes "the ironic view of human evil in history the normative one." The ironic mode views God as "a divine judge who laughs at human pretensions without being hostile to human aspirations," a position which provides the Christian historian with critical detachment, but also a place to encourage positive human action in the world. This "human irony" is sympathetic to human aspirations, yet aware of *hubris*.[12]

THE PUBLIC CHURCH

One of the most fundamental distinctions in Marty's theology of religious history is that between the "public" and "private" aspects of religion. Marty is a chronicler of "public religion," the ordering faith of the American republic. Public religion is not that which saves souls or makes "sad hearts glad"; not saving faith, but rather what he calls "ordering faith," the underlying moral and spiritual consensus of a whole people. Public religion is concerned with the *res publica*, the issues of relevance to the commonwealth. The "public church" is that "specifically Christian polity and witness" within the public religion. "Public theology" then is the "effort to interpret the life of a people in the light of a transcendent reference"; people, not just Christians, but "the pluralism of peoples with whom the language of the church is engaged in a larger way."[13]

This distinction runs throughout much of Marty's work, and provides one criterion by which he appraises religious movements. Trouble results, he believes, when people confuse public religion with saving faith. Following Luther's dictum that it is better to be ruled by a wise Turk than a foolish Christian, Marty points out that "[w]hatever saving faith is, it is not at the base of the state. Civil order, citizenship, and good morals do not depend on it. . . . The Christian, fortunately, has no exclusive claim on social justice or truth." The public realm is of the political and thus involves compromise: "Politics help separate what cannot be negotiated from what can."[14]

Marty prefers Benjamin Franklin's term of "*publick* religion" to Rousseau's "civil religion," for he considers the first open to the distinctiveness of each faith. Public religion takes into account the particularities of various faiths which "contribute their separate resources to public virtue and the common weal." Civil religion, by contrast, makes the faith of the state exclusive, in competition with traditional faiths. While admiring Thomas Jefferson and John Dewey, Marty considers them sectarian, for they insisted that Americans "should regard the civil faith or social religion as the very truth about existence."[15] In Marty's view, then, public religion is open to all who inhabit the American commonwealth.

He does not posit a simple opposition between public and private religion. Instead, Marty sees four ways of organizing religion in a modern secular society. One form is the "totalist" vision, a theocratic response to modern pluralism in which faith pervades every aspect of life. Related is the "tribalist" model, which organizes groups around exclusive identities with sharpened boundaries. Perhaps the most pervasive response is the "privatist" mode, which reduces religion to individual choice and "consumer control," with a lack of "social consequence or power." Yet this form of modern religion fuels a "hunger for wholeness," for communal expression that leaves privatist believers open to totalist or tribalist movements. Marty is a clear partisan of the public religion, seeing his goal to help people "learn to combine religious commitment with civility, spiritual passion with a public sense."

This distinction between public and private infuses his interpretation of the history of American religion. Marty sees a two-party system emerging among American Protestants in the late nineteenth century. One party, whom he calls "Private Protestantism," seized the name "evangelical," stressing "individual salvation out of the world, personal moral life congruent with the ideals of the saved," and eschatological rewards and punishments. The second party was "public insofar as it was more exposed to the social order and the social destinies of men." The former was the party of revivalism and conversions; the latter emphasized societal transformation. The numerous social upheavals of the late nineteenth century, such as economic panics, labor strikes, new immigration, and the growth of the industrial city, "led the socially oriented Protestants further into the public sphere, to ask the nation to change the circumstances that brought about the troubles. The same threats worked the opposite effect among the evangelistic camp. They withdrew progressively from involvement . . . [confining] their social message to calls for order and law and their ethical appeals to calls for repentance from private vice and change to personal holiness."[16]

Marty has been ambivalent throughout his career about this party of private Protestants, barely noticing them in his early years and only seeing them when they moved into the public realm in the early 1970s.[17] The private party separated into Fundamentalists and "New Evangelicals" in the late 1950s,[18] and Marty assesses their roles differently based upon their accommodation to public religion. His few outbursts of anger in print are against those who equate specific political positions with the will of God, such as the more militant wings of the New Christian Right in the 1980s. Significantly, he shrinks from calling Fundamentalists "public" in their move into political involvement. While mainstream Protestants were willing to see God as active "among people who did not acknowledge God as the source of that activity," the New Christian Right repudiated secularists and religious liberals, connecting partisan views and specific candidates in an essentially theocratic mode.[19] Fundamentalism, while surely "political," is not "public" in Marty's view. He considers it instead a form of totalist or tribalist faith. Evangelicalism, however, by the 1980s had come to make up one third of the "Public Church" for Marty.

MODERN AMERICAN RELIGION

Martin Marty as historian of Christianity has written only one book-length treatment of its whole history, one of his first books, *A Short History of Christianity* (1959). The disparity between the ideal of "one holy, catholic, apostolic church" and the historical reality forms his plot, yet even in Marty's early telling of the story it is the modern period that is emphasized, for here he sees something new, a "test" which the world has presented to the church: the challenge of pluralism and the secular. Since the mid-seventeenth century, and with ever increasing speed since the late eighteenth, "Christianity is no longer the motivating or impulsive center of Western life."

For Marty, the most monumental change in the church since the fourth century came in the 1780s, with its disestablishment or separation from state support in America. This was the "most profound revolution" in the entire history of the church since Constantine, for no longer would religion be enforced by the state. With the shift from compulsion to voluntaryism, new forms of holiness and faithful witness became possible. For Marty, this shift requires a fundamentally different approach than other ways of doing church history, for the coming of Christianity to the New World changed it dramatically, finally ending Constantinian Christianity. The condition of religious pluralism is one that is often seen as a threat to faith, but for Marty it is something to celebrate. He organizes his narratives around that theme, seeking not a single thread but often using a technique he calls "mapping," a topical survey of "land and landscape, . . . people and peoplescape."

Marty's theme of pluralism and the "one and the many" might sound common-sensical, yet its significance is clearest in comparison with another historian of American religion, Sydney Ahlstrom. Ahlstrom privileges New England Puritanism, seeing it as shaping the social contract of American society, and ending his story in the early 1970s, when the tradition was in disarray.[20] Rather than finding his home in Puritan New England, Marty found his first in the nineteenth century, the period of the democratization of American Christianity and the age of the "Evangelical Empire." Since the early 1980s Marty has turned towards the twentieth century, where he is in process of writing the first synthetic narrative of American religion in that century.

In his most complete history of American religion, *Pilgrims in Their Own Land*, Marty points to America's unsettled nature as an immigrant nation, essentially restless and full of pilgrims "prodded by a dream." In such a "wild diversity" of religious groups, "it is impossible to find a single ideological thread uniting the Americans in their spiritual pilgrimage." The religious history of America could be written as a series of failed attempts to establish traditional forms in a new land, but instead Marty sees it as a story of adaptation, invention and accommodation. The fundamental principle that shapes American religion is voluntaryism: "America therefore helped patent freedom *for* choice as well as freedom *of* choice in religion. As such, it can be seen as the first and most modern society." Far from seeing a progression from homogeneity to modern pluralism, Marty sees religious pluralism from the beginning in America, "from the time two men of different faiths set foot on its shore with intention to remain."[21]

After touching briefly on Native-American religion and the Spanish empire, Marty's story turns to the beginnings of Protestantism in the New World. This early history is tribal, not just of Native-Americans, but also various tribes of Europeans, who linked "race-ethnicity-religion-culture." The attempts to replicate European forms of religious empire threatened to turn the new world into the old in the mid-sixteenth century, yet fortunately the land did not allow it. Puritan New England becomes yet another tribe, more theologically literate and organized than most, yet still one whose goal of creating a model Christian commonwealth would founder as soon as the external factors—of memory, wilderness and ominous Indians—dissipated. While "the founders of the earliest American colonies wanted nothing so much as to be left alone to develop single communities for undistracted and undivided people," the "American landscape . . . almost instantly beckoned" and soon produced "nonconformist people," Baptists, Quakers, and others, to whom "belonged the American tomorrow." The heros of this reading turn out to be Roger Williams, the Calverts of Maryland and William Penn, those who demonstrated that "the spirit of exile and dissent could also issue in ordered government." These are the prototypical Americans, who, like Penn, "dreamed of an innocent and simple order but allowed for complexity and pluralism."[22]

What American pluralism did, even before the church was officially severed from state support, was to make religion a matter of choice. "For centuries godliness was supposed to be passed on with the genes: Christians were simply children of Christian parents. But that process didn't work long in America, for many chose to fall away." The Great Awakening pushed the necessity of choice even further, creating one essential of "modern faith": "[N]o longer did a particular faith simply 'come with the territory'. . . . Now Americans felt spiritually stirred to take up their own pilgrimages, to be restless about the soul in their new environment. Awakeners learned to exploit or promote this restlessness." The Great Awakening, Marty concludes, "led to competition: free enterprise had come to the world of religion."[23]

Following the revivals of the Great Awakening came three revolutions: the War of Independence, the separation of church and state, and a third revolution, of the Deist Enlightenment, which made religion more a matter of reason than of emotion. To Marty, the second revolution was the most radical, truly a *Novus Ordo Seclorum*, a new order for the ages, for it was "the most decisive element in an epochal shift in the Western world's approach to relations between civil and religious spheres of life after fourteen centuries," the end of the principle of religious uniformity as a basis for civil peace.[24] A struggle originated by religious dissenters, it found allies in people "who professed a new religion, an enlightened faith for a new nation," a republican religion. The American Founders, Marty writes, "helped produce at least two major religious innovations": (1) the view that religion was larger than individual sects, encompassing even the nation; and (2) the reduction of religion to individual opinion. This, plus the necessary corollary of separating church and state, "sundered what both tribal and church-minded people had kept bound together for thousands of years."

Benjamin Franklin was one of the first to call for a new American religion, defending "the Necessity of a *Publick Religion*" already in 1749, which would be sort of an umbrella over the existing competing sects. "Public religion to Franklin," writes Marty, "meant not the end of sects but of sectarianism, not the end of their freedoms but the increase of their duty to produce a common morality." The Founders "put their public religion to good use," for these men of the Enlightenment, like Franklin, James Madison, and Thomas Jefferson, constructed a "social fabric that assured freedom to the several churches, yet stressed common concerns of society." This new settlement, written in Jefferson's Virginia Statute of Religious Liberty, Madison's "Memorial and Remonstrance Against Religious Assessments," and later into the First Amendment, transformed religion by reducing it to opinion. Madison's arguments for a large republic were based primarily on his understanding that to preserve religious liberty and toleration, and indeed civil security, required "the multiplicity of sects." The result of this Marty sees as unambiguously positive: "After centuries of bloodshed in holy wars and after long struggles for legal power in early America, churches in the new nation were hardly ever again to leave dead bodies in the trail of their conflict." The public religion could not compete against the revivalists that sprang up in the early nineteenth century, but it did find "its true home in aspects of the American legal tradition, its established church in the public schools, its creed in the Declaration, . . . [and] its passion in the cries by citizens at the deepest crises of American life," in the idiom of America's civic piety.[25]

After Independence, the pilgrimage turned to the frontier, filling the landscape with competing sects in the great "Soul Rush" of the Second Great Awakening. The restless competition between Methodist circuit riders and Baptist lay preachers democratized American Christianity, even as it transformed religion from rational assent into fervent, emotional piety. The fervor that converted the new country into a Christian nation also pushed beyond its boundaries: "Marvelously the mission *to* America from colonial days had now become the mission *of* America to the world." Yet this impulse also turned inward, first in expanding spiritual experience into "wholly new religious outlooks," such as Mormonism or the Shakers, and second into the vast program of social reform to transform the "moral order to make it more like the Kingdom of God." Until the early nineteenth century, most religious impulses had been bounded "within inherited religious institutions." But then new movements burst the bounds of older forms and orthodox theology, movements as contradictory yet as similar as various utopians, millennialists, perfectionists, communitarians, and transcendentalists, "pathfinders beyond the bounds of existing pilgrimages."[26]

Marty does not use issues of theology, such as biblical authority or typologies of conversion, to distinguish among religious movements; rather it is their relationship to the world, to the "public." For him, the more fundamental gulf is not between the Puritan Jonathan Edwards and the neo-orthodox Reinhold Niebuhr, but rather between the public and post-millennial Edwards and the private and pre-millennial Dwight L. Moody.

After the birth of the republic, the next great age of transition in American society was the late nineteenth century, when the country passed from a rural, relatively homogeneous culture to an urban and industrial city-scape. The chronicling of this transition is the theme of the first volume of his magnum opus, *Modern American Religion: The Irony of It All, 1893–1919*. Using his favorite trope of historical irony, Marty demonstrates how Christianity consistently reinforced and exaggerated "those illusions of innocence, virtue, wisdom, and power" as America entered the industrial and imperial age. He finds the period full of irony, as consequences of human activity were so often the opposite of religious aspirations. It is especially ironic that this Progressive age "was also the era in which virtually every enduring and vital American religious conservatism was born."[27]

Marty takes a topical approach, finding five major responses to the modern challenges in this quarter century. The "modernists" were "the liberal agents of the modern, progressives who actually wanted to advance the processes of change from within the Protestant core-culture." Their archetypal event was the World's Parliament of Religions, held in Chicago in 1893, and these modernists pushed towards a universal cosmopolitanism in religion, beyond any provincial or denominational distinctives.

The "moderns" were those "gifted innovators" who developed "a distinctly modern consciousness." They were members of the first university-trained generation in America, figures such as historians Charles Beard and Carl Becker, and philosophers William James and George Herbert Mead, most of whom had struggled to free themselves from the small-town piety of their youth. "All of them repudiated the offerings of theological modernism," but were often "more respectful of historic faith" than religious modernists. The main exemplar of this tradition was John Dewey, whose book *A Common Faith* proposed faith in the democratic polity. Unlike in Europe, where philosophers of modernity, such as Nietzsche, Marx and Freud, opposed religion, in America these figures often looked backwards, to earlier, pre-industrial models for social and personal cohesiveness, contributing "to the peculiar mix of secularity and religiousness" that has survived in American intellectual life. They embraced the modern, with its evolutionary dynamism, individualism, relativism, and faith in scientific progress, but also sought to heal the fragmentation of modern life.

In the middle were those people of faith who tried to adapt to modern challenges while retaining the essence of the past, through establishing "symbolic canopies," "translucent shelters which kept threatening outside forces at some distance yet without wholly screening them out." Marty focuses on several groups: immigrants, racial minorities, and others, of whom "ethnicity mingled with religion." Many sought quickly to assimilate, yet often battled with co-religionists or ethnic rivals. He also tells the story of traditional denominations which in their quest to accommodate theological modernism, new educational developments, higher criticism and ecumenism, tried to retain the kernel of old orthodoxies.

"Countermodernism," the fourth type, is a "very modern" reaction to religious modernists, taken by many who assumed the name "Fundamentalists" in 1920. While opposing certain theological innovations, countermodernists were not afraid of modern techniques of organization and publicity. Marty considers them theologically innovative, with one of the most significant being premillennialism, especially the dispensational variety." A second innovation, in Marty's reading, was the development of "fresh rationales for biblical inerrancy as the base for authority," a mostly "fabricated" doctrine in reaction against the erosions caused by relativism, evolutionary models of history, and biblical criticism. Marty finds it ironic that "[p]roponents pictured each of these as simple repristinations or replications of timeless Christian and hence, evangelically Protestant movements." But in reality, "they were each complex innovations or inventions that refashioned elements taken from longer pasts." Marty does not consider countermodernists conservative; rather, a "radical inventive power was here at work which discovered or created a future whose threat and promise motivated people to strenuous activity." He finds this an ultimate irony as the innovators became defenders of the old-time religion.[28]

Marty sees a fifth response to the modern, the "transmodern," those who attempted to retrieve "organic models from the past" in their move beyond modern fragmentation and alienation. In this camp Marty places the rise of new therapeutic movements around the turn of the century, in religious forms such as Christian Science, but also academic psychology and its popularizations. He also considers the modern ecumenical movement and the social gospel as transmodern. Again, their aspirations were reversed, as union efforts produced more division and therapeutic models increased psychological fragmentation.

World War I unified American religion for a time, yet after the war, conflict replaced irony as Marty's major theme for the interwar period, with religious conflict anticipating and mirroring larger social conflict along lines of ideology, race, class and socio-economic doctrine. Yet it was a surprisingly non-violent conflict, one that left only four deaths from specifically religious causes between 1919 and 1941.

He interprets the schism and final cultural disestablishment of old-stock American Protestantism during the interwar period as one of the great events of American religion. Unlike a mythic view of the past as one of religious peace and homogeneity, the main drama was the "climatic struggle over the role of the once imperial Protestantism." This was the period that witnessed the last time the Supreme Court called America a Christian nation, and indeed, the last time that it was. "[N]ot since the Civil War had America been more torn. In matters specifically religious the nation had never seemed more divided than it was in these interwar years." While the main conflict was between "original stock Protestants vs. everyone else," the noise was increased by countless other battles, between "'100-percent Americans' vs. Communists and Slavs"; "old-stock

Anglo-Saxons vs. Catholic or Jewish or Asian immigrants; white Christians vs. black Christians; Fundamentalists vs. Modernists; Protestant liberals vs. Protestant realists; along with battles over Prohibition, birth control, labor rights, capitalism, pacifism, and the New Deal. "All of these conflicts," Marty maintains, "were based in religious beliefs and passions or else included profound religious motivations."[29]

At issue in all of these conflicts was a controversy that continues to divide Americans, a debate over whether "America had or needed a single center, a dominant influence, a privileged philosophy, a specified religion, if it was to promote morals, engender good values, and encourage civic virtue in the populace." The side insisting upon homogeneity stressed a Judeo-Christian tradition or Christian nationalism. While sympathetic to homogeneity, Marty finds the aspiration towards consensus "better fed on common stories and intentions than on privileging one religious complex."

All the noise of conflict then was over the power to shape the larger public culture. In this period, the formerly dominant "WASP" culture lost that power in schism and internal disarray, but also because they "yielded their hegemonic place in the culture more gracefully than one could have expected as they gradually learned to share space and power." Central, of course, to the decline of the Protestant establishment is its own internal schism, in the Fundamentalist-Modernist controversy of the 1920s. In part, Marty moves beyond interpreting the series of schisms as simply a battle between public and private elements of Protestantism, yet he does see it as a conflict which has "permanently divided Protestantism," opening up the culture for marginal and marginalized peoples.[30]

In spite of this elemental religious conflict, Marty finds almost no incidents of violence. "Americans take for granted that their own religious controversies should be verbal and bloodless, that it is too late in history for religious wars." Yet, as Marty reminds us, the twentieth century is full of religious bloodshed. The "astounding fact" of bloodless conflict makes the American situation exceptional, and hopefully spells the future for a post-Constantinian Christianity. Marty explains this phenomenon by pointing, not just to America's privatized faiths or multiplicity of sects, but also to its "culture of cross-clefts and crisscrossing" loyalties. Rather than reinforcing each other, the numerous conflicts served to knit American society together. Class lines, economic dislocation, ethnicity, and politics cut across religious divisions, yet there was no social breakdown like the Civil War, where differences in economies, population, social structure, constitutional position, and religion coalesced along regional lines. American religion, far from being the mobilizer of internecine warfare as has been the case in Europe, was "coming to be among the agencies through which conflict could be directed into ever less dangerous channels." The dominant Protestant churches, concerned with the public realm, were realizing how pluralistic America had become, and had learned what public philosopher Walter Lippmann called "the necessity of not pressing any claim too far." Marty considers this "their great contribution to civil peace, bargained for at the cost of some loss to their own self-interests." Others, such as the Fundamentalist minority and other factions, had the luxury to push their absolute claims, but only within this pluralist polity.[31]

Yet upon American entry into World War II, Marty finds a sudden quieting of the "noise of conflict in public religion," as religious leaders unified in face of a common enemy.[32] From 1941 through the early 1960s, the search for "One Nation, Indivisible" provides the dominant motif, but behind this religious consensus was the slow cultural disestablishment of mainstream Protestantism, as the dominant elite struggled to respond to religious pluralism by opening up to Catholics and Jews in a new ideology of a "Judeo-Christian tradition," but also trying to counteract a militant secularism. This consensus created one of the greatest efforts at ecumenism since the Reformation, yet, as Marty explains in a telling metaphor, this unity was like that of the ancient inhabitants of the island of Crete, who were notorious for internecine warfare but who united in the face of an external enemy: "Their coming together was strategic, not based on profound new agreements . . . As soon as the menacing forces disappeared, the [Cretan] cities had the luxury of going back to their private wars."[33]

The post-war decades were the period of "formal ecumenical advance unmatched in previous centuries," with the founding of the "paraecumenical" National Association of Evangelicals (NAE) in 1942, the World Council of Churches in 1948, the National Council of Churches in 1950, and even the Second Vatican Council in the 1960s, which opened the way for dialogue between Roman Catholics and other Christians. It is difficult, as Marty points out, to recapture the exhilarating sense of the promise of reunifying believers, especially when the dream of "The One Church in the One Nation for the One World came down to being a matter of little local councils of churches and timid interactions."[34] Still, Marty is careful to reconstruct the optimism of a period that is difficult to understand because of its very proximity.

One of the more interesting aspects of Marty's narrative is how the categories of the "public church" return in the mid-twentieth century. Earlier in his career, Marty generally overlooked the right wing of American Protestantism, but, paralleling the maturation of Evangelicalism, he now gives its early history a prominent place. Chronicling the evolution of the New Evangelicalism, from the founding of the NAE to the rise of Billy Graham, to the schism between the Evangelicals and the intransigent Fundamentalists at the 1957 New York Crusade, Marty focuses on the critical unifying role of evangelist Billy Graham and journalist-theologian Carl F. H. Henry. Graham was able to combine an openness to mainline Protestantism while retaining the orthodox distinctives of the New Evangelicalism, with Henry providing the intellectual foundation, a public theology for an emerging subculture. Henry sought to carve out space for a new movement, between modernist theology and a rigid fundamentalism, as Karl Barth and the Niebuhrs had moved liberalism towards neo-orthodoxy. "Fearful of Catholic domination," Marty writes, "disgusted by secularism, dismissive of Protestant liberalism, Henry touted evangelicalism as the single force that could properly shape national and world culture," not only by its focus on personal rebirth, but on its renewed insights into human culture that Henry was pioneering.[35] Henry's hope, of turning "the uneasy conscience of modern evangelicalism into a new reformation," was not fulfilled, though it did provide a way for Evangelicalism to move back into the public realm of religion, laying the groundwork for a renewed encounter with the secular and pluralist world beyond its boundaries.[36]

The late 1940s and 1950s were a time of culture-wide religious revival, or more accurately, a revival of interest in religion. In contrast to interpretations of the 1950s as in some way normative for the place of religion in American society, Marty sees it as one of the strangest, for it was based on a unity like that of ancient Crete, a unity in the face of militant "godless Communism," one that also combined piety with advancing secularism. To carry his own attitude towards religion in the 1950s, Marty relies on the voices of contemporary critics, chiefly Reinhold Niebuhr. Marty contrasts Niebuhr's measured Cold War politics, wherein he struggled to maintain an ironic perspective between a fallen America and a demonic Soviet Union, with the Presbyterian layman and Secretary of State John Foster Dulles, who was one of the first to call for a spiritual revival and almost called for a holy war against communism.

Communism, for all the loyalty oaths and rumors of war, was a threat outside America. The more immediate issue that mobilized the religious community after World War II was secularism, with the chief battleground the public school. "Democracy, in the final analysis, is a religious idea," as one prominent liberal Protestant commented, as he struggled with a way to maintain the broadly Protestant character of public schools in a pluralistic context. Secularist Americans took to the courts to enforce their view that religion was not a civic or public issue, but rather individual and private.

In pluralist post-war America, the attempt to be unified, especially after previous religious conflict, almost created a civil religion out of America itself. As described by sociologist Will Herberg, being Protestants, Catholics or Jews were just different ways of being American, for a broad "American Way of Life" had become "the operative faith of the American people." As one commentator analyzed at the time, "The faith is not in God but in faith; we worship our own worshipping." The religious revival bordered on the worship of democracy, success, money, security, and indeed, some even preached the explicit worship of a political system.[37]

Many Christians found this development deeply threatening, as secularism appeared to be in ascendence. Here was a common enemy that could unify, at least temporarily, battling factions. This culture war anticipated a similar religious mobilization against a militant secularism in the 1980s and 1990s, but its chief protagonists in the 1950s were mainline Protestants: "Liberals fought secularism in 1945 with fervor to match that generated by evangelicals ever after," and for liberal Protestants, "the best evidence for the decline [in Protestant America] was the change in public schools, preserves of their kind of Protestantism in days past, but now lost, or nearly lost, to secularism."[38] Jesuit theologian John Courtney Murray agreed with Protestant Liberal Charles Clayton Morrison and Evangelical evangelist Billy Graham in seeing the drift towards secularism as hostile towards religion. As Marty comments, "If that kind of critique was one day to become a preserve of religious conservatives, those who were marked as liberals first isolated it and counterattacked it on an intellectual level."[39]

In this third volume of his history, Marty relies on the critics of the revival to critique the revival, revealing his own disdain at the excesses of secularized piety. He laments the absence of a solid Christian witness: "Where now were the profound revivalists like Jonathan Edwards and Walter Rauschenbusch . . . who have fused piety and public prophesy?" Other than a few exceptions, Marty finds the 1950s rather barren.[40] But behind the tenuous consensus of the 1950s stands for Marty John Courtney Murray's question: "How much pluralism can a pluralist society stand" and still maintain coherence for "responsible action in history?" Marty's fourth volume will seek to discover how Americans addressed these questions, as the coming of the 1960s rendered the optimism of the immediate postwar period virtually irretrievable. While he does not say it, Marty finds it ironic that the vision of "One Nation, Under God, Indivisible," was about to be shattered in first radical then conservative political movements from the 1960s to the 1980s. Yet this for Marty provides hope, for it suggests a necessary openness for the actions of a God Whose ways are often hidden and Who cannot be reduced to a mere tribal deity, however large the tribe or powerful the nation.

OBSERVING FUNDAMENTALISMS

Marty's interpretations of religious countermodernism led naturally to his selection as head of the Fundamentalism Project, a five-year study, under the auspices of the American Academy of Arts and Sciences, of comparative anti-modernist religious movements around the world.[41] Marty and his associate director R. Scott Appleby coordinate numerous scholars and provide the summary essays in the multi-volume project. Marty has the careful observer's skill in discerning and analyzing contemporary trends. Early in his career, Marty concentrated on secularism, and he still sees himself close to the secular in his own spirituality. Yet since the late 1970s, when conservative religious forces began to have a greater effect on the public realm, Marty has shifted his attention towards that part of the religious spectrum.

While not strictly history, the project will be one of Marty's more influential works and thus it is important to discuss it here, for Marty's synthetic position will be the dominant interpretation of one of the most important manifestations of religion for the next half-century or so. Will this be the direction of Marty's work after *Modern American Religion*? If this project can convince policy-makers, the primary audience, that fundamentalisms must be interpreted as essentially and irreducible religious rather than spiritual rhetoric masking socio-political programs, then it will be a fitting capstone to his prolific career as a historian of public religion.

How does Marty define fundamentalism? While first coined in 1920 as a self-description of militant anti-modern American Protestants, Marty uses it generically, positing a "family of fundamentalisms" or fundamentalist-like movements.[42] Synthesizing a large variety of scholarship, Marty considers fundamentalism primarily a form of *"religious idealism . . . for the transcendent realm of the divine, as revealed and made normative for the religious community, alone provides an irreducible basis for communal and personal identity."*[43] Fundamentalism is:

A tendency, a habit of mind, found within religious communities and paradigmatically embodied in certain representative individuals and movements, which manifests itself as a strategy, or set of strategies, by which beleaguered believers attempt to preserve their distinctive identity as a people or group. Feeling this identity to be at risk in the contemporary era, they fortify it by a selective retrieval of doctrines, beliefs, and practices from a sacred past. These retrieved "fundamentals" are refined, modified and sanctioned in a spirit of shrewd pragmatism: they are to serve as a bulwark against the encroachment of outsiders who threaten to draw the believers into a syncretistic, arreligious, or irreligious cultural milieu.

While harkening back to an imagined past, fundamentalism is "vitally original" and innovative in its effort to preserve what it perceived as threatened: "religious identity thus renewed becomes the exclusive and absolute basis for a recreated political and social order that is oriented to the future rather than the past. By selecting elements of tradition and modernity, fundamentalists seek to remake the world in service of a dual commitment to the unfolding eschatological drama . . . and to self-preservation."[44] Fundamentalism reacts to the modern, specifically modern secular rationality, religious tolerance, relativism and religious individualism. While opposed to modernity, Fundamentalism exists "in a type of symbiotic relationship with the modern," finding technology, mass media and other elements "congenial to their purposes."

Marty develops a series of attributes of "pure" fundamentalism. Starting with the irreducible notion of religious identity, fundamentalists share numerous family traits. They tend to "depict revealed truth as whole, unified, and undifferentiated."[45] They are "intentionally scandalous," opposing historical consciousness, hermeneutics, developmental or evolutionary models and other canons of post-Enlightenment secular rationality, claiming instead "privileged access to absolute truth." They are concerned with setting sharp boundaries in behavior and politics, defining and even mythologizing their enemies and protecting the group from contamination. They are zealous in extending the faith, updating and modifying traditional forms of proselytism. Seeing a clear divine purpose in history, they rely on "dramatic eschatologies," often seeing themselves as divine agents to further the goal of history. Born in a spirit of crisis, fundamentalists enter into the political realm, seeking "to replace existing structures with a comprehensive system," a "totalitarian impulse" that would reorder all elements within society. While seeking to transform society, they first create their own institutions, developing controlled environments, "worlds within the world" where their ideal moral order is realized in microcosm.

While idealizing a pure past, fundamentalists are "selectively traditional and selectively modern," using certain doctrines as "ideological weapons against a hostile world," but unself-consciously employing modern technology to communicate these doctrines. This selectivity demonstrates "a closer affinity to modernism than to traditionalism," which Marty interprets as a "resentment of modern ends." Fundamentalists usually rely upon "charismatic and authoritarian male leaders," but also have mass appeal, eschewing the more elitist strategies of secular modernists.

Marty seeks to maintain scholarly objectivity in the work, seeing fundamentalists as intelligent opponents of the more destructive elements of modernity. While agreeing with some of their diagnoses, he views their solutions as a threat to civil polity. One of their shared tenets denies his distinction between the public and private aspects of religion, as is their insistence upon non-negotiable absolutes. While admitting that "fundamentalisms have a religious basis—and in fact claim to represent the pristine and most authentic religious impulses of the tradition—the authors of this volume consistently question that very authenticity." Fundamentalists "narrow and rationalize the rich historic tradition at their disposal, often robbing it of its mysteries, mysticism, magical qualities, complexities, ambiguities, and situational character." Too often they equate religion with nationalism, seeking political means to expand the boundaries of their beliefs: "They anticipate a time when the true believer will establish the rules of the game for believer and nonbeliever alike," and like nationalisms, they "possess hegemonic political ambitions and demand colossal sacrifices from the devotees."[46] Marty does see, however, a stronger influence in the realm of the personal and cultural than at the level of the state.

CONCLUSION

One of Marty's favorite quotations is from the Spanish philosopher Jose' Ortega y Gasset, "I am I and my circumstances," signifying for Marty the close interaction between personal identity and historical context. Marty has a very clear sense of his own spiritual identity, with deep roots in a historic tradition and with few personal discontinuities or crises of conviction. His career has moved from a coherent tradition outward into the public sphere, presuming the reality and truthfulness of his historic Lutheran faith. In that sense, he is perhaps perfectly situated to understand the opposite trend that those who experience the other side of pluralism miss. Most Americans, at least since mid-century, have struggled in the contrary direction, trying to find roots and their own particular spiritual identity. Marty understands the struggle, yet as an observer, not a participant. His own journey was in the opposite direction, and thus he celebrates pluralism, whereas those of us on the other side, who have struggled to discover our spiritual selves, are uneasy with his too ready embrace of a pluralism that often seems like spiritual anarchy and chaos.

As the preeminent historian of American religion, Marty's distinction between the public and private is problematic, for it leads too often to privileging the nation over against the distinctively Christian, the *polis* over the *ecclesia*. His insistence upon the distinctiveness of the American religious experience is vital, for political disestablishment has shaped Christianity more than even the Reformation, in ways still not fully understood.

His project of combining commitment with civility will be the larger challenge for Christianity in the next century, and thus his reading of the history of the church will become increasingly influential. He ends his storyteller's autobiography with a word of faith: "For the Christian there is, . . . always and only a word calling for response. It comes from One who announced little about the point of arrival but said what his followers needed to know when He declared, 'I am the way.'"[47] One wonders, however, whether Marty's commitment to civility ends up limiting the offense, the exclusivist scandal of Him who said the rest of the verse. His position is sufficient for a historian of religion in the *res publica*, but Christianity cannot be fragmented into distinct modes, in spite of modern canons of historical interpretation. Like early America, Christianity was born in the midst of religious pluralism, yet it insisted upon the scandal of a historical resurrection. In our commitment to civility, we must clearly articulate to those outside the faith that it is *true* that "all things cohere in Christ."

BIBLIOGRAPHY

There has been no complete bibliography of Martin Marty's works. His students Jay P. Dolan and James P. Wind have edited a *Festschrift, New Dimensions in American Religious History: Essays in Honor of Martin E. Marty* (Grand Rapids: Eerdmans, 1993), which contains an excellent listing of his significant books and articles. Two works, his autobiography, *By Way of Response* (Nashville: Abingdon, 1981), and *A Cry of Absence: Reflections for the Winter of the Heart* (San Francisco: Harper and Row, 1983), both contain Marty's thoughts at their most personal. His more representative and significant works, in alphabetical order, include:

PRIMARY SOURCES

The Infidel: Freethought and American Religion. Cleveland: Meridian Books, 1961.
Modern American Religion. Chicago: University of Chicago Press.
    Vol. 1: *The Irony of It All, 1893–1919.* 1986.
    Vol. 2: *The Noise of Conflict, 1919–1941.* 1991.
    Vol. 3: *Under God, Indivisible, 1941–1960.* 1995.
    Vol. 4: forthcoming.
A Nation of Behavers. Chicago: University of Chicago Press, 1976.

The New Shape of American Religion. New York: Harper, 1959.

Pilgrims in Their Own Land: 500 Years of American Religion. Boston: Little, Brown, 1984.

Protestantism. New York: Holt Rinehart and Winston, 1972.

Protestantism in the United States: Righteous Empire, 2d edition. New York: Macmillan, 1986.

The Public Church: Mainline, Evangelical, Catholic. New York: Crossroad, 1981.

Religion and Republic: The American Circumstance. Boston: Beacon Press, 1987.

NOTES

1. Martin E. Marty, *By Way of Response* (Nashville: Abingdon, 1981), 28; and *The Public Church: Mainline, Evangelical, Catholic* (New York: Crossroad, 1981), 8.

2. Martin E. Marty, *By Way of Response,* 33, and his memoir in the University of Chicago Divinity School's *Criterion* (summer, 1963).

3. See, for example, *The New Shape of American Religion* (New York: Harper, 1959), *Second Chance for American Protestants* (New York: Harper, 1963), *The Search for a Useable Future* (New York: Harper, 1968), *The Fire We Can Light: The Role of Religion in a Suddenly Different World* (New York: Doubleday, 1973), and *The Pro and Con Book of Religious America: A Bicentennial Argument* (Waco, Texas: Word Books, 1975).

4. See his *Health and Medicine in the Lutheran Tradition: Being Well* (New York: Crossroads, 1983) and *A Cry of Absence: Reflections for the Winter of the Heart* (San Francisco: Harper and Row, 1983).

5. Published by K. G. Saur, Munich and New York, 1992. This multi-volume series reprints the essential articles on American Protestantism, focusing on issues such as women in the church, foreign missions, dissenters, and others.

6. Marty, *By Way of Response,* 104, and Harold Henderson, "Martin Marty," *Chicago Reader* (27 February 1987): 18.

7. Marty, *Cry of Absence,* 6, 33.

8. Quoted in *Cry of Absence,* 10. Much of Marty's early work focused on this "intellectual solidarity" with the secular. See his *Varieties of Unbelief* (New York: Holt, Rinehart and Winston, 1964), *The Modern Schism: Three Paths to the Secular* (New York: Harper, 1969), and his dissertation, published as *The Infidel: Freethought and American Religion* (Cleveland: Meridian Books, 1961).

9. Marty E. Marty, "The Difference in Being a Christian and the Difference It Makes—For History," in *History and Historical Understanding,* ed. C. T. McIntire and Ronald Wells (Grand Rapids: Eerdmans, 1984), 43ff.

10. Martin E. Marty, "A Christian Interpretation of History," in *Conspectus of History,* vol. 1, no. 5, ed. Dwight W. Hoover and John T. A. Koumoulides, (Muncie, Ind.: Ball State University, 1978), 31f.

11. Ibid., 31–34.

12. Martin E. Marty, *Modern American Religion,* vol. 1, *The Irony of It All, 1893–1919* (University of Chicago Press, 1986), 6–7.

13. Marty, *The Public Church,* 16.

14. Marty, *By Way of Response,* 114–15, 133.

15. Ibid., 102–103; Marty, *Public Church,* 103. Marty has written extensively on the issue of civil religion. See especially "Two Kinds of Civil Religion," originally published in 1974, in which he discerns priestly and prophetic styles in two separate frameworks, "The Nation Under God," and "The Nation as Self-Transcendent." An

essential collection of his writings on church and state is *Religion and Republic: The American Circumstance* (Boston: Beacon Press, 1987).

16. Martin E. Marty, *Righteous Empire: The Protestant Experience in America* (New York: Harper and Row, 1970), 179–82.

17. Compare his earlier works such as *Protestantism* with his "Tensions Within Contemporary Evangelicalism: A Critical Appraisal," in David F. Wells and John D. Woodbridge, *The Evangelicals* (Grand Rapids: Baker, 1975).

18. The terms Fundamentalist and New Evangelical are two self-styled varieties of theologically conservative American Protestantism. While there is debate over the lineage of each branch, the two became much more distinct after evangelist Billy Graham's 1957 Crusade, for which he accepted liberal Protestant support. See Marty's account in vol. 3 of *Modern American Religion: Under God, Indivisible* (Chicago: University of Chicago Press, 1995), especially chapters 8, 10 and 25.

19. Martin E. Marty, *Protestantism in the United States: Righteous Empire*, 2d rev. ed. (New York: Macmillan, 1986), 263. See also "New-Time Religion: The Old Face of Fundamentalism Lifted," in *Religion and Republic: The American Experience* (Boston: Beacon Press, 1987; originally published in 1982 as "Fundamentalism as a Social Phenomenon").

20. See Sydney Ahlstrom, *A Religious History of the American People* (New Haven: Yale University Press, 1972).

21. Martin E. Marty, *Pilgrims in Their Own Land* (New York: Penguin, 1984), ix–x; *The New Shape of American Religion* (New York: Harper, 1959), 68.

22. Marty, *Pilgrims*, 89.

23. Ibid., 107–108, 128.

24. Martin E. Marty, "The Virginia Statute Two Hundred Years Later," in *The Virginia Statute for Religious Freedom*, ed. Merrill D. Peterson and Robert C. Vaughan (Cambridge: Cambridge University Press, 1988), 1.

25. Marty, *Pilgrims*, 158, 163–65.

26. Ibid., 175, 186–89.

27. Marty, vol. 1, *Irony of It All*, 5, 193.

28. Marty, vol. 1, *Irony of It All*, 207–19.

29. Martin E. Marty, *Modern American Religion*, vol. 2, *The Noise of Conflict, 1919–1941* (Chicago: University of Chicago Press, 1991), 2–4.

30. Ibid., 6, 13.

31. Ibid., 341–46.

32. Martin Marty graciously allowed this author to examine an advance copy of the manuscript to *One Nation, Indivisible* (Chicago: University of Chicago Press, forthcoming). As it is in press at the time of this writing, footnotes will be to chapters.

33. *One Nation, Indivisible*, chap. 3.

34. Ibid., chap. 14.

35. Ibid., chap. 25.

36. Ibid., chap. 10.

37. Ibid., chap. 23.

38. Ibid., chap. 10.

39. Ibid., chap. 11.

40. Ibid., chap. 18.

41. Martin E. Marty and R. Scott Appleby, eds., *Fundamentalisms Observed*, vol. 1 of *The Fundamentalism Project* (Chicago: University of Chicago Press, 1991). See also vol. 2, *Fundamentalisms and Society* and vol. 3, *Fundamentalisms and the State*, both 1993. The series projects at least three additional volumes, including a final volume which will discuss public policy implications.

42. More controversial is equating Christian Fundamentalism with other forms of militant religious traditionalism, yet here Marty and the Project are on solid ground in seeing family resemblances among different anti-modernist religious movements. For his defense of the cross-cultural use of the term, see the introduction to *Fundamentalisms Observed*, viii–x. He admits, though, that there is more resemblance among "people of the book," Jews, Christians, and Muslims, than among other faiths.

43. Martin E. Marty and R. Scott Appleby, "Conclusion: An Interim Report on a Hypothetical Family," in *Fundamentalisms Observed*, 817.

44. Ibid., 835.

45. Ibid., 818 (all emphases deleted). See also Marty's early attack on "integralism" and "closed" forms of faith in his *Varieties of Unbelief*.

46. Marty and Appleby, *Fundamentalism and the State*, 622–23.

47. Marty, *By Way of Response*, 143.

28

Heiko Oberman

Mickey L. Mattox

Without a grasp of the fourteenth and fifteenth centuries, the medieval history of Christian thought is not only left incomplete but, perhaps worse, Reformation and Counter-Reformation seem to appear "out of the blue," or rather out of the black night of an unknown and, therefore, unbeloved period.

—Forerunners of the Reformation, 1966

Centuries of pseudo-historical research propaganda have acquainted us with the image of a medieval Mater Ecclesia and her handmaiden Theologia straying benighted into a dead-end street on the dark and frozen eve of the Reformation; a plight from which true religion was miraculously guided into the dawn of the modern era by the morning star of the wise men of Wittenberg. . . . [T]he opposite wall of the Reformation gallery has been refitted only in recent decades with the so-called ecumenical image of Luther. Although drawn from another perspective, the new ecumenical portrait carries the same message and only confirms its Protestant counterpart. . . . Brought up under the sinister constellation of nominalism, Luther was . . . predestined by this radically "un-Catholic" theology to heresy and the destruction of the unity of the church. Thus both confessional armies have engaged in a war of words in the no-man's-land between the Middle Ages and the modern era. The shelling has disfigured the terrain beyond recognition.

—*Masters of the Reformation, 1981*

Periodization is the historian's indispensable shorthand. It enables one to use a single word or phrase to summarize—and thus to conceal—the complexity and diversity characteristic of every phase of human history. Of course, deciding just which word or phrase most accurately sums up the spirit and direction of any given era is a controversial task, for such labels tend to prejudice the way in which one understands the era. When the subject is the history of Christianity, periodization becomes even more difficult. The faith commitments that church historians bring to their work tend to run even deeper than do the commitments that all scholars have to particular research paradigms, for questions of church history impinge directly on matters of faith, matters on which the multitude of Christian communities frequently differ. Not surprisingly, given the regrettable divisions in Western Christendom, church history has been and continues to be (to borrow the metaphor cited above), the rocky terrain upon which the battles between Roman Catholicism and her estranged Protestant and Sectarian children are fought.

Heiko Augustinus Oberman, arguably the most original and influential historian of late medieval and Reformation studies in the latter half of the twentieth century, has spent nearly a lifetime attempting to revise the traditional periodization of church history from roughly 1250 to 1550. Born (1930) and educated in Holland, the precocious young Oberman had earned both the Ph.D. (1956) and Th.D. (1957) degrees at the University of Utrecht by the time he was twenty-seven. In 1958, he was ordained to the ministry of the *Nederlands Hervormde Kerk*. He then accepted a position at Harvard University, where he served as a professor in the Divinity School from 1958 to 1963, and as the Winn Professor of Ecclesiastical History from 1963 until 1967. Oberman then left Harvard to become director of the influential Institute for the Late Middle Ages and Reformation (*Institut für Spätmittelalter und Reformation*) at the University of Tübingen in West Germany. In addition, he served from 1962–1965 as a Protestant observer at the Second Vatican Council. Since 1984, Oberman has been professor of history at the University of Arizona, where he continues his teaching and research.

Over the course of his distinguished career, Oberman has produced numerous important studies of the late medieval and Reformation periods. Almost equally importantly, however, he has shaped a generation of the most gifted young historians at some of the most prestigious universities in the world, guiding their dissertation work to suit the needs of his own research program. In fact, his students' work has so closely paralleled his own that historians speak of the "Oberman school" in Reformation studies. Many of these students' dissertations have subsequently been published in what is perhaps the most helpful series in scholarly publishing in church history today, *Studies in Late Medieval and Reformation Thought*, published by E. J. Brill Press in Leiden, Holland, and edited by Oberman himself. Over fifty volumes have now appeared in this influential series. Thus, on account of the efforts of his students, Oberman's impact far outweighs even his own prodigious output.[1]

Oberman's central preoccupation has been the re-interpretation of late medieval theology. In what follows, I offer not so much a summary of Oberman's work—that would be impossible within the confines of an essay of this type—as an outline of some of his more important contributions to our understanding of late medieval and Reformation theology. In order to understand his revisionist project, and hence properly to assess the scope of Oberman's achievement, it is necessary first of all to understand the way in which the connection between the Reformation and the Middle Ages was traditionally conceived. Thus, the first part of this essay treats Oberman's work on late medieval Christianity in the context of preceding Roman Catholic and Protestant historiographies. In the second part, we consider the application of his ideas to the earliest history of the Reformation, and to the theology of Martin Luther in particular. We conclude with a tentative assessment of the success of Oberman's various projects and of his place in the history of late medieval and Reformation studies.

LATE MEDIEVAL AND REFORMATION STUDIES: OBERMAN'S CONTINUITY THESIS

TRADITIONAL APPROACHES TO THE LATE MIDDLE AGES

Perhaps no period has been more consistently maligned than has the later Middle Ages. On the one hand, Protestant historians have tended to focus upon what they consider the moral and theological failings of the late medieval church: the decadence of the Renaissance papacy, the twin crises of the Babylonian Captivity and the Great Schism, the pitiful condition of the clergy in moral and educational terms, the use and abuse of indulgences, and, perhaps most importantly, the system of meritorious works-righteousness.[2] It was precisely these crises, Protestants have argued, which caused the Reformation. Here the "heights" of sixteenth-century theology are made the standard by which to judge the shortcomings of late medieval period.

Those alleged shortcomings are the one matter upon which Protestant historians have tended to agree with their Roman Catholic counterparts. Catholic historians, like the great Étienne Gilson, came to their work with the presupposition that the theology of Thomas Aquinas produced at Paris in the mid-thirteenth century represents the apex of medieval thought, the grand synthesis in comparison to which all subsequent theological systems are judged.[3] An important, perhaps even determining, factor in this interpretation of the course of medieval thought was the encyclical *Aeterni Patris*, issued by Pope Leo XIII in 1879, which not only commended the study of the philosophy and theology of Thomas Aquinas but also had the effect of making his *Summa Theologiae* the official paradigm of Catholic doctrine. For scholars working with such presuppositions, the fourteenth and fifteenth centuries are characterized by a "failure of nerve," a fragmentation of theological system occasioned primarily by the corrosive acids of philosophical nominalism, a skeptical philosophy based upon the denial of the existence of the universal forms presumed by both the Platonism and Aristotelianism on which the great Christian theological syntheses had been built.

Gilson and like-minded scholars argued that William of Occam's destruction of Western confidence in the power of reason led to a generalized rejection of philosophy.[4] By the sixteenth century Occam's pessimism climaxed in Luther's full-scale revolt and the humanists' proto-pragmatism (a tendency to focus upon rhetoric and the "civic virtues" and avoid questions of truth). Protestant theology sans philosophy and pragmatic Christian humanism like that of Erasmus of Rotterdam became the twin heads of the hydra that ultimately resulted in the modern divorce of faith and reason. Gilson himself extended the argument to say that the late medieval divorce between faith and reason accounts for everything from René Descartes' rationalism to William James' proclamation of the individual's right to "will to believe" without sufficient evidence: reason and faith are not only autonomous, they are unrelated.[5] Gilson's views have been further popularized—albeit on a more purely philosophical level—by the late Frederick Copleston in his acclaimed multi-volume *History of Philosophy*.[6]

Professor Joseph Lortz, later an important player at Vatican II, used the results of scholarship like that of Gilson as the basis for his judgment of nominalist theology as "fundamentally un-catholic." He fashioned a new "ecumenical" Roman Catholic view of Luther and the Reformation largely by conceding that the late medieval church needed moral and theological reform.[7] For Lortz, the real tragedy of the Reformation was that Luther knew only the decadent, nominalistic form of scholastic theology,[8] implying that if Luther had known the theology of Thomas he would never have been driven to his irrational embrace of paradox as the only possible foundation for theology.[9] The problem was not so much Luther as it was the decadence of the nominalist theological tradition in which he was trained.

One of the positive results of Lortz's work was a revised interpretation of Martin Luther more conducive to ecumenical dialogue than defensive polemics. Luther on Lortz's reading is now the arch typical *homo religiosus*, the perennial religious man, an honest but misguided and un-systematic thinker who stumbled down the theological blind alley of nominalism during a time when the church had, admittedly, little capacity to offer viable theological solutions because of the theological confusion resulting from the logical conundrums of the nominalists. So for Lortz, as for previous Protestant and Roman Catholic historians, the late medieval period has little to commend it.

THE OBERMAN SCHOOL

Beginning in the late 1950s, Oberman broke into the relative calm of these interpretational waters, arguing convincingly that historians had yet to consider late medieval theology on its own terms. Late medieval nominalism, he insisted, was not primarily a skeptical philosophy, but a theology, focusing on the theme of God's sovereignty and freedom through the distinction between the *potentia dei ordinata* and *potentia dei absoluta*.[10] Indeed, the Oberman School's entire effort might well be characterized as an extended essay on the applicability of this duality to virtually every aspect of thought in the Reformation period, which they have revised considerably to include the period of roughly 1250 to 1550.

In Oberman's skilled hands Luther was transformed. No longer either the lone re-discoverer of the gospel or the ill-fated *homo religiosus* (religious man), he was, as we shall see in greater detail below, merely a faithful Augustinian, a reformer within a tradition of reform whose genius opened up new channels within the well-traveled streams of late medieval thought.[11] Part of the significance of the stream of Christian thought which historians have labeled nominalism is, in Oberman's view, that it contains the current which eventually broke free from traditional channels and formed Reformation theology, the theology of Luther and his followers.

Rather than attempting to demonstrate causal relationships between various theologians and reformers, he has focused upon those "streams" of late medieval thought, arguing for a "cradle-view of history, according to which each period gives birth to the next in such a way that its birthpangs will precede its coming of age . . . as the best theory to date which takes fully into account the coexistence of continuity and discontinuity."[12] Change and development do take place, in other words, but they are best understood when seen in prayer context. The continuity between Reformation and late medieval theology, Oberman has argued, has been obscured by the presuppositions of Roman Catholic and Protestant historians alike.[13] A non-confessional historiography (one which has not been predetermined by Protestant or Roman Catholic presuppositions) must recognize the continuity of the Reformation with late medieval calls for reform, which were first conceived as personal and spiritual, and later applied to the church as a whole.[14] Only then can the legitimate insights of the Reformers be seen in proper perspective.[15] Luther, too, must be seen through the spectacles of late medieval thought, not the colored glasses of confessional biases.[16]

Oberman's is thus a humanistic philosophy of history which does not make "deterministic" judgments about the intellectual origins of the Reformation. Instead he endeavors to reconstruct the thought world wherein the "birth pangs" of the Reformation, those unresolved intellectual and theological problems of the late medieval period, are found. Similarly, "forerunners" of the Reformation are redefined as those who dealt with the same questions rather than those who proposed similar answers.[17] The late medieval period, Oberman argues, determined the categories in which the intellectual battles of the sixteenth century were fought, the reference points to which both Reformation and Counter-Reformation had to respond. The Reformation period broke new ground in such significant areas as divine sovereignty, faith and reason, grace and works, but it did so within the basic framework of late medieval thought.

POTENTIA DEI ABSOLUTA/POTENTIA DEI ORDINATA

In his prize-winning work *The Harvest of Medieval Theology* (1963), Oberman produced the most complete full-scale study of the theology of late-medieval nominalism, focusing upon one of its most influential representatives, Gabriel Biel. The force of this monograph, together with a number of other important essays, was completely to re-write the history of late medieval theology.[18] Where both Protestants and Roman Catholics had tended—for confessional reasons—to view the late medieval period as one of decline and decay, Oberman revealed a fruitful period of meaningful theological achievement. His provocative reconstruction renders late medieval scholasticism not a period of waning—either in the Catholic, Thomistic sense or in the Protestant, moralistic sense—but a vital era of theological ferment, a period of "harvest."

That vitality was based in no small measure, Oberman has shown, on the competition between the so-called *via moderna* (modern way) and the *via antiqua* (old way).[19] The *via antiqua* stood for "doing theology" from the realist perspective, focusing on the being of God; to oversimplify somewhat, the "old doctors" tended to deduce their fundamental theological axioms from what they considered "fitting" with God's revealed character.[20] The *moderni* ("moderns") by contrast, tended to ground theology in the will (*voluntas*) of God, the significance of which will be made clear below. The *via antiqua* dates, Oberman explains, roughly from Peter Lombard (1095–1160) through Thomas Aquinas (1224–1274) and Duns Scotus (1265–1308), the "old doctors" who worked out their theologies on the basis of philosophical realism.

The *via moderna* begins with William of Occam (1285–1349) and his followers, and includes among its most important representatives Gregory of Rimini (1300–1358) and Gabriel Biel (1410–1495). In the Occamist tradition, nominalist theologians and philosophers, having rejected the objective existence of universals as archetypes of material reality existent in the mind of God, re-focused theology on the all-powerful will of God. Not content with the deductive method of theological realism, these men strove to reconstruct theology along biblical and empirical lines.[21] The *via moderna* rejected the *a priori* metaphysic of realism in favor of an *a posteriori* physic; hence Occam's "razor" (a principle which claimed that "what can be explained by assuming fewer terms is vainly explained by assuming more"[22]) set to work slicing away the speculative accretions of "meta"-theology in a manner analogous to the humanists' exhortation *ad fontes*. [23] That is, the nominalists' insistence that theology be pruned of unnecessary speculation tended to streamline theology in much the same way as did the humanists' insistence on a return to the original sources of the faith: the Bible and the writings of the Fathers.

Oberman has emphasized the importance of the perpetual conflict between the via antiqua and the via moderna, particularly on the university scene, for the development of late medieval—and, hence, Reformation—theology. The *via moderna* was a sort of step-child of the *via antiqua*, an effort to complete the "freeing" of theology only begun by the "old doctors." Nominalist theologians stressed the contingency of the created order,[24] resulting in a new focus on the all-powerful will of God, subject only to His own nature and attributes. They drew a sharp, new distinction between the *potentia dei ordinata* (the contingent order freely chosen and ordained by God) and the *potentia dei absoluta* (the absolute power of God according to which he might have done things differently).[25] For the nominalists, therefore, soteriology was approached from the standpoint of the ordained means by which God had chosen to make salvation from sin a possibility. Or, to put it in the nominalists' terms, the question of justification was understood as an aspect of the *potentia dei ordinata*, in which the covenant (*pactum*), or contractual means of salvation, was essential.[26]

In contrast to the tendency of theologians of the *via antiqua* to defend the ordained means of salvation as most "fitting" with God's character, therefore, the nominalists argued that redemption could have been achieved in any way God desired (according to God's absolute power), but that He freely chose a contractual or covenantal arrangement in which He rewards those who do the "what is in them" (*facere quod in se est*) with the grace necessary for working out one's salvation through meritorious good works. The most characteristic pastoral advice of the nominalist theologian to the struggling sinner was therefore, "Do the very best that is in you, and God will not deny you grace." The God of the nominalist tradition could be relied upon to fulfill his covenantal obligations; those who do their best are infallibly rewarded with grace. Once that grace has been made available, the Christian pilgrim (*viator*) cooperates with it and earns final salvation as a reward due in strict justice.[27] In this respect, Oberman has argued, the nominalist doctrine of justification was pastoral, an attempt not only to help parishioners apply Christian faith to their lives in meaningful ways, but also to reform medieval Christendom in the process.

The pastoral efforts of the nominalist theologians reflected, he claims, the late medievalists' attempt to integrate Augustine's insights on the relationship between grace and reason into their own "missionary" or "pastoral" theologies.[28] Relying on Augustine, "confessional" theologies of the High Middle Ages had tended to focus, quite naturally, on confession and thanksgiving. Theology was done from the "post-conversion" position of the believer; looking back through the eyes of faith, one sees the grace of God at work in one's life long before actual conversion. Such theologies tended to place a strong emphasis on God's sovereignty and the primacy of grace in salvation. But the "missionary" theologies of the late medieval period sought to understand the order of salvation from the side of the human subject (i.e., the role of reason and the human will in the turn to faith) and to integrate human responsibility with divine sovereignty in the life of the Christian. Hence, the reverse side of the *facere quod in se est* was *non facit quod in se est*—he who does not do his very best and instead persists in sin is truly guilty and is rightly punished with eternal damna-

tion.[29] Nominalist theologies thus exhorted medieval Christians to perse-
vere in good works done in a state of grace, thereby simultaneously
building up the merits necessary for final salvation and preserving and reforming medieval church and society.

Obviously, the *via moderna* stressed the individual's responsibility *coram
deo* (before God) to appropriate the divinely-ordained means for meriting
final salvation. In this respect, the nominalists' effort to clarify the role of
the human *voluntas* (will) in conforming one to the revealed will of God
within the bounds of the *potentia Dei ordinata* underscored the dignity of
humanity. *Prudentia*, the virtue of right reason by which one prepares for
the initial infusion of grace, is primary. In the theology of Gabriel Biel, for
example, *prudentia* leads through the reading of Scripture to a knowledge
of God's goodness and, hence, the prayer for His gifts.[30] The voice of natural law, speaking through *prudentia*, moves one, on account of the *synder-
esis* (the spark of the conscience), to seek after God.[31]

Biel's side of the nominalistic tradition was thus on Oberman's reading
at least semi-Pelagian. Nonetheless, even the semi-Pelagians among the
nominalist theologians were fully "catholic" in the sense that they sincerely struggled to be faithful to both Augustine and Thomas, patiently har-
vesting the insights of their predecessors and applying their pastoral
theologies to the interests and challenges of late-medieval culture. Although their doctrine of justification was ultimately rejected in 1563 at the
Council of Trent, their doctrines of tradition and church Authority
proved to be the forerunners of the formulations legitimated at Trent.
While nominalism may not represent the zenith of Roman Catholic
thought, neither is it merely a debased form of the genuinely catholic theology of the "high" Middle Ages.[32]

Of course, designating the thirteenth century the "High" Middle Ages
and the fourteenth and fifteenth centuries "Late" tends already to prejudice one's understanding of these periods and, in Oberman's view, to im-
pede one's understanding of late-medieval thought, to play into the hands
of the older historiography of decline and decay. Early in the twentieth
century Pierre Mandonnet claimed that the theology of Thomas had
dominated the intellectual world of the thirteenth and fourteenth centuries.[33] That notion is little more than wishful thinking, Oberman argues.
The philosophy of Thomas Aquinas was not "universally accepted," he
points out, even within Thomas's own Dominican Order. Scotism and
Occamism represented viable alternative *viae* to that of Thomas which
many found intellectually and theologically satisfying. Outside the universities, he claims, the influence of Hugh of St. Victor, Bonaventura and
Bernard of Clairvaux—which focused upon the "symbolic method" in

biblical study; that is, the search for typological harmonies, names and numbers—prevailed.

The thought of Thomas was used in a variety of ways by his late medieval heirs, Oberman points out, not all of which were consistent with the mature Thomas of the *Summa Theologiae*; his *Sentences* commentary, for example, was used by nominalistic theologians to support semi-Pelagian doctrines of grace, while those who defended his metaphysics from charges of Greek necessitarianism tended to portray his thought as excessively metaphysical, to the neglect of his work on Scripture and the church fathers.[34] If there was indeed a dominant school in the late medieval period, he claims, it was not Thomism, but the Franciscan *via moderna*.[35] The Franciscan movement bore fruit, Oberman argues, in the so-called *Devotio moderna* (the modern devotion). Nourished by the mysticism of Meister Eckhardt (d. 1327) and Jan Ruysbroeck (d. 1381), this movement focused upon the virtue of *simplicitas* in opposition to worldliness both within and without the church. In the *Devotio moderna*, the Franciscan campaign against dry metaphysical speculation of academic philosophy and theology reached its practical height.[36]

Taken together, Oberman believes, these streams of fourteenth- and fifteenth-century thought reveal quite a different picture than that painted by Roman Catholic scholarship earlier in this century. Rather than a "waning," Oberman sees in the late medieval period a time of vital theological foment with a visionary focus on personal and societal reform.[37]

OBERMAN'S LUTHER: MEDIEVAL OR MODERN?

Luther is to be regarded not so much as a lonely prophet—let alone as the Hercules of the humanists—but as a leading member of the Wittenberg team which, in keeping with the motto of the university, initiated its program "in the name of St. Paul and St. Augustine."

—Heiko A. Oberman[38]

The question whether the Reformation is better understood as a medieval or a modern event goes back at least to the well-known historiographical debate between two of nineteenth-century Germany's most important scholars, Wilhelm Dilthey and Ernst Troeltsch.[39] For Dilthey the Reformation was a step into the modern age, the triumph of personal religion and individual autonomy over against institutional religiosity and external conformity. Luther's elevation of secular callings vis-a-vis religious ones shattered the two-tiered structure of medieval society, he believed, and made the secular world a legitimate arena for the exercise of Christian morality. Troeltsch, by contrast, saw the Reformation, and Luther in particular, as hopelessly medieval. He disliked Luther's conservative politics and thought little of his appeal to naive faith. The result, he pointed out, was a society no less dominated by the church than it had been before.

One could gather significant evidence to suggest that Oberman's revisionist work on Luther tends to support the side of Troeltsch. For Oberman the task was to show how Luther's theology fit into the context, the gathering streams, of late-medieval thought. The result, as we shall see below, is a Luther cut somewhat down to size, a man of real genius, but a man whose achievements were made possible, perhaps even likely, by his many predecessors. That argument in and of itself is not really new, but Oberman pressed his case with more creativity and determination than had his predecessors.[40] Still, it is a mistake to attempt to fit Oberman's revisionist reading of Luther into the rather narrow either/or confines of the Troeltsch/Dilthey debate. Oberman's Luther, though in some respects a product of the late medieval period, is something altogether different, an anti-Reformer who is best understood as neither medieval nor modern, but as an apocalyptic.

ACADEMIC AUGUSTINIANISM:
LUTHER AND THE VIA GREGORII

In an intriguing article published in 1974, Oberman proposed not simply that Luther was *influenced* by the so-called Augustine Renaissance of the later Middle Ages, but that when he came to the chair of biblical studies in Wittenberg in 1512 he did so *as a representative of* an existing school of "academic Augustinianism," the *via Gregorii*.[41] While this proposal has obvious affinities with Oberman's efforts at "re-contextualizing" the Reformation within the broader streams of late-medieval thought, it has some rather startling revisionary implications for Protestant and Roman Catholic historiography alike.

Regardless of Luther's repudiation of the optimistic theological anthropology common among the humanists, Oberman claims, a strain of Renaissance humanism—yet another crucial stream of late-medieval thought—did reach him through the Augustinian Order: the so-called *schola moderna Augustiniana*, the modern school of Augustine. For this school, Oberman argued, Augustine was not merely one among many church fathers; he was the "authoritative and definitive interpreter of the one *Evangelium* located in the Scriptures."[42] Fourteenth-century theologians in the Augustinian order joined with humanists like Petrarch, he points out, in their research on the Doctor of Grace, complementing his scholarly interest in classical sources with their own theologically motivated search for authentic manuscripts of the founder of their order.[43]

According to Oberman, the greatest General of the Augustinian Order after Giles of Rome (d. 1316) was Gregory of Rimini, who became the new *doctor authenticus* (the authentic doctor) of the Augustinian Order.[44] Oberman claims that Gregory, unlike Giles, forged a powerful synthesis between the most stringent Augustinianism and Occam's theological nominalism. Unlike theologians such as Gabriel Biel, who veered off into semi-Pelagianism, Gregory of Rimini was both a nominalist and a radical Augustinian in his doctrine of grace.[45] Whereas his Augustinian predecessors, notably Bonaventura and Giles, had emphasized the *rationes seminales* (seminal reasons) over against Aristotelian abstraction, Gregory had as his philosophical starting point the nominalists' *cognitio particularis rei:* a focus upon knowledge of individual particulars. This put Gregory's thought firmly in line with the late medieval movement away from philosophical realism, the stream of thought which Oberman believes ultimately led to the experimental method of modern science.[46]

Moreover, on account of the efforts of Petrarch and the *schola Augustiniana moderna*, Gregory had at his disposal a greater number of Augustine's works—Urbino's *Milleloquium S. Augustini*, for example[47]—than had previously been available.[48] Here, Oberman claims, we find nominalism, Renaissance humanism, and a strict Augustinian doctrine of grace working together in precisely the stream of thought—"academic Augustinianism"—which Oberman believes eventually led to the Reformation, or, more precisely, to the *initia Lutheri*.[49]

The next link in the developmental chain of this academic Augustinianism, Oberman argued, was another Augustinian General, Augustinus Favaroni (d. 1443), who, some claim, anticipated Luther's evangelical doctrines by nearly seventy years.[50] In particular, Favaroni had used the term *commercium admirabile* (wondrous exchange) to describe the relationship between Christ and the Christian. According to Oberman, however, Favaroni taught a doctrine of justification *sola caritate* (by works of charity alone), not *sola fide* (by faith alone). Nevertheless, Oberman claims, Favaroni is another important link in the development of Augustinian thought between Luther's theological mentor, Johannes von Staupitz, and Gregory of Rimini; taking Favaroni and Gregory into account, Oberman concludes, "Staupitz no longer seems to arise *ex nihilo*."[51]

Staupitz's contribution, as Oberman reconstructs it, consisted in his rejection of the Thomistic notion of a created *habitus gratiae* (the habit of grace, a divine gift which enables the pilgrim to do truly good works; e.g., *gratia creata*) operative in the process of sanctification, substituting in its place the notion that the Holy Spirit (*gratia increata*) indwells the pilgrim directly.[52] Moreover, Staupitz reinterpreted the traditional doctrine of *gratia gratum faciens* (e.g., first grace, or "the grace which makes pleasing") not as the grace that makes the Christian pleasing to God, but, vice versa, as that which enables the Christian to delight in God.[53] For Staupitz, the life of the true Christian is characterized by perpetual penance. These "Augustinian" themes all played a role, Oberman claims, in the young Luther's developing theology.[54] As late as 1518, he notes, Luther could attribute "everything" to Doctor Staupitz.[55]

Thus, Luther fits into a long line of academic Augustinians, theologians long concerned with resolving certain central problems in Augustine's theology. Even at Erfurt, one of Luther's teachers, Bartholomäus von Usingen, had already pointed him toward Gregory of Rimini. But it was at Wittenberg, where the University statutes apparently allowed for a faculty representative of the *via Gregorii*—in addition to the *via Thomae* (the way of Thomas Aquinas) and *via Scoti* (the way of Duns Scotus)—that Luther encountered the Augustinian context which allowed for the development of his new theology.[56] When Staupitz left Wittenberg in 1512, Luther took his chair in the theological faculty as Doctor of Scripture; his position had been dedicated to the *via Gregorii*, so Luther was obliged to teach in accord with the *doctor authenticus* of his Order. On this basis, Oberman concludes—although he admits that the evidence is only circumstantial at certain critical points[57]—that the *schola moderna Augustiniana* provided the dynamic context for Luther's new developments.[58]

Thus Oberman gathers together the long-developing intellectual streams carrying the insights of Renaissance humanism, Augustinianism and philosophical nominalism which he claims formed the dynamic context of Luther's discovery of a gracious God. The medieval university scene, with its entrenched competition between the competing *viae*, provides the polemic atmosphere for Luther's appointment as a Doctor, and hence polemicist, for the *via Gregorii*. His appearance, though not the genius of his new theological insights, can now be understood. No longer merely a biblical theologian, Luther speaks, even on Scripture, from the medieval context of academic Augustinianism.[59]

LUTHER'S APOCALYPTICISM

Following his work on the problem of Luther's relationship to medieval Augustinianism, Oberman published one of the most original and important Luther-biographies in recent memory. In *Luther: Man Between God and the Devil*, he brought to light certain important themes in Luther's thought that make Luther appear out of step with modernity, and hence most medieval. If there is a sense in which Oberman's Luther can still be considered modern, then it is only to the extent that he participated in the nominalism of the *via moderna* which, as we have seen, Oberman believes gave birth to modern science.[60] Luther's achievement from within the context of nominalism, he claims, was to find the certain Word of God in the Scriptures and thus to free theology from its subordination to speculative philosophy.

If the question must be asked, however, Oberman's Luther is more medieval than modern.[61] His medieval roots, and hence his distance from the modern era, Oberman believes, are evidenced by his obsessions with the devil, the Anti-Christ and the like, beliefs which have become foreign to "enlightened" persons living in the modern age.[62] Such beliefs were fundamental for Luther. Oberman claims, "Luther's world of thought is wholly distorted and apologetically misconstrued if his conception of the Devil is dismissed as a medieval phenomenon and only his faith in Christ retained as relevant or as the only decisive factor.... To argue that Luther never overcame the medieval belief in the Devil says far too little; he even intensified it and lent to it additional urgency: Christ and Satan wage a cosmic war for mastery over Church and world."[63] Luther's acute sense of the warfare between Christ and Satan is not so much a kind of medieval relic in Luther's thought; it is rather an essential component of his world view, and marks him once again as a man more medieval than modern.

In the final analysis, however, Oberman's Luther is neither a typical medieval reformer nor the progenitor of the Protestant institutional church. Oberman claims that Luther should be understood in the way in which he understood himself, that is, as a prophet of the Last Days who stands poised between God and the devil, informing the world not only about the gospel of salvation by faith alone, but also about the schemes of the devil. Luther is thus neither the "gatekeeper of the modern" age nor the "last medieval man," but the prophet chosen by God to announce the Last Times.

Yet another factor that seems to increase the distance between Luther and modernity is his use of "scatological" language, the language of the privy, to shame and defeat the Devil when faced with temptations.[64] Far from the relapse of a bitter and disillusioned old man into the vulgarities of his peasant upbringing,[65] Oberman argues, Luther's "scatological language" was theologically inspired, an effort to unmask the pretensions of the devil, especially when the devil wore the mask of churchly authority or of human claims to self-righteousness. Taken together with Luther's apocalypticism, an awareness of his "scatological" side serves to increase our sense of historical distance from this man and, if Oberman is right, better to understand him in the context of his own times.

Here again we see Oberman at work against "confessional" historiography.[66] One of the reasons he wants to set Luther in context is to offset what he sees as the German Lutheran tendency to find in Luther answers to all of today's theological, moral and even political problems—what one reviewer calls the "Luther and" approach.[67] Over against the tendency of such research to enshrine Luther as a prophet and to absolutize his theology, Oberman has emphasized the extent to which Luther and his world of thought were conditioned by their historical context. If Oberman could have it his way, students of the Reformation would see Luther a bit less either as a superhuman prophet or a theological revolutionary, and a bit more as a man of flesh-and-blood, a man of his times.

CONCLUSION

Creativity—the boldness to reconceive the connections between disparate historical phenomena—is the hallmark of Oberman's work from beginning to end. But creativity should not be equated with absolute originality. Oberman's work, not unlike Reformation theology, also has its forerunners. His research on the so-called *schola moderna Augustiniana*, as we noted above, is only the latest in a long series of much-controverted attempts to ferret out the connection between certain streams of late medieval Augustinianism and the Reformation.[68] Even as Oberman did not say the first word on "academic Augustinianism," so we should not expect that his word should be the last.[69] Still, Oberman's research is nothing if not boldly revisionary. Though many would question his conclusions, few if any would take issue with the raw energy which Oberman has unleashed, particularly in regard to what is, thanks largely to Oberman, no longer the "unknown, and therefore, unbeloved" late medieval period.

Unlike the broad acceptance and scholarly acclaim which greeted much of his work on Gabriel Biel, however, Oberman's Luther research has been the subject of much controversy.[70] For all the hard work and creativity which underlies it, Oberman's reconstruction of Luther, particularly his *via Gregorii* proposal, has raised more questions than it has answered. Many still doubt even the existence of a *via Gregorii* at the Wittenberg University in 1509. As one researcher pointed out, Oberman's proposal is based upon a highly debatable "paleographical ambiguity" which leaves in considerable doubt the inclusion of any such *via* at Wittenberg.[71] The documentary evidence leaves us uncertain, in other words, whether the third *via* provided for at Wittenberg was the *via Gregorii* or merely the *via Guilelmi* (the way of William of Occam).[72]

Some would also question Oberman's emphasis upon the eschatological side of Luther.[73] If Luther was really such an other-worldly prophet, an anti-reformer, they ask, then how can we explain his efforts to insure the success of the Reformation after his death? What of his catechetical efforts, or the writing of new church orders (*Kirchenordnungen*) to serve the new evangelical parishes? How different are Luther's attitudes towards the devil from those of his contemporaries, Evangelical or Catholic? Questions such as these only serve to demonstrate, however, the ways in which Oberman's provocative revisionism has served to stimulate further research, not only by his students, but by those who take issue with him.

Of course, for his own part, Oberman continues to research and publish, and perhaps even to change his mind occasionally. The full story of his own development, and hence of his contribution to church history, cannot yet be told. His recent work focuses upon the Genevan Reformer, John Calvin, with a long-awaited monograph reported to be nearing completion.[74] If that work proves as provocative as was his work on Luther, then students of church history shall indeed be enriched.

Having worked extensively both in Europe and the United States, Oberman may well be the only truly international scholar in his field, so his impact continues to be felt on both sides of the Atlantic. Successful church historians, he once quipped, need plenty of *Sitzfleisch*, the "sitting flesh" necessary to endure the long hours of research and writing essential to the historian's task. As we have seen, Oberman himself brought *Sitzfleisch* aplenty to that task, but even more, he taught a generation of church historians the importance of reading the primary sources for themselves and inspired them all with his combination of daring revisionism and plain hard work.

A SELECT BIBLIOGRAPHY OF THE WORKS OF HEIKO A. OBERMAN

PRIMARY SOURCES

Forerunners of the Reformation: The Shape of Late Medieval Thought. New York: Holt, Rinehart & Winston, 1966.

Luther: Man Betweeen God and the Devil. New Haven and London: Yale University Press, 1989.

Masters of the Reformation: The Emergence of a New Intellectual Climate in Europe. Cambridge: Cambridge University Press, 1981.

The Dawn of the Reformation: Essays in Late Medieval and Early Reformation Thought. Edinburgh: T. & T. Clark, 1986.

The Harvest of Medieval Theology: Gabriel Biel and Late Medieval Nominalism. Cambridge: Harvard, 1963.

The Roots of Anti-Semitism in the Age of Renaisance and Reformation. Philadelphia: Fortress, 1983.

NOTES

1. Among Oberman's many influential former students, we list only some of the better known: Professor William J. Courtenay (University of Wisconsin), Professor Jane Dempsey-Douglas (Princeton Seminary), Professor Kenneth Hagen (Marquette University), Professor Steven E. Ozment (Harvard University), and Professor David C. Steinmetz (Duke University).

2. Note well, however, the assertion of A. G. Dickens and John Tonkin that "the effort to be in some sense objective began among the earliest historians of the Reformation and has steadily developed ever since." See their *The Reformation in Historical Thought* (Cambridge, Mass.:Harvard University Press, 1985), 3–4. Cf. Dickens' *Contemporary Historians of the German Reformation*, (Leeds: W. S. Maney and Sons Ltd., 1978), in which he draws attention in particular to the Lutheran historian Johann Sleidan, whose *Commentaries* of 1555 in some ways anticipated Leopold von Ranke's attempt to write history *wie es eigentlich gewesen hat*. Sleidan's *Commentaries* were reviled by Roman Catholics and Protestants alike, Dickens points out, on account of the author's stated desire to avoid partisanship.

3. See, inter alia, Maurice de Wulf, *History of Mediaeval Philosophy*, translated by Ernest C. Messenger, 2 vols. (New York: Longmans, Green & Co., 1925), *Philosophy and Civilization in the Middle Ages* (New York: Greenwood Press, 1922), *Scholasticism Old and New: An Introduction to Scholastic Philosophy Medieval and Modern*, trans. P. Coffey (Dublin: M. H. Gill & Son, 1907); Étienne Gilson's *History of Christian Philosophy in the Middle Ages* (New York: Random House, 1955), *Reason and Revelation in the Middle Ages* (New York: Charles Scribner's Sons, 1938), and *The Spirit of Medieval Philosophy*, (New York: Charles Scribner's Sons, 1940); Fernand Van Steenberghen's *Aristotle in the West: The Origins of Latin Aristotelianism*, trans. Leonard Johnston, (Louvain: E. Nauwelaerts, 1955), and *The Philosophical Movement in the Thirteenth Century* (London: Thomas Nelson & Sons, 1955); Pierre Mandonnet's *Siger de Brabant et l'averroisme latin au XIIIe siècle* (Fribourg, 1899; 2nd ed., Louvain, 1908–11, 2 vols.); Gordon Leff's "The Fourteenth Century and the Decline of Scholasticism," *Past and Present* 9 (1956); and David Knowles' *The Evolution of Medieval Thought* (New York, 1962). It was De Wulf who coined the phrase "scholastic synthesis," although he later modified it to "scholastic patrimony." See his *History of Mediaeval Philosophy*, vol. 1, 334: "At no other moment of history was doctrinal homogeneity more real than in the thirteenth century."

4. Gilson, *Reason and Revelation in the Middle Ages*, 86–97.

5. Ibid., 95–96.

6. See Frederick Copleston, *A History of Philosophy*, vol. 3: *Ockham to Suarez* (Garden City, New York: Image Books, 1985), 11.

7. See Joseph Lortz, *The Reformation in Germany*, trans. Ronald Walls, 2 vols. (London, New York: 1968). First German edition, 1939.

8. See Joseph Lortz, "Luther and the Reformation," excerpted in *Renaissance, Reformation and Absolutism: 1450–1650*, ed. Norman F. Cantor and Michael S. Werthman (New York: Thomas Y. Crowell, 1972), 126: "Luther's theological development towards the Reformation revolution was decisively advanced by a fundamentally non-Catholic Occamism, which had taken root within the Church".

9. As Oberman observes, the charge from Lortz is that " . . . whereas Luther thought he opposed *the* medieval tradition, he actually attacked only the nominalistic tradition, in this case its chief representative, Gabriel Biel." See his "'Iustitia Christi' and 'Iustitia Dei:' Luther and the Scholastic Doctrines of Justification," *Harvard Theological Review* 59 , no. 1 (January 1966): 1–26; 2.

10. See Heiko A. Oberman, "Some Notes on the Theology of Nominalism with Attention to Its Relation to the Renaissance," *Harvard Theological Review* 53 (1960): 47–76. For a helpful survey of the state of research, see William J. Courtenay's "Nominalism and Late Medieval Religion," in *The Pursuit of Holiness in Late Medieval and Renaissance Religion: Papers from the University of Michigan Conference,* ed. Charles Trinkhaus and Heiko A. Oberman (Leiden: E. J. Brill, 1974).

11. See Heiko A. Oberman, "Headwaters of the Reformation: Initia Lutheri—Initia Reformationis," in *Luther and the Dawn of the Modern Era: Papers for the Fourth International Congress for Luther Research,* ed. Heiko A. Oberman. (*Studies in Medieval and Reformation Thought* 10, ed. Heiko A. Oberman, [Leiden: E. J. Brill, 1974], 83: Regarding the creative genesis of Luther's theology Oberman says simply "In seeking to understand the emergence of a man in relation to what he was before, we can never hope to lift the veil of mystery shrouding the birth of an original mind").

12. Oberman, "The Shape of Late Medieval Thought: The Birthpangs of the Modern Era," in *The Pursuit of Holiness in Late Medieval and Renaissance Religion,* ed. Charles Trinkhaus and Heiko A. Oberman (Leiden: E. J. Brill, 1974), 3–25; 4.

13. Oberman, *Masters of the Reformation: The Emergence of a New Intellectual Climate in Europe,* trans. Dennis Martin, (Cambridge: Cambridge University Press, 1981), 5.

14. Oberman, *Forerunners of the Reformation: The Shape of Late Medieval Thought* (New York: Holt, Rinehart & Winston, 1966), 9–10.

15. Ibid., 34–35.

16. Heiko A. Oberman, "Shape of Late Medieval Thought," 21.

17. Oberman, *Forerunners,* 42.

18. See his *Forerunners* together with the seminal essays now helpfully collected in *The Dawn of the Reformation* (Edinburgh: T. & T. Clark, 1986).

19. Oberman believes that Protestant scholarship in particular is reticent to accept a connection between Luther and Occam or nominalism. See Oberman, "Headwaters," 59.

20. Heiko A. Oberman, *Masters,* 6.

21. Oberman, "Headwaters," 58–59.

22. The translation from the original Latin belongs to Steven E. Ozment. See his *The Age of Reform 1250–1550: An Intellectual and Religious History of Late Medieval and Reformation Europe* (New Haven and London:Yale University Press, 1980), 56.

23. Oberman, "Headwaters," 57.

24. For some additional support for Oberman's view, see Eugene M. Klaaren, *Religious Origins of Modern Science: Belief in Creation in Seventeenth Century Thought* (Grand Rapids: Eerdmans, 1977), and R. Hooykas, *Religion and the Rise of Modern Science* (Grand Rapids: Eerdmans, 1972).

25. For concise definitions of critical Latin terms used in nominalist medieval theology, see the glossary contained in Oberman, *The Harvest of Medieval Theology: Gabriel Biel and Late Medieval Nominalism* (Cambridge: Harvard, 1963), 457–76.

26. Oberman, "'Iustitia Christi' and 'Iustitia Dei:' ", 3–4.

27. For additional detail on the *facere quod in se est,* see He ko A. Oberman, "*Facientibus Quod in se est Deus non Denegat Gratiam:* Robert Holcot and the Beginnings of Luther's Theology," in *The Reformation in Medieval Perspective,* ed. Steven E. Ozment (Chicago: Quadrangle, 1971), 119–41; 126.

28. Oberman, *Forerunners,* 129.

29. Oberman, *Harvest,* 194–95.

30. Oberman, "'Iustitia Christi' and 'Iustitia Dei,'" 11.

31. Oberman, *Harvest,* 475.

32. Ibid., 423–28.

33. Cited by Oberman in "Fourteenth Century Religious Thought: A Premature Profile," in *Dawn*, 1–17; 2.

34. Oberman, "Fourteenth Century Religious Thought," 4–5.

35. Ibid., 8. See also Oberman, "The Shape of Late Medieval Thought."

36. Oberman, "Fourteenth Century Religious Thought," 16.

37. Ibid., 15.

38. Oberman, "Headwaters," 44.

39. On the historiography of the Reformation, see *The Reformation: Basic Interpretations*, ed. Lewis W. Spitz, 2nd ed. (Lexington, Mass.: D. C. Heath and Company, 1972). See pp. 11–24 for a partial translation of Dilthey's "Auffassung und Analyse des Menschen im 15. und 16. Jahrhundert." Troeltsch's essay "Renaissance and Reformation" follows on pp. 25–43.

40. The scholarly search for Luther's Augustinian precursors is well summarized in David C. Steinmetz's "Luther and the Late Medieval Augustinians: Another Look," *Concordia Theological Monthly* 44 (1973): 245–60.

41. This position was staked-out in Oberman's "Headwaters."

42. Oberman, "Fourteenth Century Religious Thought," 8.

43. Oberman, "Headwaters," 66.

44. The other critical figure was Thomas Bradwardine, the Archbishop of Canterbury, whose radically Augustinian *De Causa Dei Contra Pelagium* was foundational for Wycliffe. Bradwardine's influence, especially when compared to that of Gregory of Rimini, was limited by Oxford's isolation during the Hundred Years' War and, Oberman claims, " . . . [because] he tried to argue the case of God's primacy and the prevenience of his grace on the basis of a causal metaphysics in keeping with the old way, the *via antiqua*, as the university statutes of the fifteenth century would classify this tradition. Gregory of Rimini, on the other hand, succeeded in matching this central Augustinian theme with the achievements of the *via moderna*." See Oberman, "Fourteenth Century Religious Thought," 11. Cf. his comments in *Masters*, 67 ff.

45. See Oberman, "Fourteenth Century Religious Thought," 11.

46. Oberman, "Headwaters," 57: " . . . there are good reasons to claim that the beginnings of modern science can be retraced to nominalism." Cf. *Masters of the Reformation*, 41.

47. Petrarch wrote a dedicatory letter for this compilation of precise quotes from the Doctor of Grace. See Oberman, "Headwaters," 67.

48. See Oberman, "Fourteenth Century Religious Thought," 11.

49. Note that Oberman differentiates between what he calls *initia Lutheri* and the *initia Reformationis*. He argues that a different conception of Christian liberty, flowing out of Luther's *De Libertate Christiana*, characterizes the thought of such reformers as Zwingli and Bucer: they elevated *sola scriptura* to the same level as Luther's *sola gratia* and *sola fide*. See "Headwaters," 39–52.

50. Oberman cites Alphons Victor Müller's "Agostino Favaroni e la Teologia di Lutero," *Bilychnis*, 3 (1914): 1–17.

51. Oberman, "Headwaters," 70–71.

52. See David C. Steinmetz, *Misericordia Dei: The Theology of Johannes Von Staupitz in Its Late Medieval Setting* (Leiden: E. J. Brill, 1968).

53. Ibid., 84–86.

54. Oberman, "Headwaters," 72.

55. *"Ex Erasmo nihil habeo. Ich hab all mein ding von Doctor Staupitz."* Quoted in Ozment, *Age of Reform*, 232, n. 27.

56. Oberman, "Headwaters," 75. Oberman bases his case for the existence of the *via Gregorii* at Wittenberg on new manuscript evidence. He claims that what was previously thought to have been the *via Guilelmi* (the way of Occam) was in fact the *via Gre-*

gorii. In the extant copies of the statutes of Wittenberg University, the *via Gregorii* has been corrected, he believes, "by a later hand," to read *via Guilelmi.*

57. Luther did not, for example, appeal to the authority of Gregory of Rimini when in 1517 he castigated his former Erfurt teachers for wasting their time on Aristotle. See Oberman, "Headwaters," 76, n. 153.

58. Oberman, "Headwaters," 77.

59. Ibid., 82–83.

60. See Oberman's comments in his *Luther: Man Between God and the Devil,* trans. Eileen Walliser-Schwarzbart (New Haven & London: Yale University Press, 1989), 119.

61. Ibid., 61.

62. Ibid., 107.

63. Ibid., 104.

64. Ibid., 106–9. See also Oberman's "Teufelsdreck: Eschatology and Scatology in the 'Old' Luther," *Sixteenth Century Journal* XIX (1988): 435–50.

65. See Mark U. Edwards, *Luther's Last Battles* (Ithaca & London: Cornell University Press, 1983), 208.

66. Oberman, "Teufelsdreck," 447.

67. See G. R. Elton's review article, "Commemorating Luther," *Journal of Ecclesiastical History* 35 (1984): 614–19.

68. For another concise summary of the history of research on Late Medieval Augustinianism, see Denis Janz, *Luther and Late Medieval Thomism: A Study in Theological Anthropology* (Waterloo: Wilfrid Laurier University Press, 1983), 158–65.

69. The research continues. See the festschrift *Augustine, the Harvest, and Theology (1300–1650): Essays Dedicated to Heiko Augustinus Oberman in Honor of His Sixtieth Birthday* (New York & Leiden: E. J. Brill, 1990).

70. Inter alia, see Leif Grane's critical review of *Gregor von Rimini: Werk und Wirkung bis zur Reformation,* ed. Heiko A. Oberman, (Berlin and New York: de Gruyter, 1981), in *Theologische Literaturzeitung* 108 (1983): 276–79. Grane has probably been Oberman's most consistent and formidable detractor. See, inter alia, his *Modus Loquendi Theologicus: Luthers Kampf um die Erneuerung der Theologie (1515–1518)* (Leiden: E. J. Brill, 1975), in which he criticizes what he calls the "genetic method" of Oberman. The historian, he argues, must demonstrate concrete and specific relations between theologians and their context, rather than simply reciting a "spiritual genealogy." Note how the argument applies to alleged *via Gregorii.* See the helpful summary of the Grane/Oberman debates in Bernhard Lohse's "Zur Lage der Lutherforschung heute," in *Zur Lage der Lutherforschung heute,* ed. Peter Manns (Wiesbaden: Franz Steiner Verlag, 1982), 9–30.

71. See note 60 above. Janz points out that Leif Grane has argued convincingly in favor of the *via Guilelmi* reading of the disputed document. See *Luther and Late Medieval Thomism,* 163.

72. Note well, however, M. Schulze's defense of the *via Gregorii* proposal in his "'Via Gregorii' in Forschung und Quellen," in *Gregor von Rimini,* 1–126.

73. See, for example, James Kittelson, "Luther the Church Bureaucrat," *Concordia Journal* 13 (1987): 294–301.

74. Not that Oberman would be a neophyte in Calvin studies. See his "The 'Extra' Dimension in the Theology of Calvin," in *Dawn,* 241ff; and *Initia Calvini: The Matrix of Calvin's Reformation,* (Amsterdam: Koninklijke Nederlandse Akademie van Wetenschappen, 1991).

Conclusion:

HISTORICAL METHOD IN THE CHRISTIAN TRADITION

MARTIN KLAUBER

Having spanned the centuries in our perusal of classic Christian approaches to doing history, one discovers that there is no single "Christian" approach to studying history. Furthermore, our subjects do not claim that being Christian makes one a better historian, but that one's faith provides a unique perspective on the past. Christianity is in its very nature a historical religion and the Bible chronicles God's work through the Hebrew people as well as the life, death, and resurrection of Christ. The historicity of the resurrection has been by itself the subject of a myriad of scholarly studies.

Certainly, there are some consistent themes among those historians we have considered and the scholars studied here all attempted to integrate their personal faith with their discipline. There are, however, degrees of integration. On one side of the spectrum, a Christian approach to history is the process of analyzing what Christians have done in the past and allowing their actions to speak for themselves. Leopold von Ranke, for example, in his attempt to achieve complete objectivity, argued that one's faith should not interfere in historical analysis.[1] Here, the author assumes the stance of a neutral observer. The other extreme is to use faith in Christ as the governing principle of all historical interpretation. For example, William Cunningham, allowed his Calvinist perspective to color his analysis of history as he portrayed Calvin and Calvin's scholastic successors as faithful to the purity of Scripture. Calvin's followers, such as Francis Turretin, were faithful in their representations of Reformed theology and, in any deviations from Calvin, were merely responding to intellectual developments in their own era.

As the essays in this volume indicate, there has been considerable development in historical method throughout the centuries. Leonard Krieger outlines four periods of historiographical development. The ancient and medieval historian used theology uncritically in shaping accounts of the past. During the Renaissance, historians began to use more critical methods and developed the first secular histories. During the eighteenth and nineteenth centuries, historians sought universal laws of history and in the contemporary scene, historians realize that no universal patterns exist and therefore it is difficult to formulate significantly meaningful accounts of the past.[2]

This quest for historical meaning is an important aspect of a Christian approach to history. One of the most crucial elements of this quest is the role of Divine Providence, that a sovereign God is guiding all of history to His desired end. History has the purpose, therefore, of reflecting not only the actions of human beings, but also the superintendence of God. Phillip Schaff provided an example of this approach when he defined church history as the unfolding plan of God's redemption.

The providential approach to history was dominant until the Enlightenment and with the loss of providence came a corresponding search for an interpretive principle with which to approach the study of history. The French Annales school is one example of the difficulty of such an endeavor as it seeks to capture the *longue duré*, to encompass the entire picture of the past and thereby to garner some sense of meaning. However, the reader is left with an incredibly detailed picture with no overarching theme. Others in the post-Enlightenment era have attempted to replace providence with some other central principle such as the rise of nation-states or the inevitable development of the Marxist state. Peter Russell argues that the lack of meaning has led many to classify history as a social science that teaches important lessons designed to produce better citizens. He concludes that "a Christian perspective has a strong positive role to play in rescuing from the despair of meaninglessness on the one hand and on the other the adoption of false meanings in the excesses of nationalist or class-oriented claims."[3]

In developing a theory of historical providence, two approaches stand out. The first is a strict, sectarian method by which God reveals His plan for history in confirming one particular subset of beliefs within the overall framework of Christendom. One example of this is Kenneth Scott Latourette's emphasis upon the expansion of the Christian faith and his sharp moral judgments of historical figures. In the case of William Cunningham, the Calvinist way is the best and God leads the way throughout the medieval period to prepare the church for the Reformation and ultimately for the reforms of Calvin and his Reformed colleagues. Christopher Dawson argued that this providential approach to history is impossible to explain to the non-believer. This would exclude, therefore, any sense that God's work though history has anything to say to the world at large. Reinhold Niebuhr argued more sensibly that, although God is in control of history, it is not always easy to recognize His handiwork.[4]

A second method would include a more universal scope for providence which would promote unity within the Christian faith based on a common heritage. Schaff argued that divisions between denominations were caused primarily by a lack of an understanding of history. Furthermore, one cannot truly understand the nature of the church without a solid grasp of its history. Hubert Jedin asserted that the Christian historian should attempt to manifest the supernatural essence of the church.

The problem with the use of divine providence is that it is often difficult to see God's hand working directly in history. One cannot say, for example, that God favored the British fleet over the Spanish Armada. There were undoubtedly many God-fearing individuals on both sides. David Bebbington makes a distinction on this score between general and particular providence. The former would mean that God is in control of history and ensures the ultimate victory of Christ. The latter would refer to God's actions in specific instances, which is much more difficult to prove given the fallible nature of human beings.[5]

An additional difficulty with the notion of divine providence is the great number of examples throughout history of human suffering. In cases such as the holocaust, the level of devastation is almost beyond description. Then there are the many examples of natural disasters that have caused an untold number of deaths. Can God really be in control of history when such a level of suffering exists? In cases of suffering caused by human agents, one can respond that Scripture teaches the depravity of man. In the latter case, natural disasters are the unfortunate results of the Fall. Also, the Bible points to a time in the future when such suffering will ultimately cease. Jesus' suffering on the cross and resurrection point to "present liberation for the power of sin and future liberation from the power of death."[6]

A call for an ecumenical approach to church history is a second theme that is closely related to divine providence. One of the main examples of the use of divine providence is the belief that God will ultimately bring about the unity of the church. The case of Georges Florovsky is interesting on this score because he calls for an ecumenical view of church history from an Eastern Orthodox background. Florovsky views history primarily as theological, calling for a search for the ultimate significance in life. He approaches history as an encounter with living people rather than with a dead past in order to identify the purposeful character of human experience. For Florovsky, history is not cyclical because of the superintendence of God's providence.

A third major theme is the validity of religious experience in explaining the actions of individuals throughout history. This is an important point because, according to George M. Marsden, the voluntary nature of religion in America has virtually excluded "religious perspectives" from the academe. There remains freedom for individual religious practice, but the integration of religion into specific academic disciplines can be extremely difficult.[7] The importance of true spiritual motivation was the hallmark of Bainton's interpretation of Luther, who had a valid, religious experience when he "discovered" the doctrine of justification by faith. Bainton differs from the Freudian psychologists such as Erik Erikson, who attempted to explain Luther in terms of his personal identity crisis caused by an overbearing father. Salo W. Baron agrees with Bainton's approach when he explains that too many modern historians ignore the religious factor in history because they misunderstand the importance of religion in society.[8]

A fourth theme is the recent emphasis upon social history as opposed to the history of elites. Contemporary historians have ventured to discover the average parishioner's understanding of personal faith and therefore to show the extent of the impact of a revival or of a religious awakening. Heiko Oberman has argued that social history and intellectual history should complement each other to provide us with a better understanding of how people lived and what they believed.[9]

The use of quantitative methods has certainly aided the process of forming meaningful conclusions, especially in the realm of social history. Ed Van Kley argues that the use of quantitative methods assists the historian in terms of accuracy and objectivity.[10] On this score, Charles W. Brockwell, Jr. and Timothy J. Wengert point out that we should not reduce our discussion of history to "a history of ideas, liturgy, piety or social and political involvement alone."[11] They argue that a true Christian approach to history takes into account iconography, oral tradition, tracts and popular literature. This broadened approach is characteristic of a number of the subjects discussed in this present volume. Florovsky has enlightened us on the use of iconography, a source all too often ignored in Western circles. The historian, however, still must interpret the data and communicate it in a meaningful way.

Mark Noll cautions that the use of social science techniques can minimize the validity of religious experience and reduce it to a mere social phenomenon. The great French historian, Fernand Braudel, for example, views the Reformation as "only an occasion for discussing national and ethnic geography."[12] The key for the Christian historian is to apply these techniques in such a way as to maintain the validity of both the Christian faith and of religious experience. Noll laments that all too often the Christian historian practices a methodological agnosticism.[13]

This leads the historian to the question of objectivity. Jedin asserts that the historian should attempt to stay outside of the narrative. Historical conclusions should be based on the evidence of history, that is, its sources. George Marsden points out that any historian should employ a certain degree of detachment and that excessive partisanship can destroy one's credibility.[14] E. Harris Harbison adds that the Christian historian must consider the full range of political, economic, and social factors, in addition to religious motivations, when analyzing the events of the past.[15] One must be careful, however, not to allow detachment to blur the distinctiveness of Christian belief.

The Christian historian, therefore, must recognize the constant tension between God's work in history and man's own activity. One can make a significant contribution to our understanding of the past by pointing to God's work in history and to religious motivations of individuals throughout the ages with the perspective that God is ultimately in control and will bring the world to His own desired purpose.

NOTES

1. William A. Speck, "Herbert Butterfield: The Legacy of a Christian Historian" in *A Christian View of History*, ed. Frank Roberts and George M. Marsden (Grand Rapids: Eerdmans, 1975), 99.

2. Leonard Krieger, *Time's Reasons: Philosophies of History Old and New* (Chicago: University of Chicago Press, 1989). See also Shirley A. Mullen, "The Character and Purpose of History: A Review Essay," *Fides et Historia* 23 (winter/spring 1991):78–85.

3. Peter Russell, "The Challenge of Writing Christian History," *Fides et Historia* 21 (November, 1989): 9–15.

4. Reinhold Niebuhr, *Faith and History: A Comparison of Christian and Modern Views of History* (London: Nisbet, 1949): 62ff. See also David Bebbington, *Patterns in History* (Chicago: InterVarsity Press, 1979), 179.

5. Bebbington, *Patterns in History*, 171.

6. Ibid., 174–75.

7. George M. Marsden, *The Soul of the American University: From Protestant Establishment to Established Nonbelief* (Oxford: Oxford University Press, 1994), 7.

8. Salo W. Baron, *The Contemporary Relevance of History: A Study of Approaches and Methods* (New York: Columbia University Press, 1986).

9. See Heiko A. Oberman, *The Impact of the Reformation* (Grand Rapids: Eerdmans, 1994).

10. Edwin J. Van Kley, "History as a Social Science: A Christian Perspective" in Roberts and Marsden, *A Christian View of History?* 97.

11. Charles W. Brockwell, Jr. and Timothy J. Wengert, "Christian History in Ecumenical Perspective," *Fides et Historia* 24 (winter/spring 1992): 44.

12. Mark Noll, "'And the Lion Shall Lie Down with the Lamb': The Social Sciences and Religious History," *Fides et Historia* 20 (fall 1988):5–30.

13. Ibid., 23.

14. Marsden, *Soul of the American University*, 8.

15. Harris Harbison, "The Making of a Christian Historian" in *God, History, and Historians*, ed. C. T. McIntire (Oxford: Oxford University Press, 1977), 351.

CONTRIBUTORS

Michael Bauman, Professor of Theology and Culture, Hillsdale College, Hillsdale, Michigan; Lecturer in Renaissance Theology and Literature, Centre for Medieval and Renaissance Studies, Oxford, England; Visiting Professor of Christian Apologetics, Simon Greenleaf University, Anaheim, California

Joel Beeke, Pastor and Theological Instructor, First Netherlands Reformed Congregation, Grand Rapids, Michigan

Fred Beuttler, Assistant Professor of History, Trinity Christian College, Palos Heights, Illinois

W. David Buschart, Professor of Systematic Theology, Canadian Theological Seminary, Regina, Saskatchewan, Canada

Francesco C. Caesario, Assistant Professor of Church History, John Carroll University, University Heights, Ohio

Robert Clouse, Professor of History, Indiana State University, Indiana

Larry Dixon, Professor of Biblical and Theological Studies, Providence College and Seminary, Winnipeg, Manitoba, Canada

John R. Franke, Instructor in Historical and Systematic Theology, Biblical Theological Seminary, Hatfield, Pennsylvania

Steven Graham, Assistant Professor of Church History, North Park Theological Seminary, Chicago, Illinois

R. Paul House, Professor of Biblical Studies, Taylor University, Upland, Indiana

Frank A. James III, Associate Professor of Christian History, Reformed Theological Seminary, Orlando, Florida

Martin I. Klauber, Visiting Professor of Church History, Trinity Evangelical Divinity School and Lecturer in History and Religious Studies, Barat College, Lake Forest, Illinois

Caroline Marshall, Professor of History, James Madison University, Harrisburg, Virginia

Mickey Mattox, Assistant Professor of Historical Theology, Concordia College, River Forest, Illinois

Douglas McCready, Assistant Professor of Philosophy and Religious Studies, Holy Family College, New Town, Pennsylvania

Alister E. McGrath, Principal of Wycliffe Hall Oxford, England; Research Lecturer in Theology, University of Oxford, Oxford, England: Research Professor of Systematic Theology,Regents College, Vancouver, British Columbia, Canada

Donald K. McKim, Academic Dean, Memphis Theological Seminary, Memphis, Tennessee

Scot McKnight, Professor of New Testament, North Park Theological Seminary, Chicago, Illinois

Bradley Nassif, Visiting Instructor, Trinity Evangelical Divinity School, Professor of Orthodox Theology, Antiochian House of Studies, Ligonier, Pennsylvania

Richard V. Pierard, Professor of History, Indiana State University, Indiana

Richard W. Pointer, Professor of History, Westmont College, Santa Barbara, California

Stephen Pointer, Associate Dean and Professor of History, Trinity College, Deerfield, Illinois

Timothy R. Phillips, Assistant Professor of Theology, Wheaton College, Wheaton, Illinois

John S. Reist, Jr., Professor of Christianity and Literature, Hillsdale College, Hillsdale, Michigan

John B. Roney, Assistant Professor of History, Sacred Heart University, Fairfield, Connecticut

David L. Russell, Lecturer in Philosophy and Religion, Oakland City College, Auburn Hills, Michigan

Donald T. Williams, Associate Professor of English, Toccoa Falls College, Toccoa Falls, Georgia

Matthew C. Williams, Visiting Professor of Bible, Trinity Evangelical Divinity School, Deerfield, Illinois

Michael Williams, Associate Professor of Theology, Dordt College, Sioux Center, Iowa

Steve Woodworth, Associate Professor of History, Toccoa Falls College, Toccoa Falls, Georgia